*f*P

15 STARS

Eisenhower, MacArthur, Marshall:
Three Generals Who Saved
the American Century

Stanley Weintraub

FREE PRESS
NEW YORK LONDON TORONTO SYDNEY

*f*P

FREE PRESS
A Division of Simon & Schuster, Inc.
1230 Avenue of the Americas
New York, NY 10020

Copyright © 2007 by Stanley Weintraub
All rights reserved,
including the right of reproduction
in whole or in part in any form.

FREE PRESS and colophon are trademarks
of Simon & Schuster, Inc.

For information regarding special discounts for bulk purchases,
please contact Simon & Schuster Special Sales at 1-800-456-6798
or business@simonandschuster.com

Designed by Davina Mock

Manufactured in the United States of America

10 9 8 7 6 5 4 3 2 1

Library of Congress Cataloging-in-Publication Data is available

ISBN-13: 978-0-7432-7527-9
ISBN-10:   0-7432-7527-6

For Harold Segal, one of the earliest post–Pearl Harbor draftees, who finished his war at Eisenhower's SHAEF headquarters in Frankfurt, and who is in these pages.

Contents

Preface: Intersected Lives

NOT SINCE the immense fame of Grant, Sherman, and Lee at the close of the Civil War have three generals become such household names as Douglas MacArthur, George C. Marshall, and Dwight D. Eisenhower by the climax of World War II. Colleagues, and on occasion competitors, they had leapfrogged each other, sometimes stonewalled each other, even supported and protected each other, throughout their celebrated careers.

They were each created five-star generals when that super-rank was authorized by Congress in December 1944. In the public mind they appeared, in turn, as glamor, integrity, and competence. Presidential talk long hovered about them. But for the twists of circumstance, all three—rather than only one—might have occupied the White House.

MacArthur, Marshall, and Eisenhower were each featured on the covers of *Time*, when that accolade, in a pre-television era, confirmed a sort of eminence.* All three would appear on postage stamps evoking their signature traits. Their immediately recognizable faces were remarkable indices of personality. MacArthur's hawklike granite gaze conveyed his headstrong, contrary tenacity. Marshall's seamed, inscrutable look suggested the austere middle America of portraits by Grant Wood. Eisenhower's ruddy, balding head and familiar grin brought to mind less the Kansas of his boyhood than the Everyman which admirers always saw in him.

---

*Marshall and Eisenhower would each (twice) be "Man of the Year." MacArthur appeared on the cover of *Time* on December 29, 1941, in the week usually fixed for that accolade but it went the next week instead to President Roosevelt.

Collectively they represented twentieth-century America at its crest. MacArthur was always City: Washington, Manila, Tokyo, and finally New York, where he retired to the thirty-seventh floor of the Waldorf Towers. Marshall was Suburbs, with a small-town upbringing in western Pennsylvania and an unpretentious home twenty miles from the capital in Leesburg, Virgina, where he was devoted to his vegetable garden. Eisenhower was Country, out of the rural Midwest, and ended his years on his manicured swath of model farm near Gettysburg.

Their trajectories, however upward, reflected their differences. Harry Truman's last secretary of state, Dean Acheson, once said of General Marshall, "The title fitted him as though he had been baptized with it." MacArthur, son of a general, was born and bred to be one. However ambitious, Eisenhower had his stars thrust upon him. Yet their military lives intersected for decades. MacArthur and Marshall were young officers in the newly captured Philippines, seized from declining Spain. Eisenhower emerged later, as a junior aide to MacArthur in Washington and again in Manila, until World War II erupted in Europe. The flamboyant MacArthur and the unpretentious Marshall were both colonels in France during World War I, the career of one taking flight there, to brigadier general and beyond, the career of the other plunging afterward to mere postwar captain, then agonizingly creeping back up, but seemingly never far enough. Despite MacArthur's four early stars—at forty-nine—when chief of staff, he would keep the future of his contemporary, who still had none in the early 1930s, in frustrating limbo.

Serving fourteen of his thirty-seven years in the army under both men, Eisenhower was an assistant to MacArthur—invisible, and painfully aware of going nowhere—and then deputy to Marshall, who rocketed him to responsibility and to prominence. In seven years with MacArthur, laboring in the arid peacetime vineyards, Eisenhower earned a promotion of one grade, from major to lieutenant colonel, changing the oak leaves on his collar from gold to silver. In seven months under Marshall—under the vastly altered circumstances of global war—he earned a constellation of stars and a major command.

Each of the three might have coordinated D-Day in Normandy, the most complex and consequential Western military operation in World War II. All three would be army chiefs of staff, Marshall and then Eisenhower becoming in turn the ostensible superior of their onetime boss, MacArthur, who brooked no bosses.

While MacArthur was sweepingly imperial in manner, the ideal viceroy for a postwar Japan where its humiliated emperor was reduced to a symbol, Eisenhower, genial and flexible, proved the exemplary commander of quarrelsome multinational forces. The self-effacing Marshall possessed such intense respect worldwide that when he entered Westminster Abbey, unannounced, to take his seat at the coronation of young Elizabeth II, the entire congregation arose.

One often remembers people for their associations. In the cases of the three generals, these reflect and magnify their differences. One kept his court; the second kept his own counsel; the third found confidants ranging from his wartime lady chauffeur to his peacetime bridge partners. MacArthur's style was as a monarch to his minions. His closest associate since the 1930s was his erratic but devoted intelligence chief, Major General Charles Willoughby, a Great War veteran born in Germany who claimed a Prussian pedigree but discarded the unhelpful surname of Tscheppe-Wiedenbach. He affected the airs of an English officer, took an English name and what passed for an English accent, and wore a pince-nez on a silken cord. Always onstage himself, MacArthur prized an actor as much as he valued utter loyalty.

Nearly parallel in fidelity was Major General Courtney Whitney, an early army pilot who, between the wars, practiced brokerage and law in Manila and belonged to the same Masonic lodge in Luzon as did MacArthur. Recalled to duty in 1940, he landed on MacArthur's staff and accompanied him to Australia, then back to the Philippines and on to Japan. An efficient organizer, he ran, remotely, several liaison operations with guerrillas in the Philippines, but, since he commanded an office in Brisbane, he first returned to the islands with MacArthur only in a photo of the landing in Leyte, which he had doctored for his purposes by pasting his large head atop another aide's slender body. George Marshall would tell MacArthur that he had a court, rather than a staff, and Courtney Whitney, known as "Court," embodied it. Displaying his evidences of devotion to duty, he would reminisce to visitors about slogging ashore at MacArthur's side. Yet that duty was authentic even if the heroics were not. When he directed MacArthur's Government Section in the Japanese Occupation, Whitney oversaw efficiently the crash-course preparation of a democratic constitution for Japan. A fantasist himself, MacArthur appreciated kindred spirits.

MacArthur arranged for both generals, neither of whom ever commanded anyone in combat, but whom MacArthur lavishly bemedaled, to write and publish hagiographic postwar biographies of him which he freely and imaginatively dictated. Later he wrote his own lucrative memoirs, much of it drawn from their books, which were in effect his. Eisenhower sold outright, for a substantial six figures, his own World War II memoir, then dictated it, for further editing, to a stenographer employed by his publisher. Marshall refused a million dollars for his war memoirs— at a time when a million was real money.

Marshall eschewed flattery as well as fame; yet even he needed advocates. His first abettor in the White House, when Marshall was still a Depression-era colonel whose dreary, seemingly dead-end job was in part to oversee New Deal make-work projects that worked, was a reform-minded Midwestern social worker, Harry Hopkins, whose health at best was chronically frail, and income marginal, but who loved racetracks and nightclubs. (Neither venue interested Marshall in the least.) Hopkins rose from deputy director of emergency relief in Albany when Franklin Delano Roosevelt was governor of New York, to administrator of his Works Progress Administration (WPA) in Washington, then to secretary of commerce. Yet his real job was as troubleshooter and practical legs for the wheelchair-bound FDR.

Hopkins became Marshall's informal link to the White House and, although he never wore a uniform or earned a medal, was the most courageous man the general had ever known. Roosevelt's shadow, often traveling on missions with Marshall, Hopkins sometimes required blood transfusions on arrival. Not a man to employ first names easily, even for his protégé Eisenhower, Marshall called the dedicated Hopkins "Harry."

Sir John Dill, a field marshal fired as chief of the Imperial General Staff because Winston Churchill as prime minister wanted to run his own show, was marginalized overseas as liaison with the American Joint Chiefs of Staff. Despite his Sam Browne belt and British swagger stick, and a more authentic English accent than Willoughby could manage, Sir John became irreplaceable in Washington. His masterly tact, and covert conspiracies with Marshall to share confidential information from London, kept the Grand Alliance, often at cross-purposes, functioning when mutual suspicions abounded and Marshall would not suffer fools easily. Once, during the war, Dill's recall to limbo in England was rumored. Immediately, Marshall plotted a newsworthy award for him from Yale to dramatize Dill's unique transatlantic reputation, and Churchill drew back. During Dill's last illness late in the war he asked to be buried at Arlington, although the sacred premises were restricted by law to Americans. Marshall arranged for an overriding joint resolution of Congress, a state funeral, and interment as the dying Dill had wished. George Marshall would not violate a regulation, but he could make things happen.

Eisenhower was the most gregarious of his five-star peers. He needed close companions to whom he could unburden himself, unlike his remote and exacting mentor, George Marshall, who only once in their close, almost father-son relationship inadvertently called him "Ike." When Eisenhower assumed his first overseas command he took with him a CBS publicist he and Mamie knew, Harry Butcher, who, thanks to a naval reserve commission, became Eisenhower's "naval aide"—an anomaly never explained other than for its technicality. Butcher's actual tasks were to be a public relations flack, the keeper of the general's appointments, mixer of his drinks, and a spare hand at bridge. His key assignment became the maintenance of the general's "diary"—often not a list of appointments but a litany of rationalizations for why Eisenhower did whatever he thought he had to do. Eventually, the general knew, he would have to account for his actions, perhaps by becoming his own historian. But "Butch" was also ambitious. If Ike were to do great things, Butcher wanted to gain by them, and he became a personal compendium of command gossip, which Eisenhower did not know until Butcher published his mildly indiscreet *My Three Years with Eisenhower*—a Book-of-the-Month Club selection which the general cautiously refused to read in advance, and quietly disowned. In the case of his lady chauffeur, Eisenhower claimed—and that only privately—to have read only the first and last chapters of her gossipy and intimate postwar memoir.

Eisenhower also needed, as do many commanders, an efficient chief of staff: a shrewd, calculating careerist, content to rise only on the tide of his boss. In Walter Bedell ("Beetle") Smith, who had been in Marshall's stable of comers in Washington, Eisenhower found his man, and insisted on taking Smith with him on each new assignment. He was much more than a fourth at bridge. Post-Ike, "Beetle" would rise to be ambassador to Russia, and director of the CIA. Yet he never had as much power as when he ruled on Eisenhower's authority and kept his confidences—except when Eisenhower confessed that he wouldn't trade Marshall for fifty MacArthurs. "My God!" he found himself thinking aloud to Bedell Smith, "That would be a lousy deal. What would I do with fifty MacArthurs?"

Confidants who could be counted upon were hard to find, and keep. Eisenhower, who cultivated the myth of the barefoot farmboy from Abilene, Kansas who made good, always needed them and sometimes found them wanting. Not Beetle, who was the model of efficiency, if not tact. MacArthur confided in no one, and Marshall seemed beyond such need, but for a single, wistful, late letter to a beautiful young queen on a tottering European throne.

Their differences only make the intertwined careers of the three
iconic generals more poignant. Of their complex intersections over more
than five decades, many were dramatic while only a few seem, in retrospect, somewhat deplorable. Marshall would write—and even fabricate,
for effect—an unearned Medal of Honor citation for MacArthur, who
had given him no end of grief and would continue to do so. The American public, anxious for a larger-than-life hero at a time of accumulating
bad news, needed one. A midwar Marshall exchange with a reluctant
Eisenhower about his returning home to Mamie suggests much more
about Marshall's intense investment in Eisenhower's future than meets
the eye. MacArthur would allegedly disparage Ike, when he was his five-
star peer, as "the best secretary I ever had," while Eisenhower retorted, in
kind, that he had once studied dramatics under MacArthur. Yet the remarkably intersected lives of three generals who were never friends evoke
a memorable American saga while encapsulating two-thirds of the twentieth century, when the world seemed always at war. The nation needed all
three men, and each needed the other two. Would any of them have
achieved as much without the others? Only one would become president,
but it is hard to resist speculating about the other two in the White
House.

Despite the remarkable confluence of disparate personalities, and
their fifteen stars, these were men, not figures in bronze. Perfection eluded
them, as it eludes the rest of us. They are the more real for their flaws.
They did their nation proud. I salute them here for themselves, and for
their interlocking lives and achievements.

Stanley Weintraub
Beech Hill
Newark, Delaware

"Our Tails Are in the Air"

ECEMBER 7, 1941, in San Antonio was another
sultry Sunday. Exhausted in the lengthy aftermath
of the Louisiana maneuvers, the largest ever in
peacetime, Dwight D. Eisenhower, the Third Army chief of staff, now
back at country club–like Fort Sam Houston, had tucked into an early
lunch and, with a fan whirring, intended to nap the Texas afternoon away.
A new brigadier general, his first star confirmed his efficiency in overseeing mock warfare although in the equipment-short army even the
weapons were often mock.

The war games between the "Red" and "Blue" forces had ended six
weeks earlier. There were continuing lessons to be applied, and the
twenty-seven divisions of both armies, 470,000 troops, were still being
beefed up by new draftees. Overage and unfit officers identified by lackluster performance were being replaced when possible by comers rising in
the revitalized military. From Washington, General George C. Marshall
would purge thirty-one of forty-two corps and division commanders.

Overseeing much of the revamping for the Third Army "Blues"—the
"Reds" who had "lost" the sham war were Ben Lear's Second Army—was
Eisenhower. He appeared to have overshadowed his boss, Lieutenant
General Walter Krueger. Outgoing and accessible to the new breed of reporters covering the maneuvers, "Ike" not only offered good copy, but
good bourbon hard to find in a South where many counties—even entire
states—were legally dry.

Still in Depression mode, and stubbornly isolationist, Congress remained wary about funding the national defense. As late as that Septem-

ber, the widely read Walter Lippmann, a leading policy guru anxious about the escalating military budget, had published a column in the *New York Herald Tribune*, "The Case for a Smaller Army." Only on August 12, 1941, had President Franklin D. Roosevelt managed to persuade the House of Representatives to extend the first peacetime conscription bill (of September 16, 1940) by a single vote—after Chief of Staff George C. Marshall had gone to Capitol Hill to plead personally for it.

Congressional parsimony, the president told Admiral Ernest J. King, who was complaining about shortages in every kind of ship, left not enough butter to cover the bread. Troops in training were literally throwing eggs, and even rocks, to simulate grenades, and using firecrackers, when available, to hoard the live ammunition husbanded for a future battlefield. Eisenhower's tanks had often been trucks with signboards reading "tank." Many rifles had been sawed-off broomsticks. It had been tough fighting even a facsimile war so short on reality. Brigadier General George S. Patton's authentic "Blue" tanks (his armored division was "Red" in the first phase) often had to be refueled from roadside stations, the gas paid for out of Patton's well-padded wallet, as were replacement bolts he purchased from Sears, Roebuck.

Eisenhower had left instructions not to awaken him. When he sensed an aide hovering over him nonetheless, he quickly understood. He had expected war somewhere, and soon, but he had guessed wrong about where it would begin. Now war was breaking out everywhere in the Pacific, it seemed, from Hawaii westward across the International Date Line to the Philippines, where he had put in time in the 1930s, under Douglas MacArthur. The early reports withheld much bad news. It would take nearly a week before Eisenhower learned that the Japanese had crippled or sunk eight American battleships at their moorings in Pearl Harbor, and destroyed nearly five hundred aircraft on Oahu and on MacArthur's fiefdom of Luzon.

The formal American declaration of war on December 8 was followed by Nazi Germany's joining Japan on the 9th and the equivalent response of Congress on the 10th. General Marshall ordered Colonel Charles W. Bundy, War Plans Division deputy for Pacific operations, to Hawaii to survey the ruins. Bundy had reviewed the responses from commanders in the Pacific area to Marshall's cabled "war warning" of November 27, which had been taken too lightly from Honolulu to Manila. Flying with Bundy was Major General Herbert A. Dargue of the Army Air Forces, who had been posted to Oahu to replace Major General Walter C. Short, Marshall's appointee now tarnished by the failure in preparedness. In stormy weather their plane crashed into a peak in the Sierras. Marshall urgently needed a replacement in Washington for Bundy.*

Although only crucial calls were being put through to Eisenhower, on the 12th his office telephone rang insistently. He had 240,000 Third Army troops to oversee, spread out before maneuvers from New Mexico to Florida. Many were very raw. Before conscription began in 1940, only 174,000 men were in khaki, nineteenth among armies and just ahead of Bulgaria. (Another 200,000 were in the half-strength and undertrained National Guard.) But the nation was now at war across the world.

Until that second Sunday of the war, Eisenhower's task was to organize, into some level of readiness, Third Army units whose leaves and weekend passes had suddenly been canceled. They were unlikely to remain where they were much longer. Nor would Eisenhower. On the line was Colonel Walter Bedell Smith in Washington, secretary of the General Staff. "Is that you, Ike? The Chief [of Staff] says for you to hop a plane and get up here right away. Tell your boss that formal orders will come through later." Eisenhower hurriedly packed and boarded a train for Washington.

Earlier, George Marshall had turned for advice to an aide whom he had skipped from lieutenant colonel directly to brigadier general, bypassing a colonel's eagle. The lanky Mark Wayne Clark would lay out the Louisiana maneuvers. "I wish you would give me," Marshall asked, "a list of ten names of officers you know pretty well, and whom you would recommend to be the head of the Operations Division." Marshall kept a little black book of names for staffing the expanding army, and, before Louisiana, had met Eisenhower for the first time in years when Ike was in Washington in September 1938, on a mission for MacArthur to secure equipment for the frail Philippine army. Clever and ambitious, Clark had been Eisenhower's junior at West Point, and seemed to be going places.

"If you have to have ten names," said Clark, writing just one into his notepad, "I'll just put nine ditto marks below." His only recommendation—"Ike Eisenhower." Since his name kept coming up, Marshall soon asked to be taken to see Colonel Eisenhower—as he then was. The Louisiana maneuvers had begun, and it took a flight to Shreveport, and a two-hour drive to Lake Charles. There, on the second floor of a bank building which had not needed all its space since the Depression, Eisenhower temporarily occupied a room with a desk and a few chairs. On

---

*Air Forces Lieutenant General Delos C. Emmons, already in California, flew out to relieve Short on December 17.

the wall a large map of the exercise in progress was tacked, and the colonel reviewed for Marshall confidently what was supposed to happen when the Third Army "attacked" Lieutenant General Lear's Second Army.

Inevitably, not everything would work as smoothly as planned. Returning, Marshall fielded gripes that the maneuvers seemed a waste of scarce resources. "My God, Senator," Marshall told a budget-minded critic, "that's the reason I do it. I want the mistakes down in Louisiana, not over in Europe." American troops, he felt sure, would soon be at war across the Atlantic.

The briefing over, Marshall was returned to the airfield in Shreveport and flown back to Washington, where Major General Lesley J. McNair, the army's director of training, and umpire for the Louisiana games, had offered him evaluations of potential division commanders for the chief's black book. At the bottom of McNair's list of seven, but nevertheless on it, had been Eisenhower. A desk officer who had never commanded more than a battalion, he had been a balding lieutenant colonel nearly fifty when Roosevelt had jumped Marshall, with only one rather new star, over more senior generals for the top job. Having taken his own measure of Eisenhower, whom he had already approved, early in October, for his first star, Marshall ignored McNair's tepid rating.

In the June before Pearl Harbor, General Krueger had appealed to Washington for a new chief of staff for his Third Army, requesting a younger second-in-command than his retiring incumbent. He wanted someone "possessing broad vision, progressive ideas, a thorough grasp of the magnitude of the problems involved in handling an Army, and lots of initiative and resourcefulness. Lieutenant Colonel* Dwight D. Eisenhower, Infantry, is such a man. . . ." Marshall needed, wholesale, the caliber of leadership Krueger had described. Also, the obsolete between-the-wars subdivisions such as cavalry and coast artillery were being eliminated, and the new army reorganized into Ground Forces, Air Forces, and Service Forces. As Marshall liaised with Congress with his characteristic apolitical restraint that disarmed opposition, he overrode old-line generals who complained about "Soviet" tactics, for which his chief deputy, Major General Joseph T. McNarney, was often blamed. "Marshall," an associate cracked, "is the most accomplished actor in the Army. Everyone thinks MacArthur is, but he's not. The difference be-

---

*Krueger did not know that Eisenhower, then at Fort Lewis, Washington, had been promoted to colonel on March 6, three months earlier.

tween them is that you always *know* MacArthur is acting." But Marshall's probity was not a performance, and that was its strength.

When the "democratic" army burgeoned under the peacetime draft, prospects brightened for Eisenhower. Relieved to be out of MacArthur's suffocating grasp, he had written to Major General Kenyon Joyce of IX Corps in July 1941 that the "Philippine situation," already a remote memory, was puzzling. "That may be the place where the shooting starts [for the U.S.]; but even so, I don't see how it can ever be anything but a secondary theater." At war only a month, the Russians seemed to be succumbing to the Germans. Britain could again be alone opposite a burgeoning Nazi continental empire.

Busy preparing for maneuvers at Camp Polk, Louisiana, at the time, Eisenhower learned about Roosevelt's reactivating MacArthur and federalizing the unready Philippine army. The general would not cable for Ike, which he feared could happen. "I'm happy that the 'Field Marshal' didn't recall my name," Eisenhower wrote soon after to Wade ("Ham") Haislip, an old friend who was a new brigadier general and a deputy to Marshall. To a more senior general from Ike's own days at the War Department, he wrote more sourly that MacArthur must be congratulating himself on his comeback. "He had largely exhausted the possibilities of his former position but he has clearly landed, once again, on his feet!"

The assignment to Krueger had looked like the route to the division command Ike had wanted. Now Eisenhower had something potentially bigger as he headed overnight to Union Station. He was in Washington early on the 14th, the Sunday after Pearl Harbor. On the train he had encountered Sid Richardson, a Texas oil baron and stockman who would later become a close friend, and after the war would stock Eisenhower's freezers with hundreds of pounds of Texas beef, sausage, and hams. (Ike would develop a soft spot for multimillionaires, who seemed beyond greed and could offer objective advice on nearly anything.) Eisenhower could tell Richardson nothing about his mission, not knowing anything himself.

Wary that he was only being summoned temporarily for his Philippines background, he had told Mamie, who had seen him off, "I'll be back in a few days." When she predicted otherwise, he said, "That would just be my luck to sit out this war too!" Armistice Day 1918 had arrived when he was at Camp Colt, on the edge of the old Gettysburg battlefield, awaiting orders to Camp Dix, New Jersey, en route to command a tank unit in France.

Although he arrived on a weekend, Union Station was busier than Eisenhower had ever seen it, echoing with loudspeaker summonses and swarming with uniforms. His younger brother Milton, who worked for the Department of Agriculture and stood out in his civilian clothes and soft hat, met Ike and expected to drive back home to Falls Church, across the Potomac. Ike insisted on going directly to the War Department. Sundays were no longer somnolent in Washington, and the low, stucco, Old Munitions Building at 19th and Constitution Avenue, a "temporary" structure from 1917 where the War Department operated behind a deceptively modern glass facade, was now astir day and night, every day.

The similar Navy Building was linked by a second-floor overpass. To Admiral Harold ("Betty") Stark, whose tenure as chief of naval operations was about to be terminated, Marshall observed that the nonstop workweeks reminded him of his early days as an all-purpose lieutenant on Mindoro in the Philippines in 1902, where he was in effect, at twenty-two, the military governor of an isolated island the size of Connecticut. A communications boat arrived at the island every four months, and his troops labored all day long every day, whatever the weather—which was usually rain. "There was no town, no diversion, pretty much no nothing," Marshall recalled, "but always they would be singing a song as they came in at night, which had one refrain, 'Every day will be Sunday, Bye and Bye.' Now-a-days, Sundays are like Mondays and every other day in the week."

Marshall had been in his office for hours. He was aware that Winston Churchill had sailed under blackout that day, with his chief military and logistical advisers, for Hampton Roads, Virginia, on the new battleship *Duke of York* to confer with President Roosevelt. It would be a voyage of a week or more over rough seas. Marshall realized that operations had to be in the works at the War Department before decisions materialized in the White House that were more political than practical. On board the *Duke of York* the prime minister was preparing three position papers for discussion in Washington, "The Atlantic Front," "The Pacific Front," and, less confidently, "The Campaign of 1943" to retake occupied Europe. Failing thus far in fighting the Nazis, and now losing swaths of colonial territory to the Japanese—"hanging by our eyelids," as Sir Alan Brooke, chief of the Imperial General Staff, would put it—the British were coming as supplicants. Still, Churchill's legendary persuasiveness could be overwhelming.

The first time that Marshall had seen Churchill was when the service chiefs accompanied Roosevelt on the cruiser *Augusta* in early August to a conference with their British counterparts at Argentia Bay, off Newfoundland. To ensure secrecy, since the United States was not at war, the president did not tell his entourage where they were going until they were shipboard, and Marshall could not even inform Henry Stimson, secretary of war since 1940, or adequately prepare for staff talks. Roosevelt's seemingly careless management style was often a burden to Marshall, who stonily concealed his irritation.

On Sunday morning, December 7, somewhat later than usual, Marshall had been on horseback on his weekend therapeutic routine prior to leaving rambling, porch-fronted Quarters One at Fort Myer, Virginia. Although he had been ill, Marshall had been working his usual long days. Riding alone on a sorrel ironically named Prepared, with Fleet, his Dalmatian, following, he kept "a pretty lively gait" on the bridle paths around what remained of the experimental farms on the Virginia side of the Memorial Bridge. Just downstream from the National Airport, then under construction on land once part of the farms, the colossus of the Pentagon was beginning to rise.* For Marshall the hour had been a crisp interlude free from telephones and telegrams.

Returning at 10:15, he learned from Katherine about frantic messages from his office. The emergency could not be described. A car was coming for him.

At the State Department, Secretaries Cordell Hull, Henry Stimson, and Frank Knox had already been conferring without waiting for Marshall. They had learned of the open burning of papers at the Japanese embassy on Massachusetts Avenue, and from the covert breaking of the Japanese diplomatic code, of a planned severance of relations. War seemed imminent. All were to meet at the White House with the president at 3:00 P.M. Stimson's minutes noted, "Hull is very certain that the Japs are planning some deviltry and we are all wondering where the blow will strike. . . . We all thought that we must fight if the British fought." A substantial Japanese fleet, convoying apparent troop transports, had been spotted by a British Hudson bomber in the South China Sea, plowing, it seemed, toward Malaya. Furthermore, Japanese envoys in Washington who had dragged out their bargaining on keeping the peace had requested an extraordinary Sunday afternoon meeting with Hull, specifying one o'clock.

Much like everyone else in the government, Marshall had misread

---

*Groundbreaking had taken place on September 11, 1941. Colonel Leslie R. Groves, the engineer officer supervising construction, would shortly be placed in charge of the "Manhattan Engineering District," the vast coast-to-coast project to devise atomic bombs.

the signs by misjudging Japanese audacity. His staff knew from decrypts that Tokyo had ordered an assistant consul in Honolulu (surely a spy) to maintain a chart of what ships were berthed where, and which came and left. The data obtained from peacetime tourist flights over Pearl Harbor seemed intended for the Imperial Japanese Navy—perhaps to identify warships ordered to sea. After all, Oahu was too far from Japan for a strike force not to be observed somewhere en route. Besides, the navy occasionally staged maneuvers interdicting a mock carrier armada off Hawaii.

Logically, war would have to originate elsewhere, most likely against the Philippines, the focus of contingency plans "Orange" and "Rainbow." Pearl Harbor, Marshall had assured the president from navy advice, was an unlikely target. Response would be rapid. "Enemy carriers, naval escorts, and transports will begin to come under air attack at a distance of approximately 750 miles. This attack will increase in intensity until within 200 miles of the objective, the enemy will be subjected to all types of bombardment closely supported by our most modern pursuit [planes]."

Despite Marshall's confidence, based on empty assurances from area commanders, reconnaissance by air and by sea was meager, and patrol activity at Pearl Harbor itself was minimal. It was a Sunday morning. The usual on-deck religious services were being readied. Many men were on weekend shore leave. The worries were only in Washington.

Not waiting for the War Department staff car, and with an orderly with him at Fort Myer, Sergeant John Semanko, at the wheel, Marshall rushed in his stepson's red roadster through quiet Arlington National Cemetery toward the nearly empty Memorial Bridge. At the approaches they waved down the official khaki sedan driven by his primary aide, Master Sergeant James W. Powder, speeding across the Potomac in the other direction. Both jammed their brakes. Marshall transferred vehicles, and Powder made a U-turn and accelerated past the Lincoln Memorial toward the Munitions Building.

Marshall's staff assumed that whatever action was to be taken was a bureaucratic matter of service jurisdiction, base by base. The Philippines belonged to General MacArthur. The navy ran such Pacific islands and atolls as Guam, Wake, and Midway. The army had fought the navy for years for overseeing the defense of Hawaii, and had prevailed. Major General Walter C. Short, highly regarded in Washington, was well aware of his principal role but radar was primitive and, at his orders, to save fuel and wear-and-tear on scarce new planes, routine air reconnaissance hardly existed, especially on weekends. Nor was the navy flying much. Neither Marshall nor anyone else in Washington knew that a Japanese carrier strike force on an unusual path from the home islands had already lofted reconnaissance float planes toward Oahu and Maui, and that Short's primary concern for Sunday morning was a golf date at eight with his navy equivalent, Vice Admiral Husband E. Kimmel. It was already nearly dawn in Hawaii, five-and-a-half hours earlier by contemporary time zones. Across the International Date Line on Luzon, where MacArthur had largely dismissed past warnings, it was just after midnight on the 8th, and he was asleep.

Marshall scrawled an updated warning to commands in the Pacific that the Japanese had asked for an unusual meeting with State at one: "Just what significance the hour set may have we do not know but be on alert accordingly." He telephoned his nautical counterpart, Admiral Stark, to ask whether his commanders should also be notified. Stark first demurred, then called back to have Marshall postscript, "Inform naval authorities of this communication." Stark even offered radio facilities in the adjacent Navy Building, but Marshall preferred his own channels. Little coordination existed between the War and Navy departments, often rivals for funding and for influence at the White House and on Capitol Hill.

Brigadier General Leonard Gerow and Colonel Bundy, with Marshall, agreed that some hostile action against an American installation was possible at or about one in their time zone, and Gerow suggested that the Philippines should have message priority. Intelligence chief Sherman Miles thought that all recipients would understand the need to "translate it into their own time." It was 11:58 at the War Department Signals Center when Marshall's message was delivered for transmission. Forty minutes was the estimated time for all commands to have it—certainly before one o'clock in Washington. On the Japanese carriers, as darkness began to lift, dive bombers and torpedo planes were being readied for takeoff.

Ignoring Gerow's priorities, the Signals staff obtusely (but alphabetically) sent the first alert to the Canal Zone. The message to Manila went off at 12:06. No one thought of using the scrambler telephone, a new device of uncertain security—yet to be much employed several hours later. As atmospheric conditions since 10:30 A.M. in Washington had made radio traffic to Hawaii unstable, the message to Fort Shafter—army authorities could then warn navy personnel at Pearl Harbor—was sent by commercial Western Union teletype to San Francisco, and by RCA Radio from there to Hawaii. The warning was clocked out at 12:17—then 6:47 A.M. in Honolulu.

In Pearl Harbor, the destroyer *Ward*, on routine patrol, had just spotted what appeared to be the conning tower of a submarine that should not have been there. A depth charge was deployed, and the incident reported, but the episode was scoffed at onshore as "another of those false reports." It was already 7:12. The planes from *Kido Butai*—"Strike Force"—were in the air and would make landfall at 7:48. There would be no golf that Sunday morning for Kimmel and Short. Marshall's alerts would fail.

Like Eisenhower, MacArthur had also been awakened by telephone with the news from Hawaii. Just before 3:00 A.M. Manila time on Monday the 8th—two in the afternoon Washington time on the 7th yet only 8:30 A.M. that morning in Honolulu—Pacific Fleet commander Vice Admiral Thomas Hart had received a message, "AIR RAID ON PEARL HARBOR. THIS IS NO DRILL." With that, concerns about scrambler telephones had vanished. Hart sent his second-in-command, Rear Admiral William Purnell, in the darkness across tree-lined Dewey Boulevard from the Manila Hotel to the army headquarters at Calle Victoria in Intramuros, the old Spanish walled city, to alert Richard Sutherland and Richard Marshall, MacArthur's chief of staff and his deputy. Rather than awaken MacArthur, who had a posh penthouse atop the hotel, Purnell was going through channels as if no emergency existed and nothing would happen before daylight.

Sutherland and Marshall sat up in their beds in shock and took in the news. Assured that the message was authentic—Hart's duty navy radioman had recognized the "fist" (the sending technique) of his counterpart in Hawaii—Sutherland reached for his telephone and the private line to MacArthur's quarters. "Pearl Harbor! Pearl Harbor!" MacArthur repeated sleepily. "It should be our strongest point!" Sutherland clicked off, then telephoned MacArthur's air chief, Brigadier General Lewis Brereton. His aide, Lieutenant Colonel Charles Caldwell, answered on an extension but the ringing had already awakened Brereton. "General, Pearl Harbor has been bombed," explained Caldwell. "Sutherland is on the phone and wants to talk to you." It was a brief call. Sutherland knew little else but that the information was genuine.

While hastily dressing, the groggy Brereton shouted to Caldwell that all air units were to be notified and ready for action. It was still dark. He expected attacks any time after sunrise. He and many of his men had barely made it to bed. It had been a long and less than sober Sunday night of partying with pretty Filipinas under the pillars and palms at the Manila Hotel. A ladies' man who worked hard but also played hard, Brereton generated so much gossip in a later assignment that he earned a written rebuke from Marshall.

Brereton was surprised that war hadn't come sooner. Purnell had told him earlier that Hart had received an advisory from Marshall and Stark in Washington, dated November 27, that attacks from the Japanese might come any moment. It began, urgently, "This is a war warning." The same message had gone to MacArthur. Brereton expected bombs to fall that weekend, the 29th or 30th, because the last Saturday in November in the States—a Sunday in Manila—was the date of the traditional Army-Navy football game. Even the Japanese knew that officers in faraway places gathered at their service clubs then to listen, drinks in hand, to teletyped or radioed reports of the action—hours of minimal alertness. Still, nothing—then—had happened. But a week after Marshall's alert, to document a resolve that papered over the realities, MacArthur on December 3 ordered commanders in the field to hold the beaches wherever the enemy might land, and on December 5, after reports of radar tracking of obvious overflights, to shoot down any intruder sighted. No beach would be defended, and no aircraft were targeted.

On the Sunday after Pearl Harbor, Marshall's office door was open when Eisenhower arrived. He saluted formally and was waved to a chair. Having already spent some frustrating years at desks in Washington, and, realizing that careers usually depended upon combat commands, he had hoped not to be back. He knew little, personally, of the aloof, ramrod-erect Marshall. Eisenhower had first encountered him early in 1930, when as a former member of the Battle Monuments Commission in Washington under General John J. Pershing, Major Eisenhower reviewed two chapters of the general's war memoirs dealing with St.-Mihiel and the Meuse-Argonne. Since Pershing was no stylist, Eisenhower promptly drafted rewrites. Pershing showed them to Lieutenant Colonel Marshall, who was in the city on business from the Infantry School at Fort Benning, Georgia, and Marshall dropped in at Eisenhower's tiny War Department office to discuss the revisions.

Eisenhower's former mentor, Major General Fox Conner, under whom he had served in Panama, had lauded Marshall, an operations prodigy in France in 1918, as the coming man in the army—"close to being a genius." Conner's highest praise for Ike had been that something was "exactly the way that Marshall would handle it." Yet Marshall didn't appear, then, to be going anywhere. The seniority system was ingrained, and the backlog daunting.

Marshall declined to sit down. Standing, to Eisenhower's discomfort, throughout their conversation, largely one-way, he explained that while he appreciated Eisenhower's alternatives, they would be inconsistent with the diary format of the book. Further, the diary mode, whatever Pershing's after-the-fact additions, appeared less judgmental than a narrative that was more obviously postwar.

Eisenhower knew better than to argue. The diary approach notwithstanding, Pershing had vented his postwar indignation against perceived rivals, and was not about to change his tone after ten years of ponderous writing. In 1931 his book would win the Pulitzer Prize, less for its content than for its author, the aging icon of the American Expeditionary Force in France.

Impressed by Eisenhower despite their differences, Marshall on returning to Fort Benning sent an offer of a teaching post. Eisenhower, Marshall knew, had been first in his class at Fort Leavenworth's Command and General Staff School. If he went to Benning, Eisenhower realized, he would be commanding a classroom, which didn't seem career-wise. Mired in his major's rank for a decade, he hoped that the new assignment in the War Department, despite his petty title of "principal assistant to the assistant deputy chief of staff," would lead to something more. It was his immediate superior in the Department, the energetic, ultraconservative Brigadier General George Van Horn Moseley, another Pershing staffer in 1918, who had recommended Eisenhower to "Black Jack."

Under Moseley, Eisenhower's principal task was to develop an Industrial Mobilization Plan for the army. Postwar indifference about military planning in the 1920s White House had led Wall Street financier Bernard Baruch, who headed the War Industries Board in 1917–18, to push for a War Department preparedness agenda that could be regularly updated, even if unfunded. In 1927 Major Eisenhower had written an industrial planning paper while at the Army War College. It brought him to Moseley's attention. Stuck in the hidebound army with his single star, Moseley had been G-4 (supply chief) of Pershing's AEF. Thereafter he had war production on his mind, but in good times, and now bad, the army budget remained starved. Yet if war came, industry would have to be ready for reconversion.

For Moseley, Eisenhower would research potential suppliers across the country, and with West Point classmate Wade Haislip and Leavenworth classmate Leonard Gerow he prepared (it was largely Eisenhower's draft) a mobilization plan to be revisited through the 1930s. Less than helpful was the retiring chief of staff, the Mesozoic Charles P. Summerall. His undistinguished term ended in 1930. President Hoover's choice to replace Summerall was the magnetic, youngish Douglas MacArthur, who had an authentic combat record, with rows of medal ribbons.

Rather than improving prospects for a command, Eisenhower's staff work* and glib pen led to his laboring for MacArthur in Washington and afterward in the Philippines. Now, in Washington again a decade later, Eisenhower discovered that MacArthur was still dominating his life—although with a vast difference. Pearl Harbor had intervened. The general was nine thousand miles away, and despite his confident pose, soon presiding over a débacle.

Marshall put down one of his many pairs of Woolworth reading glasses which Sergeant Powder purchased for him in bulk and were regularly mislaid, and quickly summed up the calamitous Pacific news Ike had missed while on the train, as well as what he would not have learned in Texas. Although damage assessments rumbled through Congress, the disasters were far worse than reported in the press. Even anti-Roosevelt cranks like Robert R. McCormick of the *Chicago Tribune* withheld the grim statistics—that eight battleships had been sunk or crippled, that air strength on Oahu was effectively wiped out, and that but for two carriers away at sea, the fleet was ravaged. While the worst was being kept from the American public, the Japanese surely knew their successes from their aerial photos. Eisenhower was shocked.

Solutions of every sort were lacking. Hardly two years before, Eisenhower had only been MacArthur's deskbound and exploited aide. Now, operational responsibility for East Asia and the Pacific was, immediately, to be his—MacArthur included. Mamie was right.

Oahu and Luzon, Eisenhower was briefed, were both worse, militarily, than a shambles. If the Japanese wanted to return and finish the job in both places, they very likely could. After Secretary of the Navy Frank Knox's flying inspection trip to Hawaii, Roosevelt told him to get Admiral Chester W. Nimitz "the hell out to Pearl and [to] stay there 'til the war

---

*In the mid-1960s, Eisenhower recalled that however frustrating the work was, it "gave me an early look at the military-industrial complex of whose pressures I would later warn. Except at that point the pressures were exactly reversed."

is won." Nimitz's wife gushed, "You always wanted to command the Pacific Fleet. You always thought that would be the height of glory."

"Darling," said Nimitz, "the fleet's at the bottom of the sea. Nobody must know that here, but I've got to tell you."

At the same time, Earl Warren, then attorney general of California, went urgently to see Vice Admiral John Greenslade, commander of the Western Sea Frontier, whose office nearby was in the Federal Building in Sacramento. Did he know of the sinkings of two tankers just offshore? "Confidentially," he told Warren, "I have only two destroyers between here and Vancouver, British Columbia. All the rest of the fleet that was not sunk at Pearl Harbor has gone out into the Pacific."

Published accounts were so remote from the facts that the *New York Times* in its first paragraph about Pearl Harbor on Monday morning December 8 reported that the Japanese had attacked with four-engine bombers, which they did not possess, and, had they existed, could not have flown from carriers. Only the battleship *Oklahoma* was acknowledged as sunk, but "two other ships" had been "attacked." Casualties were "of unstated number."

The Philippines, within bomber range of enemy bases, now seemed indefensible, even more acutely so than before. Running supplies or men to the islands by air or by sea appeared impossible. A Japanese advance party had already landed far to the north on Luzon, and set up an airfield. Nevertheless, Marshall had radioed MacArthur tersely and more hopefully than the facts warranted just before he had sent for Eisenhower: "The resolute and effective fighting of you and your men air and ground has made a tremendous impression on the American people and confirms our confidence in your leadership. We are making every effort to reach you with air replacements and reinforcements as well as other troops and supplies." Marshall had little idea then that his lavish praise was almost entirely for the effectiveness of MacArthur's publicity apparatus. Wavering between absurd optimism about fighting off the Japanese, and desperation about the future, MacArthur had accomplished little beyond losing the best resources he had.

Although MacArthur had always claimed confidence in his troops, Eisenhower knew from experience there that they were inadequate in every way, and had been poorly equipped during the bleak 1930s. But MacArthur claimed that geography was on his side, assuring Vice Admiral Thomas Hart, whose thin Asiatic Fleet hardly deserved the designation, "My greatest security lies in the inability of our enemy to launch his air attack[s] on our islands." Marshall had seen time on his side (if any time existed), telling Admiral Harold Stark, his Washington counterpart, that more heavy bombers based in the Philippines might inhibit Japan from the "Malaysian thing."

"What should be our general course of action?" Marshall now asked Eisenhower bluntly. Although MacArthur had predicted no attack before spring, time had already run out. What little of the realities now known from Manila was all bad, however masked by MacArthurese rhetoric. Surprised by the open-ended charge, Eisenhower, still standing at Marshall's desk, asked for time to prepare some responses. "All right," said Marshall—and turned to the next bulletins from the brimming wire basket on his desk. He was not given to small talk. He had barely mentioned the death of Bundy. Eisenhower understood that he had been dismissed.

Files of contingency scenarios to respond to a Japanese attack had been prepared and updated, but only late in 1941 did Marshall order a "Victory Plan" to confront a Germany in control of the European continent and North Africa and targeting the United States. In charge of drawing it up was an ambitious major on Marshall's staff, Albert C. Wedemeyer, who had studied at the German war college in Berlin under Hitler's favorite, General Alfred Jodl, and knew outspoken America Firster Charles Lindbergh, whom he had met in Germany. Wedemeyer was the son-in-law of a former deputy chief of staff, Major General Stanley Embick. Like Embick, he was an admirer of German military expertise, and when the "Victory Plan" was leaked by isolationist senator Burton Wheeler of Montana to the isolationist *Chicago Tribune* and *Washington Times-Herald*, with headlines on December 4 charging President Roosevelt with having created "a blueprint for total war," suspicion fell on Wedemeyer. Investigating, the FBI found in his safe a copy of the top-secret plan with passages underlined in red that had also appeared in the press. His underlining, Wedemeyer claimed, had been to compare his text with the press account.

No one was ever charged with supplying the document to Wheeler, who had been a key opponent earlier in 1941 of legislation to supply aircraft and warships and vehicles to Britain as "Lend-Lease" armament. Marshall had gone to Congress to urge the passage of the symbolically numbered bill HR-1776, "An Act to Promote the Defense of the United States." Wheeler likened it sardonically to New Deal farm-subsidy legislation, in that it would "plow under every fourth American boy." Despite passage, American war industry was so unready to assist Britain, and soon Russia, that Lend-Lease, even under the tireless Harry Hopkins, would supply relatively little before Pearl Harbor.

Marshall believed utterly and perhaps naïvely in the loyalty of his staff and had Wedemeyer carry on. "I would have died for him after that," said Wedemeyer. He would rise to high command during the war, but Marshall would not assign Wedemeyer to any position confronting Germans.

A Harry Hopkins memo written on December 7 between two and three in the afternoon Washington time—the attacks on Pearl Harbor and airfields on Oahu were still ongoing—reads, cryptically, "MacArthur ordered 'execute.'" For Hopkins, Roosevelt's closest aide, who then lived in the White House like family, that meant that "Rainbow 5"—the plans for repelling a Japanese attack in the Pacific—were in effect. Marshall's radio message 736 explicitly invoking "Rainbow 5" would close hopefully but unrealistically, "You have the complete confidence of the War Department and we assure you of every possible assistance and support within our power." Yet hours would elapse before MacArthur, commander of American ground and air forces in the Philippines and field marshal of the Philippine army, executed anything.

In his Manila Hotel penthouse the bedside phone rang again. This time it was Brigadier General Leonard Gerow in Washington, once a Philippines subordinate of MacArthur and as "Gee" an old friend of Eisenhower. Marshall had been planning to reassign him from a desk to a division command, but emergencies had intervened, and Gerow was still telephoning for his chief. It was 3:40 in the Philippines, well before dawn on Monday. Ships, planes, and installations in Hawaii, he conceded to MacArthur, had suffered "considerable damage." The attack was still in progress and, Gerow warned, "I wouldn't be surprised if you get an attack there in the near future."

Stunned and seemingly confused in the predawn gloom, MacArthur asked his wife, Jean, to bring him his Bible. While the command staff was gathering in Intramuros awaiting orders, MacArthur sat on the edge of his bed, turning its pages. (Although not a churchgoer, it was his practice to read from the Scriptures for ten minutes each morning.) Finally he dressed, took the elevator six floors down, and crossed Dewey Boulevard to his office.

Soon after receiving Marshall's "war warning" the week before—it had then been November 28, Manila time—MacArthur had radioed back undismayed, and Marshall returned, "The Secretary of War and I were highly pleased to receive your report that your command is ready for any eventuality." Yet many of the mines laid in Manila Bay to repel intruders were so defective that no provocation could explode them, and the obsolete torpedoes arming Admiral Hart's few submarines would at best bump a target without going off. Antiaircraft guns in the Philippines were three-inch weapons capable only of interdicting low-flying early-1930s biplanes; the coast artillery was of Great War vintage; and the huge mortars hidden in Corregidor's hollows which gave the tadpole-shaped island protecting the bay a reputation for impregnability were embossed, if one looked closely, with an identity of manufacturer and date which made one less sanguine about the fortress's chances: Bethlehem Steel, 1898.

MacArthur's 50,000 Filipino troops and "Scouts" had few effective weapons and even fewer had real training beyond show parades. His American dimension of 20,000, whatever their ranks, were used to soft duty and servants, and led by some bright new officers, some few seniors with wartime experience in France, too many aging colonels whom Washington wanted to put at a distance, and MacArthur's contingent of adoring and protective toadies. In September MacArthur had rejected Marshall's offer to send an additional infantry division of 18,000 men, declaring that he didn't consider such numbers "necessary for defense purposes." (Realistically, he preferred to better equip his Philippines army.) MacArthur's air force included a squadron of recent P-40s that were no match for the faster and better-armed Zero, and obsolete P-36s and B-18s that were flying coffins. But he also had thirty-five B-17 heavy bombers, the strongest air capability the army had anywhere. Twenty more were en route, as well as fifty-two unassembled A-24 dive bombers and more P-40s coming on shipboard. Marshall had planned to increase B-17 "Flying Fortress" strength in the Philippines to 165 by spring 1942.

Had was the appropriate word. Despite nine hours' warning, half of the existing B-17 strength (the others had been flown south to Mindanao) was on the ground at Clark Field, north of Manila, when fifty-four Japanese Mitsubishi bombers from Formosa, in two V-formations, plunged down from 18,000 feet and ruined the crews' lunch hour and the Flying Fortresses. Zero fighters with 20 mm cannon followed, strafing the remaining aircraft and downing most of the few P-40s that managed to get airborne.

General Brereton had reported to Calle Victoria at 5:00 A.M. and (according to his published diary)* asked for authorization to have his B-17s

---

The Brereton Diaries have been called by some MacArthur biographers unreliable and even mendacious. They are corroborated only in part by official records, some lost. Brereton cannot be absolved of at least some of the blame for the way his planes were mishandled.

attack Japanese airbases on Formosa (Taiwan), from which raids could be expected. He would then follow up with the remaining Flying Fortresses, to be deployed northward from Del Monte Field in Mindanao. Sutherland told him to proceed with all preparations short of loading bombs, for which permission had to come from MacArthur. Earlier, even before the Iba Field radar screen showed incoming blips at 8:00 A.M., General H. H. ("Hap") Arnold, air force chief, had telephoned Intramuros to warn about dispersal of aircraft. The thirty-six operational P-40s at Clark Field scrambled to intercept whatever was approaching, and all B-17s there were ordered into the air.

When airmen found nothing and settled down again on the tarmac, the B-17s again had to be refueled for Formosa. There had been plenty of warnings—and sightings. From the highlands city of Baguio, where officials escaped the heat of Manila, President Manuel Quezon and his daughter Zenaida were watching, with satisfaction, seventeen silvery twin-engine bombers just overhead. Certainly they were American. He was on the telephone to his deputy, Jorge Vargas, when explosions erupted. "Jorge," Quezon shouted over the din, "tell General MacArthur that Camp John Hay has been bombed! And call the Council of State for a meeting tomorrow at nine!"

Five minutes earlier, Leonard Gerow had telephoned again to Intramuros at Marshall's instructions, asking about "any indications of attack." He wanted no repetition of Pearl Harbor, where the second wave of Japanese torpedo planes and dive bombers had left three hours earlier and, but for negligible losses, were already decked on their unseen and unlocated carriers. In the Philippines, Davao and Aparri had already been bombed, and Batan Island off the Luzon north coast occupied, but MacArthur, now dressed and at headquarters, replied casually that radar had only picked up enemy planes offshore. "Tell George not to worry. Everything is going to be all right here. You tell George that there have been some [Japanese] planes flying around for a few hours. We are watching them. You don't have to worry about us. We'll be all right." He was confident all around, he emphasized. "Our tails are in the air."

In the streets of Manila and other Philippine cities and towns, crowds emerging from daily Mass or queuing to board streetcars and buses encountered newsboys with shocking extra editions of the morning papers. They shouted, mostly in Tagalog, at street corners, "*Binomba ang* Pearl Harbor!" the headline in *Mabuhay*. "Pearl Harbor attacked!" yelled the vendors of the English-language *Bulletin* and *Tribune*. Sent home from school, Antonio Quintos and his brother José, reaching Calle Victoria, saw two American soldiers in the street. "They were crying like kids. We were too scared to cry." In the Intramuros headquarters itself, Simeon Medalla, an officer trainee, much later a colonel, recalled being assured that an American convoy with reinforcements and supplies was already en route. "MacArthur had promised, people told me, for it was a reassuring idea, that a seven-mile convoy of ships was en route with troops and tanks and guns and planes to turn the situation around. We waited three and a half years for those ships. Everybody believed that we would win, despite everything, in three or four months. People believed any optimistic statement attributed to MacArthur."

The convoy, sailing later than scheduled because of chronic inefficiency on the docks in Hawaii, and far smaller in size than the legends which grew up about it in the Philippines, would be typical of Eisenhower's first responsibilities. Escorted by the cruiser *Pensacola*, the seven slow transports carried nearly 5,000 troops, 52 A-24 bombers, 18 P-40s, 48 75mm guns, 340 motor vehicles, 600 tons of bombs, 9,000 drums of aviation fuel, and 3,500,000 rounds of ammunition. The ships had lumbered south from Honolulu on November 29. "Rainbow 5," updated on November 19, as MacArthur knew, had promised further resupply, but the Pacific had become, overnight, a Japanese pond. Washington radioed the *Pensacola* to reroute the convoy to Australia, from which efforts would be made to slip whatever was possible up through the myriad Philippine islands to Luzon.

Any assistance by sea, Marshall realized, had to come, if possible at all, via Australia, and any long-range bombers had to proceed via Africa, India, and Java, now a hazardous route. Still he buoyed up MacArthur unrealistically, perhaps because MacArthur had lied so persuasively about his readiness. Every few days more radioed promises would arrive in Manila. Another 160 dive bombers and fighters were being loaded aboard two fast transports. An additional fifteen heavy bombers had been ordered to the Philippines. Soon assurances arrived of eighty more B-17s and B-24s via India. From the fantasy world of early wartime Washington Marshall seemed less unconcerned than he should have been about the insecure supply links, ports, and airfields that in reality were nearly nonexistent. "The heavy bombers beginning to flow from this country via Africa to your theater should be able to support you materially even if compelled initially to operate from distant bases. They will be valuable also in cooperating with naval forces and smaller aircraft in protecting your line of communications. The great range, speed and power of these bombers should permit, under your direction, effective surprise concentrations against particularly favorable targets anywhere in the theater." From such messages MacArthur had every reason to assume that "Rainbow 5" was indeed working and that interdiction of enemy invasion forces was possible and even likely.

The more comprehensive "Rainbow" projections had succeeded "Orange," the much-revised 1930s blueprint for an amphibious defensive war that wrote off the Philippines, but envisioned a step-by-step return. It did not then seem absurd to envision a relief expeditionary force fighting its way to Manila Bay five thousand miles from Pearl Harbor across the Japanese-held island clusters of the central Pacific. To afford buildup time to recover the Philippines, American and local forces according to plan would have to hold Manila and its harbor for at least six months. No provision in "Rainbow" existed for an American battle fleet stationed off Manila. The navy considered the Philippines as indefensible and expendable.

The seventeen-page top-secret update commissioned by Marshall in July and delivered on September 25, 1941, emphasized the Third Reich rather than Japan as the likely primary enemy and forecast a two-ocean need for 216 infantry divisions, 51 motorized divisions, and a vastly expanded navy and air force. (Less than half that number would eventually materialize.) On the Pacific side, the plan authorized the Philippines command, if war came, "to conduct air raids against Japanese forces and installations within tactical operating radius of available bases." There was no other reason to have sent so many of the still-few heavy bombers across the Pacific, with more to come. Yet MacArthur vetoed any plans to strike at Formosa, and Brereton returned disconsolately to his own headquarters at Nielson Field, telling his staff that "we couldn't attack until we were attacked"—whatever that meant. Marshall's earlier war alert had advised that it was desirable to have the enemy commit the "first overt act," which had indeed happened at several locations on Luzon. MacArthur was pretending that none had occurred.

Although he made postwar claims that he knew "nothing of such a recommendation having been made" by Brereton, MacArthur, still in unconfessed shock, made no immediate decisions about anything, and developed an additional alibi that Japan had only attacked the United States, rather than the allegedly sovereign government of the Philippines—

which was not scheduled to be formally independent by congressional act until 1946. Although he was commanding general of American forces in the Philippines, which included all local soldiery, MacArthur was also field marshal and chief of the Philippine army. To postpone action he had donned, at least metaphorically, his gold-braided field marshal's hat to invoke an escape clause that was only imaginary.

The Air Forces summary for December 8, 1941, notes, despite MacArthur's demurrer, "07:15 General Brereton . . . requested permission of General MacArthur to take offensive action. He was informed that for the time being our role was defensive." The 09:00 log reports, "In response to query from General Brereton a message received from General Sutherland advising planes not authorized to carry bombs at this time." MacArthur continued to refuse permission until the B-17s were destroyed on the ground, after which he dismissed the bombers as "hardly more than a token force" which was "hopelessly outnumbered" and "never had a chance of winning." Further, MacArthur claimed later, despite his bravado to Washington, that he could not have made a fight of it before reinforcements expected by April 1, 1942, had arrived.

Such was the situation in which Marshall had put his new Pacific troubleshooter to work. A few hours later, having borrowed Gee Gerow's desk, the latest situation maps, and the file of messages to and from Manila since December 7, Eisenhower reappeared. On his lined yellow pad, headed "Assistance to the Far East. Steps to be Taken," he typed out, in triple space, his rationale that although the situation was close to hopeless, whatever token reinforcement of Philippine resistance was "humanly possible" should be taken. Summarizing his views, he conceded to Marshall that it would be impossible to "save the garrison . . . if the enemy commits major force to their reduction." A base of operations as close to the Philippines as could be established by sea and air had to be set up immediately, whatever the cost and the risk. This meant Australia, with Brisbane, high on the east coast, the best bet for ferrying planes, especially heavy bombers.

Eisenhower urged that the government "influence Russia to enter the war," an unrealistic bet. He also wanted a "fast merchant ship supply service" to Australia for "maintenance," presumably for supplies and spare parts. Nowhere in the document (or, apparently, in conversation) was MacArthur mentioned. "The people of China, of the Philippines, of the Dutch East Indies, will be watching us," Eisenhower exhorted his audience of one in a rhetorical lapse from terseness seldom to be repeated. "They may excuse failure but they will not excuse abandonment." In his diary he privately acknowledged that the Philippines "defied solution" but required hopeful tokens in the short term while tactical alternatives were worked out.

"Do your best to save them," said Marshall, implying full agreement and full authority.

"Eisenhower," Marshall added as his new deputy turned to leave, "the Department is filled with able men who analyze their problems but feel compelled to always bring them to me for final solution. I must have assistants who will solve their own problems and tell me later what they have done." No one could "do everything himself." In effect he was informing his new recruit to the corridors of power that he was impatient with the way that the War Plans Division was being run by Brigadier General Gerow, Eisenhower's oldest friend in the army. Eisenhower had to draw his own conclusions. When he drafted something for Marshall's signature, he would soon learn, the general would scrawl revisions—often cuts, for cogency—on everything he would hand back A staff assistant, Colonel William Sexton, remembered Eisenhower picking up and checking papers he had left with Marshall and discovering an unmarked one. As Ike closed the door, he let himself go with, "By God, I finally wrote one he didn't change!"

With his one star and the backing of his chief's four, he realized that he would be largely on his own to turn proposals into realities, and to determine his own future. "I resolved then and there," Eisenhower recalled decades later, "to do my work to the best of my ability and report to the General only situations of obvious necessity or when he personally sent for me." Anticipating Eisenhower's memorandum, the *Pensacola* and its seven transports would be only the first of many convoys bucketing to Brisbane.

Thirteen months later, from Brisbane, MacArthur would cable Marshall to ask that Walter Krueger be assigned to him to take on a command. Krueger flew to Australia with sixteen members of his Third Army headquarters staff. Had circumstances not caused Eisenhower's unexpected summons to Washington, he might have been back again under MacArthur.

2

Managing the Shop

A s EISENHOWER SETTLED IN at the refurbished World War I relic of the Old Munitions Building, he saw little daylight, literally or otherwise. In the long nights of late December (and into February) he returned to Milton's park-like home, "Tall Oaks" (Helen's family had money), well after dark. "Every night when I reached their house, regardless of the hour, which averaged something around midnight," Ike recalled, "both would be waiting up for me with a snack of midnight supper and a pot of coffee. I cannot remember ever seeing their house in daylight." Putting in sixteen-hour days, he was picked up in Falls Church by a staff car heading for the Potomac bridges before the winter sun arose. Barely visible in the wan light were billboards importuning, "WAR WORKERS NEED ROOMS, APARTMENTS, HOMES. REGISTER YOUR VACANCIES NOW." He, too, would need one when Mamie relocated from Texas.

"I've been insisting," he wrote in his diary, "[that the] Far East is critical, and no other sideshows should be undertaken until air and ground [forces] are in satisfactory state. Instead we're taking on Magnet, Gymnast, etc."* In the blur of necessities and shortcomings it was difficult to make good on Marshall's orders "to pay special attention to the Philippine Islands, Hawaii, Australia, Pacific islands, China." That the Pacific Rim would be a sideshow in a Europe-first war would soon alter his perspectives.

---

*Magnet: the stockpiling of American forces in the British Isles; Gymnast: an invasion of French North Africa to deflect the Germans from Suez and divert Nazi strength from the Russian front. Both would be renamed.

Although Eisenhower's priorities were to find ways to supply MacArthur, and to stir his old boss into action, neither effort brought tangible results. MacArthur at first seemed a gaudy success, at least from what his public relations deputy, Major LeGrande Diller, could embellish from his chief's daily handwritten communiques that imagined enemy battleships sunk, planes downed, invasion forces driven off, and battles won. Eisenhower bridled at such fictions reported as facts and published widely in the press. Marshall knew that nothing could be done about it. (Diller had been a promising student of his in 1927 in the Infantry School Company Officers Course at Fort Benning, but now brandished a typewriter and understood where his promotions would come from.) To some, like Diller, a godlike aura surrounded MacArthur, and it was the general's genius to be able to exploit adversity as much as success, appealing from afar to the conservatives in Congress whose votes the president could not do without.

Even before Eisenhower had arrived to oversee whatever meager assistance to the Philippines could be devised, the schizophrenic dimension of MacArthur's war was apparent in Marshall's offices. While calming fears in the face of imminent panic was useful, the realities of attack and failed response were visible in images of smoke and fire, and in reading between the lines of MacArthur's sanguine, radioed headquarters pronouncements. Just before eleven in the morning on December 8 in Manila, as aircraft still burned at Hickam Field and crippled warships were settling into the mud of Pearl Harbor, Diller telephoned the Associated Press offices, where silvery Mitsubishis on unhindered bombing runs could be seen from the windows, to report that the general had issued a message of "serenity and confidence" to the Philippine people, and to invite a representative to a press conference at Fort Santiago. Clark Lee raced off to represent the AP, driving into Intramuros through one of the archways in the thick stone walls.

At the end of the passageway was an open garage in which Lee saw MacArthur's gleaming black Cadillac with a red license plate on which shone the three stars of a lieutenant general. Behind it was a bomb shelter for army staff, with underground offices and a switchboard. In a small whitewashed room next to the garage, the newsmen met Major Diller, who explained that he had called them together to issue wartime press credentials. There was, as yet, no news. He did not know when MacArthur would furnish a statement, but they could return at four.

Reporters knew that there was plenty of news. They had heard the wail of air raid sirens, seen intruding enemy planes, and plumes of smoke.

"There was not much fear," Lee felt, having been fed a diet of feigned optimism, "because everybody thought the Jap planes would come over Manila and our boys would knock them out and it would be pretty as hell to watch. . . . From all over the United States those big bombers are flying to San Francisco. They'll hop to Hawaii and then on to Australia and up here. They'll be here within a week. The aircraft carriers will ferry pursuit planes from Hawaii. . . ."

MacArthur would issue his first press release before the day was out. Diller had little to do with its preparation. From December 8, 1941, until March 11, 1942, when the general left the Philippines, 109 of his 142 communiques identified only one combatant by name: Douglas MacArthur. Even units soon doing the fighting often went unidentified, and not because military secrets were involved. The Japanese knew their enemy as the newsmen did not. All troops under the American flag were "MacArthur's men," and all Philippine communiques were dated vaguely from "General MacArthur's Headquarters." It was a triumph of ego, and for many months the only triumph.

Prior to distributing the first communique, Diller held a briefing at Intramuros. He found it difficult to be upbeat, although he recited a fictitious litany of air attacks repelled in northern Luzon, and reported imaginatively that fighters had turned back a raid on Clark Field at eleven. "However," he added, "at about one this afternoon Clark Field was badly bombed. Many planes were destroyed and it appears that casualties were heavy." Reporters clamored for more details. "I don't have any," Diller claimed. "There is only one telephone line to Clark Field and that has been cut." Denial was a transparent strategy for evading bad news.

The official Manila line of optimism, hope, and certain victory, echoed in the American press, was one of Eisenhower's first dilemmas on his arrival in Washington. Anyone with a map of Luzon realized that the logical invasion site for the Japanese would be Lingayen Gulf, northwest of Manila. Eisenhower had learned the contingency plans for response years before at MacArthur's elbow. It seemed no surprise, then, when Major Diller released for the press, where it would be read even in Texas, MacArthur's report that a major landing at Lingayen had been thwarted. Most of the invasion fleet had been sunk and the beaches were littered with Japanese corpses.

Racing off in his auto to seek pictures of the dramatic aftermath, *Life* photographer Carl Mydans found the beaches quiet. No bodies could be seen. A few Filipino troops were visible and seemed to have little to do. There had been no battle. An unidentified and possibly mythical boat in the lower gulf apparently had touched off a barrage from coast defenses. The boat had vanished. "Thousands of shadows were killed that night," Colonel Glen Townsend, with the Philippine 11th Regiment, recalled. Based on Diller's handout, American newsmen who had remained in Manila worked up material for headlines in the States. Mydans returned to Intramuros and challenged Diller, "I've just been to Lingayen and there's no battle there."

"It says so here," Diller insisted, thrusting MacArthur's mimeographed communique at Mydans.

When the Japanese actually landed on the undefended upper shore of Lingayen Gulf, they moved toward Manila almost unopposed. As Major General Jonathan Wainwright put it, "The rat was in the house." Mydans and his wife, Shelley, a *Life* correspondent, were later taken prisoner. Manila was abandoned to the Japanese at Christmas, as were mountains of provisions stored in upper Luzon. MacArthur abandoned his posh hotel penthouse, and the Intramuros offices, for Corregidor, the fortified rocky speck near the entrance to Manila Bay.

Eisenhower began a new, scrappy, diary early in January. Mamie had come, visited John with him at West Point, and, once they leased a small apartment in the Wardman Tower, off Rock Creek Park at Woodley Road, returned to Texas. Until she packed and moved in February, Eisenhower remained at Milton's home and commuted back and forth across the Potomac.

Although MacArthur radioed pleas to Marshall (he did not know that it was Eisenhower who fielded them) for every kind of assistance, he and his staff were tight-lipped about losses, miscalculations, and mismanagement. However suspect, the Japanese official news agency, Domei, became a major source of intelligence. Marshall's staff could only infer that the withdrawal of what forces could be mustered into the Bataan Peninsula had not gone according to peacetime plans. Stockpiles of food and munitions to be warehoused in Bataan had never been shifted there, for MacArthur had stubbornly expected no war before April 1942. In his memoirs, writing about alleged headquarters rigidity in France in 1918 that prevented him from exploiting an opportunity, Marshall criticized "the inflexibility in the pursuit of previously conceived ideas. . . . Final decisions are made not at the front by those who are there, but many miles away by those who can but guess at the possibilities. . . . The enemy lost no time."

So it was with MacArthur and the Japanese in December 1941. Tons of recently arrived supplies burned on the Cavite docks west of Manila after the first air raids, and supplies intended for a prolonged siege of Bataan were abandoned to the enemy. Depots at Cabantuan in central Luzon held fifty million bushels of rice but troops withdrawn to Bataan would soon be down to half-rations, then even less. Although on December 23, President Quezon ordered all warehouse stocks of food to be left in Manila for the people, when the freighter *Don Esteban* steamed for Corregidor the next evening at 7:20 P.M., the ship carried not only the presidential party but Quezon's cases of fine wine and gourmet delicacies. MacArthur's headquarters staff also crowded aboard, with their trunks, food, and china, two of the general's automobiles of no use on the island, and Richard Sutherland's prized Packard. Left behind for lack of space were more essential supplies. By bright moonlight, officers on deck sang Christmas carols.

What would be called a fighting withdrawal that was reputedly one of the classics of military retreat was much less than a success. "MacArthur's men" were trapped in the small Bataan rainforest which thrust into the western edge of Manila Bay. Knowing little of the confused and contradictory orders under which troops in the Philippines functioned, Marshall nevertheless assumed the worst, hoping only to delay the inevitable.

As little could be done to delay the doom of the Luzon defenders, who actually outnumbered the Japanese, or to hold what was left of the almost undefended lower Philippines, little attention was paid to the Far East at the "Arcadia Conference" between Churchill and Roosevelt and their staffs. As the British delegation arrived in Washington on the evening of December 22, the Japanese were landing unopposed and Filipino troops were abandoning weapons and melting away. It was no different in Malaya, where ineptitude and disorganization doomed a superior British and Australian force to a disciplined army moving down the narrow peninsula on bicycles, or by foot.

At the first Anglo-American plenary session in the White House, Marshall quietly took his own notes, sizing up the British contingent, which seemed more confident than the facts everywhere their flag flew warranted. At the Munitions Building, taking whatever steps he could, Eisenhower, despite his junior status at War Plans, was managing the shop. As Marshall listened in some consternation, Churchill, downplaying the calamities still unfolding, predicted ultimate and utter victory. His reasoning was simple. America, with its preponderant industrial potential and underutilized manpower, at long last was committed to the war.

The White House now seemed to Marshall crowded, overly security-conscious, and very small. His first, rather innocent experience of the Executive Mansion had been much different. In 1900, when a cadet at the Virginia Military Institute just after the Spanish-American War, he sought approval from the minuscule presidential bureaucracy to take the examination for a commission as a lieutenant. Since there was no one downstairs, he let himself in. "The office was on the second floor, which is now among the bedrooms and the upstairs private sitting rooms. . . . I think the bedroom, as I knew it in Mr. Roosevelt's day, must have been Mr. McKinley's office. The old colored man [on duty] asked me if I had an appointment and I told him I didn't. Well, he said, I would never get in; there wasn't any possibility. I sat there and watched people go in. . . . Finally, a man and his daughter went in with this old colored man escorting them, and I attached myself to the tail of the procession and that way gained the president's office." The old retainer frowned, but Marshall "stood pat." After the pair with the appointment shook the president's hand—all they had come for in that leisurely era—"Mr. McKinley, in a very nice manner, said what did I want. I stated my case to him. I don't recall exactly what I said, but from that I think flowed my appointment. . . ."

Roosevelt assumed from Churchill's upbeat experts that the British could hang on to Singapore, long touted as a fortress island, yet the Malayan situation was as hopeless as MacArthur's. On Christmas Eve, the PM suggested to the president that if military assistance could not be forced through to MacArthur, reinforcements earmarked for the Philippines might be diverted to Singapore. When that report reached Marshall on Christmas Day—everyone was working through the holiday—he called in H. H. Arnold and Eisenhower, and went with them to Secretary Stimson's office to protest the apparent selling out of the Philippines. Stimson telephoned the White House. Reaching Harry Hopkins, he declared that if the president was going to agree to "this kind of foolishness," he would have to get a new secretary of war. Roosevelt would pass the possibility off as a rumor, which it wasn't, and offered on the record to build up a presence in Australia "toward operations to the north, including, of course, the Philippines."

Late on Christmas afternoon, the Marshalls, who did little formal dining at Fort Myer, entertained some of the British contingent at a holiday feast: Ambassador and Lady Halifax, Lord Beaverbrook, Admiral Dudley Pound, Air Marshal "Peter" Portal, and Sir John Dill. When Katherine Marshall discovered belatedly that December 25 was also Dill's birthday, she sent Sergeant James Powder, her husband's paragon of efficiency, to find a cake, and candles. Despite holiday closings, he returned with both, and also with miniature British and American flags. At the cake-cutting, Dill confided that he had not had his birthday celebrated since he was a small boy. Removing the flags to insert a knife in the cake, he discovered that they were stamped "Made in Japan." When a Western Union messenger arrived with a singing telegram—Powder had thought (almost) of everything—he was intercepted by a Secret Service detail. There was wartime security somewhere.

In further sessions, Churchill talked only (in Marshall's notes) of "aid[ing] us in some way of restoring superiority in the Pacific," although Britain had no such potential. Further, he predicted confidently that Singapore could hold out "for a matter of six months." (Under the abysmal command of General Robert Brooke-Popham and Lieutenant General Arthur Percival, both men of instant indecision, the British would surrender a garrison of 85,000 to a lightly armed Japanese assault force of 30,000 on February 15, 1942. It would be the worst defeat under the Union Jack since Yorktown in 1781.)

Psychologically and strategically, whatever the losses in the Far East, Roosevelt wanted "to have troops somewhere in active fighting across the Atlantic." He wanted a Germany-first war. Both allies proposed strategies to take some pressure off Russia in Europe, Churchill talking unrealistically of another landing in Norway (code-named "Jupiter"), where he had already failed once at Narvik, in 1940. To Churchill's alarm, Roosevelt suggested a costly feint toward occupied France, which would better get Hitler's attention. Something had to be done. It was crucial to keep Stalin from a separate peace, which could divert millions of the Wehrmacht to the West. Easier pickings as a diversion, the British suggested, would be French North Africa, controlled by the puppet pro-Nazi government in Vichy.

Unified strategy and unified command were essential for a two-ocean war over global distances. Discovering that Roosevelt only met his service chiefs on impulse, Field Marshal Dill cabled Sir Alan Brooke, chief of the Imperial General Staff, with concern that American military cohesion "belongs to the days of George Washington." In response, both Dill and Marshall proposed a Combined Chiefs of Staff. Since everyone at the table realized that preponderant American industrial and military force were future certainties in the coalition, Roosevelt and Churchill agreed to establish a combined presence in Washington. It would not be easy to maintain, as air power and sea power adherents on both sides would stubbornly resist interference, and conflicts of national interest and personal ambition would impact strategy, but Marshall, with Dill heading a British

Joint Staff Mission, would keep the Combined Chiefs functioning usefully to the end.*

On the day after Christmas, Marshall went further with unification, proposing that General Archibald Wavell, already in India, be named Supreme Commander in East Asia and the Western Pacific, and directed Eisenhower to draft "a letter of instruction" for the role. Wavell would move briefly to the Dutch Indies, then backtrack to Ceylon as the Japanese proved unstoppable. His grant of authority proved unrealistically extensive in any case, stretching from South Asia to Australia. Only symbolic unification was geographically possible. Churchill's deputy, Colonel Ian Jacob, warned in his diary, "They foresaw inevitable disasters in the Far East, and feared the force of American public opinion which might so easily cast the blame . . . on to the shoulders of a British general." MacArthur would pay no attention to Wavell, who paid no attention to MacArthur.

Although Eisenhower first appeared on his own in the White House Usher's Diary on February 9, 1942, as "P. D. Eisenhauer," consultations at his staff level late in December were held in the improvised White House map room, created for Churchill in the Monroe Room, where Eleanor Roosevelt had been holding her press conferences, with tacked blow-ups hung from floor to ceiling. (Lower-level conferences also continued in the nearby Federal Reserve Building.) Once the British left, the president ordered his own map room set up in the basement opposite the elevator he used, and had it employed further for encoding cables and decrypts.

The joint sessions were Eisenhower's introduction to the White House, sitting in at frustrating meetings to devise a combined command in the Southwest Pacific which, whatever the facade, Churchill preferred to remain bifurcated to keep his hand in from afar. Since he would rarely relinquish actual control, communications, distance, and the pre-MacArthur division of authority would make ostensibly unified operations unworkable unless they were token and small. Much of the vast expanse in Asia and the Pacific being seized by the Japanese had to be written off, and what could be saved required rare unity of purpose as well as rapport within the military bureaucracy. Washington officialdom, from Roosevelt down, would never relinquish their suspicions that underlying British strategy worldwide was the American rescue of their doomed empire. Yet the U.S. had no feasible plans other than to halt the hemorrhaging in the Pacific somewhere, and to build up forces in Britain for some

*After Dill's death in November 1944, the mission continued under his successor.

future operation that would at least worry Hitler sufficiently that he might relax some of his pressure on Russia.

As Marshall's deputy with responsibility for American support of a wide swath of southeast Asia and the western Pacific, Eisenhower realized that running a save-MacArthur strategy, however minimal, meant reaching him almost entirely through Australia. There was no other way to the Philippines, which effectively meant Luzon. The rest of the many islands to its south were worthless without it, yet Luzon was already as good as lost. MacArthur reported inventively that 80,000 Japanese in six divisions—twice the actual numbers—had already landed at Lingayen, and that additional troops were at Lamon Bay, forty miles southeast of Manila, to pinch off the city. He claimed no choice despite actual parity (or better) with the Japanese but to withdraw into Bataan, and he did not report the widespread panic among Filipino units that left them in chaos. By Christmas Eve, MacArthur was attempting to ship whatever was portable across the bay to the lonely rock of Corregidor.

Washington knew little of the realities when Air Force Major General George H. Brett, in China, was ordered, the day before Christmas, to proceed to Australia to take charge of aircraft and crews to be ferried there, or which were already en route. All the carrying capacity of available shipping was in use. Since heavy bombers could somehow, with refueling stops, fly to Australia, Brett was to establish a subcommand nominally under MacArthur, with "action to be taken in view of situation in Philippines at that time." The radioed message was signed "Marshall" but that meant Eisenhower. A one-star general who little more than a year earlier had been only a "light colonel" was now running the war and in effect was theater commander from a distance, circuitously through the South Pacific, of ten thousand miles.

Consultations at the White House were complicated by space constraints. Only small groups could meet in the map room. On occasion key meetings took place in Churchill's guest bedroom, the Rose Suite, with Roosevelt wheeled in. It became the temporary seat of the British government. The prime minister's laid-back managerial style was often literal. The December 27 session during which the British at first resisted unifying commands, Marshall wrote (as Eisenhower was too "unimportant"—in his description—to be fit in), "took place at nine o'clock one morning in Mr Churchill[']s bedroom. . . . The Prime Minister was propped up in bed with his work board resting against his knees and the usual cigar in his mouth or swung like a baton to emphasize his points, discussed the issue . . . of the moment."

"What would an army officer know about handling a ship?" Churchill challenged. The PM did not want Wavell commanding the Royal Navy in Asian waters.

"Well," said Marshall, who was nothing if not direct, "what the devil does a naval officer know about handling a tank?" The problem, he contended, was not about sailors or tankers, but about "getting control." He was not interested in the bygone era of Drake and Frobisher, Marshall said, but "in having a united front against Japan. . . . If we didn't do something right away, we were finished in the war." A directive was being formulated, Marshall went on, "to meet the onrush of the Japanese in the Southwest Pacific, where they were rapidly overwhelming an ill-prepared, pitifully equipped collection of British-Australians, Indian[s], Dutch and Indonese, Americans and New Zealanders. . . ." Someone had to be in charge, and that someone did not have to be an expert in all the particulars. Roosevelt, so Marshall explained sweepingly to his British counterparts overwhelmed by Churchill, had overall responsibility for the American war effort—"and he doesn't know about any of it."

On the morning of December 27, Churchill called for his physician, Sir Charles Wilson (later Lord Moran), complaining of pain in his chest and left arm. He had already experienced a heart attack, and this would be another unrevealed angina episode. It failed to keep him from overeating and overindulgence in brandy and champagne, and would be dismissed as a muscle strain. Churchill left the meetings as scheduled, in FDR's special railway car, for Ottawa, to address the Canadian Parliament. On returning, when a beachfront house in Pompano Beach, Florida, was made available to him by steel executive Edward R. Stettinius Jr., an FDR friend and soon a close friend of Marshall's, the Arcadia sessions went on without the prime minister.

With his doctor, bodyguard, and secretary, Churchill flew south, also accompanied at his request by Marshall, who sought no holiday and would return to work quickly. Realizing who would be running the American dimension of the war, Churchill wanted the private time which the flight afforded to press his views. Dr. Wilson had already noted in his diary on January 1, 1942, "Marshall remains the key to the situation. The PM has a feeling that in his quiet, unprovocative way he means business, and that if we are too obstinate he might take a strong line. And neither the PM nor the President can contemplate going forward without Marshall."

On the next-to-last day of the conference, January 13, Marshall had to employ his clout. The British had presented a proposal on war matériel allocations, including Lend-Lease, which divided recipient nations and colonies neither Soviet nor enemy into client countries. The Americans were only to oversee Latin America, faltering China—and Iceland. Britain took for itself its empire and Commonwealth, all French colonies, and Nazi-occupied Europe. The London and Washington committees would be independent of each other, and political at the top—under Max Beaverbrook for Churchill and Harry Hopkins for Roosevelt. Marshall was furious. The United States would largely be the supplier, but Britain would allocate the bounty.

For Marshall, suspicion of British imperial designs under Churchill underlay every wartime scheme. Unity of purpose, Marshall insisted, required that the final decisions on allocation of matériel had to be under the Combined Chiefs of Staff in Washington. Recognizing that he had overreached, Churchill stalled on signing off until he was back in London. It was clear as he left that Marshall and Dill jointly would make all crucial supply choices, with Dill the PM's "personal representative" in Washington, and head of the British Military Mission. Sir John had already become Marshall's fast friend, and Marshall, other than in conjunction with Dill, would now allocate the American arsenal yet to go into overdrive. "Strategy," Marshall insisted to the conferees at their windup session, "is dominated by matériel." Roosevelt backed him, and the PM conceded that Marshall's "machinery" could be "tried out for a month," and if unworkable "there could be a redraft." Hopkins wrote to Marshall after Churchill flew home via Bermuda in a Boeing 314 flying boat assigned to the Royal Mail, "I think we have laid the groundwork for final victory."

Giving allocations priority to the Philippines would quickly prove to be more rhetoric than reality. Ignoring the news from beyond Luzon, about which he knew only from radio, MacArthur chose to believe that reinforcements could press through the central Pacific and repel seaborne Japanese forces occupying the mandated islands and blocking all shipping lanes toward the Philippines. Unhelpfully, on his own morale-boosting initiative, Roosevelt had cabled him, as if there were no enemy impediments, that help was indeed on the way. It was—but only slowly and obliquely. Most of it would stop in Australia and remain there.

MacArthur would interpret the president's encouragement as a deception arranged by Marshall and inspired by Eisenhower. Even after the war MacArthur recalled, heatedly, Marshall's alleged "treachery." Yet when Eisenhower advised, in exasperation, that MacArthur should be allowed to die with his troops in a glorious martyrdom that would inspire

Americans, Marshall began working on extricating him. Roosevelt, whose distaste for MacArthur was total, conceded that necessity. As a hostage, MacArthur could be exploited, while as a corpse his potential leadership qualities and experience would be lost. Japanese radio beamed to the Philippines already boasted that the general, as a prisoner of war, would be taken to Tokyo to be hanged in the Imperial Palace plaza.

To demonstrate confidence in MacArthur, Marshall, before Christmas, had persuaded the president to promote him to four-star general, a rank then held only by Marshall himself. MacArthur's private reaction was that he was being restored to his appropriate level. The American public lionizing MacArthur was delighted. It did not know that, regardless of his isolation on Corregidor, he was, as if in total charge of the war, badgering Washington on global policy. By radiogram he proposed reversing the "Europe first" strategy, persuading Russia to attack the Japanese in Manchuria, and lodging bombing strikes on Japan's home islands with aircraft carriers the navy didn't yet have and could not hazard. In further blandishments he permitted a husband-and-wife team for *Time* and *Life,* Melville and Annalee Jacoby, whose publisher, Henry Luce, was then an admirer in the extreme, to file radiotelephoned reports based on misinformation which MacArthur furnished.

As undefended Manila fell, the manipulative MacArthur appeared on the cover of *Time*, turning what would be career-ending humiliations for anyone else into their opposite. "By God," the caption quoted him, "it was Destiny that brought me here." In Washington, Marshall was baffled by MacArthur's public relations successes.

On the first day of the new year, still the last day of 1941 in Washington, MacArthur had fired off a radio message to Marshall that the Philippines could be rescued if a substantial force could reach the big southern island of Mindanao and reopen communications with Luzon. While the notion was fantasy, Marshall replied discreetly on January 4, 1942, acknowledging "a keen appreciation of your situation." Roosevelt and Churchill, and "Colonel Stimson and Colonel Knox,"* had been "surveying every possibility . . . to break the enemy's hold on the Philippines." Cautioning of a post–Pearl Harbor "marked insufficiency of forces," he hoped for "the rapid development of an overwhelming air power on the

---

*Both the secretary of war and the secretary of the navy had been World War I colonels in France. Frank Knox, Republican vice presidential candidate with Alfred M. Landon in 1936, had been recruited by FDR, like Henry Stimson, secretary of war under Taft and secretary of state under Hoover, to promote a bipartisan military. Both liked to be called "Colonel."

Malay Barrier" to interdict Japanese communications—an empty dream given the British lack of hardware. Marshall also promised "a stream of four-engine bombers . . . en route with the head of the column having crossed Africa" and another stream of B-17s and "powerful medium bombers" having "started today from Hawaii."

In what was not Marshall's finest hour he predicted, improbably, "a decisive effect on Japanese shipping" from the added air power which would "force a[n enemy] withdrawal northward. . . . Every day of time you gain is vital to the concentration of the overwhelming power necessary to our purpose." If the message was to buck MacArthur up, it was futile. His troops were already withdrawn to Bataan. Almost nothing promised from Washington could get closer to Luzon than Australia. Level bombing in any case would prove utterly ineffective on moving ships.

As the Arcadia conferees argued on into 1942, Eisenhower confided to his diary that unity of command in the Southwest Pacific remained only "Talk, talk, talk." Two days later, on January 4, he added in frustration, "Tempers are short. There are lots of amateur strategists on the job, and prima donnas everywhere. I'd give anything to be back in the field." He was short on sleep, confronting a sophisticated military culture from Britain that was foreign to him, and frustrated by the give-and-take of negotiations alien to apparent strategic realities. Politics and strategy, in his perspective, didn't mix, but he was learning the hard way, as had Marshall, that war was politics by other means. "British as usual," he wrote in his diary, "are scared someone will take advantage of them even when we furnish everything." Churchill's government feared, while abandoning to the Japanese their vestiges of empire like Hong Kong and Malaya, that the openly anticolonial Roosevelt, as the price of military assistance, would seek the independence of all such colonies after the war. That prima donnas were "everywhere" suggested, beyond the British, Ike's slap at MacArthur, who seemed to hold the American war effort, and domestic politics, hostage—and who knew it.

Eisenhower's agenda was not limited to the Pacific. On one occasion a Red Army procurement officer arrived and "began throwing his weight around." He wanted the latest military hardware, but when Ike asked questions about his needs, he blustered, "I don't think that is any of your business. We want them and that is that." After asking his visitor to return later, Ike went to Marshall. "I recommend we throw the guy out," he said. "The hell with him."

Marshall recommended some pragmatism. "Our bosses believe we've just got to keep Russia in the war, and therefore we have to handle them with kid gloves—or they'll do a France on us. So treat with them. Do your best to get along with them." The Soviets had signed a pact with Hitler in 1939; they were capable of further perfidy. France had signed a dictated peace in 1940. Eisenhower learned to bite his tongue about the Russians but neither he nor Marshall ever trusted them. Much later, Marshall's representative in Moscow, Major General John R. Deane, recommended, in a long list of caveats about the Russians, "In all cases where our assistance does not contribute to the winning of the war, we should insist on a quid pro quo." Without comment, Marshall forwarded Deane's message to the White House.

The chief of staff did not want Eisenhower back in the field with a division. He had already determined to groom him for something more. Instead, he intended to send Gee Gerow, who was restless for real action, and the promotions that came with it. "We're going to put a new man in charge of War Plans, who may at some stage be destined for some pretty high command," Marshall told Assistant Secretary of War John J. McCloy, "and I'd like to have you go down and . . . give me an impression of how you think it's being run, [and] what you think of this new man." McCloy in Marshall's words was "the channel of information" for Secretary of War Stimson, and like his boss had served in France in 1918.

Although eager to be back in uniform, the canny McCloy, in his post only since April 1941, was more valuable in cutting through the Washington bureaucracy. Stimson called him "the man who handled everything that no one else happened to be handling." McCloy recalled, "So I went down to meet this man; I don't think I ever told him that I had been sent to spy on him." He reported back to Marshall, "That man Eisenhower makes more sense to me than any of the others down there." Eisenhower, McCloy also discovered in their frank discussions, was "very sensitive to the fact that he had not gotten involved in combat in World War I." Some of his peers a step ahead of him, like George Patton, had been in action. That McCloy meant what he told Marshall became obvious when the assistant secretary began spending so much time as an informal deputy to Eisenhower, an unusual reversal of functions that led Stimson, after learning of it, to remind the pragmatic McCloy, who seemed into everything, of his myriad duties. "So that put an end to my espionage on General Eisenhower and my ambitions," McCloy recalled after the war. But they were already "Jack" and "Ike," and his working with, and for, Eisenhower was just beginning.

Gee Gerow, Marshall recalled much later, and with much diplomacy, had already been at his job for two years. "I felt that he was growing stale from overwork, and I don't like to keep any man on a job so long that his ideas and forethoughts go no further than mine. When I find an officer isn't fresh, he doesn't add much to my fund of knowledge, and, worst of all, doesn't contribute to the ideas and enterprising push that are so essential to winning the war. General Eisenhower had a refreshing approach to problems."

Even before reassigning Gerow, Marshall designated another deputy, Brigadier General Wade ("Ham") Haislip, to the Fourth Armored Division. Most assistants claimed eagerness to leave their desks. Marshall's revolving secretariat—he had an instinct for picking comers—included Mark Clark, Walter Bedell ("Beetle") Smith, Matthew B. Ridgway, Maxwell D. Taylor, and J. Lawton Collins. Marshall listened to them. Once he interrupted a meeting to listen in the hallway to Beetle Smith, who explained that someone from the small Willys Overland auto firm had come in with a proposal. "This new vehicle is simple, mobile, and hardy and I think we ought to go ahead and contract for it."

"Go ahead and do it," said Marshall. No committee wrote memoranda or studied plans for the versatile, quarter-ton, four-wheel-drive vehicle before approval. Soon christened *jeep* for "general purpose," 640,000 were built during the war.

The army was expanding so rapidly that it always needed shrewd leadership at the division level. Although a few, like Mark Wayne Clark, had been jumped from field grade to a star, commanding an office cubicle was seldom the route to promotion. Earlier, Eisenhower's old pal, George Patton, now with the Second Armored Division, had hoped that Ike could join him, perhaps as his chief of staff, bringing them "together in a long and BLOODY war." With Ike at Marshall's elbow, however, Patton after a visit to Washington was beginning to sense a different and more elevated future for Ike: "You name them; I'll shoot them."

The frustrations of coping with a War Department filing cabinet, Eisenhower realized, daily, were many. With time zones in the Pacific more than half a day (or night) forward from Washington, radiograms arrived at all hours, and staff often left at ten or later, sometimes returning before seven. Exhausted, he was also fighting off flu, and worried that he might be incubating a recurrence of shingles, which could begin with flu-like symptoms. Little seemed to be going right, and he knew that he was to bring only the most extreme problems to Marshall. To keep on top of things, Eisenhower and air force chief "Hap" Arnold pored over the minutiae of maps to learn more about topography and tidewaters, discovering that geographical intelligence was so poor that not even picture postcards existed in the files of some potential overseas targets. A key intelligence resource turned out to be *National Geographic* magazine.

Before Arnold learned of it, Eisenhower was radioed that the first aircraft to arrive in Australia were nearly useless. The wing guns of A-24s unloaded from the convoy rerouted after Pearl Harbor had been hastily reassembled and flown off to the lower Philippines via the threatened Netherlands East Indies. An irate MacArthur cabled, after reports from Mindanao, that the guns failed to fire. The solenoids ("trigger motors," Eisenhower called them) feeding electrical current to the guns and attached securely to the interior of the packing crates, had been inadvertently overlooked in Brisbane and discarded. Replacements were many thousands of miles away. Everywhere, incompetence in packing, labeling, shipping, and offloading precious tons of supplies and equipment would get much worse. War was waste, squared.

Eisenhower had already summoned Brigadier General LeRoy Lutes, who had worked with him as General Krueger's supply officer (G-4) in the Louisiana maneuvers, to Washington from an antiaircraft command in California. "Just to give you an inkling as to the kind of mad house you are getting into—it is now eight o'clock New Year's Eve. I have a couple hours' work ahead of me, and tomorrow will be no different from today. I have been here about three weeks and this noon I had my first luncheon outside of the office. Usually it is a hot-dog sandwich and a glass of milk. I have had one evening meal in the whole period."

To get urgent supplies to the Philippines, such as antiaircraft ammunition for which MacArthur was desperate, Marshall authorized Eisenhower $10 million to organize smuggling operations around, and below, the Japanese blockade. "May merely lose another sub," Eisenhower wrote on January 8. Deputies in Australia and Southeast Asia were cabled to seek out skippers of any kind of craft who would attempt to slip into Manila Bay for ready cash. There were few takers. Soon the president would send another 1918-vintage colonel, Patrick J. Hurley, a former secretary of war under Hoover, to Australia as a brigadier general to organize blockade running. "If I can just help Doug," Hurley appealed to Marshall. "All right," said Marshall, "you can help him." Gerow and Eisenhower each donated a star from their uniforms to get Hurley off in his impromptu new rank. Marshall told Hurley that he would have a plane ready to fly him to Australia, and that a letter of instructions with monetary credits would be waiting for him as he boarded. At one in the morning he was airborne.

The effort would be futile. Marshall recalled, "I started Mr. Hurley

off for [Melbourne,] Australia with some . . . money [to his credit] to expedite the blockade running of supplies to MacArthur. The Japanese had
reached Borneo. Then I discovered that checks were not acceptable to . . .
those hard-bitten men [who] wanted cash on the barrel. . . . Our funds
were in the bank at Melbourne several thousand miles away. I had to find
some way to get cash in a hurry to the Celebes, Java, and Northwestern
Australia. I managed this by loading lots of $250,000 each in bombers en
route across Africa, Arabia, and India." To American commanders already
in Australia, Marshall radioed, "Use your funds without stint. Call for
more if required. Arrange for advance payments, partial payments for unsuccessful efforts, and large bonus[es] for actual delivery. Organize groups
of bold and resourceful men. . . . Movement must be made on broad front
over many routes. . . . Risks will be great. Rewards must be proportional."

   The nuts and bolts of the operation were passed on to Eisenhower,
but the abandonment of the Western Pacific was accelerating too rapidly
to arrest. "We mustn't lose NEI,* Singapore, Burma line; so we are to go
full out saving them," Eisenhower told his diary. Then a dash of realism
came to mind, although he had little idea yet how pathetic the resistance
to the Japanese already was in Malaya, Burma, and the Dutch Indies.
"We've been struggling to get a bunch of heavy bombers into NEI, but
the whole movement seems bogged down. The air corps doesn't have
enough men that will do things." The failure was fortunate. The hardware
would have become gifts to the enemy.

   In little more than two weeks Singapore would fall, all of the East Indies a month later, and the jungles and waterlogged lowlands of Burma,
invaded from Thailand, seemed increasingly hopeless to defend. The only
gain was that the Japanese in diverting troops to the NEI for its oil and
rubber delayed their final disposal of the Philippines. MacArthur's inad-
vertent boon in being able to hold out longer than expected was seen in
the U.S. as the result of inspired leadership from its hero on Corregidor.

   On January 12, Eisenhower sent a long radiogram to MacArthur formally breaking off the "command connection" between the Philippines
and Australia. General Brereton, ordered out by MacArthur after the
Clark Field fiasco he blamed on his deputy, could now operate temporarily under the distant oversight of General Sir Archibald Wavell in India.
"Today a wire from MacArthur saying fine," Eisenhower wrote the next
day. Holed up twenty-four miles across the bay from Manila, MacArthur
could command very little, and was glad to rid himself of Brereton, whose

*Netherlands East Indies, the postwar Indonesia.

new mission almost duplicated Brett's—to ready planes and air crews as they arrived in Australia. Wavell's brief involvement Down Under existed only on paper—and by radio. He was effectively as far away from the war as were Marshall and Eisenhower.

"I prepare about six cables a day," Eisenhower noted on January 19. At least one, daily, went to MacArthur, who radioed appeals from his dreary, humid headquarters in a dripping tunnel on Corregidor while his unseen troops on Bataan, on increasingly short rations, dug in, then slowly backtracked. "MacArthur is as big a baby as ever," Eisenhower told his diary. "But we've got to keep him fighting." When Admiral Hart, who had sailed to Java with what was left of his Asiatic Fleet, had been asked for submarines to ferry supplies to MacArthur, he had claimed he had none available, even though his subs were useless for anything other than supply work. Their faultily fused torpedoes had already proved ineffective against enemy shipping.

Eisenhower went to Admiral King, who hated the Japanese even more than he despised the British, to ask for two subs to slip at least token supplies to Corregidor. "You may tell General Marshall," King said in crusty bureaucratese as if Eisenhower were merely an errand boy, "that if any more drastic action is necessary than is represented in my usual method of issuing orders, such action will be taken." After Pearl Harbor the navy was overstretched and depleted. King objected to risking any resources in a losing venture. In his diary Eisenhower wrote furiously, "One thing that might help win this war is to get someone to shoot King."

Two subs were dispatched nevertheless. Their cargoes were only of minimal help. Five subs would make seven voyages in all through the blockade. Although MacArthur had 80,000 mostly ill-trained troops on Bataan, 19,000 of them (including stranded Air Forces personnel) American, outnumbering the Japanese, he also had to feed 26,000 unanticipated refugees, with supplies for far fewer. The "MacArthur Plan" overriding "Orange" and "Rainbow" had dispersed other troops and supplies over all the lower islands, where war matériel lay abandoned on the docks.

In the general's view of the situation, of course, the abandonment came from Washington. Later, in the summer of 1944, one of his tame newsmen, Frazier Hunt, published a fawning book, *MacArthur and the War Against Japan*, based largely on what MacArthur fed to him. By then the war had turned around. "You will be quite astonished to learn," Eisenhower, who had acquired a copy, warned Marshall, "that back in the Winter of '41–42, you and your assistants in the War Department had no real concern for the Philippines and for the forces fighting there—indeed, you will be astonished to learn lots of things that this book publishes as fact. I admit that the book practically gave me indigestion, something you should know before considering this suggestion further."

MacArthur's only visit to Bataan, a two-mile PT boat ride to a headquarters unit nowhere near the Japanese, had occurred on January 9, two weeks after the loss of Manila. He would write imaginatively, perhaps from photographs, in his *Reminiscences* two decades later, "My heart ached as I saw my men slowly wasting away. Their clothes hung on them like tattered rags. . . . Their long bedraggled hair framed gaunt bloodless faces. Their hoarse, wild laughter greeted the constant stream of obscene and ribald jokes issuing from their parched, dry throats. They cursed the enemy and in the same breath cursed and reviled the United States. . . . But their eyes would light up and they would cheer when they saw my battered, and much reviled in America, 'scrambled egg' cap. . . ." It was total, baleful fiction.

Occupying the general's penthouse, the enemy commander, Masaharu Homma, also took possession of MacArthur's abandoned military history library. The failure to return to the rump of mainland still in his control, although he openly endured air raids on Corregidor, left MacArthur open to diatribes from men on Bataan as "Dugout Doug," a tag which never left him. Co-opted correspondents would keep his manufactured persona fresh. John Hersey of *Time* would publish *MacArthur's Men* (1942), based on Melville Jacoby's worshipful cables,* in which MacArthur was the epitome of coolness under fire. After the general discussed "the daily press release" with LeGrande Diller "came the really enjoyable time—a visit to some command post. The men could never tell where or when he would show. He would just suddenly be there, with his brown curve-handled cane and his jaunty holder; there he would be beside a cot at the field hospital . . . or by a battery watching through binoculars as a Japanese transport train got blown up, or proud as Punch as he listened to the latest exploits of the Filipino Scouts, his boys." Hersey, who had returned to New York from Chungking in China, did not know that the general disliked visiting hospitals, that there were no Japanese trains to see from Corregidor or even from Bataan, or that the unprepared Scouts were more like Boy Scouts.

*Jacoby was killed in an airplane crash in Australia after escaping from the Philippines.

That an initial enemy barrage on forward positions on Bataan failed to dislodge the defenders led MacArthur to crow to Washington, as he seldom now did, "I have drawn the fangs of his attack." The next day, January 13, Marshall responded innocently to the first-person fraud, praising "your splendid resistance." Eisenhower revised the draft, initialed "DDE," and ordered it radioed under "Marshall." With undue optimism it referred encouragingly to "containing enemy operations" in Malaya, the Dutch Indies, and the Philippines, to heavy bombers landing daily in Australia, and to thousands of troops already arrived or in the pipeline. "Naval equilibrium," Washington prophesied, would also be restored. In closing, "Marshall" probed, "We are considering ordering you out of Philippines to exercise active command and direction over American forces now gathering in Australia. . . . Would such action in your opinion jeopardize continued resistance by Filipino troops?"

On reconsideration, the lines suggesting MacArthur's departure from the Philippines were dropped, and revived only on February 4. In the interim MacArthur's radioed theatrics evidenced increasing despair. His message to Washington on January 23 ("flamboyant" according to Eisenhower) recommended as his successor in event of "my death" newly promoted Major General Richard Sutherland, whom he had raised in rapid stages after he displaced Eisenhower in 1938. Ike loathed him, writing that Sutherland's second star showed that MacArthur "likes his bootlickers." The next day Eisenhower consulted logistics chief Major General "Bill" (Brehon) Somervell about getting more landing craft built. No offensive could ever be mounted against a coastline without them, but Somervell, whose bullying was already legendary, was up against crusty Admiral King, who had replaced "Betty" Stark. King's stern priorities ignored the other service's needs: in the aftermath of Pearl Harbor he wanted heavy armor and heavy guns and—belatedly—aircraft carriers. "The Army used to have all the time in the world and no money," deplored Marshall, who controlled no shipyards. "Now," he told Eisenhower, "we've got all the money and no time."

What coastlines were most crucial in a two-ocean war obsessed planners in Washington. Eisenhower's personal priorities kept shifting, while Marshall's had to reflect the White House. "We've got to quit wasting resources and wasting time," Ike told himself on January 22. "If we're to keep Russia in, save the Middle East, India, and Burma, we've got to begin slugging with air at Western Europe, to be followed by a land attack as soon as possible." As if that had always been his contention he added on January 27, "Tom Handy [Marshall's chief deputy] and I stick to our idea that we must win [first] in Europe." He had no idea how indirect and difficult that would be.

MacArthur's sixty-second birthday fell on January 25. Setting aside personal scorn, as the general was the hero of the moment in America, even number one on a series of posterlike bubble-gum cards propagandizing the war for kids, Eisenhower fired off a "warmest anniversary greetings" radiogram. He and former Philippines staffer Thomas Jefferson Davis, now Eisenhower's adjutant, were "proud to salute you [and] the inspiring record you are establishing. . . . Our earnest hopes for the safety and health of Jean, Arthur and yourself are with you constantly."

Four days later, consternation arose in the War Department when MacArthur radioed with his own implied agreement that President Quezon proposed the neutralization of the "Republic of the Philippines" to spare his people further death and destruction. Eisenhower called it a refusal by MacArthur "to look facts in the face, an old trait of his." Neutralization was in effect surrender, and the idea seemed to Eisenhower more like MacArthur's idea, as he had claimed prior to the Clark Field débacle that the Pearl Harbor attack was not an act of war on the allegedly sovereign Philippines, and that he could not initiate an offensive against Japan by using his B-17s to bomb Formosan bases. "Looks like MacArthur is losing his nerve," Ike added on February 3. "I hope his yelps are just his way of spurring us on, but he is always an uncertain factor." Every sector pleaded for planes, he added, realizing that there weren't many aircraft yet to allot, too few experienced pilots to fly them, and hazardous if not impossible routes to get them to where they might make a difference. "What a mess!"

The apparent acquiescence by MacArthur to the abandonment of the Philippines led to urgent conferences by Stimson and Marshall with Roosevelt. A radioed message from the president to MacArthur, drafted by Eisenhower, denied authorization to surrender "the Filipino elements of the defending forces." Roosevelt conceded the "desperate situation" and urged that Quezon and his family be evacuated, along with High Commissioner* Francis Sayre and MacArthur's wife and son. Mention of Jean and young Arthur strongly suggested that the general himself was to fight on—that it was "mandatory that there be established once and for all in the minds of all peoples complete evidence that the American determination and indomitable will to win carries on down to the last unit."

---

*Formerly governor general but with Commonwealth status, Sayre had been retitled.

By then Eisenhower had already drafted a long message to Manila in Marshall's name, responding to an earlier radiogram from MacArthur in Corregidor dated, because of the International Date Line, the next day. He had again offered his worldwide strategic thinking, describing the Hitler-first priorities of the "democratic allies" as a "fatal mistake." Downplaying the German sub menace in the Atlantic and the Mediterranean, MacArthur urged "incessant" attacks on Japanese shipping in the Pacific to loosen their grip on the island corridor to the Philippines. Yet the German submarine threat was increasingly critical. Shipping losses were shockingly high, even when vessels clustered protectively in convoys. The freighter cupboard was bare.

"Counsels of timidity based upon theories of safety first," MacArthur argued from Corregidor, "will not win against such an aggressive and audacious adversary as Japan." Marshall's cautious accruing of "supremacy" in the Southwest Pacific was dismissed as too slow a scheme: "The war will be indefinitely prolonged and its final outcome will be jeopardized. . . . No matter what the theoretical odds may be against us, if we fight him we will beat him. We have shown that here." Unfortunately, the last sentence, totally untrue as Washington knew, undercut MacArthur's thesis. Recognizing his own hyperbole, he closed, more gracefully than was his wont, "In submitting these views, I may be exceeding the proper scope of my office and therefore do so with great hesitancy. My excuse, if excuse is necessary, is that from my present point of vantage I can see the whole strategy of the Pacific perhaps clearer than anyone else. If agreeable to you I would appreciate greatly the forwarding of this view to the highest authority."

MacArthur seemed at his most persuasive, but Eisenhower and Marshall (and FDR, the "highest authority") knew that the general's point of vantage was the Malinta Tunnel deep under besieged Corregidor, which afforded a very limited global view. MacArthur knew from radio contacts that the Allied situation was desperate everywhere, and that every commander in every war wanted what tools were available to be prioritized for him.

Recognizing wartime urgencies and that Marshall was much closer to the modern military scene than Stimson, Roosevelt had made the general directly responsible to him for "strategy, tactics, and operations." Realizing the sensitivity of his relations with the secretary of war, and admiring him unstintingly, Marshall kept Stimson closely informed of all his dealings with Roosevelt. The relationship of soldier and civilian worked.

Eisenhower's delicate mission for Marshall and Stimson about

MacArthur was to undeceive him about the realities without creating additional alarm. The facts were distressing enough. Ike drafted Radio 1024 assuring "most careful study" of MacArthur's Radio 201. "Virtually the entire heavy striking elements of the Pacific Fleet" had been eliminated at Pearl Harbor. "Very heavy convoy duties" and torpedo damage to one of the few aircraft carriers available had "seriously limited aggressive naval operations." Crippling impairment by dive bombers and torpedo planes to the remaining American cruisers in MacArthur's area had occurred while aiding the floundering Dutch in the NEI, making it "obvious that surface vessels cannot operate in regions where they are subject to heavy attack by hostile land based aircraft." The litany of liabilities went on, with the only optimistic note the vague hope that "if we have an early success in checking Japanese progression and secure air superiority through employment of heavy bombers which they lack, there is the strong probability"—it was no more than wishful thinking responding to MacArthur's hopes—"that Stalin will strike against Japan." Russian intervention in Asia was years away.

Marshall redrafted Eisenhower's message and sent it off separately from the once-postponed offer to order MacArthur to Australia. Neither radiogram changed anything. Again, MacArthur promoted Quezon's quixotic neutrality idea, this time suggesting that American forces evacuate all of the Philippines if Japan would recognize its independence, and noting that High Commissioner Sayre had timidly approved the idea although it would not have spared the islands Japanese-style occupation. MacArthur suggested from his isolation on Corregidor that "the temper of the Filipinos is one of almost violent resentment against the United States. Every one of them expected help and when it has not been forthcoming they believe they have been betrayed in favor of others." A corroborating "wail" (in Ike's angry description) from Quezon followed on February 7, the day after Eisenhower moved with Mamie to the Wardman Park flat. Marshall drafted new messages, with Eisenhower, for the president's signature, to both MacArthur and Quezon. "Long, difficult, and irritating," Ike complained. "Both [MacArthur and Quezon] are babies." At 6:45 Eisenhower went to the White House and received Roosevelt's signed approval.

Realizing that there was no way to get help to him directly, MacArthur began to radio suggestions to Marshall for alternatives which were equally unrealistic. These inevitably landed on Eisenhower's desk. One after another, the myriad islands below Luzon were being swarmed over by the Japanese, who were meeting little resistance, leaving small unoccupied outposts in between, and a larger base on southernmost and increasingly precarious Mindanao. Exasperated, Ike noted on February 8, "Another long message on 'strategy' [responding] to MacArthur. He sent one extolling the virtues of the flank offensive. Wonder what he thinks we've been studying for all these years. His lecture would have been good for [West Point] plebes."

MacArthur grandstanded further to Marshall. It was OK to get Quezon and Sayre out, but he would die with his men. It was a dubious gesture given his failure to return to Bataan, an evasion which, from his press releases, the American public did not realize. Republican Party leaders like Alfred Landon, and party chairman Joseph Martin, a Massachusetts congressman, also exhorted fighting to the end in the Philippines. Wendell Willkie, defeated by Roosevelt in the presidential election of 1940, suggested one exemption to total sacrifice in a Lincoln Day speech on February 12—that MacArthur be summoned to Washington to command all American military forces. The proposal became a covert antiadministration tactic which Republicans would go on repeating, as would Arthur Krock, a conservative *New York Times* columnist and persistent critic of the president. Since aside from a doomed corner of Luzon, American troops were not fighting anywhere, the frustration reflected in the press, and reported from the British embassy in Washington to the Foreign Office, had metamorphosed into an excess of pride which the public relations–astute MacArthur could exploit, even from a tunnel on Corregidor.

As the Soviet Tass News Agency was then collecting salutes from eminent persons for the twenty-fourth anniversary of the Red Army (on February 23), its suggestion of a tribute by MacArthur, then the only high-level American hero figure, went to the War Department. Possibly some staffer there remembered the general's vociferous anti-Communism of the 1930s, for no request was radioed on to MacArthur. The PR-sensitive MacArthur, however, read the daily file of world news sent through navy communications to Corregidor, and without prompting he rushed off an encomium that "the hopes of civilization rest on the worthy banners of the courageous Russian Army" and "the scale and grandeur" of the "smashing counterattack which is driving the enemy back to his own land." MacArthur may have been sending a message to Washington rather than Moscow.

A firm order to MacArthur to "start south" to a new command (dividing Wavell's brief) was drafted on February 22. Eisenhower disagreed with Marshall over sending it, "fearful" of MacArthur's predictable theatrics if given a larger stage in Australia. Gauging the likely domestic repercussions of abandoning the general, Marshall saw no alternative. "I think he's doing a better job in Bataan," Eisenhower wrote in deepest irony, "than he will anywhere else." Roosevelt approved the reassignment and a radiogram was dispatched the next day.

Eisenhower saved further outbursts for his diary, conceding that in his biliousness he could not "even think clearly." Marshall's disciplined suppression of almost all wrath "puzzles me a bit," Eisenhower mused. "I've never seen a man who apparently develops a higher pressure of anger when he encounters a piece of stupidity than he does. Yet the outburst is so fleeting, he returns so completely to complete 'normalcy,' that I'm certain he does it for effect." Ike recalled being in Marshall's office one day when someone telephoned to recommend a promotion unlikely to go further. He heard Marshall say, "If the man is a friend of yours, the best service you can do him is to avoid mentioning his name to me."

Marshall usually kept his emotions in check to such a frigid degree that aside from the children and some wives of his colleagues—and Patton, who (in person) was always "Georgie"—he rarely employed a first name. When he inadvertently called Eisenhower "Ike," then reversed himself and used "Eisenhower" in the same exchange, the gaffe was revealing. (Over the years Eisenhower always referred to him as "General.") Intimacy to Marshall was at odds with objectivity. When Ike went to a rare Sunday dinner at Marshall's official Fort Myer residence on February 22, it was only to meet two Chinese VIPs whom Marshall was cultivating. It was no social event; Mamie was not invited. "Longest I've been out of the office in daytime since coming here ten weeks ago today," Ike wrote.

Moving to the Wardman Park meant leaving brother Milton's comfortable home in Falls Church. Soon he, too, would be leaving. Thanks to Ike's new clout, Milton was offered a job as coordinator of Executive Order 9066, on February 19, 1942, "to apprehend, restrain, secure, and remove" dangerous aliens from sensitive locations. As a result, 114,000 men, women, and children of Japanese ancestry along the Pacific coast were being uprooted and "relocated" under armed guard to remote, barren locations that were little more than concentration camps. After it was too late, Earl Warren wondered in a letter to FBI director J. Edgar Hoover whether "we are not straining out the gnat and swallowing the camel" in ignoring the very many German and Italian aliens whose loyalty might be dubious.*

All rumors about Japanese disloyalty were nonsense or worse, but Governor Cuthbert Olson of California was responding to racism cloaked as public hysteria. Lieutenant General John L. DeWitt of the Fourth Army area, who had even fantasized, after Pearl Harbor, sixty bombers identified by rising sun emblems over San Francisco, emphatically urged, in Orwellian terms, preventative removal, because "the fact that no sabotage has taken place to date is a disturbing and confirming indication that such action will be taken."

Unfortunately, DeWitt was a VMI classmate of Marshall's, an effective quartermaster-general in France during the Meuse-Argonne offensive in 1918, and "a very fine fellow." There were limits even to Marshall's objectivity. (He would coddle DeWitt throughout the war but never give him a really sensitive command.) Although J. Edgar Hoover, who had little respect for civil liberties, considered forced evacuation as based on "no factual data" and utterly unnecessary, Ike, with the hard-line McCloy, had flown to San Francisco to meet with Western officials pressing for a Japanese "exclusion" order. The attorney general of Idaho, Bert Miller, insisted, although there were few aliens in his state, that "all Japanese be put in concentration camps for the remainder of the war. We want to keep this a white man's country." The governor of Oregon and the attorney general of Washington wanted all "citizens of Japanese extraction" removed. To his later embarrassment, Earl Warren went along.

McCloy and Eisenhower accepted the assessment of a "Japanese problem," but brother Milton, it would turn out, had been done no favor, and he would resign the "relocation" appointment in mid-June, returning to Washington. His successor, Dillon S. Myer, another Department of Agriculture official, asked whether he should take it. "Yes," said Milton, "if you can do the job and sleep at night."

*By the end of 1942, 106,770 harmless Japanese internees were "relocated." More than 11,000 Americans of German ancestry and 11,600 alien Italians were also, but more briefly, interned, but they were not targets of racism like the Japanese. To encamp all Germans and Italians for the same flimsy reasons would have meant moving millions at the cost of billions, and would have created untenable outrage. Only 1,877 Japanese of the many loyal thousands in Hawaii were "relocated."

Winston Churchill had refitted the liners *Queen Mary* and *Queen Elizabeth* as troop transports, making them available to Marshall, who passed on the responsibility to Eisenhower. Marshall's thinking about their use reflected his rigid objectivity. To Secretary Stimson he noted that their capacity, including flotation gear in event of trouble, was 8,200 men, but in conversation with Churchill at the White House, Marshall and the prime minister had talked of handling twice that complement—a full division— by excluding lifeboats and rafts. Coolly, Marshall explained to Stimson that the "material difference" in the event of a torpedoing "would be in the psychological effect of the loss of the larger number of men."

Since Churchill's feeling was that one risked all in an "actual operation" but not in preparatory movement, Marshall consulted with the president through his appointments secretary, Major General Edwin ("Pa") Watson, concluding with them that any additional space would be more prudently used for "baggage." The *Queens*, which could outrace and outmaneuver subs, would make many sailings, usually alone, to Northern Ireland and to Australia. Ike's first supervision from Washington of a test run of the long Australian route, from Boston on February 18 and around South Africa via a refueling stop in Brazil, left him "in terror" (although he didn't own up to that to Marshall) until the *Queen Mary*, with 14,000 troops, docked Down Under. Like near-fascist Argentina, Brazil was full of Axis agents. "We were horrified," Eisenhower remembered, "to intercept a radio from an Italian in Rio who reported her presence . . . and upon her departure actually gave the direction upon which she set out to sea." Rome radio propagandized that the former luxury liner had been torpedoed off the Falkland Islands, but the *Queen Mary* arrived without incident.

Although "Pa" Watson contended that MacArthur was worth "five army corps," Eisenhower remained stubbornly dubious about the "psychological warfare" boost involved in extricating the general. Ike contended that MacArthur's style was effective only in simple situations, not complicated ones. "Bataan is made to order for him. It's in the public eye; it has made him a public hero; it has all the essentials of drama; and he is the acknowledged king on the spot. If brought out, public opinion will force him into a position where his love of the limelight may ruin him." Eisenhower wrote for his diary as if he were eager to preserve the hero's reputation. More likely, given his War Department and Philippines apprenticeship with MacArthur, he preferred the martyr, who would be posthumously easier to like.

By late in February, Eisenhower was in charge of the Operations Di-

vision, still called (until March 9) War Plans. His schedule had already included congressmen, manufacturers of war matériel, and military managerial types, but now would be more closely attuned to global strategy.
Ham Haislip had already left, and on the 16th, as Gee Gerow walked out
of the Munitions Building for the last time, en route to the 29th Division,
he remarked to Eisenhower, "Well, I got Pearl Harbor on the books; lost
the Philippine Islands, Singapore, Sumatra, and all of the NEI north of
the [Malay] Barrier. Let's see what you can do."

3

Sea Changes

O
N MARCH 10, 1942, Eisenhower recorded in his diary that his father, David, a Kansas farmer, had died at seventy-eight. "Nothing I can do but send a wire." He could have left Operations briefly to others, made it to the funeral, consoled his mother, Ida, who was past eighty and beginning to live in the past, and embraced his four brothers. Rather, Ike noted to himself, "It was always difficult to let him know the great depth of my affection for him," and he remained on duty. It was not that he was indispensable, or thought so. He found it difficult to unburden his feelings. He would not visit his mother until 1944.

The next evening he left work at 7:30, claiming to himself that he "hadn't the heart to go on tonight." On the day of the burial, March 12, he shut himself up briefly in his office—"for thirty minutes, to have that much time, by myself, to think of him." His eulogy for David Jacob Eisenhower was an emotional page in his diary. Distance over so many years, and the differences in their lives, had attenuated their relationship. Marshall's attachment to his own father had been closer and warmer, with shared interests, from hunting and fishing to books. The elder George Marshall was also a small-town businessman, managing, not always successfully, ventures in bricks and coal. When he sold his mining properties and coke furnaces to Henry Clay Frick and invested the returns in a Shenandoah Valley speculation, the land boom collapsed. MacArthur's father, a bemedaled general who served briefly as military governor of the Philippines, was a role model venerated by his son all his life—a spur to filial glory.*

On March 19, 1942, a week after the elder Eisenhower's obsequies, newspapers headlined that MacArthur was safely in Australia with his staff intimates he would call his "Bataan gang." Most had never set foot on Bataan. The evacuees had left Corregidor via PT boats, on a hazardous course southward on the night of March 11, to be flown from Mindanao to Australia. Unable to flee, the Dutch in the Indies were surrendering, and Rangoon in Burma had been occupied. The Japanese could now pour additional resources into the Philippines. On Luzon the end was imminent. MacArthur had summoned Major General Jonathan Wainwright from Bataan to arrange the succession, and explained with a touch of theater that he was departing unwillingly, "pursuant to repeated orders from the President. Things have gotten to such a point that I must comply or get out of the Army. I want you to make it known to all elements of your command that I am leaving over my repeated protests."

"Of course I will, Douglas," said the trapped Wainwright. MacArthur left him, as consolation prize, a box of Philippine cigars and his surplus shaving cream. Brigadier General Lewis Beebe, who would become Wainwright's chief of staff, was invited to lunch and dinner at MacArthur's house on March 9. "I found," he wrote in his diary, "that I was eating real food—properly served." Beebe and Wainwright would experience the horrors to come with their men, and would survive, reduced to emaciated near-skeletons, in a Japanese prison camp in Manchuria until released in August 1945.

Wainwright's orders from MacArthur gave him authority over troops on Bataan and Corregidor, with the remainder of the islands to be divided into subordinate commands overseen impossibly from new headquarters in Australia. Uninformed, Marshall radioed Wainwright, who was awarded a third star, that he was in full charge in the Philippines. The result would be that when he was compelled to surrender, to the dismay of MacArthur, who expected to command what was left by remote control, Wainwright formally relinquished the entire archipelago.

When MacArthur penned his *Reminiscences,* he recalled having his regiment in France in 1918 placed under General Georges de Bazelaire to be battle-trained with four French divisions. Bazelaire was reluctant to let him, as a senior officer, join a French raiding party out to capture Boche

---

*Arthur MacArthur had died in retirement at sixty-seven in 1912, never having achieved his ambition to be chief of staff. Without such dreams, George Catlett Marshall Sr., a rifleman taken prisoner by the Confederates, died in 1909.

prisoners for interrogation. "I cannot fight them," MacArthur remembered explaining, "if I cannot see them." Bazelaire authorized him to go. Later in the same memoir, he wrote imaginatively of Corregidor and Bataan, twenty-four years later, "Our headquarters, called 'Topside,' occupied the flattened summit of the highest hill on the island. It gave a perfect view of the whole panorama of the siege area. As always, I had to see the enemy; or I could not fight him effectively." But the wrenching scenes on Bataan he recalled were fabricated. In Australia and beyond he would soon travel on his personal B-17, christened *Bataan*, further fostering the illusion that he had often been with "MacArthur's men" in the steamy, forsaken jungle. But for his one brief visit, well short of troops on the line, during his seventy-eight days on Corregidor he saw only the shadowy blunt bottom of Bataan from Topside, across the bay.

On March 19, Ike's diary noted, "MacArthur is out of [the] Philippine Islands. Now supreme commander of 'Southwest Pacific Area.' The newspapers acclaim the move—the public has built itself a hero out of its own imagination. I hope he can do the miracles expected and predicted; we can use a few now. Strange that no one sees the dangers. Some apply to MacArthur, who could be ruined by it. But . . . I know him too well. The other danger is that we will move too heavily in the Southwest."

Hitler rather than Hirohito was still Washington's first objective, and while Ike moved troops in both directions, he worried about being spread too thin everywhere. Some army and navy brass wanted to plan an attack on Japan from Alaska, via the beckoning finger of the frigid Aleutian Islands. Soviet cooperation would have been needed, and would not have been forthcoming. Moreover, a difficult buildup in the vicinity of Dutch Harbor on Unalaska Island required resources not available and more good weather than ever existed there. Eisenhower recommended against it in mid-March, and Marshall backed him, but the scanty military presence across the bleak, thousand-mile Aleutians made it possible for the Japanese, on June 3, 1942, to occupy foggy, remote Attu and Kiska. Only pinpricks in the western arc of the chain, they were a threat, nevertheless, to shipping routes to Siberia and were potential stepping stones toward continental North America.

Before departure from Corregidor's Bottomside, MacArthur—the last to board—radioed Washington to recommend all army units on Bataan and Corregidor for meritorious unit citations. He excepted the marines and navy—a slight Wainwright would amend. Yet it was the navy that was extricating MacArthur's entourage. Four worn and barely operable PT boats had slipped by night from an inlet on Bataan to take on

MacArthur's wife; son; Ah Cheu, his son's Cantonese *amah*; and the chief staffers at headquarters on the Rock. Marshall had authorized the evacuation of MacArthur, and included Jean and young Arthur, then four. Later, Marshall learned that the party included Ah Cheu, fourteen senior desk officers, MacArthur's publicist Major Diller, and a staff sergeant code stenographer. All the nurses in the improvised hospital in a tunnel on Corregidor, and all the casualties, were left behind. Marshall was "astonished."

Under radio silence, traveling without lights, the patrol boats were to rendezvous at Cuyo Island on the north end of the Sulu Sea, and proceed south to Mindanao, where B-17s flown from Australia were expected. It was a frenzied dash of five hundred miles in rough seas, with the constant fear of unseen outcroppings and enemy warships. In the distance the alarming silhouette of a Japanese cruiser once appeared, creating a half-hour of extra tension. One PT had to be abandoned at Cuyo for lack of fuel. Another with engine trouble arrived at Cuyo late and also lacked enough gasoline to continue on. Slowed by overcrowding, both PT-35 and PT-41 made landfall at the small port of Cagayan de Oro on the north shore of Mindanao after sunrise on the second day.

The flight of four B-17s anticipated at the Del Monte airfield proved to be a single beat-up bomber. Two had aborted with engine trouble and returned to Australia; another had crashed into the sea on its approach to Mindanao. Spare parts were lacking in Australia, and no repair depot that could handle heavy bombers yet existed. Many aircraft there had malfunctioned, or were unflyable. Even before he arrived, MacArthur was furious at evidences of the inept buildup. From Del Monte he radioed to Marshall, and to the Army Air Forces commander in Australia, George Brett, who now had a third star, for replacements and refused to board the lone, "dangerously decrepit" aircraft, demanding "the three best planes in the United States or Hawaii." Stimson, after reading Marshall's forwarded mail, complained to Roosevelt about MacArthur's "rather imperative command," but the general, under great strain, and aware of his standing in the States, was not going to risk his small family and staff any further.

Until taking over in Australia, MacArthur had little use for aircraft but much use of high-level insubordination. As chief of staff in the early 1930s he had eliminated the position of assistant secretary of war for air. His lone vote for acquittal on the court-martial in 1925 that convicted former brigadier general Billy Mitchell for impassioned advocacy of air power when ordered to be silent came from belief that a "senior officer" should not be silenced for opinions "at variance with his superiors in rank and with accepted doctrine." No superior bureaucrat would ever silence MacArthur.

In Marshall's name, Eisenhower ordered Brett, in Melbourne, "You are directed immediately to dispatch the three best B-17s under your control to Mindanao where they will come directly under orders of General MacArthur and take their orders from him. . . . This mission shall take precedence over any other now projected for these planes, which must be operationally fit."

Just after midnight on March 17, MacArthur and his family took off in a replacement bomber from Del Monte, where the grass runway closed in by mountains ended at the sea. The general sat in the only spare chair, lashed next to the radioman. The others aboard lay in blankets on the fuselage floor, unaware that the ten-hour flight to Darwin, the northernmost city in Australia, had nearly ended abruptly over the harbor, where Mitsubishis flying southeast from occupied Portuguese Timor were spotted attacking ships at anchor. Java had fallen, and the Netherlands East Indies were no more. The three B-17s turned toward Batchelor Field, forty miles south, an emergency airstrip little more than a weed patch. There, after a scrappy breakfast, MacArthur demanded a train, as his wife would fly no farther—yet there was no rail service in the remote north of the vast Northern Territory. As an alternative he demanded a motorcade south to isolated Alice Springs, where they could meet a train coming up from Melbourne. Alice Springs was a thousand parched miles away. The impasse ended when enemy planes were reported nearby. MacArthur and party hopped on the first refueled B-17.

Across America on March 18 (it was already the 19th west of the Date Line) the media were ecstatic. The *New York Times* headlined, MACARTHUR IN AUSTRALIA AS ALLIED COMMANDER. MOVE HAILED AS TURN OF THE TIDE. The mere presence of the hero seemed to guarantee eventual victory.

Rail traffic to Melbourne from the Alice Springs terminus ran only once a week. Still, MacArthur would not fly any farther when offered a DC-3, the efficient workhorse of airlines in the United States. When told by an aide that Brett (although privately exasperated) would send a special train, via Adelaide, MacArthur shrugged, "Of course."

The rescue train was a spartan assemblage of coal-burning engine, two wooden coaches, and a caboose, but it traveled on the ground. At an intermediate stop southward an ancient sleeper was attached, and MacArthur was delivered an immaculate pair of khaki service trousers and bush jacket to wear with his signature scrambled-eggs hat. Adelaide was 1,028 miles, and seventy hours, distant.

The press began gathering as MacArthur approached, and a more posh train awaited at a junction to take him to Melbourne, where, on March 21, a crowd greeted him at Spencer Street Station. An honor guard of American army engineers was drawn up on the platform. The Australian army minister, Francis M. Forde, offered an official welcome. While sixty reporters took notes, MacArthur read from a short speech he had written en route, praising the quality of the Australian soldiery he remembered from the last war. Then he launched into a message meant more for Marshall and the Asia-firsters in Congress than for Melbourne.

MacArthur had already been disappointed by the puny and inadequate American military presence in Australia. Men and matériel came circuitously, and slowly. About 25,000 troops had arrived, less than two divisions, and 250 aircraft. Most Aussies were still in the Middle East. "No general," he warned, "can make something out of nothing. My success or failure will depend primarily on the resources which the respective governments place at my disposal. . . ." He expected to be undertaking from there "the American offensive against Japan, a primary object of which is the relief of the Philippines. I came through and I shall return."

In Washington, officials at the Office of War Information wanted to amend, for release, his "I" to "we," explaining in a radioed message that in 1812 Commodore Oliver Hazard Perry had reported, "We have met the enemy and he is ours," and that on arriving in France in 1917 with the first American contingents, a colonel,* in a phrase mistakenly attributed to Pershing, "announced, "Lafayette, we are here." Refusing, MacArthur characteristically insisted on the "I." On Bataan, hearing by radio of the Caesaresque pronoun, beleaguered GIs with little about which to laugh, began to employ such quips as, "I am going to the latrine, but I shall return."

The opening episode in Australia set the tone for MacArthur's conduct of the war. He intended to turn adulation at home and abroad into action on

---

*Colonel Charles E. Stanton had been deputed by General Pershing to speak at the tomb of the Marquis de Lafayette in Paris on July 4, 1917. In his memoirs, Pershing confessed that he could not recall saying "anything so splendid."

his behalf, forcing Washington's hand. As early as January 30, when consideration about extricating MacArthur from the Philippines began, Marshall had looked ahead to the negative as well as positive repercussions. Would the appearance of MacArthur's abandoning his doomed troops— although ordered by President Roosevelt himself—be a public relations embarrassment?

Marshall knew that if there had been anything which MacArthur craved more than the restoration of his fourth star, it was a Medal of Honor, which his father had received. Arthur MacArthur claimed he had earned it on Missionary Ridge in 1863, and was recommended by Lieutenant General Philip Sheridan. Although only enlisted men were eligible for the newly created medal, and MacArthur was duly turned down, he lobbied shamelessly for it ever after. In 1889, while a major, he discovered a loophole in the law and belatedly got his bauble.

With every other medal for valor, his son had long promoted himself for the ultimate one, first after chasing Pancho Villa in New Mexico in 1916, and again in France in 1918. Marshall saw a Medal of Honor to a military icon as a boost to domestic morale at a dark time, and an antidote in advance to predictable Axis charges that MacArthur had deserted his men under fire. (Indeed, the *Japan Times and Advertiser* in Tokyo would declare that MacArthur "fled from his post.") Eisenhower had argued against the award, contending that MacArthur had been personally reckless on numerous occasions in France in hopes of the decoration, yet blatantly and undeservingly cautious in the Philippines. That February, meanly satiric verses sung to "The Battle Hymn of the Republic" had begun circulating among the soldiers on Bataan, suggesting how they viewed their commander across Manila Bay on Corregidor:

Dugout Doug MacArthur lies ashaking on the Rock,
Safe from the bombers and from any sudden shock.
Dugout Doug is eating all the best food on Bataan
And his troops go starving on. . . .

Wainwright did inherit what was left of the best provisions brought from Manila; however the lines that preceded that charge, although equally bitter, were unreasonable. The "Rock" was raided daily, and despite the Mitsubishis high overhead, MacArthur often left the Malinta Tunnel to watch, exposing himself to enemy bombs. Yet his troops besieged on Bataan dined on dwindling three-eighths rations, and after his hasty token visit early in January he did not reappear.

The American press exhausted superlatives throughout the Philippines ordeal in extolling his brilliance as a commander, especially after supposedly impregnable Singapore surrendered, while Bataan continued to hold out. Marshall had already radioed MacArthur's toadyish chief of staff, Richard Sutherland, that the War Department intended to award MacArthur the Medal of Honor, and directed Sutherland "to transmit . . . your recommendations and supporting statement with appropriate description of any act believed sufficient to warrant this award." Unhelpfully, at much the same time an ultraconservative congressman offered a bill to authorize the medal. That was too political a route for Marshall, who intervened with Secretary Stimson, a veteran Republican, to sidetrack the legislation. By then, with MacArthur's departure imminent (and Sutherland with him), his deputy radioed that MacArthur had demonstrated "utter contempt of danger under terrific aerial bombardments," and "magnificent leadership and vision."

To ensure that the award went through, and that it would be waiting for MacArthur in Australia to defuse any local criticism of his exiting the "perilous" Philippines to escape certain capture, Marshall, who had never written fiction before, drafted the citation himself and sent it on to Stimson for approval. It cited MacArthur's "gallantry and intrepidity above and beyond the call of duty in action against invading Japanese forces," and his "utter disregard of personal danger under heavy fire and aerial bombardment, his calm judgment in each crisis, [which] inspired his troops, galvanized the spirit of resistance of the Filipino people, and confirmed the faith of the American people in their armed forces." His cameo appearances in Australia seemed sufficient to back up Marshall's particulars. No communique of MacArthur's had been so imaginative.

Unaware that Marshall had drafted the encomium himself, Henry Stimson read it and remarked, "Well, this is very well done."

"I did it," Marshall confessed, pleased with himself. He took it personally to the White House for signature. "This action was taken," he explained to the president, "among other things, to offset any propaganda by the enemy directed against [MacArthur's] leaving his command and proceeding to Australia in compliance with your orders." Roosevelt, who once labeled the greatest demagogues in America as Huey Long and Douglas MacArthur, may have privately held his nose, but he knew that the decoration would gratify the MacArthur constituency in Congress.

Much later, when Eisenhower was sounded out about a medal for himself, he told his onetime classmate at Fort Leavenworth's Command and General Staff School in the 1920s, Robert Eichelberger, who would serve under MacArthur in New Guinea and beyond, that he would have none of it, "because he knew of a man who had received one for sitting in a hole in the ground." Eichelberger did not have to guess who that man was.

The award was announced in Washington on March 25, the day (it was the 26th in Australia) that MacArthur was flown to Canberra in a former KLM Dutch DC-3 to meet with the Australian prime minister, John Curtin. There the telegram notifying MacArthur went to the room clerk of his hotel, who delivered it in error to *Time* correspondent Robert Sherrod, who had covered Eisenhower in the Louisiana maneuvers. At an official banquet in MacArthur's honor that night, ambassador Nelson T. Johnson read the citation, noting that since President Roosevelt could not be there in person, Lieutenant General Brett had been delegated by General Marshall to make the presentation. Graciously, MacArthur replied to Roosevelt and Marshall that he was sure that "this award was intended not so much for me personally as a recognition of the indomitable courage of the gallant army which it was my honor to command."

Brett would not last under MacArthur. By the end of the year he was commander of the unrewarding Caribbean Defense Command. (MacArthur had long before turned Brereton, whom he blamed for the Clark Field catastrophe, out of the Philippines, the partying general landing on his feet first in Australia, then in India, later in Europe.)

The Pacific war would have taken very different directions had MacArthur not been able to perform as only he could do from his Supreme Commander role. Although Australia was effectively rescued by the Battle of the Coral Sea early in May, in which MacArthur had no part, following that reprieve, which bought him time, he worked up his own strategy. While dominating the Australian military, although it chafed at being subservient in its own jurisdiction, he did badger his way into receiving more resources for the theater, and more independence of action, from Washington than anyone else could have managed.

Only by controlling what reinforcements and matériel he was supplied, often more than Europe-first priorities warranted, could MacArthur's complaints be reined in. The continuing superlatives lavished on him by the press and by his claque in Congress exasperated Eisenhower. Careful to keep his resentment to himself, he kept pouring it out in his diary. "Urging us in that direction," he predicted, "will be Australians, New Zealanders, our public (wanting support for the hero), and MacArthur. If we tie up shipping for the SW Pacific, we'll lose this war." The choices he had to make as Marshall's deputy were often agonizing.

There was not enough of anything anywhere. His priorities for the rest of 1942 were that the Japanese and Germans had to be prevented from linking through the Middle East and India; Russia had to be kept in the war; and Britain (now beyond invasion) had to be massively staged as the springboard for retaking occupied Europe.

MacArthur was not Eisenhower's only *bête noire*, nor Marshall's. FDR, assistant secretary of the navy in 1917–18, had always been sea-minded, often to the detriment of army needs and ground strategy. At one White House meeting, the usually restrained Marshall had enough. "At least, Mr. President," he said, "stop speaking of the Army as 'they' and the Navy as 'us.'" Privately, in a postwar conversation with Winston Churchill's wife, Clementine, Marshall told her, she recalled, that Roosevelt, with many issues competing for his attention, "would direct his mind like a shaft of light over one section of the whole subject to be considered, leaving everything else in outer darkness. He did not like his attention called to aspects he had not mastered or which from lack of time or indolence or disinclination he had disregarded."

His frustrations getting the better of him, Marshall after one White House consultation let loose a tirade at his staff that had resulted in Ike's filling a diary page on March 29 with language that he then expurgated by ripping out the sheet. Whatever his early private feelings about service adversaries, Marshall reached personal accommodations with Admiral King that worked throughout the war. With MacArthur, accommodation often meant biting one's tongue. Marshall recalled much later (April 11, 1957), "I don't think I ever said an adverse word about General MacArthur in front of the staff, though he was very difficult—very, very difficult at times—particularly when he was on a political procedure basis. . . . I do recall suppressing them."

That March, soon after the White House episode, Marshall was preparing a rebuttal to a barb from the president. Roosevelt had been hearing from politicians that there were too many generals in Washington and too few in the field. Marshall wrote to FDR's principal secretary, Marvin H. McIntyre, that it was nothing like 1917–18, when there were "6,000 officers" in Washington, including "a great many" generals. The United States was now in a "vast and complicated" military expansion "for which the old AEF had no counterpart." That meant, he wrote, "a large number of officers with very high and responsible positions. Almost without exception, the officers of the line of the Army—air and ground—wish to get out of Washington. They feel that their advancement is penalized, which it is, by staying here. For example, I have three Assistant Chiefs of

Staff with the rank of Brigadier General, all of whom would be Major Generals and division commanders were they not held on duty here." All of them, he added, would do their duty regardless of rank, but it was "against the public interest" to hold back earned promotions.

Referring to the elevation of combat commanders at the expense of those at desks around him, Marshall had told Eisenhower, privately, "Take your case. I know that you were recommended by one general for division command and by another for corps command. That's all very well. I'm glad they have that opinion of you, but you are going to stay right here to fill your position and that's that!" Then he added, with an asperity not directed personally at Eisenhower, "While this may seem a sacrifice to you, that's the way it must be." He had told the General Staff, Marshall confided, that "the men who are going to get the promotions in this war are the commanders in the field, not the staff officers who clutter up all the administrative machinery. . . . The field commanders carry the responsibility and I'm going to see to it that they're properly rewarded so far as promotions can provide a reward."

For the only time in his relationship with Marshall, Eisenhower turned on his chief, who cultivated a protective veneer of aloofness at odds with his humanity. "General, I'm interested in what you say," Ike recalled answering, "but I want you to know that I don't give a damn about your promotion plans as far as I'm concerned. I came into this office from the field and I am trying to do my duty. I expect to do so as long as you want me here. If that locks me to a desk for the rest of the war, so be it!"

Having worked up his quota of resentment he rose and walked toward Marshall's door in what seemed suddenly "a long march." The closer he came to exiting, the more sheepish he felt about his outburst, and began to grin at his own expense. Something impelled him to look back in Marshall's direction. "A tiny smile," Ike thought, "quirked the corner of his face."

Their relationship was certified in the code names which Hopkins and Roosevelt contrived for private use in cables and calls, all drawn from the president's Hyde Park estate. Marshall was "Plog," as William Plog was the superintendent who went back so far on the grounds that he still called Roosevelt "Mr. Franklin." Eisenhower was "Keuren," Hopkins's misspelling for Plog's primary assistant, Van Curan.

A few days after Eisenhower's exchange with his boss he found on his desk a copy of Marshall's recommendation to Roosevelt that the assistant chief be promoted to major general. Splitting hairs, Marshall explained to the president that as the Operations officer, Eisenhower was not merely in a staff job. He also commanded from afar the army's presence in Britain. On March 28, Ike pinned on his second star. "Maybe I'll finally get out of this slave seat [in Washington]," he wrote to George Patton, "so I can let loose a little lead with you. By that time you'll be the 'Black Jack' [Pershing] of the dam[n] war."

The prediction would go wildly awry, but the star encouraged Eisenhower to hope once more for a division. Still, his role remained what it had been—the devising, from a desk, of means to plug strategic holes everywhere. MacArthur's unlucky successor in what remained of the Philippines, Jonathan Wainwright, who shared Bataan's misery with his men, had little left with which to fight. From Washington, Eisenhower was helpless. Except for stealthy and inadequate supply by a few subs, he realized, "there's not much chance." Wainwright was expendable.

Both Marshall's and Eisenhower's offices were wired with dictaphones at the chief of staff's instructions. Conversations were instantly transcribed by a secretary in the next room. All visitors were informed that the system was in place for prompt communication, and execution of business. Conferences thereafter would never bog down in gossip or trivia.

One of Eisenhower's rare meetings with the president, accompanying Marshall and Stimson, and with Hopkins and Admiral King present, occurred on April 1. The subject was Europe. A War Department analysis prepared by Eisenhower and Colonel (later General) Thomas T. Handy, described as the Marshall Memorandum, was on the table. A cross-Channel operation in France, it contended, was the only geographical possibility to commit an Anglo-American force which might have air and ground superiority. "The United States can concentrate and use larger forces in Western Europe than [anywhere else] due to sea distances and the existence in England of base facilities." Marshall's projection was unrealistic for 1942, and perhaps for 1943. The Germans could move reinforcements quickly by road and rail. Their airfields dotted the countryside. At the time, the American buildup in Britain had hardly begun.

The document conceded that there was no way yet to "concentrate on Japan." Although King was a Pacific-first advocate, Roosevelt wanted the admiral in the discussions to resolve a way to get American troops arriving in Britain into action against Germany. There could be no movement into France without massive sealift. On FDR's instructions, Marshall, Hopkins, and King were to fly to London with the memorandum. Eisenhower, with his new second star, was to manage the shop.

The trio, with aides, all in civilian clothes for secrecy, left by Boeing flying boat for Bermuda on April 4, then to Northern Ireland. In London on April 8, they began a week of meetings with Churchill and his staff in their hideaway bunker forty feet below Great George Street, east of St. James's Park. At Roosevelt's urging, Marshall proposed the cross-Channel assault as the best way to end the war quickly while the Germans were preoccupied with Russia, but Alan Brooke, aware of Allied unpreparedness, snapped, "Yes, but not the way we want it to end!" Marshall had "great charm and dignity," Brooke conceded, but he had a lot yet to learn about "strategic implications."

Eisenhower was still Pacific-focused. Despite recognizing that occupation of the Philippines could not be thwarted, he looked for every means, as a moral imperative, to assist his former station. "We've literally squandered money," he admitted to his diary; "we've wrestled with the navy; we've tried to think of anything that would give even a modicum of help. I'll go on trying. . . ." On April 8, a date which arrived earlier in Australia than in the U.S., MacArthur radioed to Marshall that the end was near on Bataan. "I regard the situation," he noted, and Eisenhower read, "as extremely critical and feel that you should anticipate the possibility of disaster there very shortly." Crossing his message was Eisenhower's to Marshall in London: "Surface ships now on the way to Bataan carry a total of 13,500 tons of supplies. 4,500 tons are on the leading ship, 1,500 tons on each of six others following at intervals. Reports on blockade clearly indicate little possibility of any of these ships arriving." At dawn on April 9, Major General Edward P. King Jr.'s couriers carried the white flag of surrender to General Masaharu Homma on what was left of Bataan. Americans and Filipinos alike death-marched into the horrors of Japanese captivity. All that remained on Luzon other than pockets of futile resistance in impenetrable areas, was isolated Corregidor, bombed day and night.

From Australia, MacArthur now saw no need to keep the ailing Manuel Quezon, also evacuated, nearby, complaining to him daily as president-in-exile. The general radioed Washington for some diplomatic White House excuse to send his former benefactor—and the godfather of young Arthur MacArthur—packing. Ike fielded the general's messages for Marshall, who was still away in England, and consulted Roosevelt. FDR approved.

It was April 20. The Philippines was almost off the charts and it would be a long way back for MacArthur. Still he demanded, and received War Department sanction, that all "press releases" from isolated Corregidor be radioed to him first for approval. Wainwright, however, did not ask permission from Australia when he radioed Roosevelt on May 5, with the Japanese having landed, and penetrating Corregidor's tunnels, that he was preparing to surrender "with broken heart and head bowed in sadness but not in shame."

Eisenhower wrote the next day, "Poor Wainwright! He did the fighting in the Philippine Islands; another got such glory as the public could find in the operation. Resistance elsewhere in the P.I. will quickly close. . . ." Ike saw no loss for MacArthur in turning over that page of his history. "But he's a hero! Yah!"

To Washington, MacArthur cabled his feigned disbelief that, contrary to explicit orders, Wainwright had capitulated, and that his voice had been broadcast on Manila's KZRH. Commercial radio in San Francisco had picked it up through the transoceanic static and transmitted it to Marshall. It meant the imminent end of all organized resistance in the Philippines.

Just before the surrender, Eisenhower sent a handwritten note to Marshall, who made changes in the draft and sent it on to the president, recommending that Wainwright, who had "done all he could without uttering a word of complaint" should be awarded a Medal of Honor. As Wainwright's theater superior, MacArthur meanly quashed it.

At Camp O'Donnell, above San Fernando, northeast of Manila Bay, to which officers and men were marched into captivity, and where conditions were already atrocious, and the dying escalated, Brigadier General William E. Brougher, commander of the 11th Division before the surrender, wrote a bitter memorandum to himself. Who had the right, he asked, to condemn, by "colossal military blunder," 20,000 Americans to a hopeless prison camp existence?

Was he not an arch-deceiver, traitor, and criminal rather than a great soldier? Didn't he know that he was sentencing all his comrades to sure failure, defeat, death, or rotting in a Prison Camp? If our friends in the States are not aware of these facts and are not doing something about it for our relief, we are the victims of the crime of the century. For nothing more than doing our duty as good soldiers, we have been sentenced to penal servitude of the vilest sort. That was not included [in] my oath of office as an officer of the U.S. Army. A foul trick of deception has been played on a large group of Americans by a Commander in Chief and small staff who are now eating steak and eggs in Australia. God damn them!

Brougher concealed the paper throughout his forty months of incarceration in Luzon, Taiwan, and Manchuria, and had every opportunity to destroy it, during, or after, the war. He did not.

Marshall had returned from London on April 20. Despite strong private misgivings, he had presented Roosevelt's proposals for the long-discussed "Sledgehammer," a token cross-Channel incursion into occupied France, first suggested during the December 1941 "Arcadia" conference. Both Marshall and Eisenhower realized that the president was chafing at inaction in the European Theater, yet any premature operation would expose inadequate, undertrained, and ill-equipped American troops to certain reverses. Marshall insisted later that British criticism overlooked the reality "that the Germans had little in the West and that little was of poor quality." To Secretary of the Treasury Henry Morgenthau, Roosevelt observed, much as he had done to Marshall, "Nothing would be worse than to have the Russians collapse. . . . I would rather lose New Zealand, Australia, or anything else than have the Russians collapse." But a potential fiasco seemed the wrong way to offer the Russians a "Second Front."

General Brooke remained skeptical. Marshall was "a pleasant and easy man to get along with," Brooke had sized him up in his diary on April 9, "[but] rather over-filled with his own importance. . . . I should not put him down as a great man." Later in editing his diary for publication he added in a further put-down, that Marshall was "a big man and a very great gentleman, who inspired trust, but did not impress me by the ability of his brain." He had, then, "only touched the fringe of all the implications for re-entry into France. In the light of the existing situation his plans for September of 1942 were just fantastic!" A thwarted second front would not help Russia, Brooke insisted. Privately, he was also impatient with the Soviets, confiding to Sir Alexander Cadogan of the Foreign Office that they asked for everything and offered nothing. "Of course the Russians are fighting—but for themselves and not for us."

Working committees and late dinners had filled Marshall's time in England. Churchill had Hopkins, King, and Marshall for dinner and overnight at Chequers with the three British chiefs of staff, who had reviewed Marshall's unpersuasive proposals that afternoon. "We were kept up till 2 A.M. doing a world survey," Brooke wrote, "but little useful work." He was amused at American discomfort with the PM's late hours, Marshall confiding that he frequently didn't see Roosevelt "for a month or six weeks." Brooke often received six hours a day—or night—of Churchill's strategic wisdom. After two hours with Marshall on April 15, he gauged him as "a good general in raising armies and providing the necessary links between the military and the political worlds," but saw his lack of "strategical ability" as "dangerous." A landing in France was not the crucial factor; it was what might follow. Brooke wrote that he asked Marshall

> to imagine that his landing had been safely carried out and asked him what his plans would then be. Would he move east toward Germany exposing his south flank? Would he move south to liberate France and expose his left flank? . . . I found that he had not even begun to visualize the problems that would face an army after landing. . . . I found [later] that his stunted strategic outlook made it very difficult to discuss strategic plans with him, for the good reason that he did not understand them personally but backed the briefs prepared by his staff.

Marshall acknowledged to Brooke privately that Admiral King had been "a drain on his military resources, continually calling for land forces to capture and hold bases," while MacArthur in Australia "constitutes another threat by asking for forces to develop an offensive from Australia." Proposing a Second Front across the Channel was partly "to counter these moves," and "fits in well with present political opinion and the desire to help Russia." Brooke suggested alternatives in the Mediterranean, while Churchill "in impressive pronouncement," Marshall cabled Secretary Stimson, had "declared a complete agreement" in principle with a Second

Front. The general had much to learn about Churchill's duplicity. His enthusiasm was phony and only rhetorical. He understood that the impetu-
ous Americans had no amphibious lift capacity to cross the Channel
successfully anytime in 1942, and perhaps even in 1943. Having it both
ways, he was agreeing with principle rather than practice.

In his devious manner, Churchill intended to subvert the operation
by proposing a more cautious, and different, scenario that promised more
chance of success. His single-minded strategy throughout the war would
be to confront Germany indirectly from the Mediterranean, avoiding the
catastrophe of another Somme or Passchendaele. In the eastern Mediterranean, he quietly speculated, an Allied presence in the Balkans might
block a resurgent Russia from determining the future of central Europe
while protecting a British-dominated, and oil-rich, Middle East. More
open (but not openly imperial) British concerns offered to Marshall were
that a German spring offensive in Russia could push into the Caucasus oil
fields, and that Erwin Rommel's Afrika Korps might strike beyond Egypt
into Asia, possibly linking up with the Japanese, who seemed likely to occupy Burma and threaten unstable India.

Churchill's indirect road back to Europe began with Vichy North
Africa, discussed off and on since "Arcadia" in December 1941. To the
American military, it contributed nothing to keeping Russia in the war.
Brooke dismissed a landing in France, and a costly raid in force across the
Channel, still to come, at Dieppe, would be the only vestige of a Second
Front in Europe during 1942. Intended in part to divert the Wehrmacht
from thinking about North Africa, it may have also been a bloodily cyn-
ical object lesson to the Americans (largely at Canadian expense) that a
landing in France would be a watery Somme. Although "Bolero" would
continue—the American buildup in Britain—the British saw French
Africa as the only possibility for fighting Germans.

Since Marshall had just returned from England and had much on his
plate, he would send Eisenhower back to survey for him how the American military could activate the president's expectations, for political and
psychological reasons, to be attacking somewhere. Renewed pressure had
come from British reverses. The Afrika Korps had penetrated deep into
Egypt from Libya, and the surrounded port enclave of Tobruk seemed
likely to become a British Bataan.

For Eisenhower to fly to Britain meant leaving the Operations desk,
and MacArthur, to others. Officially, as of mid-April, MacArthur had
been designated commander in chief, Southwest Pacific Area, dividing
the vast ocean between his oversight and that of Admiral Chester W.

Nimitz, who was mandated command of the Pacific Ocean Area. The line dividing them was established as the 160th degree of east longitude, soon corrected to the 159th degree, to put the then little-known island of Guadalcanal in the Solomons under Nimitz. That meant that Admiral Robert H. Ghormley and then Admiral William F. Halsey would be operating at times under the general. It was an added irony that the directive to MacArthur outlining his powers was written by his former subordinate, who in Marshall's absence had liaised with Stimson and Roosevelt, wrote messages for the president's signature, and in effect—but for the sea dimension under Admiral King—was running much of the war.

While Marshall was abroad, Lieutenant Colonel James H. Doolittle's squadron of fifteen B-25 twin-engine bombers took off from the deck of the carrier *Hornet* to harass Japanese cities, intending, if possible, to land in unoccupied China. A test pilot with a Ph.D. in aeronautical engineering from MIT, Doolittle had flown with the Air Corps in 1917–18 and retired as a major in 1930 to work for Shell Oil on aviation fuels. Returning to duty in 1940, he first oversaw the conversion of automobile factories to aircraft production, but chafed at inaction. Early in 1942 he had his wish, planning and directing—and then commanding—for Hap Arnold an operation that had been considered technically and strategically impossible.

Because Japanese picket vessels were discovered farther offshore than expected, hazarding the precious carrier, Doolittle's eighty fliers took off prematurely, without sufficient fuel to reach deep into China. Even the weather worsened. Landing even under the best conditions would have been daunting, and Eisenhower, writing as Marshall and preparing for Doolittle's arrival, had his first contretemps with Generalissimo Chiang Kai-shek. The haughty, stubborn Chiang, who sought American aid more to line the pockets of local warlords and block Mao Zedong's Red Chinese rebels than to fight the Japanese, wanted to ward off expected enemy retaliation by preventing the mission. Eisenhower had to resort to an abject apology in advance, promising for the United States to undertake no further flights into or out of Nationalist China except under "your complete control and in conformity with your desires."

Whether the rigid, laconic Marshall would have written as humbly is unlikely, but Eisenhower wanted to keep the unreliable Chiang and his apathetic troops in the war. In a radiogram to Lieutenant "Vinegar Joe" Stilwell, then in Chungking, the next day, April 18, as Doolittle's B-25s were crash-landing in occupied China, Eisenhower cautioned that no publicity was to follow. "It is our purpose to maintain an atmosphere of complete mystery including origin, nationality, destination, and results of this type of effort. . . . You are directed also to make earnest request upon the Generalissimo to observe this policy." Chiang complied. Marshall asked Stilwell further for a report "through survivors or otherwise."

Most aircraft made it through, including Doolittle's. One B-25 landed in Siberia and the crew was interned since the Russians were not at war with Japan. Several captured crewmen were beheaded by the Japanese; five others, near starvation, would narrowly survive imprisonment. Asked at a press conference about the flight's origin, Roosevelt offered "Shangri-la," the make-believe Tibetan city in James Hilton's novel *Lost Horizon*. (Citing fiction for the only time in warship history, an aircraft carrier would shortly be christened *Shangri-la*.) Doolittle, soon a brigadier general, would return to receive an authentically earned Medal of Honor at a White House ceremony, and go on to a command under Eisenhower—and then under MacArthur.

However unfortunately the hazardous mission ended, and however token were its bombs, the attack on Japanese cities established that they were not invulnerable. In part to safeguard the home islands, the Japanese leadership rushed preparations already under way for a broad attack eastward that would lead in June to unanticipated catastrophe in the central Pacific.

The surrender of Corregidor occurred just after the first major sea engagement in the Southwest Pacific, in the Coral Sea east of Australia. MacArthur was still in temporary headquarters in Melbourne, in the best suite in the Menzies Hotel, where he had switchboard operators take calls by announcing, "This is Bataan." When the Australians asked Jean MacArthur to christen a destroyer, it was named *Bataan*. It was almost as much fiction as *Shangri-la*. But for one overnight stay in Canberra, he remained at the Menzies for four months.

Marshall wanted Australian and Dutch officers represented on MacArthur's senior staff, to suggest an Allied look, and the stubby, rumpled Australian general Sir Thomas Blamey, who had served in France in World War I, was recalled from the Middle East to be chief of ground forces. MacArthur accepted Blamey nominally but largely ignored him. All eleven major headquarters assignments otherwise would be American, including eight senior officers MacArthur had brought with him from Corregidor.

In the same week that MacArthur pronounced a maudlin requiem over Skinny Wainwright and his men, he found a diversion from gloom and a rare victory to claim. The Coral Sea affair below New Guinea was in reality a draw, fought in the air over warships that never encountered each other, some of which on both sides would be disabled or sunk. Fearing that the encounter had jeopardized their air and sea superiority, the Japanese postponed attempts to occupy New Guinea and threaten Australia. MacArthur happily began referring to warships not under his command as "my navy" and the Fifth Air Force as "my air." He would later insert his absent self into news releases about SWPA ground operations. With the war inching closer, he arranged, for efficiency, to relocate his headquarters to Brisbane, five hundred miles northeast of Melbourne, just below the Barrier Reef and the Coral Sea. On July 20 he and Jean would move into Lennon's Hotel, the city's best hostelry, and MacArthur commandeered an eight-story insurance company building for his burgeoning military bureaucracy.

Another, less remote headquarters was also on Marshall's mind. He was dissatisfied with the handling of the American buildup in Britain, and had dispatched Eisenhower to survey the problem. Prior to Pearl Harbor an American liaison group had been ordered to England. Now coordinating a burgeoning but disorganized buildup, the pre–Pearl Harbor "Special Observer Group," headed by an air forces officer, Major General James E. Chaney, seemed out of touch with Washington. His staff still viewed Britain as a defensive theater likely to be air oriented and operating under local control. Chaney's post-observer achievements were a small bomber command in East Anglia and a "Northern Air Route" that ferried aircraft, even fighter planes, via Maine, Newfoundland, Labrador, Greenland, Iceland, and Scotland.

"My own particular reason for going," Eisenhower told his diary, "is an uneasy feeling that either we do not understand our own commanding general and staff in England or they don't understand us. Our planning for Bolero—the UK build-up—is not progressing." Chaney, however, had little authority over ground troops other than to watch them debark from transports in Northern Ireland and to settle them into training camps.

With "Bolero" higher on Marshall's agenda than Brisbane, he planned to dispatch Major General Robert C. Richardson Jr., Seventh Army commander in California and close geographically and in outlook on Pacific matters, to confer with MacArthur and brief him personally on Washington's priorities. MacArthur would not be pleased. Marshall sent for Richardson, he noted to Eisenhower in a memorandum, and discussed "whether or not he should inform General MacArthur regarding BOLERO. I think he must do this, otherwise we would lose the one safe opportunity of making MacArthur aware of the general situation. . . ." If

Russia succumbed and Britain teetered on the margins, the United States would have to fight a two-ocean war almost alone. Yet handling MacArthur, and his influential domestic constituency, was a delicate matter. Allocating the resources MacArthur demanded was impossible. Although the public wanted MacArthur to go at the perpetrators of Pearl Harbor and the conquerors of Bataan, and Europe-first had not evoked substantial popular feeling, the White House still sought action in what was, to the Russians, at least, the West.

"Bolero" could be accelerated without "Sledgehammer" (the proposed limited landing on the French coast) but Roosevelt insisted to Marshall and King, "I do not believe we can wait until 1943 to strike at Germany." Churchill, supported as always by his military chiefs, resisted a Channel operation that seemed premature and sacrificial. Eisenhower's mission to England was in part to persuade the PM to reconsider. Arriving with Mark Clark and logistics chief Brehon Somervell at Prestwick in Scotland, Ike observed a landing craft exercise using vessels "that could cross the Channel only in very calm weather." The Channel was seldom calm. If the assault-craft show was to demonstrate the impracticality of "Sledgehammer" it contributed to the desired effect.

In the south of England the Americans were observers at a field exercise run by the mercurial, sweater-and-beret clad General Bernard Montgomery, described diplomatically in Eisenhower's diary as "a decisive type who appears to be extremely energetic and professionally able." He did not tell Marshall, or confide to his own diary, that the ascetic Monty, incensed at his visitor's compulsive smoking, humiliated him by a public dressing-down. Sheepishly, then, Eisenhower stubbed out his cigarette. En route back to London, according to their Motor Transport Corps driver, Kay Summersby, Ike "was furious—really steaming mad," and he railed at Montgomery as "that son of a bitch." The generals would continue to hit it off badly at best, and Ike nervously intensified his nicotine habit.

In London he conferred with the British chiefs of staff, and General Chaney. In more private meetings it became clear that although Eisenhower had described Chaney as "the representative here of General Marshall and . . . the administrative and operational commander of all United States troops in the United Kingdom," the British, Ike realized, saw nothing in Chaney to inspire any confidence. In fact they saw little potential whatever, at every level, in the naïve and untested American leadership, including Eisenhower.

General Brooke had dismissed all American senior officers in Britain as lightweight. His misgivings included the abrasive, Anglophobic Admiral King, and almost every other American military figure he had encountered anywhere. (When Brooke first met the courtly, cautious Secretary of War Stimson, an artillery colonel in 1918 and now seventy-five, he dismissed him as "one of the strong adherents of breaking our heads in too early operations across the Channel.") Following Marshall in London, Eisenhower seemed to Brooke an amiable mediocrity lacking command experience and strategic sense. Further, Ike promoted, as ordered, a "D-Day" bridgehead in France in "spring, 1943." Hopes of an assault in that direction in 1942 were gone, but for what Marshall had downplayed as a "limited objective operation." Even if that came off it could employ few American troops, who were unready to confront blooded Germans. Yanks, it was made clear, could not dominate strategic thinking if the players remained predominantly British. With all the talk of buildup of forces in Britain, the Americans had fewer than three divisions equipped and in training. General Chaney had little with which to work.

The conferees discussed potential commanders of a future joint operation. Eisenhower suggested Vice Admiral Lord Louis Mountbatten, who, he had heard, was "vigorous, intelligent, and courageous"—and indeed at forty-two and related to the royal family, he outranked many of his elders and was already a popular hero. A favorite of Churchill, the PM had jumped him three ranks. Breaking the abrupt silence that followed, Brooke said, "General, possibly you have not met Admiral Mountbatten. This is he, sitting directly across the table from you."

Returning to Washington on June 4, 1942, Eisenhower recommended that "the present incumbent"and his staff be replaced by his old friend Mark Clark (to whom he owed much), to lead an American corps to train in England, and that Marshall's shrewd War Department deputy, Major General Joseph McNarney, direct what was planned to be an "exceedingly complex" new American command that would be integrated into a unified Anglo-American headquarters. Ever sensitive to army politics, Patton, however distant, seemed to know who would make it happen. "From the rumors I heard," he wrote a colleague, "it now seems that Eisenhower and Clark will have the big jobs."

In the corridors of power it appeared by then that the first major strike in the West would be the long-debated and renamed "Torch"—an invasion of Vichy-administered North Africa. Given the hatred of the British following the fall of France, when to keep its navy out of Nazi hands the British had attacked and sunk five warships near Oran in Algeria; and the accusations that the British had run out on the French at Dunkirk, the operation would have to be fronted by an American. The Nazified Vichy French, Roosevelt thought, "will offer less resistance to us than they will to the British." But that meant at least the facade of an American commander, and substantial American input.

Marshall resisted, seeing the Mediterranean, with all its possibilities to squander resources from Gibraltar to Cairo, as not only a Churchillian empire-related diversion from the inevitable front in France, and a delay in winning the war, but a remote, high-risk operation. North Africa was not across the English Channel, twenty miles away at Dover. Forces would have to be conveyed long distances in waters infested by German submarines. Transporting one armored division required forty-five troop and cargo ships plus escorting combat vessels. The prime minister promoted his strategy as a victory on the cheap— aggressive action against the Axis that would end quickly if the collaborationist French would cooperate and quit. He neglected to mention that the German Control Commission at Wiesbaden, which monitored French military activity in North Africa, was empowered to intervene and almost certainly would do so.

Roosevelt presided over a nation now addicted, since Pearl Harbor, to newspapers and the radio. No further embarrassing reverses in the Pacific were likely, but no serious movement against the Japanese either. And where was the war being taken to the Germans? Marshall recalled ruefully, about an operation he deplored, that he had "failed to see that the leader in a democracy has to keep the people entertained. That may sound like the wrong word, but it conveys the thought." To keep Congress and the electorate in a positive frame of mind to support the costs of a two-ocean war, Roosevelt had to show visible progress somewhere.

Since Churchill was about to return to Washington to confirm future plans, Eisenhower worked on a directive establishing a European Theater of Operations that would be in place when the prime minister arrived. On June 8, he completed for Marshall a directive outlining to General Chaney the parameters of the redefined ETO. At a conference with Marshall three days later, Ike was asked, "In your opinion, are the plans as nearly complete as we can make them?"

"Yessir," said Eisenhower.

"That's lucky," said Marshall, "because you're the man who is going to carry them out."

In his diary, Ike penned without further comment, "The chief of staff says I'm the guy." His command would be effective as of June 24, 1942.

He may have recalled, then, an exchange of letters with his former boss, General MacArthur, initiated when Ike wrote from Fort Lewis, Washington, on December 11, 1940, months after the fall of France and the likelihood of many bleak years ahead for the Continent. Airmail by Pan Am Clipper to Manila then cost fifty cents, and Eisenhower, still a restless and impecunious lieutenant colonel, offered advance Christmas greetings and an update on his post-Philippines assignments. "So far as the U.S. is concerned," he had closed diplomatically, as MacArthur was far away in what seemed a backwater, "the guns, of course, are not yet roaring. But how long they can keep silent becomes more of a guess, it seems to me, with every day that passes. Once they really open up I'll expect to see you in the thick of it."

In return, Eisenhower apparently received a letter from MacArthur boasting of a remarkable message from President Roosevelt. Ike showed MacArthur's letter to his son, John, soon to be a West Point cadet, and visiting from school on holiday leave. In it Roosevelt was quoted as promising that should the United States become involved in the war across the Atlantic, MacArthur would be summoned to command American forces in the recovery of Europe. John remembered vividly the last line: "Of course this pleases me very much."

MacArthur's confidences are untraceable. The letter would not have ended in a wastebasket; however a footlocker with some of Eisenhower's files was lost when he was next transferred.* Roosevelt may have penned a private letter, as he sometimes did, putting the stamps on himself, for no copy of the alleged offer to have MacArthur oversee a visionary D-Day from England survives at Hyde Park. The president told Churchill's Cabinet crony, Lord Beaverbrook, in January 1942, that he didn't write "over a dozen long-hand letters in a year—and even then they do not average a page and a half apiece." Was one to MacArthur? Or was MacArthur's claim triggered by Ike's prediction that another Pershing might be needed across the Atlantic? One wonders.

When Eisenhower returned to Fort Myer, and Mamie, after his meeting with Marshall he was uncharacteristically quiet. After dinner Mamie asked him what was up. He was returning to London, Ike said.

"What post are you going to have?"

"I'm going to command the whole shebang."

---

*Another Eisenhower footlocker was lost en route to England. Ike wrote to General Somervell on July 27, 1942, about the disappearance of the baggage, "God knows I need my trunk!!"

Although it was unclear what the whole shebang entailed, as Churchill had a habit of changing his mind, Eisenhower drafted, again under Marshall's signature, a cable (#1197) letting the hapless Chaney down. His relief, Ike wrote, "does not imply dissatisfaction with your performance. . . . I deem it of urgent importance however that the commanding general in England be an officer . . . completely familiar with all our military plans and affairs and who has taken a leading part in the military developments since December 7. I am assigning Eisenhower to the post. He will leave here in about ten days. . . ." To Brigadier General Spencer Ball Akin, an old friend who was MacArthur's signal officer and who had left Corregidor for Australia on the same day as his boss, but on another PT boat, Eisenhower wrote, four days before flying off, to inform him of the new assignment. "Please pay my respects to General MacArthur when you see him," Ike closed. It seemed prudent to inform MacArthur indirectly.

4

Dreaming of Commands

Much later in 1942, from a temporary tunnel headquarters as his first offensive loomed, Eisenhower confided to his crony, Harry Butcher, now his all-purpose and purely nominal "naval aide," of the "ridiculous situations" brought about in wartime. "I've often thought or dreamed of commands of various types that I might one day hold," he confided, "—war commands, peace commands, battle commands, administrative commands, etc. One I now have could never, under any conditions, have entered my mind even fleetingly. *I have operational command of Gibraltar!!*" He had already exercised effective if indirect command of his four-star former boss, Douglas MacArthur. Almost the last thing Eisenhower did from Washington before he left for his "Torch" assignment was to assure Field Marshal Sir John Dill for the British Chiefs of Staff that MacArthur was being furnished adequate forces in Australia "to carry out his directive."

Never imagining in palmier days that he would be commanding a backwater, but recognizing ruefully the Europe-first priorities in Washington and London, MacArthur was employing every dimension of his domestic prestige to reverse the view that Japan would have to wait its turn. "We feel that both the ground and air forces projected for Australia," Ike replied to Dill under Marshall's signature, "are sufficient for the operations now visualized in that area, . . . a defensive mission with the task of preparation for an offensive. This conforms to our basic strategy. To be able to take positive action in any theater, it is necessary to hold forces in defensive theaters to a minimum and, in doing so, to recognize the acceptance of certain calculated risks. The measures General MacArthur advocates would be highly desirable if we were at war with Japan only."

After the Coral Sea standoff, Japanese air and sea forces had vanished beyond American reconnaissance from Australia. Soon they would reappear, augmented by carriers and capital ships, in the central Pacific approaching Midway Island. Crucially, navy cryptanalysts had broken the Japanese operational code, enabling a victory unexpected in scope. Early in June, Admiral Nimitz's fleet and air arm from Pearl Harbor, back in business under Vice Admiral Raymond Spruance, ended the surge of Imperial advances for good. Despite a heavy cost in American pilots, within a few minutes on June 4, 1942, three of Admiral Chuichi Nagumo's four aircraft carriers were sunk with their planes still on deck. The tide was turning.

MacArthur saw the reversal as an opportunity for his new command. Marshall answered that he would discuss it with the navy. That meant cajoling the stubborn Admiral King, who advocated gradual island-hopping toward Japan itself, while leaving the Philippines an inconsequential tangent. Shrewdly putting his ego behind him, MacArthur cabled back to Marshall that he was aware of "the extreme delicacy of your position and the complex difficulties that you face there."

MacArthur would not have to cope much longer in Washington with the continuing yet obscure presence of Eisenhower. Three days before his flight, Ike received a visitor in his Munitions Building office who evoked the difficult old days in Manila. Manuel Quezon, now exiled from Australia to Washington at MacArthur's request, arrived at the War Department early in the morning on June 20. He brought with him an honorarium to accompany a citation for services rendered by Eisenhower in the 1930s. Ike knew that MacArthur, from Corregidor on February 13, had accepted for deposit in his American account (arranged by radiogram) a staggering bonus of half a million dollars in Philippine funds. Sutherland had been given $75,000, and lesser staff who accompanied MacArthur to Australia received smaller five-figure Commonwealth checks. Eisenhower also knew from Quezon's aide, Basilio Valdez, that the awkward gift was coming. Although intending to refuse it as gracefully as possible, Ike had discussed its questionable ethics with Marshall.

As Ike was exiting the Philippines in December 1939, Quezon had offered him $100,000. Ike diplomatically turned it down. It had been standard practice for American officers in the Philippines to receive small additions to their pay from the Commonwealth: Ike had accepted five hundred dollars a month, MacArthur vastly more. The bonuses violated regulations, but MacArthur could have claimed that until he was reactivated he was only receiving retirement pay and was no longer under army discipline, and that the cash reflected that technicality. (The members of his "court" had no such exemptions.) As Ike knew, Marshall had consulted Stimson and Roosevelt, who advised ignoring the bonuses in hopes that they would remain a wartime secret. "I carefully explained," Ike wrote in his diary, ". . . that I deeply appreciated [Quezon's] thought . . . but that it was inadvisable and even impossible for me to accept a material reward." He blamed the explosive possibility of "gossip on such a matter," given his position in Washington, and was relieved that Quezon understood. "To refuse a gift from anyone raised in the Far East," Eisenhower wrote afterward, "especially if a point of ethics has to be pled, is quite apt to develop into a serious matter."

Eisenhower's seven years with MacArthur had not begun in the Philippines, but in the War Department in Washington, reporting for duty on November 8, 1929, after working for the Battle Monuments Commission. Only on February 20, 1933, two weeks before a new president was inaugurated to replace Herbert Hoover, was he formally made special assistant to MacArthur and given a cramped cubicle behind a slatted door adjacent to the general's suite. MacArthur summoned Major Eisenhower by raising his voice.

A major since 1924, in the crisis month of July 1932, D. D. Eisenhower was still "Assistant Executive, Office of the Secretary of War." In reality he worked for the chief of staff on analyses, memos, and speeches. In the ornate Old State, War, and Navy Department Building at 17th and Pennsylvania Avenue, across the street from the White House, he learned to be a patient listener. While MacArthur moved splendidly about Washington in a chauffeured limousine, his assistant went on errands for the chief by streetcar or taxi, filing vouchers for reimbursement. "Never once," Eisenhower remembered, was he offered a ride in, or use of, MacArthur's car.

The failed Hoover presidency was winding down. Begun during the most prosperous decade in American history, it was ending in the nation's worst economic depression. An index to Hoover's accumulating troubles was the "Bonus Army" dilemma about which Eisenhower was called into his chief's office to discuss. It was a political problem, not a military one, but MacArthur considered himself adept at public relations. No ordinary peacetime bureaucrat, a wartime general at thirty-eight, then the youngest superintendent ever to run West Point, MacArthur wore the additional stars of a full general, two beyond his permanent rank, while serving at the pinnacle of his profession.

At fifty-two, he was only ten years older than his ruddy, balding assistant. In the underfunded and undermanned between-the-wars army, rising in rank was slow if it happened at all. Since Eisenhower bore only a gold leaf on his shoulder tabs, he aspired for a troop command to improve his prospects. He seemed to have reached his career limits as a paper-pusher. Exploiting Ike's desk talents, and a geniality that masked his anxieties, evident largely by his compulsive smoking, MacArthur had persuaded Eisenhower that rewards often came to those close to the sources of power. Justifying his role to himself in a diary entry on February 15, 1932, Eisenhower wrote, "Gen. MacA was very nice to me—and after all I know of no greater compliment the bosses can give you than I want you hanging around." But on June 14 he noted, bleakly, as the Depression deepened further, "All salaries are to be reduced—apparently about 10%. The outlook for an army officer on 'city' duty is none too cheering."

Eisenhower tried to put a gloss on working with such a "romantic" figure as MacArthur. In a series of notes written then about War Department staff, Ike described the chief admiringly, almost as if he expected the pages to be peered at over his shoulder, as "very appreciative of good work, positive in his convictions—a genius at giving concise and clear instructions." He assumed innocently that MacArthur avoided "social duties" because his interests were "almost exclusively military." Divorced in mid-1929 from peripatetic socialite Louise Cromwell Brooks,* whose father was a multimillionaire partner of J. P. Morgan and whose Jazz Age appetites excluded the military life, MacArthur lived with his elderly mother, the possessive "Pinky," at the chief of staff's spacious quarters at Fort Myer.

The general's interests, despite Ike's guesses, were not "exclusively military." Long estranged from Louise, he quietly kept a pretty, if bored, Eurasian mistress, then eighteen, at the exclusive Castleton Hotel on 16th

---

*In Paris, and then in Washington, Louise, already a divorcée, had been the "hostess" (and mistress) of General Pershing, a widower. When she threatened to leave if he eschewed matrimony, he told her, "Marrying you would be like buying a book for someone else to read."

Street, NW, near the White House. Isabel Rosario Cooper had been imported from Manila when she was sixteen. The unsubmissive "Baby Girl" proved dissatisfied by jewels, furs, a chauffeur-driven car, and the furtive hours of "Daddy's" presence. Apprehensive about exposure, with ambitions beyond what Eisenhower assumed, MacArthur had little time to spare—or to risk—for opportunistic social diversions.

Few knew anything of Isabel until 1934, when political columnist Drew Pearson, to help quash a $1.75 million libel suit inspired by his charging MacArthur with "dictatorial leanings," gained access to her letters from him. To buy Isabel's silence, MacArthur would pay her $15,000 for the letters and include a return ticket to Manila in the envelope to her which he marked "From the Humane Society." She decamped instead to Hollywood, where her career failed to take off. Years later she died, far more forgotten than MacArthur, of a barbiturate overdose.

MacArthur's fancied postmilitary career included politics. "I shall never forget the time in Washington," Ike recalled in his diary in 1937, from the Philippines, "when receipt of instructions [in mid-1932] to report to the President, led him to conclude, in the greatest seriousness, that he was to be invited to be the President's running mate in the succeeding election." Impulsively, MacArthur had confided that Hoover, desperate for a popular figure to run as his vice presidential candidate, was likely to offer him the nomination. That wishful thinking had arisen from almost nothing. An appointment with Hoover at the White House turned out to have a more disappointing agenda—the army budget. Still, political ambition in MacArthur would run long and deep.

Hoover would have improved his slipping reelection chances only slightly with the general on his ticket. No politician eager to climb craved a losing campaign, and the president would be stuck once more with former senator Charles Curtis of Kansas, a nonentity of seventy-two, whose penchant for laws protecting poultrymen had earned him the tag, "Eggie Curtis."

As early as 1931, MacArthur had placed a "special commendation" in Ike's personnel file which was so fulsome (yet characteristically egomaniacal) in acknowledging Major Eisenhower's "excellent work of a highly important nature which you have just completed under my personal direction" that Mamie, in wifely pride, had it framed. The general had assured him, so Ike wrote in his diary, that "as long as he stays in the Army I am one of the people earmarked for his 'gang.'" Nothing in the annual evaluation, including the enigmatic "as long as he stays in the Army," seemed to suggest to Eisenhower, narrowly immersed as he was in military matters with MacArthur, that the boss could then harbor political ambitions after his term as chief of staff ended. Generals with such aspirations usually emerged soon after the close of a successful war. That season had long ended.

Eisenhower speculated that MacArthur would not be content to relinquish his temporary stars and submerge himself in a footling assignment as he waited out mandatory retirement. "In my opinion," Ike wrote before the general's uncharacteristic disclosure, "he has the capacity to undertake successfully any position in govt. He has a reserved dignity—but is most animated in conversation on [nonmilitary] subjects interesting him. I doubt that he has any real political ambition—and in these days of high-powered publicity and propaganda—I do not expect to see him ever prominently mentioned for office outside the W[ar] D[epartment]."

The "Bonus Army" fiasco would have dampened anyone else's sense of destiny. Not since "Coxey's Army" had marched on Washington in 1894 to demand help for aging and desperate Civil War veterans had there been anything like the pathetic, ragtag petitioners encamped at the capital in June and July 1932. In the middle 1920s, thousands of war veterans untouched by stock market boom times had campaigned for a small share of the ongoing prosperity, describing it as adjusted wartime compensation—partial payback for what they had lost on puny service pay in 1917–18 while nonveterans earned large industrial wages. Congress grudgingly voted small bonuses in 1924, averaging about a thousand dollars each, but these were promised only in 1945 or to their beneficiaries upon their deaths. Many veterans now were jobless; few could imagine surviving the full twenty-one years. Opposed to spending public money, Calvin Coolidge had signed the bill contingent on payment being deferred until the veterans had likely gone on to their posthumous rewards. "Patriotism which is bought and paid for," he declared smugly, his hands in his shallow pockets, "is not patriotism." The ungrateful legislation quickly became known as the "Tombstone Bonus."

In 1932 there were few veterans who saw any likelihood of making it into 1945. Many other Americans were also out of work, but ex-soldiers felt that they had a special claim, long recognized by law. Self-described as the "Bonus Expeditionary Force," about twelve thousand of the three million eligibles, some with their ragged families, arrived in the capital, making their way from as far off as California. They camped in shantytowns constructed from abandoned crates and cardboard on the mudflats across the Anacostia River, or in abandoned old government buildings in central Washington awaiting the wrecker's ball. In such "Hoovervilles" they

cooked skimpy meals on fires made from discarded lumber, raised plac-
ards describing their plight, and picketed on Pennsylvania Avenue. "We
Done a Good Job in France," read one crude sign, "Now You Do a Job in
America." Despite their vigils in legislative offices, and a House-passed
bill, the Senate on June 17 refused to go along and adjourned for the summer on July 16. Stubbornly, 11,698 Bonus marchers hung on.

Although well disciplined but for a few loud agitators, their presence
disturbed the summer tranquility of the seat of government. Prodded by
Hoover subordinates, local health authorities declared the encampments
unsanitary and recommended their removal. Although the marchers eschewed radical rhetoric, conservative congressmen (as well as General
MacArthur) denounced the throng as Bolsheviks awaiting some provocation to rise. As three of the thirty-six alleged leaders arrested later were
known Communists, the party boasted improbable credit for the protest.
Most veterans were loyal capitalists without capital.

Alleging that new government construction was being impeded, District police tried to clear the Capitol area. Seeing only a pretext to get rid
of them, the veterans refused to budge, and heaved bricks. Through Secretary of War Patrick J. Hurley, Hoover called on MacArthur to disperse
the squatters. "I don't want to hear them and I don't want to see them,"
Hoover told Hurley. Although Brigadier General Perry Miles was in
charge of the local garrison, MacArthur, bored with desk work and visu-
alizing admiring newspaper accounts to come once he restored order, told
Eisenhower that he would oversee the 600 soldiers himself, "not with a
view of commanding the troops but to be on hand as things progressed, . . . [to] issue necessary instructions on the ground."

Dismayed by the perception of a four-star general directing a battalion to put down a street protest, Eisenhower politely wondered aloud to
his boss about the misapplication of the staff system and the potential for
embarrassment if the affair got out of hand. Many years later he recalled
acidly, "I told that dumb son-of-a-bitch he had no business down there. I
told him it was no place for the Chief of Staff." Rather, he thought, it was
a "damn fool" reaction.

MacArthur disagreed. Federal authority was involved, he reminded
Ike, warning of "incipient revolution in the air." Further, in preparation for
the action which he had determined upon before asking for advice he had
no intention of accepting, he ordered Eisenhower into uniform. In peacetime Washington, officers wore civilian clothes—in July, summer whites.

When Ike reported back on the sweltering afternoon of July 28,
MacArthur already had collected additional aides, including the spiffily

attired Major George Patton. Also at the ready were a few of Patton's clanking tanks never employed in 1918 and now little more than museum pieces. Eisenhower realized that they were meant for intimidation rather than use.

It was already late in the day. By 6:30 the veterans in what Eisenhower would later call the "Communist area" in the report he wrote in MacArthur's name had begun drifting back. Offering no resistance, they were nudged across the Anacostia River toward the mudflats where their jerry-built encampment stood. Jeering the soldiers, as did several thousand supportive onlookers, the motley remnants sullenly retreated toward the 11th Street Bridge.

As MacArthur watched from the Ellipse below the White House, debonair and splendid for press photographers in his gold-braided cap and tunic with eight rows of ribbons, two messengers from the War Department turned up, looking for him. On further orders from the president, to avoid any violence, Secretary of War Hurley forbade troops to cross the bridge into the shambles of the Bonus Army bivouac. To furnish added authority, the message was carried by Colonel Esmund White of the General Staff. Brigadier General George Van Horn Moseley, an executive assistant to the secretary, reputedly mean and malicious, sent the second courier deliberately late. When MacArthur objected that he was too busy to be "bothered by people coming down and pretending to give orders," their messages were read at him.

Later, both MacArthur and Eisenhower would deny receiving orders from anyone. In his memoirs, MacArthur admitted, "I received words from the Secretary of War as we were in the midst of crossing the river, to suspend the operation at my discretion." Blatant insubordination was already a MacArthur hallmark. He would get away with many more of them.

In his ghostwritten report, Eisenhower mentioned neither order, nor that the troops brandished intimidating bayonets. He did observe, perhaps for MacArthur's appreciation, the potential of tanks "in quelling civil disorder." Merely by being there, the sputtering antiques had created "an impression of irresistible and inexorable power." Further, Eisenhower condoned employing tear gas on the vets, as "this harmless instrument quickly saps the will to resist," and possesses, as well, "moral suasion" to "run from rather than toward the scene of its use." Still, he added with a touch of diplomacy, using troops was a "disagreeable and repugnant" last resort, as the "riot" was "rapidly assuming alarming proportions."

Accompanying the column of soldiers, MacArthur and his aides, including the anxious Eisenhower, kept going along Pennsylvania Avenue and then across the bridge. It was already dark. A municipal fire truck with a searchlight probed into the gloom as soldiers were greeted by a shower of rocks. Tear gas drove the protesters back, but by then the troops discovered, to their surprise, they claimed, that the shacks and tents were in flames. Reporters with flashbulb-equipped cameras were already snapping away at the ragged, routed women and children.

After eleven, leaving a few foot soldiers to guard the bridge approaches, MacArthur ordered the troops dismissed and returned to barracks. A bugler blew "Assembly." What was left of the smoldering encampment had emptied. As the general summoned a staff car to take him back to the War Department, Eisenhower warned that whatever the hour, there would be reporters poised to question him, and that "it would be the better part of wisdom, if not valor, to avoid meeting them. . . . Political officials only should talk to the press."

MacArthur thought otherwise. Although it was well after eleven, he spoke with a crowd of reporters, claiming that the rout of the rabble was Hoover's idea, and that constitutional government would have been in jeopardy had the president "not acted with the force and vigor that he did." MacArthur, allegedly, was only the agent of that force and vigor. He had saved the country from "incipient revolution." He could never keep the civilian and the military sectors separated, and would not live down the Bonus Army embarrassment, which had at first seemed an opportunity to enhance his conservative credentials.

In New York, glancing at the morning papers, Governor Franklin D. Roosevelt, the Democratic presidential candidate nominated only weeks before, observed to future Supreme Court justice Frankfurter, a political adviser, "Well, Felix, this elects me."

MacArthur instantly became almost as unpopular as Hoover. The victims got little of Eisenhower's sympathy. He saw the episode as lamentable, the outcome of mobocracy and the misuse of authority. But MacArthur remained his chief, and Ike had to live with that career realization, as well as with his responsibility for concocting, in MacArthur-style prose, cover-up language about which he could not be very proud. Only in 1967 would he set down, with obvious chagrin, his own self-serving account of the affair.

At the close of 1932, Eisenhower again drafted MacArthur's annual report and edited those of the outgoing secretary of war and the assistant secretary. He did so again late in 1933 under the new administration, when the new secretary, in a political payoff of Roosevelt supporters, was the "slow, ponderous" former governor of Utah, George H. Dern. Eisenhower was not sorry to lose Hoover, confiding to his diary that he had "no definite leanings toward any political party" as it was clear MacArthur had. Ike (who had never voted) thought nevertheless that, in Depression-ridden times, it was "a good thing the Democrats won." Newspaper accounts of Fascist achievements in Italy had made him a closet admirer of Benito Mussolini, and he thought that "more power" had to be "centered in one man's hands"—even "virtual dictatorship"—to extricate the country from its internal problems. That he had said as much, privately, even before the presidential election, he confessed, had caused cronies to label him "Dictator Ike."

Conferred just before the change at the White House and bringing no rise in rank, Eisenhower's new title was "Senior Aide to the Chief of Staff." It validated what he had already been doing. Uncomfortably, on the other side of his cubicle from MacArthur, as deputy chief of staff, remained the openly ambitious and unlikable Major General Hugh Drum, already a brigadier general on the Western Front in 1918 when Eisenhower got no farther than Pennsylvania. (Ten years into the Roosevelt presidency, his career stalled, Drum would be retired with the sop of an additional star to become commander of the New York National Guard.) When MacArthur led the inaugural parade for FDR along Pennsylvania Avenue on March 4, 1933,* stylishly riding a grey gelding, Eisenhower remained behind his slatted door.

MacArthur's year-extended term was due to end in November 1934. His new boss in the White House had been an activist assistant secretary of the navy while the general was acquiring glory in France. A military innocent whose appointment suggested the priorities of the peacetime army, Secretary Dern had asked Roosevelt to retain MacArthur an extra year to utilize his administrative expertise. Visiting the White House with MacArthur to seek restoration of Hoover's budget cuts, Dern encountered fiscal resistance. Congress, Roosevelt said, would not vote the money. MacArthur recalled weighing in melodramatically with "something to the general effect that when we lost the next war, and an American boy, lying in the mud with an enemy bullet through his belly, and an enemy foot on his dying throat, spat out his last curse, I wanted the name not to be MacArthur, but Roosevelt."

---

*It would be the last March 4 inaugural. Beginning in 1936, the date was moved forward to January 20, recognizing belatedly improved postelection travel and communications since Washington's day and costing Roosevelt six weeks of his first term.

"You must not talk that way to the President!" FDR shouted back. Realizing his error, MacArthur apologized. When he offered his resignation, and arose to leave, Roosevelt said, "Don't be foolish, Douglas. You and the budget must get together on this." The advice worked; MacArthur's next request was better received. So was MacArthur, who was also sounded out on matters unrelated to his military role, as he had influential conservative connections on Capitol Hill. "Douglas," blandished the president, "you are my American conscience."

As a New Deal emergency measure, Congress had legislated a Civilian Conservation Corps to create practical work opportunities for unemployed young men. Roosevelt wanted 275,000 of the jobless recruited within months. Only the army seemed qualified to cope with the challenge. Although MacArthur stayed on with his chief's stars, and with him, Eisenhower, actual CCC oversight was left to backwater brass like George Catlett Marshall. The end of the war in 1918 had thwarted Marshall's hopes for a star. He had been on the postwar recommended list while assistant chief of staff, First Army, and a temporary colonel. MacArthur went to West Point as a brigadier general, keeping his star. Marshall was downgraded to his permanent prewar captaincy, rising only to major in 1920 while aide-de-camp to General Pershing. It was in that reduced status that, in 1921, he published a cautionary essay for future commanders in *Infantry Journal*, warning them from his experience not to assume that warfare of the future would be anything like their testing in 1918 against a demoralized German army exhausted by four years of attrition. They had to assume that a likely enemy would be first-class in every way, and that such a challenge had to be anticipated. His predictions would be correct on both counts. Future adversaries would be formidable indeed, yet many of his colleagues who had drifted through the interwar army remained complacent and unready.

As a lieutenant colonel, Marshall served with the 15th Infantry Regiment in Tientsin, China from 1924 to 1927, under a nominal commander who, addicted to the bottle, had allowed the regiment to fall into disarray. Marshall ran it, assisted by a young lieutenant, Matthew B. Ridgway. Returning to temporary duty at the Army War College, Marshall was then posted, as assistant commandant, then commandant, to the Infantry School, Fort Benning, Georgia, from October 1927 to June 1932. More than two hundred men he schooled at Benning would become generals. Marshall discarded the outmoded field manuals and produced *Infantry in Battle* (1934), proposing a "triangular" division of three regiments as more efficient than the World War I "square" division of four, and adding battalions of heavy weapons firepower (and, soon, tanks).

Going nowhere in rank, he wore only an insignificant silver leaf on his epaulets, yet Marshall was not completely beneath MacArthur's notice, for the chief of staff reviewed all senior officers' postings, and had a special and vocal distaste for the "Chaumont Crowd" of Pershing's staff of 1917–18 (headquartered at Chaumont, southwest of Nancy). When the CCC began functioning in 1933, Marshall was commanding, on assignment from MacArthur, stagnant Fort Screven, Georgia, where he was also handed District F of the New Deal labor corps. Moved to Fort Moultrie in South Carolina that June, he also received CCC District I. Supervising nineteen CCC camps in addition to regular troops was not much of an improvement in status, but in September 1933, after fifteen years, he would finally be back to full colonel. Later, as chief of staff himself, he recalled CCC assignments for young officers as useful training "in matters of administration and supply on a large scale." Though he had no need for that himself, having efficiently moved hundreds of thousands of troops and their equipment about in France, he was only being reassigned from one unpromising location to another.

Marshall's next posting, in October 1933, was to the 33rd Division, an Illinois National Guard unit, as "Senior Instructor." That indignity seemed too much to bear quietly. It was a career-busting job, although MacArthur faint-praised Marshall to Major General Frank Parker, commander of the Sixth Corps area in the Midwest, as an officer "with no superior among infantry colonels." To Marshall, MacArthur wrote that the new assignment was more important than it appeared, and included a raise in pay. Economic depression and unrest had created "incipient revolution," and a firm hand was needed to create a well-disciplined force in the populous Midwest. Still, mandatory retirement for age-in-rank reasons loomed.

In despair, Marshall, who realized that National Guard service would not count toward attaining his long-deferred first star, wrote the first letter in his military life asking to have the posting changed. It does not appear in MacArthur's surviving papers, but Katherine Marshall recalled that her husband told the chief of staff that he had never made any request to higher authority before. "He had always accepted what was given him. But, he pointed out, he . . . couldn't get his generalcy without having been so many [additional] years with troops."

When retired general Charles G. Dawes, former vice president under Coolidge and a Chaumont staffer, learned of the dead-end assignment to

Chicago, he objected passionately to Pershing that MacArthur "can't do that. Hell, no! Not George Marshall. He's too big a man for this job. In fact he's the best goddamned officer in the U.S. Army." The long-retired and ailing Pershing appealed to MacArthur, who explained unconvincingly (as he would no longer be chief of staff) that an appointment in the War Department itself was possible for Marshall in two years or thereabouts, once a vacancy occurred, as chief of infantry, which came with a star. Pershing told Marshall as much, but that desk job seemed vague and tainted. Paper pushing did not lead to much more than a pension, and time was running out. He explained that he sought "command duty, with the attendant possibilities for the future. . . . As I will soon be 54, I must get started if I am going anywhere in the Army." MacArthur replied with a curt "All requests refused." Via time-in rank, Marshall's promotion to colonel took effect just before he took the train to Chicago.

For years, Douglas MacArthur counted upon his assertive mother, "Pinky," to promote the son of a famous father to senior generals who had been junior officers under Arthur MacArthur, but she was now feeble and out of the picture. Marshall still needed Pershing, who might have done something as early as 1919, but did not. This time Marshall interceded with Roosevelt, who asked Dern to put the colonel "on the list of next promotions" to general, only to have an army selection board refuse to make any exceptions to strict seniority. "I can but wait, grow older, and hope for a more favorable situation in Washington," Marshall wrote to Pershing.

MacArthur was pondering his own army future after relinquishing his temporary chief of staff's stars. For a time he was despondent. An aide, Lieutenant Thomas Jefferson Davis, recalled MacArthur's sitting theatrically in a railway car with a revolver in hand. Davis was accompanying the chief on a dull journey through the middle South, and trying to doze off. "We are nearing the area, Davis," MacArthur intoned in the semidarkness, "where my father won his Medal of Honor. I've done everything I can in the army and life. As we pass over the Tennessee River bridge, I intend to jump from the train. This is where my life ends, Davis."

"T. J." had endured MacArthur's histrionics before, and barked, although he knew it might cost him, "General, would you hurry up and get it over with so I can get back to sleep?"

Connections in the Philippines he made in the 1920s solved MacArthur's problems. Serving at a reduced rank under someone else inevitably his inferior was not his style. Instead, he would head the American military mission to Manila at the invitation of Commonwealth president Manuel Quezon. The general intended to exploit his outsized reputation to build a Philippine army, then hardly more than a constabulary, while double-dipping in earnings. Self-rule required self-defense, and the Philippines by congressional mandate was to become fully independent in 1946. The arrangement was approved by Roosevelt, who saw the general as dangerous if at loose ends and left at home. MacArthur understood that he could wait for his moment, especially if he could do so in the public eye as commander of some other army with American connections.

As a final assignment while the general's aide, Eisenhower wrote MacArthur's "Farewell to the Army," much admired as in his inimitable style. At a time when a dollar had real buying power, the Philippines deal added to MacArthur's salary $3,000 as head of the mission, a further salary of $18,000 from the Philippines plus an expense account of $15,000, and a penthouse atop the luxurious Manila Hotel. He also secretly negotiated a commission of $46/100$ of 1 percent on military spending into 1942 if the Quezon government accepted his defense budgets. Quezon considered that as incentive pay to wheedle money from Washington, and it implied a likely performance bonus in six figures. In effect it was corporate executive compensation.

Eisenhower accompanied his chief, who valued him enough to write into his personnel file, "This is the best officer in the army. When the next war comes, he should go right to the top." Despite Ike's failure to appreciate MacArthur's pretentious verbal style, which he could pen in pastiche (he could not yet type), he remained as loyal as he was ambitious, recognizing that in the small army bureaucracy there were few paths to advancement, and that he would remain only a cubicle away from authentic clout. In the early 1920s he had confided to another young officer, Bradford G. Chynoweth, that the way up was through the "strongest and ablest man" at hand. "I forget my ideas and do everything in my power to promote what he says is right." Yet unless he was determined to remain in the army, he did not need MacArthur.

Eisenhower's reputation as a writer for the general (who according to Ike added only the "purple splendor") had reached into the private sector, leading to an offer from the Hearst press to become its military correspondent. A new war in Europe seemed inevitable. As a civilian, he could escalate his salary to $15,000 a year—serious money. Yet he and Mamie enjoyed the army ambience. He was not desperate for funds although after Hoover, citing hard times, had cut service pay by 10 percent, Roosevelt had reduced service pay by another 10 percent. The Eisenhowers lived modestly, and Mamie's well-fixed father in Colorado furnished whatever they needed beyond their income, even her car.

Life in the Philippines, they knew, would be cheap and good. They could even save money. In addition, there would be a Philippines government pay supplement and expense account. He would have preferred to command troops like his friend George Patton, who benefitted from combat experience in France, but as adviser to the American military mission, Eisenhower would finally be promoted to lieutenant colonel (effective July 1, 1936). The desk detail would only be "for a year or so," MacArthur encouraged. He said, Ike recalled, "that he and I had worked together for a long time and he didn't want to bring in somebody new." Ike could even invite a Regular Army colleague as assistant—and he thought immediately of Major James Basevi Ord, a jolly West Point classmate who was helpfully fluent in Spanish.

MacArthur had requested a nominal further extension of his term as chief of staff in order to arrive in Manila in full four-star dignity, and he assured as much in War Department travel orders he wrote for himself which relieved him "as of date Dec. 15, 1935." Early in October, however, en route via Chicago to the West Coast, as the train paused at Cheyenne, Wyoming, MacArthur, traveling in civilian clothes with his mother, now eighty-two, was handed a War Department telegram. Ike watched him read it, anger spreading across the general's face. Only one four-star position in the army existed. His temporary stars as chief of staff had automatically vanished with the confirmation of a successor he deplored, Major General Malin Craig.

MacArthur had boarded the rails west on October 1. Realistically, then, as of that date in Washington he was no longer in charge and had no further claim on four stars. Craig's appointment became effective October 2. Suspecting that the ploy to keep his temporary rank until his arrival in the Philippines had been quashed by Roosevelt, MacArthur ignored the presence of bystanders on the station platform, including Eisenhower, and began abusing the president loudly—to Ike "an explosive denunciation of politics, bad manners, bad judgment, broken promises, arrogance, unconstitutionality, insensitivity, and the way the world had gone to hell. Then he sent an eloquent telegram of congratulations to his successor."

Just before the Philippines mission entrained through, Marshall's name was put on the promotion list by Secretary Dern, who was then ailing and about to retire. On August 24, 1936, the day that Dern died, Marshall was informed by the new secretary of war, Harry Woodring, another political nonentity, that his first star would be effective on October 1. With it came a transfer from Chicago to the Third Division at Vancouver Barracks, Washington. He had finally inched up. The "political influences involved in the officer corps," he recalled, were a heavy burden in overseeing the National Guard, and in "the handling of the [enlisted] men" it was "very difficult, short of a war basis, to have men discipline their neighbors." He was relieved to turn that over to someone else. With the Washington assignment came the inevitable parallel duty of director of the CCC district in the far Northwest.

Marshall and Katherine drove cross-country on a wide southern arc in a new Packard that replaced their Ford. The general, whose curiosity ranged beyond military matters, wanted to find what Katherine recalled as "an isolated spot in Arizona"* where there was a meteor impact crater nearly a mile in diameter that he had once read about in a *National Geographic*. An elderly caretaker emerged from his shack with surprise. Few visitors had sought out the Barringer Crater since exploratory drilling ceased in 1928. From Flagstaff they drove north to Vancouver Barracks. A band and guard of honor greeted them. It was Marshall's first encounter with authentic status.

The CCC connection proved, unpredictably, to be one of the most useful in Marshall's life. The Federal Emergency Relief administrator for Roosevelt was Harry Hopkins, who supervised agencies like the CCC, WPA, and PWA,† and productively employed six and a half million formerly out-of-work Americans. When federal appropriations for the armed forces were meager, New Deal agencies rescued many army posts and naval stations from obsolescence, and built highways, airports, and bridges. (About $250 million was spent on War Department projects from 1935 through 1939.) The gaunt, chronically ailing but tireless Hopkins would get to admire Marshall's civic efficiency and sensitivity. They would work together in peace and later in war.

Marshall was ailing himself at the time, but kept his condition quiet to avoid jeopardizing his career chances. Since 1923 he had known of his need to have surgery for an overactive thyroid. By February 1937 he could postpone it no longer and went to San Francisco, where at Letterman Army Hospital the malfunctioning areas of both lobes of the gland were excised. Resuming normal activity, including fishing, hunting, and riding,

---

*Erroneously, she wrote "New Mexico" in her memoir of their marriage.
†Civilian Conservation Corps, Works Progress Administration, Public Works Administration.

he found that his altered body chemistry reduced his stress level. To outsiders he seemed as imperturbable as always.

Marshall's link to the president remained indirect, through the selfless, troubleshooting Hopkins, but it would get better. "The only thing I really want to do, as my contribution to the success of this war," Hopkins later told Brigadier General Raymond E. Lee, military attaché at the American mission in London, "is to arrange for General Marshall to establish and maintain free access to the President." What Lee described as "this war" was not then formally America's. The date was July 25, 1941, months before Pearl Harbor.

MacArthur's own relationship to Roosevelt, never warm, was frigid after his unexpected loss of rank. From Manila he would loudly predict FDR's "landslide" defeat for reelection in November 1936 by the governor of Kansas, the likable Alfred M. Landon, even after Eisenhower warned that Landon would not even carry his own state. That led to a "terrible bawling out," but when the general learned that Wall Street odds were four-to-one on Roosevelt, he worried to Ike that Roy Howard, the United Press head in whom MacArthur long confided, would "tell on him" in Washington. "Boy, did the General back pedal rapidly," Eisenhower wrote after the election. MacArthur was concerned that his outspoken animus would reach the White House and get him recalled into military limbo.

In San Francisco the Philippine mission personnel boarded the liner *President Hoover*. While "Pinky" accompanied her son, Eisenhower traveled alone. Mamie remained in Washington, where John would be at school until the end of term in June. On disembarking, Ike moved into a stifling hotel room. MacArthur received a cool, seven-room suite atop the best hotel in Manila, having insisted on accommodations equal to those of the high commissioner. Headquarters would be a short walk away, in the old Walled City. Although his staff suggested that he schedule a weekly visit to Manuel Quezon so that the nominal president would learn to depend upon him for information and advice, MacArthur loftily informed Ike and the others that "it was not in keeping with the dignity of his position to report to Malacañan [Palace]." The Philippines, nominally a "Commonwealth," was in fact an American colony.

MacArthur's upkeep as military adviser would become a major expense of the strapped commonwealth. The semiautonomous nation was poor; its financial assistance from Washington was inadequate, and the perks that Quezon's officials expected (as did MacArthur, now one of them) were overly costly. Eisenhower and T. J. Davis, now a captain, and also imported from Washington, even advised the general to decline "for the present"—as counterproductive public relations—the rank of field marshal in what Ike called "a virtually nonexisting army." MacArthur insisted that the idea was not his but Quezon's. As titles were cheap, Quezon also offered Ike and Ord general's rank, which they declined as appearing ridiculous.

Equipping an army was more crucial than its commandant's title. In 1936–37 the Japanese, pushing into the vastness of China, had obvious designs on all of Southeast Asia. Only a massive American response in arming the Philippines could be intimidating. Some semblance of a national military force had to be assembled to ward off, or at least slow down, an aggressor until American help arrived from across the Pacific. The navy had a file of "Orange" and "Rainbow" options to go after the Japanese fleet to clear a path for resupply of the Philippines, but these implied a predictable sea conflict and a powerful force in readiness. Late in 1937, when an American gunboat (named *Panay* for a Philippine island) was attacked in the Yangtze by Japanese aircraft on the warpath in China, American domestic reaction was feeble. The incident was too trivial for a war, and too far away. Besides, the nation was isolationist-minded and its military was still enfeebled by Depression cutbacks. In Manila, MacArthur grumbled to Ike of a "pacific, subversive element that surrounds the President," but that element was farther down Pennsylvania Avenue, in both houses of Congress.

Suggesting a bit of theater to prop up local morale while realistic rearmament was on hold, MacArthur proposed to Eisenhower and Ord a demonstration of national military strength, bringing newly formed units from all over the islands to a staging area near Manila for several days. Filipinos could visit the cantonments; the press would publicize the circus, and a grand parade into Manila would climax the propaganda show. Without enthusiasm Eisenhower and Ord furnished the general with a pessimistic cost estimate far in excess of available funds, which were already allocated for more crucial needs. The entire authorized Philippine army was only 920 officers and 10,000 men, most of them still without basic uniforms or even obsolete 1918-vintage weapons. MacArthur, however, had only wanted his aides to listen, not to furnish advice. He ordered them to arrange for local shipping firms to ferry such troops as already existed elsewhere in the islands to Manila Bay.

When Quezon telephoned to inquire angrily about a rumored demonstration, Eisenhower realized that the president of the Philippines hadn't been consulted. MacArthur was next on Quezon's call list, and within the hour "an exceedingly unhappy" general summoned his staff. He had never intended to proceed with the event, he claimed—only to explore the possibilities. Brazenly, he denied giving any such orders—"which was certainly news to us," Ike wrote, and "there was nothing to do except stop the proceedings." Following the fiasco he told MacArthur with the safest bluntness he could muster, "General, all you're saying is that I'm a liar, and I am *not* a liar." Diplomatically, MacArthur reached an arm out over Eisenhower's shoulder and said, "Ike, it's just fun to see that damn Dutch temper.... It's just a misunderstanding, and let's let it go at that." But there was "considerable resentment—and never again were we on the same warm and cordial terms."

When Ike had learned from MacArthur that the appointment as field marshal of a barely visible Philippine army, complete to a gold, eleven-ounce marshal's baton courtesy of Quezon, was actually going through, the self-discipline that was one of Eisenhower's strengths temporarily vanished. Forgetting his insignificance, he exploded ungrammatically, "General, you have been a four-star general. This is a *proud* thing. There's only been a few who've had it. Why in the *hell* do you want a *banana* country giving you a field-marshalship? This . . . looks like you're trying for some kind of—" Bluntly, MacArthur cut him off.

"Oh, Jesus!" Eisenhower later remembered. "He just gave me hell!"

Stories would surface that MacArthur had designed a gaudy field marshal's uniform for himself, but these came from the dissidents irritated by MacArthur's vanity. The army summer dress uniform for officers was ornate enough, and MacArthur added additional "scrambled eggs" gold braid to his cap. In Manila, as in Washington, army gear in peacetime was reserved for military functions. Usual attire was a white cotton or linen civilian suit, and straw hat.

Late in 1936 Pinky MacArthur died. Her son kept the body chilled in a Manila morgue until he had an opportunity to return to the States to bury her at his father's side at Arlington. That came when former Indiana governor Paul McNutt was appointed Philippines high commissioner and MacArthur accompanied Quezon to Washington in April 1937 for the swearing-in ceremony. MacArthur would not set foot in the United States again until 1951.

While Ike and others maintained the mission at Intramuros, MacArthur sailed to the West Coast, and quietly took the train to New York. There, in a civil ceremony at City Hall on April 30, 1937, he married Jean Faircloth, thirty-seven, an attractive, wealthy Tennessean and a Daughter of the Confederacy whom he had first met on shipboard en route to the Philippines late in 1935. The groom was fifty-seven. No one had known of his interest in her. They returned to Manila on the *President Coolidge*, where on February 21, 1938, she gave birth to their only child, Arthur.

The general had barely settled in to his late-rising marital routine, in which he spent even fewer hours at work than before (office hours in sultry Manila ended at 1:00 P.M.), when on August 23, 1937, he learned from General Malin Craig that the appointment in the Philippines as senior military adviser would end after two years. MacArthur would be expected to return on a transport scheduled to depart Manila in October, and take up a new command. The wire from the War Department had arrived the day after he had been formally presented by Quezon with his marshal's baton.

To Eisenhower, MacArthur blamed his recall on the vindictiveness of Roosevelt and the jealousy of Pershing's lingering Chaumont cronies. MacArthur raged that he would sooner retire than be pushed around by his inferiors. Ike noted in his diary, "I find myself, sooner or later, bearing the brunt of the General's displeasure, which always manifests itself against anyone who fails to agree . . . with his theories and hypotheses, no matter how astounding they may be."

Making good his vow, MacArthur cabled a request for retirement, which the War Department approved effective December 31, 1937. Then he lobbied Quezon to retain him as military adviser. MacArthur would keep, in addition to his general's pension, Ike wrote, "a 66,000 peso salary [equivalent then to $33,000], plus penthouse and expenses"—and also his secret arrangement for a percentage of the military budget. MacArthur was now, according to Eisenhower, "a free agent" on a "munificent salary" and required to "do no work" while protected from punitive transfer by the Washington military bureaucracy. The hated Roosevelt sent what Ike described as "a flowery telegram," which the field marshal promptly released to the press.

With Eisenhower's own career stagnating at a level too low to fund his own retirement, he grumbled that only "egotism [and] exclusive devotion to one's own interests" was motivating his chief, who was "raised in the conception of Douglas MacArthur superiority. . . . The barest mention of his name in the gossip column of the poorest of our universally poor daily periodicals [in Manila] sends him into hysterical delight or deepest despair, depending upon its note of praise or condemnation. He . . . displays an exaggeration of glee when he believes things are shaping up to glorify his name, or increase his income."

"For some months," he reasoned early in October 1937 as the next ship from the States came and went, "I've remained on this job, not because of the Gen—but in spite of him." He believed that he was seriously involved in trying to develop a Philippine army "capable of running itself" and that it was better work than to "mark time" somewhere else. He also knew that on a lesser scale he was also earning extra salary and expenses on the Quezon budget, and that dollars went a long way in Manila. "But now I'm at a cross-road. If the [Field] Marshal is to persist in his arbitrary methods, and is going to make things as unpleasant, if not impossible, as his today's homily [on "adequacy of security"] indicated, then I'm [opting] for home."

His attitude altered when on October 12, MacArthur showily appointed "Lt. Col. Dwight D. Eisenhower"—he had been promoted the year before—"Senior Assistant to the Military Adviser, and Chief of Staff to the Military Adviser to the Commonwealth of the Philippines." The job, Ike decided, had become "personally agreeable as well as professionally interesting." He was learning how to navigate American interests with a foreign government, and coping with the frustrations of trying to build an army from scratch. Yet 1938 was approaching, and war in Europe looked close. Since 1918 he had spent only six months with troops. He had attended four advanced army schools and commanded several desks. Any comparison of careers with that of MacArthur suggested that Ike's own military future was hopeless. He was forty-seven and nowhere. In wartime, younger men rose to high rank.

His bridges burned over and over again after six years with MacArthur, Eisenhower impulsively announced in May 1938 that he had to return to the States for his health. He had been ailing with gastrointestinal discomfort* and was in the hospital that January when his closest friend, Jimmy Ord, was killed near Baguio in an airplane crash. Devastated, Ike returned home to Mamie and John, telling them as he paced their small parlor, "The only reason left for me to stay in this place is the extra money the Philippine Government is giving me. Other than that, there's not much to keep me here." Then he learned that Mamie needed surgery for a uterine fibroid tumor, a procedure which she wanted accomplished near her parents' home in Colorado.

It was Quezon, not MacArthur, who persuaded Ike to hang on further. He had a second desk at Malacañan Palace, to which Quezon came to beg him to remain. Having unsuccessfully offered Eisenhower a

---

*The illness, which became chronic, led to an ileitis attack, and surgery, finally, in 1956.

brigadier general's star in the Philippine army, Quezon would write confidentially for Eisenhower's personnel file, "In time of war this officer should be promoted to general rank immediately." Ike settled for a three-month leave in the U.S., and a year's extension of duty—but no more. On orders to shop for arms for the Philippine army, he left with Mamie for the States via Shanghai and Yokohama, stopping in Honolulu and detouring on the West Coast to Fort Lewis, Washington, to visit his bean-pole friend Lieutenant Colonel Mark Wayne Clark and try to find a new posting. As he went from factory to factory on procurement missions as far east as Rahway, New Jersey, he renewed useful garrison contacts and let it be known that he wanted to be back—and with troops—before imminent war passed him by.

At the War Department in September he met, for MacArthur, with officials ranging from lackluster timeservers to alert Hap Arnold, already assistant chief of the Army Air Corps (soon Air Forces) and a major general, and the newly arrived George Marshall. Eisenhower had left behind in Manila a brainy and manipulative new deputy whom he had known from War Department days, Major Richard K. Sutherland, a Yalie regular officer imported from a China station, whose father was an archconservative Supreme Court justice. ("We got him on my recommendation to Gen," Ike boasted to his diary.) To Sutherland and MacArthur he reported back via telegrams and detailed airmail letters, while keeping careful track of his expenditures ($1.35 for a cable, fifty cents for a stamp), on the quality of equipment available for the needs of the small Philippine army—such weaponry as efficient mortars and modern rifles. There wasn't much to be had.

Apprehensive, too, about likely war in Europe spilling over into Asia via colonial territories at risk to Japan, MacArthur issued a hurried paper, bypassing Ike's usual preliminary draft. In it he explained convincingly to himself, possibly hoping that Tokyo's many spies in Luzon would pilfer it, why it would be folly for Japan to attack the Philippines and draw America into the war. Although by the time that war came, not a single division of the Philippine army was fully mobilized, MacArthur would report progress "exceed[ing] original anticipation."

Returning to Manila with Mamie and John on November 5, 1938, Eisenhower "found a vastly different situation, so far as it affects me and my work." Richard Sutherland had usurped all of Eisenhower's major roles, including liaison with President Quezon. A ruthless climber and courtier, Sutherland had left Eisenhower superfluous. On November 10, 1938, in one of the longest and most vituperative entries in his diary, Ike exploded at MacArthur. "I'm no longer his C. of S. But only another staff officer." The purpose of Sutherland's elevation, Ike wrote heatedly, was "to rob me of any influence." That "make[s] certain that I'll get out as soon as I decently can." Now he regretted "the campaign I conducted everywhere in the States" to promote MacArthur as "a wise counsellor, an asset to the Philippines, and a splendid man in his present post." After "writing every word he publishes, keeping his secrets . . . , he should suddenly turn on me, as he has all others who have ever been around him. He'd like to occupy a throne room surrounded by experts in flattery. . . ."

His pent-up anger would flood out again in a long entry on December 12, on MacArthur's penny-pinching trainee instructions for Filipino recruits, largely perfunctory, "to preserve outward evidence of progress, which he thinks will get by with laymen who know nothing of [military] efficiency, the Gen., as always, is willing to scuttle anything and everything real. Will I be glad when I get out of this!"

During his stateside mission the looming European war had brushed the Philippines in the form of new refugee communities in Manila and in the Cebu city of Iloilo. As Eisenhower got to know some of the 1,200 émigrés who had fled Hitler but who could find no sanctuaries in the uncaring West, including his own country, he was made a surprising and hugely remunerative offer. Almost certainly it came from Alex Frieder, one of three brothers from Cincinnati who had opened a cigar factory in Manila, and who played bridge and poker with Paul McNutt, Manuel Quezon, and Ike. "I was asked to take a job seeking in China, Southeast Asia . . . and every country where they might be acceptable, a haven for Jewish refugees from Nazi Germany. The proposed pay would be $60,000 a year, with expenses. . . . The offer was, of course, appealing for several reasons. But . . . I had become so committed to my profession that I declined."

In early 1939 Eisenhower saw, nonetheless, his "constructive action on this job" as finished, and had little contact now with Quezon's functionaries. "Further, there is no head of this office—except the General— who is here only an hour a day." Eisenhower played a lot of bridge.* He read more of his favorite escape fiction—Westerns. He also continued to care about the future of the Commonwealth, delivering the commencement address to the ROTC graduates of the University of the Philippines on March 24, where he laid out his ideas about the young men as poten-

---

*He would stop mentioning poker, although he was very proficient at it, and made money. Bridge seemed more gentlemanly.

tial leaders in the future nation. He urged them to place "pride of service above personal convenience, duty above immediate economic gain."

Soon after, Quezon called him in confidentially to ask about military reorganization, speculating, according to Ike's diary, as to whether a call-up of twice as many men as could be effectively trained, was based upon MacArthur's desire to get more men into uniform so that his field marshal status "would have some basis in logic." The appointment, Quezon confessed, "made his government look ridiculous," and he had only gone along because MacArthur "wanted it." Someone has lied, Ike thought. "The Gen. said that he accepted the appointment with *great reluctance,* and only because refusal would have mortally offended the Pres[ident]!! Wow!! . . . I told the Pres. I wanted to go home."

When war broke out in Europe, Eisenhower's extended year was almost over. With Mamie and John, he visited the apartment of a friend whose shortwave radio picked up from London Prime Minister Neville Chamberlain's address declaring, on September 3, 1939, that Britain was at war with Germany, which had invaded Poland two days earlier. There was also change in Washington. Long invisible, Malin Craig was to retire officially on September 1, but effectively he had already been replaced. Ike had written a fulsome letter to him on August 3, identifying Craig with "the brilliant group" that had directed the war in France in 1918, and recalling seven then and future generals that included George Catlett Marshall. He failed to mention MacArthur.

With the quiet backing of Harry Hopkins, President Roosevelt had prevailed on the War Department to summon Marshall from Vancouver Barracks to become assistant chief of staff, War Plans Division, in July 1938. He became deputy chief of staff, displacing Hugh Drum, that October. On November 14, 1938, Marshall was invited to the White House with other high-ranking officials to discuss a budget proposal for vastly increasing aircraft production. It was the first time he had met the president, but after the meeting Roosevelt asked Marshall whether he agreed that a strong case had been made for Congress: "Don't you think so, George?"

Planes without pilots did not appeal to Marshall. "No, Mr. President," he said, bluntly. "I do not agree with you at all." Written all over Marshall's stony face was also the reality that he did not like being Georged.*

---

*But for two or three times in writing, FDR never "Georged" Marshall again.

Although Marshall bore only one star, on April 23, 1939, he was jumped over thirty-three more senior generals as acting chief of staff. Other than the politically influential Drum, only three were realistic aspirants, for a War Department proviso required that the chief of staff be able to serve out a four-year term before mandatory retirement age. The army was top-heavy with desk generals sixty or older, prepared to fight the last war.

Soon after Marshall's confirmation as heir apparent, the president received a letter from Katherine Marshall. "It is difficult for me to put into words what I really feel," she began. For years, she confided, she feared that her husband's brilliant mind and outspoken opinions "were hopelessly caught in more or less of a tread-mill. That you should recognize his ability and place in him your confidence gives me all I have dreamed of and hoped for. I realize the great responsibility that is his. I know that his loyalty to you and to this trust will be unfailing."

On July 1, Roosevelt called in his military chiefs, the Army-Navy Munitions Board, and fiscal aides to go over his preparedness budget. It was as close to centralization of effort as the president would get. In order to maintain control, he liked to keep as few people as possible fully informed, including his own service secretaries, but Marshall would always keep his Cabinet chief in the loop. There was too much to mobilize. Scattered over 130 posts, camps, and stations, the underfunded and undermanned army Marshall had inherited was short in everything but obsolescent equipment. On one of his many pre–Pearl Harbor visits to beg appropriations from Congress, his list of requirements included "overseas caps," the familiar soft, wedge-shaped, wool garrison hat. Isolationalists pounced upon "overseas" and charged covert preparation for foreign wars. Leaving Capitol Hill, the general confessed to an aide, "If I can only keep all personal feelings out of my system, I may be able to get through with this job."

On September 1, 1939, the day that war in Europe began, Marshall became a major general and then immediately, as chief of staff, a full general with four stars. He could move from a small house at 2118 Wyoming Avenue, just off Connecticut Avenue, to official quarters at Fort Myer, Virginia, where Colonel George Patton, resplendent in tailored cavalry togs—he was independently wealthy—commanded the post. (Marshall thought that Patton was being wasted and within months would give him command of a new Second Armored Brigade, and soon a division, as well as a desert training center in California.) With the additional stars, Marshall's pay rose from $625.00 per month to $808.33 plus $2,200 per year in additional allowances as chief of staff. The promotion did not put him in MacArthur's fiscal league, nor even in Patton's.

Hundreds of congratulatory letters and telegrams flooded his office in the Old Post Office Building on Pennsylvania Avenue from which he would soon relocate. One declared the signer's "great pleasure to have our association during my official tour of duty in your country. Please be good enough to extend to us your courtesies officially as well as privately." It was from Major General Masafumi Yamauti, military attaché at the Japanese embassy.

Calling on MacArthur to seek a release and an early sailing date, Eisenhower laid out his agenda. "General, in my opinion the United States cannot remain out of this war for long. I want to go home as soon as possible. I want to participate in the preparatory work that I am sure is going to be intense." MacArthur tried to persuade him that it would be a mistake. The work which Ike was doing in the Philippines far exceeded what a mere lieutenant colonel in the States would be assigned. Then Quezon offered him a new contract in which the emoluments line was left blank. "You will write that in," he suggested, unsuccessfully. Eisenhower booked passages to San Francisco on the *President Cleveland,* sailing on December 13, 1939.

At the pier to Ike's surprise were both MacArthurs, with a bottle of whiskey as a going-away gift. "Such a gesture was uncommon for this normally thoughtless and egocentric man," John Eisenhower, then a lanky teenager, later wrote. Yet he had already seen what a bundle of paradoxes MacArthur was. That summer the Eisenhowers had finally moved out of the torrid heat into an air-conditioned apartment at the Manila Hotel. Just before leaving, Mamie asked John to take the elevator up to the penthouse level to say goodbye to the MacArthurs. Not realizing how little time the general spent on the job, John expected to see only Jean MacArthur, but as he turned to leave, "she exclaimed that the general would be terribly sorry if he missed me." She took John out to the roof terrace where MacArthur paced back and forth, his hands clasped behind his back. (He would smoke his strong "Manila rope" cigars there—a predilection replaced later by his trademark corncob pipe.) Immediately, John recalled, his theatrical impulses manifested themselves. He walked over and shook hands—in his typical fashion with his left hand on my right shoulder—and recited in detail the positions I had been elected to for my senior year. . . . We both completely ignored the fact that the senior class would consist only of five pupils, only two of whom were boys, and all these jobs were reserved for seniors. But the general's memory, his charm, and his ability to show interest in an inconsequential boy always impressed me and explained to a large degree how he was able to mesmerize any individual he wanted, even including my recalcitrant Old Man.

Aboard ship, Ike prepared at the request of Jorge Vargas, executive secretary to Quezon, an evaluation of the infant Philippine army, and suggestions for a defense plan for the islands. In it Eisenhower had insisted, in lines that would have haunted MacArthur in 1941, had he read them, and worry Ike himself in 1942, 1943, and 1944, "Successful penetration of a defended beach is the most difficult operation in warfare. . . . The enemy must be repulsed at the Beach."

Vargas came in Latin fashion with a parting bonus for Eisenhower—per diem payments for nothing—a thousand American dollars to add to the ten thousand Ike had accumulated on low-overhead duty. He prefaced the report with a proviso that it be cleared with MacArthur before it went to Quezon. More than twenty years passed before he saw Vargas again and learned that the evaluation had never been shown to the general. Vargas conceded that all he did was hide it from the Japanese. Yet the Japanese would not come for two more years. The postwar Ike understood. Malacañan Palace had asked for advice from a mere lieutenant colonel, who was nearly fifty and nowhere. How could such a low-status document be offered to the imperial MacArthur?

5

Counterparts

B Y JUNE 1942 both MacArthur and his once-obscure
former assistant were both theater commanders.
MacArthur may not have taken the turnabout with
much satisfaction. "Best clerk I ever had," he would say later about Eisenhower. "I learned dramatics under MacArthur," Ike allegedly bad-
mouthed. Privately, they detested each other. Publicly, they remained
businesslike and mutually admiring. Both would always deny any rancor.

As 1940 opened, Eisenhower felt relieved that MacArthur was now
behind him. Other bondage was not. When the *President Cleveland*
docked in San Francisco on January 5, Ike was immediately waylaid by a
sergeant paging him with a radio message from Lieutenant General John
DeWitt, the imperious commander of the Fourth Army at the nearby
Presidio. He had altered Ike's orders to Fort Lewis while the latter was
shipboard because the general (as Ike's diary put it) had a "rush job and
needed someone to do some pick and shovel work." (There were now
three-star generals authorized for command of field armies, and Marshall
would ask Congress to authorize even more lieutenant general openings
as the army expanded. MacArthur remained ineligible: he had retired.)

"DeWitt's order," Eisenhower recalled, "blew up a sizeable typhoon
in the family." Firmly but courteously, Eisenhower explained that he had
to command troops if he was to move his career along. DeWitt did his
own explaining. It was temporary duty. Eisenhower's own 3rd Division at
Fort Lewis, to which he had been assigned, was being shipped down to
northern California for maneuvers for which he was to do the planning.
Marshall considered the exercises scheduled across the country for early

1940 as crucial to the modernization of the army. Ike remained, and Mamie was put up in a hotel. Their belongings went north to Washington, where, in Tacoma, John would stay with his uncle Edgar and attend school.

In assisting DeWitt to get the complex operation at Monterey Bay organized—mounting a simulated invasion at the beaches to be resisted ashore—Ike again encountered George Marshall, whose presence as chief of staff lent significance to the maneuvers. Knowing from his own Philippine experience how cheap personal servants were there and how little real work most officers had to do, Marshall greeted the returnee with, "Eisenhower, have you learned to put your pants on again by yourself now that you're back in the States?"

"Yes, Sir," said Eisenhower, wrinkling into a grin. "I'd never lost the knack. It's tying my shoelaces that bothers me."

Early in February he was released to accompany his 15th Infantry from Fort Lewis to Fort Ord,* newly constructed on the heights overlooking Monterey Bay. For the exercises lasting into the first days of May, Eisenhower, the new executive officer, was the regiment's chief umpire, evaluating its performance. "I hope the students don't know it," he wrote to his West Point classmate Omar Bradley, then a lieutenant colonel on the War Department staff, "but I learn more than they do."

Through 1940 the first peacetime draft act squeaked slowly and with difficulty through a reluctant Congress, passing narrowly in September during Roosevelt's campaign for an unprecedented third term. (An anti-FDR campaign button warned, "Draft Roosevelt and he'll draft you.") France was occupied, and Britain reeled under *Luftwaffe* bombing. The United States seemed closer to being drawn in, but much of America remained stubbornly isolationist. Although the army had nothing to spare, Roosevelt gambled that Congress would come around, and ordered Marshall to aid Britain by stripping the arsenals. The evacuation of Dunkirk had saved most of its soldiers but at the cost of abandoning most weapons. By October the U.S. had sent across the Atlantic 970,000 rifles of World War I vintage, 87,500 machine guns, 895 French "75s" and millions of rounds of ammunition. Useful in England in a home defense emergency, they would be useless to train and equip a new American army—should there be one.

Since conscription's most effective advocate on Capitol Hill was Mar-

*Named for the late Jimmy Ord's grandfather, Major General E. O. C. Ord, a Civil War corps commander under Grant. Ord took Richmond in April 1865.

shall, Secretary of the Treasury Henry Morgenthau had advised the president to send no one else to speak for it. "Mr. Roosevelt had many Republican and Democrat opponents," Marshall recalled. "I could get many things, if I asked for them, which he couldn't. . . . More than one Democratic leader and Republican leader would ask if I wanted it or if I were speaking for the President. Roosevelt resented this fact when his own people would ask that I go." When FDR signed the Burke-Wadsworth Bill on September 16, 1940, Marshall, at the ceremony, remarked, "Grenville Clark should have been here instead of me." Clark, a New York lawyer influential in World War I preparedness, had mobilized influential Americans outside government to press for a draft.

Burke-Wadsworth initiated a mandatory national registration beginning in October 1940 for a draft lottery involving all American males aged twenty-one through thirty-five. Because of the intense opposition from isolationists, Congress obligated draftees to serve only one year, ostensibly limited to military training. But after thirty-six rancorous public hearings, it became the foundation for national preparedness. Some 600,000 men would be called up before the legislation would expire, a deadline that would be a continuing dilemma for Marshall through much of 1941. By late 1945, 10.1 million men would be drafted, mostly for the army.

Marshall had to cultivate the public sector as well as a reluctant Congress. In December 1940, to defuse press criticism that the army was rushing expansion of facilities beyond fiscal prudence, he sent twenty newspapermen on a tour of training camps; when cranky columnist Westbrook Pegler aired similar concerns early in 1941, Marshall offered his own plane to ferry Pegler to such new posts as Fort Bragg. Soon, Major General Jacob L. Devers had a report from Marshall that Pegler's "reversal of form is almost revolutionary." On the morning after Pearl Harbor, when Marshall needed forty-eight hours in the day, he kept a scheduled meeting with the Conference of Negro Newspaper Editors. When the buildup of troops was accelerating in the British Isles, and Yanks were receiving not only higher pay than their British counterparts, but a larger meat ration, some local dismay was evident. Marshall explained that reducing the ration would lead to thousands of service mothers writing to their Congressmen that the army was not providing properly for their sons. Taxpayers were financing the war.

To promote the military budget, Harry Hopkins urged Marshall to cultivate Roosevelt more, to find excuses to visit him at Hyde Park and on his recuperative stays in Warm Springs, Georgia. Marshall would not lobby that way. "Never got too friendly with Roosevelt; made a point of never laughing at one of his jokes." The president, he recalled after the war, "was accustomed to dealing with so many political factors, where you have to be so careful and possess such a wide background of knowledge of the people involved, that it was quite understandable [that] for a long time he hesitated about taking me into his confidence. Also I had to be proven. . . ."

Marshall would prove himself in his own fashion. When in May 1940, he met at the White House with Treasury Secretary Morgenthau and the president to present a request for a $657 million appropriation for the army, Roosevelt turned Morgenthau down and waved them out of the office. Expecting to run for a third term, the president would campaign, clearly dissembling, on keeping America out of the war. Although a Nazi blitzkrieg had begun tearing through France and the Low Countries, a massive boost in military spending seemed the wrong signal to a nervous electorate. "Mr. President," Morgenthau appealed, "will you hear General Marshall?"

"I know exactly what he will say," Roosevelt brushed off Morgenthau as if Marshall were not in the room. "There is no need for me to hear him at all."

Marshall realized that he would get the money after the election, but the authorization could not be postponed by politics, nor by a more desperate downturn in the war. He rose and walked over to the president's chair. "Mr. President," he said, "may I have three minutes?"

Roosevelt had no choice. He listened to Marshall's litany of critical requirements that could not wait. Much more than three minutes passed, but no pause in the particulars permitted any interruption. "If you don't do something," the general concluded, "and do it right away—I don't know what is going to happen to this country."

Marshall was ordered to return the next day with a budget request for the Congress. He would not get all he wanted, but he could continue building and equipping an army that soon would be burgeoning with recruits from the first peacetime draft in the nation's history.

Since Roosevelt had an extraordinary admiration for General Pershing, who long had entreé to the White House, Marshall exploited that connection. Chronically ailing now, Pershing spent more and more of his days in a suite at the Walter Reed Hospital, keeping *au courant* largely through Marshall's visits. After a rare chat at the White House when FDR did most of the talking, largely about rushing aircraft production, Pershing mentioned it to Marshall, then left for San Antonio. Since Marshall needed a higher priority for ammunition manufacture, he got hold of Pershing's stationery, drafted a letter under his name to the president observing that in the hurried visit, the general had failed to urge strongly enough the urgencies of munitions supply. It was flown to Pershing, who signed it and had it mailed. The strategy was "intricate," Marshall remembered, but it had "a tremendous effect."

His appearances on Capitol Hill in behalf of appropriations for rearmament and conscription were personal successes as well as effective politics. His austere manner and straight talk contrasted dramatically with isolationist rhetoric and hostility toward an allegedly warmongering president. With the party nominating conventions imminent, Senator Harry F. Byrd Sr. of Virginia, averse to breaking the two-term tradition, drafted an article calling for Marshall to become the Democratic candidate. Learning of it before publication, Marshall persuaded Byrd to quash it. (For MacArthur, confined to the small stage of the prewar Philippines, it would be the last quadrennial election in decades without his self-promotion for the presidency.)

Although Marshall preferred understatement, few if any military men had his experience of coping, in war, with great numbers of troops and the intricate logistics involved. Most officers likely to lead the reborn army had been small fry only in brief combat like Patton, or—like Eisenhower—had never heard an enemy shot fired. "Dear George," Eisenhower wrote to Patton, now a one-star general, on September 17, 1940, "I am flattered by your suggestion that I come to your outfit. It would be great to be in the tanks once more, and even better to be associated with you again. . . . I suppose it's too much to hope that I could have a regiment in your division, because I'm still almost three years away [in seniority] from my colonelcy. But *I think* I could do a damn good job of a commanding a regiment."

Despite Ike's pessimism, the old promotion rules were crumbling. The long-stagnating military needed all the Eisenhowers who were now proving themselves in readying the army, and it told in his shifting assignments—to chief of staff, Third Division, then chief of staff of IX Corps, the umbrella administration for the Northwestern states. When he acquired the eagles of a full colonel in March 1941, he was about to leave to become General Walter Krueger's deputy in

Texas.* Little more than a year later Eisenhower had one star, and then two (for his assignment to London required more status), yet he was almost always commanding from inferior rank. The British had field marshals and air marshals, beyond American titular possibilities.

As Eisenhower was taking charge of the burgeoning American presence in England, and MacArthur was pondering how to respond to the news that his former functionary was now his counterpart, Churchill and Alan Brooke, his chief of the Imperial General Staff, arrived in Washington via Gander, Newfoundland. Their Boeing sea clipper carried a party of military advisers and the PM's entourage of doctor, military aide, clerk, butler, and special detective—a euphemism for bodyguard. On June 21, 1942, before an afternoon meeting with Roosevelt, Harry Hopkins noted to Churchill, "There are a couple of American officers the President would like you to meet," and at five, in Churchill's White House quarters, he was introduced to Eisenhower and Mark Clark.

The PM later claimed to have been "immediately impressed by these remarkable but hitherto unknown men," and to have talked with them about plans for the cross-Channel operation "on which their thoughts had evidently been concentrated." Much of that must have been ex post facto fiction, for his mind was elsewhere. At the meeting with the president, Marshall had appeared with a piece of pink notepaper confirming the capitulation of the Libyan port of Tobruk, which had been long under siege by General Erwin Rommel's Afrika Korps. Aside from the surrender of Singapore in early February, also fallen to a much smaller force, it was the most embarrassing British defeat in the war. The threat to the Nile Delta seemed real.

The president offered sympathy to the shocked British. Marshall suggested sending the partially trained First Armored Division to Egypt. When Brooke worried about the complexities of establishing an "American front," Marshall proposed instead to rush 300 Sherman tanks and 100 self-propelled 105 mm cannon despite his depriving a division which had just received them. As Marshall put it pragmatically, "We had to calculate which was the quickest thing. We decided to send the equipment and we ripped into our own organizations, took it away from the troops—could

*Later assigned to an army under MacArthur, Krueger would be the only senior general inherited by Marshall to receive an overseas combat command. Since he had been Eisenhower's superior in 1941, it was a matter of delicacy not to send Krueger to Europe or North Africa. Ben Lear, who had commanded the Second ("Red") Army in the 1941 Louisiana maneuvers opposite Krueger, did go overseas in early 1945 as deputy to Eisenhower, but not in a combat capacity.

give no explanation. I know that in some cases they'd only had the equipment two days and it"—the cannon—"had been developed personally by the commander of those troops going right down to industry to get it done. Just as he got it all, we took it away from him."

Recognizing the certain disappointment of the men awaiting the arms, Brooke realized the "depth of kindness that lay behind this gesture." The Tobruk episode as it played out in the Oval Office, he later judged, despite much carping in his diaries and conversation, "did a great deal towards laying the foundations of friendship and understanding built up during the war between the President and Marshall on the one hand and myself on the other." Tobruk would also revive discussions of an urgent North African initiative. "Gymnast" would become "Torch."

As before, Eisenhower failed to impress the British brass. "If I had been told then of the future that lay in front of him," Brooke recalled, "I should have refused to believe it." On July 8, he had a visit from the new American commander, to "put him into the picture," but Sir Alan's preoccupation remained the Middle East, and Churchill asked crankily why 750,000 men listed on its "ration strength" meant only 100,000 men mustered to fight. Egypt was, Brooke tried to explain, "a vast base for operations." In modern war, support personnel of every kind backed the relatively few who fired weapons.

Brooke had hardly made his point to the PM when he learned that Marshall, King, and Hopkins were again flying to Britain. Supported by Secretary Stimson, Marshall had sent a parting message to FDR on July 10, 1942, that if Churchill continued to evade a cross-Channel buildup, he and Stimson were "definitely of the opinion that we should turn to the Pacific and strike decisively against Japan; in other words, assume a defensive attitude toward Germany, except for air operations, and use all available means in the Pacific." With the air-sea victory over the Japanese near Midway Island only five weeks earlier, suddenly crippling Imperial carrier strength beyond replacement, there was momentum to exploit. The American public would have supported putting Japan first, and placing MacArthur, who had nothing to do with Midway but was still an all-purpose hero to the press, in charge.

Briefing Marshall by cable on July 11, Eisenhower reiterated that the British were opposed to any Channel landing "that could not remain permanently on the continent." Further, their planning delays, he contended, arose from "clumsiness in their organization." They were far less clumsy in suggesting to Ike that Marshall command the vague operation: "Some British officers have been outspoken to me in their desire to have you as supreme commander even though they realize that in view of the enormity of your present duties you would have to operate largely by long distance methods for a considerable time." Such distancing, Eisenhower may not have realized from their eagerness, would afford local generals and admirals actual control—a good thing for British interests if their commander anywhere had to be an American.

Forwarding much of Eisenhower's message to Field Marshal Sir John Dill, head of the British Joint Staff Mission in Washington, Marshall edited the cable extensively, then, suspicious of British motives and still hostile to the North African compromise, added a line of his own, as if Eisenhower's: "Gymnast logistically and from an air and naval point of view is impracticable and in any event would be a sponge absorbing our growing strength with little possibility of decisive returns." Then, reconsidering the White House position, he deleted it.

Rarely at strategic odds with his military leadership, Roosevelt considered Marshall's Pacific-first response as only bluff. Despite Pearl Harbor and Emperor Hirohito, despite press lionization of MacArthur, and public eagerness to go after Japan, it was Hitler who mattered. Further, Marshall offered no other operational plans for the remainder of 1942 to content Americans with the conduct of the war as he built up troop strength across two oceans. To both Marshall and King, the president sent a crisp chiding of the sort a stern teacher might have appended to a term paper:

> I have carefully read your estimate of Sunday. My first
> impression is that it is exactly what Germany hoped the
> United States would do following Pearl Harbor. Secondly,
> it does not in fact provide use of American troops in
> fighting except in a lot of [Pacific] islands whose occupa-
> tion will not affect the world situation this year or next.
> Third: it does not help Russia, or the Near East.
> Therefore it is disapproved as of the present.
>
>   Roosevelt, C in C

Unaware yet of Roosevelt's rebuke, Eisenhower again pressed on the British the White House contention that it was of "transcendent importance" to keep Russia in the war—that in event of the Red Army's collapse the United States would have to "go on the defensive throughout the Atlantic and build up offensive operations against Japan." The British position, Ike explained to Washington, was that the cross-Channel (but very limited) "Sledgehammer," unless it impossibly lived up to its code name, would have little if any effect on the Russian front, while if the foothold failed (Brooke realistically dismissed it as a "sacrifice" operation), it would "adversely affect" the balance of forces.

Marshall realized that any campaign elsewhere across the Atlantic preliminary to an invasion of occupied Europe would delay that operation into 1944, granting Germany a dangerously long recuperative respite. To prop up imperial interests as well as to stave off what promised to be—so Marshall worried—a grave failure in every sense of the word, the British seemed to him eager to evade northern Europe altogether while proceeding with a safer strategy elsewhere to involve untested Americans in actual combat.

Before Marshall (with Wedemeyer as deputy), King, and Hopkins left for London, Roosevelt gave them a two-page handwritten memorandum to consider en route. He wanted some European operation mounted somewhere in 1942. Congressional elections were coming in early November. If a cross-Channel landing were necessary "to save Russia this year," it should be executed, whatever the risks. "If SLEDGE-HAMMER is finally and definitely out of the picture, I want you to consider the world situation as it exists at that time, and determine another place for U.S. troops to fight [Germans] in 1942." The president was defining the war in the West as an incremental series of operations to thrust America and Americans into military reality.

Hopkins embodied Roosevelt abroad, and given his surrogate's fragility, it was rare that Hopkins arrived anywhere without needing immediate medical intervention to keep him going. The president cabled Marshall in London, where they were put up at Claridge's Hotel in Mayfair, "Please put Hopkins to bed and keep him there under 24-hour guard by Army or Marine Corps. Ask the King for additional assistance if required on this job." Still, Hopkins's presence meant that Roosevelt was listening as Brooke tried to persuade Marshall once more that an assault on France with "raw" American divisions required realizing that the Germans by land could reinforce their troops "some 3 or 4 times faster than we could," and that Allied movement was limited by a "crippling shortage of sea transport."

A special train from Prestwick airfield in Scotland brought the party to London shortly after dawn on July 18, where Eisenhower, looking exhausted, but now with a third star to boost his status, was waiting at Euston Station. Sixteen guest rooms on the fourth floor of Claridge's had been converted into a military headquarters, with communications gear and sentries at every door. They had passed up an invitation to dine and stay overnight with Churchill at Chequers, in Buckinghamshire, as Marshall had not wanted to be subject to the PM's persuasion.

On July 20 Brooke met again with Marshall and King, with Eisenhower and Hopkins there but unrecorded, and argued "that there was no hope of such a bridgehead surviving the winter." Hopkins passed a message to Marshall on 10 Downing Street notepaper: "I feel damn depressed." Marshall conceded that a premature Second Front in Europe was basically a "desperate" contingency to counter, if necessary, German thrusts into the Don River basin toward Stalingrad that could impel Russia toward a separate peace. Again Brooke proposed "alternative operations in North Africa," but the American chiefs, knowing that FDR wanted to attack Germans, claimed that they preferred Pacific operations to a Mediterranean adventure against the Vichy French. As before, Churchill described southern Europe as the soft underbelly of Hitler's empire, and like Brooke he preferred gnawing at it indefinitely to risking a new Dunkirk.

Later, Marshall would comment wryly that the "soft underbelly" in reality "had chrome steel baseboards. Mountainous country." He was willing, instead, to divert more resources to the two Pacific theaters, King's (through Nimitz), and MacArthur's. No attempt would ever be made by Marshall to unify the zones. The area was too vast, and the prima donnas in command were at war with each other as well as with Japan.

As Eisenhower confided to his diary, the British attitude was that a serious cross-Channel operation depended on "the existence of an effective Russian Army," for a waterborne invasion "can never be executed unless and until the whole German position experiences a very great deterioration." Unlike the Americans, the British preferred pragmatism to idealism. They were out to save Britain and its empire, not the Soviet Union.

By cable, Eisenhower briefed the president for Marshall that Churchill's staff remained hostile to a premature cross-Channel landing anywhere, even as a feint, under any circumstances. Brooke himself had not forgotten that as commander of the stranded Second Army in France in June 1940, his own Dunkirk had been an ignominious evacuation by trawler.

On the 23rd Roosevelt acknowledged the military realities he had anticipated in his memorandum. He wired his approval of French North Africa as an immediate target, and Marshall set up yet another meeting for the next day at noon to confirm what would now be code-named

"Torch." The president had considered the domestic implications of delay into 1943 and beyond. He had to answer to an impatient voting public. Millions were being drafted and billions voted for armaments. Americans wanted their forces engaged in a real fight. Newspapers had only MacArthur's imaginative communiques from the Southwest Pacific to suggest ground action. Since the party in power usually lost midterm seats, Roosevelt wanted "Torch" to jump off no later than October 30.

Marshall was up before breakfast at Claridge's the next morning to draft the response for Roosevelt. Military men, he recalled more than a decade later after holding an ambassadorship and two Cabinet offices, "lack knowledge of political factors which political leaders must keep in mind. . . . I recognized that we couldn't do SLEDGEHAMMER and that there was no immediate prospect of ROUNDUP.* What was the least harmful diversion? Always bearing in mind that we didn't have much. Much of what we had [in Britain] was in an amateurish stage, particularly air." He put together a proposal to do largely what Churchill and Brooke wanted—"an expedition into North Africa" but with hopeful limits on its reach. "Just as I was finishing, King came in. It is remarkable now, but King accepted [it] without a quibble."

As Eisenhower was establishing himself in London, he met at an off-the-record dinner with American correspondents who knew little about him other than that he had worked for Marshall, and earlier for MacArthur. They wanted to know about the remote, near-mythic MacArthur. Eisenhower leveled with them about the general's ego-driven personality, then conceded, "Yet, if that door opened at this moment, and General MacArthur was standing there, and he said, 'Ike, follow me,' I'd get up and follow him."

Having achieved "Torch" despite American discontent, Churchill urged a mid-October strike. Eisenhower predicted that it would take until early December to prepare. High-level give-and-take was also involved. By early 1943, American troops and hardware were likely to be prepon-

*"Roundup" was the planned operation against the French coast which would undergo a code change to "Overlord." "Sledgehammer" was the abandoned limited bridehead across the Channel intended to divert German troops from the Russian front.

derant. Conceding that reality to broker acceptance, Brooke and his staff proposed a "USA Supreme Commander with British deputy. Under him two Task Force Commanders, one USA for Casablanca front, and one British for Oran front." The beachheads would expand beyond two, but the principle of shared powers was agreed upon, with a politically expedient American to preside.

To make amends for bypassing Chequers, the Americans visited the PM en route home. Brandishing his cigar before a map, Churchill used the opportunity to lecture them on the military realities. He was his own minister of defense. All the armed services were under his ultimate command. Hopkins argued back that American troops and military hardware would inevitably overwhelm the British beginnings. It could not always be a Churchill show, Hopkins insisted. Churchill, however, listened largely to himself.

Since Marshall's party had to return via Scotland, he arranged with Brigadier General Robert A. McClure, military attaché at the London embassy, to visit the American camp for new army arrivals at Belfast. Then they flew to Port Patrick, a coastal village in Scotland across the North Channel of the Irish Sea. Even telephoning the next Scottish hamlet with big copper pennies was difficult, but Marshall and Hopkins tried to place a call to President Roosevelt. The awesome request led to one line supervisor after another, and finally to Downing Street, where Lieutenant Commander C. R. ("Tommy") Thompson, Churchill's aide, heard McClure refer cautiously to "the two friends who are with me." While a hookup to the White House was arranged, Scotland Yard operatives, alerted to the outsiders, closed in on the Port Patrick Hotel. No arrests followed.

In confirmation, as scrambler phones did not exist in Port Patrick and the telephone exchanges were guarded, Roosevelt cabled Hopkins to tell Churchill that "we will go ahead full speed." With the necessary compromises accomplished, Marshall hoped that the decisions were irrevocable. (With Churchill, nothing was.) On July 26 the Americans boarded the long flight back to Gander and Washington on a Clipper flying boat from nearby Stranraer.

For a few days before Marshall's return, the supreme command remained officially open. He told Eisenhower that at worst he would be deputy to a more prestigious designee, if one could be found, and, whatever, that he should "take the bull by the horns and endeavor to push through the organizational set-up." On August 6, the British chiefs of staff, as expected, swallowing their private misgivings, recommended the unblooded Eisenhower to command "Torch."

FDR formally agreed. "I can say that when I went to him with TORCH," Marshall recalled, "he put up his hands [prayerfully] and said, 'Please make it before Election Day.' However, when I found we had to have more time and put it after the election, he never said a word about it."

The delayed November 7, 1942, target date was predicated upon simultaneous assaults, including a Patton-led landing in Morocco with troops convoyed across the Atlantic from the United States. The congressional elections would go on without the boost the president hoped for, and the Democrats, charged by the opposition, many of them pre–Pearl Harbor isolationists, with lack of vigor in fighting the war, lost seats in both houses.

There was a fair chance in any case of disastrous failure in North Africa, especially if the collaborationist French resisted. With unfortunate accuracy, it would turn out, Eisenhower forecast that "overall success in the operation, including the capture of Tunis before it can be reinforced by the Axis," would be "considerably less than 50 per cent." Landings could be attempted only within supporting aircraft roundtrip range from Gibraltar, and the fragmented French dimension was unpredictable. No assault date could be imparted to "Free French" General Charles De Gaulle in London, Eisenhower understood, as deception and secrecy were crucial. Marshall warned the president, who despised De Gaulle as even more vain and imperious than MacArthur, and seemingly with less reason, that Gaullists had a reputation for being "leaky" in their self-interest. Indeed, by September 1, Gaullist agents in Vichy, Tangier, Gibraltar, Syria (controlled by the Free French), and Washington were unhelpfully gossiping about an imminent North African landing. Furthermore, De Gaulle had no credentials. No one anywhere had elected him to anything.

Intended as a probing of German coastal defenses, and to divert attention from French North Africa, Admiral Mountbatten's Combined Operations staff had been planning a raid across the Channel at Dieppe. Scheduled for July 4, it had been postponed by bad weather and pushed to the next phase of favorable tides. Launched on August 19 and utilizing mostly Canadian troops who were hurled back, Combined Operations took more than 3,300 casualties out of 5,000 men involved. Hitler's vaunted "Atlantic Wall" looked very real. Conspiracy theorists would suggest that the inevitable result was to unnerve American cross-Channel advocates.

Away for conferences in Moscow and then Cairo, Brooke limited his diary reference to "recent telegrams about the Dieppe raid." The fiasco, however, gave the British more reason to criticize American eagerness for a bridgehead on the Continent as a price too steep to pay. Eisenhower and Marshall would see that eventuality pushed further and further back.

While the buildup for "Torch" accelerated, MacArthur made no secret of his frustration that the vast Southwest Pacific theater was not only being shortchanged by European priorities but by a rival Pacific command. From Pearl Harbor, Admiral Chester Nimitz oversaw what his mentor, Admiral King, intended to be the major Pacific operations, island-hopping westward by sea and by air. MacArthur's overwhelming presence in Australia overshadowed not only the prime minister, but also blustering, hard-drinking army chief General Sir Thomas Blamey, whose troops were blunting the first Japanese thrusts into New Guinea.

By contrast, Eisenhower's genial and unpretentious personality seemed likely to keep friction in his integrated future command to a minimum. He also recognized his inferiority in experience. British generals had already fought in France and in Egypt. Some, like MacArthur across the globe, even had combat commands in an earlier war. In hotel suites first at Claridge's and then at the Dorchester on Park Lane, close to his Grosvenor Square offices, Eisenhower indulged his anxieties, sleeping restlessly, rejecting English cooking for American candy bars, smoking more, and enduring novocaine injections for neuritis in a shoulder. A volatile temper exposed his insecurities to subordinates. Publicly he radiated confidence and charm to visiting officials and journalists, although he had little to impart but his privately shaky conviction in the inevitable success of Anglo-American cooperation. To Fox Conner, a World War I associate of Marshall on Pershing's staff and a mentor to Eisenhower since his early service in the Panama Canal Zone, Ike had already written, on July 4, acknowledging his stress, "More and more in the last few days my mind has turned back to you and to the days when I was privileged to serve intimately under your wise counsel and leadership. I cannot tell you how much I would appreciate, at this moment, an opportunity for an hour's discussion with you on problems that constantly beset me."

Early on, Conner had been crucial to Eisenhower. Going nowhere after the Armistice, he thought of leaving the army, but Conner pulled him back, asking whether he would like to be the general's executive officer in Panama. When his wartime commanding officer at Camp Colt denied the transfer, Conner wrote to Pershing's aide, George C. Marshall, asking that he have Pershing override the Tank Corps chief, Brigadier General Samuel D. Rockenbach. It was the first time that Marshall had heard of Eisenhower, who arrived in Panama in January 1922, but Marshall's mental personnel index would file anyone who impressed Fox Conner.

MacArthur would have been irritated that Eisenhower had appealed to a member of the anathematized Chaumont group. The 1917–18 war remained as close to him as his chestful of ribbons, which he continued to exhibit until he saw a photo in the Australian press of Eisenhower in uniform with no decorations at all. Quietly, MacArthur put his rows of ribbons in a drawer.

When the war MacArthur was symbolically putting aside began twenty-eight years earlier, both MacArthur and Marshall seemed destined for quick promotions to fill leadership gaps in an army suddenly forced to expand exponentially. While Marshall had been little more than an average student at VMI, MacArthur was the most brilliant student in his class at West Point—and to make sure he fulfilled his promise, his determined mother followed him and watched over her son's career from a nearby hotel. Despite early Philippines service at much the same time, MacArthur and Marshall hardly knew each other when both, afterward, were lieutenants at Fort Leavenworth, Kansas. Young officers were so poorly paid then that they were cautioned not to marry before achieving a captaincy, which meant age forty, if at all. A lieutenant for fourteen years, Marshall early on would violate the code. MacArthur bided his time.

"Pinky" MacArthur continued steering her son's career, intervening with her late husband's associates to ensure that Douglas received postings that would move him ahead. He got into the Mexican border affair in 1916, even to a hazardous, and frowned upon, exploit which he thought should have earned a Medal of Honor, denied by an allegedly obtuse awards board. What he did win, nevertheless, was attention. Ironically, Marshall was already back in the Philippines, where he became chief of staff of a unit planning the defense of Bataan and Corregidor against a mythical Japanese enemy.

The army burgeoned from 28,000 in 1914 to a wartime 2 million. In

1917 the two contemporaries, rising with the tide, shipped out separately to France to serve in Pershing's AEF. Soon both were temporary lieutenant colonels. Having shown his fighting mettle, MacArthur won a combat assignment to the 42nd Division. Marshall's organizing experience got him a staff job with the 1st Division—the "Big Red One." Although he was close to the opening American encounters, at Château-Thierry and Cantigny, he nearly missed them. As he was cantering toward the front lines, his horse slipped in the mud. Dragged down, Marshall fractured a leg. Insisting on overseeing the operation, he had his leg bound on the spot, and despite considerable pain he remained with his troops. Commended for his performance, he was given a field promotion to colonel and promised command of a brigade.

A star loomed if he remained in the fighting, but Pershing had now heard of Marshall. After six months in the line he was shifted to the AEF General Staff. Six days later, he recalled in a memoir, the division "dashed into the great counterattack which precipitated the retreat of the German Army, and within seventy-two hours every field officer of the infantry, excepting three colonels, had fallen. . . . All four of the lieutenant colonels were killed, and every battalion commander was a casualty, dead or wounded."

Regimental command might have done Marshall in—or moved him up. Instead he shared, at Chaumont, below the action, a comfortable farmhouse with Fox Conner, AEF chief of operations, and LeRoy Eltinge, deputy chief of staff. Marshall spent the last months of the war drawing up operations orders, his first against the German-held St.-Mihiel salient. One of the attacking divisions would be his former "Big Red One." Another would be the 42nd, where MacArthur, also now a colonel, was chief of staff but operating forward, sans helmet, and making a case for his own command.

At division level Marshall would have been in immediate contact with the enemy. His oversight would have ranged from supply to "marching and fighting"—he "trained replacements to fill the thinning ranks, [ordered] more ammunition and horses; [and endured] less frequent visits from staff officers in limousines." Now he was a brass hat from headquarters, arranging for the movement of hundreds of thousands of men and trucks and artillery which moved at radically different speeds to be accounted for in planning; and for the evacuation of sick and wounded—tens of thousands at one point. His office was an upstairs room in the town hall of Souilly, southwest of Verdun, where he had a telephone usable when field wires were not inadvertently cut by vehicles, troops, and shelling. Charting the Meuse-Argonne offensive intended to press the weakening Germans into surrender, he wanted to prevent their orderly withdrawal eastward by forcing them into rugged Ardennes country in which mobility seemed unmanageable.

Ironically it would be Eisenhower rather than the experienced Marshall who would be in command in 1944 when the Ardennes again arose as a strategic quandary. "The gaining of ground counts for little," Marshall told Pershing; "it is the ruining of his army that will end the struggle." Because of coalition operations and publicity-minded generals, it was a lesson he and Eisenhower would find difficult to apply the next time.

To the men in the line in 1918, Marshall's mandate, and situation, were remote from the real thing—without anxiety and violence. They were contemptuous of headquarters lifestyle, and lack of hazard. So, too, MacArthur. Although only colonel of the 48th Regiment of the multistate 42nd ("Rainbow") Division, he was effectively the division commander. Passively, Major General Charles Menoher left everything to him, and MacArthur blamed Chaumont for undercutting him although he was quickly elevated to brigadier general, at thirty-eight the youngest, then, in the army.

In his memoirs MacArthur dramatized his Great War glory with dialogue right out of boys' books about wartime heroism. Visiting his candlelit command post then, he recalled, was the corps commander, Major General Charles P. Summerall, to whom he offered "a cup of steaming black coffee, strong enough to blister the throat."

"Give me Châtillon, MacArthur," said Summerall, allegedly. "Give me Châtillon, or a list of five thousand casualties."

"All right, General," MacArthur promised, "we'll take it or my name will lead the list."

Twelve hundred casualties later, with MacArthur himself lightly wounded and again recommended for a Medal of Honor, the target was taken, "but the Awards Board at Chaumont disapproved." He was seen as showboating for glory, adept at co-opting war correspondents, and swaggeringly unheedful of the rules. Colonel Enoch H. Crowder, once an aide to the general's father, recalled, "Arthur MacArthur was the most flamboyantly egotistic man I had ever seen—until I met his son."

As the war wound down, while Marshall at Chaumont quietly did his job, MacArthur saw an opportunity to take coveted, German-held Metz, but GHQ intervened. Unaware of the infighting among the commands early in November 1918, Marshall sent MacArthur's Rainbow Division as well as the "Big Red One" to strike across the Meuse toward Sedan. Armistice negotiations were imminent; both sides wanted the best possible strategic position from which to initiate a cease-fire and to billet troops for the winter. Sedan, also, was too suffused with symbolism for the Germans to relinquish it willingly or for Allied—especially French—forces to resist trying to retake, although an end to the war would make the case moot. At Sedan in 1870, Napoleon III had lost his throne and with it Alsace and Lorraine. (At the peace table in Versailles, the French would get the provinces back.)

Consulting with Fox Conner, Marshall was assured that the French Fourth Army—assigned the objective by Marshal Ferdinand Foch—was not positioned to seize Sedan before the shooting stopped. Rationalizing the town into a legitimate American target, Conner exceeded his authority and directed Marshall on November 5 to prepare instructions for an immediate American attack. Divisions jumping off would include MacArthur's. Despite his brigadier general's star he was still refusing in his theatrical style to operate from the rear, and was the subject of complaints to GHQ "that I wore no helmet, that I carried no gas mask, that I went unarmed, that I always had a riding crop in my hand." Pershing, who had served under Arthur MacArthur, as Pinky regularly reminded him, dismissed the complaints as irrelevant nonsense. (In Australia, now, MacArthur put aside the cane he had been using as a prop, concerned that it made him appear less vigorous.)

When Conner began dictating to Marshall a message that Pershing "desires that the honor of entering Sedan should fall to the First American Army," Colonel Marshall was impolitely skeptical. "Am I expected to believe," he asked sharply, "that this is General Pershing's order, when I known damn well *you* came to this conclusion?"

"That is the order of the Commander in Chief," Conner snapped, "which I am authorized to issue in his name. Now get it out as quickly as possible."

Pershing, so Marshall directed, dutifully, "has every confidence that troops . . . will enable him to realize this desire." Then, to emphasize the urgency of the order, he added a second paragraph. "In transmitting the foregoing message, your attention is invited to the favorable opportunity for pressing the advance throughout the night." Although Marshall realized that the American advance would overlap the flank of the French Fourth Army, he rationalized that when a tactical advantage might be gained, it was acceptable to ignore "a theoretical line drawn on a map." It took until that evening before Major General Hugh Drum, Pershing's chief of staff, agreed to the dispatch of the order, adding a further open-ended sentence, "Boundaries will not be considered binding."

MacArthur would blame Marshall for the entire episode, which "narrowly missed"—he exaggerated—causing "one of the great tragedies of American history." The result was a free-for-all toward Sedan. But MacArthur had prudently postponed his own attack until daylight because he did not want troops pushing ahead in darkness into "unfamiliar and rough ground." Other U.S. commanders did not hesitate, crossing into one another's fields of fire and even encroaching into the sector held by the French 40th Division.

Realizing the hazards of friendly forces firing into one another's areas, MacArthur riskily set off near dawn to try to prevent it, again exposing himself beyond what was appropriate. The "Big Red One" was already getting tangled with his units and with the French. Striding ahead, MacArthur was taken prisoner "at the point of a pistol" by an American (16th Infantry Regiment) patrol, which mistook his floppy hat—he had removed the stiff wire grommet from his officer's cap—and his flowing nonregulation scarf for German officer's garb. In his memoirs he claimed that he was "recognized . . . at once" and there was no embarrassing capture, but in reality, after strenuous protests he effected his release, with apologies, then learned that his division was being relieved by the 77th—he had not been around to argue for keeping it in the fight.

On the night of the 9th he reluctantly led the 42nd into reserve status near Buzancy, to the south. From Sedan, enemy fire was still intense, but MacArthur would see no more of the war. His division had been only three miles from Sedan and from heights across the river could look down into its streets. Although MacArthur afterward claimed to see comedy in the affair, he had little sense of humor. Ambition was serious business. He was already the most decorated officer in the AEF. The order that had sent units through each other's lines was a desk-drafted blunder seemingly committed by one George C. Marshall, a colonel he knew vaguely who represented all that MacArthur found wrong with Chaumont. Despite his reputation for recklessness, he felt that he had been the cautious one in the affair, and Marshall—however under orders and even guiltless of the last line in the instructions—was the perpetrator of the chaos. Many years later Marshall dismissed the recriminations as "senseless. . . . The thing was we were succeeding. . . . There's going to be all sorts of turbulence on the battlefield, and this thing was carried back to old animosities. I didn't have much patience with it."

Perhaps it was nostalgia that caused him to recall, as melodramatically as MacArthur, the last pushes, as the armistice approached and every casualty had become unnecessary, in a way that does not suggest the judicious World War II chief of staff. The eleventh-hour attacks in 1918, Marshall remembered, were "a typical American 'grandstand' finish. The spirit of competition was awakened in the respective divisions to such an extent that the men threw aside all thoughts of danger and fatigue. . . . Soldiers dropped dead from exhaustion, wonderful examples of self-sacrifice and utter devotion to duty. It requires far less of resolution to meet a machine-gun bullet than it does to drive one's body to the death. The men in the 6th Division, which lacked thousands of draft animals, substituted themselves for the missing horses and mules and towed the machine-gun carts and other light vehicles. In six days the army had advanced thirty-eight kilometers, and had driven every German beyond the Meuse from Sedan to Verdun. It was a wonderful and inspiring feat of arms. . . ."

For MacArthur, the reason for being there vanished with the peace. He was ready to accompany his division home, milk his glory, and fulfill his further promise. Pinky's pride would be overwhelming. Stopped short of a star but keeping his temporary colonel's eagle while still on duty abroad, Marshall stoically accepted an assignment as chief of operations for U.S. forces in Germany. His wife, Lily, expected him back, at the least on leave, but his entire marriage had been, apparently, celibate, as only on their wedding night in 1902, just before Marshall as a young lieutenant was posted to the Philippines, had she told him of her heart trouble—a mitral valve insufficiency—that would, Lily claimed, require that she abstain from sex and children.* Marshall's taut bearing may date from that deprivation. Although the marriage survived and he was devoted to the beautiful Lily (four years his elder), Marshall decided to remain with Pershing into the Occupation.†

The Armistice was to become effective at 11 A.M. on November 11, 1918. At First Army headquarters, Marshall had been telephoned the news at six. He rushed to cancel orders for four divisions scheduled to push off at 6:30. Two divisions were already on the march; it took him

---

*In Ford Madox Ford's novel *The Good Soldier* (1915), the American-born English gentleman Edward Dowell learns on his wedding night that his beautiful wife, the former Florence Hurlbird, alleges a similar cardiac insuffiency, and until her death he experiences "twelve years of the repression of my instincts."
†Three years after Lily's death, Marshall married, in 1930, Katherine Tupper Brown, a widow, acquiring three stepchildren to whom he became very close. Not knowing what to call him, they settled on "Colonel," which stuck.

two hours to communicate with them and turn them back. Then he wearily went back to sleep, assuming that he had done all that was to be done on his watch.

Breakfast for his staff in Marshall's headquarters farmhouse awaited his awakening again, which didn't happen until 10:30. At the table a French liaison officer was voicing his frustration that he could not go into wicked Germany firing away at the Boche while leading a regiment of fierce Moroccans. As his British equivalent began to air his own grievances—about permitting freedom of the seas to the defeated Germans—there was a shattering explosion just outside the only window in the room. Marshall was thrown against the wall, stunned. "I thought I had been killed," he remembered, "and I think each of the others had the same idea, but we picked ourselves up and found that aside from the ruin of the breakfast, no particular damage had been done. Soon afterwards a young aviator hurried in to see what had happened. He explained that he had been out in his plane with some small bombs, all of which he thought he had released, but . . . one stuck to the rack and as he sailed down just over our roof to make his landing in the field beyond our garden wall, the remaining bomb jerked loose and fell just ten yards outside our window." Had the walls of the old house been less sturdy, a different chief of staff would have led the American armies against the Germans in the next war.

Marshall's post-Armistice tasks, which required improvisation and reserves of patience, lasted only a few months. As Pershing's aide in postwar Europe, with headquarters in Paris, he accompanied the general on official visits to Allied capitals, for which Marshall would handle the logistics and share the welcomes. With his career at stake, he worked to establish bonds with the man most likely to represent the future of the army.

In the downsizing army, Marshall's temporary rank of colonel would be suspended on his return. He faced being a permanent—and seemingly elderly—captain. Congress, however, awarded four permanent stars to Pershing, now a hero, two more than the irate chief of staff, Peyton March, his ostensible boss. As Marshall was a Pershing man, he would see no favors from March. Pinky MacArthur may have had something to do with her son's next position, as Peyton March, too, had served under her husband in the Philippines. March's priority, when the prized West Point superintendency was his to fill, was *not* to appoint a Pershing man.

All that Marshall had going for him was to be on the periphery of a national "inspection tour" by Pershing, a celebratory interim, made in two luxurious railway cars with an entourage that included Fox Conner and other men of Chaumont. Pershing would soon succeed March as chief of staff, but in a shrinking postwar army the connection did Marshall little good.

Reverberations from the earlier war persisted as plans for "Torch" proceeded. As late as two weeks before the assault, on October 20, Eisenhower had to radio Marshall that he took "definite exception" to instructions to the First British Army, about to embark, which emphasized "the degree in which the Army Commander [General Kenneth Anderson] would be exempt from the authority of the Allied Commander, rather than insisting on unity. . . ." The British chiefs of staff then "apologized for the crude way in which they had attempted to express their instructions. They had merely paraphrased the instructions to [General Douglas] Haig, written in the spring of 1918." Marshal Ferdinand Foch had become Allied generalissimo on the Western Front and Haig had resisted dilution of his independence.

The Pacific dimension of World War I had been a minor affair. German island colonies were seized easily, largely by Japan, which entered the war for such spoils. Now, 1942 priorities left the Pacific, although crucial to Americans remembering Pearl Harbor, lagging behind. Admiral King argued that leapfrogging oceanic stepping stones toward Japan was more vital than pulling Churchill's colonial chestnuts out of the fire in the Mediterranean. Roosevelt insisted nevertheless on the political and strategic necessity of fighting Germans, and correctly saw the Japanese as reaching their logistical limits. Most of the assets which King wanted would go to his surrogate, Chester Nimitz. To mollify MacArthur, the president offered substantial resources, but not enough personnel and matériel to mount a campaign north and west across a thousand miles of islands and sea to retake the Philippines. MacArthur would even lose some promised heavy bombers to "Torch."

Unlike any other general in the Allied forces, MacArthur was permitted to keep his wife and son with him in a war zone. He also wanted a personal plane and was given a precious new B-17 which he ordered his personal pilot, Major Henry Godman, to pick up at Wright-Patterson Air Corps Base in Dayton, Ohio. "Godman," he instructed, "I want the plane named *BATAAN*, and the artist is to paint a map of the Philippines on the side of the nose and then to have the word *BATAAN* painted across it." MacArthur was given wide latitude to promote officers in his entourage and fire others. Since he saw his venue ruefully as a tertiary fiefdom, as long as an enemy threat seemed remotely credible, even after the Coral Sea and Midway, he would warn of a Japanese invasion of Australia. "I wish to invite attention," went a typical message to Marshall in the summer of 1942, "to the acute danger which is rapidly developing in the Pacific theater. . . . The enemy . . . is rapidly moving the center of gravity of his forces in this general direction." Claiming a crisis, he urged that "the Atlantic and Indian oceans be temporarily stripped" of ships and planes for his command to head off a series of looming "disasters."

While momentum for "Torch" was building in England, MacArthur cabled Marshall in rage about even closer competition: "It is quite evident that the Navy contemplates assuming general command control of all operations in the Pacific theater, the role of the Army being subsidiary and consisting largely of placing its forces at the disposal and under the command of Navy and Marine officers." In Washington, Marshall had to intercede with King to placate MacArthur with a more prominent role, yet Major General Richard Sutherland would goad his boss on. "You see," he told MacArthur, "Marshall and his boy, Eisenhower, they're just cutting your throat." Unaware, Eisenhower would confide to Brigadier General Ralph Coane, in Australia to command the 41st Division's artillery, "Should you happen to run into General MacArthur, please remember me kindly to him. I served under him for many years and, of course, watch the accounts of operations from his theater with the keenest interest."

To veteran editor of the *Army and Navy Journal* John Callan O'Laughlin, an old friend, MacArthur would complain, although he bad-mouthed the Australians, "Probably no commander in American history has been so poorly supported. If I had not the Australians I would have been lost indeed. At times it has looked as though it was intended that I should be defeated." Later in the war he would claim that decisions in Washington handicapping him were "corrupt." Marshall had to chide him on August 10, 1942, that he was damaging his case by abetting ill-feeling about war priorities. "Under dateline from your headquarters of August 6," went Marshall's radiogram 664, "the *Washington Post* [on August 7] and other papers have published an article by Lee Van Atta. He stated that his information was from 'authoritative military and civilian circles,' the spokesmen for whom"—the source was entirely MacArthur—"made seven points . . . designed to deprecate the part played by the United States in aiding the war effort in your theater. This press release from your headquarters can only serve to fan . . . indignation and resentment."

MacArthur had used an earlier story, in the *New York World-Telegram*, possibly again his own plant, as a springboard to comment that it had been "featured in all Australian papers and has caused a tremendous upheaval of bitter resentment throughout this country." The editorial had charged that earlier in the war, when Australia seemed in immediate danger, resources intended for other areas were diverted there, but now Roosevelt and Churchill had other priorities. "If two-thirds of our bombers are going to England to strike at Hitler, if enough are going to the Hawaiian-Midway-Aleutian line and to China to hold our major defensive-offensive bases against Japan, and if we are to keep our pledge to Russia not to mention Egypt—Australia can no longer count on priority." Although by the end of 1943 the U.S. had committed more troops and resources to the two Pacific theaters than to Europe, MacArthur's political moves had nothing to do with it. A central Pacific strategy to seize potential air bases from which to bomb the home islands of Japan divided a very large pie.

"Your problems," Marshall assured MacArthur, "are appreciated by the Combined Chiefs of Staff and by the Secretary of War and me personally." MacArthur turned the criticism and the assurances on their heads, replying, "You are entirely correct that this Headquarters is not by indirection attempting to influence strategic control from higher Headquarters." It was the American press, he complained, although he was trying to manipulate it, that was out of line.

A Pacific survey trip by Hap Arnold for the Combined Chiefs of Staff, concerned about the New Guinea barrier to Australia threatened by the Japanese, gave MacArthur the opportunity to ask again for more aircraft. (Arnold had warned Marshall of "unplanned demands from all directions.") MacArthur criticized Washington's priorities, contending that "no second front can possibly be established from England," and that landings in French North Africa would be "a waste of effort." Hitler could be left to Russia while he went after Japan.

Intelligence intercepts had revealed Japanese plans to occupy the island of Guadalcanal to dominate the Solomons, and to seize Port Moresby, on the southern coast of Papua New Guinea, an operation at first thwarted at the Coral Sea. A month later, carrier losses at the Battle of Midway blunted Japanese sea and air power, but planners in Tokyo would not give up on New Guinea and the Solomons, both fragments of the fraying British colonial empire.* MacArthur proposed bypassing New Guinea to seize Rabaul, to the northeast on the island of New Britain, being built up as a major enemy base. As that was far too risky for his resources, Washington advised focusing on New Guinea, where the Japanese controlled the northern coast. For MacArthur, the proposal seemed attractive, as only a few hundred miles above northwestern New Guinea lay Mindanao, the southernmost of the Philippines. Port Moresby, however, was far to the southeast: New Guinea was one of the largest islands on the globe. Much of it was nearly impenetrable and had to be bypassed. The effort would consume many frustrating months.

On July 21, 1942, as Marshall was flying to London to work out compromises on "Torch," 16,000 green-clad Japanese troops crossing the tropical, treacherous Owen Stanley Mountains toward Port Moresby and Milne Bay, occupied the village of Buna on the jungle trail south. MacArthur ordered the Australian 7th Division, returned from the Middle East, to New Guinea. Given the appetites of swarming tropical insects, Aussie desert gear was utterly useless, but it was what they had. Then MacArthur sent the inexperienced American 32nd Division, while deprecating Blamey's veterans to Marshall by radiogram, "The effect on the Australian soldier of aggressive action by even a small American unit would be of enormous value." When the Aussies finally got to Milne Bay, in knee-deep mud, he denigrated them as not up to the Japanese. "The enemy's defeat at Milne Bay," he cabled Marshall, "must not be accepted as a measure of the relative fighting capacity of the troops involved. . . . The decisive factor was the complete surprise obtained [over the enemy] by our preliminary concentration of superior forces." It was entirely the product of his remote strategic genius.

At almost the same time as the first of 117,000 Allied troops, three-quarters of them American, were landing in French North Africa in early November, the complex inter-service logistics in that theater receiving their first test, omens in the Pacific improved. Vice Admiral† William Halsey's fleet off Guadalcanal drove off an enemy convoy attempting to reinforce the island, the beginning of a costly effort (some of it hidden by the navy) to retake the Solomons, while Australian and American troops

*The western half of New Guinea had been a Dutch colony, part of the NEI.
†Halsey was promoted to full admiral on November 18, 1942.

under MacArthur's Brisbane command attacked the Buna-Gona beach-head on the north shore of New Guinea.

The former National Guard troops landing in Guadalcanal were from South Dakota, Ohio, and Massachusetts. For public relations reasons, Marshall planned to announce their presence. In a message "From Marshall for MacArthur's Eyes Only," the chief of staff requested, "It would be very helpful to the Army's position in relation to Naval and Marine Corps publicity . . . if you could make it known that Michigan and Wisconsin units (that is the 32nd Division) are operating between Kokoda and Buna." Press releases from Brisbane had only identified "MacArthur's men." Marshall would have to appeal to MacArthur again and again to permit the release of the identities of divisions and the names of their commanders. In 1918, ironically, pressing to keep his 42nd from being picked apart for replacements to understrength divisions, MacArthur had made a publicity plus of their multistate origins—a "Rainbow" division. The clever ploy worked. But this was a new war and he was a Supreme Commander intending to stay supreme.

MacArthur had visited the 32nd's encampment before troops shipped out to New Guinea, offering those GIs up front who could hear him, some slogans to rally them. As his intelligence chief, Brigadier General Willoughby, later dissembled in a biography of MacArthur, much of which came from the theater commander's dictation, "MacArthur . . . moved into Port Moresby personally, along with his staff, to join a handful of Australians and local Europeans who had come to New Guinea to prospect for gold and who remained to fight." The "handful" of Australians were his major force. Actually then in Brisbane, MacArthur was driven daily in his Humber limousine, licensed USA-1, three city blocks to his office in the requisitioned AMP Building, from which in off-the-record press conferences he held correspondents spellbound with graphic images of the military situation he had yet to see for himself. At Lennon's Hotel, where he appropriated three adjoining suites on the fourth floor, and came home for lunch and a nap, he would leave again for his office at four, remain for radiograms from Washington where it was still the day before, and return for late dinner and often a film. "Any yearning he had for high adventure," a disgruntled Australian journalist wrote, was "assuaged . . . by watching western movies in the theatrette which had been constructed in the hotel for his private use."

Preparing for Hap Arnold, MacArthur on September 19 flew in his B-17 over Port Moresby and the Kokoda Trail. On September 25 in Brisbane he briefed Arnold, who had arrived to look over the Guadalcanal operations to the east. MacArthur ridiculed the Germany-first strategy and the practicality of a Second Front. Marshall had already heard concerns from aircrews in the SWPA. Even before Arnold's visit, he had dispatched a deputy to investigate complaints that airmen were flying too much without relief, and that their fighters, largely the upgraded P-40, were less maneuverable than the Japanese Zero. Knowing that the extra weight the planes carried was armor (the Zero had none) to protect the pilots, Marshall instructed his emissary to tell the young fliers, "Just say the word, and I will have the planes stripped." Unanimously, they decided to keep the P-40s as they were.

On October 2, MacArthur paid his first on-the-ground visit to Port Moresby. Driven by jeep to Owens Corner, where there was an Australian artillery position, and dressed in his suntans and his trademark cap, he had a Signal Corps photographer snap his picture for the papers. The tropical rains held off. There, MacArthur upbraided Major General Arthur ("Tubby") Allen, a veteran of the desert campaigns, that his 21st Brigade had not moved rapidly enough after the Japanese, although Australian radio correspondent Chester Wilmot had noted candidly how "uncanny" a war it was. "You never see a Jap even if he's only twenty yards away. They're masters of camouflage and deception. I should say about 40 per cent of our boys wounded in these engagements have never seen a Japanese soldier."

Allen resented MacArthur's "insinuation," retorting that when the green American troops just arriving "proved to be as good," he would take MacArthur more seriously. After a night in Government House, the irate MacArthur flew back to Brisbane, where it was announced that Tubby Allen had been relieved. Wilmot was banned from broadcasting from New Guinea on grounds of "implied criticism of military direction." He had also reported the destruction of MacArthur's undispersed aircraft on the ground at Seven-Mile Airstrip, and his refusal to permit correspondents to talk to irate aircrews or to go beyond the official communiques from Brisbane. Wilmot would relocate to Eisenhower's war, where Ike would fare no better under Wilmot's pen.

For Eisenhower's operation, now gathering momentum, Marshall had already recruited some officers from the Southwest Pacific, from whom the staff in London heard tales about MacArthur's high-handed management of his war. Still, his remote direction meant that officers whose names MacArthur hardly knew had commanded some real fighting.

On November 6, just as "Torch" was about to jump off halfway across the world, MacArthur established a second headquarters in Port Moresby. Government House was being refitted for him, complete to the first flush toilet in New Guinea. While the battle for Buna went on across the rank thickets of the Owen Stanley Mountains, neither he nor his senior staff went to look. He put in the same hours as he did at Brisbane, complete to a two-hour dinner, after which he would write the day's communiqué for LeGrande Diller to distribute.

Worried about German submarines endangering "Torch" convoys, Marshall insisted to the British that the Portuguese Azores had to be occupied "without delay." An Atlantic area nearly a thousand miles wide was in hazard because of Portuguese neutrality, which benefitted both sides. Each used Portugal itself as civil airstrip, covert seaport, and communications center for spies. Seizing the islands could jeopardize a good thing. Marshall "put it up" to Churchill, declaring, "By God, we had to do it." Anthony Eden, Churchill's foreign secretary, was opposed in principle to interference in another nation's neutrality, "but decided," Marshall recalled triumphantly, "it could be done under an English treaty with Portugal of the 1600s."*

Weather delays would dog all of Eisenhower's D-Days. On September 19, 1942, he had radioed Marshall that the landings were definitively set for November 8. (FDR the politician exerted no pressure to move it up.) In the first days of November, after three days of travel postponements as rain and a blanket of fog settled on southern England, Eisenhower was anxious to get closer to the action. He insisted that the pilot of *Red Gremlin*, his B-17 (of six in the group), Major Paul Tibbets, later to fly the *Enola Gay* and its atomic bomb over Hiroshima, take off from Bournemouth, in hazardous near-zero visibility, for Gibraltar. In the darkening afternoon of November 5, battling dangerous crosswinds after wave-hopping much of the flight, the plane touched down at an airstrip

---

*The Anglo-Portuguese treaty actually dated from 1373. Under it, after many weeks of negotiations, British and American military aircraft were permitted to operate from the Azores, and the Germans lost their facilities.

adjacent to "the Rock." It was three days before the assault across the Mediterranean was scheduled to begin. Allied fleets were approaching Africa.

With his staff, Eisenhower holed up in one of the dank, poorly lit caves under Gibraltar fitted up as a command center, eerily reminiscent of the humid Malinta Tunnel under another "rock" he knew, Corregidor. MacArthur had left his own tunnel in early March and the Rising Sun now flew there. Eisenhower's underground command post, beset by faulty communications, feeble electric bulbs in block-long passages, and the drip of surface water, was an ironic echo.

6

Turning to Offense

ITLER WOULD BE SPARED a Second Front in
Europe in 1942. The West was far from ready.
North Africa was the trial run, and on several
fronts. General Montgomery's Eighth Army in Egypt had launched an
offensive, long in preparation* and overwhelming in firepower, on October 23 at El Alamein, in the desert west of Cairo. It seemed logical, also,
for Erwin Rommel, a field marshal since Tobruk, to anticipate an Allied
landing somewhere in the Afrika Korps' rear. The buildup of shipping in
British ports hinted a large operation, and De Gaulle's Free French, kept
out of the planning loop, spitefully leaked what they knew. The Germans
suspected Allied disinformation, yet realized that something was up.

Eisenhower was anxious, as he cabled to Marshall, about German
ability to reinforce North Africa via Sicily and the projecting "elbow" of
Tunisia. It was the shortest water crossing. Axis subs and planes controlled the central Mediterranean, leaving isolated Malta at risk and hazarding supply of British forces in Egypt. The Vichy French were also
expected to resist. French hatred of their former allies for contributing to
the catastrophes of 1940 was unforgotten. Eisenhower had to portray
"Torch," now imminent, as largely an American affair.

MacArthur's problems, mostly of his own making, were with his

---

*Hype for Montgomery's offensive obscured the reality that it was a "second
Alamein." Although replaced afterward by Churchill, Sir Claude Auchinleck in July
had stopped Rommel at Alamein. By November 1942 the Afrika Korps was irrepara-
bly weakened by resupply failures.

Australian allies. In his grandiose fashion he dismissed them as second-class soldiers in their own country—even those returned from the Middle East with the experience that his raw troops from the States lacked. General Blamey offered him Lieutenant General Sydney Rowell and his 7th Australian Division as the core of a New Guinea force. Although MacArthur, regally remote, needed the Aussies, who operated in abysmal conditions with plodding but real success, he radioed to Marshall disparagingly, "The Australians have proven themselves unable to match the enemy in jungle fighting. Aggressive leadership is lacking." The Aussies were under a different dimension of discipline than the enemy. Japanese troops lived off the land, endured wretched climate and terrain, and ignored their losses to hunger and disease.

To get at the invaders, MacArthur accepted a suggestion from General George C. Kenney that an airstrip be built secretly, sixty miles south of the enemy-occupied port of Lae on the north coast. "How are you going to protect it?" MacArthur asked. By flying in some Australian troops, Kenney said, after dark. He did, and Lae would fall. When air force chief Hap Arnold visited MacArthur in Brisbane after the Kokoda Trail and Milne Bay episodes, MacArthur delivered a two-hour monologue claiming that the pick of the Japanese army was fighting him, that they were superior to the Germans, and—belittlingly—that the Australians (according to Arnold's notes) "were not even good militia." In his diary, Arnold noted that he had "the impression of a brilliant mind—obsessed by a plan he can't carry out—frustrated—dramatic to the extreme—much more nervous than when I formerly knew him. Hands twitch and tremble—shell shocked." Yet Arnold had witnessed a performance which left him in some awe of MacArthur.

Although American troops had not seen action, MacArthur's communiques suggested that "his" forces were rolling back the Japanese. He never identified the Australian units doing the mucky job and taking the casualties, and he refused to place Australian officers on his headquarters staff, claiming they were unqualified. Vainly, Marshall's chief deputy, Major General Thomas T. Handy, protested, "The Australians have 350,000 troops [in the SWPA] and a little [appreciative] break for them seems to be necessary." A former National Guard division from the Midwest, the 32nd,* that had yet to fire a shot, allegedly (Hap Arnold's notes quoted MacArthur's assessment) "knew more about the New Guinea jun-

---

*Michigan and Wisconsin in origin. MacArthur thought that the hastily trained division came from Massachusetts.

gle in two days than the Australians in two years." Yet MacArthur soon sacked its commander, Major General Edwin Harding, whose troops arrived on the Buna front in mid-November and were broken up into task forces. When Harding protested that his men, on Sutherland's orders, were being sent into combat without their artillery, Kenney, who had converted MacArthur to air power, contended, "In this theater the artillery flies." Kenney offered to bomb what seemed necessary.

Without criticism of MacArthur, Marshall transferred the misused Harding to Panama. Recalling the inheriting of eighteen National Guard divisions, "among whom there were only one or two competent commanders," Marshall noted, "it took me a whole year to get rid of the bad ones." Later, he held back Omar Bradley's appointment to a corps command four times "so he could stay with the [Pennsylvania] 28th Division and get it straightened out." The division had been under a political appointee, Edward Martin, who was likable but ineffective. "He came to me one day and said he had been asked to run for governor, but felt he owed it to me and the army to stay on." Relieved, Marshall urged, "Take it!" The division would fight in France under Eisenhower, with a new commanding general.

Marshall's military challenges often overlapped his civil responsibilities, for his portfolio inevitably involved Congress and the public. Only Marshall could have persuaded the Senate and House, aware of the wrath of American mothers, to amend the Selective Service Act to permit the employment of eighteen-year-olds in combat—no problem in any other country. With that success in November 1942, just as "Torch" took off, the president sent a note to Marshall,

> Dear George:
> You win again.
>
>   F.D.R.

Marshall put aside his displeasure at being Georged.

MacArthur's most insistent problems were neither the New Guinea jungle, which he sometimes saw from the air, nor the Japanese, but the intrusions of crusty Admiral Ernest J. King, who exerted his clout from Washington. To King, the war against Japan would only be won at sea, and MacArthur was only to maintain the southwest barrier and supply what he protested to Marshall was "subsidiary" backup from his meager forces to support the South Pacific objectives of Admiral Nimitz, whose instructions came from the detested King. Service rivalries had not diminished under the demands of war. The summer and fall of 1942 were months of cautious accommodation by Marshall to keep MacArthur in the game.

MacArthur also had a card of his own to play from deep in his deck. "By using Army troops to garrison the islands of the Pacific under Navy command," he cabled Washington, "the Navy retains Marine forces always available giving them inherently an army of their own and serving as the real bases for their plans by virtue of having the most readily available unit[s] for offensive action. This Navy plan came under my observation accidentally as far back as ten years ago when I was Chief of Staff and senior member of the Joint Board." Having been inside the Washington whale, he could charge, with some credibility, that the Pacific plan "envisions the complete absorption of the national defense functions by the Navy, the Army being relegated merely to base training, garrisoning and supply purposes. I cannot tell you how completely destructive this would be to the morale of the Army both air and ground units. . . . [However] I shall take no step or action with reference to any components of my Command except under your direct orders."

The message displayed MacArthur at his most persuasive. Marshall soon leaned on King, cautioning that "unity of command" was more important than jurisdictional "lines drawn on a map"—a phrase echoing his 1918 experience. King conceded that operations east of New Guinea could "pass" to MacArthur's authority after the planned seizure of the island of Tulagi, just north of Guadalcanal in the enemy-occupied Solomons. Predictably, that failed to satisfy MacArthur, who warned that a shift of command during tactical operations could occur when it would be "impossible to predict the enemy's reaction, and [the] consequent trend of combat" would "invite confusion and loss of coordination."

Marshall forwarded the cable to King with a detailed draft of a "joint directive," which King accepted reluctantly after first proposing that the navy and marines go it alone. The long-term result would be greater cross-services authority for MacArthur, and increased support. He banked upon his ability to get his way. "It is unnecessary for me to tell you," MacArthur responded confidently in a radiogram, "that you can count on my complete cooperation with regard to the directive delivered to me today. . . . I am inviting Admiral [Robert] Ghormley and his Marine Division Commander and their Staffs to unite temporarily with me here [in Brisbane] to coordinate on details and phases. I shall suggest that Admiral Ghormley continue as the Commander of all Forces afloat during the entire operation. I shall ask him to establish his Headquarters with me up to the moment of his going to sea."

Some weeks later, Marshall reminded MacArthur by radiogram, "The defense of the Pacific areas particularly in air and naval matters will depend to a large degree upon the closeness of the cooperation and coordination of the forces now available to you, Nimitz, and Ghormley." MacArthur's "complete cooperation" in shifting to the offensive would be assured thereafter whenever he was at least nominally in charge. His campaign for more resources for his command continued by other means while Marshall was preoccupied with assembling the essentials to make the North African operation, expanded by planned landings on the Atlantic coast north and south of Casablanca, viable.

His own best lobbyist, MacArthur kept issuing his usual hyperbolic, and mendacious, press releases. Also, he covertly fed favored newspapermen with seemingly exclusive material, mostly exaggerated or invented, intended to fan indignation in America about Washington's priorities. Home front anti-Japanese sentiment remained far stronger than anti-German feeling, as editorial pages and radio commentary made clear. Although MacArthur's propaganda reached willing ears, Marshall rebuked him in a lengthy "eyes alone" cable for "objecting to our strategy by indirection." The scolding, predictably, failed. Unmoved, MacArthur lied, "The complete opposite is the case." Even so, despite what would become more and more a Eurrope-first priority, in late 1942 more combat forces were deployed against Japan than against Germany.

An emissary dispatched without Marshall's knowledge to further admonish MacArthur was onetime World War I flying ace and Eastern Airlines impresario Eddie Rickenbacker, who was quietly troubleshooting for Secretary of War Stimson. After a tough inspection of the Eighth Air Force in England, Rickenbacker was called in by Stimson to fly, via Australia, to MacArthur's Southwest Pacific Area headquarters in Port Moresby. Closing his office door so that Marshall would not overhear, Stimson swore Rickenbacker to secrecy and asked him to write nothing down, as the mission involved the chief of staff's difficult relations with MacArthur.

Near the end of the long flight, navigational errors by the crew left Rickenbacker's Seventh Air Force plane so short in fuel that it had to ditch in the Coral Sea. The survivors spent twenty-four days bobbing on life rafts before they were spotted. Learning of the rescue, MacArthur sent his B-17 to take the gaunt Rickenbacker, once he recovered from exposure, to New Guinea, where, on November 26, 1942, the general met him at an airfield near Port Moresby. "God, Eddie, I'm so glad to see you!" said MacArthur with genuine feeling. Recriminations dating back to the Billy Mitchell court-martial in 1925 were forgotten, as, for the moment, were the purposes of Rickenbacker's mission. MacArthur offered to put his guest up at what he called "my shack"—literally a grandiose structure (with outhouse) as temporary quarters while Government House was being stylishly renovated.

Looking vaguely familiar to Rickenbacker was one of MacArthur's senior staff, Charles Willoughby—"but I did not place his name. Then it came to me. He had been one of my fellow officers at the flying school at Issoudun during World War I, but then his name had been 'Wiedenbach.'"

Realizing that he had better deal directly with his mission before MacArthur's cordiality overwhelmed him, Rickenbacker told the general bluntly that Secretary Stimson insisted that MacArthur cease his self-promotion at the expense of everyone else in his theater; lower the tone of his whining radiograms and press leaks about being deprived of resources for his command; cease his badmouthing of the navy as he needed its cooperation to win his war; and end his indirect attacks on George Marshall. Keeping his promise to Stimson, Rickenbacker confided nothing to his letters or memoirs, but his biographer found the evidence in unpublished papers.

Accepting the reproofs without comment, MacArthur entertained Rickenbacker at dinner, exchanged reminiscences about mutual military acquaintances, and discussed the future of air power in war, about which the general, thanks to George Kenney, was now an enthusiast. He lauded the progress of his troops toward Buna, which would be faster, he conceded, if he wanted to accept more casualties than necessary—a message he hoped that Rickenbacker would take back with him—and only the day after he departed New Guinea did MacArthur sack General Harding.

For Marshall, his distractions in managing the war included swatting down a host of indiscretions almost daily. Among them were contemptuous remarks about the British by Americans in Eisenhower's command, and about Australians (and Washington) by MacArthur and his coterie. Marshall warned about "ill feeling" demonstrated by the ranks against seamen in the merchant marine, who were often at more hazard than uniformed personnel, and against civilian laborers working abroad, "because of differences in pay." Bad blood between the army and navy overflowed from service rivalries into the halls of Congress, and Marshall rebuked higher commanders lax in discipline whose subordinates sometimes seemed more "schoolboys than commissioned officers."

One consistent offender, predictably, was MacArthur himself, who apparently ignored a message that Secretary of the Navy Frank Knox, with Admirals Nimitz and John McCain Sr., planned to visit Brisbane, and commented superciliously—and was overheard—that "no useful purpose would be served by such a conference." (MacArthur denied everything, including receiving the message.) Uncowed, he would keep warning falsely that large Japanese naval and land forces were within striking distance of Australia. Frank Knox had to issue a public denial. Other high brass, exploiting the opportunities of rank, were sometimes conspicuously indiscreet in relations with female subordinates. In September, Marshall had admonished the pleasure-loving General Brereton, who had been ousted by MacArthur but landed on his feet as commander of the Middle East Air Force in Cairo, for indiscretions with his secretary, and ordered her "return . . . to her permanent residence." Soon Marshall would receive rumors about others on MacArthur's and Eisenhower's staffs, and about Eisenhower's own relationship with his lissome British driver, Kathleen ("Kay") Summersby, thirty-four and a divorceé, whose duties and employment status kept changing visibly for the better.* Allotted only one sentence early in Eisenhower's own war memoirs, she is described as "corresponding secretary and doubled as a driver." As obvious as his preoccupation with Kay became, all that Marshall felt able to do was to keep anxious watch.

As "Torch" materialized—*extemporized* might be closer to the realities—on Sunday November 8, Eisenhower remained headquartered in one of the twenty-five miles of tunnels bored into the limestone rock of Gibraltar. The Casablanca landing, by troops under Patton convoyed directly from the U.S., was a muddled success, as transports anchored gingerly too far offshore to ground landing craft. Although the Vichy French resisted briefly, Patton's naval escorts, including the battleship *Mississippi*, intimidated the defenders with their big guns. Yet an Atlantic coast beachhead was not the strategic prize that Bone, near the Tunisian border, would have been. Marshall refused to expose Patton's green troops to likely hazard from German subs and aircraft over a long, slow Mediterranean haul. He also worried that if the Vichyites prevailed and with-

---

*Soviet generals became known for taking "war wives" from among their uniformed women. Eisenhower would leave himself open for increasing gossip.

drawal became necessary, an Atlantic harbor had to be available. However reasonable, such caution may have cost Tunisia and lengthened the campaign.

Before embarking from Virginia, early on the morning of October 21, 1942, Patton had spent forty-five minutes with Marshall in the last days of the Old Munitions Building. Marshall would move his office three weeks later to the huge new Pentagon, and was already distracted by the noisy transfers in progress. In his diary Patton, often averse to caution, wrote, "Marshall lacks imagination but has an unusual mind." Later in the day Patton went to Walter Reed Hospital to see Pershing, who gave him his "start" in the Mexican campaign in 1916. "He looks very old," Patton wrote. "It is probably the last time I shall see him, but he may outlive me."

On November 8, Marshall begged off going to the Washington Redskins football game, pleading press of business, and asked Katherine to take Hap and Bee Arnold as her guests. When the public address system at Griffith Stadium broke into the play to report, "The president of the United States of America announces the successful landing on the African coast of an American expeditionary force," the football players, she recalled, "turned somersaults and handsprings down the center of the field; the crowd went wild.... We had struck back." Striking back somewhere made Roosevelt's point. The many operational and political mistakes that followed would prove how premature was Marshall's uncharacteristic impetuousness about attacking France itself. The real thing was a painful learning process. After a long day, when Marshall returned home with further news, Katherine telephoned Mamie Eisenhower and Beatrice Patton.

Of the 117,000 troops initially committed to "Torch," all but 23,000 were American. While an American force commanded by Major General Lloyd R. Fredendall, sailing from Scotland, landed at Oran, and Anglo-American troops commanded by Major General Charles W. Ryder seized Algiers, Ike remained in touch by radio from damp, uncomfortable Gibraltar, where Patton flew from Morocco to report on November 17, impressed that the Supreme Commander of the operation (initiating his remote control style) still "lives in a cave in the middle of the rock." Eisenhower, he wrote to Beatrice, "spoke of lunch as 'tiffin,'* of gasoline as

*A British Indian term.

'petrol,' and of antiaircraft [fire] as 'flak.' I truly fear that London has conquered Abilene."

In England as well as the United States, Eisenhower was an instant celebrity, although he had yet to set foot on captured soil. The unalloyed adulation, however, would not last. He was out of his depth politically as well as militarily, and had to learn his job from scratch. As he began to cope, at first while not even on the scene, with the first amphibious operations ever attempted by American generals, and ambitious in its scale, the "Darlan Deal" intruded. For the Vichy forces, convoluted by betrayal and counter-betrayal, to stand down, Eisenhower, even before the invasion, had entered into bargains with unsavory French authority figures who would embarrass him. Smuggled out of France to Gibraltar, and then to Algeria, General Henri Giraud aspired to glory, but proved pompous and ineffective, unable to command the loyalty of the collaborationist French. More crucial was the Anglophobic and fascist Admiral Jean Darlan, commander of the Vichy armed forces. Discovered in Algiers, he was put under house arrest. Then, on Eisenhower's orders, he was offered by Mark Clark the post of high commissioner for North Africa in exchange for ordering a cease-fire by forces loyal to him.

Vichy repudiated Darlan; the Germans reacted by storming into the "Unoccupied Zone" of France under Petainist administration; French naval commanders stubbornly scuttled their ships at the Toulon base near Marseilles rather than surrender them to the Germans or sail them to the Allies. Confused fighting continued near Oran and Casablanca, ending only on the eleventh. Luckily for "Torch," Hitler was entraining to Munich as it opened, for his annual rant on the anniversary of the failed 1923 Beer Hall *Putsch* that had vaulted him into notoriety. Still, after hurried consultations with him, the OKW (General Staff) began airlifting troops to Tunisia before Eisenhower could consolidate his positions in Algeria and move eastward himself.

The bargain with Darlan outraged the American press and the Congress, and was a massive distraction to Eisenhower and Marshall. De Gaulle in London huffed, "The U.S. can pay traitors but not with the honor of France." Churchill claimed to be "disgusted," and suggested, "Darlan ought to be shot." CBS radio correspondent Edward R. Murrow, a much-listened-to voice from London, asked, "Are we fighting Nazis or sleeping with them?"

Marshall arranged a meeting with the House and Senate military affairs committees to explain in confidence Eisenhower's motives and broad authority to make expeditious and sometimes sleazy temporary deals.

Blindsided, Eisenhower began to recognize how much of his mission was political, and that however much of North Africa was bleak desert, it was also a jungle of greed and intrigue. Marshall's continued backing was crucial, for Roosevelt could have removed Eisenhower to protect his reduced and unstable consensus in Congress. (Republicans had gained forty-seven House seats and ten in the Senate.) "I know you understand," Ike's radiogram from Algiers to Marshall conceded, "the necessity for dealing with turncoats and crooks is as distasteful to me as to anyone else."

In a tepid supporting statement, Roosevelt, in 450 cautious words, used *temporary* or its equivalent six times. Marshall told Stimson that the bargain was bound to cause further trouble for Eisenhower, who did not expect any loyalty from Admiral Darlan but still needed his cooperation. Reacting to Roosevelt's assertion, Darlan told Mark Clark, "I am only a lemon which the Americans will drop after they have squeezed it dry."

Marshall suggested in a radiogram on November 22, as Eisenhower was settling down in Algiers, that since critics of the deal "have no conception of the serious nature of the fighting and therefore feel free to embarrass the President the War Department and you by superficial assaults on what we are doing," the grumbling might be defused by releasing casualty figures. It would "prove the seriousness of the situation and the tremendous advantage we gained . . . by Darlan's orders." The next day a preliminary combined services tally was released: 360 confirmed dead, 1,050 wounded, and 500 missing and presumed drowned in the heavy surf during the landings. In Washington, Marshall then put his spin on the figures by comparing them to the worst-case planning estimate of 18,000 casualties. It made the dubious deal look good.

Logistics were even more problematic than politics, as resupply had to be accomplished with almost no railway lines or adequate roads, a shortage of ships, a dangerous German sub presence offshore, and the hammering of ports by the Luftwaffe, now quickly established near Tunis and Bizerte, five hundred miles from Algiers. In the rain and mud of late autumn, the delayed advance into Tunisia bogged down. Whatever timetable Eisenhower had assumed for taking all of French North Africa, he was mired by weather and balked by Field Marshal Albert Kesselring's improvised battalions flown in from Italy and permitted by Vichyites to land unopposed. Rommel may have been routed in the Egyptian desert near El Alamein just before "Torch" opened, but he, too, knew how to backtrack cagily. The Axis loss of North Africa was now inevitable, but the vast spaces and Montgomery's slow pursuit granted the Afrika Korps time to regroup and combine forces with the Tunisian reinforcements.

Given the certainty that Tunis would be no cakewalk, General Brooke in London was scornful of Eisenhower's juggling opportunistic Vichy losers while mismanaging strategy and tactics. To his private satisfaction, Brooke reminded himself that Eisenhower had never even commanded a battalion in action, and was distracted not only by the impossible Darlan and *la gloire*–obsessed Giraud, but also by the rigidly Vichyite Pierre Boisson, the collaborationist military governor of French West Africa, who controlled Dakar. Eisenhower's chief seemed no better to Brooke. "This evening," he confided to his diary on December 11, "[I] received wire from Dill [in Washington], giving insight into Marshall's brain: apparently he considers we should close down operations in the Mediterranean once we have pushed [the] Germans out, and then concentrate for preparing for re-entry into France. . . . I think he is wrong and that Mediterranean gives us far better facilities for wearing out German forces, both land and air, and of withdrawing [Wehrmacht] strength from Russia."

Brooke had obviously absorbed an earful from Churchill, who, despite his denials to Washington, objected totally to a future Channel beachhead. Given the inexperience of the Americans, and even the British, and the competence of the Wehrmacht generals, the combat skills of their troops, and the superiority of their artillery and armor, the Germans would have made hamburger of a cross-Channel invasion force. The Allies had much to learn, and would be educated by frustration and failure, and trial runs in cooperation and command. "Torch" did open a new front long before any other possibility emerged.

Expecting a long interlude in North Africa, Eisenhower had his aide Harry Butcher lease Villa dar el Ouard in Algiers, considered compatible with his rank, and, soon, for weekends, a white stucco, red-tiled "farmhouse" ten miles from Algiers which Butcher claimed was called "Sailor's Delight." It had horses and stables, a tennis court, a lawn level enough for golf practice, and a view of the Mediterranean. Eisenhower moved in Kay Summersby, imported from his English entourage. She had survived the torpedoing of the transport *Strathallan* and landed in Oran needing new clothes. (Eyebrows were raised when Ike was seen cantering with the attractive lady who was ostensibly his chauffeur.)* The "farm" would receive his many official visitors, both civilian and military. Nearby was an airfield from which he could fly the nearly three hundred miles to Constantine, near the Tunisian border yet a two hours' drive to forward positions.

---

*Billeted nearby with several WAC officers, she resided otherwise with Eisenhower.

Although Eisenhower may have wanted Tunis for Christmas, he received an alternative gift in Algiers itself. On Christmas Eve a young Frenchman who claimed to be a royalist shot the odious Darlan. Even Marshall diplomatically cabled a message to the unconscious admiral deploring the attempt on his life. Darlan died on Christmas Day, grieved over formally by most of the powerful in Algeria—who were actually delighted at his removal from the scene. Eisenhower looked the other way as the French military authorities summarily executed Fernand Bonnier de la Chapelle for murder.

Cabled for advice about a replacement for Darlan, Marshall recommended the pretentious Giraud. After all, the general was spirited out of France, at great hazard, for his potential as a leader. Further, Roosevelt despised De Gaulle, who might not have accepted any restrictions on his role. Giraud, who had no following in French North Africa, would prove useless, and *le grande Charles* would ignore him. The opportunity, however slender, of co-opting the vain De Gaulle foundered on the outspoken dislike of Churchill and Roosevelt. The damage was irreparable, and would last for decades.

Although Darlan's disappearance relieved Eisenhower of a political burden, the military outlook remained unpromising. It would be the first of his bleak Christmases of the war. The hoped-for quick fix of regaining the initiative in the Mediterranean, and destabilizing Italy, had vanished with the chill winter rains and the failure to take Tunisia. His troops were low in everything, from armor and aircraft to command decisiveness. The Germans were building up forces to defend Tunis and Bizerte. With his anxieties at a high level, he smoked more and more, confessed as much in his letters to Mamie, yet rationalized to her that it was the only bad habit he had.

Eisenhower was not alone in his disappointments with the inadequacies of the first joint Allied operation. Since neither RAF nor American air missions in North Africa seemed better than "fumbling," he brought Major General Carl ("Tooey") Spaatz from England to alleviate the disorder and establish forward airfields. Even Brooke in London realized that his own top general on the Tunisian front, the plodding Kenneth Anderson, disdained "cooperation" with other army commanders. (An historian of the Mediterranean campaigns, Douglas Porch, wrote that Anderson "cast a pall of scrupulous melancholy" over operations.) Brooke's agent visiting Algeria, General Ian Jacob, claimed that Mark Clark, Eisenhower's crony and Marshall's former aide, was so "ambitious and unscrupulous" in seeking to take charge of the Tunisia operation, rather than (in a balancing of authority) a British general, that Eisenhower distanced him to command reserve forces in Morocco. There, also, the impatient George Patton, another old friend, idled frustratingly in a commandeered sheik's palace. Both were promised leading roles in "Husky"—the Sicilian operation to follow. Pleased at the reduction of Clark's role and in increasing British dominance, Brooke faint-praised Eisenhower's "high quality of impartiality"—that while he had no tactical ability, he "shone" in managing "inter-allied forces."

The first serious test on the ground for Eisenhower, foreshadowing the "Bulge" disaster in the Ardennes nearly two years later, came embarrassingly just after a summit conference in Casablanca. In the relative limbo prior to new moves, military and political leaders from Washington and London gathered to determine future strategy. (As a courtesy, knowing that he would not travel far, if at all, from Russia, Stalin was invited.) Confidently—and naïvely—they assumed that clearing the Axis from North Africa required little more than good weather. Concerned more that Stalin considered "Torch" an evasion of the promise of a Second Front in Europe, and that the Darlan Deal suggested that the Anglo-Americans might broker a separate peace with Hitler to avoid a cross-Channel bloodbath, Roosevelt closed the Casablanca conference with a manifesto, which surprised Churchill, promising to end the war with the Axis powers only upon "unconditional surrender." Despite quiet misgivings, Churchill agreed.

Kremlin bosses suspected nevertheless that some influential politicians in the West, assuming that Russia was only an ally of opportunity, were promoting a policy of plague on both the Nazi and the Soviet houses.* Churchill as well as Roosevelt remained concerned that Stalin might make his own deal with Hitler, as once before with the flouted Nonaggression Pact of August 1939. However essential it seemed at the time, the Casablanca manifesto would mean a war without compromise, possibly even post-Hitler—should that happen—to the bitter end.

Brooke had already rejected for the British what he described as "a very bad plan" to follow up the dislodging of the Germans from Tunisia and from western Libya, where Rommel's retreating forces were regrouping. The American choice had been an invasion of Sardinia. Marshall and

*One was Senator Harry S Truman, who told the *New York Times* two days after Hitler's attack on Russia in June 1941 that "if we see that Germany is winning we ought to help Russia and if Russia is winning we ought to help Germany and that way let them kill off as many as possible although I don't want to see Hitler victorious under any circumstance[s]."

Eisenhower saw the big island below the French southern coastline, and Corsica, in terms of a second front in southern France. Backing Churchill, Brooke had proposed instead to invade Sicily as the back door to Italy. It was not merely that Italy was midway across the upper Mediterranean, but that the big lake was central to unconfessed British imperial interests. To Churchill, Sicily was a "glorious opportunity . . . we must not fail to seize."

After Casablanca, Marshall stayed briefly in Eisenhower's Algiers villa, a visit begun inauspiciously when Ike's pet Scottie, Telek, peed on the chief of staff's bed. Deflecting Eisenhower's embarrassment, Marshall remarked with a grin, "Apparently the dog doesn't realize who's to sleep here—or maybe he does!" Far from obtuse, Marshall was more concerned about Eisenhower's relationship with Kay Summersby, who shared custody of Telek, and perhaps more. The chief chatted with Harry Butcher ostensibly about Ike's health—that he was pushing himself too hard and smoking too much—but he may have also been hinting about Kay. She would remain on Marshall's mind—and also on that of Eisenhower's administrative aide, Colonel Ernest R. ("Tex") Lee, who told her bluntly although with embarrassment, "There's a lot of gossip about you and the Boss. People are saying that you . . ."

"That we what?" she asked, when he fumbled for more words.

"That you, uh—well, that you sleep together when he goes on trips."

Kay explained that she was engaged to a remote American captain. "It's ridiculous." The rumors would continue, even crossing the Atlantic to Washington—a very obvious matter after Eisenhower, the month after landing in North Africa, tucked into a list of recommended early decorations a Legion of Merit for a little-known British civilian employee, Kathleen Summersby. Marshall's deputies recognized the name and with some consternation brought the proposal to him. As her services were credited as "above and beyond the call of duty," the staff wondered what that really meant and whether Eisenhower realized how improper the request—and the situation—seemed to be.

Marshall had a General Staff memorandum sent to Eisenhower's adjutant on January 5, 1943, observing blandly that Mrs. Summersby was "not qualified for the Legion of Merit by virtue of not being in the Military Service." That indirectly disposed of the matter.

The charming and efficient Kay Summersby, now in a tailor-made uniform resembling that of an American WAC officer, had, since England, seen nothing of her American captain, Richard Arnold, who would shortly be killed by an exploding mine in Tunisia. She hardly knew him but mourned at the news. "I went where Ike went," she would confide. Omar Bradley called Kay "Ike's shadow." When she began typing, at his dictation, letters to Mamie, to which he dashed off signed postscripts, Mamie suspiciously wrote back that she wanted, henceforth, only his handwritten letters.*

Once the Casablanca sessions concluded, Churchill invited Roosevelt to Marrakech, a four-hour drive, where the PM wanted to relax and paint with the snowcapped Atlas Mountains as backdrop. "It's the most lovely spot in the whole world," he explained. There, at a dinner arranged by Churchill's staff, conference papers were formally signed, toasts made, a message to Stalin about future operations agreed upon, and, as Averell Harriman recalled, "Winston sang."

One unlovely matter intervened for Churchill: Eisenhower's "horrible bad temper" at the VIP dinner because the general's "lady chauffeur had not been asked too."

After Casablanca, Marshall—who was not at Marrakech—had left North Africa with some disquiet. "I always had the distinct impression," Mrs. Summersby remembered, "that General Marshall would have been just as happy if I did not exist. He always shook hands when we met. . . . Certainly he never addressed a personal word to me. . . . I thought Marshall was a cold fish."

Aside from Kay, the chief of staff's many concerns included the open British desire to keep extending the war farther into the Mediterranean and to delay if not scuttle a cross-Channel operation. An inveterate reader of history as he logged hours on airplanes, and irritated by Churchill's proposals, which seemed only covert imperial designs, Marshall would learn more about British tenacity in behalf of empire on the five thousand miles back via Dakar and Trinidad. Air Marshal John Slessor had given him Arthur Bryant's *Years of Endurance, 1793–1802,* on the Napoleonic wars. (Marshall also finished H. J. Haskell's *This Was Cicero.*)

While the top guns had parleyed in Casablanca, Patton invited Marshall to dinner, hoping to promote his prospects after North Africa. After two days of action early in November, Patton lived in style but felt unemployed. "Never asked a question and talked steadily about South Pacific," he complained to his diary about the chief of staff. Marshall's thoughts were elsewhere, especially about the distant but unforgotten MacArthur. While action lagged on the Tunisian front, Marshall checked cables about SWPA progress in New Guinea, MacArthur's messages suggesting that

---

*In nearly five years of war Mamie received 319 letters from Ike.

he was personally directing "his" troops through the Papuan jungle. Marshall knew better. His Pentagon agents were constantly flying to various theaters to be Marshall's eyes and ears. He had noted early in December in a talk to the National Association of Manufacturers, "In a single morning a few days ago I interviewed two General Staff officers just in from [the] Kokoda Pass and Milne Bay in New Guinea and from Guadalcanal; another from Chungking, China, and New Delhi in India; and still another from Moscow, Basra, and way points." He could separate photo-ops and phony communiques from reality.

MacArthur had ordered his replacement for Harding in New Guinea, Lieutenant General Robert Eichelberger, a former West Point commandant like his new chief, to "take Buna or not come back alive." If successful, Eichelberger was promised the rare accolade of having his identity made public, and a medal awarded by the Supreme Commander himself. At the height of the fighting, which became costly in dead and wounded, MacArthur edited down a communique piously to "On Christmas Day our activities were limited to routine safety precautions. Divine services were held."

Japanese resistance was tenacious, as were New Guinea's swarms of malaria-bearing mosquitoes. Nearly half of Eichelberger's troops were medical casualties. He began to realize why the sacked Harding's pace had been "pallid." In mid-January, however, as the Allied summit convened in Casablanca, the Japanese evacuated Buna and withdrew westward, opening a path across the more traversable upper coast of the big island. Somehow a few press reports escaped ahead of MacArthur's communiques, and flattering articles about Eichelberger appeared in *Life* and the *Saturday Evening Post*. MacArthur summoned the general to threaten, so he wrote to his wife, "Em," to "reduce you to the grade of colonel tomorrow, and send you home."

"Of course you could," Eichelbeger agreed supinely. Stealing MacArthur's limelight, Eichelberger explained in a letter to his wife, might "prove more dangerous than a Japanese bullet." When Robert Sherrod of *Time* asked to interview him for a cover story, Eichelberger responded, "Do you want to get me sent home?" He wrote to a colleague who handled public relations for the War Department, "I would rather have you slip a rattlesnake in my pocket than have you give me any publicity." Keeping a low profile, Eichelberger would survive the war with MacArthur.

Despite his hunger to manipulate the media and imply that he was commanding troops in the field, MacArthur had not done so since 1918. In any case, front-line action was not the job of a theater commander. Still, one of his aims was to overshadow, if possible, the ongoing drama in the nearby Solomons, where costly naval losses around Guadalcanal were covered up or minimized, and marine and army forces fought at considerable cost to take, and maintain, an airfield that might dominate the archipelago. Of the 33,000 troops in eastern New Guinea, 8,546 became combat casualties; 3,095 of them died. Employing his own count, MacArthur claimed a "low . . . expenditure of life and resources," but the cost was far greater than the 2,000 dead* at Guadalcanal, where army Major General J. Lawton Collins and marine Major General Alexander Vandegrift, both later chiefs of staff of their services, displayed striking personal valor and urged on their men to memorable levels of heroism.

Since the Guadalcanal struggle seized press attention far more than did unromantic New Guinea, MacArthur withheld Eichelberger's promised medal and mention in a communique, even cabling the War Department meanly that the general deserved no decoration and had mishandled the fighting. MacArthur's subsequent news releases, nevertheless, estimated imaginatively huge numbers of enemy dead—upwards of 150,000 killed. Yet he still badgered Marshall that his men lacked weaponry of every kind and could barely defend themselves.

With the capture of Buna—only a way station—MacArthur prematurely announced the end of the Papua phase of the New Guinea campaign in order to preempt the continuing drama of Admiral Halsey's forces on Guadalcanal, and of Eisenhower's divisions in North Africa. Fighting had three more weeks to run, but it was a typical MacArthur ploy. Similarly, he would announce, in March, a great air victory over the Bismarck Sea above northeastern New Guinea, with enemy ship and plane losses far in excess of realistic assessments later brought to him. "It

---

*The Japanese lost two-thirds of the 31,400 troops committed to Guadalcanal.

wasn't up to me," LeGrande Diller later shrugged, "to verify the communiqués."

"Bob," MacArthur would recall to Eichelberger, "those were great days when you and I were fighting at Buna, weren't they?" And he laughed. It was a warning that whatever MacArthur told visiting politicians and newsmen, not to disclose his absence. But he had himself photographed in a jeep with Eichelberger at the wheel, at Rockhampton, north of Brisbane. Signal Corps prints were sent to newspapers in the U.S. captioned, "General MacArthur at the front with General Eichelberger in New Guinea." Such was Eichelberger's promised publicity.

Listening to the exaggerations as broadcast on armed forces radio often furnished soldiers with the only kind of fun possible in the miserable climate and terrain. In many sardonic verses, GIs in New Guinea sang of "Doug's Communique," for its spin on a reality

> . . . seldom tarnished with
> The plain unvarnished truth.
> It's quite a rag; it waves the flag . . .
> And while possibly a rumor now,
> Someday it will be fact
> That the Lord will hear a deep voice say
> "Move over, God—it's Mac."
> So bet your shoes that all the news
> that last great Judgment Day
> Will go to press in nothing less than
> DOUG'S COMMUNIQUE!

MacArthur blamed the poor bargaining power he allegedly suffered in Washington on Eisenhower, who was "enhancing his own position by feeding the White House with anti-MacArthur data." Eisenhower's victories, he charged, were "a sham." The North African landings, he told Eichelberger, were a pointless diversion. Japan, not Germany, was the principal enemy, for life could be "tolerable" under Hitler, who represented "a civilized race." The Japanese, however, were "a total menace to civilization," and life under the Rising Sun would be "impossible." MacArthur may have been echoing Charles Willoughby. Speaking on behalf of his boss to Lieutenant Colonel Gerald Wilkinson, Churchill's liaison to SWPA headquarters, MacArthur's Prussian-born G-2 suggested that Allied priorities ought to be to seek a cease-fire in Europe and "let

Naziism mellow," then encourage the Germans and Russians "to kill each other off."* After leaving Australia for England in mid-1943, Wilkinson summed up MacArthur himself shrewdly in a bundle of negatives:

> He is shrewd, selfish, proud, remote, highly strung and vastly vain. He has imagination, self-confidence, physical courage and charm, but no humor about himself, no regard for truth, and is unaware of these defects. He mistakes his emotions and ambitions for principles. With moral depth he would be a great man; as it is he is a near miss which may be worse than a mile. . . . His main ambition would be to end the war as Pan-American hero in the form of generalissimo of all Pacific theaters. . . . He hates Roosevelt and dislikes Winston's control of Roosevelt's strategy. He is not basically anti-British, just pro-MacArthur.

Wilkinson also noted that MacArthur, in his insubordinate hatred of Washington, claimed that Churchill (whom he had never met) was "his only ally," and that despite orders that he was justified in going past the Pentagon to "Curtin, Queen Wilhelmina, and Churchill," as he had Australian, Dutch, and British forces under his command. On one occasion he offered his views on European strategy to Churchill through Major General R. H. Dewing, British military observer in Brisbane. A cross-Channel assault, MacArthur advised, would be a "costly failure." Rather, he would "throw all the reserves of America and Great Britain on[to] the Russian front," on the southern sector where lines of supply might be established through the Caucasus and Persia. Dewing informed Churchill, who observed to his military deputy, Hastings "Pug" Ismay, "The General's ideas about the European theatre are singularly untroubled by considerations of transport and distance." They were also untroubled by politics. Stalin would not even permit American pilots to ferry desperately needed Lend-Lease aircraft into Russian airspace.

When MacArthur relented and recommended Eichelberger for a Distinguished Service Cross, he issued a pompous order of the day announcing eleven recipients, as if the battle for Buna, a blip on the map, had been a Gettysburg. Although the DSC was intended for exemplary courage in combat, MacArthur included similar baubles for such mo-

---

*Later, to Eisenhower's embarrassment, the idea would also obsess the outspoken George Patton.

mentary visitors to the line—if even that—as Sutherland, Kenney, Blamey, and Willoughby.

For Marshall, public relations was part of his everyday job, and not a covert operation, and he acted selflessly in the role. On February 13, after his return from Casablanca, he spoke in Washington off the record to the American Society of Newspaper Editors. His subject was the sensitivity of what news could be released, and on what basis newspapermen might form their editorial comments. "You are familiar with the Darlan incident," he began, and observed that other potential embarrassments lurked in North Africa, where there was "probably no more fertile field in the world for racial and political confusions and Axis propaganda." Since there were insufficient Allied troops to maintain a military occupation, Eisenhower had coddled more than one collaborationist Frenchman, and still needed some of them, at least temporarily, to keep the dysfunctional territories quiet. Carefully, Marshall did not cite chapter and verse. The editors understood. He left unmentioned the local Arab hostility and the continuing Vichy miasma that kept in force racist laws which oppressed Jews who had lived for centuries in Algeria and Morocco. Pacifying the region came first.

Roosevelt justified Eisenhower's compromises to a press conference with what he claimed was an old Bulgarian proverb of the Orthodox Church: "My children, you are permitted in time of great danger to walk with the Devil until you have crossed the bridge."

Marshall also voiced cautious pride in Eisenhower's leadership as an American "of a great Allied force." It was the first such time in history, and he declared that the British War Cabinet's instructions to its commanders, some of them outranking Eisenhower, "were models of their kind and those officers have given him the most loyal and warm-hearted support." If Marshall knew how grudging and hostile some of that support was, he cautiously conceded none of it. Problems admittedly existed. A difficult logistical situation seemed endlessly ongoing. However much momentum there already was in war production, it was never enough, nor did worldwide transport of war matériel suffice. America needed to supply resources "not only in New Guinea, we must have them in the Solomons, we must have them in the Aleutians, we must have them supporting the battle in Tunisia." The U.S. was also supporting the British

Eighth Army as it pursued Rommel, and arming British, and willing French forces, in North Africa. Using aircraft—he could have substituted trucks—as a hardware example, he observed, "Russia must have planes, transport, and combat [types]. China must have planes, transport, and combat. The British and Australians must have American planes."

To determine where the needs were most crucial in the Pacific, Marshall went on, obviously now for the eyes and ears of MacArthur and his press and legislative claque, "I send a constant stream of officers from the War Department . . . traveling to this theater. They follow our troops into Buna, into Guadalcanal, and into the westernmost islands of the Aleutians, and bring back to me first-hand reports of local conditions and the requirements as they see them. . . . As you must realize, the man on the ground, or the commander in each area, clearly sees his own problems but can know but little of what is happening elsewhere unless it directly affects his battle." Each commander, Marshall observed, "usually wants more than we can give him in planes, troops, and ships, and our problem is to see that he does have the necessary additional means at the critical moments."

In further diplomacy a week later he drafted a letter to MacArthur under Roosevelt's signature commending him for the "tremendous and remarkably efficient bombardments launched by your air forces" in support of the Solomons operations, "which command our enthusiastic admiration." He also praised "the arduous and difficult land campaign" in New Guinea, which "must have a demoralizing effect on Japanese confidence in the fighting efficiency of their ground troops." Apparently feeling that Marshall's buttering-up gave MacArthur too much undeserved credit, the president deleted "tremendous and remarkably."

Marshall would also laud MacArthur's belated and long-urged offloading of vessels at his forward bases. The stagnation had created vast congestion, continued shortages of shipping, and reduced supplies to troops. At a later point MacArthur was holding up more than 140 cargo ships, claiming, when questioned, shortages in personnel and facilities. Marshall offered, hardly seriously—the outcome would have been catastrophic if followed through—to send 50,000 coolies from China *each month*, by way of Calcutta, to unload SWPA cargo. Relieved when MacArthur, who usually distanced himself from the realities, hastened to keep the coolies out, Marshall praised his "vigorous and effective action in the solution of a difficult problem." At a White House meeting with the JCS, Roosevelt observed that at the rate of MacArthur's progress, it would take two thousand years to reach the Japanese home islands. At that,

Marshall suggested, so Hap Arnold recalled, leapfrogging and isolating enemy strong points, a strategy proposed by Naval War College staff planners who were anticipating war, and Japanese successes, as early as 1940.

Marshall was always fending off appeals and excuses from commanders. Earlier, in Casablanca, at a one-on-one dinner laid out for him, and just as Patton felt his opportunity was arising to voice a personal plea to return to action, a courier turned up. The chief of staff was to dine urgently with "A-1" (Churchill was "A-2" in American code). The president had arrived by air, and at 8:10, Marshall, modest at best in his eating and drinking, had to go off to a second dinner.

As Patton learned details of the summit from Mark Clark, his disappointment grew. The British would receive an increased command role, with Harold Alexander, a Churchill favorite, shifted from the Middle East to become Eisenhower's deputy (replacing Clark). Eisenhower in the prime minister's "stratosphere" scheme would attend more to inter-Allied affairs, planning, and oversight of the theater: "Ike will be a sort of War Department." Patton was unhappy at the likelihood of being ordered about by Alexander, whose charm, he felt, exceeded his competence, and who was abetted by the arrogant Montgomery and the mediocre Anderson. "It will be one hell of a bloody mess, with no credit to us."

The bloody mess came sooner than Patton anticipated, before the unwanted British oversight arrived. On an inspection tour after the German presence had been augmented to the south by Rommel's troops from Tripoli, which had been taken by Montgomery's Eighth Army, Eisenhower found the four divisions of the American II Corps in Tunisia undisciplined and unprepared either for offense or defense. The only person clearly ready for the Germans was the Corps commander, Lloyd Fredendall, who had ordered two hundred engineer troops to blast a bombproof underground headquarters for him far to the rear. "One of the things that gives me the most concern," Eisenhower suggested indirectly, "is the habit of some of our generals in staying too close to their command posts."

The hint went unheard. To Fredendall's subordinates, only his reputation for a foul mouth suggested any ferocity. Even more remote from the action, Eisenhower already had a surplus of nonfighting bureaucratic brass. Headquarters in Algiers had swollen to fourteen hundred personnel, managed by Walter Bedell Smith, who had moved from London to be chief of staff, and by logistics chief J.C.H. (already widely known as "Jesus Christ Himself") Lee, a West Point classmate of Patton's and already an expert at rear-area indulgence. Eisenhower loyally overlooked

Lee's lifestyle, depending on his supply schemes, which always came second, after Lee himself. "Beetle" Smith was a demon for paperwork. Ike seemed to have acquired an affinity for comfortable distancing from his old boss in Manila, Douglas MacArthur.

Although General Jürgen von Arnim had commanded Axis troops—the Fifth Panzer Army—holding Bizerte and Tunis since the Allied advance had been blunted, Rommel, moving north into central Tunisia, now turned away from Montgomery, combining with Arnim in a two-pronged attack on Eisenhower's largely unblooded troops. Perched below the Mareth Line in southern Tunisia, strongpoints which had been built by the French years earlier to protect the colony from the Italians in Libya, Montgomery could be expected in his unhurriedly methodical fashion to accumulate superiority in armor and artillery before mounting a renewed offensive. Improved weather would make it possible, Monty thought, by the third week in March.

In mid-February, while Arnim struck at the Faid Pass in central Tunisia, Rommel's Afrika Korps, supported by Stuka dive-bombers, routed the unready Americans and the rearmed French to the south and penetrated the Kasserine Pass. The intelligence failure was complete. Of 7,000 American casualties, nearly 3,000 were taken prisoner with embarrassing ease. Motorized equipment and supplies were abandoned as Fredendall's panicked troops fled. Eisenhower's aide, Harry Butcher, conceded frankly in his diary that "the outstanding fact" after Kasserine was "that the proud and cocky Americans today stand humiliated by one of the greatest defeats in our history. This is particularly embarrassing to us with the British." Eisenhower would only learn of Butcher's remark after the war.

Following Buna, MacArthur's victory communique halfway across the world had boasted, "Our losses . . . are low. As compared to the enemy they are less than half that of his ground force losses. . . . These figures reverse the usual results of a ground offensive campaign. . . . Losses to the attacker are usually several times that of a defender." It was false in MacArthur's case, and only unreliable brag, but it did reflect the German toll on Eisenhower's unprepared and surprised II Corps. By February 21, 1943, the rampaging Germans, who took few casualties, had driven a fifty-mile breach into the Allied lines, threatening the crucial supply port of Constantine to the north. Montgomery told Brooke that "the Bosche does just whatever he likes with the Americans." In early April he added, on reflection, that Eisenhower is "a very nice chap. I should say he is probably quite good on the political side. But I can also say, quite definitely, that he knows nothing whatever about how to make war or to fight battles; he should be kept right away from all that business if we want to win the war."

MacArthur shared few messages with subordinates, especially if mentioned by name. "Please give General Kenney and his fliers our warmest congratulations on their splendid performances of the past few days," Marshall radioed with futility on March 3 about successes in the Bismarck Sea off Papua. Estimates of kills—both ships and planes—were always on the high side, and often overlapping, but MacArthur added supplementary excess. "Japanese morale," Marshall added, "must deteriorate as they come to realize that this is but a foretaste of the rapid growth of United States air power in skill and daring even more than in constantly increasing numbers." After the navy questioned MacArthur's claims, because he had boasted publicly (and erroneously) of the superiority of land-based bombers to carrier aircraft, Marshall had Hap Arnold make a quiet investigation. The reports of twenty-two ships sunk and an estimated 15,000 enemy soldiers drowned proved to be twelve ships and about 2,800 dead.

Both MacArthur and Kenney challenged the figures, even years later after postwar research in Japan confirmed the War Department's estimates. Ten days earlier, Marshall had written a message in Roosevelt's name praising MacArthur and "the officers and men of the Australian and United States forces who carried the fight to the enemy on all levels and over great distances. . . ." It seemed essential to keep flattering MacArthur to prompt his cooperation with rival commands whose resources he resented, but it is unlikely that any encouragement from Washington was communicated very far down the line.

While resupply of Eisenhower's losses became a strategic priority, calls in Congress continued for investigative committees to junket to the fronts to see whether MacArthur's theater and other allegedly neglected areas like China should receive more resources. Exasperated, Marshall declared that he would even obey orders, if from Stimson, to transport the whole of Congress to the fighting fronts. North Africa received the most headlines, but some adverse news never appeared, although the arrival of General Alexander to command, ostensibly under Ike, had its implications. Eisenhower did not know of Alexander's six-page "most secret" letter to Brooke in which he charged that the Americans, "from the General to the private soldier," did not "know their job. . . . If this handful of Divisions here are their best, the value of the remainder may be imagined." Alexander wondered how "these same men's grandfathers fought like heroes in the Civil War." Even worse was the subterfuge secretly recommended by Churchill's political adviser at Eisenhower's headquarters, Harold Macmillan—that the British should pretend that the Americans are "running the show. This will enable you to run it yourself. We . . . are the Greeks in this American empire. . . . We must run [Allied headquarters] as the Greek slaves ran the operations of Emperor Claudius."

Summoned grudgingly by Eisenhower to take charge of ground forces in Tunisia, Alexander flew from Cairo to Tripoli, and on into Constantine, assuming ground command on February 19. Belatedly sacking II Corps commander Fredendall two weeks later, Eisenhower did not wait to write the relief orders before sending for Major General Ernest N. Harmon, Patton's deputy, to take over, temporarily, the American forces in disarray. Harmon, who would direct a counterattack that would clear Kasserine, reported to Patton unsurprisingly that Fredendall had been "a physical and moral coward."

Although Patton itched to be on the scene himself, for excitement he had to be content with sitting through the Bob Hope–Bing Crosby film *The Road to Morocco.* Fredendall, who was at least right about the weakness of American firepower against German armor, would be remembered for little more than his remark that "the only way to hurt a Kraut with a 37 mm. anti-tank gun is to catch him and give him an enema with it." The Germans used a formidable 88.

Before Harmon, and then Patton, were sent for as fighting replacements for Fredendall, none of his failings seemed sufficient in the self-protective culture of the military bureaucracy to remove him immediately—although a MacArthur would not have hesitated. Instead of making a tough call, Eisenhower had fudged to Marshall that Fredendall, one of the chief of staff's rare recommendation mistakes, was "a good fighter, energetic and self-confident." To Fredendall himself, the Supreme Commander wrote a peculiar admonition about regrouping his disorganized units, assuring "my complete confidence on your leadership. I meant every word of it but we must not blind ourselves to the serious defects that exist in our training, and perhaps . . . our organization." After returning from another flying visit to the area Eisenhower sent from Algiers a hardly believable "*Secret. Personal*" message to Fredendall avowing, timidly, "I would not leave you in command . . . one second if you did not have my confidence. You may be perfectly certain that you have it—you have it to such an extent that I feel I can tell you frankly about the things that worry me a bit as well as those things that please me immensely. Among the things that please me the most is . . . that after several days of rough handling [by the Germans] and constant retreat you were able—through your efforts and your personality—not only to hold the position that had to be held but were able to stage at least minor counter-attacks that showed that the subordinates under you had not lost their fighting spirit."

Following that increasingly faint praise, Ike finally confessed to Marshall on March 3 his "moments of doubt about Fredendall" and the hopeless general's disturbing but unidentified "idiosyncrasies," admitting finally the urgency to find "a good substitute."* Avoiding a bad press at home—as it was the first American transatlantic operation publicly gone sour—Marshall would shabbily promote Fredendall to lieutenant general (rather than eliminate his two stars) while banishing him as a "training officer" to Memphis, Tennessee, to command the Second Army. Perhaps as consolation prize, the quirky but relentless Patton would also get a third star.

At Marshall's urging (Roosevelt preferred waiting for "some damn good reason"—actual performance), Eisenhower would get a fourth star because so many of the British brass in the Mediterranean outranked him. After Casablanca, at a White House Correspondents Association dinner in February, Roosevelt had referred to spending "many hours with this young general—a descendant of Kansas pioneers. I know what a fine, tough job he has done and how carefully and skillfully he is directing the soldiers under him." At Churchill's suggestion, he added, Eisenhower would have "the supreme command of the great Allied operations which are imminent." Then unidentified, they would continue with Sicily, and then Italy.

Although Marshall would send further commanders to Eisenhower, he told him with the Fredendall blunder in mind that Ike was free to reassign or return any who performed poorly. "This principle will apply to the letter, because I have no intention of ever giving you an alibi for failure on the excuse that I forced unsatisfactory subordinates [on you]. I

---

*In his *Crusade in Europe* Eisenhower blamed himself rather than Fredendall for the Kasserine defeat and claimed that he "recommended" the general for a training command.

hold you responsible." Few would get an early ticket home. Fredendall's name would come up again—once. "Vinegar Joe" Stilwell unwisely proposed him as deputy supreme commander for the China-Burma-India Theater. Marshall (September 9, 1944) replied that he was "somewhat shocked"—and left Fredendall in Memphis.

In effect confirming Marshall's point about logistics in his confidential talk to the newspaper editors, Eisenhower had radioed urgently and without embarrassment to Washington on February 24 that "a very considerable quantity of equipment"—tanks, half-tracks, and artillery destroyed or abandoned in the Kasserine Pass—"must be made good as rapidly as possible." (Losses were estimated at 200 tanks and 1,000 other vehicles; German losses were about 10 percent of that.) Also that American antitank guns were "completely outmoded" and unable to "harm" German armor. He had stripped rear area units for immediate needs. Emergency shipments were rushed out, but that took time. General Brehon B. Somervell's logistical assistant, Major General Wilhelm D. Styer, cabled back, "If you should happen to want the Pentagon shipped over there, please try to give us about a week's notice."

A "bitter lesson" Eisenhower conceded to Marshall was that troops had learned that war was not "a child's game" and that they had to "perfect . . . their own battlefield efficiency." To accomplish that he had to acknowledge his humiliation and secure, through Alexander, "a number of highly experienced British officers to serve as liaison . . . in our units." (Resentment among American brass was extreme.) In effect Eisenhower's clout at the command level was also diminished. As London quietly wanted, and Washington accepted, he became the coalition's board chairman. Omar Bradley later wrote that only the need for an American facade saved Eisenhower's job. "Ike led an extraordinarily charmed life."

With sensitivity, Marshall in a radiogram on March 1, 1943, offered what he called "merely a suggestion" for Patton's resuming the offensive in Tunisia with fresh units. "MacArthur," he explained, actually meaning Kenney, "transported an entire division by bomber plane *with* equipment though a large portion of the heavy guns followed by boat, but he transported those large forces, even tanks and 105 [mm] guns, and supplied 2 ½ divisions entirely by air and mostly by bomber, so there is a great deal [that] can be done particularly if all but personal equipment is eliminated. It is also possible that economy of air transport could be realized by some movements by rail of personnel only from the Casablanca region to the vicinity of Oran, and there picked up by air transport. I offer this in a purely personal manner and wish you to feel no necessity for explanation of why you do not consider it practical." Eisenhower radioed on March 5, "Not practicable at this time."

Enemy momentum had slowed as the Germans suffered fuel shortages and poor weather. After the Kasserine Pass was reoccupied, Eisenhower telephoned Patton on March 4 to take over II Corps. Supposedly the summons came because operations to follow would be "primarily a tank show," and Patton knew "more about tanks" than anyone else available. He would keep his command in Morocco, and return to it. Then Omar Bradley was to step in. Patton flew to Constantine, consulted with Alexander, who suddenly (but only briefly) impressed him "a lot," and talked with Marshall's visiting troubleshooter, John McCloy. The next morning he had breakfast with the departing Fredendall, who was, Patton decided, "a little nuts or badly scared."

His job, Eisenhower cautioned Patton on March 6, was to revitalize American forces, forgo "personal recklessness," and "to respond to General Alexander's orders exactly as if they were issued by me. I want no mistake about my belief in unity of command." Patton would have four divisions and about 90,000 men, and operate in tandem with the equally flamboyant Montgomery, whose show, after his film-star visibility at El Alamein, it would be. An "Andrew Jackson type," Patton thought: "small, very alert, wonderfully conceited, and the best soldier—or so it seems—I have met in this war." Now that he was in on the action, Patton liked everyone.

After visiting Montgomery's command post, Eisenhower, putting aside memories of his rebuke on their first meeting, was also impressed, but wrote to Marshall shrewdly that there was a flaw in the jewel. It would emerge often, later, to furnish Ike grief. "Montgomery," he judged, "is of a different caliber from some of the outstanding British leaders you have met. He is unquestionably able, but very conceited. For your most secret and confidential information, I will give you my opinion which is that he is so proud of his successes to date that he will never willingly make a single move until he is absolutely certain of success—in other words, until he has concentrated enough resources so that anybody could practically guarantee the outcome. . . . Unquestionably he is an able tactician and organizer and, provided only that Alexander will never let him forget for one second who is the boss, he should deliver in good style."

The desert graveyards of wrecked vehicles in Tunisia were not the only ruins Patton would encounter. "Whole country [is] full of ruins," he wrote in his diary on March 8, 1945 "—great stones and pillars sticking up like the ribs of wrecked ships, or dead men through sand." The next day, Rommel would fly secretly to Italy, then Germany, recommending that the overmatched Axis troops, their resupply interdicted by sea and by air, be evacuated from North Africa rather than risk becoming prisoners of war wholesale. Kasserine, he contended, had only delayed the inevitable. Hitler derided Rommel's defeatism and refused to let him return. Captured instead was General Jürgen von Arnim, whom Eisenhower refused to meet, declaring, "The only German generals I'm interested in are the ones we haven't captured yet."

For Patton, the Germans were not the only enemy on the field. He despised the French and deprecated the British. After the débacle under Fredendall, the British made slighting remarks about American competence and courage, and Patton's anglophobia revived although he had been warned to control it. (He had been in the American Expeditionary Force in France in 1918, when AEF to some Yanks stood for "After England Failed.") "I would rather be commanded by an Arab," he fumed. When his G-3 (Operations) complained about "total lack of air cover," which the British were to provide, Air Marshal Sir Arthur Coningham called the criticism an alibi for troops that "are not battleworthy." Patton did not contain his outrage. When Alexander's G-3 counterpart telephoned with instructions about where Patton should order his battalions, Patton replied directly (and "respectfully") to Alexander "that in the United States Army we tell officers what to do, not how to do it; that to do otherwise suggests lack of confidence. . . . I feel that, for the honor and prestige of the U.S. Army, I must protest."

Patton would have been furious had he known of Montgomery's warning to Alexander about the Americans, "Don't let them be too ambitious and spoil the show." On April 12, 1943, writing of the former National Guard 34th Division, a Midwest outfit* accused earlier of a "poor showing" under fire, Patton told his diary scornfully, "After we had drawn off the Germans, the British came in and took their hill." He was crankily sure that Eisenhower would do nothing about it. "Ike is more British than the British and is putty in their hands." To Marshall, Eisenhower philosophized, perhaps validating Patton's concerns, that American sensitivities toward the British had existed "ever since we had read our little red school history books."

When Alexander's patronizing of American troops sufficiently incensed Marshall (who learned of the practice from Bradley), he intervened to have Eisenhower allocate the Patton-led, then Bradley-led, II

---

*From North Dakota, South Dakota, Minnesota, and Iowa.

Corps a greater role in finishing off the Germans. Then the contretemps between Patton and Coningham, only one of the continuing crises in Anglo-American relations in the campaign, left Eisenhower, often on a short fuse and fed up with friction and fence-mending, feeling that he had utterly lost management control. According to Air Chief Marshal Arthur Tedder, who considered Coningham's contempt "ill-judged," and "dynamite," he was handed by Eisenhower a draft of a cable to Marshall conceding that his failure to control subordinates meant that he was ineffective as their commander and that he "would ask to be relieved." Only Bedell Smith's intervention kept Eisenhower's career from being abbreviated.

After more than a month of nearly constant action, taking considerable casualties, II Corps was turned over to Omar Bradley. Some troops had fought to exhaustion because that was what one did for Patton. When the 10th Panzers attacked, he noted, as a "fine thing," that one of his platoons "died to a man. The last thing they were heard yelling was come on you hun bastards." Returning to Morocco, he would begin to prepare for "Husky," the cross-Mediterranean invasion of Sicily urged by Churchill and Brooke and accepted without enthusiasm by Roosevelt and Marshall. Commending "the successful completion of that phase of the Tunisian operations for which I placed you temporarily in command of the II Corps," Eisenhower offered Patton his "sincere congratulations upon the outstanding example of leadership you have given us all." Ike was undoubtedly relieved that the vision of Patton erect in his speeding command car, his three stars gleaming on his helmet, his pearl-handed revolver visible at his hip, and outriders on motorcycles roaring ahead, was at least temporarily in the past tense. The final phases would be the ambitious yet self-effacing Bradley's.

"The people who count," Patton explained to Beatrice from Casablanca in his curious phraseology, "know why what is. George [Marshall] sent me a wonderful telegram all by himself." Washington and London had pressed for an April 30 conclusion to the Tunisian campaign in order to release resources for Sicily. On May 7, 1943, Anderson's troops finally entered Bizerte. On May 13, the remaining 275,000 Axis troops, abandoned for lack of shipping, surrendered, more than half of them German. Rommel had been right.

The North African adventure had been costlier than predicted and had taken much too long. Of the 71,810 Allied casualties then acknowledged, 10,820 were killed, 39,575 were wounded, and 21,415 missing or captured, one of them Patton's son-in-law, Lieutenant Colonel John K.

Waters Jr. "You set a stiff pace for Bradley," Marshall had cabled Patton on May 4, 1943, "but he seems to be following through in excellent style. I realize that the planning you are now occupied with is a poor substitute for active combat, but it is of the utmost importance, and, as you know, your turn will come soon again."

The next day Marshall reported by courier to Eisenhower (it was always "Dear Eisenhower" on one side and "Dear General" on the other) that a letter of "urgent advice" for him had arrived in Washington from John Petroskey in New York. He had read reports that Eisenhower "takes cold water with his meals." Rommel, Petroskey advised, "would not have been the successful desert fox if he was caught with a cylinder or two missing in his brain by bad digestion." He suggested stronger drink for Eisenhower. "After you have cut out the cold water," Marshall added in rare humor, "I expect to see the modified HUSKY go through with a bang." To his public relations deputy, Major General Alexander Surles, Marshall sent a memorandum castigating a *Washington Post* editorial lauding the Tunisian victory as a "truly Allied triumph" yet failing to credit Eisenhower:

> See if you can't do something with the news writers and the broadcasters to register an appreciation of the magnificent job Eisenhower has done and the great contribution he has made to the Allied cause in demonstrating, under the most conceivably complicated circumstances, a successful unity of command.
>
> You can tell some of these newsmen from me that I think it is a damned outrage that because he is self-effacing and not self-advertising that they ignore him completely when, as a matter of fact, he is responsible for the coordination of forces and events which brought about the success. . . .

From London, Churchill cabled the White House that Australian prime minister Curtin felt that MacArthur's victories in New Guinea, which had kept Down Under secure, deserved the royal award—honorary in the case of Americans—of the Order of Knight Grand Cross of the Bath. Kept out of the loop, Curtin had been seduced by MacArthur's communiques. Churchill thought that the bauble would not be objected to by Marshall or King, as it was for military action. Harry Hopkins replied dryly for Roosevelt, "Decorations for bravery in combat are all right but most people believe that the decorating should stop there. If, however, you decide to give a decoration to MacArthur, neither the world nor the war will come to an end any sooner and I doubt if Marshall, King, or Nimitz will lose any sleep because of it. The Tunisian news is great."

Churchill took the hint. On May 26, King George VI conferred the GCB on MacArthur (via Curtin) and also on Eisenhower.

7

Running a War, and Running for Office

A S THE BUILDUP FOR "HUSKY," the invasion of
Sicily, was ongoing, the fighting in North Africa
had ceased. Hostilities among the coalition part-
ners continued, although joint conferences papered over the differences.
As Sir Alan Brooke complained in his diary on May 8, 1943, "Running
a war seems to consist in making plans and then ensuring that all those
destined to carry it out don't quarrel with each other instead of the
enemy." While MacArthur intrigued from Brisbane for his Southwest
Pacific theater and King, from Washington, argued for more resources to
move across the central Pacific, Brooke wanted only to "hold Japan." For
Britain that meant fighting off "diversion of force" until Germany was
out of the war. Lost colonies in East Asia remained largely an unspoken
embarrassment, worth the price of preventing a cross-Channel operation
in 1943, if ever. Sicily and the margins of Europe were the British priorities.

MacArthur sent staffers to Washington to lobby for him. One was
Colonel Philip La Follette of the Wisconsin political family. "He came
back, I suppose, for the trip [home]," Marshall recalled wryly, "and also to
see what he could root up for General MacArthur, who was always in dire
need of everything. . . ." La Follette's appointment was at 8:30, which happened to precede Marshall's nine o'clock daily briefing. "The presentation
of the world picture was of great importance to me and to the principal
staff, because we had so many theaters operating at once, and along with
that, the stormy times with things at home." A Pentagon crew "got up at
four o'clock in the morning and worked on the cables of the night, which

always poured in, particularly from the Pacific. . . . Just prior to that hour this special force came into my office, no matter what I was doing or with whom I was talking, and set up all the machinery, and then they started. . . . Just went off like a theatrical thing. . . . You saw the whole war up to the last minute."

When La Follette arose, Marshall offered, "Would you like to see this?" La Follette stayed for the world survey and took his leave when it was over, abandoning what remained of MacArthur's mission. Only "after the peace" did La Follette see Marshall again and asked, then, "Did you keep me back there purposely to see that?" The update had "changed his whole state of mind the minute he saw the enormity of what was going on and what its requirements were and what the demands were. He began to see the picture in the light of the real circumstances." Marshall was amused. "I did keep him for the purpose, but I let it just fall into place . . . because if these fellows could see what the [global] thing is, they would understand more what the impossibility was of many things they were talking about."

Post-Tunis, Churchill, Brooke, and a large supporting party had arrived in New York on the *Queen Mary*, which also carried 5,000 German prisoners bagged in North Africa. Greeted by Harry Hopkins, the British conferees entrained for Washington, intent on postponing any cross-Channel commitment by suggesting dire visions of beaches covered with corpses. Marshall understood that for political as well as military reasons, troops following a campaign could not vegetate in place for a year or more. But he did not want them "sucked in" to lengthen the war where it would not be won.

To circumvent Churchill and Brooke, he argued for more resources for the Southwest Pacific, where MacArthur was "operating on a shoe-string and where great results could be achieved by relatively small additions." A Mediterranean campaign, Marshall warned, "would mean a prolongation of the war in Europe, and thus a delay in the ultimate defeat of Japan, which the people of the U.S. would not tolerate."

After ten days of disharmony Marshall remained insistent that operations which did not contribute to a Second Front across the Channel by May 1, 1944, long promised to Stalin, risked a separate peace that could leave Hitler in central and western Europe. "The Americans," Brooke deplored, "are now taking up the attitude that we led them down the garden path [in] taking them to North Africa! That at Casablanca we again misled them by inducing them to attack Sicily!! And now they are not going to be led astray again. Added to that the swing toward the Pacific is stronger than ever and before long they will be urging that we should defeat Japan first!"

In the American heartland, as Marshall realized, Japan remained the primary enemy, especially among ex-isolationists who had energized the America First Committee imploded by Pearl Harbor. Some of its die-hards remained in Congress. A few were deep into the Pacific war through industrial connections. The pragmatic Hap Arnold was using those he could, notably aviation hero Charles Lindbergh and the Sears, Roebuck chairman, retired Brigadier General Robert E. Wood. Given Roosevelt's antipathy, Marshall knew better than to seek a new commission for Colonel Lindbergh,* who had accepted the Cross of the German Eagle from Hermann Göring in 1938. Lindbergh nevertheless worked for curmudgeonly Henry Ford, tinkering with production of B-24 Liberator bombers at Willow Run, and testing the Republic Aircraft P-47 Thunderbolt. "If George Marshall ever took a position contrary to mine," said Arnold (who Marshall, breaking his usual rules, always called "Hap"), "I would know I was wrong." Marshall looked the other way even when Lindbergh as technical adviser to United Aircraft flew combat missions in the Pacific.

When Marshall attempted, on Arnold's behalf, to have the president order Robert Wood (long a MacArthur-for-President stalwart) back on active service to deal with aircraft production, Roosevelt refused, retorting that the former head of America First was "too old, and has, in the past, shown far too great approval of Nazi methods." Roosevelt, however, permitted his unpublicized use. (Marshall again brought up the subject of activating Wood, in June 1943; Roosevelt again disapproved.) The general could do nothing to improve relations with Senator Arthur Vandenberg, Republican of Michigan and crony of Lindbergh and Wood, for whom Pearl Harbor had ended isolationism but not his criticism of Roosevelt and his "private war." Further, *Chicago Tribune* publisher Colonel Robert McCormick and his newspaper-owner cousins in New York and Washington persisted in charges that Europe-first priorities left the United States the tool of British colonialists and Russian communists. The same crowd also argued that a hero allegedly abandoned by dangerous New Dealers to wither in the boondocks should be brought home to save the nation—Douglas MacArthur, whom army regulations prevented

---

*Under fire for his views, Lindbergh had resigned his Army Air Force Reserve commission in April 1941. He claimed that he was unaware he would be bemedalled by the Nazis, but he did not return the bauble.

(as he was on active duty) from becoming a formal candidate for political office.

The restrictions long in place had been recalled without any naming of names by Secretary Stimson. They were quickly interpreted in the Congress and in the press to be directed at MacArthur, yet the 1944 presidential primaries were still a year away. As Vandenberg, who had never met the general, maintained his right to run, MacArthur wrote to his champion, ambiguously, while his troops were on their slog across the northern coast of New Guinea, "I am most grateful to you for your complete attitude of friendship. I only hope that I can some day reciprocate. . . . In the meanwhile I want you to know the absolute confidence I would feel in your experienced and wise mentorship."

Vandenberg, who considered his one and only message from MacArthur, who wrote from Australia, as "supremely historic," began organizing an informal candidacy, enlisting as moneybags General Wood (who had already met with MacArthur in Brisbane), and as campaign facade former president Herbert Hoover. The campaign was so little a secret that the May 17, 1943, issue of *Time*—its publisher, Henry Luce, no longer shared his wife's enthusiasm for the general—included a fantasy, with a cartoon of Vandenberg, depicting the senator asleep in his office and dreaming of a procession in a great hall in 1944, led by prewar isolationist Representative Hamilton Fish, "magnificent in khaki and gold braid" and on a white horse, trumpeting the drafting of MacArthur on a "win-the-war platform." Over the cheers of the crowd, the slumbering Vandenberg hears the tune, "There's something about a soldier." A columnist close to the senator, *Time* claimed, had let it be known that a MacArthur-for-President movement was under way, out of Vandenberg's senatorial office. The case for the general was simple. No politician could defeat Roosevelt, "but the people will be voting for a Commander in Chief rather than for a President, and there are no credentials equal to MacArthur's upon that score."

Using the SWPA intelligence chief as intermediary, MacArthur concocted military excuses in the summer of 1943 to send Charles Willoughby to the States to meet with Vandenberg and other potential supporters, including Clare Boothe Luce, who on a reporting trip had been bedded in Manila by Willoughby before the war. The strategy cooked up would be for MacArthur to deny political ambitions but to encourage a covert candidacy in case events would derail a run by Governor Thomas E. Dewey, who seemed, despite Wendell Willkie, the feisty loser in 1940, a clear favorite. Mrs. Luce wrote to MacArthur shrewdly, "I believe you should allow the MacArthur sentiment here to grow unchecked. . . . Let people talk of MacArthur-for-President when such talk is of material help to your theater by helping to focus the public's attention on its problems and needs. . . . This political talk, painful as it may be to you, is of military value to the SWPA." In her view, MacArthur could claim that his supposedly unwilling candidacy was only to extract resources from Washington to win the war against Japan.

Stimson told his diary that MacArthur, "who is not an unselfish being and . . . a good deal of a prima donna," was "sending people here"—like his aide Sid Huff, and generals Kenney and Sutherland—"who carry a message from him that he was not a presidential candidate, thereby playing into the hands of the people who would really like to make him a candidate." In Port Moresby, MacArthur confided to General Eichelberger that the "only reason I want to be President . . . is to beat that S.O.B. Roosevelt." Struck by MacArthur's intensity and candor, Eichelberger concluded, "I can see he expects to get it, and I sort of think so, too."

As the invasion of Sicily loomed, the press had made MacArthur the most admired soldier in America. Marshall remained self-effacing and directly commanded no troops; Eisenhower, although much in the news, was still on probation. The stench of the Darlan Deal lingered; the botched North African operation had dragged on too long. Yet the public liked what it knew of Ike, and for the three top generals there was no one else of their stature.

At Casablanca, on January 23, 1943, Eisenhower had been directed to undertake an invasion of Sicily from Tunisia, "with the target date as the period of the favorable July moon." Although Marshall considered the Mediterranean a sink of unnecessary expenditure, he saw promise in opening the sea lanes through Suez in order to supply Russia through Middle Eastern ports. In actual command of the Sicily operation would be Alexander, assisted by Montgomery and Patton. Distracted by continuing North African political complications, Eisenhower left the planning largely to Alexander, which in effect meant that the domineering Montgomery took the major role for himself. Patton was in effect to hold Monty's coat.

Marshall suggested a surprise seizure, preemptive and possibly airborne, of a key site with a small force before the Axis recognized preparations which could not be hidden, and reinforced the island, as had happened in Tunisia. Eisenhower preferred, cautiously, "to capture HOBGOBLIN"—code for the tiny Italian island of Pantellaria between Tunis and the tip of Sicily—in order to safeguard shipping lanes. While Pantellaria was bombed into easy submission, the Germans rushed troops into Sicily by air. "Hobgoblin"—which meant mischievous goblin—belied its name. Its garrison prepared to surrender even before the British 1st Division went ashore without incident on June 11. The real hobgoblin would be Sicily.

After the Washington conference, Marshall had flown with Churchill to North Africa rather than to the South Pacific as he had planned, because he worried about Eisenhower's succumbing to Churchill's blandishments. American priorities could be undone in the claims of Allied amity. Churchill wrote to Clementine that he had asked FDR to permit Marshall to accompany him, so that "there should be no suggestion that I had exerted a one-sided influence. I think very highly of Marshall. He wrote a paper . . . in the airplane on general strategy. It was one of the most masterly I have seen, and with which I am in the fullest accord. There is no doubt he has a massive brain and a very high and honourable character." When closeted with General Brooke, Churchill's opinion was markedly different.

Touching down at Gibraltar, which Marshall had not visited before, he was shown about the fortifications, including new artillery mounts cut deep in the limestone, which Churchill thought would fend off any attack by General Franco, for Hitler, on the narrow, three-mile-long spit from the Spanish mainland. Undiplomatically, Marshall observed to Gibraltar's governor-general, Sir Frank Mason-MacFarlane, that MacArthur had prepared similarly for coastal defense at Corregidor, but the Japanese quickly refocused their guns. In two or three days, the impregnable sites had been blocked by rubble. Churchill seemed appalled, but recorded only that "all the smiles vanished from [Sir Frank's] face." Marshall would constantly bring up the Pacific war to remind the British that there was one, and that it might not be easy to win.

On May 28, 1943, on landing in Algiers to be greeted by Eisenhower, Churchill pulled Ike away to spend the day selling him on Mediterranean strategies. Something of a hostage to circumstances, all Marshall could do was to extract a promise that France remained fixedly on the agenda—for 1944, once the American buildup in the British Isles made a massive landing practicable. The manipulative PM's enthusiasms, Marshall knew, often faded in the face of political priorities.

Pantellaria and its sister islands of Lampedusa and Linosa were the first bits of Italian soil to fall, presaging the collapse of Mussolini's cardboard regime. To Churchill, all of Italy beckoned after Sicily, opening a back door to Hitler's empire. Although Marshall met with the commanders for "Husky" in Algiers in early June, he had multiple misgivings, and much else on his plate, worldwide. His concerns ranged from General Wood and General MacArthur to the reassigning of racist General John DeWitt (one of the few, like Patton, who got away with calling Marshall "George"); and subduing salacious rightist slanders against the Women's Army Auxiliary Corps (the "auxiliary" soon dropped), which impeded recruitment throughout the war. He also had to cope with Roosevelt's refusal to let Eisenhower deal with the vain De Gaulle, whom the president charged with unreliability and obstruction.

Marshall had to engage in some obstruction himself. Senator Harry S. Truman's war investigative committee wanted to look into the unprecedented start-up expenditures for a huge and mysterious manufacturing installation to be managed by E. I. Du Pont de Nemours along the Columbia River at Pasco, Washington. Truman had to be diverted from the nuclear operation without exciting suspicions. DeWitt, who commanded the Fourth Army from San Francisco, had opposed the return of "relocated" Japanese-Americans from their detention camps set up in the climate of post–Pearl Harbor fear he had abetted. Marshall named him commandant of the Army and Navy Staff College, prompting accusations of Washington "skullduggery." DeWitt was assured that his "knowledge of combined operations" was behind the appointment, which had "nothing to do with the Japanese situation"—although indeed it had.

In the case of the tenacious Senator Truman, Marshall instructed his Legislative and Liaison director, Brigadier General Wilton Persons, who knew nothing of plutonium extraction, to request that Truman and his committee "ask no questions whatsoever" about Pasco. "This is a matter of great importance and one in which I am exercising a direct personal supervision." The first $100 million for the "Manhattan Project" was granted to Marshall with no proviso to account for it—an indication of the chief of staff's standing with Congress, and why he was essential to the White House. Stimson also told Truman to trust him personally about the project, and the senator (according to the secretary of war's diary) "said that was all he needed to know." Although he inferred a good deal from his own sources, Truman would not learn the facts about atomic bomb development until April 13, 1945.

Marshall traveled to Columbus, Ohio, on June 21, 1943, to be the featured speaker at the thirty-fifth annual Governors' Conference, where he aired the WAAC issue. The accusations that female recruits were to be issued contraceptives (according to Cissy Patterson's reactionary *Washington Times-Herald*), a slur intended to keep women out of uniform, were, Marshall said, an abuse of precious American liberties. "Some seem intent on the suicide of our own war effort, not to mention the defamation of as fine an organization of women as I have ever seen assembled. . . . If we can't be decent in such matters we at least should not be naive enough to destroy ourselves."

Among other matters, he dealt daily with the logistic complexities of worldwide war, and "unity of operations among the Allies." For example, he noted to the governors, in General Eisenhower's residence near Algiers "you will [also] find . . . a British Planning Officer with him." It was a good cover story, for Eisenhower and his immediate staff were actually then in Malta to oversee the invasion of Sicily. There, he proposed optimistically that if Sicilian defenses collapsed, his forces should move quickly across the narrow Strait of Messina. Otherwise, no decision could be made to take Italy out of the war unless an internal collapse opened access to the toe of the "boot."

Marshall had been asked to delay his departure from North Africa long enough to attend a Memorial Day ceremony in Tunisia, at the bivouac site of Major General Charles Ryder's 34th Infantry. A tedious affair, it was presided over by a battalion chaplain who kept the torrid afternoon sun out of his eyes by positioning the troops, whom he kept standing, into it. Marshall knew he was to say a few words, and, an effective motivational speaker despite an austere initial presence, "faced the men away from the setting sun," he recalled, "and had them sit down, and gave them a talk describing what was going on with the American forces in the various portions of the world, trying to take the curse off this miscast ceremony."

Since Marshall could not meet with the entire army, he found an indirect way to get his messages across. One of his global emissaries, Lieutenant Colonel Russell ("Red") Reeder, who had combat backround, was deputed to interview a sampling from all ranks he encountered in Guadalcanal and find out what they had learned from the real thing, and to report it in their own words—as GI as possible. Reeder, soon a colonel, worried that he had gone too far, but Marshall approved the colorful colloquialisms and ordered a million copies of *Fighting in Guadalcanal* printed. He wrote in a foreword, "Soldiers and officers alike should read these notes and seek to apply their lessons. We *must* cash in on the experience which these and other brave men have paid for in blood." On his next trip for Marshall, to the Mediterranean, Reeder was told by General Alexander that the booklet was "the most impressive training instruction" he had seen, for it was something "soldiers will read—the ordinary instruction bores them."*

Later, feeling that wounded soldiers while mending should be given an opportunity to read about the events in which they had become casualties, Marshall ordered another writing program. The War Department's Historical Branch would be directed to assign combat historians to prepare action reports in pamphlet form. Twenty writers—former lawyers, newspapermen, novelists, and academics—would fan out to Europe, Africa, and the Pacific.

The invasion of Sicily began six weeks after Marshall left Tunisia. Despite overwhelming force—even when augmented from Italy, the Axis defenders were vastly outnumbered—the Allies bungled away their initial opportunities. Early in the morning of July 10, troop-carrying gliders ditched at sea when tow-plane pilots became disoriented by German searchlights and prematurely cut the gliders loose. Panicky "friendly fire" from warships in the poor light of dawn downed twenty-three aircraft and targeted 82nd Airborne parachutists as they drifted helplessly. A surviving battalion commander, Lieutenant Colonel William P. Yarborough, was so vocal in condemning the faulty flight plan that Eisenhower relieved him. (As a lieutenant general Yarborough later led the postwar "Green Beret" Special Forces, devising its distinctive beret.)

The losses from Allied guns, ground and sea, earned the unhappy and innocent Patton a scolding from Eisenhower, who was ferried close to the beaches in a British destroyer, for "disorganized executive management." Although the landings were nearly unopposed, many ships in the 2,590-vessel armada were scattered by unexpected gales. Confusion seemed everywhere in and around Sicily. In Washington, Marshall was appalled. Distrusting explanations, he dispatched a Pentagon aide for firsthand findings.

---

*As a regimental commander, Red Reeder would lose a leg on Utah Beach, earning the first DSC in Normandy. He retired after the war to a position at West Point, and to writing.

Field Marshal Albert Kesselring's shrewd improvisations in Sicily survived the many Allied mistakes, including the failure of the British command to collaborate with the supporting Americans. Outnumbered three to one, Kesselring's troops, many of them usually ineffective Italians, would hold back thirteen Allied divisions for thirty-eight days. He would soon replace Rommel in Italy. In Hitler's doghouse, but grudgingly respected for his abilities, Rommel would be dispatched to supervise the vaunted Atlantic Wall along the Channel and the North Sea, and build it up from mere metaphor. Italy, the Führer, realized, was not the Second Front.

Mussolini ceased to be a factor. Deposed on July 25, he was arrested by order of the puppet king, Victor Emmanuel III. Rescued then at Hitler's orders, the former *Duce* set up a symbolic if useless Fascist government at Salò, far to the north, on Lake Garda. With German efficiency, as in Tunisia, the Nazi occupation of most of mainland Italy followed.

By then, Eisenhower had returned to Malta, then to Tunis, following—rather than directing—events by radio. With no one apparently minding the shop in North Africa, an ammunition ship blew up, or was blown up, in Algiers harbor, setting nearby tankers ablaze. Such blunders matched the actual operations in eastern Sicily. Expecting quick glory in a dash to the port of Messina, opposite Reggio di Calabria, on the "toe" of Italy, Alexander and Montgomery misdirected the British advance, pushing Patton's unwanted troops aside to the west rather than exploiting them on their flank. Montgomery planned to move up the contested coastal road east of Mount Etna and into Messina. Splitting his forces, he ordered his principal thrust west of Mount Etna, in the path of Bradley's troops, who had to turn aside.

Forced further westward to conduct a sideshow, Patton's divisions rapidly occupied central Sicily and beyond, taking Palermo on July 22, where thirty-four scuttled ships blocked the harbor, endangering resupply. Despite German tank counterattacks, Bradley also drove to the north coast. Deprived, still, of the prize of Messina, which Patton, turning east, would take, Monty's divided army saw much of the fabled slopes of Etna. Lauding Montgomery nevertheless, the BBC claimed that while the British did the real fighting, the Americans had "nothing to do except walk through Sicily, eating melons and drinking wine." Patton and Bradley were outraged, and Eisenhower protested to Churchill by cable, "A soldier is apt to class the BBC and the British Government as one and the same thing." Churchill did not respond.

To Washington, Eisenhower excused British sluggishness up the wide northeast of the triangle-shaped island as due to "the difficult nature of the country," and conceded "the possibility of some delay in capturing Messina—possibly until mid-August. . . . We cannot yet discount the possibility of a substantial German reinforcement of southern Italy." Patton entered Messina on August 16. Enemy withdrawal toward the strait, two miles from the toe of Italy at its narrowest, was almost unopposed as the Germans demolished sections of the road in the path of the British. Many of Kesselring's troops which would defend Italy had benefitted from Montgomery's lack of progress.

Two weeks before Messina fell to Patton, General Alexander had alerted Air Marshal Tedder and Admiral Andrew Cunningham of Eisenhower's staff that "the full weight of navy and air power" should interdict the evacuation. "You have no doubt coordinated plans to meet this contingency." Yet they hadn't. Still, Alexander radioed Churchill dramatically, "The last German soldier [has been] flung out of Sicily." The operative verb was a lie. Allied air power and sea power went unused. Despite the slow Italian barges, the tough Hermann Göring Panzer Division, among others, complete to tanks and artillery, crossed the Strait of Messina unopposed. From August 10 through August 16, one-armed Lieutenant General Hans Hube (a casualty in Russia) evacuated 39,569 Germans and 62,182 Italians, and tens of thousands of tons of vehicles, guns, ammunition, and supplies to renew the fight.

Allied combat casualties, mostly British because of Montgomery's bizarre shortcomings, were about 20,000. The Germans took 29,000 casualties, including 6,663 captured, while the Italian losses were mostly prisoners of war—troops fired on by both sides while they were eagerly trying to surrender.

Infuriated by British aspersions and the denial of quick victory, Patton took out his frustrations during ostensibly morale-boosting visits to military hospitals for awarding Purple Heart medals to the wounded. He turned two inspections into obscene tirades during which, on August 3 and August 10, he recklessly cursed and slapped two patients evidencing no signs of wounds. (They were suffering from dysentery and shell shock.) News of the incidents, which came late to Eisenhower, was suppressed on his appeal to reporters, until he learned in November that the story was about to surface anyway. He then reprimanded Patton in writing and, "more than a little annoyed," directed that he "make in the form of apology or otherwise such personal amends to the individuals concerned as may be within your power." Evasively, Patton spoke to divisional officers who were requested to carry his remorse to the ranks. Unrepentantly but privately he called the two soldiers "skulkers" and Eisenhower "timid."

Until the hushed-up story broke (in a broadcast by columnist Drew Pearson), Patton, described by Eisenhower to Marshall as the "mainspring" of the Sicilian drive, had been the hero of "Husky" and the prime candidate to lead American troops across the Channel. He, rather than Monty, had taken the surrender of Messina, effectively ending the campaign. But with his future now uncertain, Patton would languish without an active role for months.

Eisenhower had disregarded advice to tip off Marshall, for a disciplinary reassignment to the States would have destroyed Patton and embarrassed the command. Marshall learned details of the affair from Eisenhower only months later amidst widespread public resentment which complicated the chief of staff's ongoing efforts to direct the weeding out, everywhere, of potential "battle fatigue" cases. The burden of disability ineffectives was enormous. During the war, 1,225,230 service personnel were lost to nonbattle injuries, disease, and breakdowns. Placing a press blackout on the problem to ward off a contagion of psychiatric discharges,* and inevitably adverse publicity, Marshall would order the army to seek ways to keep such men in uniform, but in less threatening assignments. As for Patton, Marshall offered Eisenhower, despite his timid cover-up to Washington, extraordinary, almost paternal protection, advising, "If it is your decision that General Patton be relieved from duty, allow me to do that. You have far more difficult and searching duties and decisions before you to be further troubled by the outcry that would follow. . . . Let me do it."

On August 9, before the second Patton incident, Marshall had met with Roosevelt and reached agreement that sending seven new divisions to the Mediterranean by early 1944 as requested by Churchill would only encourage his further adventures in the area, possibly extending to the Balkans. On the Italian mainland, Roosevelt wanted no more than "bases," not the absorption of impoverished millions.

Possibly unaware as commander-at-a-distance of the limitations of his hands-off style, Eisenhower had assured Marshall that southern and central Italy could be occupied without additional forces better stockpiled

---

*MacArthur's SWPA had the highest rate of neuropsychiatric breakdowns in the American armed forces (44 per thousand), a factor of jungle terrain and oppressive climate.

for "Overlord," the cross-Channel operation. As a result, Marshall even ordered seven of Eisenhower's existing divisions pulled from the Mediterranean and redeployed in England for the invasion of France, which further diminished possibilities in Italy—a strategic cipher but a resources sinkhole. Back from Britain and North Africa, Stimson also warned of further "pinprick warfare" encouraged by Churchill.

How much of Stimson's urgency came from recognizing that Sicily, then still an unfinished operation, was a badly run affair, exposing further the weaknesses of coalition warfare, is unclear. Pressure from Stalin, who dismissed the Mediterranean as marginal, was unremitting. According to *Red Star* war correspondent Vasily Grossman on the Russian front, troops still awaiting a real offensive in the west would joke bitterly whenever Soviet artillery fired short into their own lines, "Here we are, the Second Front has opened at last."

Although Eisenhower claimed that he could move up the Italian boot with ground troops he had ("Avalanche," the landing at Salerno, was scheduled for September 9), he did ask Marshall to release, temporarily, four heavy bomber groups with the Eighth Air Force in Britain to soften up German installations and disrupt communications. At ETO headquarters in London, Lieutenant General Jacob Devers, who had replaced Frank Andrews, killed in May in an air crash in Iceland, objected, as did Major General Ira Eaker, the Eighth Air Force commander. Reduction of their bomber arsenal by a third, they claimed, would cut into efforts to smash German war industry and to draw out the Luftwaffe for destruction.

Marshall realized, too, that additional investments in Italian operations were more in Churchill's interest than a cross-Channel buildup. Further, the B-17s and B-24s might not come back. A massive heavy bomber attack, from Mediterranean bases, on the Ploesti refineries in Romania was imminent. The casualty toll was expected to be high—and it was. Although Eisenhower warned that landings in Italy without increased bomber support would be "skating on very thin ice," Marshall turned him down. Ike would blame Devers, and not forget.

On Patton's capture of Messina, Marshall had dutifully radioed congratulations to Eisenhower for the "triumphant conclusion." He also ordered Omar Bradley to England to command American forces preparing for France. (Patton, as yet publicly untainted, seemed too risky, and Devers was a stand-in for a future "Overlord" designee.) Eisenhower's response to Marshall on August 18 thanked him for the "generous message." The chief of staff had lauded the "brilliant success," which it was not. Eisenhower had replied, "We are all proud of the smooth functioning ... of the Allied team, among all services. The aggressiveness, determination, skill, and cooperative spirit of all naval, air, and ground units were exemplary." Although the reality was a travesty of the language Eisenhower employed, and the sweeping German escape scandalous, he ordered cheap Distinguished Service Medals for many of the command brass. Yet unlike MacArthur's example, Ike's "fruit salad" (a common service reference to ribbons on the tunic) did not misuse combat DSCs.

Despite MacArthur's communiques, it was clear to Marshall, who had yet to personally survey the SWPA region, that moves against the Japanese in the area were bogging down. With depleted forces and diminishing air support, the Japanese cagily exploited the cover of the New Guinea jungle and the willingness to take casualties—which Marshall described dryly as "the sacrifice of the individual who is prepared to impose the maximum of delay." Malaria and dysentery were also taking a heavy toll of Australian and American troops. One casualty was Archibald Roosevelt, youngest son of Theodore Roosevelt. Archie had served in France with Marshall in 1918 and despite being classified as 100 percent disabled, persuaded Marshall to reactivate him. Marshall offered him to MacArthur, who as a lieutenant forty years earlier was briefly assistant military aide to the first Roosevelt. In New Guinea, Archie was seriously wounded, then incapacitated by malaria, the only American serviceman to suffer 100 percent disability in both world wars. His brother Theodore Jr. ("Ted"), a brigadier general, had already been dispatched by Marshall to Eisenhower.

To MacArthur's advantage, he continued to exploit a superior air technician who was no Bataan gang sycophant. Lieutenant General George C. Kenney, a young flier in France in 1918, had air forces chief Hap Arnold's ear, and molded a motley collection of planes into an air umbrella that, when weather permitted, pinned down Japanese troops while protecting American and Australian forces. His coverage made leapfrogging of enemy strongpoints possible, leaving such formidable Japanese bases as Rabaul, with its garrison of 135,000, entrapped and fated to wither the war away. Ever the military impresario, MacArthur would claim to have invented the bypassing strategy that gave him momentum toward the lower Philippines. Nothing new, the tactic was also being employed by Nimitz in the central Pacific, who would bypass such bastions as Truk in the Carolines, the Japanese prewar equivalent to Pearl

Harbor. Blockaded and left to atrophy, Truk could be resupplied only by submarines.

To cope better with the Japanese and their contempt for casualties, Marshall radioed MacArthur that he was sending Colonel William A. Borden, an ordnance expert, with a staff, after testing new weapons for the theater "under me independently of normal War Department channels." Borden developed an array of weaponry, including 4.5-inch aircraft-fired rockets to hit enemy coconut-log bunkers, 105 mm and 155 mm mortars, flamethrowers, ground-launched rockets, and skid pans for hauling heavy artillery in mud. MacArthur's improved menu would keep his casualties down as enemy casualties went up. Still, Americans lacked a mobile weapon as efficient as the German *Panzerfaust* (panzer-fist), a more powerful bazooka.

On September 3, 1943, ten days later than Eisenhower had hoped, his unfocused forces crossed at three places to southern Italy. Seven landings had been planned before the Germans exploited new defensive positions, he explained in a radio to Marshall, and even the Allied hold on Taranto and Brindisi, "where no Germans were present," was reported as "precarious." Marshall had long urged an opportunistic landing to seize Naples, but Eisenhower had worried that the Italians were too untrustworthy for him to absorb quickly a large, seething population. He settled only for Mark Clark's beachhead near Salerno, south of Naples—an operation almost repulsed and for which "precarious" was not a strong enough description. Eisenhower was still dickering with Marshal Pietro Badoglio's uncertain post-Mussolini regime on a surrender, signed at Malta on September 28 after it was too late to move inland quickly and control southern Italy.

The situation, Eisenhower cabled the combined chiefs of staff, was "tense but not unexpected." His immobility was actually so thoroughly unanticipated that it seemed ironic for Eisenhower, at the request of Lord Louis Mountbatten, about to be Supreme Commander for Southeast Asia, to prepare a lengthy memorandum of "straight talk with you" (as Mountbatten put it) "on the duties and tribulations with which a Supreme Allied Commander is faced." Eisenhower began (September 14) by discussing "unity of command," which was based upon "earnest cooperation of the senior officers assigned to an allied theater." Real unity required "patience, tolerance, frankness"—and "firmness," some of which he failed to concede were lacking in the Mediterranean. He felt that internal channels of communication should be intruded into from outside the command as little as possible. Yet, encouraging external meddling, his British subordinates—not to Ike's liking—sent "special daily telegraphic reports" to London, which "differs from the U.S. habit," he explained. "I do not even send General Marshall any information concerning operations other than what is contained in the daily sit[uation] rep[ort]s to the Combined Chiefs of Staff."

Ike continued on for pages, probably realizing as he went how imperfect and different each command structure had to be, where even common goals, other than ultimate victory, failed to exist. Had MacArthur offered parallel advice to Mountbatten, it would have been very different. MacArthur accepted no limiting factors, brooked no non-American subordinates whose authority amounted to anything, and communicated little to higher authority because he effectively acknowledged none. The compromises of coalition warfare did not bind him. The Australians, despite hosting his theater headquarters, remained largely ignored.

Protecting Mark Clark, whose Fifth Army beachhead at Salerno remained in jeopardy, Eisenhower radioed Marshall cautiously, just after offering advice to Mountbatten, that Alexander was "most favorably impressed by Clark and by his calmness and serenity under adverse circumstances." In reality, the previously unblooded Clark, who had no command experience in North Africa and Sicily, had raised further concerns that American leadership had not matured beyond Lloyd Fredendall and the Kasserine Pass. (As late as Sunday evening, September 5, a few days before his Salerno landing, Clark, leaving preparation to subordinates, was playing bridge in Eisenhower's villa in Algiers.)

Preempting criticism, Clark blamed the VI Corps commander, Major General Ernest J. Dawley, who had objected in advance to the botched operations, reducing Dawley two ranks to colonel and ordering him home; blasting the efficient and imaginative Lieutenant General Richard McCreery as a "feather duster"; and disparaging Dawley's replacement, Major General John Lucas, who was consolidating his shaky beachhead under fire, as lacking aggressiveness. Eisenhower remained distant in Tunis and Algiers.* Marshall did not intervene.

*On September 12, 1943, Eisenhower commiserated with Dawley ("Dear Mike") over the "great blow" to him. By February 1944 he was commandant of the Tank Destroyer School at Camp Hood, Texas, and later commanding general of the Ground Reinforcement Command in Europe. He retired in 1948, again a major general. Later, Lucas would also be scapegoated.

Nearby Naples seemed in the circumstances tantalizingly remote, a political objective inspired by Churchill's eagerness to seize Rome. Yet the slog up the Italian boot, and the slugging match to enlarge the beachheads, at the least tied down formidable German divisions which might have reinforced the Channel coast or confronted Russians on the Eastern Front. Behind ridges and rivers, and dug in on reverse slopes, the armies of Albert Kesselring exploited tactically an unwelcoming terrain and the miserable weather which would get even worse as the seasons changed. Italy as autumn arrived seemed mired in a war of attrition reminiscent of 1914–18, impossible for the Germans to win yet delaying defeat. To make matters worse for Eisenhower, he had an unreliable Italian government as a new ally, and restless millions to feed and to police as the Germans withdrew.

Marshall seldom interposed any criticism once an operation began, or pointed to squandered opportunities, but before the Italian slog was four weeks along (on September 23) he had gently admonished the risk-averse Eisenhower that "it would seem that you give the enemy too much time to prepare and eventually [you] find yourself up against a very stiff resistance." On October 9, Eisenhower felt it necessary to cable regrets to Churchill (as his own defense minister) that "drastic changes" in the situation—the German buildup south of Rome—did not permit taking the capital cheaply, or at all.

The consequences of Marshall's futile warning were materializing rapidly. It would be a long winter in Italy, and the graveyard of reputations as well as, literally, of the ranks. But not for Eisenhower, who carefully prepared long diary apologias for Harry Butcher's file to explain away his courses of action. Cautiously, Butcher prefaced the newest entry, "The Allied Commander-in-Chief has, after many interruptions, dictated and edited a 'piece' for the diary, this one being especially significant because of scattered criticism at home that landings were made at Salerno when we were already making good if slow progress up the Toe."

It was November 12, 1943, when Ike noted to Butcher for the record that he had made three trips to Italy and was about to begin a fourth. Perhaps the most revealing aspect of his opening paragraphs was that remark. With homes in North Africa after two and a half months of the Italian campaign, his primary mission, he had not relocated to Italy and still operated by remote control. "Command," he explained, "has become extremely difficult because the Air Commander feels he must be in Tunis with the bulk of his forces, the Naval Commander is back at Algiers, and [the ground commander] Alexander is in Italy. Every problem that arises involving the three services requires an enormous amount of communi-

cation because the holding of Commanders-in-Chief meetings in the
Tunis area is a laborious affair." That Foggia, perhaps Italy's finest air base,
was his, as well as the major naval harbor at Taranto (after serious shipping and personnel losses to mines, some unrevealed), had not altered the
inefficient separation of commands. Posh villas appropriated by top brass
in salubrious Algiers and Tunis may have had considerable influence on
how the war in Italy was run. The Dwight Eisenhower of the fall of 1943
was not yet the Eisenhower who would command D-Day nine months
later.

MacArthur made do with two headquarters and two comfortable residences—his family home occupying an entire floor of Brisbane's best
hotel, and the former governor general's modernized mansion in Port
Moresby. Yet his refrain to well-connected old associates in the U.S., as he
wrote to old crony Robert Wood, was his "working on such a shoestring."
To a Washington deputy of a decade earlier, George Van Horn Moseley,
MacArthur lamented "the weakness of my forces. . . . It is truly an Area of
Lost Opportunity." To Major General George P. Duncan, a World War I
associate, he employed his usual images. "From the very beginning we
have had a hard time. No resources and no supplies made the situation
precarious from the start. I have done the best I could with what I had,
but no commander in American history has so failed of support as here.
We have come through, but it has been shoestring stuff."

In reality his strength against what the Japanese could bring to bear
against him compared very favorably with what Eisenhower could summon against the Wehrmacht. By December 1943 MacArthur had received 700,000 American ground troops to augment his Australians, far
more than the March estimates. The two Pacific theaters already employed 1,878,000 air, ground, and naval forces, while Americans committed across the Atlantic were 1,810,000. In aircraft the Pacific had slightly
fewer resources, particularly in heavy bombers; but in fighting ships vastly
preponderant numbers plied the Pacific.

Although the balance was fairly even, MacArthur knew that the
cross-Channel operation scheduled for 1944 would draw the greater share
of new deployments. He hardly needed troops on that scale even to retake
the Philippines. Coping with Japan itself was another matter for a later
phase. The Germany-first priorities ensured that MacArthur would have

it all once Germany was defeated and Hirohito replaced Hitler as target.

Speaking to the American Legion convention in Omaha on September 21, 1943, and recognizing the strong MacArthur constituency in the Midwest, Marshall emphasized long-range plans for Japan. Eliminating the "Axis navy" in the Mediterranean, he declared, would divert even more naval power to the Pacific. "We are similarly engaged in planning regarding other forces, particularly air, and it will probably interest you as much as it will discourage the Japanese to learn that our most difficult problem is to find sufficient bases from which to operate the vast forces which are to be poured into the Pacific for the rearrangement of the affairs of the Son of Heaven with his military clique." Broadcast nationwide by NBC radio, the message was meant as much for MacArthur as for the Mikado.

MacArthur, nevertheless, always had some alternative controversy with Washington going. In September 1943 the navy objected to his boasting of the sinking of a transport, as established policy was that such reports were to come from the Navy Department. Marshall relayed the protest, and MacArthur snapped that there were no exemptions to his control of SWPA information. Then he complained that the Australian press had carried a report that Vice Admiral Thomas Kinkaid was being assigned to SWPA naval forces without his (and Australian) prior concurrence. (Richard Sutherland had spoken with Marshall about a preference for a different appointee, but Marshall had cabled MacArthur that the admiral in question had retired the previous December.) In an unusually conciliatory gesture, Admiral King apologized for the premature leak—but not directly to MacArthur. Marshall had to relay the message and request assurance that the highly efficient Kinkaid was suitable.

In effect, Marshall had to cosset two MacArthurs, one in each hemisphere. His equivalent was Charles De Gaulle. Both were autocratic, ambitious, and endlessly insensitive. Both would prevail with similar strategies. As De Gaulle put it in his memoirs, the Anglo-Americans "came to terms with what they could not prevent." (Eisenhower also had two lesser prima donnas in Patton and Montgomery, as well as the pontifical Churchill, who operated *ex cathedra*.)

As the MacArthur constituency claiming that Lord Mountbatten was too lightweight for his future role in India began promoting the idea of a single Supreme Commander for the Asia-Pacific area, the general hinted at his candidacy for an even larger role. The presidency was still on his mind, and that of his admirers, and also the nonexistent Pacific super-command. When a party of American senators visited him at Port Moresby for three days beginning September 9, 1943, he entertained them lavishly at Government House and opened the door to discussions of future global strategy and the presidential campaign of 1944. In a deliberate snub, when later in the month Eleanor Roosevelt visited Australia, General Eichelberger was delegated as her host. The peripatetic First Lady was not permitted to travel to Port Moresby or to see the excessively busy MacArthur anywhere.

Influential friends and pseudofriends aware of the looming appointment in the West visualized for MacArthur a title, at the least, to be coordinate with the expansive one talked about in the European Theater as likely for Marshall, and assumed to be in the bag for him by almost everyone but Marshall and Brooke. It might be a springboard for a presidential candidacy in 1944. Early in August, Secretary Stimson had shown the chief of staff a message he was sending to Roosevelt recommending that since the majority of forces in a cross-Channel attack would be from the U.S., the "Overlord" command, once assumed as British, should go to "our most commanding soldier," George Marshall. When Marshall handed the letter back, declining any role in the decision, Stimson remarked that it was why he had signed it in advance. At the White House on August 10, going over the text with the president, Stimson observed that "the shadows of Passchendaele and Dunkirk" still afflicted the leadership in London, making it inadvisable that the command be British. "I see no other alternative." Roosevelt agreed on all points. The decision seemed closed.

The New York correspondent of London's *Daily Mirror* made the command issues, worldwide, public in the issue of September 30, 1943. A group of senators unhappy with the Mountbatten appointment, he began, felt that the entire "Asiatic" area should be placed under MacArthur. H. Styles Bridges of New Hampshire, a former isolationist and a backer as well of MacArthur for president, claimed "new support in the Senate." The *Mirror* quoted the *Ohio State Journal* as lamenting that "it would be a tragic thing if MacArthur were to be shorn of his authority while a London glamor boy is elevated." The absurdity of the contention would have been obvious to anyone with a map, but the *Journal* predicted that if MacArthur were subordinated to Mountbatten (who was being given an onerous and parallel assignment), "a wave of anger will sweep this nation that will bode certain Washington people no good."

Churchill protested the newspaper campaign to Roosevelt, and in a press conference on October 5 observed that the indignation revealed "an extraordinary ignorance of geography" and "malice aforethought." For what would now be called a photo opportunity, Churchill showed a guest an immense globe at his official residence, Chequers, and estimated the distance between Mountbatten's future headquarters in India and MacArthur's own: it was 6,600 miles. (To encourage a worldwide perspective, General Marshall in 1942 had given identical globes to Roosevelt and Churchill.) On October 9, Bridges, a member of the Senate military affairs committee, assured Roosevelt with transparent dishonesty that he had not been party to the controversy: "As a matter of fact, I have never given this matter any thought."

Sutherland was again in Washington in November as proxy for his chief—"with my full authority," MacArthur cabled Marshall—to covertly check the political winds and urge Marshall's Joint Staff planners to give priority to an advance on the Philippines via bases in New Guinea. Threatening Mindanao, he explained, to coax Admiral King into his strategy, would force the Japanese fleet into the open, and invite its destruction. To make MacArthur's point, Sutherland disparaged the navy's plans to strike across the central Pacific, with Nimitz as the general's counterpart, to develop air bases from which to attack the home islands of Japan. Marshall remarked privately that Sutherland was "the chief insulter of the Navy."

Ignoring the British but for formal notification, Pentagon planners adopted two concurrent strategies—Nimitz's toward the Marshalls, Carolines, and Marianas, and MacArthur's toward the Philippines from New Guinea, describing them as "mutually supporting." The central Pacific thrust was estimated as "more likely to precipitate a decisive engagement with the Japanese fleet." Ironically, in future Philippines operations, MacArthur would be proved more prophetic. Until such confrontations occurred, many months away, he could only seethe that Washington as usual bypassed him.

Had he made his case in person, MacArthur's overwhelming presence could not have been ignored, and he might have propelled his further ambitions as well. In that failure to contend, except by indirection and from afar, lies a mysterious dimension of the MacArthur enigma. Was he concerned that, beneath his grand geopolitical pronouncements, damaging weaknesses in operational and technical details might be detected? Was he worried that if he returned to the "Z.I."* he might not be

*Military parlance for "Zone of the Interior"—the continental United States.

authorized to resume his command? He would be sixty-four in January 1944, by regulation the army retirement age. Yet it was politically impossible for Marshall, or Stimson, or even Roosevelt, to shelve him.

The mountain would have to come to Mohammed. MacArthur had not been to the United States since April 1937. Marshall had sent senior colleagues, even Hap Arnold, to visit the SWPA and consult with MacArthur. Every high-level occasion had been frustrating, and even futile, as the general exploited captive audiences to dramatize himself. Planning to be halfway there for the summit conferences coming up in Cairo and Teheran, Marshall determined to continue on to New Guinea, and Government House.

8

The Best Man

A LTHOUGH CHURCHILL had promised "Overlord" to Alan Brooke, chief of the Imperial General Staff, who knew France from the Dunkirk spring of 1940, neither grasped the imminent political realities. Originally code-named "Roundup," which sounded American, it was renamed to be more English, perhaps to market the huge and hazardous operation to the more reluctant of the partners. By D-Day or soon after, the American dimension would be dominant and public opinion across the Atlantic would be a factor in its command. For Roosevelt, now pressed urgently by Stimson for a decision, that appeared to ensure naming George Marshall. However celebrated Dwight Eisenhower had become in the American press, global management of the war emanated largely from Marshall at the Pentagon.

From the Darlan débacle on, there had been political miscalculations and strategic failures on Eisenhower's watch—in Algeria, in Tunisia, in Sicily, and in Italy. Still, the Anglo-American forces learned expensively from them, and pressed ahead in what had become a war of attrition that might lead, Churchill hoped, to an enemy collapse. The cross-Channel attack, destined to be the largest combined operation in history, required the organization skills at which Eisenhower was now experienced. He lacked only the obvious authority that "Overlord" appeared to require. In mid-1943, short of recalling MacArthur, there seemed only the inevitable Marshall.

There is no evidence that MacArthur was even remotely considered. Brooke contended sourly that Marshall himself failed to understand Europe. "I could never get him to appreciate the very close connection that existed between the various German fronts. For him they might have been separate wars, a Russian war on the one side, a Mediterranean war on another and a cross Channel one to be started as soon as possible. I have often wondered . . . how different matters might have been if I had MacArthur instead of Marshall to deal with. . . . He certainly showed a far greater strategic grasp than Marshall. I must confess that Winston was no great help in the handling of Marshall, in fact the reverse. Marshall had a holy fear of Winston's Balkans and Dardanelles ventures, and was always guarding against these dangers even when they did not exist." Yet they did exist. Later, Brooke would disown them.

Would MacArthur have leaped at the appointment? An outsider to what seemed the main contest, he understood that New Guinea and even the Philippines had, relative to Europe, almost no geopolitical significance. Even Japan might be defeated without dislodging the Rising Sun from the vast occupied territories to its south. "It is a desperate time for me," MacArthur had confided to an old friend. He exaggerated, for the war was clearly turning in his direction, that he was "always the underdog," with "destruction just around the corner. I am sick at heart at the mistakes and the lost opportunities that are so prevalent."

A closer and more logical candidate for "Overlord" was Eisenhower, although Brooke dismissed him as a competent functionary who let others command his divisions. Brooke also downplayed Marshall as a colorless desk officer in contrast to his own experience, not only with troops in France in 1940 but also in 1914–18. Brooke had risen from lieutenant to lieutenant colonel with the 18th Division during the carnage on the Somme, earning a DSO. Marshall never boasted about his more brief experience on the line in 1917–18, but in 1945, speaking off the record in behalf of the postwar military, he recalled, "I sailed for France in the last war on the first transport of the first convoy along with one of the most complete exhibitions of utter unpreparedness I have ever imagined. . . . As a member of the 1st Division I saw our first dead on the ground where they fell. I was the only officer present at the burial of the first American soldiers to die in battle in 1917. Also, it was my duty, in my position later on, to write the order that stopped the fighting in the Meuse-Argonne." In 1943 his goal was to win the war as soon as it could be won, with the fewest possible fatalities.

As Marshall recognized, casualties were a delicate matter in a democracy, where military appropriations depended upon votes in Congress, and public opinion could sway strategy. *Life* magazine (as censorship altered policy) pictured its first American battle dead in September 1943, nearly two years after Pearl Harbor. Few war films from Hollywood until then even showed any combat wounded. As defeats gave way to victories, their price could, cautiously, be acknowledged. John Huston's documentary film shot in the Liri Valley of Italy, the grim *The Battle of San Pietro*, which showed battle dead being wrapped in mattress covers, would have its training camp screenings, and public release, objected to by army commanders until Marshall overruled them, declaring that it might make soldiers take their training more seriously.

On June 15, 1943, on the brink of the Sicilian operation, Churchill, following a chiefs of staff meeting in London, called in General Brooke. "He wanted me," Brooke confided to his diary, "to take the Supreme Command of operations from this country across the Channel when the time was suitable. He said nice things about having full confidence in me. . . ." Although he had objected to the operation all along, Brooke was elated. It was "the perfect climax" to his guidance of war strategy. Several days later, General Ronald Forbes Adam, fresh from talks with Eisenhower in Algiers, told Brooke that Eisenhower, assuming that General Harold Alexander was in the running, confided that he did not feel that "Alex" was "fit to take on the Supreme Commander's job. . . . He considered that there were only two men to take on the Supreme Command in this country and that one was Marshall and the other was myself." Brooke quoted the accolade to himself from Ike in his diary, but, sworn to secrecy by Churchill, told Adam nothing.

On July 7, the PM again assured Brooke of the assignment, suggesting that "if it looked pretty certain the operation was possible," Brooke should step down from the Imperial General Staff in January or February of 1944 "to take over." Three days later Eisenhower's forces were landing in Sicily, and Brooke was fending off Marshall's proposal to strike at Naples and cut off much of Italy rather than to slog up the boot from the bottom. Marshall wanted a quick end to the Italian campaign, seizing only what could be taken cheaply, in order to prepare for France. Despite his own aspirations for "Overlord," the "soft underbelly" alternative—the term was Churchill's—again animated Brooke's pen. "Marshall absolutely fails to realize what strategic treasures lie at our feet in the Mediterranean, and always hankers after cross Channel operations. He admits that our object must be to eliminate Italy and yet is always afraid of facing the consequences of doing so. He cannot see beyond the tip of his nose and is maddening."

Preparing for the "Quadrant" summit conference in Quebec, Marshall on July 16, 1943, had again suggested to Eisenhower that if the Italian government collapsed, an immediate landing near Naples could be risked with existing resources. The *coup de main* might head off German reinforcements to southern Italy, as had occurred in Tunisia. "Existing" framed Marshall's approach. In a memorandum to Quebec planners, to which Secretary Stimson signed on, Marshall emphasized the need "to concentrate forces and hold to decisions," for shipping more resources to the Italian front was "uneconomical and assists Germany to create a strategic stalemate in Europe." Churchill's strategy, he charged, was to abandon the Channel for the Mediterranean, "which did not offer an opportunity for decisive military action."

Although General Sir Frederick Morgan was already preparing detailed plans for "Overlord," Brooke predicted "hard fighting with our American friends" over it. Like Churchill, he preferred indefinite postponement. A cross-Channel operation, he disparaged, was "a good plan but too optimistic as to rate of advance to be expected" and would succeed "only if we pin Germany in Italy" so that the Wehrmacht would be unable to meet all its commitments.

Just prior to Quebec, Stimson made his first pitch to the president to name "our most commanding soldier in charge of this critical operation at this critical time." To keep "Overlord" from being derailed by Churchill, whose newest diversion toy* was Norway, required Marshall's "towering eminence of reputation as a tried soldier and as a broad-minded and skillful administrator." The downside to losing Marshall, Stimson recognized, would be "the loss in . . . organization and worldwide strategy centered in Washington," but he saw "no other alternative."

Speculation that Marshall might be exiting the Pentagon for another role, perhaps even a diminished one, took on a transatlantic life of its own. Even the calendar hinted at it. His four-year term as chief of staff would end (if Roosevelt wanted it to end) on September 1.† A shipboard rumor that Brooke found personally encouraging was "that a movement was on foot in America to replace Marshall with [Brehon] Somervell," and that Admiral Ernest J. King was among the "conspirators." Such canards would continue to surface as long as the Supreme Command remained unsettled. Rather, King told Eisenhower on a European visit that he "dreaded the consequences" of relinquishing Marshall to "Overlord."

Docking in Halifax, and changing trains several times, Churchill

---

*Brooke at Quebec referred in his diary to Churchill on strategy as "a spoilt child that wants a toy in a shop irrespective of the fact that his parents tell him it is no good."
†Roosevelt would soon announce an indefinite extension of Marshall's term.

traveled to New York City and then to Hyde Park on August 12. After private meetings there, he and FDR entrained together in drizzling rain for cold and bleak Quebec City, Churchill attempting all the way to persuade Roosevelt and Hopkins to accept Brooke for "Overlord"—perhaps, cagily, to delay or diminish the operation. Before formal conferences began on August 15 at the Château Frontenac, the grand neo-Gothic Victorian railway hotel on a bluff overlooking a broad bend in the St. Lawrence, the prime minister conceded that all his rhetorical powers had been unavailing. Brooke felt crushed when Churchill confided that it would be Marshall.

"Winston gave in," Brooke wrote despairingly in his diary, "in spite of having previously promised me the job!" Eisenhower, Brooke was told, would replace Marshall in Washington, and Alexander would take Eisenhower's place in the Mediterranean. As a concession to the British side, Montgomery would have a senior role in "Overlord" and, despite his junior status, Lord Mountbatten, whom Brooke considered a lightweight dilettante, would be Supreme Commander in Southeast Asia, as expected, where British Empire interests were paramount.

Mountbatten owed his appointment indirectly to Marshall. Churchill had preferred one of the heroes of the Battle of Britain in 1940, Air Marshal Sir Sholto Douglas, then RAF commander in Cairo. Sir John Dill alerted Marshall, who had a large file about Sir Sholto's open anti-Americanism. Marshall explained to Dill that no Yankee-basher would be permitted to command troops likely to include Americans, and Dill reported to Whitehall that Marshall had "somehow" learned of the unannounced appointment, already accepted by Roosevelt, and hinted that the chief of staff would resign if it were confirmed. Sir Sholto's "capacity for successful command of American units" was in question. By telephone, Roosevelt and Churchill backed down. Marshall was not expendable. The job went to the surprised Mountbatten.

Although the "Overlord" appointment remained unsettled, an American designee had become inevitable. In Churchill's unreliable postwar memoirs he wrote that Brooke "bore the great disappointment with soldierly dignity." Not so, Brooke confessed later. It took him "several months to recover." Yet in Quebec he had to go almost at once to what would now be an agonizing conference of the Joint Chiefs. "It was a most painful meeting and we settled nothing. I entirely failed to get Marshall to realize the relation between cross Channel and Italian operations, and the repercussions which one exercises on the other. It is quite impossible to argue with him as he does not even begin to understand a strategic problem! He had not even read the plans worked out by Morgan," Brooke charged, falsely, "and consequently was not even in a position to begin to appreciate its difficulties and requirements." What animated Brooke was Marshall's "threat" that expanding Mediterranean objectives on Germany's periphery might lead to America's reducing its British buildup and reorienting its share of the war effort more toward Japan. Many hundreds of thousands of American troops were idling (if training) in the British Isles, Marshall warned, and thousands of planes and landing craft that could be employed elsewhere were being warehoused on the wrong side of the Channel.

"Unfortunately," Brooke exploded in his diary as usual on August 16, while the conferees continued to clash, "Marshall has no strategic outlook of any kind, and King has only one thought and that is based on the Pacific." Ignoring Marshall's daring—and risky—Naples proposal, Brooke charged that the Americans lacked opportunism, and tried to run the war "on a series of lawyer's agreements, which, when once signed, can never be departed from." The sessions grew so acrimonious that, to argue further less publicly, the principals emptied the Château Frontenac's largest drawing room of sixty of their subsidiary staff.

While deliberating off the record, "Dickie" Mountbatten, still chief of Combined Operations and a relentless experimenter with military gadgetry, had attendants bring in a sample section of his proposed "Habakkuk,"* an aircraft carrier deck to be built atop icebergs with a resilient form of ice created by mixing it with wood pulp, and the massive hulks somehow towed into combat position. To demonstrate that the proposed platform would not splinter like ordinary ice, also carried in for his demonstration, he pulled a revolver from his pocket and fired at the conventional block. The leaders of the free world—the wheelchair-borne Roosevelt in steel leg braces, and the portly and less than agile prime minister—dodged a shower of ice splinters.

"There!" said Mountbatten happily, "that's just what I told you. Now I shall fire at the block on the right to show you the difference." A shot echoed through the room as the second bullet, Brooke recorded, "rebounded out of the block and buzzed round our legs like an angry bee!" Churchill was charmed. In the adjoining room an ejected staffer shouted, "Good heavens, they've started shooting now!"

---

*Churchill, who loved military tinkerers, had chosen the code name from a biblical text attributed to the apocalyptic Hebrew prophet Habakkuk: "I will work a work in your days which ye will not believe, though it be told you."

Many conferees would be grateful for Mountbatten's posting, very far off, to the Supreme Command in India. No "Habakkuk" would be constructed, not even later for the fictional James Bond, whose then little-known creator, Ian Fleming, worked for naval intelligence. Support for Mountbatten was tepid among MacArthur's loyalists in Congress and the anti-Roosevelt press. The acronym for the admiral's Southeast Asia Command, SEAC, was pilloried as "Save England's Asiatic Colonies." Despite authentic heroism in action,* his royal connections left him open to attack as a "princeling" whose inventive selection over MacArthur—allegedly entitled to all of East Asia as well as the SWPA—proved the influence of the British over American decision-making. John O'Donnell, whose *New York Daily News* columns reflected the McCormick-Patterson press points of view, however removed from reality, wrote that "higher-ups in Washington" who have been "starving" MacArthur of men and supplies, had ordered him "to play second fiddle to Lord Louis Mountbatten, who will launch the spectacular main attack on Japan while the Hero of Bataan fights a third rate holding war in the islands north of Australia."

Republicans seeking to embarrass the administration seized upon the Mountbatten appointment as another opportunity to promote MacArthur for the presidency. Representative Hamilton Fish, a former America Firster, and from Roosevelt's own congressional district although not of his party, proposed MacArthur as the only credible opponent of a fourth FDR term if Governor Dewey begged off. Oxford philosopher Isaiah Berlin, at the Washington embassy to evaluate the American press for Foreign Secretary Anthony Eden and take confidential soundings among American power brokers, advised that the general "should not be overlooked," and that a "President Dewey or President MacArthur" candidacy was being promoted by some influential Republicans "to protect the Western World against Russian influence."

It was premature for a British diplomat to suggest Eisenhower in that context, but that June, United Press correspondent Virgil Pinkley, a Californian from Glendale who would become more and more intimate with Ike, sounded him out on the presidency. If a general making headlines and likely to make more were to become a political rival to MacArthur, why not Eisenhower? "My reaction," Ike recalled from the White House

*Noel Coward's film epic *In Which We Serve* was based on Mountbatten's bravado and exploits as commander of a destroyer flotilla in which his own flagship was torpedoed and sunk.

sixteen years later, "was of course completely negative." The idea was "more than ridiculous."

Leaving icebergs behind, the Quebec conferees discussed the central and southern Pacific but left major decisions for their next parley. Admiral King, however, was authorized to island-hop westward across the Japanese island mandates, leaving some enemy strongholds to wither in isolation. Similarly, the big Japanese base at Rabaul in New Britain, east of New Guinea, and coveted by MacArthur, was also by JCS mandate to be "neutralized rather than captured"—for which MacArthur would later take credit. And a "Two-Stage Ending" from south and east was approved to achieve victory over Japan within a year after the defeat of Germany.

Realizing before the voyage to Canada that decisions to be reached would leave MacArthur presiding Supreme Commander over nearly nothing of importance to winning the war, Churchill wrote a rare, and sensitive, letter to the general, explaining that "when, having cleared up our troubles here, we can come with all our needful forces and aid you in your great task." Once the Italian fleet in the Mediterranean was rendered harmless, Churchill promised, he would "constitute a powerful Eastern British Fleet in the Indian Ocean." He felt that Stalin, whose Red Army had already "cut a good part of the guts" out of the Wehrmacht, "will most likely come into the War against Japan, whose hyena attitude he has thoroughly understood. This of course would open very large possibilities for the attack upon Japan itself."

"Rolling forward into the future," Churchill added that he was "under no delusions" about the "terrible foe" they were facing in Southeast Asia and the Pacific. "Their military qualities extort admiration from the most reluctant minds." The next day he sent a memo to his War Cabinet predicting gloomily that subduing Japan might take "several years" further, and require "a large proportion" of Britain's best troops freed from Europe, which might cause "heart-burnings" among the British public.

Making post-conference rounds of Mediterranean bases, Secretary of the Navy Frank Knox mistakenly told Eisenhower over lunch at an air base near Tunis on October 1 that Marshall at Quebec had been officially named Supreme Commander for "Overlord." Ike, he thought, would be assigned to Washington. Immediately after, Eisenhower prepared a long memo for Marshall which he directed "Beetle" Smith to hand-carry to the chief of staff, assuming his relocation to London. Ike recommended troop and staff redispositions for the Mediterranean and for England, including a plea to use Patton (who was not yet on probation) as an "assault" commander, and the much-respected Tedder as his air deputy "although it would be a bitter blow for me to lose him" (in Italy). Beetle would corroborate from Mountbatten that Churchill had agreed to Marshall, after which Harry Hopkins suggested that the new Allied commander in the Mediterranean be British—either Brooke, who had aspired for "Overlord," or another Churchill designee. Yet the "Overlord" appointment remained unconfirmed.

With no expectations for the plum assignment in the West, Eisenhower told Harry Butcher that he was unhappy at the idea of losing a field command to a desk job in which he would be "a failure," as he was "not a politician." He asked Beetle Smith to suggest that should the Mediterranean post go to a Brit, his own preference would be to command an army group under Marshall. Smith went on to talk with Roosevelt at Hyde Park, returning on October 21. By then, King George VI had written to Churchill to urge that Britain "be [only] the base from which all bombing operations will take place in an ever increasing intensity over Germany," and Churchill had cabled Roosevelt, again warning about a Channel crossing, "The campaign of 1944 will be by far the most dangerous we have ever undertaken, and personally, I am more anxious about its success than I was about 1941, 1942, or 1943."

If "Overlord" were to be his own assignment, Marshall had told Beetle, an army group would be a step down for Ike. The president, Beetle learned, was "sold on" Eisenhower and most likely would recall him to be chief of staff. Rushed Beetle's findings, Eisenhower cabled Marshall unhappily on October 24 that Smith had given him "some indications of possibilities involving changes in certain positions." He asked only that Smith not be reassigned away, but remain as his deputy, "maintaining our existing relationship." At the least Ike hoped, Butcher noted in his diary, that he could win a major victory over the Germans in Italy before Christmas—and before transfer to the Pentagon.

Even small victories then were few. Operations from Sicily into Italy through October were disappointing. German resistance on the narrow front of the "boot" was abetted by failures in Allied planning and generalship. Brooke would blame lack of resources—their diversion toward France. Now that the assignment had eluded him, he badmouthed "Overlord" as "very problematical" and charged that the quagmire in southern Italy—"the full beauty of the Marshall strategy," he sneered—

was the price of American "insistence to abandon the Mediterranean."

However solid the Allied lodgment in lower Italy, the war had stag-nated. "The attitude of Ike's HQ," Brooke deplored, was "not encourag-ing. I knew that he never really appreciated the strategic advantages of Italy, and that the American blindfolded cross-Channel policy must ap-peal to him as being easier to understand." By early November he had convinced himself that if Marshall and Eisenhower had agreed to land-ings on Crete and Rhodes, and then invaded Greece, as Churchill pro-posed, the Turks would have stood aside at the Dardanelles, and "we should have the whole Balkans ablaze by now, and the war might have been finished in 1943!!! . . . It is heartbreaking." The unpromising lessons of Gallipoli, and 1915, had, for the moment, vanished. Angrily, in his diary, Stimson described as "Dirty Baseball" the persistent British at-tempts to undermine the Channel operation.

Late in September, Marshall had been quietly told by the president that he would assume the supreme command of "Overlord" while retain-ing his position in Washington. Eisenhower would return only to be act-ing chief of staff. Yet when Roosevelt began asking other members of the Joint Chiefs of Staff for what he expected to be their enthusiastic ap-proval, the plan began unraveling. The Joint Chiefs of Staff had itself been Marshall's device to coordinate services effort. When Admiral Harold E. Stark had left for England in March 1942 to command Amer-ican naval forces in Europe and Admiral King took Stark's title of chief of naval operations while remaining commander of the fleet, Marshall had convinced the president to appoint a former chief of naval operations, Ad-miral William D. Leahy, as Roosevelt's personal chief of staff. Leahy, an FDR intimate, had briefly been ambassador to the rump Vichy govern-ment. Marshall's aim was an army-navy balance in the JCS, as he and Arnold represented the army. Leahy presided over JCS meetings, but its leadership effectively remained Marshall's, as the others recognized him as first among equals. Leahy and Arnold advised FDR that Marshall was irreplaceable. Even without another title, they claimed, he was effectively Supreme Commander everywhere. His range of action would be reduced. More outspokenly, King charged, "We have the winning combination here in Washington. Why break it up?" King also warned that if Eisen-hower were chief of staff, as Robert Sherwood, playwright and presi-dential speechwriter, put it from the inside, "the regrettable but real lack of cordiality which characterized the relationship between him"—Eisenhower, he meant—"and MacArthur could become a source of major embarrassments."

An editorial in the influential *Army and Navy Journal*, very likely by an insider at the Pentagon, suggested that unnamed "powerful influences" were plotting to "eliminate" Marshall from Washington by kicking him upstairs, which "would shock the Army, the Congress, and the nation at large." Even Pershing weighed in from Walter Reed Army Hospital, where he now seemed to be awaiting his end,* writing to Roosevelt of his "deep conviction that the suggested transfer of General Marshall would be a fundamental and very grave error in our military policy."

"You are absolutely right about George Marshall—and yet," the president replied to Pershing on September 20, "I think you are wrong too! ... I think it is only a fair thing to give George a chance in the field—and because of the nature of the job we shall still have the benefit of his strategical ability. The best way I can express it is to tell you that I want George to be the Pershing of the Second World War—and he cannot be that if we keep him here."

Embarrassingly for the tight-lipped Marshall, the most crucial American command decision of the war seemed openly aired in the service journals, apparently from deliberate leaks. A few days later, the "unofficial" *Army and Navy Register* charged that "some military circles" wanted Marshall out of developing overall operations from Washington because he was known "to have had some differences over strategy" with Churchill. Also, it claimed, "It is understood that Harry Hopkins prefers General Brehon B. Somervell" as chief of staff, rather than Eisenhower, because the hard-driving logistics chief had been associated with Hopkins's 1930s New Deal projects. The anti-FDR *Times-Herald* screamed, GLOBAL W.P.A. SEEN AIM IN MARSHALL PLOT. When Senator Truman, from the opposite political side, warned Marshall that such schemes were rumored, the general assured Truman that Somervell was completely loyal. Somervell himself told Marshall that the rumormongers were "swine."

Hopkins, who had devised no such plot, had also learned from Beetle Smith that Ike did not want the bureaucratic, multitasking entanglements of the Pentagon. He preferred a combat command under Marshall. Hopkins informed the president of Eisenhower's reluctance, but FDR saw no one else out there who was up to Marshall's global responsibilities.

In the House of Representatives, former isolationists who had only changed their labels charged that a "sinister" pro-Roosevelt clique of Justice Felix Frankfurter, Judge Samuel I. Rosenman, and Hopkins associate

---

*Pershing would live on at Walter Reed into 1948.

David K. Niles (to the far right it was notable that the three were Jewish) were plotting "to turn the War Department into a global political organization" with a Bolshevik taint. Yet the *Chicago Tribune*'s anti-FDR Walter Trohan, who like his boss Colonel McCormick was passionately Anglophobic, praised Marshall's "experience and ability," claiming that the plot was British rather than Bolshevik—to install someone more pliant to Churchill's purposes. Marshall hardly needed that kind of perverse support. Roosevelt had told a press conference frankly that the emergency therapy of "Dr. New Deal" had long been supplanted by "Dr. Win-the-War."

Also unhelpful while the leadership of "Overlord" still openly simmered was a Nazi propaganda broadcast from Paris, exploiting the brouhaha in Washington. "General George C. Marshall, the U.S. Chief of Staff," German radio fantasized, "has been dismissed. President Roosevelt [himself] has taken over his command. This occurred two days ago, but has not yet been commented upon in Washington." When the radio transcript came to Marshall's desk from an intelligence listening post he passed it on to Hopkins with a scrawled, breezy comment, "Dear Harry: Are you responsible for pulling this fast one on me? G.C.M."

Hopkins took the intercepted message to Roosevelt, who pencilled on the note, again in rare first-name fashion, "Dear George—Only true in part—I am now Chief of Staff *but* you are President. FDR."

Among other complications was that the joke seemed no joke. Political pressures were growing, a year before the 1944 presidential elections, to jettison the allegedly flaky and ultraliberal vice president, Henry A. Wallace, for a more acceptable successor to Roosevelt, about whose health disquieting rumors floated. Further, MacArthur, from afar and despite public denials which a newsman from New Guinea described as MacArthur's "humility," was still encouraging talk among Republicans that he was available as a candidate. As early as the aftermath of reverses in the November 1942 off-year elections, worried anti-Roosevelt Democrats with conservative biases had begun discussing Marshall. Although his political views were unknown, a few saw him as an alternative to a Roosevelt fourth term, or, prudently, as a vice presidential candidate. "This is a time to draft men," Senator Edwin C. Johnson of Colorado declared sanctimoniously. "In this grave crisis the Democratic Party owes it to the people to draft Gen. Marshall for President. He is not a candidate and will emphatically say so, but no patriotic American from George Washington down can refuse such a call. George Marshall is not only a very great soldier and military leader, he is a fine Christian gentleman and a statesman in the highest concept of that much abused term. He has depth and he has capacity. He is firm and he is courageous. He has tact and he has the respect and confidence of the Congress and the people regardless of party. He is the man of this tragic hour."

Passing on such newspaper clippings to Henry Stimson, Marshall asked him to observe at his next press conference that such proposals were "embarrassing" to the general and made "his present task more difficult. . . . Further, that he will never permit himself to be considered as a possible Presidential candidate. His training and ambitions are not political." Stimson politely declined to intervene, assuming that silence would defuse the speculation.

As the Marshall boom faded, a boomlet arose for Eisenhower. On September 29, George Van Horn Moseley, whom Eisenhower, as a seemingly dead-end major, had assisted in the War Department fifteen years earlier, sent Ike a surprising letter. "In his broadcast last Sunday evening," the retired, archconservative general wrote, "Walter Winchell stated that if the Republicans ran MacArthur for President, Mr. Roosevelt would take you as his running mate. I have no respect whatsoever for Mr. Winchell, but sometimes he gets the news quite accurate." He advised Eisenhower to keep his distance.

"You need have no fear about my being tempted into indiscretions concerning politics," Ike assured Moseley. "I not only know nothing about such things, it is an honest fact that I am so deeply engrossed in the job given me that I do not even have time to read the general news from home." Winchell, Ike wrote, was "to say the least, badly misinformed. . . . When this war is won, I will be glad of the chance to take things easy. In any event, I can scarcely imagine anyone in the United States less qualified than I for any type of political work."

Winchell was not alone in proposing Eisenhower for 1944. Republican Senator Arthur Capper of Kansas, Ike's home state, suggested either MacArthur or Eisenhower for the GOP ticket, and the World War I Tank Corps Association duly passed a resolution touting Eisenhower, whose party affiliation, if any, was unknown, for president. Edward J. Price of the U.S. Leather Company of Chicago, the association's head, even paid a visit to the general's brother Arthur seeking an endorsement. Arthur Eisenhower wrote to his brother hoping that he would "deny emphatically to his commander in chief that he has any interest whatsoever, irrespective of what newspapers say or what various organizations do in passing resolutions." MacArthur's failure to spurn such political ambitions, Arthur felt, impeded his military role. "Met Senator [Harry] Truman at the Kansas City Club today noon," he added, "and we commented briefly on this subject. He agreed with me there was only one man today whose suggestion or intimation [that] you be the next president was worth a continental* and that man is President Roosevelt. I hope all the rest will keep their mouths shut. . . ."

On October 20, Ike responded that he had seen "a few careless and ill-considered items in the newspapers" but he thought that issuing any statement "would, I think, be merely making myself ridiculous." There was no danger in his "becoming mixed up in politics." If a time should come when it was useful to produce a public denial, "you may be sure that my language will leave no room for misinterpretation." What Eisenhower had seen was a clipping from the *Washington Post* of October 5, sent by his friend George Allen, then involved in political fund-raising. The headline read "Eisenhower Urged for President," and it reported a resolution of Tank Corps Post No. 715 of the American Legion supporting the Price proposal. Members of the post claimed "no knowledge or concern as to the political affiliations or beliefs" of the general, but considered him as presidential timber because of his proven "leadership qualities."

"How does it feel to be a presidential candidate?" Allen asked. "Baloney!" Ike penciled on the letter, which he had Harry Butcher return. "Why can't a simple soldier be left alone to carry out his orders? And I furiously object to the word 'candidate'—I ain't and won't!"

Despite his difficulties in Sicily and in Italy, little was known of them in the U.S., and Eisenhower's domestic standing remained high. Assuming, like Secretary Knox, that General Marshall would command the cross-Channel operation and that Eisenhower would replace him in Washington, Stimson urged Roosevelt to ask Congress to confer five-star status on Marshall. He was outranked by British field marshals who would serve under him. Both Marshall and Roosevelt opposed the idea, as the field marshal title, despite MacArthur's adopting it briefly in the Philippines, had never existed in the American military.

Since "Marshal Marshall" seemed absurd, Stimson suggested instead employing the rank Congress conferred only on Pershing—General of the Armies. Marshall denied any need for it. "I didn't want any promotion at all," he told biographer Forrest Pogue years later. On the British side, the highest brass "were already field marshals, so they would be senior to me [in date of rank] whatever I was made. . . . I didn't want to be be-

*Continentals were paper currency issued by the Continental Congress (rather than the individual states) during the American Revolution.

holden to Congress for any rank or anything of the kind. I wanted to be able to go in there with my skirts clean and with no personal ambitions concerned in it in any way. . . . But that was twisted around and somebody said I didn't like the term *marshal* because it was the same as my name. I know Mr. Churchill twitted me about this in a rather scathing tone."

While Eisenhower now held the temporary wartime rank of general, his rank in the permanent military establishment since 1936 had been lieutenant colonel. Whether he remained a field commander or relocated to Washington, the anomaly was personally awkward. Finally, on September 15, 1943, the president submitted to Congress Eisenhower's nomination as a permanent major general effective from August 30. Since it would be a recess appointment in Congress's absence, Marshall cautioned, with MacArthur in mind, "Don't be upset if a small political attack is launched against the President. . . . This may be connected up with some further attack along the lines of favoring the European Theater and slighting the Southwest Pacific."

"I do not think we can safely postpone the date of [Marshall's] taking command," Stimson reminded Roosevelt, "beyond November first. The fatal delays and diversions which may sabotage Overlord will begin in the U.K. this autumn and nothing but his direct presence and influence will save us from them." Then came a confidence which would contribute to dooming Marshall's chances for the command. "No one dreads more than I do the loss of his influence in theatres other than the European theatres," Stimson added, "but I hope that the rank and title which I have suggested will help to preserve that influence indirectly in those faraway theatres even if not directly. I have talked this matter over with Harry [Hopkins] and I think on most of these points he is in full sympathy with me." Without Stimson's spelling it out, he was contending that no one other than Marshall could keep the abrasive and Anglophobic Admiral King cooperative, and MacArthur from insubordination—and that Eisenhower, who had been only a lowly aide to MacArthur, might find that relationship too difficult to handle.

Since Roosevelt had still not made up his mind, Churchill telephoned on September 30 to suggest hopefully that a joint statement be "timed after our next good success in Italy." He was anticipating the fall of Rome, yet that occasion appeared remote. German resistance remained stiff, although the Italians were desperately trying to abandon the war. Optimistically, Eisenhower intended to explain at the "Sextant" summit conference, planned for Cairo, that it would take until early spring in 1944 to reach much farther northward. Traversing the hip of the boot of

Italy, the river Po seemed to him "the most important land objective in the Mediterranean" because ground and air forces there would be "extremely threatening to the German structure in the Balkans, in France, and in the Reich itself." Yet the military assets needed to accomplish that "would delay Overlord from sixty to ninety days." Otherwise "we . . . would have to content ourselves on land with a line covering Rome."

The "Overlord" decision lingered—Ike's British visitors still promoted Brooke—as the next summits loomed. Cabling Roosevelt on October 22, Churchill recommended, in effect committing himself to the Channel operation, "To give 'Overlord' the best chance, the Commanders should be at it now. The eye of the master maketh the horse fat." He was quoting Xenophon—that a supervisory eye was urgent.

The conferences at Cairo and Teheran were to coordinate strategy with distant allies. Yet Stalin was playing his own game and Chiang, no serious ally, was hardly playing at all, except to evade suicidal cooperation with Mao's disciplined Red forces intent on taking over postwar China. Stalin would not risk travel far from Russia, and could not meet with Chiang, whom he regarded anyway as a paper lion, for the Soviets were not at war with Japan. Despite FDR's disabilities, Chiang and Stalin required arduous separate sessions.

Still assuming that he would command "Overlord," Marshall penned a confidential memorandum for his deputy, General Tom Handy, on November 8, as preparations were nearly complete for the two summits. "Informally I have been told that our Ambassador in London, Mr. Winant, suggests turning over half his Embassy to me if I go to London. I don't know how serious the proposal is, nor its implications." Facilities for the Supreme Commander were also being readied in Norfolk House, in St. James's Square. Following Cairo and Teheran would come a formal appointment, and John Winant was certain it would be Marshall.

Katherine Marshall was so confident that her husband would be leaving Fort Myer that she began moving, in a trailer and under a green tarpaulin, her most precious possessions, including Chinese vases and rugs bought by Marshall in the 1920s, to Leesburg. Since 1940 they had owned, but rarely used, Dodona Manor, an unpretentious Revolution-era white-brick house that was their sometime weekend retreat. Mrs. Marshall had reconnoitered the suburban Virginia property and bought it months before her preoccupied husband even saw it. Had the press picked up what she was doing, the rumor mill in Washington would have churned further.

Hopkins, busy planning for Teheran, was one of the few in the West who received more than nominal respect from Stalin. Barring "further diversions or delays," Stimson updated Hopkins, if the president remained "steadfast," the "Overlord" operation would proceed on schedule. "I believe," he wrote, "that Marshall's command . . . is so much the most important thing on the world horizon . . . in spite of all the counter reasons which I can envisage. . . . I anticipate that his European command will be extended in future to all auxiliary movements in Western Europe even if that is not now agreed upon." He felt that no successor to Marshall "should be appointed for the present but that post should be carried on by an acting chief." Shrewdly, Stimson added, "Marshall's presence in London will strongly tend to prevent any interferences with Overlord even if they were attempted, and as to other theaters of operation we shall have to take our chances of carrying on along the present plans which have been pretty well laid out. . . . Good luck!"

Three days later, just after midnight on November 13, 1943, Roosevelt embarked for "Sextant" from Hampton Roads, Virginia, aboard the new battleship *Iowa*. His party included Hopkins, Marshall, Arnold, Leahy, King, and Somervell, and their discussions aboard focused on fending off Churchill's predictable alternatives to "Overlord." Attrition on other fronts, they agreed, would not bring down Germany. To counter Churchill's evasions, the Joint Chiefs proposed to Roosevelt, implausibly, that although the supreme command would devolve ultimately on an American, the initial commander might be British—"provided the man named is Sir John Dill." He had presided over the Imperial General Staff until Churchill became prime minister. Although replaced by Churchill, who considered Dill obstructive to the PM's strategic flights, he had led the "Arcadia" military contingent to Washington after Pearl Harbor and remained to work intimately with Marshall. The memorandum to Roosevelt emphasized Field Marshal Dill's "integrity of character and singleness of purpose. He understands our organization . . . and our way of doing business." He had also long furnished Marshall with confidential cables not shared by Whitehall with the American Joint Chiefs, and had the general collaborate secretly on replies to London. But the Dill suggestion was a nonstarter.

On the second afternoon in the Atlantic, a torpedo jarred loose by heavy seas from an accompanying destroyer hurtled toward the *Iowa*. An emergency warning from the bridge aborted an exhibition of balloon target shooting from the deck, and Roosevelt, in white fisherman's hat and sunglasses, was wheeled about by Chief Petty Officer Arthur Prettyman to watch as the ship turned right full rudder and a battery of the battleship's five-inch antisub guns fired. The missile veered aft, exploding harmlessly in the great wake of the *Iowa*.

The remainder of the voyage was anticlimactic. The *Iowa* docked at Oran on Saturday, November 20, met by Eisenhower and his senior staff. After welcoming ceremonies, the presidential party flew to Tunis in a four-engine C-54 transport (the DC-4 of postwar commercial aviation) christened *The Sacred Cow*.

On Sunday morning, Eisenhower escorted Roosevelt about nearby battlefields, from the recent expulsion of the Germans to the site of ancient Carthage. It was the first prolonged opportunity which the president had to appraise the affable Eisenhower. As they motored about, Roosevelt told him casually, "Ike, you and I know who was the Chief of Staff during the last years of the Civil War"—it was Henry W. Halleck—"but practically no one else knows, although the names of the field generals—Grant, of course, and Lee, and Jackson, Sherman, Sheridan, and the others—every schoolboy knows them. I hate to think that 50 years from now practically nobody will know who George Marshall was. That is one of the reasons why I want George to have the big Command—he is entitled to establish his place in history as a great General." Then FDR mused, as if thinking aloud, "But it is dangerous to monkey with a winning team." When he added that he planned to bring Eisenhower back as acting chief of staff, Ike evidenced little enthusiasm, saying only that as a soldier he would follow orders.

When Eisenhower mentioned the conversation to Admiral King, the navy chief said that although he would welcome Ike to the Joint Chiefs of Staff, he still believed (and hoped) that Roosevelt would change his mind and keep Marshall in Washington.

Late Sunday evening the president's C-54 took off for Egypt. There the principals and their aides, ensconced at the sumptuous but barbed-wire fenced Mena House hostelry, eight miles from Cairo in the shadow of the Sphinx and the Pyramids, met through the week, accomplishing little. The presence of Chiang Kai-shek irritated the always irascible Alan Brooke as Chiang had nothing to contribute to the defeat of Germany, nor even, Brooke thought, to the defeat of Japan. Disagreement surfaced as to how much could be accomplished by costly fighting on the mainland of Southeast Asia, or recovering the occupied Andaman Islands below

Burma, and what resources could be transferred to Asia if Italy were freed from the Germans. Although China had to be assisted in driving out the Japanese, Chiang was fighting more against Maoists than against the common enemy. A dozen Chinese generals and their American advisers on the conference tab further exasperated Brooke. When the Chinese were finally excused, Brooke turned to Marshall, saying, "That was a ghastly waste of time!"

"You're telling me!" Marshall agreed, but he and Brooke clashed over almost everything else. Brooke also argued with King over priorities, as it was already clear that his Pacific fleet intended to confront Japan with only token involvement wanted from the British. Burma, Malaya, and China, in King's view, needed only to wither in stalemate, to be retrieved when Japan capitulated. King claimed (although battling for Pacific atolls was proving expensive in lives) that sea power could strangle Japanese supply routes, while the unlikable Richard Sutherland, flown to Cairo as MacArthur's deputy, stressed assaulting Japan via the Philippines.

Had the aloof MacArthur appeared in Cairo himself as his own spokesman, the postwar world might have been radically different. Still formidable at sixty-three, MacArthur may not have wanted to seem an appellant, a posture at odds with his grandiosity, nor to share the same platform with those with whom he felt no rapport and were hardly (in his view) his peers. The *ifs* of history here remain worth pondering, although ironies rather than realities. His imposing presence might have drawn support for his Pacific Rim strategies far beyond anything an abrasive surrogate, whatever Sutherland's three stars, could have managed. Even more, the oft-postponed decision on the supreme command for "Overlord" might have suddenly closed, begging all previous questions, with the near-legendary MacArthur's dramatic appointment. No divas in the wings could have stood up to him: no Montgomery, no Patton, not even De Gaulle, and relations with Stalin and the Red Army might have been altered. The war in Europe might have taken an unpredictable turn. And the inevitable momentum of "Overlord" might in time have made Douglas MacArthur president.

Sutherland was heard, duly thanked, and returned to Brisbane. Marshall argued for MacArthur that plans for a return to the Philippines be kept on the table, but accepted that a summer 1944 amphibious assault on the Marianas, to seize jumping-off facilities in the western Pacific for bombers to Japan, should receive priority. Then the Europe-first litany resumed. Churchill wanted more investment in Italy and the eastern Mediterranean, contending yet again that he had not lost his zeal for

"Overlord," but that "whoever holds Rome holds the title deeds to Italy," and that the Balkans could be destabilized as a back door to Germany. If Marshall were overall commander for Europe such dreams were dead. Churchill insisted to Roosevelt that "Overlord" was not to overlap into the Mediterranean. That command would have to go to a British general.

Marshall dined privately with Churchill. Mentioning in passing that on the Atlantic voyage he had been reading the speeches of Churchill's great predecessor, the elder William Pitt, Marshall triggered a performance by the prime minister, who strode about the Mena House gardens reciting from memory quotable lines he recalled from Pitt's orations. To further blandish Marshall, Churchill embellished his strategic arguments with colorful rhetoric. "They sat into two in the morning," Marshall recalled, succumbing neither to the prime minister's Mediterranean persuasions nor his vintage port. Rebuffed on strategy and flushed with wine, Churchill became "red hot." By house phone he summoned his generals from bed. Marshall called in Eisenhower, but signaled that Ike was not to involve himself. "All the British were against me. It got hotter and hotter." Finally, Churchill seized his own lapels for effect and declared, unable to suppress his desire to land on Rhodes, that he could not have His Majesty's troops "standing idle" while the buildup for "Overlord" continued. In alcoholic emphasis he shouted, "Muskets must flame!"

"God forbid if I should try to dictate," Marshall said emphatically, "but not one American soldier is going to die on that goddamned beach." The British generals looked horrified. No one spoke to Churchill that way. Marshall thought they also appeared relieved, and said nothing in the PM's support, for "they didn't want the operation [either], and were willing for me to say it."

After the encounter, Churchill's personal representative to his chiefs of staff, General Hastings Ismay, "had to stay up with him all night." Unforgiving if correct toward the prime minister thereafter in Cairo, Marshall reminded a top-level group consulting on moves toward Japan after the German phase had ended that Churchill had "clouded and hampered all our preparations for the cross-channel operation," weakening "the resolution" of his military chiefs.

Before the sessions, supporting the prime minister, Brooke had carped in his diary that he could not make the Americans "see daylight." Now he brooded, "to satisfy American shortsightedness we have been led into agreeing to the withdrawal of [some] forces from the Mediterranean for a nebulous 2nd front." Churchill could no longer renege on "Overlord" but he would continue stonewalling it. To move the Normandy operation forward, and assuming that Teheran would change nothing, the American conferees agreed as expected on a British commander for the Mediterranean. No American troops would fight east of Italy.

Eisenhower did not accompany Roosevelt's mission to Teheran on *The Sacred Cow,* which took off from Egypt on Saturday, November 28. Marshall advised Ike to take a few days off for relaxation. Eisenhower and his party, which included several women so that Kay Summersby could accompany him, visited Luxor and the Pyramids, then detoured to Jerusalem. Wandering biblical sites and the bazaars, he picked up, among his postcards, one with its own envelope labeled "Souvenir from the Garden of Gethsemane." Before retiring he scribbled something on it and gave it to Kay. "Good night!" he wrote, seemingly discreetly. "There are lots of things I could say—you know them. Good night."

Kay tucked the card away and said, for the others to hear, "Oh, thank you, General. Thank you so much. And thank you for a lovely day." Prudently, Eisenhower spread out the rest of his postcard haul and told the two WAC officers with Kay, "Take what you want. You should have some remembrance of the trip. . . ."

In Teheran, the talks relocated the day after arrival at Stalin's request to a villa in the Russian compound—he had claimed the urgencies of security—the American party talked cautiously, realizing that there were listening devices planted everywhere, even in the gardens, and that all the servants were very likely NKVD agents. At their sessions, participants discussed a United Nations organization, and Russian reservations about it, and the future occupation and partition of Germany. With the most powerful ground army in history, Stalin could overrun whatever he wanted, even up to the Rhine. The Allies wanted assurances of Russian intervention against Japan, which would come with a large price tag. Stalin wanted a commitment that a Second Front was coming—and soon. To British discomfort, he approved Marshall's "Anvil" proposal of a second landing in the south of France. In his diary Brooke deplored that an additional front was "already an impossibility." Again he dismissed Marshall as having no "strategic vision." As late as July 7, 1944, Churchill, his own prejudices unchanging a month after D-Day, would comment to an approving Brooke, "The Arnold-King-Marshall combination is one of the stupidest strategic teams ever seen." Then he added condescendingly (and concerned, perhaps, that his tart tongue would lead Brooke to gossip), "They are good fellows and there is no need to tell them this."

A morning meeting of top brass included Brooke, Marshall, and Klimenti Voroshilov. The second plenary session, a late-afternoon meeting at a large round table in the Soviet Embassy that seated twenty-eight, began at 3:30. Following a review of the morning exchanges, Marshal Voroshilov suggested that the Americans and British study, for "Overlord," how the Russians traversed large rivers like the Dnieper in force. Marshall took up the question bluntly. "The difference between a river crossing, however wide, and a landing from the ocean," he explained, "is that the failure of a river crossing is a reverse, while the failure of a landing operation from the sea . . . means the almost utter destruction of the landing craft and personnel involved." It was a reply meant as much for the British as the Russians. Voroshilov answered, to Marshall's satisfaction, "If you think about it, you will do it."

Stalin raised the expected question: "Who will command 'Overlord'? Nothing will come out of the operation unless one man is made responsible." When Roosevelt conceded that the decision had not yet been made, Stalin responded that without it he could not believe in the reality of the operation. Roosevelt rejoined that until the decisions made at their conference were complete, he could not determine the appropriate designee for the supreme command. To him, "supreme" still implied all of western Europe, but Churchill again launched into his familiar refrain of Italy, Yugoslavia, Greece, Turkey, and Rhodes. Rome, Stalin dismissed, was not worth any delay for "Overlord." It would be useful, he added, to be able to confirm the Supreme Commander before leaving Teheran.

Once more, Churchill dredged up the eastern Mediterranean, clearly intending to deter the Soviets from designs there. Stalin interrupted with what he confessed was an indiscreet question. Did the British really believe in "Overlord" or was the operation merely strung out to reassure the Russians? Conceding the inevitable, Churchill offered to hurl his best forces across the Channel, but the acrimony remained—which Roosevelt softened by reminding everyone that Stalin was to be hosting a grand dinner for which they would have to prepare their appetites, and that the Combined Chiefs of Staff would settle the "Overlord" command in the morning. Satisfied, Stalin offered to coordinate an offensive in the east with the launching of the Second Front.

The issue would not be settled the next morning, nor for several more. Brooke liked nothing of what he had heard in either Cairo or Teheran. "I feel more like entering a lunatic asylum or a nursing home than continuing with my present job," he complained to his diary on November 29. But he consoled himself in Churchillian fashion that by again stalling the start of "Overlord" he had assured "that it would not cripple the Italian campaign."

Early the next day at a private meeting which Churchill requested, he explained to Stalin that his attitude toward a Second Front was being misrepresented, arguing that since the British had the preponderance of troops in the Mediterranean, he wanted to keep them usefully occupied throughout the region. Stalin carefully did not ask why they were not further employed in Italy itself, where the going remained hard. (In his diary, Brooke would confess, "The [Italian] offensive is stagnating badly.") Roosevelt, added Churchill, had finally agreed (at the prime minister's insistence) that the imbalance of forces likely to continue was good reason for separate commanders for "Overlord" and for the Mediterranean, one American, the other British. Yet Churchill still hoped that if the Turks could be induced to enter the war, the Channel crossing he feared would fail might prove unnecessary.

At lunch the three, with interpreters, discussed "Overlord" yet again, and Roosevelt told Stalin that the Joint Chiefs (despite Churchill's misgivings) had settled on June 1 for the invasion of northern France, with a landing in the south soon after. With the decisions beyond further argument, the tension dissipated, and the conferees thereafter attempted to charm each other.

Delays, political and logistic, over forcing paths into France, long deplored by Roosevelt and Marshall, would continue to afford Stalin crucial advantages in time and space to work more of his territorial will on the Continent. The pace of advances would make little difference to future frontiers agreed upon, from dismembering Germany to other proposed occupation and national boundaries in central Europe and East Asia. The understandings arrived at in Teheran, anticipating a belated "Overlord" and purchasing coexistence in advance, would be the basis of the postwar settlement, but for Stalin's unspoken ambitions about the home islands of Japan.

A final dinner on December 1, hosted by Stalin, concluded the sessions. The closing communique pledged postwar goodwill. Roosevelt, Churchill, and their parties flew back to Cairo, where the principals conferred with Turkish premier Ismet Inonu. Cagily, Inonu asked as his price for going to war military assistance well beyond anything he knew that Britain or America could provide, and which he wanted more for protection against Russia than intervention against Germany. Since neither Roosevelt nor Marshall expected nor wanted more than anxious neutrality from Turkey, FDR remained politely aloof. Churchill and his foreign minister, Anthony Eden, accompanied Inonu to the airport, where the Turkish president in his country's style embraced Churchill and kissed him. "Did you see," Churchill remarked hopefully to Eden as they left, "Ismet kissed me?" Eden observed that was all they got out of him.*

While still in Cairo, Harry Hopkins came to see Marshall early one evening before dinner, probably on December 4. Always the bearer of the president's private thoughts, Hopkins confided that Roosevelt remained anxious over Marshall's imminent appointment as "Overlord" Supreme Commander. As big as the task was, Roosevelt may have had misgivings not only about losing Marshall at his right hand, but about the assignment's reduction, at Churchill's insistence, from oversight of driving the Germans from all of the ETO to a separate theater command. In substance rather than visibility it would be a demotion. Marshall had given the position of army chief of staff a dimension that was unique. "They had this idea that they should have Marshall in command of everything," Churchill raged to the compliant Ismay. "I won't have it." From Roosevelt's standpoint, that closed the matter—unless Marshall still wanted "Overlord."

As Hopkins later told Robert Sherwood, he explained to Marshall privately what he thought Roosevelt's "point of view" was. "I merely endeavored to make it clear," Marshall recalled his response, "that I would go along wholeheartedly with whatever decision the President made. He need[ed] to have no fears regarding my personal reactions. I declined to state my opinion." Marshall, Hopkins knew from the start, would ask for nothing.

The next morning Roosevelt summoned Marshall, and "in response to his question," the general recalled, "I made virtually the same reply I made to Hopkins. I recall saying I would not attempt to estimate my capabilities; the President would have to do that; I merely wished to make it clear that whatever the decision, I would go along with it . . . ; the issue was too great for any personal feelings to be considered." Relieved, Roosevelt conceded, "I feel I could not sleep at night with you out of the country." Personal glory would have to go. To the president, Marshall's grasp of global strategy and his bipartisan respect in the Congress were irreplaceable.

Back in Tunis on December 6, Eisenhower confided to his diary that in Cairo and after he had "seen quite a bit of Colonel Elliott Roosevelt, who is apparently quite close to the president in family councils." (He had been at the conference in Egypt, as had Eisenhower, and had gone on to

---

*Turkey would enter the war more than a year later, when its intervention was of no military usefulness, in order to stake a claim as a founding member of the United Nations.

Iran.) "He feels that the president is quite undecided as to what is the best thing to do, especially since the meeting at Teheran, where it is understood that Stalin insisted both upon Overlord in the spring and upon the utmost pressing of the Italian campaign during the winter." After talks with his father, Elliott Roosevelt felt that the president remained troubled that despite Marshall's "great contributions," a chief of staff "will never be remembered in history." Future annals "entitled" him to a more visible "field command."

In Cairo, conferring alone with Marshall, FDR dictated a secret radiogram to Stalin: "The immediate appointment of General Eisenhower to command of Overlord operation has been decided upon. Roosevelt." As the austere Marshall wrote out the extinguishing of his dream, the inner drama can only be imagined. Stimson would quote in his journal from *Proverbs,* "He that ruleth his spirit is better than he that taketh a city."

The next morning, Marshall penned and dated below FDR's signed message, a note to Ike: "Dear Eisenhower, I thought you might like to have this as a memento. It was written very hurriedly by me as the final meeting broke up yesterday, the President signing it immediately. G.C.M." Eisenhower would describe it, certainly in understatement, as "one of my most cherished mementos of World War II."

Later in December, Major General "Lightning Joe" Collins checked in at the Pentagon to see Marshall. Highly regarded as a fighting commander with the 25th ("Tropic Lightning") Division at Guadalcanal, he was on his way to England, to command a corps, at thirty-seven, in the cross-Channel invasion to come; he now knew it would not be led, as everyone had assumed, by the chief. Marshall, Collins wrote in his diary, "showed no signs of disappointment that Eisenhower, and not he, had been chosen by the President." Marshall had discussed the matter with no one other than his wife, yet from Guadalcanal to Reggio Calabria, everyone in khaki seemed to sense that the obvious designee had been let down.

Early on the morning of December 7, 1943, Churchill and Roosevelt had parted at the Cairo airport, the president flying to Tunis. They would meet again, as a pair and with Stalin, but the relationship, despite mutually friendly rhetoric, was cooling. Churchill's lengthy distancing from "Overlord" for reasons he could never bring himself to explain to Roosevelt, and his deviousness about it, had made the difference.*

---

*Churchill had told Stimson that he visualized beaches stacked with bloody corpses, and the secretary understood that the PM saw the real price as the hemorrhaging of the British Empire.

That afternoon at Tunis, Eisenhower met the president's C-54, conducting Roosevelt back to the Villa Casa Blanca, where the president had stayed while en route to Egypt. Once aides had seated FDR in the general's staff car he wasted no time with preliminaries. "Well, Ike," the president said, "you'd better start packing. You are going to command 'Overlord.'"

9

Goodenough Island
to Grosvenor Square

"HAVE THE RETURNING COURIER," Marshall instructed the secretary of the General Staff, Colonel William Sexton, "bring me a summer cap and my khaki kepi, also a waist belt—none were included in my baggage. Tell Mrs. Marshall I am well and the weather has been fine and the scenery magnificent. I cannot say more for reasons of secrecy." With the summits at Teheran and Cairo over early in December 1943, and "Overlord" settled, Marshall boarded a long-range transport almost in the shadows of the Pyramids and with a staff of three left for New Guinea by way of Karachi and Colombo. Flying eastward rather than via Washington as first planned, a grueling return of 10,500 air miles via Cairo, Dakar, and Natal, he would miss seeing his stepsons, Clifton and Allen, who had often advised him how to win the war. Both in uniform, they had orders overseas.

Cabling Marshall, Sexton reported that the *Washington Times-Herald* (an echo of the *Chicago Tribune*) had editorialized that if MacArthur were not the Republican candidate for president in 1944, the successful nominee, to win, would have to "promise that MacArthur would be appointed Secretary of War upon his election." Although the general had spent only forty-six days in New Guinea since the close of the Buna operation in January, he intended to show that he was on top of events by meeting Marshall closer to the action than downtown Brisbane. On December 12, MacArthur flew with several subordinates to Port Moresby, then hopped to Lieutenant General Walter Krueger's headquarters on Goodenough Island, just above eastern Papua on the edge of the Solomon Sea. Krueger, commanding the Sixth Army, and at the time of Pearl Harbor Eisenhower's boss in Texas, was one of the few senior generals MacArthur permitted to be assigned to him. About to launch an amphibious assault on the Arawe islands on the far western end of New Britain, Krueger wanted to further outflank the big Japanese base to the east at Rabaul.

Marshall's C-54 touched down at Port Moresby on December 14, after seventeen hours in the air. He, Tom Handy, Frank McCarthy, and Vice Admiral Charles Cooke were met by General Kenney and flown two hundred miles across New Guinea to Goodenough Bay, to lunch with MacArthur. Working in Hollywood, the wiry, tireless Colonel McCarthy, a VMI product like Marshall, had learned how to handle prima donnas. Long after the war, Marshall's deputy would earn an Academy Award as producer of *Patton,* a subject acquired from personal experience.

Whether by design or coincidence, that morning Krueger's "Alamo Force" had landed on Arawe. Marshall received a briefing in which, as usual, MacArthur complained about "the paucity of men and materiel" he was receiving. One issue that came up was Admiral King, who considered the Central Pacific theater ostensibly under Chester Nimitz as his own, and allegedly tried to shortchange the SWPA. The president, MacArthur had charged to one of Marshall's emissaries, Brigadier General Frederick H. Osborn, remained "Navy minded. . . . Mr. Stimson must speak to him, must persuade him. Give me central direction of the war in the Pacific, and I will be in the Philippines in ten months. Time is against me."

Recovery of the Philippines obsessed MacArthur. His "I shall return" declaration was broadcast to the Philippines from Australia by every means possible, and radios and small weapons were slipped into the islands by sub and dropped from planes to reach guerrilla groups across the archipelago. The promise sustained many Filipinos. Itsurō Horiguchi, a Japanese soldier in a Manila hospital, was told by a nurse unafraid to be assertive, "MacArthur will certainly return and save us." For Filipinos, the word they remembered with hope was "return."

MacArthur blamed Admiral Leahy as well as King for influencing the White House on army-navy priorities, and told Marshall that, once chief of staff himself, he realized that "professional and objective matters" could seldom be decided "on the basis of merit and common sense." Marshall might have agreed in principle. Stimson recalled a Joint Chiefs meeting when King's open hostility to MacArthur caused Marshall to rap the table, declaring, "I will not have any meetings carried on with this hatred." King's overreaching may have influenced decisions that went MacArthur's way later in the war.

In what Krueger recalled as a heavy tropical downpour, Marshall "took time out to drive with me . . . to some of our troop units and installations." On the steamy morning of December 16, the Marshall and MacArthur parties returned to Port Moresby, and before midnight the very weary Marshall took off again for Guadalcanal, nine hundred miles to the east.

The only wartime meeting of the generals lasted little more than two days, but it was amicable and to MacArthur's advantage. He worked his persuasive powers to the full. Marshall on his return would cable praise of "the admirable organization and fighting force you have under development there. I was greatly impressed by all that I saw. Already this morning I have talked to Arnold about some of the air matters and probably will have a little encouraging news for you in a few days." MacArthur recalled in his memoirs that Washington became "more generous" thereafter and sent fifty twin-engine P-38 fighters beyond the aircraft complement already destined for the SWPA, and also increased bomber deliveries. In a "fireside chat" on Christmas Eve, Roosevelt would tell a nationwide radio audience that Marshall's meeting with MacArthur "will spell plenty of bad news for the Japs in the not too distant future."

At much-fought-over Henderson Field on Guadalcanal the Marshall party was met by Lieutenant General Millard F. Harmon and flown over the northern Solomons to view the ongoing action on Bougainville. Then they continued to Munda, on New Georgia Island. As Marshall told a reporter for *Yank* in Hawaii, he went on to the New Hebrides, and visited service hospitals, then flew to the Fijis, where he watched troops embarking and visited more hospitals—a duty (he did not tell the *Yank* writer) from which MacArthur always shrank. After refueling on Canton Island,* a coral atoll just across the International Date Line, Marshall's C-54 reached Honolulu on the morning of December 19.

On Oahu he watched jungle-fighting maneuvers, and told troops assembled for him, "We have got the Japs beaten but we have to keep pushing. The Japs had jungle training before the war and we didn't. . . . Our great advantage is our enterprise and resourcefulness. Your training here is the best that can be given and it is up to you to push the enemy

*Now Kanton, in the Phoenix Islands, part of the mini-republic of Kiribati.

through the jungle." Recalling the efficient small-unit tactics the Germans were employing in Italy, he challenged the trainees, "You men have to do the same and better, and you have the initiative and the leadership to do it." His talk was covered by the press, and the *New York Times* report was one of the rare occasions in the war when newspapers reported command praise of the enemy from anyone. Few but Marshall could get away with it.

Impatient for the general's return, Churchill knew that Roosevelt would confirm nothing before consulting with Marshall. "Do hasten back to the Capital," the PM had cabled to Honolulu, "as much necessary structure hangs in mid-air pending your arrival. . . . The war in Italy languishes and the Turk is stalling." Marshall expected the former and cared little about the latter.

With the announcement of the "Overlord" appointment still on hold, Eisenhower left Algiers for Italy with Beetle Smith and aides on December 18, for an unadmitted farewell tour of his command. After Cairo and Teheran, Algiers had been awash with rumors that Ike was going to replace Marshall in Washington, but Italy required attention. Temporary quarters had been set up for him in a grand if unkempt palace at Caserta, northeast of Naples, where Harold Alexander had his army group headquarters. The fighting for small gains toward Rome remained as bitter as the weather. In cold rain, fog, and mud, movement had bogged down. Wherever Eisenhower went, he passed by posh residences appropriated by senior officers willing to wait out the winter. "Tooey" Spaatz had taken over an estate targeted as a rest center for the ranks. He and Mark Clark had made lush Capri off-limits except for air force officers; seductive Sorrento was reserved for army officers. Enlisted men had the run of back streets in Naples teeming with pimps and prostitutes adept at emptying pockets.

The most shooting in which Eisenhower was involved during the war came, in Italy, from his own service revolver. At exiled Crown Prince Umberto's former hunting lodge where the general was established, the fireplaces worked poorly and in the dim light a rat was discovered perched stubbornly on his toilet seat lid. A small crowd gathered at the lavatory entrance. "I can handle this," Ike assured Sergeant Mickey McKeogh, his aide. Eisenhower put on his glasses, reached for his pistol, fired—and missed. Plaster flew. As the rat scampered to a pipe, he fired again, clipping its tail. On a third try he tumbled the rat, which was then dispatched by an orderly with a fireplace log.

"Great marksmanship, Chief," Harry Butcher gibed. "Just what we'd expect from the Supreme Commander."* Very likely they were the only shots ever fired by Eisenhower in a combat zone.

On December 21 Marshall was back from the Pacific and in California, hoping to depart after visiting aviation plants and dining with aircraft manufacturers. When weather delayed him, film mogul Louis B. Mayer improvised a party. (Marshall had met at lunch with producers and directors to discuss further war projects.) The general found himself at a late supper with a hundred rounded-up celebrities, sitting between Greer Garson and child star Margaret O'Brien, and laughing at impromptu skits. Groggy after little sleep, he left Los Angeles early on December 22 and by ten in the evening, after logging 35,000 miles, he was back in Washington.

The next morning, before meeting with the president and Stimson at the White House, he cabled MacArthur from the Pentagon and wrote a note to the wife of MacArthur's communique-writing amanuensis, Colonel LeGrande Diller (risen from major), conveying her husband's Christmas greetings; another went to the wife of Major General Charles Thompson, who commanded troops on Fiji, and "was most comfortably established, though in surroundings quite different from yours." A third was posted to Virginia Stettinius, wife of the new undersecretary of state, accompanying a signed place card acquired in Honolulu—their ten-year-old twin sons wanted the autograph of Admiral Nimitz. Marshall also wrote Christmas letters to his stepsons, both now in the ETO. Then he drafted a memorandum for the president on their reluctant acceptance of Montgomery to command "Overlord" ground forces, to be cabled to Churchill for his announcement, and another to Eisenhower about replacements for Italy. (One command shift proposed by Ike's largely British senior staff was scorned by Marshall as "selfish and not purely objective.") Yet he pressed Eisenhower to keep Sir Frederick Morgan—"a very capable officer" who "almost seems more American than British"—in charge of "Overlord" planning in London. On Christmas Eve, FDR broadcast the appointment of Eisenhower. Alerted, Ike listened on the radio, six time zones away.

---

*Butcher, McKeogh, and Summersby (in accounts much separated in time) tell the story slightly differently, the earlier versions probably intended to keep Kay remote.

Employing the good offices of the Red Cross, whose work he admired, Marshall had long before sent a message offering his Christmas wishes to American prisoners of war, wherever they happened to be, hoping that it would get through, along with mail and token packets:

> Wherever you are this Christmas message goes to you
> with my heartfelt thanks and with my prayer for your
> wellbeing and safety. God bless you all. May your Christ-
> mas be a cheerful one.
>   G. C. Marshall, Chief of Staff

In a prison camp at Shirakawa, Taiwan, on January 23, 1944, the lines were read to General Brougher and his fellow POW officers. There was no other mail.

Lieutenant General Morgan, Eisenhower would recall gratefully, "had, long before my arrival [in London in 1944], won the high admiration and respect of General Marshall. I soon came to place an equal value upon his qualifications. He had in the months preceding . . . accomplished a mass of detailed planning, accumulation of data, and gathering of supply that made D-Day possible." Diplomatically, Morgan wrote to Eisenhower, "I feel that your selection has done everything possible to discount the disadvantages of the lateness of your arrival." Morgan would be a key cog in the works.

Once Morgan had received his assignment, he flew to Washington to discuss his manpower and matériel needs, and was put up at Fort Myer in a style that "seemed like Paradise itself" after English austerity. Marshall urged him to take some time to see the country, and asked where he would like to go. Morgan confessed that he had always admired Stonewall Jackson, and hoped to visit the Shenandoah Valley, where Jackson had secured his fame. "If you had thought it out for a hundred years," said Katherine Marshall, "you couldn't have given a more tactful answer. It is where we live."

After Morgan had his Jackson immersion, he toured infantry, artillery, and airborne training sites, and the port of embarkation in New York harbor, seeing "profusion on an unlimited scale," where a Liberty ship "was fully loaded, it seemed, almost before our eyes." He was also invited to the White House to be charmed by the president, whose concerns about "Overlord," he detected, came from the continuing misgivings of Winston Churchill.

Marshall was back in Leesburg late in December, in snow and sleet that snapped tree limbs, for a family Christmas dinner which included his stepdaughter, Molly Winn, and her husband, an army major. They toasted the absent boys. One of Marshall's unexpected Christmas gifts was very likely at the table. When he was senior instructor for the Illinois National Guard, the commander of the 58th Field Artillery Brigade in Chicago had been Major General Frank R. Schwengel. On retirement he became director of U.S. operations for Seagram's Ltd. For Christmas, he sent Marshall a case of the firm's products.

Thanking Schwengel, Marshall wrote, "I might confess that for the first time in my life I have felt the need of a drink occasionally. Mrs. Marshall and I work very hard on our place down at Leesburg and by work I mean the pickaxe or pitchfork, the shovel and the wheelbarrow, and at times a crowbar—no labor ordinarily being available. As our work hours as a rule start at about 7:30 A.M. and we run up to about 6:00 P.M. whenever I am able to get away from Washington, both of us now find ourselves much in need of a pick-up and here is where you come into the picture. As a matter of fact I seemingly need at times to be completely picked up, though I find that on Monday morning my brain works at top speed."

Eisenhower and his party were in Algiers for Christmas. On December 26, he wrote a rare letter to his fading mother in Kansas hoping that "by the time another Christmas rolls around I can come home to see all of you, at least for a brief visit." He had no idea that he would be in the U.S. much sooner. Marshall had been pressing him to return, more for domestic reasons than discussions with American policy makers. Fending him off, Eisenhower would cable, "With regard to my visit home I feel for the moment it is an impossibility. I truly hope that February or early March will afford me such an opportunity."

Although he operated under great tension, Eisenhower relished his lifestyle and looked forward eagerly to his new command, although it meant giving up his several residences in North Africa—a seaside villa in the Tunis suburb of La Mersa, a house in Algiers, and what he called "the farm," outside of Algiers, where he entertained grandly. Wherever he was, there was Kay Summersby, who in her last years described the arrangement as a "strange love affair, if one could call it an affair." One day that December, Everett Hughes, a brigadier general in supply services, and a longtime friend of Eisenhower, asked him about Kay. "I don't know whether Ike is alibiing or not," Hughes penned in a diary note. "Says he wants to hold her hand, accompanies her to her house, doesn't sleep with her. He doth protest too much. . . ." Kay claimed decades later that the only time they tried to make love, Eisenhower proved not up to it, but their liaison appeared intense nevertheless. When another officer who was an old friend overheard gossip about them he snapped, "Leave Kay and Ike alone. She's helping him win the war."

At the Maison Blanche, Eisenhower's first "white house," Churchill, describing himself as one of the ruins of Carthage, and greatly susceptible to pneumonia, was recuperating from another illness and holding his usual bedside conferences. His wife, Clementine, wrote to their daughter, Mary, "A little gun-boat patrols up and down in front of the house in case a German submarine should pop up its nose and shoot up the villa."

From there Churchill called a conference for Christmas Day to discuss "Shingle," the proposed Anzio beachhead south of Rome, which now interested Eisenhower far less than an "Anvil" landing on the French Riviera, which would be completely an American enterprise supporting, then linking with, operations across the Channel. Happily, he had no further responsibility for what Churchill called "half-finished" Italy, still his obsession and very far from half-finished. In part the meeting was to establish portly Sir Henry Maitland ("Jumbo") Wilson, drawn from Egypt, into the hierarchy as Eisenhower's successor in the Mediterranean.

Wilson, Alexander, Tedder, and Cunningham, with Eisenhower as the lone American participant, listened to Churchill's blandishments that "Overlord" and "Anvil" would only succeed if the effort to take Rome worked, to "possibly achieve the destruction of a substantial part of the enemy's army." He was even willing, the PM claimed, to abandon dreams of Rhodes and an Aegean campaign, and of luring Turkey into the war, in order to open the road to Rome. In truth he would keep pressing, if more subtly, for an Aegean operation, worried that otherwise, Russia would intrude into what he considered an historically British sphere of influence. Urged by Marshall, Roosevelt continued to say no. "I doubt that I did anything better in the war," Marshall would recall, "than to keep Churchill on the main point (he always wanted to take side shots). I was furious when he wanted to push us further in the Mediterranean."

Often mesmeric enough to move Eisenhower in his direction, Churchill got the general to concede that "the right course was to press on in Italy, where the Germans were still full of fight." A "bold venture" like Anzio would "quicken up" the war. Churchill raised the issue of postponing the transfer of fifty-six landing craft to the U.K. (if they survived) until the two divisions intended for Anzio made their beachhead, but he claimed that he would let nothing interfere with "Overlord." "Various expedients" could recover the lost three weeks. He knew very well that his Italian designs would delay preparations for France.

After two hours of talk Churchill dictated a cable to Roosevelt embodying the decisions he had extorted from the group. For the press he concocted a fictitious bulletin on his health, ostensibly from his doctors. He also urged FDR to agree formally to the major appointees for "Overlord," as Montgomery had already left for England in a deal to have him command all cross-Channel ground forces until Bradley took over the American dimension. Eisenhower preferred the less abrasive and more effective Alexander, but Churchill cabled Roosevelt, "The War Cabinet desires that Montgomery should command the first expeditionary group of armies. I feel that the Cabinet are right, as Montgomery is a public hero and will give confidence among our people, not unshared by yours." The final phrase, hedged in the negative, was certainly false. In any case it was the PM's personal choice, abetted by Brooke. Churchill itched to make the announcements quickly and personally.

The clever management scheme seemed Anglo-American but was contrived by London to create a Supreme Commander who was not to command. Rather, he would be an American chairman of a corporate board delegating actual authority to deputies for air, land, and sea who would be British, and to field generals who would be largely British until a preponderance of U.S. forces required Americanized subordinate commands.

A festive luncheon followed—turkey and plum pudding—with the prime minister presiding in a padded silk Chinese dressing gown decorated with blue and gold dragons. It was Churchill's first meal outside his bedroom since his illness.

Although Churchill cabled thanks to Roosevelt for the landing craft diversion, he realized that he owed the concession permitting "Shingle" to happen to Marshall's reluctant give-and-take. Few tangential operations would cause Marshall as much anguish as the Anzio operation. Pleased by his ploy, the PM considered the Teheran "contract with Stalin" for a landing in France "during May" effectively fulfilled if a few days late. Privately, he would concede ruefully to Brooke later about Anzio, "We hoped to land a wildcat that would tear out the bowels of the Boche. Instead we have stranded a vast whale with its tail flopping about in the water!"

The "June moon around 6th June" seemed likely to offer the tidal conditions equivalent to early May. But it would not actually be May, as promised in Teheran. Stalin growled about the slippage in date and about the delayed delivery of seized Italian warships and transports promised to Russia but which the Western allies wanted to withhold for possible use, first, against Japan.

Exasperated by Eisenhower's bland refusal to fly to Washington, Marshall responded by radiogram on December 29, directly ordering that Ike return on grounds that the respite would ease the pressures on him before they became more insistent. Marshall was precise about his intentions. Earlier in the year, when in Algiers, he took Harry Butcher aside and told him to make his boss "relax. . . . He may think he has troubles so far, including Darlan, but he will have so many before this war is over that Darlan will be nothing." Butcher understood the implied as well as the declared reasons. While Eisenhower did relieve some tension with Kay Summersby, Marshall worried about what that augured for his planned postwar successor at the Pentagon. Gossip, or worse, could undo Eisenhower's future.

Preparations for "Overlord," Marshall cabled, would continue very well for a few additional days without its designated commander. "Things have been going ahead in the UK for a long time and under a wise and aggressive man[, General Morgan]. . . . You will be under terrific strain from now on. . . . I am not interested in the usual rejoinder that you can take it. It is of vast importance that you be fresh mentally and you certainly will not be if you go straight from one giant problem to another." Then came the key, and unambiguous, line in Marshall's cable: "Now come on home and see your wife and trust somebody else for 20 minutes in England."*

Reluctantly, Eisenhower arranged a return to Washington, first cabling Bedell Smith in London to arrange for a house "in which three people, including my driver and secretary could live." At Marrakech, en route to the States, he again saw Churchill, then made a stopover in the Azores and another at Gander in Newfoundland. Before departing Tunis, Eisen-

---

*Eisenhower rewrote Marshall's phrase for his memoirs as "allow someone else to run the war for twenty minutes." He excised the "see your wife." But in *Crusade in Europe*, his return to Mamie was described, despite his protests to Washington, as "a treasured opportunity."

hower was asked for his new year predictions about the defeat of Germany. "I believe," he declared, "we will win the European war in 1944."

The *Time* "Man of the Year" accolade in its New Year issue might have gone to MacArthur or Eisenhower. The face on the cover dated January 3, 1944, was the austere one of George Catlett Marshall, with the caption, "He armed the Republic." In the background of Ernest Hamlin Baker's portrait was part of an American flag, with its stripes metamorphosing into arrows pointing at western Europe. The accompanying story observed that although the American people "do not usually like or trust the military, they like and trust General Marshall. . . . The secret is that American democracy is the stuff Marshall is made of." He was "trustee for the nation" and "the indispensable man."

Time was already on the newsstands on December 31, 1943, Marshall's sixty-third birthday, when Stimson hosted a party for him, at which the secretary prophesied that Marshall would become the first American army chief since George Washington to shepherd the armed forces through an entire long war. With hilarity certainly more feigned than real, Marshall coaxed General Somervell into a circle of colleagues to lead a chorus of "Now We're Working on the Railroad."* That morning, Marshall had told an off-the-record press conference that railway unions then threatening a strike over wage freezes were assisting German propaganda about America and sabotaging the war effort. A walkout was temporarily averted later in the day, before Somervell, with Major General Charles P. Gross, his chief of transportation, would have operated the rail lines, but the delay was brief. The president would soon order the War Department to take over the rails and Roosevelt himself would arbitrate a settlement.

A week after Marshall's remarks appeared in the press, unattributed, a Florida newspaper disclosed his identity, which moved him from his usual position beyond criticism. Yet, inevitably, someone with conservative credentials and high visibility would consider Marshall's stiff stand against industrial shutdowns as further proving his presidential caliber. After the newest railway imbroglio the admirer was airline executive Eddie Rickenbacker.

Marshall's deputy, Frank McCarthy, met Eisenhower's plane at 1:30

---

*Marshall's improvisation for the occasion of "I've Been Working on the Railroad."

A.M. on the 2nd, a useful hour to ensure that his arrival would be unpublicized. At the Wardman Park Hotel, to preserve secrecy, he was driven to the service entrance and taken up to Mamie on the freight elevator. She had not seen him for eighteen months. Ike seemed withdrawn, lined, and overweight. The homecoming was awkward. They had little to say to each other. He smoked incessantly, was intolerant of small talk, and told Mamie very little about his life abroad.

At the Pentagon, which he had never seen completed, he met with Marshall. Eisenhower and Mamie were then escorted to a snowy rail siding in Maryland to board a private Pullman car for an overnight journey to West Point, where John, in his third and final year in the war-abbreviated curriculum, was a cadet sergeant. On returning, Eisenhower was asked by the president to the White House, after which Marshall hosted a dinner for the general and Mamie at the Alibi Club with high-level military and congressional guests who were asked, impossibly, to keep the session secret. Happily, the press, encouraged by Marshall, cooperated. (Ike was at the White House again on the 4th.)

The Alibi Club, at 1806 I Street, occupied an old house which had been purchased and rehabilitated by seven members of the better-known Metropolitan Club. Through retired ambassador Robert Woods Bliss, Marshall convened discreet VIP dinners at the Alibi. The December 3 event was perhaps his largest. Admiral Harold "Betty" Stark had returned from London, and Generals Kenney and Collins were back from the Southwest Pacific. Collins told the group about fighting for Guadalcanal; Kenney (who would return to the SWPA) reviewed operations in New Guinea and New Britain; Stark talked about protecting convoys crossing the North Atlantic. Eisenhower, called last, described the difficulties in slogging up the boot of Italy.

Then came a brief, awkward stay for the Eisenhowers arranged by Marshall at a cottage on the grounds of the Greenbrier Hotel at White Sulphur Springs, West Virginia, taken over as an army convalescent hospital. Despite the renewed intimacy, Ike would not discuss his new assignment with Mamie and more than once inadvertently called her "Kay." Yet he had written to Mamie as far back as March 2, 1943, nearly a year before, to defuse persistent rumors that had reached her, that he was "an old duffer" and had "no emotional attachments and will have none."

Alone but for an aide, he flew to Fort Riley, Kansas, on January 8. At Manhattan, his brother Milton was now president of Kansas State College. Ida, eighty-two, but cheerful as well as tearful, was brought there to be with "Dwight" briefly, and his brother Arthur arrived from Kansas

City. Then Ike flew back to Washington, and Mamie, and meetings at the Pentagon. From Marshall he learned that Maitland Wilson and Churchill, at Marrakech, had set the "Shingle" (Anzio) operation prematurely for January 22. From Montgomery in London he discovered that Churchill and the British chiefs of staff were still plotting to cancel "Anvil," ostensibly to reserve landing craft for "Overlord" but actually to hoard ground forces for the failing push up Italy, now in winter stagnation. Its narrow boot, efficient for the Germans to defend yet expensive to attack, had become a Churchill obsession.

During Eisenhower's twelve days in the U.S., the president asked to see him for a third time. Mamie complained about losing a rare evening with him. He found Roosevelt in bed with the flu (yet with the inevitable cigarette in a long holder). After many such sessions with Churchill, Eisenhower was used to bedroom conferences. Whatever Roosevelt's agenda, Eisenhower's first item of business was to have the president autograph a photo for Kay.

Assuming industrial supremacy and inevitable victory, and willing to leave "Overlord" decisions to the generals, Roosevelt wanted to talk about the postwar viability of Germany.* Zones of occupation troubled Eisenhower. What territory under Russian control would ever be relinquished? The president implied that zone partition was, since Teheran, a done deal. Since the Red Army could not be rolled back, it was only a matter of which nation administered what after the peace. He wanted northwest Germany for the Americans. Although Eisenhower explained that invasion strategy would almost certainly put the British there, Roosevelt considered that only a personnel rearrangement, not a postwar problem. Eisenhower wished the president well, and took his leave.

With Marshall, privately, Eisenhower discussed coping with the British dimension of "Overlord." Despite the concession to let Montgomery command ground forces for the initial stages of the assault, Churchill and Brooke remained cool, when not covertly hostile, to the entire operation. Postscripting a message for his chiefs of staff, the prime minister wrote cynically that "it may be that we need not recant on

---

*Meeting with Republican Party advisers on July 29, 1952, as a presidential candidate, Eisenhower told them untruthfully that he had made a secret flight to Washington early in 1944 "to protest vigorously . . . against the Allied plans for the postwar division of Germany that left Berlin isolated inside Soviet-occupied territory. . . . In talking to Mr. Roosevelt about these things, he just laughed, 'I can handle Uncle Joe.' That is exactly what he told me." Yet he had been directly ordered by Marshall to make the flight home—for very different reasons.

OVERLORD except as regards emphasis and the balance of effort." It was code for disrupting the invasion timetable and starving it of resources. Later, when Churchill was preparing a postwar memoir, Robert Sherwood wrote to Marshall, who had contended with the PM's duplicity, "As you probably know, Mr. Churchill now takes the position that he was always whole-heartedly in favor of OVERLORD, and presumably he intends to write his own record that way." (He did, often altering documents to do it.)

The continuing shortage of sealift, Eisenhower learned, compromised the breadth of the proposed beachheads. (King at first had given landing craft a low shipbuilding priority, then withheld many for the Pacific.) Weaponry matters were next. With Stimson, Marshall updated Eisenhower on the use of handheld rockets as antitank artillery, and discussed the possibility of rocket mountings on half-tracks and tanks. The Germans were ahead of the game on rockets, great and small. A December intercept from General Hiroshi Oshima, the Japanese ambassador in Germany, to Tokyo, detailed his inspection tour of the "Western Wall" defenses with Field Marshal Gerd von Rundstedt's chief of staff, while another decrypted intercept to air attachés assured them that "reprisal installations" (for "V" weapons) along the Channel and North Sea coast had not been affected by Allied bombing. Eisenhower confessed, "You make me scared."

Saying goodbye to Mamie, Ike was shocked when she told him, bluntly, "Don't come back again till it's over, Ike—I can't stand losing you again." She would not fly to him: an inner-ear condition kept her from poorly pressurized planes. He would not see Mamie for eighteen more months.

With Eisenhower's departure from London to manage "Torch," the European Theater of Operations had become an administrative command. Jake Devers tried to keep his hand in Frederick Morgan's "Overlord" planning, but Morgan was formally Chief of Staff to the Supreme Allied Commander (Designate), or COSSAC. The "Designate" had not yet been named, but it was clear from the separation that it would not be Devers. Marshall expected that the efficient Devers, a West Point classmate of Patton, and thus senior to Ike, would be offered an "Overlord" opportunity, but in likely payback, neither Eisenhower nor Bradley wanted him.

Eisenhower dismissed Jake Devers as ".22 caliber." On returning to England, Ike had him shunted from ETO to the Mediterranean. Excessively loyal, Bradley derogated Devers as "egotistical, shallow, intolerant, not very smart, and much too inclined to rush off half-cocked." His effective leadership of the Sixth Army Group in southern France would prove the antithesis of such derision. Although Marshall's confidence in Devers was considerable, he did not press him on Eisenhower. When Devers was in Italy, Marshall sent him a Pentagon aide being reassigned, with the admonition, "I want him attached to a . . . division in the line in Italy, not as a liaison or observer but on duty with artillery. What I want is to give him the experience in fighting as a final step to offset his long service to me in this office. After that he is on his own." It said much for Devers, who would be in to the end on the ruin of the Third Reich.

On the day Eisenhower arrived in Britain, nearly a million Americans were already there. An associate of Henry Luce remarked in a cable to the Time Inc. chief, "There is not a single square inch of London on which an American is not standing, and add to that fact that, if he is standing after dark, he is standing unsteadily." Traveling from the air base at Prestwick, Scotland, in a private railway carriage code-named *Bayonet,* Eisenhower arrived in blacked-out, crowded London on January 15. Waiting late at night in a winter fog to drive him was Kay Summersby. To lead the way to Hays Lodge, a town house off Berkeley Square, two men paced ahead, on either side of Kay's car. It was a short walk from the house in Mayfair to his office at 28 Grosvenor Square, soon to become known informally as Eisenhowerplatz. (Operational headquarters was a longer walk away at Norfolk House, St. James's Square.) Kay shared quarters nearby with WAC officers transferred with her to London. Whenever Eisenhower decamped for privacy to Telegraph Cottage, a slate-roofed house in a ten-acre wooded tract near Richmond Park, she was with him as driver and companion. He had used Telegraph Cottage for privacy when planning "Torch," and his staff had secured it for him again.

Still a civilian employee (Eisenhower would arrange for Kay's commission as a WAC lieutenant later in the year), she had no security clearance but sat in on his confidential meetings. At one strategy session in North Africa, Patton had hinted strongly that she should leave the room, and Eisenhower snapped, "We have no secrets from Kay." When Patton struck back, "Well, I have secrets from her," it was not a career-enhancing response. A *Chicago Tribune* correspondent, John "Beaver" Thompson, commented, "I've never before seen a chauffeur get out of a car and kiss a General good morning. . . ." James Gavin, then a one-star general, observed, "Chauffeurs do not normally join their generals for tea." Rumors from Algiers and Tunis quickly revived in London.

Like Kay, most of Eisenhower's early support staff was British. He struggled to find Americans who suited him for command and head-quarters positions, preferring those he and Beetle Smith knew from the Mediterranean. Some, like J. C. H. Lee, soon a lieutenant general, and appointed as deputy commander of U.S. ground forces and logistics chief, were less than inspired choices. (Lee's unearned third star would keep him parallel with MacArthur's Richard Sutherland.) Jake Devers, high on Marshall's list but low on Eisenhower's, was exiled as Jumbo Wilson's deputy, then assigned by Marshall to "Anvil." Devers would get somewhat even, frustrating Eisenhower by refusing to part with combat-tested subordinates in the Mediterranean even after Ike urged Marshall to intervene.

Marshall also sent J. Lawton Collins and Charles H. Corlett, both expert in amphibious operations in the Pacific, to bolster Eisenhower's command, but they were first ignored by Omar Bradley and by Eisenhower himself. "Pete" Corlett, a major general who Marshall said "approached perfection," had ably commanded the Seventh Division in the capture of Kwajalein Atoll in early February, and Joe Collins, who had been at Marshall's dinner for Eisenhower in December, had been brilliant in securing Guadalcanal. "Corlett's early arrival here will be of great advantage to us," Eisenhower cabled Marshall on February 19. Yet Corlett would write, tartly, "I felt like an expert according to the naval definition: 'a son-of-a-bitch from out of town.'" In the end, both received corps commands.

Although Marshall questioned salvaging Patton for "Overlord," suggesting relegating him at best to "Anvil," Eisenhower brought him to Britain, where, slated for a top command, Patton again self-destructed. Asked to say a few words at the opening of a British Welcome Club for American soldiers in the market town of Knutsford, Patton turned out a few too many. "The only welcoming I have done for some time," he began, "has been welcoming Germans and Italians into hell. I have done quite a lot in that direction. . . . I agree with Bernard Shaw," Patton went on, "that the English and American peoples are separated by a common language. The idea of these clubs could not be better because undoubtedly it is our destiny to rule the world, and the more we see of each other the better." Privately, Patton had a low opinion of local pulchritude, but he added, diplomatically, he thought, "The sooner our soldiers write home and say how lovely the English ladies are, the sooner American dames will get jealous and force the war to a successful conclusion and then I shall have a chance to go and kill the Japanese."

The insensitive—perhaps only jocular—"destiny" line was reported in the *New York Times* on April 26, and the hostile *Washington Times-Herald* christened him "Chief Foot-in-the-Mouth." The War Department had to quiet the stir in the national press with a statement that Patton's remark was not the policy of the United States government. Marshall radioed Eisenhower that the promotion, now ill-timed, was "killed."*

Ike regretted that Patton had "broken out again," and claimed that the general had actually included Russia in the "destiny" brag, and was misquoted. When asked about possible disciplinary action, Marshall suggested a "business basis" for coping with the flap. Patton had real experience against Rommel, who was defending Normandy, and Marshall wanted his best fighting general involved. "You bear the burden of the responsibility as to the success of OVERLORD. . . . Between us we can bear the burden of the present unfortunate reaction."

It was a bad day for Eisenhower. He had just received word—to be suppressed by press censorship—that fast German "E-boats" had slipped into night maneuvers of VII Corps at Slapton Sands, off Lyme Bay, sinking two loaded LSTs, and blowing the stern off another. (LST—Landing Ship, Tank—was one of an alphabet soup of military abbreviations, which included DUKW, or "duck"—an amphibious truck—and "jeep," from GP, or general purpose vehicle.) Exceeding the future cost of D-Day operations at "Utah Beach,"† 197 sailors and 441 soldiers were drowned. The security failure was overwhelming and the Supreme Commander had to take appropriate action. Were any of the missing officers picked up by the Germans for interrogation about the likely assault beaches? Montgomery's headquarters investigated, and sent boats out to pick up bodies bobbing in their flotation Mae Wests. Every officer corpse was found.

Among the many problems to anticipate—the disruption of maneuvers had not been one of them—was when and how to beach landing craft, and which needed low tides to evade being impaled on "Rommel asparagus" (steel obstacles planted between the high-tide and low-tide locations to rip apart the shallow craft). To see the spikes, yet not be exposed to fire, troops had to land near dawn. Operational dates had to permit months of preparation, and follow-up months before winter set in. Only three windows in time existed, whatever the weather—the first days

---

*It was approved in August after Patton had been creditably in action.
†Relatively speaking, the cost was minor compared to aircrew losses. Between April 1 and June 5 the RAF and USAAF lost over 2,000 aircraft and 12,000 men in pre-D-Day operations. By the end of August aircrew casualties supporting the Normandy operations would pass 28,000. The RAF was no longer changing the oil in bomber engines, assuming that it wasted fuel to replenish a plane certain to be downed.

of May and several days in the first and third weeks of June. It was a hairy combination of hazards.

Eisenhower was also now overstretched in landing craft and in experienced leadership. Still, he followed up a message to Marshall with an order to Patton to report to him. He had "begun to doubt your all-round good judgment" and was "thoroughly weary of your failure to control your tongue." Patton went to Grosvenor Square the next morning to seek a reprieve. "When I came out [of Ike's office]," he wrote in his diary, "I don't think anyone could tell that I had just been killed. . . . I feel like death, but I am not out yet. If they let me fight, I will; but if not, I will resign so as to be able to talk, and then I will tell the truth. . . ."

Eisenhower was jumpy and restless as D-Day neared. The brilliant F. W. Winterbotham called on him at Norfolk House to brief him and Clark professorially on ULTRA, a system of decrypted intelligence of such vast potential that it could only be applied if the user did not hint at the source. While Clark sat in, bored, Eisenhower impatiently left. He would learn almost too late. Winterbotham recalled that Mark Clark "didn't appear to believe the first part and after a quarter of an hour, he excused himself . . . on grounds that he had something else to do."

Since much was left unlearned, and time was short, Marshall arranged with MacArthur to have more key officers from his command transferred to Eisenhower to gain their experience of landing operations—their "innovations, flexibility, and imagination," as Hap Arnold put it. The SWPA had even come up in the diary of the Pacific-resistant Brooke, when he was visited on February 14 by his liaison officer in Brisbane, Lieutenant General Herbert Lumsden, who conveyed dubious, MacArthur-influenced confidences from his headquarters. "Apparently Nimitz and MacArthur have never yet met," Lumsden gossiped, "although working [at] side by side [theaters]! King and MacArthur are totally opposed in their plans. Marshall and King are frightened of MacArthur standing for [the] presidency; Marshall hopes for vice-presidency and consequently won't fall foul of King. General feeling is that King has finished serving his useful period [as navy chief]. All military plans [are] shadowed by political backgrounds. God knows how this will straighten itself out!" A War Cabinet meeting followed, and Brooke very likely brought to it Lumsden's intelligence from the Pacific.

The dilemma for the Cabinet over Pacific strategy was how to contribute in a face-saving way to what increasingly appeared to be a smashing American victory over Japan. Only marginally did it seem a British war. Should "Dickie" Mountbatten be offered support to slog through

Burma and invade Sumatra? "Winston," Brooke would write after a later meeting, "is determined Mountbatten must be given some operation to carry out." Should a campaign with MacArthur, via Australia, push northward "through New Guinea towards Philippines, Formosa, etc.?" In mid-March, Churchill told the Cabinet that he had "discovered a new island," insignificant Simeuluë, in the Indian Ocean below Burma, that might be a jumping off place to reach "the top of Sumatra." Brooke complained that the prime minister "lives for the impulse and for the present, and refuses to look at lateral implications or future commitments."

Although Churchill was always "stepping in and muddling things badly," Brooke felt he had to offer support in the Cabinet "irrespective of the degree of lunacy." Yet for both Brooke and the PM, the most "lunatic" matter remained the very logical "Anvil," and both he and Churchill, protecting the Italian quagmire, continued to nag for "Anvil's" cancellation. Marshall was "quite hopeless" in promoting "the South of France" invasion, Brooke carped in a familiar refrain. "Abolition" was necessary. Marshall "cannot see beyond the end of his nose."

Expelled from SWPA reporting by MacArthur and in England awaiting "Overlord," Chester Wilmot would see the American effort though a myopic Brooke lens, ignoring the deception plans* now exploiting Patton (the Germans were already referring to *Armeegruppe Patton*), and the flanking movements in France that would leave the dilatory Montgomery in the dust. "An organizer rather than a strategist," Wilmot disparaged Marshall, "he applied to the problem of defeating Germany the directness and determination which he had mobilized the resources of the U.S. for war. . . . His military thinking was essentially simple and direct. To him the problem of defeating Germany was one of production and organization. He thought that if sufficient driving power were put behind Allied forces . . . , then momentum would carry them across the straits of Dover† into France. It was a matter of extending the production-line techniques into the field of strategy. There was no question of finesse or manoeuvre, of weakening or distracting the enemy, but merely of building up until you had overwhelming might." Wilmot flew the flag.

---

*The nineteen ghost divisions simulated troop movements, encampments, and radio nets, and even had fabricated shoulder patches reproduced openly in *National Geographic*.

†Busy belittling Marshall, Wilmot—who was there—forgot in the immediate postwar that Dover was in the deception strategy and that the landings would be far to the west, in Normandy.

Since MacArthur knew of the resources poured into Italy, and the continuing buildup for crossing the Channel, Marshall had realized since his Pacific trip that more than aircraft had to go to MacArthur. Always aware of the general's sensitivity to perceived slights, Marshall had evaded one potential problem when Frank Murphy, then a Supreme Court justice and a reserve officer, had asked to be assigned to service in the Pacific during a long recess of the court. Once high commissioner in the Philippines, Murphy assumed that temporary service in Australia might be appropriate, but Marshall proposed Alaska or Hawaii to him in view of Murphy's "feelings regarding MacArthur while he was High Commissioner."

One morning at the Pentagon in mid-January, Marshall asked Tom Handy, "What do you think of a DSM for MacArthur on his birthday?" MacArthur would be sixty-four on January 26. In peacetime that would have meant mandatory retirement. Another oak-leaf cluster to his Distinguished Service Medal might have waited, Marshall continued, until the capture of some major prize—but "Rabaul is a long way off maybe." Thus two days in advance he wrote a citation under the president's name to be radioed to MacArthur "in the clear" (the Japanese were invited to intercept the message), along with Marshall's own birthday wishes for "the great satisfaction and reward of a succession of victories on the road to Japan." Soon came another gift: a presidential ruling that "regular officers of the armed forces can accept such nominations for political office as come to them without solicitation by themselves." Conceding Republican realities, Roosevelt was permitting MacArthur to bid for the White House as long as he did not overtly authorize his candidacy.

FDR's own birthday, his sixty-second, came on January 30. Marshall sent another birthday message, adding his thanks "for the strong support you have given me personally and to the entire Army in the past twelve months." Any disappointment over the European command, never voiced, was now history. Victory was assured, he implied. "I anticipate some very hard knocks, but I think these will not be fatal to our hopes, rather the inevitable stumbles on a most difficult course."

The first hard knocks came, despite Marshall's efforts, from an unanticipated direction. MacArthur's rather amateurish presidential boom had struggled into 1944. Henry Luce had sent a *Life* correspondent to Brisbane, perhaps at his wife's urging, to assess MacArthur's presidential chances. The reporter had returned without a story. A Gallup Poll credited MacArthur with only 15 percent of the likely Republican vote, Dewey well in the lead with 40 and Willkie next with 20. John McCarten, once a Luce editor, in an article in the January issue of the liberal *American Mercury* which harshly judged MacArthur's military record since the war began, described his presidential hopes as literally misguided. "It may not be his fault," McCarten wrote, "but it is surely his misfortune that the worst elements on the political Right, including its most blatant lunatic fringe, are whooping it up for MacArthur." Although dispatches critical of the general from the SWPA had been quashed before by censors, probably because MacArthur's name was in the title, McCarten's was automatically listed by the Army War College's library service in its monthly bulletin to service libraries as relevant reading.

On the Senate floor on March 9, 1944, Arthur Vandenberg of Michigan attacked the War Department for recommending "smear" literature to the troops. On March 11, MacArthur cabled the War Department to describe the article as "scandalous in tone and libelous in essence." Marshall and Stimson were guiltless, but apologized for an administrative oversight many rungs beneath their purview, and ordered the endorsement expunged. The War Department had already, the month before, prevented *Harper's Magazine* from publishing an article critical of MacArthur by the *London Daily Express* correspondent Walter Lucas, who had covered the SWPA for eighteen months. A War Department underling dubiously claimed "security. The article as written undermines the confidence of this country, Australia, and particularly the troops in that theater in their commander and his strategic and tactical plans." *Harper's* editors charged that MacArthur was "protected by censorship from adverse criticism." Later they would protest, "No candidate for the Presidency, tacit or otherwise, should be hidden behind a veil of censorship."

Uncensored, the total of adulatory books on MacArthur since 1942 would soon reach twelve, some resembling campaign biographies. MacArthur would peak in the polls in mid-April at 20 percent, the same month in which in the early primaries he gained three delegates in Wisconsin (which he claimed as his home state) and won the Illinois vote against negligible opposition. Unfortunately, a minor Republican congressman, Arthur L. Miller of Nebraska, trying to keep the modest boom going, chose that week to release two letters from the general in response to two from him, one of which promoted MacArthur as "Commander-in-Chief and President of a free America." In a letter dated February 11, MacArthur had replied, coyly, that Miller's denunciation of the New Deal was "sobering" and his suggestion that the general let his name be placed in nomination was "flattering." Miller deserved "the thoughtful consideration of every true patriot."

One immediately arose. Senator Gerald P. Nye, an isolationist Republican from North Dakota, called in reporters to observe that the letters to Representative Miller "mean that if the people of the United States want General MacArthur for President, they can have him." They could also have Jean MacArthur for First Lady, according to a newspaper campaign promoting her as a Tennessean and a heroine of Corregidor who could assist Republicans with "wavering southern elements."

On the same day as Vandenberg's February speech in the Senate, Marshall had responded in a radiogram to MacArthur's petty demarcation dispute with Admiral Nimitz over tiny Manus Island, north of central New Guinea, in the Bismarck Sea. MacArthur claimed that the shift in theater lines was an early effort to deny him "control of the campaign to recapture the Philippines." He demanded an "early opportunity personally to present the case to the Secretary of War and to the President before finally determining my own personal reaction in this matter." Clearly exasperated, Marshall wrote, calling MacArthur's bluff, "I do not feel that we should be unnecessarily restricted by boundaries on a map. . . . Furthermore I cannot see that a change in the boundary of your area, in itself, could be regarded as a serious reflection upon your ability to command. . . . Your professional integrity and personal honor are in no way questioned or, so far I can see, involved. However if you so desire I will arrange for you to see the Secretary of War and the President at any time on this or any other matter."

"I appreciate greatly your prompt and full reply," MacArthur responded vaguely but contritely. His bluff had been called. Although a threat had been clearly implied, he neither resigned his command to run openly for the presidency, nor flew to Washington. Instead, he met in Brisbane with Admiral Halsey and—the admiral recalled—"lumped me, Nimitz, King and the whole Navy in a vicious conspiracy to pare away his authority. . . . Unlike me, strong emotion did not make him profane." When MacArthur paused, Halsey observed that personal attacks would be "hampering the war effort." Talking back was unheard of. MacArthur's staff, Halsey thought, "never expected to hear anyone address him in those terms this side of the Judgment Throne." When they met again the next day, MacArthur put his arm round Halsey's shoulder, saying, "Well, you win, Bill." Future boundary adjustments were amicable.

The hard knocks Marshall had anticipated in his message to Roosevelt began with a painful reassessment of manpower requirements. Draft deferments for occupational, medical, and family reasons had left the army short by 200,000 men at the end of 1943. Of the 5 million occupational deferments for industry and agriculture, one-third of the men in question were either not yet fathers, or were under twenty-six. Marshall wanted such cases reassessed. Further, he had discovered that medical deferments included two prominent athletes turned down by army doctors, and a former major league catcher placed on limited duty because he had once broken two fingers. It was scandalous, he objected to Colonel Sexton at the Pentagon. If a man who can catch a fast ball "can't handle a machine gun, I am no soldier."

In January he had asked General McNarney to look into the exemption of Frank Sinatra for a punctured eardrum that did not affect his nightclub performances. It seemed puzzling to Marshall, as ears were "vital to a musician, vocal or instrumental." Although he had to accept the full medical report, Marshall grumbled anyway about deferments that seemed "damned nonsense." He also knew that service athletic teams rescued many football and baseball stars, college and professional, at least temporarily, from throwing grenades or brandishing rifles. They heaved footballs and swung bats. Few became combat casualties. No other nation eliminated such military potential for so little cause. Marshall was frustrated. Popularity in the national pastimes was power.

Brains were easier to deal with than brawn. One drastic manning decision he made, although it disturbed Roosevelt, was to wash out much of the Army Specialized Training Program, which had sent 145,000 soldiers after basic training to college campuses to study such subjects as languages, medicine, and engineering. While it preserved some intellectual capital, it was highly elitist. All but 35,000 would be reassigned to Army Ground Forces. ASTP troops soon abroad had referred hopefully to the academic assignments as "All Safe 'Till Peace." Marshall, however, had to balance public and private perception of wartime risks taken and avoided.

Only days before, he had learned of the death in action of Private Stephen Hopkins, eighteen and a marine, in the landing on Kwajalein Atoll. Young Hopkins had been killed in his first day in combat, carrying ammunition to a machine-gun unit.

Marshall broke the news to Sir John Dill in Washington, and both wrote to Harry Hopkins, then in Florida recuperating from what would be a long illness and further surgery at the Mayo Clinic. Dill himself, now failing, was still hard at work reconciling Churchill to American priorities and had only a few months left. Replying to Marshall, Hopkins hoped that he would not, in sympathy, retrieve his son Robert from action in the Mediterranean. (A third son, David, was on a carrier in the Pacific.) "The blow was hard and biting," Hopkins conceded, "but I am overwhelmingly proud of Stephen. . . . I am sure he died as gallantly as he lived through a short but happy life. As for Robert, I hope you will not send for him. The last time I saw him in Tunis he told me he wanted to stay until we got to Berlin—in fact we have both agreed to meet there."*

While Anzio, Cassino, and Salerno stalled expensively, affecting the reputations of some American subordinate commanders, Alexander and Wilson—their British planners—remained unscathed. Churchill conceded to Montgomery that Italy had turned into a very bloody war, not merely a contest for a symbol labeled Rome. Marshall cabled Eisenhower sharply, "At long range, it would seem that you gave the enemy too much time to prepare and eventually find yourself up against a very stiff resistance." Defending himself by throwing Churchill, the chief proponent of Italy, into the fray, Eisenhower, stung by the accusation, untypical of Marshall, put aside breakfast and lunch until he could think out a response. Since Churchill had been elated by a foothold up the Italian boot, Eisenhower cabled back unpersuasively, "As a matter of interest to you, I

---

*Worn out by his own wartime service, Hopkins, who would himself die only months after the victory over Japan, was attacked viciously by an anti-FDR newspaper for recuperating at the Army's Ashford General Hospital in White Sulphur Springs, questioning, "Who entitles this representative of Rooseveltian squandermania to treatment and nursing in an Army hospital?" The War Department observed that Hopkins was entitled to medical care as chairman of the Munitions Assignment Board and that the secretary of war had authorized his admission.

received this morning from the Prime Minister a telegram congratulating me on the success of my 'policy of running risks.' I feel certain that some . . . look upon me as a gambler."

In the case of Mark Clark, a Marshall protégé and an Eisenhower crony, the ongoing disasters left Clark embarrassed yet in no risk of removal. Before leaving Italy, Eisenhower persuaded Marshall that Clark "must be left with a tactical command." Paying for it would be Major General John Lucas. Exhausted at Anzio, a poorly conceived operation with which he became saddled, he was replaced by the aggressive Lucian Truscott, whom Eisenhower would soon pluck from Italy for France. "This brings up the question of Lucas," Marshall queried his personnel chief, Lesley McNair. "He has had a wealth of experience and quite evidently is tired out. I want to save his pride. I want to protect his reputation, and, at the same time, get the best benefit of his service. Would you have a place for him? It might be that Eisenhower would like to have him in England to check . . . on the various plans and training they are now in the process of carrying out."

Marshall also sent Jake Devers a list of twenty-three colonels and lieutenant colonels for lower-level replacements as the attrition in Italy remained deep. When Eisenhower, very likely unwilling to face Lucas again, turned Marshall down, he reassigned the general taking the fall for Clark's failures to the Fourth Army at Fort Sam Houston, Texas. In Britain, the press was almost gleeful at American embarrassments, playing up widely a photo of Montgomery leaning down from a tank to shake hands with an obviously displeased (and entrapped) Clark, whose fat Monty was allegedly pulling out of the fire. Clark, a publicity hound nearly a foot taller than Monty had they been standing together, took out his humiliation on subordinates. Alexander's American deputy, Lyman Lemnitzer, thought that Clark should be relieved—an impossibility given his close ties to Marshall and Eisenhower.

The repercussions of stalemate and stagnation in Italy began to raise suppressed misgivings in Eisenhower, who was nagged by Churchill about unutilized assets held in abeyance for "Anvil." Weakening, Eisenhower even began suggesting to Marshall that keeping "Overlord" at designed strength (what the cautious Montgomery called "a good margin all round") might require abandoning a Riviera beachhead. Fighting two wars simultaneously, he complained, was hazarding "Overlord." Although Nimitz continued drawing landing craft from American shipyards, Marshall's deputy Tom Handy reminded Ike that there would be no diversions of LSTs from other operations. Distance and time—and need—

precluded that. In both its theaters, the Pacific was an ongoing, and seaborne, war.

As "Anvil" remained the unwanted stepchild of the Mediterranean command, Eisenhower was persuaded for the moment by Churchill's military secretary, "Pug" Ismay, that Italy should have "the overriding priority over all existing and future operations" in the region. Brooke, who had received a consolation prize from Churchill (for losing "Overlord") of promotion to field marshal, and was committed to the attrition in Italy, charged in his diary, not for the first time, "Eisenhower has got absolutely no strategical outlook and is really totally unfit for the post he holds from an operational point of view." For Marshall, Tom Handy had to warn Eisenhower over the transatlantic telephone about "Anvil," "We better hang on to that as long as we can. I am afraid that you are the people who are going to regret more than anybody else cancelling it in the long run." Marshall would not allow a struggle on the margins to thwart the main event.

With Churchill and Brooke obsessed with Italy and Eisenhower's Supreme Headquarters (SHAEF) in London feeling much less than supreme about sealift, Marshall conceded on March 25 to delaying but not canceling the Riviera landings. Covertly, Churchill's "Mediterranean strategy," he understood, was intended to postpone into oblivion both the Normandy and the Riviera operations. Although realizing that Rome's alleged political significance would vanish with success in France, Marshall agreed to order all newly manufactured landing craft to the U.K., for reshipment after "Overlord" to "Anvil," now moved grudgingly to July 10. After the war, veteran British military critic J. F. C. Fuller identified three stages in the war in mismanaged Italy: the reasonable (occupying Naples), the political (seizing Rome), and "the Daft, from the occupation of Rome onwards." Stages two and three still loomed.

Intuiting that Eisenhower, an outsider in Britain, had an almost obsessive desire to be accepted by the Establishment, Marshall worried frankly in language which closed more strongly than he intended when he began, "I merely wish to be certain that localitis"—British influence—"is not developing and that the pressures on you have not warped your judgment." To reduce the influence of Whitehall, Eisenhower moved SHAEF headquarters from central London to Bushy Park in the southwest suburbs, ostensibly to secure more space. Dated February 12, 1944, and bearing the mark of Marshall, his directive from the Combined Chiefs of Staff began, "You will enter the Continent of Europe and . . . undertake operations aimed at the heart of Germany and the destruction of her armed forces. The date for entering the Continent is the month of May, 1944." The months-old mandate was testing all of Eisenhower's organizational skills.

Although "Overlord" seemed now unstoppable, Marshall felt compelled to cable Churchill, "We appear to be agreed in principle, but quite evidently not as to method." Marshall saw "Anvil" as a link to cross-Channel operations and an opportunity for decisive strategic options on the ground. To divert landing craft from their Pacific destinations was a "sacrifice" only to be made with "complete faith" in crucial alternatives in Europe. Churchill found the shortage of LSTs "absurd." (Clearly Marshall did, too, as shipyards were turning out vast numbers of freighters and even larger and more complex vessels, but Admiral King dominated naval procurement policy.) "How it is," Churchill deplored, with reason, "that the plans of two great Empires like Britain and the United States should be so much hamstrung and limited by a hundred or two of these particular vessels will never be understood by history."

Echoing Churchill, Brooke was sure that the "South of France operation" was pressed by Eisenhower only "to please Marshall," whose "foolish idea" it remained. "It is quite clear to me from Marshall's wire that he does not begin to understand the Italian campaign. . . . He cannot realize that to maintain an offensive a proportion of reserve divisions are required. He considers that this reserve can be withdrawn for a new offensive in the South of France and that the momentum in Italy can still be maintained. Eisenhower sees the situation a little more clearly, but he is too frightened of disagreeing with Marshall to be able to express his views. . . . " Yet there was no momentum in Italy to maintain. Only the depletion of German forces for lack of replacements, and the requirements of defending the Channel coast while holding off the Russians, would create the conditions to restart any movement north. In the end, Maitland Wilson's instructions for Italy would be to contain enemy troops rather than gain territory.

Eisenhower confessed anxiously to Marshall in mid-April that the problems of preparation for "Overlord" were "intricate and difficult beyond belief." Omar Bradley wanted paratroops used behind the expected German lines, and RAF Air Marshall Sir Trafford Leigh-Mallory predicted severe losses in daylight, but conceded, "You'll do it in spite of my opposition." Marshall and Arnold proposed a more ambitious operation—a landing near Evreux, seventy-five miles east of

Caen, to capture airfields that could jeopardize the German hold on Paris and possibly end the war. In a rare objection to Marshall, Eisenhower begged off. It would take all the airborne forces available, he insisted, to support the amphibious operations beyond the beaches. Warned about a repetition of the Sicilian aircraft losses from confused friendly fire, Ike assured Arnold of "new and most distinctive markings" to be painted on planes. On the ground, beach obstacles like hidden bunkers and "Rommel asparagus" at water level might be beyond blasting. But the primary barrier was the Channel itself, seldom less than rough, and often stormy.

Aircraft to protect the landings had to devastate enemy rail facilities in advance, inhibiting reinforcement of shore defenses, and the British War Cabinet (in Churchill's words) "took rather a grave and on the whole an adverse view of the proposal" for concentrated bombing because of the likely deaths of civilians in the impact areas. Paul-Henri Spaak, foreign minister of the exiled Belgian government, had already protested an American strike over a densely populated area. Through an aide, Charles De Gaulle conveyed similar misgivings to Marshall. Eisenhower had Bedell Smith consult Major General Pierre Koenig, head of French forces in the U.K., who, Smith reported to Marshall, remarked despite De Gaulle, "This is War, and it must be expected that people will be killed. We would take twice the anticipated loss to be rid of the Germans."

"There was a French village wrongly bombed by us during the D-Day operation," General Handy recalled, "and it was badly damaged, people killed." He consulted Marshall, who said, "Just tell them you're sorry it happened, and give them a million dollars." Handy procured the funds from the many millions Congress had authorized to Marshall for the supersecret atomic bomb start-up budget, and, just as quietly, the State Department later provided reimbursement.

Casualty estimates by the anxious British exceeded a hundred thousand, but in the end only a tenth of that number of French civilians were killed or injured. When the Royal Navy claimed that it did not have enough warships available for fire support of the American segment of the beachheads, Eisenhower cabled Marshall that "a few more battleships would be very comforting." Marshall turned to Admiral King, who diverted three American battleships from the Mediterranean, supplementing them with two cruisers and thirty-four destroyers. Still another perplexing matter was Roosevelt's continuing antipathy to the obstructionist De Gaulle (and his "Jeanne d'Arc complex") although

Eisenhower needed the Free French to administer liberated French territory.

Alexander's spring offensive in Italy, optimistically code-named "Diadem," and directed at intractable Cassino, opened just after midnight on May 12. One objective was to draw enemy attention, and troops, from Eisenhower's Channel preparations. Since the débacle at Slapton Sands, the Germans had little doubt as to what was coming—the question was where the primary thrust would be. Joseph Goebbels's *Reich* for May 7 declared, "The fortune of war is still in the balance. An unsuccessful invasion would mean final defeat for the enemy. The German nation is more worried in case the invasion does not come, than if it does come. Should the enemy . . . really intend starting an operation, on which everything depends, with such frivolity, well, good night!"

Briefing Secretary Stimson, Marshall minuted, "We are about to invade a continent, and have staked our success on our air superiority, on Soviet numerical preponderance, and on the high quality of our ground combat units." There was no question of the first two. The invasion force would have a preponderant air umbrella. The Red Army kept two-thirds of the Wehrmacht at the Eastern Front. Yet largely untested American foot soldiers, officered mostly by former civilians, were seldom drawn from the top of the top of the quality barrel, and the number of infantry divisions was rigidly limited by Marshall in order to keep the domestic manufacturing and agricultural and transport dimensions at the highest possible level. The United States furnished much of the wherewithal of war for all its allies. Even the Russians moved on American trucks and railway cars pulled by American locomotives, shipped at great hazard past ravenous U-boats. Marshall counted upon a relatively quick conclusion to the war once Germany, its resiliency sapped by mounting attrition, took a hammering from east and west. He had no idea of the resiliency of the *Reich*. In a police state, people were too cowed to demonstrate their disillusionment, and many key war industries were manned by slave labor, and housed underground. Railways, constantly interdicted from the air, were restored by night.

Despite the blackout relating to "Overlord," which was inadvertently broken, but not dangerously, by a few braggarts and inebriates,* a major briefing was planned for May 15 on Eisenhower's return from another inspection of Allied divisions. He had already visited twenty-two. His invariable question to an enlisted man was, "Where are you from?" His next was usually, "What did you do before the war?" (MacArthur's inspections were rare, and generally silent.)

At the imposing redbrick St. Paul's School in the comparative safety of Hammersmith in west London (and since relocated), more than 150 senior officers and political elite gathered on the morning of May 15, a Monday, for a review of final "Overlord" plans. In the audience were the King, Churchill, the War Cabinet, the British chiefs of staff, and what the confidential minutes boasted were "the greatest assembly of military leadership the world has ever known." The school (its students had evacuated to Crowthorne) was also the temporary headquarters of General Montgomery's 21st Army Group. He was an old boy of St. Paul's. Now he had taken it over. Somehow, neither invitees' gossip nor German intelligence breached the security of the lengthy session, which lasted until 5:15 P.M. In his diary Brooke badmouthed every presenter but the "excellent" Montgomery, and George VI ("a few well-chosen remarks").

Presiding was Eisenhower, who was dismissed by Brooke as "no real director of thought, plans, energy or direction! Just a coordinator—a good mixer, a champion of inter-allied cooperation, and in those respects few can hold a candle to him. But is that enough? Or can we not find all qualities of a commander in one man?" (The conference coincided with a meeting of Commonwealth prime ministers, including Australia's Curtin, who "is entirely in MacArthur's pocket [and] was afraid we were trying to oust MacArthur!") Summoning Brooke as usual to a bedroom discussion two days after St. Paul's, Churchill complained about the swollen rear-area logistics described by Lieutenant General Humfrey Gale, which in-

*One was Major General Henry J. F. Miller, a West Point classmate of Eisenhower, overheard in the hotel dining room at Claridge's on April 18. Despite a personal appeal, he was reduced to his permanent grade of colonel by Eisenhower, and sent to the U.S. for medical observation. Ike told Marshall (May 21, 1944) as further cases surfaced that he could "cheerfully shoot the offender[s] myself." It was "almost enough to give one the shakes." MI5 investigated military writer Captain (Ret.) Basil Liddell Hart for possessing details of the landing sites, even to their code names. Although he claimed unconvincingly to General Hastings Ismay and Brigadier Ian Jacob of Churchill's staff that he had worked it all out for himself, they could pin down no source for the security breach. Liddell Hart was later privy to official secrets, and even knighted.

cluded a thousand clerks and, allegedly, "one lorry for every 5 men." Compared to American backup, it was trifling.

As "Overlord" neared and Eisenhower began turning for weather forecasts for the Channel from the senior meteorologist for SHAEF, RAF Group Captain James Stagg, briefly the most important person in Britain, he received news from Italy that Marshall's stepson Allen Tupper Brown had been killed at Anzio. One of the last messages that Ike wrote before D-Day was a cable of condolence to the Marshalls. The costs of Cassino and Anzio were heavy. Not until June 3 was resistance broken at Anzio. On May 29, as Lieutenant Allen Brown had led his tank platoon against heavy resistance south of the Alban Hills, he rose in his turret to survey the German line. A sniper fired. Brown died instantly. At his stepson's urging, Marshall had hastened Allen's assignment to North Africa. When the First Armored Division went to Italy, Allen went with it.

Allen's first letter to him had come in the summer of 1930 when the boy was twelve, and his mother wanted Marshall to visit her family to ensure that the children would approve of her remarriage. Allen thought he was wonderful. "I hope you will come to Fire Island," he wrote. "Don't be nervous. It is O.K. with me. A friend in need is a friend indeed." Marshall wrote to him every few days, noting in April 1944, "Your mother seems to take the situation with considerable calm, though I imagine it is largely a matter of repressing feelings. In any event she never refers to it." On May 29, Katherine had heard from both sons, who were briefly together before Allen left for the Anzio beachhead.

Unaware, Marshall was at the Capitol for a morning meeting with congressmen. He then left with Admiral King for the annual Governors' Conference at Hershey, Pennsylvania, chauffeured by Marjorie Payne, a WAC. Forty-four of the forty-eight state chief executives attended. Marshall had already appeared before the American Society of Newspaper Editors, the Business Advisory Council, and other national organizations since the beginning of the year. King spoke first, and briefly, from a prepared script and received polite attention. Marshall used no notes. As Brigadier General Robert Cutler, who also accompanied them, recalled, the chief of staff needed none. "In his low but clear voice, speaking carefully articulated and exactly formed sentences, he gave an accounting of the military activities in each theater of war all over the globe." After an hour and a quarter, Marshall sat down, and Governor Leverett Saltonstall of Massachusetts asked his colleagues to give a standing vote of thanks to both speakers. Once Marshall and King were seated again, the governors broke into applause.

The next day, Memorial Day but with work as usual, just after Sergeant Payne delivered Marshall to the Pentagon and waited in the outer office to ensure she had no further instructions, the general strode out again grimly. Cora Thomas, his secretary, who had been with him since his first days as chief of staff, realized that it would be an untypical morning. "You'd better run," Miss Thomas said. "Something is up."

As Sergeant Payne turned the key in the ignition to return Marshall to Quarters One at Fort Myer, he closed the car door and told her what she had already understood.

Allen had died, Katherine Marshall would write, "on the road to Rome."

10

"A Satisfactory Foothold"

As "Overlord" loomed, gale-force winds and gloomy, low clouds kept the Channel impassable. Thousands of waiting aircraft, from heavy bombers to engineless gliders, were fueled and armed, or packed with jittery paratroops. From battleships to landing craft, a constellation of vessels heaved at anchor; tens of thousands of infantrymen crowded wallowing transports, their days and nights of waiting anxious and often unfed. June 4 came and went.

Awaiting opportune D-Day weather, Eisenhower released an announcement to "Soldiers, Sailors, and Airmen of the Allied Expeditionary Force," but meant as much for the press, about embarking on a "Great Crusade" for which they had prepared "these many months." Although their task "would not be an easy one," he had full confidence in success. Perhaps that was implied in the code signal for the operation: "Mickey Mouse."

Early on the 5th, as the invasion paused on hold, Eisenhower, in the main hall of the Naval War College in Portsmouth, the "Overlord" command center, drafted a message of a different sort. Every contingency had to be anticipated. His uneven capitalization and shaky prose betrayed suppressed emotions less assured than the traditional proclamation. "Our landings in the Cherbourg-Havre area," he began, "have failed to gain a satisfactory foothold and the troops have been withdrawn." Then he began again, eliminating the passive voice and its evasion of responsibility. Rewriting, he took charge of his reputation with ". . . and I have withdrawn the troops. My decision to attack at this time and place was based on the best information available. The troops, the air and the Navy did all that Bravery and devotion to duty could do. If any blame or fault attaches to the attempt it is mine alone." He folded the paper and slipped it into his wallet for possible use, putting it aside a week later. At 4 A.M. he had to order the operation under way for early on June 6, or cancel, and risk its unraveling. "Okay," he told the officers awaiting a signal, "we'll go."

What remained of June 5 was hectic with conferences and inspections. After Kay Summersby covered the four stars on Eisenhower's red license plate for security, he visited airborne troops that evening. They were preparing to jump off. At 1:15 A.M., already Tuesday, June 6, he returned with Kay to spend the few presummer hours of darkness that were left in his command "caravan" (to Americans a "trailer") in the woods at Southwick,* just north of Portsmouth, tensely awaiting the first telephoned reports from the beachheads. "All you can do is be there [with him]," she wrote in a memoir published after his death, "—and bite your tongue. It meant a lot to me that I was the person he chose to be with in those crucial hours. If Ike had wished, he could have been surrounded by top brass . . . , by any of the important personages who were gathered just a few miles away in Portsmouth. But he preferred to wait in solitude."

Fifteen minutes later—it was 7:30 P.M.† in Washington on Monday—George Marshall was at the Soviet Embassy to accept the Order of Suvorov from Ambassador Andrei Gromyko. Russia's highest military decoration for foreigners, it recognized an early hero of the Napoleonic wars. Although Marshall knew that the first paratroops were then touching down in Normandy, he betrayed no anxiety. As soon as he could escape the lengthy vodka reception he returned to Fort Myer, and to bed. There was no reason to stay up sleeplessly for news. It would come.

In the Berghof eyrie at Berchtesgaden, Hitler appeared confident as he awaited "the Second Front." Even the pullback from Rome, with German troops withdrawing to establish a new redoubt along the Apennines, failed to discourage him. Unlike Churchill, Hitler considered Italy a sideshow. Eisenhower's deception, disinformation, and diversionary tactics, intended to spread the Wehrmacht thin in the west, suggested landings from Norway to Calais to Cherbourg, at the tip of the Cotentin Peninsula, which projected into the Channel. To Ambassador Oshima, who soon radioed the exchange to Tokyo, and unknowingly, also, to an

---

*Southwick House itself, a mansion just above Portsmouth, was the headquarters of Admiral Sir Bertram Ramsay, naval commander for "Overlord."
†Britain was on war-mandated Double Summer Time, two hours advanced from Greenwich Mean Time.

American intercept station, Hitler boasted, "No matter when it comes or at what point, I have made adequate preparations to meet it. In Finland we have seven divisions; in Norway twelve; in Denmark six; in France and the Low Countries sixty-two. . . . I have gotten together as many armored divisions as possible, including four SS divisions and the Hermann Göring Division. But how vast is that sea coast! It would be utterly impossible for me to prevent some kind of landing somewhere or other! . . . I would just like to see the Anglo-Saxons come on and try to stage an invasion!"

"Does your Excellency have any idea where they may land?"

"Honestly, I can only say that I don't know. The most effective area would be along the Straits of Dover [at Calais], but to land there would require much preparation and the difficulties would be great. I don't think that the enemy will run such a risk." Patton had been put in command of a fake army poised to cross to Calais, and German generals took it seriously. Why else would a Patton be assigned to it?

"Of course," Hitler reminded Oshima, "everything which I am telling you is said in the utmost confidence, but I can assure you that I have plenty of plans. . . . Besides, don't forget our coming retaliation against England. We are going to do it principally with rocket artillery. Everything is now ready. . . . We also have ready two thousand *Schnellbomber*." The "fast bombers" (at 250 miles an hour) were not conventional aircraft. A primitive cruise missile, soon christened "doodle-bug" by the ordinary Brit, who was the target of the fear offensive, the "V-1" was a cheaply constructed pilotless jet, little more than a flying bomb, targeted at London and southern England. Sixty-seven ramps were being readied from the Pas de Calais to Holland. British intelligence had known of the devices, intended primarily to provoke terror, and had bombed concealed concrete launching sites unsuccessfully for months. Only their seizure could neutralize them.

In the expected invasion week, despite Hitler's hopes, the V-1 ramps were not yet ready. Instead, the Luftwaffe sent twin-engine bombers over London. "With all these [secret weapons]," he claimed, "I believe we can gradually regain the initiative and, seizing our opportunities, turn once again against Russia." When Oshima expressed his satisfaction, Hitler assured him, "I, for one, believe that this is the year that will decide who wins and who loses, and I have plans and calculations that will turn the tables by this fall."

Since the weather in the Channel seemed likely to get worse, reducing the imminence of a landing, Field Marshal Rommel chanced going home to Ulm for the birthday of his wife, Lucie. His staff meteorologist forecast Force 7 gales in the Cherbourg sector and Force 6 in the Pas de Calais. Even if the heavy skies cleared and the winds abated, the tides would not be right for an assault for another two weeks, if then.

At two in the morning on June 6, six gliders with airborne troops landed near two bridges spanning the Canal de Caen and the River Orne, capturing the spans intact. A half-hour later, parachute troops began landing east of the Orne. By dawn, after hours of air strikes and shelling by warships offshore, British, Canadian, and American divisions were disembarking from landing craft on the Cotentin Peninsula below Cherbourg, and the Normandy coast. The Führer had warned of attempts to lure defending forces away from what he anticipated would be the primary landing areas, and his adjutants worried that awakening him early with news of beachheads in Normandy would be conveying premature information. Dummy parachutists had been dropped in some areas. Patton's phantom army might cross to the Pas de Calais.

Russian and German offensives in the east had involved far greater masses of men and matériel, but they had been land operations. For D-Day, more than two thousand aircraft had to be coordinated so that they did not strike each other in flight nor rain fire (as some did) on Allied forces. Nearly seven thousand vessels with nearly 200,000 naval and merchant marine personnel had to cover and disembark 156,000 troops close enough to the beaches to give them a chance to make it ashore. Fifteen hospital ships stood by, and emptied landing craft were to be reutilized if necessary to convey more wounded. Eight thousand doctors were with the divisions. Since it took, usually, eight or nine rear area personnel for every fighting man to support an operation, far more than a million soldiers, sailors, and airmen were involved.

The magnitude of the mission, and its complexity, guaranteed that things would go wrong and that the unexpected would happen. Some landings proved perilously on the edge of disaster. Troops too heavily laden, or debarked from LSTs too far offshore, drowned; others were casualties to mistaken friendly fire; tanks and artillery were swamped in the strong surf. Only five of the first thirty-two amphibious tanks launched toward Omaha Beach made it ashore. The veteran U.S. 1st Division and a regiment of the 29th met fierce resistance from the German 325th Division, forcing troops to disembark under fire in rough water.

Some things went according to plan. Utah Beach on the Cotentin eastern coast was subjected to the least opposition and the U.S. 4th Infantry Division quickly secured a beachhead. British and Canadian troops securing Gold, Juno, and Sword beaches to the east fared better. American casualties approached 7,000, including 1,465 known dead and 1,928 missing, half of them from the two U.S. airborne divisions, most of the others at Omaha. The airborne drop to secure roads and bridges from the interior involved 13,000 paratroops in 822 transports, flying hazardously in darkness to jump beyond Utah at 1:30 A.M. Missed drop zones, scattering of units, lost equipment, and strong German resistance were all anticipated—and happened.

British and Canadian casualties on the first day were about 3,000. The losses, though painful, and marked for days by corpses washing ashore, did not approach Churchill's sanguinary prophecies made at nearly every planning conference as he attempted to doom "Overlord" by indefinite delay. Unable to do anything across the Channel but listen to reports of how prearranged moves were playing out, Eisenhower cabled Marshall at 8:00 A.M. London time that preliminary reports were "satisfactory."

Eisenhower had not been able to persuade De Gaulle, who stubbornly pulled 200 French National Committee liaison officers from the operation, to accept the invasion forces as a temporary civilian authority. Meanly, he sent messages to his agents warning the French not to accept Allied military currency, but to treat it as counterfeit. His envoy in Washington went to Marshall nevertheless to ask that De Gaulle be conveyed to France on a battleship as head of state. According to Marshall's deputy, General Tom Handy, "He shot the paint off the walls," exploding, "No sons of Iowa will fight to put up statues of De Gaulle in France." But Iowans were about to fight and die anyway. In time, images of De Gaulle would materialize in Normandy, but he would arrive, like Allied troops before him, on a landing craft.

In Italy, another irate general, Mark Clark, complained about the invasion, "The sons-of-bitches—they didn't even let us have the newspaper headlines for the fall of Rome for one day!" Yet Rome had its day—the 5th. By the next day, Pope Pius XII's appreciation to both belligerents for leaving Rome intact appeared in small print in the *New York Times*, which headlined, ALLIED ARMIES LAND IN FRANCE. . . . GREAT INVASION IS UNDER WAY. In Belorussia (now Belarus), where the massive "Operation Bagration"—for Prince Peter Bagration, who bested Napoleon at Borodino—was being readied, to begin on June 22 (the third anniversary of the German attack), correspondent Vasily Grossman noted some brief excitement among the troops. "On the subject of the Second Front. Great enthusiasm on the first day. Spontaneous meetings, shooting, saluting, then a sharp decrease of interest."

Montgomery failed in his D-Day objective of taking Caen, the gateway to the River Seine. Pausing stalemated on its outskirts for more than a month he dithered away his chances of taking the crucial Falaise Gap. He reported to Eisenhower by radio nevertheless that all units were on the ground to stay. Disappointingly too, Cherbourg, urgently desired as a supply port, would not fall to Bradley and Collins until June 27, its harbor by then rendered unusable by the surrendering Germans, who hung tough. Without inland terrain where runways could be built, Allied air support in the overcast had to come from bases in southern England. Nonetheless, Eisenhower confirmed on the BBC that all beachheads were in place.

On the morning of June 7, he crossed from Portsmouth to Omaha Beach on the minelayer HMS *Aurora*, to confer on board with local commanders. Maneuvering in too close, the *Aurora* grounded on a sandbar and the high brass aboard transferred gingerly to another Royal Navy vessel. Ashore, where Montgomery joined the group, mountains of equipment and supplies were being unloaded and a "Mulberry" artificial harbor towed into place. The floating artillery of Allied warships still boomed salvos beyond the steep slopes to drive defenders back. Boarding a destroyer for his three-hour return, Eisenhower slept hard.

In England on the 8th, he held an off-the-record press conference, describing the beachheads as still "hazardous." By June 11 they had merged into a shallow but continuous sixty-mile front. The Germans had not driven the Allies off, but would reinforce their defenses across the natural barriers of rivers and *bocage*—hedgerows—more quickly than planners of the massive bombing and shelling preliminaries thought possible. Now eager to associate himself with the landings he had resisted, Churchill, with Brooke, crossed to Normandy on a British destroyer on D+6, through what he cabled to Stalin was a fifty-mile "city of ships" that had already landed more than 400,000 troops. In his postwar memoirs, reinventing his history, he wrote that he returned "full of confidence in the execution of our long-cherished design."

Flying to England, Marshall, King, and Arnold boarded the U.S. destroyer *Thompson* at Portsmouth. Transferring to a PT boat close in, they reached the Omaha and Utah beachheads, serviced by the huge, anchored "Mulberry." The relentless activity resembled an overturned anthill. Plowing back across the Channel with Eisenhower, Marshall confided that his own job was in Ike's future. "Why do you think we have been pushing you? When the war is over I expect you will have ten years of hard work ahead of you." Ike was just short of fifty-five.

Drained by the unremitting tension of "Overlord" preparations, Eisenhower responded wearily, "General, I hope then to have a long rest."

Returning from Portsmouth, Allied brass dined with the PM on Churchill's special train en route to London. Aboard, intent on recognizing Mountbatten's Combined Operations elements that had helped "Overlord" to succeed, Marshall drafted an appreciative cable to the admiral, who had long been a target of skeptics. All the brass signed it.

Satisfied by the "remarkable scale of efficiency" of organization on the beaches and the unexpected, yet temporary, brilliant weather, Marshall radioed to Roosevelt and Stimson, "Eisenhower and his Staff are cool and confident, carrying out an affair of incredible magnitude and complication with superlative efficiency. I think we have these Huns at the top of the toboggan slide, and the full crash of the Russian offensive should put the skids under them. There will be hard fighting and the enemy will seize every opportunity for a skillful counter stroke, but I think he faces a grim prospect." Marshall also prepared a statement for the service *Stars and Stripes* expressing pride in the "aggressive action, skill, and high morale displayed by the American soldier."

In some matters, the British quickly exceeded American efficiency. A major who had been in the first tank assault wave wrote to a colleague in England, "Some of the troop leaders had no trouble recognising their parts of the beach. They said the aerial photographs showed a gun in a certain spot and there it was, but neither the air force nor the bombardment had taken it out, so they did." Since D+5 they had been "living well, with our mess lorry nicely outfitted, and it is good to see a well set up mess table with linen and silver and, not the least, the operational whiskey which we saved."

Some of the action was occurring on the English side of the Channel. Just after Marshall's party returned to London for meetings with their British counterparts, three waves of flying bombs crashed down. It was a week after D-Day. Although Eisenhower dismissed the no-longer-secret weapon to Marshall as "very much of a nuisance," it seemed more than that when one exploded near his quarters. Only four of the first twenty-seven reached London, one of them killing two people in Bethnal Green. That night more than 150 more were launched, fifty landing in the London area. Only twenty were intercepted by AA-fire or fighter planes. Sixty worshipers were killed when a V-1 fell on the Guards Chapel during a service. To suppress panic, as the blind, impersonal weapon offered little warning but the cutoff of its buzz, air raid sirens were no longer sounded.

Meeting with Rommel and Rundstedt near Metz, just below Luxembourg, on June 17, Hitler rejected appeals to permit troops to withdraw beyond the range of Allied artillery in order to prepare a counterattack, ordering them to relinquish nothing, and "fight to the death." After radioing for panzer reinforcements from the Eastern Front, he slipped back to Berchtesgaden, where he remarked to his coterie that Rommel had "lost his nerve."

Through June 18, seven hundred flying bombs were launched. About two hundred of them were shot down. In the first sixteen days of the terror offensive, until stockpiles of the V-1 needed replenishing, nearly 2,000 civilians were killed and 6,000 injured, and hundreds of houses destroyed. Hitler hoped that his lines in Normandy would hold long enough to gain time to devise and produce more, and further, "miracle" weapons which might turn the war around.

The Combined Chiefs of Staff met on June 14 and June 15 in Churchill's underground war rooms ("No. 10 Annexe"), where Brooke as the PM's spokesman urged "the possibilities of exploiting the Italian situation by an advance eastward, based eventually on Trieste." Marshall rejected it as another ruse to substitute the Balkans for the south of France, but Eisenhower would be badgered after Marshall and Arnold departed for the Mediterranean. There they endured more Churchillian evasions from Maitland Wilson, who wanted to delay "Anvil" to August 15 if he could not do away with it altogether.

At Ike's request, Marshall had orders cut for John Eisenhower on graduation from West Point, to join his father. The two Eisenhowers flew with Air Marshal Tedder to Normandy on June 15, to newly liberated Bayeux, and to a conference with Montgomery north of Caen. The new lieutenant was struck by Monty's peculiar garb ("his only concession to proper uniform was the black tanker's beret") and his "chirping, birdlike voice." After a second visit, this time to Omaha Beach and Omar Bradley, John was flown home—London to Prestwick to Reykjavik to Bangor to Washington—in his father's personal B-17, accompanied by Ike's aide, Colonel Ernest R. ("Tex") Lee, and Kay Summersby, who was carrying papers endorsed by Ike for her commission in the Women's Army Corps. As irregular precedent, three Australian women in MacArthur's Brisbane headquarters had been commissioned before Washington could intervene, one the mistress of General Sutherland.

Eisenhower's request that Kay be made a WAC lieutenant—he intended to have her personally sworn as an officer in Washington—was objected to by WAC Colonel Oveta Culp Hobby and Marshall's senior staff. Frank McCarthy sent a message to Marshall on July 8 explaining why Kay should not be commissioned—and that Eisenhower had "specifically" told his aide "that you were not to be troubled with this." Considering "the *personal* aspects of the appointment," McCarthy added, leaving the interpretation to Marshall, he believed that his attached draft memorandum as if written by Major General M. G. White, an assistant chief of staff, would keep Marshall out of the loop and "accomplish the purpose." Eisenhower was cabled the next day by McCarthy in WAR62711 that with Summersby's case on hold, she had been sent briefly to Florida on a holiday. White would be sending by air to London, with Colonel Lee, a confidential message. "There are some complications as a result of which General White thinks it best to bring you a personal memorandum from him."

White's lengthy memorandum (WDGAP210 1WAC), silently revised by Marshall, explained that WAC enlistees had to be American citizens and that the existence of a lengthy Officer Candidate School waiting list would require the double exception of a direct commission that would be "so embarrassing, not only to me, but to the Chief of Staff and to you." Still, if the matter was "of such importance" as to ignore all the rules, General White (as if Marshall were not involved) would recommend a waiver. That such high-level handling, on both sides of the Atlantic, of an essentially indiscreet and improper trifle took priority amidst the most massive combined military operation in history boggles the mind.

On July 16, 1944, Eisenhower cabled, "Please drop the matter." Kay returned, and Ike raised it again later in the year, personally, to Frank McCarthy. Marshall overruled further objections, remarking, Mrs. Hobby recalled, that "he never felt like telling a man who was responsible for winning a war not to do little things that he thought would help him win the war." In any case it was a belated quid pro quo for MacArthur's lack of oversight in Australia.

Mamie had been present in July to greet John, and—awkwardly—Kay. Much later, John's daughter Susan contended that the pairing for the flight with John proved that the most lurid gossip already current about Eisenhower and his glamorous aide could not be true. "It is inconceivable that Ike would have sent his 'lover' to the United States in the care of his son." By that reasoning, it may have been a clever gambit on Eisenhower's part, and when Mamie treated her briefly in Washington (so Kay later wrote) "like a favorite niece," the colorful rumors allegedly diminished. In October, after her reapplication, Kay Summersby was commissioned as a WAC, and in December Eisenhower promoted her to first lieutenant.

After Normandy, Marshall visited Rome and Naples, and in the co-pilot's seat of a "puddle-jumper" he flew in stormy weather over the current lines, and the Salerno-Anzio area. With his brother-in-law Colonel Tristram Tupper, Allen's uncle, who was with General Devers's headquarters, Marshall paid his respects at his stepson's grave. "I see by the papers here," he wrote to Allen's widow, Madge, from his hotel in Rome, "that I am being criticized because they turned on the hot water in honor of my arrival. Also they apparently moved one or two newspaper men out of their rooms to accommodate our party, which didn't please."

Returning to Washington after two weeks in motion, Marshall radioed MacArthur about relevant discussions in London, commenting obliquely on the latest Japanese decrypts. The enemy, Marshall warned, could figure out where MacArthur's next attacks were likely to be, possibly Palau and Mindanao, because of their geographical inevitability. "There will be less opportunity to move against his weakness and to his surprise, as has been the case in your recent series of moves." Marshall implied the strategic virtues of doing the unexpected, and MacArthur would follow through.

"Accelerating operations" as described to MacArthur was Pentagon code for bypassing the Philippines, and he had objected to that as "unsound." He wanted to land on Mindanao by mid-October and then leap to Leyte, just to the north. Using the former Japanese invasion route via Lingayen Gulf, he planned to reach Luzon early in the new year, to establish heavy bomber bases there, he claimed—but Marshall almost certainly remembered MacArthur's refusal to use Luzon on the day after Pearl Harbor to order air strikes toward Formosa. Although he knew that MacArthur wanted to recover the Philippines, especially Manila and Corregidor, for personal as well as political reasons, what price should pride play in Pacific strategy?

Even had there been no military considerations, such as cutting enemy communications "to the South and to secure a base for our further advance," MacArthur insisted, rewriting, like Churchill, his own history, and adding some intended blackmail, "Philippines is American Territory where our unsupported forces were destroyed by the enemy. . . . We have a great national obligation to discharge. Moreover if the United States should deliberately bypass the Philippines, leaving our prisoners, nationals, and loyal Filipinos in enemy hands without an effort to retrieve them at earliest moment we would incur the gravest psychological reaction." Again he implied a threat he had no intention of carrying out, fantasizing further a hero's welcome on American soil that he would orchestrate to the discomfort of the War Department and the White House. "I request," he closed sharply, "that I be accorded the opportunity of personally proceeding to Washington to present fully my views."

Unpersuaded, Marshall suggested in return, identifying concerns about "the collapse of resistance in China," MacArthur's bypassing the Philippines for Formosa (Taiwan) "about November 1." That could lead, he cajoled, to operations against the Japanese homeland itself, "the southern tip of Japan proper, Kyushu." Luring out the remaining strength of the Japanese fleet that way, and delivering "a crushing blow" to it, Marshall suggested in all seriousness, would "shorten the war, which means the reconquest of the Philippines." Since he realized that MacArthur would not return to America unless ordered to do so, Marshall "saw no difficulty about that and if the issue arises [I] will speak to the President who I am certain would be agreeable. . . . Meanwhile we are waiting for a statement of Nimitz' views."

★   ★   ★   ★   ★

On June 22, Marshall's first day back, he radioed to Eisenhower, "We appreciate your problems resulting from the bad weather in the channel," and confirmed that "Anvil" would proceed despite the contrariness of the PM. The weather off Normandy was now bad—far worse than Marshall realized—the worst Channel storm in twenty years. RAF Group Captain Stagg had sent Eisenhower a memorandum noting that had "Overlord" been postponed and rescheduled for the next propitious tides, not only would the catastrophic chaos of debarkation and reembarkation have ensued, the problem would have reoccurred, and in spades. Skies were completely overcast and winds of near gale force began to blow from the northeast early on June 19, wrecking the Cotentin "Mulberry" port and halting resupply. "Thanks," Eisenhower wrote across the bottom of Stagg's memo, "and thank the gods of war we went when we did!"

Although German ability to improvise a stubborn resistance exceeded Allied estimates, Normandy was not a topographical mystery to

Eisenhower's planners or the ground forces commanders. Still, the natural barrier of the deeply rooted *bocage* seemed worth divisions to the Germans. Allied infantry was immobilized by hidden fire from the hedgerows, and neither artillery nor aircraft made much of a difference. During all of July, Bradley's troops advanced less than ten miles into the countryside. Yet it might have been worse. SHAEF cabled Marshall on July 6, a month after the landings, that the "Fortitude" deception was still keeping the German 15th Army north of the Seine at almost full strength, expecting another crossing. "Reliable intelligence," Cable S-55125 reported, "indicates that enemy is [still] preparing for decisive Allied effort by 1st U.S. Army Group in Pas de Calais area under the command of Patton."

Marshall had pressed for a real, not a bogus, diversion elsewhere in France in July, but "Anvil" kept receding as Churchill manipulated deadlines to keep alive his hopes for other adventures in Italy and eastward. "Anvil," the PM insisted, could not "directly influence the present battle in 1944." Urging further intervention, Eisenhower cabled Marshall on June 20, "Wandering off overland via Trieste to Ljubljana is to indulge in conjecture to an unwarranted degree." Exasperated, Marshall drafted a sharp message to Churchill for Roosevelt's signature that squandering "practically all the Mediterranean resources to advance into northern Italy and from there to the northeast is unacceptable to me."

Keeping FDR's political consciousness raised, Marshall sent him every few days, without comment, "a statement of our casualties, . . . graphically and rather in colors, . . . because you get hardened to these things." The president reinforced the cable by adding to Marshall's line "and I really believe we should consolidate our operations and not scatter them." Then, pretending a mutual need to overcome a delaying deadlock in the "Combined Staffs," Roosevelt continued, "You and I must prevent this and I think we should support the views of the ["Overlord"] Supreme Allied Commander. He is definitely for ANVIL and wants action in the field by August 30th preferably earlier." Roosevelt and Marshall had enough of Churchill's Balkans intrigues.

"Anvil" would finally be realized—as a joint American and Gaullist French operation. On July 13, Maitland Wilson reluctantly authorized an army group under General Devers to undertake the invasion of southern France. Eisenhower radioed to Marshall, relieved, "If you want to arrange the American affairs in the Mediterranean so that [Devers] can be free to command ANVIL . . . , I will accept the decision cheerfully and willingly." The operation was renamed "Dragoon"—a mounted British infantryman in earlier wars—to mask the lingering British negativism. Churchill carped that he had been "dragooned" into accepting it.

On July 13, Marshall's memories returned to an earlier July in France. Brigadier General Theodore Roosevelt Jr., brother of the twice-wounded Archie, had died the day before, of a heart attack, at the Fourth Division command post in Normandy. Learning of it the next day, Marshall wrote to Roosevelt's widow of the "close bond" which he and "Ted" had established in July 1918. "The first raid in the Ansauville sector which he directed and Archie led, the early days in the Toul sector and the heavy fighting around Cantigny and later at Soissons, . . . marked him as one of the great battalion and regimental commanders of that vast Army. And in this war, in Tunisia and on the beachhead at Gela [in Sicily], he displayed the same fighting, courageous spirit. I am happy in the thought that he had the satisfaction of going into France in the first wave and that if he was to be stricken down it should come in the midst of the fighting."

Later Marshall recalled to her that, as two sons of the former president were in the same unit, he had been ordered "to see that . . . Ted, personally, did not participate [in the Ansauville operation], in addition to his brother." Yet their father had asked Colonel Marshall to help get Ted back into action, and when, although badly wounded, he went AWOL from the hospital to rejoin his regiment, limping at the head of his men as they advanced toward Sedan, Marshall had covered for him. It was OK to "pull strings," he told Ted's widow, "if what you wanted was a more dangerous job than the one you had."

Following the fiercely contested landing in Normandy, the division commander, Major General Raymond O. Barton, had recommended Roosevelt, who led his men with a walking stick, for a Medal of Honor and a division command. Eisenhower and Bradley had reduced the citation to a DSC, a decision affirmed by the War Department's Decorations Board. Marshall went to Stimson. In mid-August the two quietly overruled the board. Marshall redrafted the now-posthumous accolade. After the presentation at the White House on September 21, Mrs. Roosevelt (another Eleanor, like Mrs. FDR) wrote to Marshall, perhaps guessing the answer to her question, "Ted's citation was one of the most beautiful pieces of writing I have ever seen, especially the part referring to 'his seasoned, precise, calm, and unfaltering leadership.' I wonder if I might know someday who wrote that." Until the first Roosevelt was voted by Congress the same decoration seventy-five years posthumously for his "Rough Riders" feat in 1898, the Medals of Honor to the two MacArthurs had been the only such awards to father and son.

Marshall would learn of the death of another friend and associate on July 25. General Lesley McNair, for years his trusted training chief, and now Patton's bogus-army replacement, was killed in Normandy when American bombers dropped their loads short of the German lines. Marshall would radio Eisenhower on August 1 that he was reining in McNair's pilot and aide, who were revealing the unpleasant facts on their return to Washington. "We are endeavoring to suppress the story here in line with your desire to avoid an[y] air-ground antagonism but this will be futile unless more care is taken on your side." The bungled attack fatally injuring McNair killed 111 Americans and injured 500, although lines had been pulled back more than a mile after a misjudged bombing the day before had killed 25 and wounded 131, prompting enraged GIs to fire on their own planes. According to Bradley, Eisenhower was "completely dejected." Often covered up, many more deaths "in action" would result from misnamed "friendly fire" in every war than a little-forgiving public would ever know.

★　★　★　★　★

Although MacArthur had twice offered to visit the White House to persuade Roosevelt to a Philippines strategy which overruled the navy, he had backed away each time. Yet a chance to meet Roosevelt halfway was coming, and in a way that underlined the president's political opportunism. The major threat to FDR's reelection chances seemed public perception of his declining health. Governor Thomas Dewey of New York, his Republican opponent, was a vigorous forty-two. Campaigning required exposure, and Roosevelt's weight loss showed in his loose-fitting clothes. His heart and lungs were failing, aggravated by the physical demands of his paralysis, and his heavy smoking. Responding to rumors, columnist Dorothy Thompson took to the radio to observe that although FDR was a tired old man, at least as tired and old as Mr. Churchill and Marshal Stalin, Mr. Dewey was obviously not tired. Why should he be?

Demonstrating a continuing ability to govern required some dramatic evidences of active leadership. Roosevelt chose to confer with MacArthur and Nimitz at Honolulu, and would arrive on July 26 on the heavy cruiser *Baltimore*. Marshall and King would remain in Washington. FDR wanted to deal with MacArthur openly and alone. On travel orders, Marshall had him fly as "Mister Catch"—almost certainly Roosevelt's meaningful code identity—and specified no staff. "Purpose," Marshall radioed, "general strategical discussion." To inhibit MacArthur from any political display, Marshall informed Lieutenant General Robert C. Richardson Jr., commander in Hawaii, "I wish you to see that no reference is permitted regarding General MacArthur's presence . . . except in strict accordance with the President's instructions."

No chance then remained for MacArthur to be nominated on the Republican presidential ticket. Dewey had swept the Republican convention, and the colorless, ultraconservative John Bricker, governor of Ohio, had been given second place as a sop to Robert Taft's loyalists. Roosevelt would exploit the meeting in Hawaii to charge his reelection campaign. He arrived in a special train at the San Diego naval base on July 20, as Democratic delegates in Chicago were nominating him by acclamation for a fourth term. He had agreed to Senator Truman of Missouri, considered a political moderate, as his running mate.

From a railway car that evening the president acknowledged the nomination by radio, declaring that he accepted his draft like a soldier. "Today Oklahoma and California are being defended in Normandy and Saipan," he said, "and they must be defended there—for what happens in Normandy and Saipan vitally affects the security and well-being of every human being in Oklahoma and California."

Listeners knew much about Normandy but little about Saipan. Captured by Nimitz's marine and army forces in June and July at a hideous price of 14,111 casualties, the island in the Marianas group became the grave of tens of thousands of Japanese, soldier and civilian. Rather than surrender, some, including women and children, leaped from cliffs into the sea. But Japan was now within bombing range of the new, long-haul B-29s, reserved for Pacific operations.

Since Roosevelt's renomination on July 20 was no surprise, press coverage was easily overtaken by the attempted assassination, on the same day, of Adolf Hitler at his East Prussian headquarters. A bomb hidden in a briefcase under a map table had deafened an ear and lamed his right arm. German radio screamed about dozens of conspirators and alleged conspirators, who were quickly rounded up. Many were horribly executed. To avoid embarrassment, one high-ranking suspect, Field Marshal Rommel, wounded earlier when his staff car was strafed by enemy aircraft, and now recovering, was compelled to take poison. His death was explained away by his injuries. Von Rundstedt presided at his state funeral.

The *Baltimore* anchored at Pearl Harbor on July 26. As Nimitz came aboard to greet the president, who asked whether MacArthur had arrived, a bright red convertible, its siren blasting, pulled up at dockside. It was borrowed through General Richardson, a West Point friend, from the Honolulu fire chief. In familiar leather flight jacket and scrambled eggs cap, the general sat proudly in a rear seat awaiting press cameras. Roosevelt had not seen him since 1937.

From the quarterdeck, FDR shouted, "Hello, Douglas, what are you doing with that leather jacket on? It's damn hot today."

"Well," said MacArthur, who had been with Richardson at Fort Shafter, "I've just flown in from Australia. It's pretty cold up there." At about the same distance below the Equator as Palm Beach is above it, Brisbane was down rather than up, and had never seen a snowflake.

That Marshall, King, and Arnold remained in Washington suggested to MacArthur that he had been summoned only for a political show. He was right—in part. Roosevelt had already made up his mind about where to attack next in the Pacific. MacArthur would have his Philippines route and Nimitz a coordinate path, and MacArthur was to attack well before the election. In November 1942, Eisenhower's push into North Africa, delayed by logistics until just after the midterm election, had cost Roosevelt seats in Congress. A few days had made a difference. The president was not going to have *this* operation delayed beyond the balloting.

MacArthur had spelled out his Philippines case to Marshall by radiogram CX-13891 on June 18. The president had already reviewed it. "Douglas," Roosevelt announced, "I'm taking that car," and for six hours in the fire-red convertible, with other vehicles fore and aft, he and the general toured sites already in place to prepare troops for the invasion of Japan. They talked at length, with MacArthur calling the president, as if an intimate friend, "Franklin."

The impromptu tour of Oahu took the president's security detail by surprise, as it did anyone who recognized the pair. When MacArthur and Roosevelt drove through the naval air station at Kaneohe Bay on the northeast coast, Aviation Machinist's Mate Tom Pitoniak, formerly a Westfield, Massachusetts, farmboy, looked up to see two of the most famous men in the world tool by in one of the most unlikely of vehicles for their status. Few others bothered. "It was payday," he remembered, "and the guys playing craps on the Quonset hut porches didn't even bother turning around to see."

At Richardson's posh Waikiki spread that evening, Roosevelt began, as if he did not already know the answer, "Well, Douglas, where do we go from here?" MacArthur offered to land in the Philippines in three months and complete the occupation six months after. He would isolate Japan from its sources of oil and other war matériel in the Netherlands East Indies, strangling the enemy without the bloody frontal assaults on island approaches planned, on King's behalf, by Nimitz. Further, MacArthur contended, a proposed offensive toward Formosa that bypassed the Philippines would leave American invasion forces nakedly open for assault.

Although MacArthur was shocked by Roosevelt's pallor and frailty, their talks went on amiably until nearly midnight and resumed in the morning. In his memoirs MacArthur quoted himself from memory certainly colored very liberally by fiction. No one, not even the imperious MacArthur, would have spoken to his president and commander in chief as he later reconstructed his argument. "Mr. President," he quoted himself (forgetting the "Franklin" and blaming Roosevelt personally for the loss of the Philippines), "the country has forgiven you for what took place on Bataan. You hope to be reelected President of the United States, but the nation will never forgive you if you approve a[ny] plan which leaves 17 million Christian American subjects to wither in the Philippines under the conqueror's heel until the peace treaty frees them. You might do it for reasons of strategy or tactics, but politically, it would ruin you."

In their further chatter he recalled asking, "What chance do you think Dewey has?" Roosevelt quipped that he was too busy with the war to think about politics, and both laughed. Then FDR said, seriously—and here MacArthur seems utterly genuine, as pithy rejoinders often lodge in the memory—"If the war with Germany ends before the election, I will not be reelected." The remark strikingly prefigures the electoral fate of Winston Churchill in 1945.

When MacArthur left Oahu for Brisbane he knew he had won his case. On August 9, having sailed to the naval base at the Aleutian island of Adak and then eastward toward California, Roosevelt radioed MacArthur, "As soon as I get back I will push on that plan [of yours], for I am convinced that as a whole it is logical and can be done. . . . Some day there will be a flag raising in Manila—and without question I want you to do it." He added, warmly, that it was "a particular happiness" to see MacArthur again. "I wished very much in Honolulu that you and I could swap places—and personally I have a hunch that you would make much more a go as President than I would as general in the retaking of the Philippines."

By the time that Roosevelt returned to Washington, the renamed "Dragoon" was on in the south of France—yet Churchill had tried one last time to abort it. Late on August 5, the PM telephoned Eisenhower to invite himself for lunch the next day at Ike's Southwick headquarters. Ike had yet to relocate across the Channel. Churchill argued again to cancel the landing and augment troops in Italy. Eisenhower cabled Marshall afterward, "I will not, repeat not, under any conditions agree to cancellation of Dragoon."

Finally launched on August 15, the early action by Jake Devers's Sixth Army Group was followed from the destroyer HMS *Kimberley* by Churchill, who intended to identify himself with the unwanted operation now that it was succeeding. "I had at least done the civil thing to Anvil," he claimed falsely in his memoirs, "and indeed I thought it was a good thing I was near the scene to show the interest I took in it."

What "Dragoon" furnished, in addition to a rapid route into the French interior, was a major harbor which resistance and destruction in the north had denied. Marseilles was captured quickly and undamaged. Through December it would unload more tonnage than any other Allied port. Within two weeks, Devers's forces had made contact with Eisenhower's troops from the north. Since, in his deliberate command style, Montgomery had vacillated about capturing Caen, claiming as always insufficient force—although by July 4 there were already over a million men in Normandy—the breakout had to come from Bradley's (and Collins's) troops moving toward the base of the Cotentin Peninsula and beyond. Although Monty—"a tired little fart," Patton scoffed—had the political clout to set the boundaries between his 21st Army Group and Bradley's command, on August 1, Patton's Third Army under Bradley was turned loose, driving eastward with the First Army of Courtney Hodges on his left, below Caen. The toll in German prisoners—and dead—was great, and in the British press, which knew nothing yet of Patton's presence, the successes were credited to the nonexistent enterprise of Montgomery.

Stalin's cable to Churchill, "Congratulations on your brilliant victory at Caen," was made much of by London newspapers. Yet Monty's sluggishness prompted Eisenhower to remind him that Churchill had "repeated over and over again that he knew you understood the necessity for 'keeping the front aflame.'" To Marshall, Eisenhower explained Montgomery's lack of progress as topographically handicapped in every way—across difficult hedgerows and marshes and ditches; through rain and mud and under overcast skies; and on underpowered artillery, tanks, and ammunition. Yet the hedgerow country was largely on Bradley's side of the command boundary.

The advance of the American armies threatened to outrun supplies, but Marshall resisted J. C. H. Lee's appeals for direct shipments from the U.S. He ordered Lee (through Eisenhower) to draw from the millions of tons of matériel in Britain, which otherwise would have to be liquidated after the war. Yet what was stockpiled in Britain was often not what was needed.

With the breakout from Normandy under way, Marshall and Arnold took a week for fishing in the High Sierras, using the president's plane and keeping in touch by radio and by courier. When a pouch with classified messages was mistakenly dropped in the woods two miles from their camp, Marshall was furious. Search parties were ordered in several directions, one setting off several fires in trying to signal. The pouch was found intact and sealed just before their return to Washington, where FDR, exasperated by Montgomery's lack of progress and Eisenhower's remoteness in England, told Marshall, "Tell Ike to get over there."

The perception, Marshall recalled, was Eisenhower "wasn't in the show and Montgomery was the sole, dominant figure." But the move was not easy. Communications had to be reestablished and a temporary headquarters erected. For two days, the Supreme Commander was only physically in France, more out of touch than in London.

Once Eisenhower moved his command post of tents and trailers to an orchard southwest of Bayeux, Marshall also urged Ike to take overall command. The move and its purpose was no secret. Reacting to preemptive protests in the British press about the forthcoming "demotion" of Monty, Churchill raised him on no military grounds to field marshal. "I consider this step necessary from the point of view of the British nation with whom Montgomery's name is a household word," Churchill informed Eisenhower, adding dishonestly, "It, of course, makes no difference in the military relations prevailing between Montgomery and other high-ranking American officers." But Monty now outranked them all, even Marshall and Monty's own ostensible boss, General Brooke.

On August 28, Brooke carped to his diary that Eisenhower's assumption of ground command as of September 1 was "likely to add another 3 to 6 months on to the war!" Yet Paris had fallen—like Rome, little damaged, its liberation not expected by Churchill before Christmas. On August 25, De Gaulle reentered with a symbolic, U.S.-supplied and U.S.-equipped French force backed by an umbrella of Allied might. To Eisenhower's discomfiture De Gaulle immediately began shameless fabrication of the myth that France had liberated itself by its own massive resistance, and that the humiliating surrender in June 1940 and the collaborationist Vichy regime had merely been inconveniences, as were the Allied armies.

There was no complementary symbolism in the convening of a second summit conference in French-speaking Quebec ("Octagon") on September 13. By September 11, Patton's troops had approached objectives, Brooke notwithstanding, that SHAEF projections did not expect to reach until May 21, 1945, halting only because—lacking Antwerp—they had run out of supplies. In Quebec the many local Vichyites lay low, and the meetings evidenced a Churchill enervated by what Brooke called another "go of pneumonia" yet "impossible to argue with." What also weakened the PM was the reality that troops in France were now overwhelmingly American, and that his obstinacy about forcing the Balkans was now useless. Brooke conceded in his diary, "Winston hated having to give up the position of predominant partner which he held at the start. As a result he became inclined at times to put out strategic proposals which he knew were unsound, purely to spite the Americans." He even described the PM privately as "a public menace," but for political advantage he was now eager for "a Dominion Task Force under MacArthur" to shore up a postwar position protecting colonies in East Asia.

As the chiefs conferred, the Pacific war took a new turn when Halsey's carrier-focused Third Fleet struck hard at the western Carolines and at Mindanao. Nimitz radioed Quebec that further operations could expose Leyte for invasion. As Marshall recalled, "General MacArthur's views were requested and 2 days later he advised us that he was already prepared to shift his plans [from Mindanao] to land on Leyte 20 October, instead of 20 December as previously intended. It was a remarkable administrative achievement. . . . Within 90 minutes after the signal had been received in Quebec, General MacArthur and Admiral Nimitz had received their instructions to execute the Leyte operation."* Luzon could be set forward, and the navy could open a second path toward Japan in early 1945 via the Bonin Islands (Iwo Jima) and the Ryukyus (Okinawa).

Also during the conferences, Marshall and Arnold were pulled out of a dinner. As the Red Army had neared Warsaw, the underground Polish Home Army under General Tadeusz Bór-Komorowski, on August 1, had risen against their occupiers, but were now in desperate straits. Stalin had cynically halted the Russian advance to let the rebel Poles, no Communists, wither, and an Allied airdrop of supplies had fallen short, into German hands. By radio to Averell Harriman, the American ambassador to Moscow, the desperate Poles had appealed for practical aid. Harriman had forwarded the plea to Marshall, who with Arnold agreed to make another try if the Soviets permitted it. Since Stalin had written off the Poles, he let General Spaatz hazard another drop. It, too failed, and remnants of the Home Army would surrender on October 2.

The Reich itself appeared doomed if supply shortages slowing Allied progress could be overcome. To the tirelessly badmouthing Brooke, who saw no quick solution, Marshall seemed "boring" in his eagerness to exploit German exhaustion. Romania, Bulgaria, and Finland were negotiating for peace. Even Turkey had broken diplomatic relations with Germany. Discussions at Quebec continued on tribunals to try German war criminals, on how to treat a defeated Germany, and on occupation zones. Confidently, Eisenhower had cabled the Combined Chiefs of Staff on September 4, "Enemy resistance on the entire front shows signs of collapse." He viewed the enemy divisions northwest of the Ardennes forest as "weak" and "in full retreat." Below the Ardennes, although most of the German divisions were "poor," they were stubbornly holding areas in Belgium and Holland to prevent Allied resupply and to protect missile sites.

The detail Eisenhower transmitted to Marshall, a mixed bag of optimism and caution, was summed up in a self-protective memorandum to himself: "For some days it has been obvious that our military forces can advance almost at will, subject only to the requirement for maintenance. Resistance has largely melted all along the front. . . . With this advance we should use our Airborne forces to seize crossings over the Rhine and be in a position to thrust deep into the Ruhr and threaten Berlin." His assumptions required "maintenance, in which we are stretched to the limit,"

---

*Leyte preparation would be massive. Excluding aircraft, warships, and troop transports, 1,500,000 tons of general equipment, 235,000 tons of combat vehicles, 200,000 tons of ammunition, and 200,000 tons of medical supplies were to be deployed from nine staging bases.

and adequate "lines of communication," which remained handicapped by Montgomery's failure to take the crucial Belgian port of Antwerp. No alternative existed.

After Antwerp finally fell on September 4, its harbor demolished by the Germans, their troops still held on in the lowlands of the Scheldt Estuary, including Walcheren Island, keeping Antwerp harbor unusable and protecting launch sites for the V-1 and the V-2. The newest victory weapon arced into the stratosphere over the North Sea and plunged without warning onto British soil. Some were even targeted, short, at Antwerp.

Marshall had warned Eisenhower not to put everything "in the Antwerp basket," but Ike had urged Montgomery to make the capture of Walcheren his priority, and assumed that he would. Instead, Montgomery planned an audacious airborne leap to Arnhem, a Dutch city on the Rhine behind enemy defenses and on a possible northern path into Germany. He assured Eisenhower he could accomplish both, but while working on an Arnhem quick fix he dithered about Walcheren.*

Without a usable Antwerp, the other offensives, lacking ammunition and fuel, slowed. Still, elements of Hodges's First Army reached Aachen, on German soil, on September 10. A repeat of the breakdown in October and November 1918 seemed possible. Then the Germans had signed an armistice before Allied soldiers had set foot on the Fatherland, and Marshall braked the American armies to a cease-fire. He would soon revisit Aachen, taken expensively on October 21, 1944, after a month of heavy fighting and sustained bombardment.

The 1918 Armistice had spared Germany physical devastation but led to the political fantasy that revolutionaries had stabbed a still-victorious Reich in the back. Hitler had vaulted to power on that myth. But unlike Wilhelm II, who abdicated into comfortable exile two days before the shooting stopped, Hitler intended to take all of Germany down with him. And he was not yet finished. His terror weapons were working, and he had planners devising more of them. Also, he was hoarding forces for a blow that might push the Western allies into a separate peace.

Contemplating a bold stroke to end the war, Montgomery wanted Eisenhower's approval to seize bridgeheads across the Rhine in the north with airborne divisions augmented by ground forces, then break into the German interior. Yet Walcheren still languished. Bradley wanted to take

*Eisenhower fudged in *Crusade* that Monty had "set about the task energetically." In a diary entry much later, on September 10, 1959, Ike recalled that Monty's grandiose strategy to race to Berlin had been "preposterous."

troops into Germany south of the Ardennes, exploiting Patton's Third Army, as long hauls from inadequate harbors in Normandy, by miles-long SHAEF truck convoys, could not resupply the increasingly expanding and remote fronts. The first Allied freighters able to dock at Antwerp would not make it through until November 28. Marshall estimated that each division required 900 tons of supplies a day. Allocations now had to include De Gaulle's newly recruited French, who needed everything from uniforms to tanks.

Patton told Bradley melodramatically that he preferred fuel to food: "Give us gasoline; we can eat our belts." Seeing deference to Montgomery as a sop to coalition war, Patton snapped to a correspondent, in a favorite metaphor, "Now, if Ike stops holding Monty's hand and gives me the supplies, I'll go through the Siegfried Line like shit through a goose."

Although Eisenhower had injured a knee while helping to push a small plane carrying him which had crash-landed along a beach, and could hardly walk, he agreed to talk strategy with Monty, who insisted that the Supreme Commander come to him. As Ike's British G-4, General Humfrey Gale, described it, "The object of the meeting was to discuss Montgomery's proposal to rush to Berlin at the expense of the immobilization of the rest of the Allied Armies. This was a fantastic proposal viewed from any angle and was highly unsound logistically."

Escorted by four Spitfires, Eisenhower flew in his B-17 to Brussels, liberated on September 3. Aboard the parked plane, Montgomery condemned any "broad front" plan that would keep other armies than his own in motion as "balls, sheer balls, rubbish!" His patience ebbing, Eisenhower tried to quiet Montgomery, tapping his knee and warning, "Steady, Monty! You can't speak to me like that. I'm your boss."

"I'm sorry, Ike," conceded Monty in a rare withdrawal. But he would keep exploiting any indecisiveness he perceived.

General Gale's "own view" was that Montgomery "never really intended to go to Berlin—that it was merely a manoeuvre 'off the record' to show that he had been prevented from ending the war in a few days by the Supreme Commander himself." Air Marshal Tedder telegraphed Brooke to expect a dishonest report from Monty "so that any possibility of Montgomery queering the pitch in London would then be scotched."

Montgomery's "Market Garden" operation, approved by the usually cautious Eisenhower as a shortcut to victory, and launched on September 17, was a débacle. Monty's forces were commanded by Lieutenant General Frederick ("Boy") Browning, and included American airborne troops. The drops to seize the bridges at Arnhem fell short and ran into tough German resistance. Despite "Ultra" decrypts warning him, Monty had stubbornly downplayed German strength. Supporting ground troops were unable to reach the pinned-down airborne units. Casualties were enormous. The remnants retreated. Of the 10,000 men in the First British Airborne Division alone, 1,400 were killed and 6,000 taken prisoner.

In his memoirs, Montgomery fictionalized that he had been "ninety percent successful." Churchill also reinvented the gross failure as "a decided victory."* As a consoling token, Eisenhower early in October misguidedly allotted American medals to Montgomery for the most courageous of the British troops to survive "Market Garden." According to Humfrey Gale, Monty, in a MacArthuresque gesture, gave them instead to his headquarters staff.

Eisenhower now began to hedge his optimism about a German collapse. Marshall conceded "that your greatest difficulty is maintenance and that the closer you get to the Siegfried line the greater you will be stretched . . . and eventually a period of relative inaction will be imposed on you. . . . I should be much more disposed to bring [logistical] pressure from here on the Mediterranean," he radioed, suggesting immediate alternative sources from Italy, "than to see you weaken your supply capabilities at such a vital moment in the great European battle." But the "Market Garden" misfire had given Germany a winter to delay defeat, regardless of what urgent resupply from Italian stockpiles might be arranged through Marseilles.

Eisenhower claimed his lame knee as reason to withdraw from on-the-scene oversight through September and October and remain near Paris. Despite a forward trailer headquarters in Reims, his primary office was an annex of the Hotel Trianon (J. C. H. Lee usurped most of the grand establishments in Paris for his swollen staff) and Ike lived in a small chateau in St.-Germain-en-Laye once occupied by Rundstedt. As autumn came and the weather again worsened, grounding the dominant Allied air arm and slowing truck traffic, the initiative vanished. Humfrey Gale had written while still in Normandy with Eisenhower on July 22, "The effect of weather on all kinds of operations . . . has to be seen to be believed." He also added then, "I think the Americans, although achieving great results, are doing it in a much more muddled way than the British."

---

*One of its secondary failures was Allied inability to reach and reduce V-2 launch sites in Holland, as the big rockets were still harassing London and southern England.

By October everything appeared muddled everywhere, and the Westwall and the Rhine seemed unreachable.

While Patton, fuel-starved, was chafing in relative inaction in Lorraine, Marshall had radioed, in unfortunate jocularity, "When you have nothing else to do except invade Germany, have one of your people stop by Gondrecourt between Neufchateau and Barleduc and look up Madame Jouatte, formerly [on] Rue Sourcy, my landlady in France. . . . Find out what her necessities are if any without committing me. But give her a very personal message from me and a contact with your headquarters." Apparently Patton was to improvise the personal message, but found it was no tax on his imagination when he arrived "reinforced," he replied to Marshall on September 27, "by three pounds of coffee and five pounds of sugar," and found she had moved long before to Mountauban. Patton got her new address, posted a letter to her, and told Marshall that he would send a staff officer to visit Madame Jouatte "when the situation in southern France clears up." For Marshall, France in 1918 remained yesterday.

For the Republican opposition in Congress, Pearl Harbor and 1941 was always yesterday. As the presidential election heated up, yet another inquiry into the events of December 7 was convened—"largely political," Stimson thought, in "trying to embarrass the President." Marshall was called once more to be asked whether "the contemplated severance of diplomatic relations [was] practically a declaration of war." Since the Japanese were so "devious," he was "not certain of that." General Gerow, on his staff in 1941, was recalled from France to testify.

More worrisome was the coordinate attempt to bring into the campaign the revelation that Japanese diplomatic codes had been broken before the war, and exploited since. Since Governor Dewey was leaked the information, even that Baron Oshima's inadvertently helpful radiograms from Germany to Tokyo continued to be decrypted while the Japanese remained unaware, Marshall worried that conduct of the war could be compromised. With Admiral King's concurrence he wrote cautiously to Dewey that no one else had knowledge of the correspondence, and asked that the codes matter be kept out of the campaign. But Dewey brushed Marshall off with "Franklin Roosevelt knows all about it. He knew what was happening before Pearl Harbor and instead of being reelected he ought to be impeached." That the codes then broken revealed diplomatic moves, not military ones, meant nothing to a political opponent, and less, even now, many decades later, to purveyors of conspiracy theories.

Marshall's confidential aide, Colonel Carter W. Clarke, flew to Tulsa, where Dewey was campaigning, with a second letter warning of the "utterly tragic consequences if the present political debates regarding Pearl Harbor disclose to the enemy, German or Jap, any suspicion of the vital sources of information we possess." Clarke returned with no commitment from Dewey, who charged, ignorantly, about Japanese retention of the codes, "Why in hell haven't they changed them, especially after what happened at Midway and the Coral Sea?"

Clarke made a second effort to see Dewey, this time going to Albany, New York, and conveying Marshall's assurances that only King knew of the appeal to keep codebreaking under wraps, and that no political trickery was involved.* Abruptly Dewey left the room to discuss the matter with an adviser, Elliot V. Bell, returning after twenty minutes to say, "Well, Colonel, I do not believe that there are any questions I want to ask you nor do I care to have any discussion about the contents of the letter." To the governor, no differences existed between diplomatic and military codes.*

Although Dewey did not afterward bring up Pearl Harbor, Marshall remained concerned because MacArthur was about to launch the Leyte operation, and Marshall's own forthcoming flight to France would fuel speculation in the press about a possible new Allied offensive to break into Germany. Putting the presidential campaign, in which he would not be involved but for the Dewey affair, behind him, he flew (in nineteen hours) in Roosevelt's C-54, *The Sacred Cow*, to Paris via Newfoundland. After conferring with Eisenhower he boarded a light plane to see Bradley, ordering the pilot to fly low over the Meuse-Argonne battlefields of 1918. By staff car he went to Étain to see Patton, and even visited his old wartime billet in Souilly. "The right of Patton's Third Army," he wrote to a Pentagon deputy, Major General Frank R. McCoy, "was in the village, and No Man's Land in the exact spot that I found in October, 1917, when I arranged for the induction of separate battalions of the First Division into a French front."

On Sunday, October 8, with Bradley, Marshall flew to Eindhoven in the Netherlands to confer frustratingly with Montgomery. Although the supply crisis continued, much of it through Monty's own failures, he complained about Eisenhower's poor "operational direction." Because of Ike's "lack of grip" they were "now in a real mess." Montgomery saw "no plan,

*Roosevelt learned of Marshall's action later, with surprise, telling Hopkins that he felt confident that Dewey, for political purposes, would not divulge vital information that would benefit the enemy. Besides, it "would be bound to react against him."

and we moved by disconnected jerks." His orders to clear the Scheldt Estuary and open Antwerp had only been trivialities* to bypass while he intended seizing Hitler's war-making potential in the Ruhr and racing on dramatically to Berlin. His own ambitions overshadowed coalition war.

Coping with him, Marshall realized, was Eisenhower's task, but Montgomery's "blowing off out of turn" and "overwhelming egotism" were difficult to sit through. "I came pretty near to blowing off [myself]," he recalled, but "overcame an urgent compulsion to whittle him down. It was very hard for me to restrain myself. . . ." Marshall abruptly took his leave, then flew to Luxeuil, from which Gaullist general Jean de Lattre de Tassigny had just begun pushing into the mountainous Vosges north of Belfort, terrain also remembered from 1918.

Drastically shortchanged in fuel and ammunition, Patton remained bogged down, his momentum gone. Forrest Pogue, a tanks sergeant although a Ph.D. in history (and later, Marshall's biographer), observed in his service diary that Patton "(although he is disliked by many) is greatly admired. I think . . . it may be possible for people to argue in years to come that a desire to keep him in his place may have led to a [headquarters] failure to allot sufficient material to him for the drives he might have been able to make."

De Lattre, as if he were singled out punitively as a Gaullist, complained to Marshall of supply shortages, but Marshall lacked sympathy. De Lattre was expending precious gasoline on "triumphant" processions in retaken cities and villages to flaunt the Tricolor. When he continued to pout in the presence of French reporters, who were his real audience, Marshall recalled twelve years later, "I just stopped the thing right where it was and walked out."

Marshall could do that. Eisenhower could not. Commanding a multinational force, Ike was continually faced with problems for which he had few political directives. He understood that politics was not for generals, but everything from strategy to supply was also a political matter. Ostensibly if not actually, Marshall represented only the United States Army, but to further investigate the supply breakdown, he asked General Somervell to send over a high-level troubleshooter. When Major General Henry S. Aurand arrived, he found stonewalling at every level to cover up cronyism, corruption, and incompetence. In Versailles, Beetle Smith—as

---

*When Montgomery belatedly assaulted the Antwerp area, the Germans were ready for his British and Canadian troops, who experienced 27,633 in dead, wounded, and missing.

Eisenhower must have known—even threatened protectively to have Aurand demoted to colonel if he sent tough recommendations home. Aurand didn't.

Returning to Washington, Marshall found more pleasant news. "A solid hold on Leyte," he cabled Patton, "with minimum losses to date. Now if we can open up the port of Antwerp," he wrote overconfidently, "the European picture will change rapidly." Still, he warned Eisenhower again about banking wholly on "the Antwerp basket." SHAEF, he said, needed two contingency plans: an "all-out effort to crush German resistance" by the beginning of the new year and strategy "for carrying on the battle beyond 1 January" if the Germans hung in. Aided by missed opportunities, the Germans would interfere with both alternatives.

On the same date that MacArthur's forces seized footholds on Leyte, Eisenhower had reported to Washington that his shortage of artillery ammunition was "not merely one of port capacity and distributional facilities; it likewise involves limitations in production." War matériel shortages were the fruits of apparent success. With seemingly imminent victory, factory workers had begun abandoning war employment for industries already retooling for civilian needs, or otherwise protecting former jobs before the influx of returned veterans. Strikes over salary caps escalated and shut down production lines. To keep troops from merely watching the war not get won, supplies shipped directly to French ports were offloaded onto quartermaster "Red Ball Express" long-haul trucks which roared with lights on through the darkness on highways cleared of all other traffic. Yet there was never enough.

Manpower crises had also increased with higher casualties in the push toward the Rhine. As the enemy backed toward the *Heimat,* resistance intensified. Reports that the Germans were drained of reserves fed press optimism about imminent victory, but Eisenhower, too, needed fresh troops. The British were cannibalizing from existing divisions. Marshall offered infantry replacements from the States dispatched, without waiting for additional shipping needed for their equipment and rotating them into action to rest and refit exhausted units.

As Eisenhower learned, "instead of replacing tired troops with fresh ones," obtuse army commanders he did not identify (but protected) "assign[ed] a special sector to the new troops." The exhausted units remained, and "the requirements of the front allowed us to do nothing else." Brooke on October 26 mocked Marshall's hope for a decision by Christmas as "wonderful." The British chiefs of staff estimated that the earliest date for an end of the war with Germany was January 31, 1945, and the latest was mid-May. Japan might last into 1946.

★　　★　　★　　★　　★

MacArthur's dramatic return to the Philippines may have increased Roosevelt's reelection pluralities. While Dewey was charging that Roosevelt had shortchanged the Hero of Bataan, backed by the most powerful battle fleet in history, MacArthur was wading ashore into the massed lenses of press photographers. At Shibe Park in Philadelphia on October 27, a week after Leyte, a seemingly tireless Roosevelt told a cheering campaign crowd in a stadium usually seating baseball fans that in the previous twelve months, twenty-seven successful landings had been made on enemy soil, some thirteen thousand miles apart. "And, speaking of the glorious operation in the Philippines—I wonder what became of the suggestion made a few weeks ago, that I had failed for political reasons to send enough forces or supplies to General MacArthur?" In Leyte, the general's PR man, LeGrande Diller, suggested to correspondents, "The elections are coming up in a few days, and the Philippines must be kept on the front pages back home."

Although Roosevelt's margin on November 7 of 432 electoral votes to 99 seemed overwhelming, Dewey secured 46 percent of the popular vote, few from servicemen. If more of the millions in uniform had participated (most were disenfranchised by distance and perhaps a tenth had cast absentee ballots), it is unlikely that they would have voted for a candidate described by Alice Roosevelt Longworth (TR's daughter and no friend of FDR) as "the bridegroom on the wedding cake." Marshall sent the president "warm congratulations on your great victory." He had no party affiliation and like many career servicemen did not cast a ballot. But he despised Dewey. Neither Eisenhower nor MacArthur found it appropriate to write. Eisenhower, of a family of Kansas Republicans, had never yet voted. Privately, he had opposed a third term for Roosevelt, but openly favored a fourth term.

MacArthur already controlled the 1,300-mile northern coastline of New Guinea. The Japanese had expected him to strike next at Mindanao rather than bypass it for Leyte. After Ranger detachments seized outlying islands on October 17 and 18, MacArthur's main force came ashore on Leyte on October 20 ("A-Day" to the command). At the widening beachhead, to which he arrived via the cruiser *Nashville* and a "whale boat," wading knee-deep the final yards, the general grasped a waiting microphone, more for the newsreel cameras than the few Filipinos with clandestine radios, to announce his return. A radar technician watched an adjutant, "like Mac's puppy dog, helping to set the tilt of his cap, removing his wet and dirty leather boots and substituting a fresh pair. . . . He jutted out his jaw and proclaimed, 'People of the Philippines, I have returned! . . . Rally to me! Let the indomitable spirit of Bataan and Corregidor lead on. As the lines of battle roll forward . . . , rise and strike! . . . In the name of your sacred dead, strike!'" Since Filipinos were a pious people, he closed melodramatically, although possibly with some confusion between the Almighty and himself, "The guidance of divine God points the way. Follow in His name to the Holy Grail of righteous victory!"

It had not helped Governor Dewey's campaign that the first letter which MacArthur sent from "the freed Philippines" via a Signal Corps courier was to President Roosevelt, ostensibly for his stamp collection. "Please excuse this scribble," he exaggerated from the command post of Major General Frederick Irving of the 24th Division, three hundred yards in from the beach, "but at the moment I am on the combat line with no facilities except for this field message pad." Roosevelt replied, "I know well what this means to you. I know what it cost you to obey my order that you leave Corregidor."

Although MacArthur reported "minimum" losses, by Christmas there were 15,584 American casualties on Leyte. Central Pacific island-hopping cost much more. Mopping up would take six months, and further casualties, but the Japanese, opting for death rather than surrender, lost many times that, and further thousands on sunken troopships. They would lose, through sinkings, many more in the Battle of Leyte Gulf, beginning on October 23, in which the Japanese used, for the first time, *"kamikaze"* suicide pilots against the American armada. With the employment of Halsey's Third Fleet under Nimitz's distant command, and Kinkaid's Seventh Fleet, under MacArthur, the first effective coordination on a large scale between commanders worked. Together the fleets mustered twenty aircraft carriers and a dozen battleships, a myriad of cruisers and destroyers, and transports conveying 175,000 troops. Five of Kinkaid's renovated battleships had been sent to the muddy bottom of Pearl Harbor on December 7, 1941.

With a symbolic piece of Philippines geography in American hands,

Roosevelt asked Stimson whether he should name MacArthur high commissioner. In his diary, Stimson noted that he was "disturbed" by the suggestion, and asked Marshall's advice. The appointment was one MacArthur had desired in the 1930s. It "might be a good thing," Marshall returned, if it did not terminate MacArthur's command function. He suggested putting the appointment on hold.

Now a WAC lieutenant courtesy of Eisenhower's clout, Kay Summersby had gone with him from England to France, and presided over the upscale chateau at Versailles to which he had moved from Rundstedt's former residence. MacArthur soon found that Richard Sutherland's inamorata, Elaine Clarke, now also a WAC officer, had been quickly installed on Leyte, where the chief of staff had headquarters engineering personnel build her a house. Although Kenney and assistant chief of staff Richard Marshall had also imported Australian WAC "assistants," the arrogant Lieutenant Clarke had always been a disruptive presence, and MacArthur was especially livid that Sutherland had disobeyed instructions to leave her in Brisbane.

When last in Washington, preceding the Summersby appointment, Sutherland had requested the War Department, without MacArthur's knowledge, to commission the three female noncitizens. Colonel Hobby objected, but Sutherland took the matter to General McNarney in George Marshall's office and lied that they were "personally desired by General MacArthur as essential to headquarters operation." Although they were not, and MacArthur ordered Elaine back to Australia, he ignored the George Kenney and Richard Marshall affairs, even transferring to Marshall many of Sutherland's responsibilities, which were now punitively reduced. He needed Kenney's air expertise, although the general's prediction that the Leyte airfields would be advantageous was premature. The ground was soggy, and the airfields abandoned by the Japanese could be used without runway grids only by light planes. While Tacloban air base in northernmost Leyte was only 195 miles below Manila, to reach Formosa and Japan from the south MacArthur still had to take Luzon.

One of Kenney's showpiece pilots was Richard Bong, who was recommended after his thirty-sixth aircraft kill for a Medal of Honor. Kenney asked his boss to decorate Major Bong himself, for press photographers. "I'm not running for any office," MacArthur joked; "I don't want the publicity."

11

Victory Delayed

CHRISTMAS 1944 was, for American troops in the ETO, the most bitter since Valley Forge. The war almost obliterated Christmas. Yet army post exchange officials, certain that the war with Germany would end before the holidays, had already distributed a memorandum reporting that they were arranging to return to the United States those Christmas presents already in the European mail pipeline.

On October 11, 1943, Eisenhower had bet General Montgomery five pounds that Germany would be beaten by Christmas 1944. Allied troops had crossed into the boot of Italy the month before, and Mussolini's faltering government had collapsed. Ike's wager looked even better in October 1944. Although the July bomb plot by German army officers against Hitler had failed, the Führer had been injured and at fifty-five he was a bent, somewhat deaf old man. Allied and Soviet armies now threatened the German heartland. On October 23, General Marshall had cabled Eisenhower urging maintenance of the momentum of early autumn— that "an immediate supreme effort . . . may well result in the collapse of German resistance before the heavy winter weather limits large operations and facilitates [enemy] defensive strategy." Strong pressure might "contribute to defeating Germany by 1 January 1945."

Any observer on the ground a month later would have classified Marshall's optimism from Washington as hopeful fantasy. Supply shortages, and the fog, rain, and ice of late autumn had slowed the Allied advance to a near stalemate. Seeing the window of German vulnerability closing, Patton, stalled for lack of fuel, wrote to his wife in frustration, echoing the familiar Coca-Cola slogan, "Books will some day be written on that 'pause which did not refresh.'"

Although its defenders were often improvisations from the Wehrmacht scrap heap, the Hürtgenwald, southeast of Aachen, took painful weeks to seize. Overage reservists of sixty, and teenagers, some under sixteen, made up the *Volkssturm* divisions. Ernest Hemingway, who was there, drank far too much, and flouted restrictions on correspondents, later wrote bitterly, "Who could love the authors of that national catastrophe which killed off the flower of our fighting men in a stupid frontal attack?" An American officer conceded, "We are taking three trees a day, yet they cost us about 100 men apiece."

Exhausted divisions had little opportunity to rest and refit, except in supposedly quiet, fog-shrouded areas—like the Ardennes. They were now at the edges of Germany, and occupied much of Belgium and Luxembourg. But on December 19, Major Tom Bigland, a liaison officer deputed by Montgomery to Lieutenant General Courtney Hodges of the First Army in Spa, the historic resort town in Belgium, found neither Hodges nor any of his staff. Bigland did not know that an erroneous report received by Hodges at 4:00 P.M. the previous day had placed a Panzer division nearby. In panic the staff had burned files, abandoned their offices, and fled.

Bigland claimed that he "walked into the H.Q. to find literally *not one single person* there except a German [cleaning] woman. Breakfast was laid and the Christmas tree was decorated in the dining room, telephones were in all the offices, papers were all over the place—but there was no one there. . . . I found them again at their rear H.Q. and here they had even less control of the battle than the day before." Major William Desobry, commander of the 20th Armored Infantry Battalion, and who soon would be captured, passed through a nearby Belgian town in a thick fog. He was looking for Germans reportedly in half-tracks. "You could see an American unit had been there, abandoned all their stuff, their bedding, their bunks, and had written on the wall, 'We shall return,' like MacArthur."

Eisenhower's bet seemed lost. Montgomery had requested permission from Eisenhower the day before to return to England to spend the school holiday with his son, David, then sixteen. Monty's front was quiet. Without comment, he had enclosed Eisenhower's signed memorandum from Italy, "Amount £5. Eisenhower bets war with Germany will end before Xmas 1944—local time." From the beginning of November into mid-December, Montgomery's forces in Belgium had advanced just ten miles.

Eisenhower conceded stubbornly, "I still have nine days, and while it seems almost certain that you will have an extra five pounds for Christmas, you will not get it until that day. At least you must admit we have gone a long ways toward the defeat of Germany since we made our bet. . . ."

When decrypts from German sources revealed Luftwaffe reinforcements reaching the Rhine, and *Reichsbahn* troop trains bringing new divisions west, SHAEF intelligence ignored both, despite Hitler's intercepted boasts to Japanese ambassador Hiroshi Oshima of a coming counteroffensive to obstruct the breaching of the homeland.

Eisenhower had made a tour of the lines from November 8 through November 11. An army photo shows him at Major General Troy Middleton's VIII Corps forward post at Wiltz in Luxembourg, southeast of Bastogne. With him are Middleton; Bradley, with a revolver slung under his left armpit; and Major General John Leonard of the 9th Armored Division. Eisenhower is perched on a battered desk, coffee in a chipped cup in one hand, in the other a cigarette from the three packs he burned daily. His report to Marshall on the day before he returned to Versailles began, "I am getting exceedingly tired of [the] weather." He reported "floods in Patton's area," caused by heavy rains which eliminated air support. "Then the floods came down the [Moselle] river [a mile wide at one point] and not only washed out two fixed bridges, but destroyed his principal floating bridge and made others almost unusable." Eventually, he assured Marshall, "Patton will get ahead all along his front." He did, briefly, encircling Metz on November 18 and capturing it four days later.

Accompanied by Bradley, Eisenhower had visited every division in Courtney Hodges's First and William H. Simpson's Ninth Armies, finding morale "surprisingly high" and troops "rather comfortable" with "no signs of exhaustion." In the hills, snow had already reached six inches. Below, it "melted rather rapidly." Marshall's own Ardennes experience must have caused him to wonder, since his October euphoria, about what further progress could be expected so late in autumn.

The Germans were receiving weather data radioed from North Atlantic outposts on Greenland and Spitsbergen and from surfaced subs, and were counting on continuing poor skies. "All of us keep hoping," Eisenhower closed, hoping that he sounded upbeat, "that some little spell will come along in which we can have a bit of relief from mud, rain, and fog so that tanks and infantry can operate more easily on the offensive and so that we can use our great air asset. In spite of difficulties, no one is discouraged and we will yet make the German wish that he had gone completely back of the Rhine at the end of his great retreat across France." Eisenhower wanted to keep movement going "to the extreme limit of our ability," believing that the commander "who took counsel only of the gloomy Intelligence estimates would never win a battle."

In mid-December the static Ardennes front erupted. Downplaying it at first, Eisenhower wrote to Marshall's logistics chief, "Bill" Somervell, that the Germans had launched "a rather ambitious counterattack east of the Luxembourg area where we have been holding rather thinly." Forested and riverine areas seemed unlikely to sustain serious troop movements or offer terrain for armor, and Eisenhower had concentrated his forces, he explained, at more "vital points." Still, he was "closing in on the threat from each flank. If things go well we should not only stop the thrust but should be able to profit from it."

On recovering sufficiently from the failed July bomb to ponder a reversal of fortune, Hitler had consulted the highest authority in the Third Reich—himself. Since the Allied advance, although slowing down, seemed unstoppable, he hoped to offer Stalin a deal to keep the West from dominating Germany to Soviet disadvantage. If it seemed too late for that, putting the Reich's remaining resources into denying the Anglo-Americans victory might buy time to deploy new "miracle" weapons and force them to reconsider their war.

The first twenty-five V-2 high-altitude rockets, launched in early September, were a beginning. There was no defense against them. Thousands more were being manufactured by slave labor. Revived pessimism might stir anti-Communism in the West, and a compromise with Germany could keep the Soviets at a distance. A counteroffensive in the Ardennes, however, had to succeed before the Russians penetrated the homeland through Poland. That meant exploiting weather that was nullifying Allied air power.

While still bedridden in late September, Hitler had called in *Generaloberst* Alfred Jodl to examine maps of the Ardennes, lightly manned by the Americans because it seemed a natural barrier to armor. For the Wehrmacht to thrust westward to the Meuse and to Antwerp, 125 miles to the north, would require hoarding fuel for armored vehicles at a half-gallon per mile, at best, for each. After the first few days troops would have to tap enemy supplies.

In mid-October, to overthrow a coup in Budapest intended to take Hungary out of the war, Hitler had ordered paratroop major Otto Skorzeny, who had rescued Mussolini, to take hostage the son of Hungarian dictator Admiral Nikolaus Horthy. When, after his new success,

Skorzeny arrived at Hitler's bunker headquarters in East Prussia, soon to be evacuated ahead of the Red Army, the Führer promoted him on the spot to the SS equivalent of lieutenant colonel. "Don't go, Skorzeny," he said. "I have perhaps the most important job in your life for you. So far very few people know of the preparations for a secret plan in which you have an important part to play. In December, Germany will start a great offensive, which may well decide her fate." He explained that Skorzeny was to create disarray as the Ardennes breakout began by leading a brigade of 3,300 commandos disguised in captured American uniforms, fluent in American idiom, and supported by vehicles with American markings.

Earlier in October Jodl had offered Hitler a scheme for a break-through to Antwerp in seven days. Details were finalized on November 3. Sixteen divisions, half of them armored, the others foot soldiers largely cobbled from now-surplus *Kriegsmarine* and Luftwaffe ranks, and con-scripts from factory jobs, would penetrate the thin Allied lines. Although the Germans planned to muster about 200,000 troops and 800 tanks against an expected 80,000 Americans with 600 tanks, no one in the Wehrmacht command thought the forces, and dwindling fuel, were ade-quate for extended winter warfare, nor that reaching Antwerp was realis-tic. Jodl reminded the generals nevertheless that more limited gains would not suffice "to make the western powers ready to negotiate." He banked on bad weather, and surprise.

Delays in organizing troops and equipment pushed the start to De-cember 16. To keep tight control of operations, Hitler left Berlin on De-cember 10 to establish headquarters in bunkers at Ziegenberg, near Bad Nauheim. There, at what he christened *"Adlerhorst"* (Eagle's Nest"), he spoke to a gathering of top officers. "Wars are finally decided," he said, "through the recognition by one side or the other that the war as such can no longer be won. To get the enemy to realize this is therefore the most important task."

On December 15, First Army intelligence picked up a signal that the Wehrmacht targeted Aachen, on the border—a very limited offensive to retrieve the only German city then lost to the Allies. On December 16, the topmost brass in the American military, however distracted by other events, received an early Christmas gift. Congress had passed, and the president had signed, legislation advancing to five-star rank seven senior generals and admirals.

Marshall had long deplored the elevation as unnecessary. "I didn't want any promotion at all," he recalled in 1956. "I didn't need it. . . . I didn't want to be beholden to Congress for any rank or anything of that kind. I wanted to be able to go in there with my skirts clean and no personal ambition concerned in it in any way, and I could get all I wanted with the rank I had."

Marshall also thought that parity with other armies was useless. British field marshals were already senior to him and the Soviets used six stars for super-ranks. Under pressure from Roosevelt and Stimson, Marshall finally accepted "General of the Army," with the navy equivalent as "Fleet Admiral." Advanced in order of seniority were Leahy, Marshall, King, MacArthur, Nimitz, Eisenhower, and Arnold.

MacArthur's date of rank would precede Ike's by two days. Pleased with the star, and that he would outrank Eisenhower if only fractionally, MacArthur rushed a saccharine radiogram to Roosevelt, "My grateful thanks for the promotion you have just given me. My pleasure in receiving it is greatly enhanced because it was made by you." Unwilling in Leyte to wait for official insignia, he had a circlet of five small stars crafted for him by a Filipino silversmith in Tacloban, using American, Australian, Dutch, and Philippine coins to symbolize the national elements of his command. Two of his generals ceremoniously pinned the circlets on his lapels.

Marshall wrote a laconic two-sentence appreciation of the president's "confidence." Eisenhower cabled Marshall to thank Roosevelt for him, but the real trust in Ike's capacities came from the intentions of Marshall, Stimson, and the president to leave Eisenhower free from nagging by Washington. "I shall merely say now," Marshall cabled, "that you have our complete confidence." He "kept down" the messages to Eisenhower, Marshall remembered. He even recalled one from the Pentagon before it was transmitted, saying, "Don't bother him." The attitude of the White House especially pleased Marshall. "Roosevelt didn't send a word to Eisenhower nor ask a question. In great stress Roosevelt was a strong man."

At a press conference on December 22, one week into the German offensive, the president refused any comment other than that "the end was not yet in sight." Afterward he summoned Secretary Stimson and Major General Leslie R. Groves of the supersecret Manhattan Project, and asked whether an atomic bomb could be rushed into readiness if urgently needed to close the salient. (Even had the Bomb been completed, it would have been useless as a tactical weapon.) Groves advised that no trigger mechanism yet existed, but he hoped that the device would be ready by summer—perhaps by August. "If we can't test it first, the mechanism might not go off. Then the Germans might find out how it works." Despite later allegations of racism, the weapon was not being withheld for use against Japan.

There was also a war going on across the world. MacArthur's divisions in Leyte were pushing the Japanese deeper into the island. Mindoro would be next, and then Luzon. Tacloban, the Leyte capital, and its airfield, had long been in American hands, and MacArthur had taken over the elegant, stucco Japanese officers' club, once the home of an American they had killed, as his headquarters. (Four prefab structures were added for his staff.) From there he let Generals Krueger and Eichelberger run the war while he smoked his corncob pipe on the veranda, watched movies in the evening, turned civil administration over to the rather reluctant President Sergio Osmeña (successor to Manuel Quezon), wrote communiques for Colonel Diller to distribute, and entertained visiting correspondents.

Chief press celebrities were Turner Catledge and Arthur H. Sulzberger of the *New York Times,* to whom MacArthur reviewed the presidential election and criticized Eisenhower's handling of the war. To Catledge, MacArthur "was variously the military expert, the political figure, the man of destiny. Sulzberger and I later agreed we had never met a more egotistical man, nor one more aware of his egotism and more able and determined to back it up with his deeds." To correspondent Bert Andrews, MacArthur predicted sweepingly that "the lands touching the Pacific will determine the course of history for the next ten thousand years."

Without a home in the U.S., MacArthur indulged his edifice complex wherever he was. After Manila, Brisbane, and Port Moresby, and before Tacloban, he claimed the top of a hill in Hollandia (now Sukarnapura, just across the West Papuan border of Indonesian New Guinea). Overlooking Lake Sentani, the peak of Mount Cyclops, and a spectacular waterfall, the area had been occupied for three months when, in the late summer of 1944, MacArthur had engineers bulldoze a road a thousand feet above the heat and stench of the swamps, where among the Quonset huts for Seventh Fleet headquarters, sheet metal warehouses, and brown tents for army personnel, they erected a large structure for his staff and himself. Kenney flew in rugs and furniture from Brisbane. GIs called it extravagantly a "million-dollar mansion," but it was relatively spare, and the planning venue for the Leyte operation.

Communicating by cable from Australia, MacArthur left most of the planning to staff. He spent three weeks in September and early October with Jean and Arthur in Brisbane. On October 16 he was back in New Guinea to board the *Nashville* for Leyte. The million-dollar mansion had been his for less than two months.

On Christmas Eve in Leyte, as he paced after dark on the veranda with his corncob, reminiscent of Manila Hotel days before the war, a GI group gathered below to sing carols in a climate and locale that hardly resembled a traditional American Christmas. He paused to listen. Several Japanese nuisance raiders in low-flying planes buzzed the compound, and the singing stopped abruptly. The soldiers sought cover in the hedges. Searchlights caught one of the intruders in crossbeams and a burst of antiaircraft fire brought it down. MacArthur leaned down to thank the carollers, and resumed his solitary pacing.

On Christmas Day he cabled rather blandly to Jean, with instructions that the message be delivered on the 27th, her birthday, "Many happy returns of the day. The entire command joins me in saluting our staunchest soldier." It was quieter than the evening before, and far quieter than in the snowbound but chaotic Ardennes. The Japanese command on its remaining corner of Leyte had been ordered to conduct "strategic delay." On Christmas morning General Tomoyuki Yamashita in Luzon radioed that he was shedding "tears of remorse" for the doomed troops on Leyte. Lieutenant General Sosaku Suzuki's forces were then moving westward to the coast when a battalion of the 77th Division landed at one of the few remaining ports still open. A regiment of the 24th then landed above them and on December 28 took the northernmost port of San Isidro. The Japanese were trapped but not finished.

Always given to premature announcements of victory, MacArthur declared Leyte taken. Nearly 3,000 Americans had died—and 56,000 Japanese. What communiques lightly called "mopping up" was, to Eichelberger, ruefully, "several months of the roughest kind of combat. . . . Between Christmas Day and the end of the campaign [in May 1945] we killed more than 27,000 Japs. . . . I never understood the public relations policy. . . . It seemed to me, as it did to many of the commanders and correspondents, ill advised to announce victories when a first phase had been accomplished without too many casualties." But that was MacArthur's intent. Although troops were bitter about the fur-

ther cost, premature communiques looked good. Luzon would repeat
the formula.

When the Germans struck the Ardennes, Marshall was busy rethinking
deployments from Europe to the Pacific, and new roles for airborne
troops. Major General Matthew B. Ridgway, commander of the recently
created XVIIIth Airborne Corps, had sent Major General Maxwell D.
Taylor, who led the 101st Airborne Division, to Washington to discuss
more effective use of what the War Department conceived narrowly as
small combat groups which only went into action by parachute or glider.
To retain that distinction they were often underutilized, but Ridgway
wanted them available "to fight on the line . . . when not being employed
as an Airborne Unit." Although Eisenhower had used paratroops in Sicily
and in France, Ridgway knew he preferred infantry, which brought more
firepower with them on the ground. After Eisenhower's paratroop problems in Sicily he had written to Marshall flatly, "I do not believe in the
airborne division." Yet they had been effective, if expensive, in Normandy.

"Just now," Marshall cabled Ridgway two days after the German
breakthrough in the Bulge, realizing that chutists were more than mere
manpower, "it would appear that you could not leave the theater. In January the situation should be much clearer. . . . The courage and dash of
airborne troops has become a by-word and is a great inspiration to all the
others." Courage and dash were already called for, and the need for more
men on the line had emerged by the time Ridgway read Marshall's message in England. He later wrote that Marshall "never forgot the man with
the rifle, the man whose task it was to kill and be killed."

Confident that the Germans "cannot stage offensive operations,"
Montgomery still retired every evening at 9:30. Bradley, on the southern
edge of what was being dismissed as a "Ghost Front," had put up at the
Hotel Alfa in Luxembourg City, the quiet capital of the duchy, and well
below the fighting. He was about to travel to Versailles to ask Eisenhower
for infantry replacements to be drawn from rear-area units. Bradley's own
bloated headquarters area barracked 5,000 service troops who had no expectation of ever firing a rifle.

Eisenhower had flown to Maastricht in southern Holland to meet
Monty, Bradley, and Tedder early in December to discuss how to reactivate the stagnating war. Brooke in London saw no end in sight, com-

plaining to his diary about "the very unsatisfactory state of affairs in France, with no one running the land battle." After Arnhem, however, Montgomery had returned to England briefly to plot with Brooke a scheme "to counter the pernicious American strategy of attacking all along the line," with northern and southern commanders—Monty and Bradley—and allegedly "splitting an army group with the Ardennes in the middle of it." Monty, in command in the north, wanted control of the entire ground war, from which he claimed Eisenhower remained aloof and distant.

Brooke also charged Eisenhower, very likely based on gossip from Monty, with failing to take charge, for Ike "does not hope to cross the Rhine before May!!!" Rather, he was "by himself with his lady chauffeur on the golf links at Reims—entirely detached from the war and taking practically no part in the running of the war! Matters got so bad lately that a deputation of [Major General John "Jock"] Whiteley, Bedell Smith, and a few others went up to tell him that he must get down to it and RUN the war, which he said he would. Personally I think he is incapable of running the war even if he tries."* Beetle himself, Brooke added, lived in Paris with a huge SHAEF headquarters entourage, leaving the war "in a rudderless condition." J. C. H. Lee's sprawling logistics empire in Paris was even larger, and Lee thought nothing of flying in fresh oranges from Algiers for his breakfasts.

American divisions had already bled a lot in the hilly and heavily wooded Hürtgenwald, where air support seemed useless. Farthest east was the Schnee Eifel (Snow Mountains), wooded hills and rushing streams, with German villages nestled in the valleys. The Hürtgen, eight miles deep by twenty miles wide, had cost 25,000 American casualties in October and November. A driver-interpreter with the 28th Division, George Nakhnikian, recalled that his company, its numbers continually reduced, then reinforced with replacements, "suffered 300% casualties" before being transferred to Wiltz in Luxembourg, in the supposedly quieter Ardennes.

The larger Ardennes, overlapping France and southern Belgium, and extending to the meandering Meuse and Aisne rivers, stretched over 2,015 square miles of forest. Under the cover of miserable rain, mud, and sleet, German *Kampfgruppen* were assembling.

---

*When historian Arthur Bryant published an edition of the last years of Brooke's diaries in 1959 as *Triumph in the West*, he cut the last sentence, but even so what remained caused widespread outrage in the U.S. Eisenhower then occupied the White House.

Routine patrolling had been minimal in the poor weather and forbidding terrain. No unusual activity had been identified. The dozens of troop trains in and out were misinterpreted as rotating replacements. Intelligence assumed the usual disinformation expected from prisoners. Civilian claims were also suspect, as the area included Nazi sympathizers and resettled Germans, and Belgian border areas had been loyal to Leon Degrelle's fascist movement. The clamor of motors and the clanking of tracked vehicles far off was muffled by the forest.

At 5:30 A.M. on December 16, the Ardennes front awakened to the flash and roar of German artillery. Few surface telephone wires survived, and radio communications were jammed as the Germans played phonograph records to interfere with known American wavelengths. After an hour the guns fell silent. Searchlights, casting ghostly reflections landward, probed toward the clouds in the predawn drizzle and fog, as white-sheeted forms in camouflage moved forward toward the dazed Americans. Some fled; other platoons were overrun; a few companies stuck to their positions and returned fire. The front was too sparsely held to maintain a continuous line, and enemy infantry, even inexperienced garrison soldiers drawn from Denmark and Norway, or just mustered into service from overage civil defense units, slipped through.

Refitted Panzer and *Volksgrenadier* divisions from the Eastern Front, soon identified, made it clear that Bradley's divisions were not facing what he dismissed as "just a goddam little spoiling attack." Leonard Gerow, returned to V Corps in the north, took it seriously, at eleven that morning telephoning Hodges in Spa, urging, "I'd like to halt my attack." He needed to reassemble his forces. "Keep your attack moving," Hodges insisted—before withdrawing himself. Although the Germans had massed forces to push toward the Meuse, as planned, and northward toward Antwerp, as no one expected, the realization that more than a local attack was in progress had not yet sunk in. Hodges would soon be despondent. From Versailles, Eisenhower had just sent off his message to Montgomery that he had nine days left to win his wager. Monty was off at golf.

Out of touch with events on the line, Bradley had left by staff car for Versailles to consult with Eisenhower about replacements. Attrition had reduced divisions below authorized levels. Driven about in his armored Cadillac, Bradley had been escorting the sinuous Marlene Dietrich to USO appearances. Troops were loudly appreciative. He did not know that, with no time to apply makeup, she had just fled the 99th Division sector. Slightly less out of touch than Bradley, Hodges had spent some of his time with morale-boosting baseball heroes Frankie Frisch, Bucky

Walters, Dutch Leonard, and Mel Ott. Eisenhower had been occupied on the 16th at the Saturday morning wedding of his valet, Mickey McKeough, to WAC sergeant Pearlie Hargrave in the Louis XIV Chapel in Versailles, then in having his staff toast, in the ubiquitous Reims champagne, his elevation to five stars.

Although slowed by icy roads, Bradley lunched at the Ritz in Paris with his aide, Major Chester Hansen, then was driven to Versailles in midafternoon. While conferring with Eisenhower as dusk came, they were interrupted by a message for Eisenhower's British G-2, Major General Kenneth Strong: "This morning the enemy counterattacked at five separate points across the First Army sector." Bradley had contended about an earlier warning that the German threat was exaggerated. Now he scoffed, from a distance, "Let them come!"

Patton's staff was preparing a push into the Saar through southern Luxembourg. Hodges was planning a thrust toward four dams on the Rur (Roer) River east of Aachen. Eisenhower concluded that a "local attack" would not be made "at our weakest point." He asked Bradley to shift two armored divisions to the area. "Where the hell has this sonofabitch gotten all his strength?" Bradley wondered, having disregarded evidences of a German buildup. Later, a deputy G-2, Noel Annan, would explain that intelligence officers at SHAEF "were regarded as defeatist if they did not believe the end of the war was in sight."

Although communications were confused, and Bradley had learned little about the quiet front during the poor weather, he understood that a broad attack against Hodges's First Army positions was under way. Eisenhower wanted the 10th Armored Division, in Patton's Third Army, moved in. Bradley warned that Patton wouldn't like that. "Tell him," Eisenhower scowled, "that Ike is running this damned war!" Bradley telephoned that the division had to be turned toward Bastogne, a crossroads market town just west of the Belgian border with Luxembourg.

"God damn it!" said Patton in his deceptively unsoldierly high voice. All the Germans wanted to do, he objected, was to delay his push, but he conceded the redeployment. Bradley then telephoned his own headquarters to ask that Lieutenant General William H. Simpson's Ninth Army send down the 7th Armored from the panhandle of southern Holland that dipped between Belgium and Germany near Aachen. Simpson, unprotesting, wouldn't like it either.

Rumors spread from tank to half-track that the European war was over and that troops were really being redeployed to the Pacific. Crews in some tanks and trucks scrawled in chalk on the sides of their vehicles,

PACIFIC BOUND. The next morning the division awakened to rain and darkness and Germans, on the road which led west to St. Vith, a junction town west of the Schnee Eifel and in the path of the First SS Panzer Division. On the fourth day of the offensive a German artillery lieutenant would write in his diary, "The roads are littered with wrecked American vehicles, cars, tanks. Another column of prisoners passes. I count over a thousand men. Nearby there is another column of 1500, with about 50 officers, including a lieutenant-colonel who had asked to surrender." The 28th Division, formerly the Pennsylvania National Guard, had a red keystone shoulder patch, called by its troops since 1917 the "bucket of blood." Its casualties were living up to it. Reports spread that the Germans were murdering captives. At least 350 Americans and 100 Belgians were killed, 86 in the "Malmédy massacre." Further shootings, hangings, and beatings occurred in the sweep west. An SS machine-gunner in *Obersturmbannführer* Jochen Peiper's strike force emptied his rounds into a house as his armored vehicle clattered by, killing the Gengoux family.

Among others at the Versailles meeting with Eisenhower on the 16th had been Brigadier General Bruce Clarke, just posted to Combat Command B of the 7th Armored. He was planning on leave in Paris. Instead, Bradley ordered him to Bastogne, which Clarke questioned, as it seemed then almost a rear area. As a colonel with Patton's 4th Armored he had acquired a reputation for pugnacity. On a Marshall visit to France, Patton had asked for a first star for Clarke and the chief of staff confessed, his black book now obsolete, "I don't know him." Marshall apparently then checked, as a Patton recommendation was rare. Clarke was promoted.

After fresh reports arrived, Bradley sent Clarke instead to Vielsalm, a village well north of Bastogne and to the west of St. Vith. Thousands of troops were already on the road but few, as in the 7th Armored, knew their destinations, which kept changing on reports of enemy thrusts. Despite the narrow, congested roads, the Germans were moving fast. In St. Vith, Brigadier General William Hoge's 9th Armored Division was already feeling the pressure. Two regiments of Major General Alan Jones's 106th Infantry, the 422nd and 423rd, their earlier losses in the Hürtgenwald replaced by former ASTP men good at books but still green on infantry tactics, were in danger of being cut off in the Schnee Eifel. The division had been assigned to the Ardennes because it seemed safe. Some GIs were so new to their outfits that sergeants failed to learn their names before they had to report them killed or missing.

Employing 88s, mortars, and *Panzerfaust* rocket launchers with his tanks, wrecking lightly armored American Shermans, Field Marshal

Walther Model's troops pushed back the "Amis" farther in two days than they had moved forward in two months. Allied forces had stalled in most places before the German Westwall, a series of bunkers and natural barriers like rivers and forests that largely followed the prewar border with Belgium, Luxembourg, and France.

Editors at home had little conception of the realities. In the fat Sunday papers in the States on December 17 the gravity of the counteroffensive in the Ardennes was underplayed. Buried on page 19 in the *New York Times* was Harold Denny's story, GERMAN ASSAULTS ON 1ST ARMY FIERCE. The contradictory subhead reassured, "Enemy Pays Heavy Price in Futile Blow to Stem the Advance of Hodges." Denny claimed from a briefing that the attacks were "to delay and harass us and make every yard of our advance as costly as possible. . . . These counter-attacks were checked everywhere, usually after hours of severe fighting, and they cost the enemy heavy casualties." The *Times's* front page ignored the Ardennes. Rather, General MacArthur received top billing: AMERICANS CAPTURE AIRFIELDS ON MINDORO AS SAN JOSE IS WON IN 9-MILE ADVANCE; SEVENTH ARMY DRIVES DEEPER INTO REICH.

Lieutenant General Alexander Patch's Seventh Army had captured Wissembourg, on the prewar French border with Germany north of Strasbourg and was hardly "deep" into Germany, but readers without maps would have their optimism about a quick end to war boosted. Only in later papers did the German attacks mushroom. Revised headlines in the *Times* on the 18th balanced the foreboding with apparent MacArthur successes in the Philippines: NAZI OFFENSIVE PIERCES FIRST ARMY LINES; CHUTISTS AND LUFTWAFFE SUPPORT PUSH; AMERICANS ADVANCE 6 MILES ON MINDORO. On the front page, but still not in the lead story, Harold Denny wrote, "It now looks like the real thing."

From Versailles, Eisenhower ordered more redeployments. Nineteen German divisions had already been identified. The few roads through the Ardennes were so crowded with troops and vehicles that Nazi generals had to stand in open staff cars directing traffic. To counter the pressure, two airborne divisions, the 82nd and the 101st, at Reims to refit with replacements after Arnhem, were ordered forward as light infantry. The 82nd was settling into its billets at Suippes and Soissons and some already had brief leaves to Paris. A staff officer at SHAEF commented to a colleague, "Those paratroopers are the smartest, most alert-looking soldiers I have seen."

"Hell, man," said the other, realizing that they had been in Montgomery's botched "Market Garden" operation at Eindhoven, "they should be. You are looking at the survivors."

In advance of his troops, Brigadier General Anthony C. McAuliffe, artillery commander of the 101st and acting in the absence of Maxwell Taylor, left Reims by jeep on the 18th. Pausing at Bastogne for an update, he learned that his instructions had been changed. The town was to be held, and the 101st was to do it. Orders from Major General Gavin, acting for Ridgway, were to prepare the area "for all-around defense and to stay there until . . . further orders." As historian Russell Weigley would put it, "In an old American army tradition, the 101st would have to form a circle to fend off the Indians until the cavalry reinforcements arrived, in this instance in the form of [old cavalryman] George Patton's Third Army tanks."

Bastogne was the only key junction in the region still in Allied hands. To the east, St. Vith had been evacuated. Later, German General Hasso von Manteuffel would concede that the four days' delay at St. Vith had been a crucial "disadvantage," stalling the offensive until the Americans could form a defense along the Amblève and Salm rivers. Yet the fall of St. Vith released more Germans to invest Bastogne. Artillery fire hammered the town. Locals lived in their cellars. On the morning of December 22, General Heinrich von Luttwitz offered to end the standoff with a surrender ultimatum he had delivered. McAullife's one-word rejection—"Nuts!"—became the byword of the Bulge.

Montgomery's troops in Holland and upper Belgium were repositioned as backup without actually joining the fighting. Having downplayed German potential only a few days earlier, Monty now forecast that the Wehrmacht would be "bounding the Meuse and advancing on Brussels." The British 6th Airborne was dispatched from England. Manpower reserves, after years of war, were low. The British were already cannibalizing infantry divisions in Italy. Perversely pleased that Eisenhower's "broad front" strategy of pressing everywhere was not working, and that only he had the proper formula, Montgomery watched and waited.

Since even generals had to attend to their appetites, Eisenhower and his guests, including Arthur Tedder and Beetle Smith, had dined on the 16th on stewed and fried New England oysters, with champagne. Afterward, despite grim initial reports, over five rubbers of bridge, they drank scotch and bourbon past midnight. It suggested a misplaced confidence, for by darkness on the first day of the Bulge, thousands of American stragglers from service units and from units broken in the first assaults had begun clogging roads rearward, along with refugees from endangered villages. Some vehicles were abandoned when an officer at a fuel dump panicked on hearing rumors of approaching Germans, and ordered the axing of four thousand drums of gasoline. In the U.S., newspaper headlines had become larger and more gloomy, although the Pacific still furnished some balance: GERMANS DRIVE 20 MILES INTO BELGIUM; ALLIED FLIERS POUND TANK SPEARHEADS; 742 JAPANESE PLANES SMASHED IN ONE WEEK.

The inflated statistics about Japanese losses reflected the navy's role in MacArthur's moves up the Philippines. Mindoro, the stepping stone to Luzon, had been invaded on December 15, just before the Bulge balloon went up. Unlike Leyte, where fighting dragged on, Mindoro did not become a quagmire. The Japanese intended that for Luzon. But their desperate new secret weapons—*kamikazes*—harassed the American fleet, one suicide plane striking MacArthur's former flagship *Nashville*, causing 323 casualties, 133 of them dead. Japanese technology was not up to the German V-1 or V-2 but no human weapons were spared. Soon, suicide attackers materialized in manned bombs, small boats, and torpedoes. (MacArthur watched from the cruiser *Boise*, which an enemy midget sub attacked—and missed. A dive bomber also crashed wide of the *Boise*.)

A typhoon on December 19 caused more damage than the Japanese, capsizing three destroyers, destroying 186 exposed carrier planes, and taking the lives of nearly 800 men. In the Philippine Sea, enemy losses of aircraft and ships to overwhelming American firepower were catastrophic, but *kamikazes* kept coming. It required no maps for the Japanese to realize that MacArthur's forces would invade where they themselves had in December 1941, at Lingayen Gulf. MacArthur's own D-Day for Luzon was planned for January 9, 1945, postponed from December 20 because of the slogging pace across Leyte. The Japanese could not miss observing the massing of nearly a thousand ships, but their tremendous losses left them unready.

Far off in Paris (always a party) the bad news from the Ardennes got out quickly as officers on pre-Christmas leave were alerted, if they could be found, to return to their units. At a posh restaurant, General "Tooey" Spaatz was hosting a dinner on the seemingly limitless SHAEF tab for visiting brass. Aides with anxious faces kept sidling up to him with messages. His guests realized that something was indeed up, but Spaatz remained for dessert.

As the German bulge into the Ardennes deepened, divisions beefed up with untested recruits or replacements reeled back. German armor and artillery were reason enough, and Americans, seldom defensive-minded and preparing to resume the attack, had done little digging in, nor mining. Dismaying reports arrived about enemy paratroops landing behind them, and commandos in American uniform. Skorzeny's mission used forty captured American jeeps and German tanks painted with U.S. markings. Teams were to seize bridges across the Meuse and create suspicion and confusion. Squads sent false messages, shot up command posts, cut telephone lines, changed directional road signs, misdirected American traffic, and created a frenzy of changed passwords drawn from baseball, comic books, and the movies. ("Where do the Dodgers play?" "What is Superman's real name?" "Who is Betty Grable's latest husband?")

Some unexpected successes occurred. One *Kommando* when captured claimed imaginatively that their mission was to kidnap Eisenhower. When that frightening intelligence got to Versailles, the general became a virtual prisoner of his security detail. Beetle Smith offered the misinformation to Eisenhower at his morning staff conference on the 20th. Rumors then escalated. Soon, allegedly, there were sixty mythical Germans en route to seize Eisenhower. He was persuaded to move from his villa in St.-Germain-en-Laye. It was too remote from SHAEF headquarters. A lookalike, Lieutenant Colonel Baldwin Smith, was chauffeured about in Ike's overcoat, wearing five stars, to distract the ghost kidnappers. From a guest villa on the grounds of the Trianon Palace Hotel, Eisenhower was driven by circuitous routes to his office.

By the time Bradley had returned to Luxembourg City, below the action, German divisions were pushing deep wedges into the American lines. Since armored columns required roads, Eisenhower's staff, spreading a large blow-up map of the Ardennes on the floor, identified two towns where east-west routes toward the Meuse converged: St. Vith and Bastogne. Soon St. Vith was gone. If the Germans could break through into the Belgian lowlands, they could split the British and American armies, and either retake Antwerp or render it unusable. Eisenhower called for a meeting of top brass on December 19 in Verdun. Predictably, Monty sent a deputy.

In an old French stone barracks, warmed inadequately by a potbelly stove, and with large easels to display maps, Tedder, Bradley, Patton, Devers, Montgomery's second-in-command Freddie de Guingand, and their aides met with Eisenhower. He described the crisis as an opportunity rather than a "disaster," asking unsuccessfully for "only cheerful faces at this conference table." To the east, his divisions were being mauled. Patton, thinking big as usual, offered, "Hell, let's have the guts to let the sons of bitches go all the way to Paris. Then we'll really cut 'em up and chew 'em up." Some laughed, but Eisenhower, in no mood for irony, said sharply, "George, that's fine. But the enemy must never be allowed to cross the Meuse."

The penetration had to be blunted and narrowed. Containing the bulge north to south would tie up the few decent roads by which the Germans could move reinforcements and supplies. Juggling army boundaries, Eisenhower wanted Devers's Seventh Army to move into areas from which Patton had hoped to jump off into the Saar, and Patton to attack the southern flank of the bulge below Bastogne. Inevitably, Bradley would become a minor player, as the salient split his zone. "George," said Eisenhower, "I want you to command this move—under Brad's supervision, of course—making a strong counterattack with at least six divisions. When can you start?"

"As soon as you're through with me," said Patton, noting that he had left three alternative plans with his staff in Nancy, anticipating the next move. All he had to do was telephone a coded signal. He could initiate an attack "in forty-eight hours. The morning of the 21st, with three divisions." Patton noted in his diary about the instructions from Eisenhower that it "didn't enter his head" that the other three of the six divisions "exist[ted] only on paper." They had been battered in the Hürtgenwald in November. Patton's aide, Lieutenant Colonel Charles R. Codman, recalled "a stir, a shuffling of feet, as those present straightened up in their chairs. In some faces skepticism. But through the room a current of excitement leaped like a flame." Taking tens of thousands of troops facing east, swiveling them north, and moving them, with their armor and supplies set up for a different thrust, over inadequate and icy roads to counterattack two days later, seemed logistically problematic. Patton was confident he could do it.

Later, German General Erich Brandenberger recalled that he expected "a speedy reaction from the enemy." The few good roads leading north through Arlon, just west of the Luxembourg border, would be used to move American troops north toward Bastogne, but "not earlier than the fourth day of the attack. The fact that these forces would probably be commanded by General Patton made it quite likely that the enemy would direct a heavy punch against the deep [southern] flank of the German forces." In striking southeast out of Normandy, Brandenberger boasted in ironic self-congratulation, "Patton had given proof of his extraordinary skill in armored warfare, which he conducted according to the fundamental German conception."

From radio intercepts,* Brandenberger already knew that the 101st Airborne was to move toward Bastogne from the west. He expected his own Seventh Army to face Patton's Third Army as well, from the south. Unfortunately for German plans, tough resistance from the first day, even from broken divisions in the Bulge, had slowed the advance. Hitler hoped to have troops cross the Meuse by the third day, but they struggled at St. Vith and then at Bastogne.

At 4:15 A.M. on the 20th, Montgomery radioed London offering to take charge in the north. The general on night duty explained that it was "no good" arousing Brooke, as London could not order Eisenhower about and would have to consult Washington, where it was just after midnight.

Some German troops remained wedged in traffic jams which tailed back to the Westwall. In Verdun, Patton had contended coldly that the Germans could afford attrition much less than the Americans. Looking up at Bradley as he outlined on a map his plans for the southern shoulder of the Bulge, Patton said, "Brad, the Kraut's stuck his head in a meat-grinder. And"—he turned his fist in simulation—"this time I have hold of the handle."

"Don't be fatuous, George," Eisenhower had warned, reining in Patton's brag. But in two hours, the redispositions were worked out and settled. As the meeting broke up, Eisenhower walked to the door with Patton. Referring to his new fifth star, Eisenhower said, "Funny thing, George, every time I get another star, I get attacked." His fourth star had come just before the Kasserine Pass embarrassment in Tunisia.

"And every time you get attacked, Ike," said Patton, "I have to bail you out." Bailing out the Bulge would become Patton's finest hour. Yet

---

*The Germans routinely intercepted Allied communications, even exchanges between the president and the prime minister. Perhaps it was fortunate that there were so many radioed messages that only a fraction of them could be digested in time, and utilized.

Bradley and Eisenhower remained uneasy about entrusting major operations to Patton, while continuing to show confidence in Hodges. "I trust,"
Eisenhower would write to Marshall as late as March 12, 1945, "that the
Secretary of War will wait for my recommendation before putting in Patton's name for promotion. There is no one better acquainted than I with
Patton's good qualities and likewise with his limitations. In the past I have
demonstrated my high opinion of him when it was not easy to do so. In
certain situations both Bradley and I would select Patton to command
above any other general we have, but in other situations we would prefer
Hodges."

In Washington, Stimson noted in his diary, "By this morning they"—
the Germans—"had made quite a good deal of progress. So I had a talk
with Marshall over that. We agreed [from reports received] that the Germans could not get very far. . . . Our people do not seem to be rattled and
the American forces are closing around the German salient and I think
will stop it."

Hodges, who had abandoned his First Army command post at Spa in
panic, had not even been invited—or ordered—to the Verdun conference.
He remained unexplainably unavailable for two more days, and his chief
of staff, Major General William B. Kean, was in de facto command.
Later, Kean claimed that Hodges had been "confined to his bed, barely
conscious with viral pneumonia," a diagnosis denied by a headquarters officer who saw Hodges "sitting with his arms folded on his desk, his head
in his arms." Bradley communicated with Kean by telephone. "First Army
had a very bad staff," the impolitic Beetle Smith later wrote, and "Hodges
[was] the weakest commander we had."

Having failed to get London to intervene, Montgomery used Major
General Jock Whiteley at SHAEF to suggest to Eisenhower that
Bradley's armies be put temporarily under Monty's 21st Army Group.
The Bulge had separated Bradley's 12th Army Group headquarters in
Luxembourg City from the north. Later, Bradley claimed that the loss of
two-thirds of his command was Eisenhower's idea, and that he was "completely dumbfounded—and shocked." Instead of "standing up to [Bedell]
Smith," telling Beetle that SHAEF "was losing its head, that I had things
under control, and reassuring him that Hodges was performing magnificently under the circumstances," Bradley wrote, Eisenhower "knuckled
under." Hodges's "magnificence" was a mystery, and Bradley refused to
concede that he had lost control of his front. It was a matter of personal
and national pride. Ken Strong could overhear, in Versailles, Bradley
shouting to Eisenhower, "By God, Ike, I cannot be responsible to the

American people if you do this. I resign." Very likely he worried that after
Montgomery took over, he would give nothing back.

"Well, Brad," Eisenhower replied wearily, "those are my orders." He
would shield Bradley, who continued to make a show of appearing involved. Chester Hansen, his aide, wrote on December 20, "[12th Army
Group] Headquarters continues to be a madhouse, with too many people
running in and out—too many telephone calls. Traffic is heavy, too, with
the new divisions coming to reinforce our effort. . . . They have helped at
least to abate the alarmist sentiment that was so evident yesterday."
Bradley also worried about the Skorzeny scare that had nearly immobilized Eisenhower. "We have removed the [three-star license] plates from
the General's jeep," Hansen wrote. ". . . No more sedans."

Bradley did not try to visit Hodges, telephoning him instead several
times, or more, a day. Montgomery was employing his more physical intelligence system to liaise with other commands: officers who carried information back and forth from headquarters to headquarters in their
heads. He checked in personally before turning over Hodges and Kean to
them. Flanked by motorcycle outriders, in an armored car flying British
pennants, Montgomery, with his aide, Major Carol Mather, arrived showily at the unpalatial Palace Hotel in the relocated Hodges command post
in Liege at 1:30 P.M. on the 20th. He had asked Simpson to join them. It
was, an aide to Hodges recalled resentfully, like "Christ come to cleanse
the temple." Montgomery declined lunch and rather than have the generals brief him, spread out his own maps on the warm "bonnet" of his
Humber staff car. Turning to Mather, much lower in rank than the American generals, he barked, "What's the form?" The term was graceless, as it
was a Britishism for what was happening, or required, possibly unknown
to Hodges or to Simpson. Mather recalled, "Our American friends . . .
looked severely discomfited. It was a slight uncalled for."

One visit sufficed for Montgomery to suggest that Hodges should be
replaced. With unusual tact, however, he added that Eisenhower should
give the matter some overnight thought. The next day, Freddie de Guingand telephoned Beetle Smith and quoted Monty as advising, in faint
praise, "Hodges is not the man I would pick, but he is much better [at the
moment]." To Brooke, Montgomery telegraphed, "There is a definite lack
of grip and control; no one seems to have a clear picture as to the situation. . . ." Soon he added, with his usual vanity, "I think I see daylight now
on the northern front, and we have tidied up the mess and got two American armies properly organised. But I see rocks ahead and no grounds for
the optimism Ike seems to feel. Rundstedt is fighting a good battle." The

next day, as Patton began wheeling his troops about, Montgomery telegraphed Brooke again, gleefully, "I do not think Third US Army will be strong enough to do what is needed. If my forecast proves true, then I shall have to deal unaided with both Fifth and Sixth Panzer Armies. I think I can manage them, but it will be a bit of a party."

Eisenhower rationalized to Montgomery that Hodges, who was being demoted by Monty in every way but rank, was "the quiet reticent type and doesn't appear as aggressive as he really is. Unless he becomes exhausted he will always wage a good fight." Ike radioed both Simpson and Hodges, separately, "In the recent battling you and your army have performed in your usual magnificent style." As if they were children he added, "Now that you have been placed under the Field Marshal's operational command, I know that you will respond cheerfully and efficiently to every instruction he gives." Although Bradley had worried about Montgomery's tendency to "tweak our Yankee noses," the tweaking first came unsubtly from Eisenhower. Patton noted scornfully in his diary that the rearrangement was "either a case of having lost confidence in Bradley, or having been forced to put Montgomery in through the machinations of the Prime Minister or with the hope that if he gives Monty operational control, he will get some of the British divisions in[to action]. Eisenhower is unwilling or unable to command Montgomery."

Almost as if a campaign had been orchestrated to wrest command from the Americans, London papers printed gloomy and even scarifying reports about how operations were being bungled by Eisenhower. A *Daily Express* headline asked, MONTHS ADDED TO WAR? Possibly that was accurate, but not the story, drawn from a German broadcast that Liege had been reached—which would never happen—and that fighting was under way "in the city's suburbs."

Although Montgomery was reorganizing at Bradley's expense what the British called the "Northern Wing," and Churchill's Cabinet reacted with pleasure, Brooke remained skeptical of any management of troops left to mediocre American generals who had "mishandled" the war. "If only the Americans are up to it," he confided to his diary. "Ike is a hopeless commander." On the 22nd he added, "German offensive appears to be held in the north, but I am a little more doubtful about the south. Patton is reported to have put in a counter-attack. This could only have been a half-baked affair and I doubt it's doing much good."

Getting updated, Stimson sat in on a staff conference at the Pentagon with Marshall, writing afterward, "The news from France was bad again today still, although our troops seem to be slowing up the breakthrough somewhat. Still, it is a very formidable threat. . . . It may lengthen the war." A redeeming aspect of the crisis which Marshall and Stimson clung to, was that even exhausted and shattered American divisions had slowed, if not blunted, the German offensive beyond expectations on both sides.

Pentagon concern remained what was *not* happening in the east. In a winter freeze, the Russian front remained relatively quiet. Both Marshall and Eisenhower realized that Hitler, banking on efficient rail lines, could still risk temporary withdrawals of forces and matériel to force the Bulge. To Marshall on December 21, Eisenhower had fudged, "Bradley has kept his head magnificently and has proceeded methodically and energetically to meet the situation. In no quarter is there any tendency to place any blame on Bradley. I retain all my former confidence in him." Less confidently, Stimson held his weekly press conference, assuring newspapermen who saw a dark Christmas ahead, "We will have them."

In the face of the facts, Eisenhower cabled the War Department that he wanted both Spaatz and Bradley to receive four-star rank. It would have "a fine effect," he argued, in being seen as evidence of "calm determination and courage in the face of trials and difficulties." Having no idea how little involved Bradley was, or how overshadowed Spaatz was by Eisenhower's British air advisers like Tedder, Marshall replied cautiously that as Congress was recessed for the holidays, no action would be feasible. Eisenhower conceded on December 23 that he understood.

On the 23rd Ike also issued an Order of the Day meant more for newspapers at home than for troops in the field who had no opportunity to read it. It was his first since D-Day. He urged troops to turn Hitler's "great gamble into his worst defeat," and exhorted them "to rise now to new heights of courage, of resolution, and of effort. Let everyone hold before him a single thought—to destroy the enemy on the ground, in the air, everywhere—destroy him!" He also dictated a long self-protective diary memorandum to Harry Butcher, summing up the first week of the Ardennes war for a report to the Pentagon. Ike had just received Christmas greetings from Marshall, who expressed cautious appreciation for a "magnificent job." It seemed tailored for release to the press: "Largely through your leadership, in force, in wisdom, and in patience and tolerance, you have made possible Allied cooperation and teamwork in the greatest military operation in the history of the world, complicated by social, economic and political problems almost without precedent. Good luck to you in the New Year. May the Lord watch over you. You have my complete confidence."

With obvious relief, Eisenhower replied from Versailles that Marshall's Christmas letter was "the brightest spot in my existence since we reached the Siegfried Line.* Short of a major defeat inflicted on the enemy, I could not have had a better personal present."

The Christmas gift that Patton desperately wanted was clearing weather, to better move his armor and for air support of his operations. On returning from Reims, as his divisions were about to turn toward the Belgium-Luxembourg border, he told his Third Army senior chaplain, Colonel James O'Neill, that he was going to use the prayer he had the chaplain write earlier when rain was delaying the now-aborted attack into the Saar. "Do you have a good prayer for weather?" he had asked then. "I'm tired of these soldiers having to fight mud and flood as well as Germans. See if we can't get God to work on our side."

"May I say, General," the chaplain ventured, "that it isn't a customary thing among men of my profession to pray for clear weather to kill fellow men."

"Are you teaching me theology or are you the Chaplain of the Third Army? I want a prayer." As Father O'Neill realized that Patton did everything over the top, he duly wrote something. The rains had largely changed to snow, and the Saar offensive for which the earlier supplication had been intended had been canceled. When O'Neill reminded him of that, Patton said, "Oh, the Lord won't mind. He knows we're too busy now to print another prayer." Printed locally in 250,000 copies, it was distributed in wallet size, with a holiday greeting on the other side. The entreaty for good weather was also reproduced in a box on the front page of the *Stars and Stripes*, which irked commanders in the north who hadn't Patton's public relations instincts. He would also go to a chapel in Luxembourg City and pray for good weather personally, addressing God—as if the Deity were a senior general—as "Sir."

He wanted "four clear days," Patton appealed, so that supporting aircraft could fly (*Jabowetter*, the Germans called it), and reconnaissance could pick out artillery targets. "You have just got to make up Your mind whose side You're on. You must come to my assistance, so that I may dispatch the entire German Army as a birthday present to Your Prince of Peace."

To Beatrice, Patton had written with typical swagger, "We shoot the works on a chestnut pulling expedition in the morning. . . . Yesterday I again earned my pay. I visited seven divisions and regrouped an army alone. It was quite a day and I enjoyed it." Optimistically, he added, "Re-

*The Westwall fortifications, based upon the prewar Siegfried Line.

member how a tarpon always makes one big flop just before it dies?" His Third Army had "progressed on a twenty mile front to a depth of seven miles." He had "hoped for more but we are in the middle of a snow storm and there were a lot of demolitions. So I should be content which of course I am not." Still they had "moved over a hundred miles . . . With a little luck I will put on a more daring operation just after Xmas." He combed 8,000 replacement infantry from his "rear echelons" and made "doeboys" out of clerks and cooks and bandsmen and other service personnel: "If others would do the same"—he knew how swollen the support staffs were from Paris to Brussels—"we could finish this show in short order."

Patton now had, he noted in his diary, 108 battalions of infantry and artillery in his combined attacking force, with "1,296 guns of 105 [mm] or bigger. I don't see how the Boche can take this much artillery." The Germans, however, bent without buckling, and the advance slowed. In the snow, a battalion of the 4th Armored, whose III Corps commander, Major General John Millikin, a former cavalryman, was ordered to "drive like hell," lost thirty-three tanks to two tough German units, and was still twelve miles from Bastogne. Patton told him to get close enough to hear the bullets "whistle," and push on, if he could, through the night.

The Germans had already bypassed Bastogne, assuming that the garrison and the townspeople would give up after running out of food and fuel. The Panzer Lehr Division was left to deal with the siege while other troops pushed on toward St. Hubert, twenty miles from the Meuse. On December 23, the skies cleared briefly, and 1,200 American support and supply sorties were flown across the humpbacked front. On the day before Christmas, Allied planes flew more than 5,000 sorties and the Luftwaffe 1,088—with losses that sapped German air strength and left few experienced airmen. Major General Ludwig Heilmann of the 5th *Fallschirmjager* (Paratroop) Division reported, "One could see from Bastogne back [eastward] to the Westwall, a single torchlight procession of burning vehicles."

By Christmas Eve a spearhead of the 2nd Panzer Division had reached Celles, well beyond Bastogne and only a few miles from a bend in the Meuse. Sixty miles from the start line on December 16, it would be as far as the Bulge would extend. At a chateau near La Roche, General von

Manteuffel telephoned General Jodl at Hitler's headquarters. "Time is running short," he explained. The Führer had expected to exploit surprise and reach the Meuse in three days. December 24 was far beyond their fuel limits. His left flank was not covered: the salient was too narrow to be useful. He expected further attacks from Patton. "You have to let me know what the Führer wants. The time has come for a complete new plan. I can't keep driving toward the Meuse and still take Bastogne. . . . We've been delayed too long. . . . Besides, by this time the Allies are sure to be on the other side of the Meuse in strength."

Following Hitler's expected refusal, von Rundstedt came in person to appeal for his "limited solution," eliminating Antwerp, now an impossible objective. "When all goes well, people are on top of the world," Hitler said, "but when everything starts to go wrong they just fold up and give in."

Although the edges of Bastogne were fraying, especially in the south and east, McAuliffe now counted on holding on. Near the Meuse at Celles, capture of thirteen German self-propelled guns abandoned for lack of fuel suggested that the 2nd Panzers had gone as far west as they could go. At *Adlerhorst*, Jodl said cautiously, realizing that he also faced a rebuff, "*Mein Führer*, we must face the facts. We cannot force the Meuse."

"We have had unexpected setbacks," Hitler conceded, "because my plan was not followed to the letter, but all is not lost. The war cannot last as long again as it has already lasted. Nobody could stand it, neither we nor the others." In his tortured reasoning, he explained, "The question is, which side will crack first? I say that the side which lasts longer will do so only if it stands to lose everything. We stand to lose everything."

At Montgomery's command post on Christmas Day, Bradley, looking humiliated, arrived to be updated on the northern shoulder of the Bulge. Monty expressed pessimism about the delayed reassembly toward the Rhine. Although he now had the U.S. First and Ninth as well as his own troops for a counterattack, he preferred waiting for more reinforcements. He asked what Eisenhower proposed, as he had heard nothing from Versailles since the shift in command. Bradley had no idea. He had not seen Eisenhower for weeks, and claimed not to have heard from him. The Germans, Monty told Bradley, and repeated to Brooke, have "given us a real bloody nose. It was useless to pretend that we were going to turn this quickly into a great victory and we had better much admit it. . . . The enemy saw his chance and took it." (Eisenhower, he recalled, had claimed that the turnaround would result in "our greatest victory.") "Poor chap," Monty reflected, Bradley was "such a decent fellow" but over his head. He had never before commanded anything larger than a corps and he had permitted Patton to go too far.

On returning to Luxembourg City, Bradley quoted Monty to Patton as estimating that it would take three months to straighten out the situation—that only he could mount a fresh attack but that his forces were still "too weak" for that. "Personally," Montgomery told his aides, "I am enjoying a very interesting battle." Smugly, he anticipated taking over the ground campaign in the west for the remainder of the war. The British press was loud in promoting that. The *Daily Mail* criticized Bradley in an editorial, "A Slur on Monty," for insisting that Montgomery's assignment over him was temporary and that Monty soon would be back commanding only his 21st Army Group. When the emergency was over, the *Daily Mail* predicted, Montgomery would "again be pushed back into the semi-obscurity that was his lot before the Ardennes. . . ."

In his diary, Patton wished that "Ike were more of a gambler, but he is certainly a lion compared to Montgomery, and Bradley is better than Ike as far as nerve is concerned." He found Montgomery "disgusting" and eager to impugn "the valor of our army and the confidence of our people. . . . If ordered to fall back, I think I will ask to be relieved." In Versailles, according to General Gavin, word had already gotten to Ike "that Patton's staff was saying that Eisenhower was the best general the British had."

Headquarters mess on Christmas Day at Versailles put on roast turkey with all the traditional trimmings. Ike's hostess was Kay Summersby, who had written to Frank McCarthy at the Pentagon about her WAC commission, "If you think it appropriate, I should like to ask you to give an expression of my thanks to General Marshall." (The letter had arrived on December 21; very likely the discreet Colonel McCarthy kept it to himself.) Eisenhower unwrapped his gifts early, wore fancy slippers which Mamie had sent him, and smoked some of the king-sized cigarettes she included, which, he wrote to her, would give him more time "to devote to the job," as he would not have to pause as often to light another. Lieutenant Summersby noted that "E. is a bit low in his mind" because of unabated worries about abduction, and stayed close to his office.

Eisenhower would soon break free. Although delayed further by bad weather, he would fly to Brussels to meet again with Montgomery. Press criticism in London continued, and Marshall and Stimson were furious about it, as it seemed to them the only evidence of British pugnacity. It prompted Marshall to write an "eyes only" radio message to Eisenhower confessing that he was violating his own orders to Pentagon staff about not bothering him "while you are in the turmoil of this German offensive." Still, without mentioning Montgomery by name, Marshall wanted Eisenhower to keep his backbone rigid. Articles in "certain London papers" had proposed "a British Deputy Commander for all your ground forces," Marshall wrote, ". . . implying that you have undertaken too much of a task yourself. My feeling is this: under no circumstances make any concessions of any kind whatsoever. You not only have our complete confidence but there would be a terrific resentment in this country following such action. I am not assuming that you had in mind such a concession. I just wish you to be certain of our attitude on this side. You are doing a grand job and go on and give them hell." But crediting Patton, too often in trouble, for the turnaround, Marshall observed to WAC Colonel Oveta Culp Hobby, "Don't you love to see a man come rushing out of a doghouse?"

Fighting everywhere in the Bulge was as intense on Christmas Day as it had been since the breakthrough began. German grenadiers in white capes and sheets blending in with the snow fired into doors and windows in villages, and took fire from Americans in foxholes and behind barns. Woods and ravines and riverbanks changed hands, then changed hands again. Although the weather was again worsening, American P-38s and British Typhoons, landing only to replenish fuel and ammunition, worked over clearings in the woods harboring suspected tanks and trucks.

On Christmas night in the north, the 19th Panzer Grenadier Regiment of the 9th Panzer Division, ordered to break across the Salm River at Vielsalm, again hit the 82nd Airborne's 508th Regiment. After a three-hour firefight the Germans were beaten back. Screaming and yelling in a mass attack they would return again but were finally stopped. To the south, the Christmas attack on Bastogne began at four on a cold and clear dawn when an assault party clad in white crept toward the perimeter village of Champs. By daylight the attempt had failed amid artillery crossfire that cost the 15th Panzer Grenadiers its tanks and the dismounted foot soldiers they had carried. McAuliffe's artillerymen frustrated renewed assaults, and the German 5th Parachute Division and 39th Regiment failed to close the corridor being opened by Patton's armor. Four miles south of Bastogne on December 26, units of the 4th Armored Division pushed into Bastogne from the southwest.

McAuliffe jeeped with an aide to see the arrival of the 4th Armored for himself. Other paratroopers followed. At 4:50 P.M., the first tanks threaded through a hastily laid and ineffective German minefield, and fifteen minutes later, opening their hatches, the relieving tankers observed with surprise that the 101st command had ensured that its greeting party was well dressed and clean-shaven. Their casualties had been 105 officers and 1,536 men, while the 10th Armored had lost 25 officers and 478 men, but McAuliffe was going to show that his division and supporting units had everything under control.

Captain William Dwight climbed out of his tank, strode up the hill to McAuliffe's observation post, saluted, and asked, "How are you, General?"

"Gee, I am mighty glad to see you," said McAuliffe.

In January Edgar Eisenhower would write to his brother from Tacoma about criticism of "generalship" in the Ardenes. Dwight (as he signed his letter) would respond that he was not disturbed by unwanted advice from the press. If he had taken all the suggestions offered, the army would be running around in circles. The Germans, he wrote, had "gambled a lot," and lost—as they were "sure to lose"—hundreds of irreplaceable tanks and more than a hundred thousand of their "best remaining fighting men." They had not regained the initiative. Yet even in victory, the Bulge would continue to haunt him.

12

Reclaiming the Lost Ground

DRAFTING FOR ROOSEVELT on January 2, 1945, a citation to be presented posthumously to the widow of Sir John Dill, George Marshall warmly described his late colleague, representing the British in Washington since Pearl Harbor, as having been an antidote to "the bickerings that are inevitable at this stage of the war."* Bickering in the plural reflected the complications piling up at the end of the tunnel. Among them were exchanges with MacArthur, who intended to bar the British from exploiting his successes in order to reclaim their Asian colonies and a role in the peace in the Pacific. Nor did he want the American navy to outrace him, after the Philippines, to Japan.

Marshall and Eisenhower were already contending with De Gaulle's perverse myth that France had liberated itself. As Russian-French novelist Irène Némirovsky, lost to the Holocaust at Birkenau, predicted in 1942, "There will be such a conspiracy of lies that all this will be transformed into yet another glorious page in the history of France." Although with diminishing resources to employ and little role in reversing the Ardennes bulge, Churchill hoped, at the least in appearance, to dominate the defeat of Germany in the west, with Montgomery commanding all Allied forces across the Rhine, and Eisenhower a facade. While at home, looking suitably grim on its cover, Eisenhower was *Time*'s "Man of the Year," in Britain he was the whipping boy for victory delayed.

*"He really loved you, George," Lady Dill wrote to Marshall on December 22, 1945, "and your mutual affection meant a great deal to him—he always trusted you implicitly."

Eisenhower would remain anxious about the Bulge, writing to Secretary of War Robert Patterson a year later, "I am unalterably opposed to making any effort to publicize at this time any story concerning the Ardennes Battle, or even allowing any written explanation to go outside the War Department." He objected to defending "something where no defense is necessary." It was "a mere incident to a large campaign." He could not keep a lid on the realities, however, and reassessments, including his own, would emerge for decades. Among them would be MacArthur's later claim that the Bulge "resulted in approximately as many casualties as were sustained in the entire Southwest Pacific Area campaigns from Australia to Tokyo." SHAEF commanders, he told Bert Andrews of the *New York Herald Tribune* without naming names, "made every mistake that supposedly intelligent men could make."

Certainly one commander under Ike made no serious mistakes. Patton on December 27 had again addressed God, reporting "complete progress," and now crediting the weather supplied from above as making it "possible for the German army to commit suicide. That, Sir, was a brilliant military move, and I bow humbly to a supreme military genius." In a letter to Beatrice Patton he confirmed, "My prayer seems to be working."

As the Ardennes salient was being reduced (at considerable cost), Eisenhower planned to further shorten his lines by withdrawing from exposed Strasbourg—until De Gaulle confronted him angrily on January 3, 1945, to warn of the consequences. Whatever the hazard, *le grande Charles* threatened, should that symbol of Franco-German contention become "a terrible wound on the honor of our country," he would interrupt Allied lines of military communication and unsettle all of France. "If we were at *Kriegspiel*"—war games—"I should say you are right . . . but retreat in Alsace would be a national disaster!" (With Devers also disapproving, Eisenhower backed down, he explained to Marshall, on grounds of "necessity.") "Next to the weather," Ike would confide on February 29, after further exasperation, "the French," meaning De Gaulle, "have caused me more trouble in this war than any other single factor."

With unbending arrogance, De Gaulle, while blackmailing Eisenhower, was utterly dependent on American resources. Tom Handy called him "an ungrateful son-of-a-bitch. We gave him everything, including a pillow on which to lay his head." Knowing how much Roosevelt detested the prickly De Gaulle, Marshall could not coddle him. "If you want a man to be for you," he told Handy, "never let him feel he is dependent on you. Because he is then not going to like you at all. If you really want the guy to be for you, find some way to make him feel you are in some way dependent on him." The homily was not easy to employ.

Complications grew as the war ground to a close. Although Russian liaison officers were attached to Eisenhower's SHAEF, Stalin rejected all reciprocity, and Allied aircrews making emergency landings in Soviet space were interrogated, humiliated, and detained. Once the Red Army returned to the offensive, Stalin—an ally only in adversity—could be expected to claim any winnings he wanted, and won, in Europe, and to ignore Allied exasperation.

Realizing that a final agonizing summit meeting was planned before the European war wound down, Marshall cautioned Eisenhower, perhaps too mildly, about inadvertently giving anything away in communicating with Soviet authorities. "In future," he wrote, "I suggest that you approach them in simple Main Street Abilene style. They are rather cynically disposed toward the diplomatic phrasing of our compliments and seem almost to appreciate downright rough talk."

Furnishing Germans with his own new year message, Hitler no longer promised further "wonder weapons" but contended that although the Reich might not win the war, its enemies would also fail. Leaving *Adlerhorst* he assured his senior commanders, "We shall yet master fate." The Ardennes surprise had created "a tremendous easing of the situation. The enemy has had to abandon all his plans for attack.... Already he has had to admit that there is no chance of the war being decided before August, perhaps not before the end of next year." Pulling his SS Panzer divisions* for return to the Russian front while ordering a stubborn, fighting withdrawal behind the Westwall, Hitler confided to an aide, Captain Nicolaus von Below, "I know the war is lost. Their superior power is too great. I've been betrayed." But he insisted, "We'll not capitulate. Never. We can go down. But we'll take a world with us."

Roosevelt's new year message claimed that the rapidity of recovery in the Ardennes was "because we have one Supreme Commander in complete control of all the Allied Armies...." Although the Allies were regaining the initiative, the Bulge would not be entirely blunted until the end of the month. And while Eisenhower remained nominally in authority, he had handed the armies in the north to Montgomery, whose sweeping vanity in claiming ("I took certain steps myself . . .") that he had

---

*American troops were so furious at SS atrocities discovered as the Germans fell back that on New Year's Day 1945, soldiers of the 11th Armored Division murdered 60 prisoners picked up, 21 of whom were lined up and executed.

personally reversed the German drive was only exceeded by his further ambitions. "American GIs [are] great fighting men," he explained, "when given the proper leadership." A dispatch from Hugh Schuck of the *New York Daily News* following Montgomery's unhelpful press conference closed with the blast, "To borrow the expression of American general Tony McAuliffe, 'Nuts to you, Monty!'"

Perhaps as an indirect slap at Montgomery, Eisenhower, in MacArthur style, awarded Omar Bradley, the chief victim of the field marshal's humiliation, a Bronze Star. As it was unclear what achievement Ike had in mind, one of Bradley's staff explained to a correspondent cynically, "Omar received the medal for continuing to breathe through the battle."

Abetted by Brooke, who nursed his resentments, and by Churchill, who saw his grip irreversibly weakening, Montgomery still argued to personally take the war all the way to Berlin. Only Marshall's continuing pressure to stiffen Eisenhower's spine kept the Allied command from imploding. Although Brooke had warned that "unfortunate" remarks would antagonize Eisenhower, Monty's contrariness would become a boon to Russian ambitions in central Europe.

Eisenhower had appealed for additional troops for the pushes to the Rhine and beyond, and was furnished two unallocated American divisions. He also asked Marshall, very likely as only a rhetorical exercise, for "a hundred thousand Marines," as he shied away from using black soldiers beyond service units, considering only Jim Crow "separate battalions" to be attached to existing divisions. With Beetle Smith's backing, he claimed that giving blacks guns would be politically inexpedient at home. Having had good relations with Filipino soldiers over a lifetime, MacArthur was not as fussy, and had long utilized black (but segregated) troops successfully.

Stimson had forwarded to Marshall a query from the president: out of a million and a half troops in Europe, why were only half a million actually fighting? In fact, there were more than 2 million in uniform, 400,000 of them airmen. Half of the ground army was employed in support services. (In Paris alone, J. C. H. Lee had taken over 651 hotels.) By May 1945 there were 2,909,602 Americans in Europe, including Britain and the Mediterranean.

Considering the buildup necessary for invading Japan, Stimson again urged Marshall to create ten more divisions from the pool of undrafted men. Marshall resisted, contending that the war everywhere would be over before they could be inducted, trained, and deployed. Effectively there were, already, substantially more than the ninety divisions Marshall mandated, as the equivalent of additional divisions circulated through the pipeline as replacements. Until the offensive in the west had stalled, he and his staff had assumed that the war in Europe could be won with the men and matériel in place in the high summer of 1944. Additional troops necessary to defeat Japan could be moved from the ETO to the Pacific.

It was Stimson's major wartime clash with Marshall, and on the chief of staff's part a calculated risk. Marshall saw a diminishing will for sacrifice on the home front, from increasing industrial disputes to a political reluctance to see the draft extended into previously deferred categories. Marshall cabled Eisenhower about "a terrific drive . . . against the use of 18-year-old men in combat which has been fulminated by a speech by Senator Taft on the floor of the Senate." After casualty figures through February 7 were published four weeks later—782,180 dead and wounded, including 693,342 for the army alone—the president ordered a cessation of further listings. For many Americans, rationing and other restrictions into 1945 were hardly noticeable, and evaded when possible. The realities conveniently remained oceans away.

The costs of the remote war, nevertheless, were piling up. Weather, supply, and the problems of coalition compromises had stagnated the drives east. As the Wehrmacht withdrew closer to home, it gained the advantages of proximity to sources of manpower and matériel. After Montgomery's failures at Walcheren (to open Antwerp) and at Arnhem, the Westwall could no longer be outflanked. With little more than half the American population, the Germans also employed captive peoples as slave labor, and satellite nationalities to fight. One of Patton's subordinates dismissed an ineffective enemy formation as "nothing but Poles with ulcers," but the Wehrmacht had an uncanny ability to turn men unacceptable by Allied standards—"from the depths of the barrel," Stimson marveled—within weeks into dangerous *Volkssturm* divisions.* Now pressed into the *Heimat,* but for Norway, Denmark, and much of Holland, the German command could also deploy troops by bus or rail, or even by foot.

---

*As noted earlier, American manpower shortages were exacerbated by military standards, some of which outraged Marshall. More than 5 million men, one out of every three examined for service, were rejected for "physical, emotional, mental, or moral disability." Millions more had occupational deferments, largely for agriculture and war industry.

Just as Eisenhower ordered Ridgway's XVIII Corps to retake St. Vith, despite snow and ice and fierce resistance, MacArthur's Luzon force was landing at Lingayen Gulf, at first to little response on the ground. From the air, the invasion fleet, the largest yet committed to a Pacific operation, had been swarmed over by *kamikazes* as it approached. Dozens of Rear Admiral Jesse Oldendorf's ships were hit, including an escort carrier, the *Ommaney Bay* (which sank) and the battleship *New Mexico*, on which was Churchill's shrewd SWPA liaison officer, Lieutenant General Herbert Lumsden. Hundreds of sailors—and General Lumsden—were buried at sea.

The cruiser *Boise,* carrying MacArthur, narrowly escaped a bomb. Undeterred, he was eager to get ashore, boarding a landing craft with his headquarters brass, including his physician. At about two in the afternoon on January 9, 1945, four hours after the first troops went in, Admiral Kinkaid recalled, "The Seabees ashore had taken a bulldozer and pushed out a little sort of pier. . . . But when . . . MacArthur saw what they were going to do, he said, no, he wouldn't land there. So they bypassed the pier . . . and he jumped out in[to] the water and waded ashore. He didn't want to step out on dry land." Ever the showman, and aware of the publicity extracted by wading into the camera lenses at Leyte, he would not miss another photo opportunity. He felt constantly in competition with Eisenhower, who never thought of it. After the embarrassments of the Bulge, MacArthur told Robert Eichelberger confidently, "Eisenhower's curve had gone down . . . and he is not considered the great leader he formerly was."

The next day MacArthur returned briefly from the *Boise* via an LST, inspected four of General Krueger's divisions, and prepared a communique. "The decisive battle for the liberation of the Philippines and the control of the Southwest Pacific is at hand," he announced, adding in the imperial third person, "General MacArthur is in personal command at the front and landed with his assault troops." Yet he remained comfortably on the *Boise* until the afternoon of January 13, when he occupied a headquarters set up in a provincial office building and adjoining school on the south shore of the gulf. The Japanese had spent their Philippines air force. Fewer than a dozen enemy aircraft remained on Luzon. They were hoarding suicide planes now for immediate threats closer to the home islands: expected landings on Iwo Jima and Okinawa, which the Japanese intended to make so horrifically costly that the Americans would back off and settle for a peace deal short of invading Japan proper—the peril now imminent for Germany.

General Yamashita, the conqueror of Singapore and now in command of 275,000 isolated troops in Luzon, intended to tie up and destroy as much American shipping, aircraft, equipment, and troops as possible to delay, even forestall, an invasion of the home islands which he expected MacArthur to mount from the Philippines. While Eisenhower worried little about chewing up infrastructure in the *Heimat*, as his goal was destruction of the enemy's ability to resist, MacArthur intended to preserve what could be used by a recovering Philippines, including bridges and dams. As his forces pushed closer to Manila, resistance became savage, but until it did, MacArthur followed Krueger's Sixth Army toward Clark Field, which Kenney badly wanted in order to have a major air base. Often MacArthur sat in the front passenger seat of a dusty open jeep, Patton-style, clamping down his scrambled eggs hat, readjusting his sunglasses in the sultry heat, and gripping the windshield post with his right hand. From Clark Field southward the Japanese were dug in with artillery. Casualties mounted, and Krueger worried about his exposed eastern flank, as his orders were to bypass central and northern Luzon.

MacArthur even tried to make a competitive race of it to Manila, as Eichelberger's Eighth Army, after landing in southern Luzon, was pushing northward. MacArthur had his public relations eye on the calendar. On January 21 he ordered Krueger to get troops into Manila by February 5—since he had assured the Joint Chiefs of Staff that he would have Manila within four weeks of landing. The unspoken reason seemed different. MacArthur read all transmissions that reached him. The Big 3 summit to take place in the Crimean resort of Yalta would convene in early February. He knew that the windups of both the German and the Japanese wars would be on the table, and the glory of liberating Manila might establish how central his role would be. He did not want to be an also-ran to Nimitz and the navy, or to watch an end to the war with Japan by air power managed from Washington that eliminated any need for his ground forces.

The last summit, in Teheran, had concluded with a preliminary agreement on occupation zones in Germany, and a promise by Stalin that once Germany was defeated he would enter the Pacific war. Only with the Japanese preoccupied with a Russian threat did an invasion of what would be fanatically defended home islands appear practical. As Yalta approached, both military and political planners in Washington and London realized that whatever the territorial price demanded by Stalin for his sending the Red Army against Japan, it would have to be paid. Even if Russia remained cynically on the sidelines while Americans died on

Japanese beaches, Stalin could still take his pickings from the Imperial corpse—at least on mainland Asia.

MacArthur's competition for primacy in the Pacific came from naval and air commanders who, in parallel with him, had compressed the vast ocean into a broad moat behind which was Japan. Eisenhower's strategic conflict came as, in January, his armies were fighting to restore the lost ground and reach the German moat of the Rhine, from British backers of Montgomery, who still argued for a single thrust—led by him—toward Berlin. Yet when the Red Army behemoth, already only sixty miles from Berlin, renewed its final offensive, which it did on January 12, it would swarm toward Berlin at whatever cost. Casualties inhibited the West far more than they did the Russians.

The Teheran agreements, to be confirmed at Yalta, recognized the facts on the ground. Although Yalta became a political tag for sellout, a political division of Europe was inevitable and irreversible. The Western allies were to withdraw from whatever territory they might overrun which had already been conceded at the conference table, including all of Berlin but their own occupation sectors in the city.

Bradley and Patton, with Hodges, threatened to resign if Montgomery in the north exploited preponderant military assets at American expense, whether or not targeted at Berlin. Seeing their own advances into the Reich as a "sure thing," Eisenhower's top generals even rebelled at sending some divisions south to help Devers, their colleague, eliminate the Colmar "pocket" west of the Rhine between Strasbourg and Mulhouse. They preferred to let the Germans wither there. Only "a sideshow," Colmar was not a potential Bulge, Bradley shouted into his phone at Eisenhower. "Take any goddam division or corps," he threatened, ". . . and those of us that you leave back will sit on our ass[es] until hell freezes." Patton kept his divisions. He and Bradley struggled in mud and snow and flooded rivers through another month of winter. Simpson's Ninth Army remained with Montgomery, who in mid-February gained only seventeen miles in two weeks.

Eisenhower wanted "a broad front," pushing the Germans back against the Red Army until a mutually agreed-upon demarcation, preferably a broad river, was reached. "As an added thought," he argued to a selectively deaf Montgomery, who still sought a solo strike toward Berlin, "the more Germans we kill west of the Rhine, the fewer there will be to meet us east of the river." Eisenhower could not allow, after the Ardennes débacle, the Germans "to hold great bastions sticking into our lines at the same time as we invade his country." He had radioed Marshall about "a noticeable and fanatical zeal on the part of nearly all [German] fighting men as well as the whole nation of 85,000,000* people, successfully united by terror from within and fear of consequences from without." Marshall warned Brooke that Eisenhower would ask to be relieved—in effect withdrawn—as Supreme Commander unless the jingoist British contrariness ceased. Eisenhower had wavered again and again under pressure from Churchill and Brooke, once agreeing with them that Berlin was the main prize, then arguing that its symbolic value was not worth its cost. Churchill's circle still dreamed of a dramatic, British-commanded close to the war in the west, however borrowed were its American logistics, to bolster claims to continuing Great Power status. Facing facts was hard.

On January 28, Eisenhower met with Marshall in Marseilles, then sent Beetle Smith to joint pre-Yalta discussions in Malta. Ike knew that much of the agenda would focus on his leadership, or lack of it, in the Ardennes, and that it was best that he be represented by a canny surrogate. Marshall had too much invested in Eisenhower to make replacing him more than a threat—although the British would understand that if they wounded Ike sufficiently they might get, for their pains, G.C.M. himself. He left Eisenhower at Marseilles with a warning that henceforth he had to evade in every way "the direct influence of the PM."

Beetle Smith called Brooke "stubborn as Hell" on insisting that Montgomery push to Berlin from the north. Further, Brooke contended that Eisenhower needed a British deputy to make the strategic decisions. Marshall, Brooke wrote, "was opposed to cramping Eisenhower's style by issuing any directive to him," which he considered "quite unacceptable." Marshall soon had enough, and demanded a closed session. "At Malta [on February 1] we had a very acid meeting," Marshall recalled more politely than the actuality. "[Brooke] said the British chiefs of staff were very much worried by the influence on General Eisenhower of General Bradley, and I think he mentioned General Patton. And I said, 'Well, Brooke, they are not nearly as much worried as the American chiefs of staff are by the immediate pressures and influence of Mr. Churchill on General Eisenhower. The President practically never sees Eisenhower, never writes to him—that is at my advice because he is an Allied commander—and we are deeply concerned by the pressures of the prime minister and the fact of the proximity of the British chiefs of staff, so I think your worries are on the wrong foot.' We had a terrible meeting."

---

*The inflated estimate apparently guesses at many millions of imported slave labor.

Marshall prevailed. Eisenhower would not suffer a British nanny. Brooke wanted the pliable Harold Alexander brought from Italy, as after Kasserine in 1943, but to placate the British, Montgomery, with no increased prerogatives, would nevertheless get lavish additional resources. Later, at Yalta, when Alexander was as patronizing as ever about American military effectiveness although Eisenhower's Americans had beaten back the Bulge while Montgomery's British largely watched, Marshall lost patience. "Yes," he snapped, "American troops start out and make every possible mistake. But after the first time, they do not repeat their mistakes. The British troops start in the same way and continue making the same mistakes over and over. . . ."

Prepared with Marshall's position papers, Roosevelt arrived in Malta aboard the cruiser *Quincy* to confer with Churchill. It turned out, Brooke wrote with chagrin, that the PM "as usual" had not examined the British staff folder. "He made [the] most foolish remarks about it which proved he had not read it." It was an inauspicious beginning for the imminent meetings with Stalin, as Roosevelt, pallid and physically failing, and Churchill, only intermittently alert although making a public show of energy, would be overmatched by the crafty Russians, experts at betrayal. Despite the presence of the generals, and the reality that strategy often had a political context, political decisions remained the province of the politicians.

Early on February 3, twenty aircraft, departing ten minutes apart, flew the Allied party to the Crimea under fighter escort. Under a tent at Saki airfield, General Alexei Antonov, Red Army chief of staff, hosted a huge breakfast, and Marshall found to his surprise that a large tumbler that he assumed held fruit juice proved to be potent Crimean brandy. Yalta, eighty-five miles distant via a fleet of Lend-Lease automobiles, had only been cleared of Germans eight months before. Two czarist winter palaces and a Victorian-style mansion were only partly rehabilitated. In the Livadia Palace, Marshall had the czarina's bedroom and Admiral King her boudoir. Lesser delegates had improvised quarters—sixteen colonels in one large bedroom with buckets by their cots. Soviet intelligence bugged all the rooms as well as the gardens.

Vodka, and fulsome toasts, were plentiful. Dinners were lavish, and enormously lengthy. Communist surface friendliness only foreshadowed serious differences. Claiming republican sympathies, Stalin refused to drink to the health of George VI, toasting Churchill instead for supporting Russia when attacked by Hitler. Western leaders asked for coordination of strategy for closing on the Germans, from a demarcation boundary for strategic bombing and a junction line in mid-Germany to a liaison group in Moscow. Only token concessions were forthcoming.

The British became equally grudging about liaison with Red Army commanders on the Eastern Front, insisting on contacts between forces only through the Combined Chiefs of Staff. Marshall deplored the bureaucratic obstinacy. The Russians were now forty miles from Berlin. He attended only the first and ninth plenary sessions with heads of state, confining himself to military matters. For Soviet ears he noted that Antwerp was open and accepting seventy-five to eighty thousand tons of cargo daily, and described the success of airborne supply routes between Burma and China, where 44,000 tons of cargo had been delivered over the daunting Himalayas in January, as "the greatest [such] feat in all history." Given that achievement, he suggested hopefully, "cooperation by the staffs now seated around the table should be relatively easy."

Many painful issues had been settled in principle earlier: zonal boundaries and the reshaping of Poland to give it German land to compensate for the territory which Russia retrieved—it had been Russian (much of it ethnically Polish) until 1917—in its cynical deal with Germany in 1939. But whatever Poland's new dimensions, it would be Communist. Stalin had no intention of permitting the London-based government in exile to return. Its troops and airmen who had fought courageously against the Nazis in the West would be rejected by the Lublin puppets set up in Moscow. Baldly lying, Stalin claimed no special interest in Berlin, then sent his armies to seize it whatever the casualties. To the west, beyond the end in Europe loomed Russia's role in Asia. Stalin promised that ninety days after the end in Germany the Red Army would attack Japan, and that he would begin moving twenty-five divisions across Siberia. His asking price was irrelevant. Allied concurrence only ratified what he would seize anyway.

With no certainty yet that there would be an atomic bomb to shock the Japanese into ending the war, Roosevelt, Stimson, and Marshall were willing to purchase casualty insurance from Stalin. An invasion of the home islands would generate a fanatical, *kamikaze* defense costing hundreds of thousands of American lives, and more than one landing might be necessary. Planners were working on two, possibly three, amphibious operations, against Kyushu and then Honshu, which might drag the Pacific war well into 1946 and even beyond.

In the first weeks after Pearl Harbor, MacArthur had cabled Marshall that Russian involvement would be "a golden opportunity" for a "master stroke" against Japan. Leonard Gerow, when at the Operations desk before Eisenhower replaced him, had concurred, recommending that "every effort" be made to bring the Soviets in. Speaking off the record to correspondents in Leyte just before receiving his fifth star, MacArthur predicted hopefully that Stalin would intervene to reverse the terms of the 1904 peace settlement with Japan that cost Russia territory and prestige in East Asia. After Yalta, a spokesman for MacArthur in Luzon told correspondents that a Red Army attack on Japan remained "essential," and that American forces—presumably MacArthur's—"must not invade Japan proper unless the Russian army is previously committed to action," and that "get[ting] Russia into the Japanese war" would end it. After conferring with the general in February 1945, the new secretary of the navy, James Forrestal (Frank Knox had died in 1944), wrote in his diary that MacArthur believed "that our strength should be reserved for use in the Japanese mainland, on the plain of Tokyo," which could not be done "without the assurance that the Japanese would be heavily engaged by the Russians." MacArthur took this to mean "sixty divisions" to invade Manchuria, where he guessed that the Japanese deployed a million troops. At dinner with the general, Forrestal asked, "Do you wish to hazard a guess upon the end of the war in the Pacific?"

"I predict," said MacArthur, "that it will terminate this year." As Marshall had counted upon attrition to force Germany out of the war, MacArthur was looking at possibly fatal Japanese air and sea losses, and oil strangulation. Washington foresaw a stubbornly suicidal defense of the home islands, a cultural ethos that was already in grim practice elsewhere. When there was nothing left for the Japanese to lose but lives, what did lives matter? Nearly a decade later, when still nursing presidential ambitions, MacArthur charged to conservative Republicans that the Yalta agreement with Stalin on Japan was "fantastic" in what it gave away. His views "were never solicited," for he would have "most emphatically recommended against bringing the Soviet into the war at that late date." He never had to be consulted. MacArthur had declared his eagerness for Russian involvement throughout the war, into 1945.

On February 5, as Yalta proceeded, participants learned from a MacArthur communique dated a day later because of time zones, "Our forces are rapidly clearing the enemy from Manila. Our converging columns . . . entered the city and surrounded the Jap defenders. Their complete destruction is imminent." He made the sensation he intended. Foreign Minister V. M. Molotov proposed a toast at luncheon; laudatory messages followed from heads of state. Marshall drafted one for Roosevelt beginning, "Congratulations to you personally and to your commanders and troops on the liberation of Manila. This is an historic moment in the reestablishment of freedom . . . in the Far East, and the celerity of movement and economy of forces involved in this victory add immeasurably to our appreciation of your success."

MacArthur included the "personal message" from the president in his *Reminiscences,* although the "celerity" and "economy" language would prove premature. The battle for the ruins of Manila would take nearly a month more; casualties would be high. Although the haste was humanitarian, the rush to exploit the victory was not. Bilibid and Santo Tomás prisons held gaunt and starving military and civilian prisoners of the Japanese. MacArthur, who shied away from hospitals, visited the scrawny survivors, who had been too ill to be shipped to work camps in Manchuria, Korea, and Japan. Those who could speak murmured, "You're back," or "You made it," or "God bless you," and MacArthur replied, "I'm a little late, but we finally came." Yet the triumphal parade through Manila, it was announced, was "put off indefinitely" because of continued resistance, and never rescheduled.

Even the paratroop assault on Corregidor took far longer than anticipated. MacArthur's trusty intelligence chief, Charles Willoughby, estimated 850 defenders. Six thousand hunkered down in its tunnels and bunkers. Clearing them out took two bloody weeks.

MacArthur's grand penthouse flat in the Manila Hotel, occupied by General Yamashita for much of the war, had burned along with the rest of the building.* According to MacArthur's unreliable memoirs, the Japanese "had fired it. I watched, with indescribable feelings, the destruction of my fine military library, my souvenirs, my personal belongings of a lifetime." Yamashita had abandoned the city to fight on in the Luzon highlands, but he had no authority over the 30,000 grounded sailors and marines under the fanatical Rear Admiral Sanji Iwabuchi,

---

*Although MacArthur blamed the Japanese for torching the Manila Hotel, it was done by 75 mm shells from five tanks of the American 754th Tank Battalion which blasted the building, including the general's suite, on February 22, misunderstanding a signal *not* to fire. From a distance, MacArthur, who wanted to save the hotel, watched in shock. The penthouse has since been replicated, minus several unnecessary bedrooms, as a memorial to the general and as a VIP accommodation, atop a tower addition to the rebuilt structure.

who intended to incinerate everything. Wherever Japanese naval contingents could fight in the rubble of the city, they did. Ruefully, an infantry officer told Major General Joseph M. Swing of the 11th Airborne Division, "Tell [Admiral] Halsey to stop looking for the Jap Fleet. It's dug in on Nichols Field."

Japanese atrocities were widespread. Even hospitals were set afire. A hundred thousand Filipinos perished. Few major buildings survived, notably—and curiously—Malacañan Palace, perhaps because it was remote from the action. Most streets were blocked by rubble and ashes. Yet in the U.S., *Time* would prematurely headline its Philippine story, "Victory! Mabuhay!"—the Tagalog word for "hurrah!"—and *Newsweek* would headline, "Prize of the Pacific War. Manila Fell to MacArthur Like a Ripened Plum." The *Philadelphia Evening Bulletin* headlined an Associated Press dispatch from "MacArthur's Headquarters" on February 7, "U.S. Troops in Manila Clean Out Snipers, Push Ahead to Free all of Capital." GHQ censors would not permit correspondents to file the facts.

When Roosevelt radioed more realistic congratulations on March 1, on "the virtual culmination of a flawless campaign," the key word was "virtual." MacArthur replied to Marshall's own message with evident insincerity and in the imperial third person, "Nothing pleases us so much as your praise." On the morning of February 27, three weeks and more after the victory announcement, MacArthur officiated unilaterally in restoring the powers of the Philippine Commonwealth to Sergio Osmeña at Malacañan, where the red-carpeted halls remained unblemished by war. Never a churchgoer but ever an actor, the general asked Filipino exiles who had returned to express with him "gratitude to almighty God for bringing this decisive victory to our arms." His voice faltered and he wiped his eyes on his sleeve. Then he asked the audience to rise "and join me in reciting the Lord's Prayer." The loyal exiles would not rule alone. From Baguio, the relatively cool summer capital above Manila, MacArthur had Manuel Roxas, a power in the Japanese puppet regime, flown with several other collaborators to Manila. They were part of the prewar oligarchy which MacArthur again embraced, permitting Roxas to reopen his family's *Manila Daily News* and campaign for the presidency. Roxas was elected leader of the restored Senate, and prosecution of turncoats would depend upon their prewar relationship to the proconsul.

With some of the major islands in the Philippines largely free of the Japanese—it would take many months to mop up the rest—Jean MacArthur and seven-year-old Arthur (and his Cantonese amah) sailed

on the *Columbia Express* from Brisbane to reunite with her "Sir Boss."*
She arrived on March 6, the day after Manila was finally declared secure.
MacArthur had not seen them since October 14, 1944.

Soon after Manila became quiet, writer Robert Sherwood flew in on
Pentagon business, bringing proposals relating to military government for
an occupied Japan. He had heard "that even generals from the War Department on inspection tours were refused permission to enter the Philippine Theater and those that did were carefully chaperoned as if they were
attempting to visit the Russian front." Although "hospitably received," he
was "shocked by the inaccuracy of the information held by General
MacArthur and his immediate entourage about the formation of high
policy in Washington." He saw "unmistakable evidences of an acute per-
secution complex. . . . One would think that the War Department, the
State Department, the Joint Chiefs of Staff—and possibly, even the
White House staff—are under the domination of Communists and
British imperialism." It was "an obviously unhealthy state of mind." Marshall received similar reports from others. "The [army] surgeon general,"
he recalled, "got as far as Leyte and then was not permitted to go into
Manila." But Marshall balked at overriding MacArthur.

Fighting would go on in the north of Luzon for months, but while
waiting for the next move toward Japan, MacArthur, flouting Pentagon
instructions, began organizing the recovery of Dutch and British colonies
in the East Indies, claiming that their oil would be needed to support operations against the home islands. From his listening post at the Washington embassy, Isaiah Berlin would cable Anthony Eden, "If we
prosecute [Far] Eastern War with might and main, we shall be told by
some people that we are really fighting for our colonial possessions the
better to exploit them and that American blood is being shed to [no] better purpose than to help ourselves and Dutch and French to perpetuate
our unregenerate colonial Empires; while if we are judged not to have
gone all out, that is because we are letting America fight her own war with
little aid after letting her pull our chestnuts out of [the] European fire."

From Yalta, Marshall had warned MacArthur that no American
troops were to be used to retrieve colonies. While assuring Washington
that he would utilize Australians, who were not involved in the Philip-

---

*The Connecticut Yankee in Mark Twain's 1889 burlesque of his times, set in the
court of King Arthur, is addressed by his minions in Camelot, where the transplanted
American, applying late-Victorian technology to medieval England, takes over, as
"Sir Boss." However adoring Jean MacArthur was, her constant use of the title was
tongue-in-cheek.

pines, MacArthur built a case for disobedience. He radioed Marshall that the U.S. had been "obligated under the international agreement establishing the Southwest Pacific Area" to restore the status quo, and to do otherwise "would represent a failure . . . to keep faith." MacArthur could always be counted upon to do what he wanted to do and find an excuse.

Leaving Yalta before the rest of the American party to go on to Italy to see the situation there for himself, Marshall came away impressed by German resilience in what had become an expensive backwater of the war. In some ways MacArthur's experience in Luzon was much like the tough Italian campaign—an enemy delaying action with no hope of their relief, to tie up as many attacking troops as possible. Characteristically, Marshall wanted no fuss on flying in. As his assistant, Frank McCarthy, put it to Mark Clark, "Usual form holds good for the Chief; that is, no aides, no orderlies, no flags, no auto plates, no escort, no fanfare of any kind. He . . . is unwilling to commit himself to a press conference and wishes no advance heralding of visit." Still, Clark had a large honor guard in Florence standing at attention at his 15th Army Group headquarters. He wanted to risk making a point: that twelve disparate nationalities comprised his forces. Marshall first frowned, then understood. He even prepared a handout for the press noting the "spirit of common purpose" in the campaign to drive the Germans from Italy.

President Roosevelt had radioed Eisenhower that he would be "passing through" Alexandria on his return from Yalta. "If you have anything you particularly wish to see me about and the military situation permits, I will of course be glad to see you." Eisenhower sent regrets that he was in the midst of strategic "changes . . . that no one except myself can authorize." The president replied, "Much as I would like to see you, I of course do not wish to interfere with your duties at the front. I am following your grand offensive with the greatest attention and I want you to know how constantly the battle and the armies which you command are in my mind."

In reality, although Eisenhower was seldom close to the lines, he had been bedded for treatment of his gimpy leg, and to remove a benign but painful cyst from his back. His last chance to summon Roosevelt's vast prestige against chronic Churchillian interference had vanished.

The rest did some good. At a press conference on February 24, Ike's first in several months, which Steve Early, returning from Yalta, attended, FDR's veteran press secretary watched him grin a lot while offering nothing of substance. Asked about his relations with Montgomery, Eisenhower at length said "absolutely nothing but the boys and girls of the press acted as if they heard Einstein explain relativity." To Early it was a "magnificent performance."

At home again late in February, Marshall spoke off the record to the Overseas Press Club in Manhattan on the evening of March 1. Without referring directly to the frustrating impact of industrial strikes and slowdowns, he contended, "Military momentum is the greatest single factor in shortening this war. Nothing should be permitted to interfere with it. To do so is the greatest form of extravagance in men and materiel." He made yet another futile pitch for postwar universal military training, urging that the nation never again face war crises unprepared. The American public would never buy the concept, then or later. "Making war in a democracy," he would cable to Eisenhower on March 6, "is not a bed of roses." Marshall had little to say about Yalta other than that the German dream of splitting the wartime allies would not happen.

Roosevelt had addressed Congress about Yalta earlier in the day. Judge Samuel Rosenman, often a drafter of Roosevelt's speeches, had flown to Algiers to meet the *Quincy*. He was "disheartened" by the president's "all burnt out" frailty. Harry Hopkins had been in the party but was again gravely ill, more so than Roosevelt realized. Unable to assist Rosenman, Hopkins left the cruiser to recuperate at Marrakech. Admiral Leahy, who had sat in on all plenary sessions, filled Rosenman in, and the speech sounded like authentic FDR.

On March 1, 1945, when Roosevelt entered the Capitol for the first time in two years, it was, openly, in his White House conveyance—a simple Hyde Park kitchen chair with no arms or cushion, and fitted with wheels. As a seat of power, it emphasized dramatically how much he had overcome. But it also frankly revealed his decline. He apologized genially for the "unusual posture" and spoke from the wheelchair, microphones taking his voice by radio round the world. Reviewing the next moves (including the new United Nations Organization to be formed late in April) as well as the war, the fragile president defended his insistence upon unconditional surrender on military grounds rather than the unsaid need to allay insistent Soviet suspicions that the Western allies might sign a separate peace. He referred to the return to the Philippines, and the massive invasion of Iwo Jima, on the edge of the Japanese homeland. Then, Franklin Delano Roosevelt, chief executive for more than twelve years, was wheeled off a public platform for the last time, having given his last address.

Born in 1880, two years older than the president, Douglas MacArthur had hardly been ill a day in his life. His only exercise was his restless pacing back and forth in his living quarters and offices. He would not submit to routine medical examinations. His wartime physician, Colonel Roger O. Egeberg, recalled only one time, flying at 20,000 feet in an unpressurized cabin, when MacArthur permitted a stethoscope on his chest. His pulse was "perfectly normal." Roosevelt's physician, Vice Admiral Ross McIntyre, examined the president daily but had little control of such counterproductive habits as his smoking. Despite his patient's sieges of respiratory infections, alarmingly high blood pressure, and weakening cardiac function, as well as the strain of his wheelchair existence since 1921, McIntyre had certified him, half a year earlier, as fit to seek a fourth term. But at Warm Springs, Georgia, on April 12, 1945, sitting for a portrait painter, Roosevelt suddenly lost consciousness—a fatal cerebral hemorrhage.

Although the nation plunged into shock, the Constitution provided continuity. Former senator Harry S Truman, vice president only since January 20, and left in the background of executive affairs, succeeded to the presidency. Truman barely knew Marshall; he knew far less of MacArthur and Eisenhower other than by rumor and report. Truman would get to know all three, but would get on only with Marshall, whom he had first met in the summer of 1942 through the senator's war-effort investigating committee.

MacArthur's claim on combat vessels for Philippine operations had handicapped the Iwo Jima expeditionary force. He refused to return some of the assets of the Pacific Fleet, contending that his "retention of these two veterans"—older battleships—"could hardly affect the success of the massive undertaking." Lieutenant General Holland M. Smith, the Marine commander, complained later that the weakening of preliminary gunfire support added to his casualties. Although Iwo, 775 miles from Tokyo, proved extremely costly (6,821 died, 20,000 were wounded), its occupation put American forces much closer to Japan than did Luzon. Exploiting the casualties to boost MacArthur, William Randolph Hearst editorialized, "Why do we not use him more, and indeed, why do we not give him supreme command in the Pacific war, and utilize to the utmost his rare military genius of winning important battles without excessive loss of American lives?" About a hundred Marines invaded the offices of the *San Francisco Examiner,* Hearst's flagship paper, demanding a retraction.

In an irony entirely unconnected, one of Roosevelt's last significant military visitors had been MacArthur's reliable General George Kenney. On March 20, as he departed the White House, the president waved Kenney out with, "You might tell Douglas that I expect he will have a lot of work to do well north of the Philippines before very long." As soon as Truman, an artillery captain in the earlier war, became president, his cantankerous and often embarrassing military aide, Major General Harry H. Vaughan, was quoted as telling Washingtonians, "During the Roosevelt administration, the White House was a Navy wardroom, we're going to fix that!" There was nothing to fix. Technology had already accomplished that. The B-29 squadrons in the Marianas, which comprised the 20th Air Force, could fly bomb loads to Japan, and had begun massive raids in March. Although Guam, Saipan, and Tinian were within Admiral Nimitz's sphere, the big aircraft were controlled through the Joint Chiefs of Staff.

Okinawa, the major island in the Ryukyu chain, was administered as part of the Tokyo prefecture although 350 miles distant. The bloodiest setting of the Pacific war, it was a portent of the price of invading the home islands. Landings began on April 1, 1945; combat consumed three bloody months; 1,465 *kamikazes* sank 26 ships and damaged 368. The island war, from Tarawa in the Gilbert Islands in November 1943 to Okinawa, proved enormously costly in lives on both sides. Suicidal defenses spared no one. Few Japanese physically able to take their own lives surrendered. The Bushido code valued honor above life, and a prisoner of war, if identifiable to home authorities, was declared dead to his family. Even the *Yamato,* the largest warship afloat, was sent out without air cover on a one-way suicide mission toward Okinawa. Attacked en route, it took 3,000 sailors to the bottom.

Comparing his own SWPA casualties to Nimitz's, MacArthur told Major General James G. Christiansen (as he remarked also to others), "The way they handled the fighting on Okinawa was awful. The Central Pacific command just sacrificed thousands of American soldiers because they insisted on driving the Japanese off the island. In three or four days after the landing, the American forces had all the area that they needed . . . for airplane bases. They should have had the troops go into a defensive position and just let the Japs come to them and kill them from a defensive position, which would have been much easier to do and would have cost less men."

Although MacArthur charged that casualties in taking Okinawa and Iwo Jima were excessive, in 1942 he had ordered Lieutenant General Jonathan Wainwright, from Australia, to fight on Bataan to the last man. In 1944 Admiral King had argued that a campaign to liberate the Philippines served no strategic purpose as the islands could be bypassed to wither militarily. MacArthur had maintained a moral obligation to recover "American" territory, and argued that it would be cheap. It would not be cheap, but his pride in returning was paramount. After Leyte and Luzon, where losses were large, liberating the other southern and central Philippines cost less than a thousand lives, as the Japanese saw no military value in them, but on Cebu, beyond the dead, the 23rd (American) Division alone suffered 2,000 wounded and 8,000 hepatitis cases.

Luzon cost MacArthur about 10,000 dead, relatively little compared to the 205,000 Japanese who would not return, but the 30,000 wounded and tens of thousands invalided by hepatitis and malaria did not even include the airmen and sailors lost to *kamikazes*. "Mopping up" suggests light-duty operations but the term is as deceptive as is the dismissive "pockets of resistance." Fighting on Luzon and Mindanao would continue even following the final Japanese surrender ordered by Emperor Hirohito, prompting one of Walter Krueger's generals to observe wryly, contending that the price for the package was too high, "MacArthur violated the principles of shopping." In the American press he was hailed as "a master strategist."

But for coal, mined mostly by prisoners of war and turned into synthetic oil, the Japanese, dependent upon resources from the captured colonies, were being cut off from resources to continue fighting. Only the expanse of China, with Manchuria, remained. That the Germans, with their occupation economy also largely gone, continued to fight multifront defensive campaigns against demographically and materially overwhelming adversaries was an achievement of generalship, technology, and the ruthless employment of slave labor. These also had their limits. Reaching the Rhine, Eisenhower's eighty divisions—fifty-six American, twelve British, three Canadian, eight French, and one Polish—cut off the industrial Ruhr and the North Sea V-2 sites in Holland. By then Hitler, increasingly manic, was commanding his own fantasy war from his bunker beneath the Chancellery in the riddled shell of Berlin. "We are vomiting up our victories," a disillusioned German officer conceded.

Another fantasy war also proceeded. Eisenhower found it difficult to rein in his generals, who seemed to be conducting independent pushes toward the Rhine. Backed by Whitehall, Montgomery still campaigned to unleash his 21st Army Group toward Berlin. Hodges and Patton had their own agendas, aborted by the Bulge, to restart, and Devers was pushing past the Westwall from Lorraine. To the dismay of American generals, Eisenhower gave in to Brooke, allocating Montgomery extravagant resources. Moving slowly if at all, Monty left the isolated Dutch to starve, hoarding his wherewithal for a showpiece crossing of the Rhine using airborne troops preceded by a vast preliminary barrage. At the same time, Eisenhower pleaded to Marshall for urgent shipments of hundreds of thousands of tons of additional bombs, and oceans of fuel.

The Germans now expected no bold strokes from the west, but to be worn down by massive firepower while holding off Russian hordes from the east. Reflecting the mood in London that costly heroics could no longer be afforded by a declining manpower pool, a British officer frankly told his troops that he wanted no Victoria Crosses. Yet Churchill was still eager to score propaganda successes on the cheap. The Germans also had to fight on the cheap. Between the Westwall and the Rhine, the Wehrmacht, improvising units from officer-candidate schools and Hitler Youth, army service troops and factory workers without work, sailors without ships and airmen without planes, fought desperately and hopelessly, delaying advances and making every kilometer costly.

Patton reprimanded the commanding general of the 94th Division for its excess of noncombat injuries, suggesting a reluctance to fight. In February, taking heavy losses, Hodges's troops finally seized, through floods, the opened Roer dams that had been targets since October. But all the American pushes were hostage to the deliberate Montgomery, Eisenhower excusing the slow pace on grounds of continuing poor weather and his own claim that it was more important to destroy German armies west of the Rhine than merely to occupy hills and fields. Montgomery, with Simpson's Ninth Army of 120,000 and his own huge army group, reached the Rhine on March 10. He planned to take two weeks to prepare a crossing at Wesel, well to the north of Dusseldorf. With him were 60,000 combat engineers for multiple bridgings of the river, and hundreds of thousands of tons of supplies, landing craft, and amphibious vehicles.

Collins and Hodges had already met at the Rhine on March 7, at the ruins of Cologne, to the south. Just below, early in the afternoon on the same day, the 9th Armored Division reached Remagen, south of Bonn. The Ludendorff rail bridge was still intact, as Germans were still retreating across it on improvised wooden planks. A local German reported that explosives had been planted to go off at four in the afternoon, and soon after that, as the 27th Armored Infantry Regiment rushed its approaches, an explosion shook, without toppling, the thousand-foot span. Despite enemy fire from the right bank, troops went forward across the Rhine.

Eisenhower's Operations chief, Major General Harold ("Pinky") Bull, was at Bradley's 12th Army Group post when Hodges telephoned. "Hot dog, Courtney," said Bradley; "shove everything you can across it." To Bradley's dismay, Bull bureaucratically downplayed the opportunity. "You're not going anywhere down there in Remagen. It just doesn't fit in with *the* plan." Eisenhower's plan. "Right now his mind is up north [with Montgomery]."

Astonished, Bradley asked, "What in hell do you want us to do—pull back and blow it up?" He telephoned Eisenhower, who—while Bull stubbornly objected—obviously agreed that the crossing should be held, and reinforced. "It's the best break we've had. . . . To hell with the planners." Yet Ike did not want Bradley to advance any further, especially in the rugged area beyond Remagen, until all Allied armies had reached the Rhine. He remained haunted by the Bulge. Battered enemy forces still isolated in their rear might surprise them again. He was also waiting for Montgomery to move, maintaining the "broad front." In effect Bull got his way.*

---

*Years later, Bull, then commandant of the National War College in Washington, was embarrassed by Bradley's memoir when excerpted in *Life*, claiming that it damaged his reputation. Insisting that he was not "your thoroughly stupid G-3," he explained to Eisenhower (May 31, 1951) that he had no intention of interfering with "an accomplished fact" but only to learn "how this new action would affect your over-all plans."

Already, with Eisenhower's reluctant permission, Patton's 4th Armored Division had struck southwest from Trier to reach the Rhine at Coblenz on the 7th, then occupying Mainz. As Montgomery's plodding but prodigious operation neared, Patton quietly collected bridging matériel, determined to beat Monty across.

Pressed by the cross-purposes of his top generals; interference from Brooke and Churchill, who had their own agenda; and an imminent linkage with the Red Army, approaching overwhelmingly from the east, Eisenhower approached physical and emotional exhaustion. He had suffered from several episodes of flu and had recurrent high blood pressure. Beetle Smith pushed him into a mid-March rest at a luxurious villa in sunny Cannes rented by the army for high brass from its absentee American owner. As if the war were over, Bradley joined him, as did the inevitable Kay Summersby and her service cover of Ruth Briggs and Ethel Westermann. J. C. H. Lee left the Hotel Majestic in Paris to fly to Cannes, his Packard limousine and cases of whiskey following by special train. Tooey Spaatz brought an English lady he kept. The terrace at Sous le Vent was as far from the villa as Eisenhower would go, but his five-star presence was hardly a secret. Drained by responsibility, he even declined rounds of bridge as involving "damned thinking." As he conceded to Kay, "All I want to do is sit here and not think."

On March 23, he reoccupied his headquarters in Reims, a sprawling redbrick former technical training school. Bradley had already left Cannes for Montgomery's big show. A day earlier, units of Patton's Third Army crossed the Rhine on pontoon bridges at two points below Mainz. Patton telephoned 12th Army headquarters. "Brad," he urged, "for God's sake tell the world we're across. . . . I want the world to know Third Army made it before Monty."

The high-decibel extravaganza mounted by Montgomery opened the next night, heralded by days of smokescreen to conceal the obvious, a barrage from two thousand guns at a thousand shells a minute, and carpet bombing of the west bank of the Rhine by 1,406 B-17s. Nearly a million combat and support troops were involved in a grandiose operation intended for the newspapers. While dozens of correspondents and guests watched, including Churchill, Brooke, Eisenhower, and Simpson, who observed from a church tower, the river was breached at nine in the morning on the 24th, with only 31 casualties. Leapfrogging the ground troops were two divisions of paratroops and glider infantry in 1,696 transports and 1,348 gliders escorted by 1,800 fighter planes. German ground fire downed 44 transport planes and 22 C-46 troop-carrying aircraft, damaging a further 332. The 17th Airborne took 1,500 casualties; the British 6th Airborne 1,400. However grossly the spectacle gratified Monty's vanity, the censored dispatches permitted to the press concealed the price and hyped the producer.

After a splendid VIP dinner set up in large tents, Montgomery held an audience utilizing his now-legendary liaison officers. "From their reports there is no doubt," Brooke wrote in his diary, "that the operations have been an outstanding success," although the "ferry and bridging process" seemed "far behind" schedule. The next day, the 25th, was a Sunday. Monty held "a small Headquarters service" with hymns and a Presbyterian chaplain who preached a war sermon. Since Eisenhower, Bradley, and Simpson attended, Brooke again urged going for Berlin, suggesting that with the Germans "crumbling, . . . we certainly have the necessary strength for a double envelopment strategy which [earlier] I did not consider applicable." Churchill was in high spirits as they walked along the Rhine, telling Eisenhower, "My dear General, the German is whipped. We've got him. He is all through." Eisenhower recalled Brooke's confiding (quoted in *Crusade in Europe*), "Thank God, Ike, you stuck by your plan. You were completely right, and I am sorry if my fear of dispersed efforts added to your burdens. The German is now licked. It is merely a question of when he chooses to quit. Thank God you stuck by your guns."

"I was misquoted," Brooke charged on reading the page in Eisenhower's memoirs three years later. ". . . I congratulated him heartily on his success, and said that as matters had turned out, his policy was now the correct one, that with the German in his defeated condition no dangers now existed in a dispersal of effort." Brooke's use of *now,* twice, subtly altered his argument. "I am quite certain," he went on, "that I never said to him 'You were completely right,' as I am still convinced that he was 'completely wrong,' as proved by the temporary defeat inflicted on him by Rundstedt's counter-stroke [in the Ardennes], which considerably retarded the defeat of Germany." Montgomery's unmentioned futility at Caen, failure at Arnhem, and footling progress elsewhere allegedly had little to do with retarding victory.

Now ebullient, Montgomery was intent upon his "bold drive to the Elbe." After Patton's coup at crossing the Rhine without Montgomery's overkill, Eisenhower lauded the Third Army as a great outfit, and added, "George, you are not only a good general, you are a *lucky* general, and as you will re-member, in a general, Napoleon prized luck above skill." Patton called that the first (if dubious) compliment he ever had from Ike, and repeated it to his chief of staff, Brigadier General Hobart Gay, who wondered why Eisenhower had said it. "That's easy," Patton guessed. "Before long, Ike will be running for President. The Third Army represents a lot of votes. You think I'm joking? I'm not. Just wait and see." Showily, Patton peed in the Rhine.

. His audacity further elevated, Patton would take a costly risk. He kept up with the news from other fronts, and had learned of MacArthur's plaudits for having liberated 513 POWs at a camp near Cabanatuan in central Luzon by sending a Ranger raiding party thirty miles through enemy territory. Reportedly declaring he would make MacArthur look like a piker, Patton ordered a force to slip forty miles northeast to Ham-melburg, where Lieutenant Colonel John K. Waters Jr., Patton's son-in-law, who had been captured in North Africa, and 1,290 other officers were being held. Generals Manton Eddy and William Hoge expressed misgivings, but in predawn darkness on March 26 Patton sent out Cap-tain Abraham J. Baum, with 307 officers and men in tanks, half-tracks, and support vehicles. By March 30 Patton conceded that the shoddy affair was "a bad guess."

Task Force Baum was overwhelmed. Waters and other prisoners were wounded. Nine GIs in Baum's small column were killed and he and 31 others wounded and captured—a hairy business for Baum as his dog tag identified him as Jewish. Suppression of the reckless affair failed. Marshall was outraged. Eisenhower had put in fulsome new recommendations for four-star rank for both Hodges (". . . a model of boldness and daring . . . ; tactical masterpieces . . .") and Patton ("resourceful, courageous, and de-termined . . .") which Marshall had approved for Patton on April 14 and for Hodges on April 15. Eisenhower explained "the little expedition" lamely on April 15, the day *after* Patton's promotion, as "a wild goose chase in an effort to liberate some American prisoners. The upshot was that he got 25 prisoners back and lost a full company of medium tanks and a platoon of light tanks." Patton is "a problem child," Eisenhower ad-mitted to Marshall, "but he is a great fighting leader in pursuit and ex-ploitation."

Patton escaped discipline. Eisenhower had more acute problems. He had to rein Monty in, as he still wanted to take his troops as well as Simp-son's Americans toward Berlin into the path of the Red Army. Instead, Eisenhower wanted Monty to press to the northeast, blocking any attempt by Stalin to occupy Denmark. Bluntly, Eisenhower told Mont-gomery that Berlin was now "only a geographical location." In London, Brooke was outraged. "Now that Ike has explained his plans," he com-plained to his diary on April 1, "it is quite clear that . . . he directs his main axis of advance on Leipzig instead of on Berlin. He also transfers 9th [U.S.] Army back to Bradley as soon as the Ruhr [in the American rear] is surrounded, and delays further advance whilst sweeping up this place. Most of the changes are due to national aspirations and to ensure that the USA effort will not be lost under British command." Brooke's claims in-verted the obvious. Churchill did not want Britain submerged in the final weeks of the European war, and beyond, by what were now the two world superpowers. The "Big 3" were realistically two.

However grotesquely absurd, Nazi foreign minister Joachim von Ribbentrop held a reception early in April, in the ruin into which Berlin was disintegrating, where he assured the dwindling diplomatic corps, "Germany has lost the war but still has it in her power to decide to whom she lost." Unconditional surrender remained the only condition on the table for Hitler. Surrender could have blunted the Red Army's relentless drive on Berlin. That the West might get there first bedeviled Stalin, who would squander entire divisions in a race that was only between two of his own armies, whose commanders he egged on. When Ike visited the com-mander of the 84th Division, Major General Alexander Bolling, who had just taken Hanover, on April 8, he asked, "Alex, where are you going next?"

Bolling said they were ready to push ahead. "We have a clear go to Berlin and nothing can stop us." But they were 170 miles away, the Rus-sians thirty. "Keep going," Eisenhower said, putting a hand on Bolling's shoulder. "I wish you all the luck in the world and don't let anybody stop you." In reality, Berlin was merely a metaphor for continuing into Ger-many. The real aim was linkage at the Elbe with a Red Army wreaking a terrible vengeance.

With Berlin still a bee in his beret, Montgomery continued to nag Eisenhower, who now considered him terminally insufferable. "I consider that Berlin has definite value as an objective," Monty persisted, "and I have no doubt whatever that the Russians think the same; but they may well pretend that this is not the case!!" Whatever Stalin's designs, for Marshall and Eisenhower the price was too high in lives and in likely confrontation—rather than junction—with the Russians. The most seri-ous encounter had been verbal, when Stalin suggested Western collusion in turning the bulk of German resistance toward the Red Army. In an exchange with Roosevelt initiated by Stalin on April 3, he questioned sus-piciously why secret (and futile) talks in Berne, Switzerland, between American intelligence chief Allen Dulles and SS General Karl Wolff about surrendering Wehrmacht forces in Italy did not include a Soviet representative. When Stalin charged that a separate peace was being planned with the Nazis, Marshall angrily drafted a letter for the presi-dent's signature, fired off the next day. Both knew how many promises and guarantees had already been broken openly by Stalin.

"It would be one of the great tragedies of history," Marshall wrote for FDR, "if at the very moment of victory, now within our grasp, such mis-trust, such lack of faith, should prejudice the entire undertaking after the colossal losses of life, materiel, and treasure involved. Frankly, I cannot avoid a feeling of bitter resentment toward your informers, whoever they are, for such vile misrepresentations of my actions or those of my trusted subordinates." He copied Churchill.

"I had and have no intention of offending anyone," Stalin assured Roosevelt in a rare apology. It was Marshall's last message in the presi-dent's name.

In a brief meeting in London with Churchill to discuss zones of oc-cupation, the PM again forced the issue of Berlin. Eisenhower changed the subject to his fears of Nazi retrenchment into a last-ditch "southern redoubt"—*Alpenfestung*—in the Austrian Alps. Marshall urged wariness, noting that "in a situation where Germany is breaking up, rapid action might prevent the formation of any organized resistance areas. The mountainous country in the south is considered a possibility for one of these." Eisenhower thought afterward that such resistance "existed largely in the imagination of a few fanatic Nazis" and it would—almost—not materialize.*

After Eisenhower communicated directly with Stalin to inform him that he had no plans to take Berlin, and Stalin lied that Berlin was also unimportant to him as a strategic target, Churchill was livid. The general allegedly had no business communicating directly with a head of state. With Marshall's backing, Eisenhower replied that just as Winston was his own Minister of Defense—his excuse for meddling into purely military decisions—Marshal Stalin was commander in chief of the Red Army.

---

*A joint U.S.-French operation in April 1946 involving elements of the 9th Infantry Division did flush out an SS unit in the Tyrol near Wildbad Kreuth, Austria, eleven months after the surrender. Unreported in the press, it nevertheless concluded the European war.

Soon Marshall added that he saw no reason, either, to push uselessly toward Prague, as the Czech state would inevitably fall under Soviet influence. "Personally," he cabled Eisenhower bluntly, "and aside from all logistical, tactical, and strategic implications, I would be loath to hazard American lives for purely political purposes."

Once the Rhine ceased to be a barrier, there seemed no useful German purpose in fighting on, and much to be gained from surrender before succumbing to the Red Army, and—at very best—becoming slave labor in Siberia. Yet what was left of the Wehrmacht fought on, even its 120,000 troops bypassed in Holland, where they manned the only remaining V-2 sites and kept the Dutch close to starvation. Rockets there were launched eastward, as well as over the North Sea,* the only time that the Nazis fired on German soil from across a frontier. Little was left to protect otherwise but the unraveling horror of the death camps, which Eisenhower experienced on April 15. Belsen and Buchenwald were liberated on April 12. Nothing revealed more the material and moral ruin of Germany. "The things I saw beggar description . . . ," he wrote to Marshall. Inexplicably he added—perhaps it was true only of Belsen—"George Patton would not even enter. He said he would get sick if he did so. I made the visit deliberately, in order to be in a position to give *first-hand* evidence of these things. . . ."†

Writing on April 12 from Patton's Third Army headquarters, Eisenhower urged Marshall to come over and see his army for himself, and also to confirm the professionalism of the overwhelming army he had built from nearly nothing five years earlier. At dinner, with Bradley also present, Patton again urged pushing to Berlin. Eisenhower told him that it was wholly inadvisable. "I hope political influence won't cause me to take the city. It has no tactical or strategic value and would place upon Amer-

---

*The last rocket to reach England impacted on March 27, 1945.
†Patton did enter Buchenwald when it was liberated. Officers and soldiers alike wept. "This is the camp," he wrote, "where we paraded some fifteen hundred citizens of Weimar to give them a first-hand knowledge of the infamy of their own government." Earlier in April he had been with his Third Army when it liberated the Ohrdruf Nord slave labor camp, which he called in a letter to John McCloy "the most horrible sight I have ever seen." Eisenhower's comments to Marshall are baffling, as the allegation suggests Patton's refusal to confront the reality he already knew.

ican forces the burden of caring for thousands and thousands of Germans, displaced persons, and Allied prisoners of war." Even so, Western armies, moving on momentum, and Wehrmacht collapse, seized territory designated for Russian occupation, which Eisenhower relinquished after the German surrender.

A few hours later in Virginia, Marshall had just settled on his porch at Fort Myer when Frank McCarthy arrive, with news from Warm Springs, Georgia, of Roosevelt's death. He drove Marshall to the White House, where Eleanor Roosevelt asked him to manage the funeral arrangements. At Third Army in Germany, before retiring, Patton had clicked on the BBC to reset his watch. Hearing the opening bulletin about the president's death, he awakened Ike and Brad. Sitting about until two in the morning, they wondered about the impact FDR's passing would have on the playing out of the war, and then the peace. They knew little about his successor, and Bradley recalled that "from our distance, Truman did not appear at all qualified to fill Roosevelt's large shoes." To Patton it seemed "very unfortunate that in order to secure political preference, people are made Vice Presidents who were never intended, neither by Party nor by the Lord to be Presidents." Eisenhower remembered returning to bed "depressed and sad."

On Berlin radio, Propaganda Minister Joseph Goebbels described the news as "a miracle," as if it would rescue Germany. Clicking off his microphone, he called for champagne.

Rather than fly to Germany to witness the dissolution of the Reich, Marshall had to organize the complex obsequies which took FDR's body from Warm Springs to Washington to Hyde Park. His imposing orderly, Master Sergeant James W. Powder, commanded the pallbearers and walked behind the caisson bearing the late president's body. Conveying her gratitude, Mrs. Roosevelt wrote to Marshall, "I know it was all as he would have wished it. He always spoke of his trust in you & of his affection for you."

When the military chiefs met with President Truman on the first morning of his presidency, Marshall and King filled him in on the latest developments in the war, and Stimson took him aside to discuss the atomic bomb, the hidden expenditures for its manufacture which Marshall had persuaded Truman when he was a senator not to investigate. Returning by car to the Pentagon together and discussing the new president, Marshall told Stimson, "We shall not know what he is really like until the pressure begins to be felt."

The pressure came instantly from many directions, and Marshall was at the White House almost daily to explain the complexities of ending one war, redeploying troops to the unfinished war, and dealing with difficult allies about military moves that were also inherently political. Since De Gaulle and Churchill were almost as difficult as Stalin, the untried Truman might be bullied. As the Germans crumbled in the West, Stalin seemed more paranoid than ever that the Wehrmacht surrenders—even negotiations about surrenders—would lead to connivance with the enemy to resist Russian expansion. Domestic pressure was already building to bring troops home, to close surplus bases among the three thousand in use, to return factories to civilian production even before consideration of defeating Japan or policing shattered Europe and caring for helpless populations. Turning its focus to the Pacific, the Joint Chiefs of Staff prepared a directive to MacArthur "to execute OLYMPIC"—the invasion of Kyushu—"not later than 1 November."

On April 25, 1945, the 69th Infantry Division under Major General Emil F. Reinhardt, which had captured Leipzig the week before, reached the Elbe—the first ground contact with the Red Army. Superficially friendly, Russian officers were under orders to be deeply suspicious of the Americans and the British, and to restrict contacts by the ranks other than for propaganda purposes. Since resistance had weakened in the west and intensified in the east, where Red Army enormities were considered by Stalin only as payback, opportunities arose for cheap gains, and Eisenhower cabled Marshall on April 29, "I shall *not* attempt any move I see as militarily unwise merely to gain a political prize unless I receive specific orders from the Combined Chiefs of Staff." He knew that Marshall would resist pressure from the British to grab territory destined for postwar Soviet occupation.

One of Eisenhower's few kudos to Montgomery came on May 3. The day before, Monty's army group entered Lubeck on the Baltic, sealing off the neck of the peninsula toward Denmark. Keeping the Russians out ensured that the Danish resistance could secure the surrender of the German occupiers. It took some doing. Eisenhower had spent "some weeks"—he cabled Marshall—"waking up" Churchill to the "danger" that the Red Army could occupy Denmark, and then Norway. The PM had remained stubbornly intent upon unattainable Berlin; without his intervention on April 27, Montgomery would not move. The same day, Field Marshal Albert Kesselring agreed to a surrender in Italy, asking for a forty-eight-hour delay in the announcement to give troops a chance to escape capture by the Red Army already in Austria. Eisenhower learned from Harold Alexander that German radio in Bolzano was already broadcasting the terms. Although the Russians were overrunning pitilessly what was left of Germany east of the Elbe, each Wehrmacht surrender in the west added to Stalin's suspicion of Allied intentions.

Rigid sticklers for Nazi legitimacy, some German generals felt that their oaths to the Führer precluded submission until their sworn fidelity had become void—as would occur with Hitler's suicide, on April 30, in the depths of wrecked Berlin. On March 13 he had visited the Oder front, where at a closely guarded manor house near Wriezen he met with commanders and urged them to keep fighting. Hitler's glittering eyes and decrepit gait suggested a mad old man. He would not emerge from the Chancellery bunker again. The captain was not so much going down with his ship as taking the ship down with him—a *kamikaze* conclusion.

Hitler's Supreme Command, the OKW, had fled north on April 22 to Schleswig-Holstein in the few planes left, low-flying liaison "Storks." On May 1, as the Red Army was ruthlessly storming the last few blocks in central Berlin, German radio in Plön, just below Kiel, announced Hitler's death and his legacy of the isolated rump of the Reich to Admiral Karl Dönitz.

On May 4 the surrender of Admiral Hans von Friedeburg to Montgomery at Lüneburg covered all German forces in Holland, northwest Germany, Norway, and Denmark. With Jodl, Friedeburg was escorted, in a British plane, to Reims to sign, for Dönitz, a full capitulation. Eisenhower would not sign for SHAEF. Effectively he was a head of state, master of a grand coalition. The German admiral, who broadcast emptily, "We fight on," represented a stateless entity and possessed doubtful credentials only his for a few days. Besides, Eisenhower knew little German and preferred to leave Friedeburg and Jodl to Beetle Smith and Kenneth Strong.

Playing for time, so that further hundreds of thousands might evade the Red Army to surrender to the West, the Germans dragged the negotiations into the next morning. Waiting anxiously in a nearby room, often pacing up and down, Eisenhower turned the pages of his favorite bedtime reading. He had a pulp Western by William Colt MacDonald, *Cartridge Carnival,* in the oblong two-columned Armed Forces Edition. Writing to Mamie with some of the book's leaden pages still to go, he summed it up as "terrible. I could write better ones, left-handed." Warned about deliberate delays, Eisenhower finally abandoned the novel to insist through deputies that the Germans sign immediately or Allied lines would be closed to their troops attempting to surrender. Dönitz telegraphed back that it was "sheer extortion," but gave in.

Just before 3 A.M. on May 7, in the presence of British, American, French, and Russian witnesses, Jodl duly signed, then made a brief plea to treat the German people "with generosity." The effective date was to be midnight the next day, although Stalin insisted on another, symbolic, signing in Berlin the day after. Marched into Eisenhower's office under Strong's escort as interpreter, the Nazi brass (including Jodl's aide) saw Eisenhower standing rigidly behind his desk, Arthur Tedder at his side. "Do you understand the terms of the document of surrender you have just signed?" Eisenhower asked. *"Ja, ja,"* Jodl said, not requiring a translation. After another sentence or two, Eisenhower said curtly, "That is all." Jodl bowed stiffly for the delegation, turned, and left the room to the waiting newsreel and press photographers, and a radioman preparing a recording. Kay Summersby, who had come in from her anteroom, appears behind Beetle Smith and Eisenhower. In some photos as published, she is air-brushed out.

"I suppose this calls for a bottle of champagne," Eisenhower re-marked once the pressmen had left. "There was no triumph in his voice," Kay remembered, "none of the elation he had shown when the photogra-phers were there. . . . We drove back to the château where he lived in Reims—there were about ten or twelve of us—and drank champagne and discussed the events of the last few hours until dawn showed through the window. It was a somber occasion. No one laughed. No one smiled. It was all over."*

When Jodl and Friedeburg were returned to Schleswig with the sur-render documents, with them also was the service newspaper *Stars and Stripes*, which had published stark photographs taken in Buchenwald. Dönitz would later claim that for most Wehrmacht officers it was the first revelation they had of the death camps, which were under SS control.

To the Combined Chiefs of Staff, as Cable FWD 20798 and SCAF 355, Eisenhower, rejecting drafts of grand victory statements, dictated a message memorable for its studied brevity: "The mission of this Allied force was fulfilled at 0241, local time, May 7th, 1945."

Marshall responded, "You have completed your mission with the greatest victory in the history of warfare." He went on to note the "un-precedented complications" of national interests, logistical problems, and military obstacles which Eisenhower had surmounted, selflessly, soundly, tolerantly, yet decisively. "You have made history, great history for the

---

*In his memoirs Eisenhower writes, "We had no victory celebrations of any kind, then or later. When Jodl signed we merely went to bed for some much-needed rest."

good of all mankind, and you have stood for all we hope for and admire in an officer of the United States Army. These are my tributes and my personal thanks."

To Marshall, separately, the next day, came Eisenhower's reply, clearly composed earlier for the occasion but no less heartfelt for that. "Since the day I first went to England, indeed since I first reported to you in the War Department, the strongest weapon I have always had in my hand was a confident feeling that you trusted my judgment, believed in the objectivity of my approach to any problem, and were ready to sustain to the full limit of your resources and your tremendous moral support, anything we found necessary . . . to accomplish the defeat of the enemy." Marshall's unstinted backing, Eisenhower contended, especially his resisting "interference from any outside sources," did "far more to strengthen my personal position throughout the war than is realized even by those people who were affected by this circumstance. . . . Our army and people have never been so deeply indebted to any other soldier."

On the morning of V-E Day in Washington, May 8, Henry Stimson called Marshall into his Pentagon office, in which he had assembled the General Staff. Nearly seventy-eight, Stimson had first been secretary of war in 1909 during the presidency of William Howard Taft, successor to the first Roosevelt. Movingly, he spoke of the debt the nation owed Marshall for his selfless services. "Seldom can a man put aside," he judged, "such a thing as being the Commanding General of the greatest field army in our history. This decision was made by you for wholly unselfish reasons. . . . I have seen a great many soldiers in my lifetime and you, sir, are the finest soldier I have ever known." The war might only be half over now, Stimson thought, considering the tenacity and fanaticism of the enemy in the far Pacific. "I may not live to see the end of the war with Japan but I pray that you do."

Characteristically for Marshall, he took only two sentences to reply.

Colonel Marshall as aide to General John J. Pershing, commander-in-chief, American Expeditionary Force in France, 1918. CREDIT: MARSHALL LIBRARY AND FOUNDATION

MacArthur in 1918 being decorated by General Pershing with his second Distinguished Service Cross. MacArthur was the most decorated officer in the war. CREDIT: MACARTHUR MEMORIAL AND ARCHIVE

MacArthur in summer whites and straw hat in foreground at a ceremony in Manila, probably in 1935. Behind him to his right, and similarly dressed, is Eisenhower.
CREDIT: NATIONAL ARCHIVES

George and Katherine Marshall fishing, 1938.
CREDIT: MARSHALL LIBRARY AND FOUNDATION

Eisenhower and Marshall conferring in North Africa, May 1943.
CREDIT: NATIONAL ARCHIVES

Marshall with Churchill and Montgomery in North Africa, May 1943, to confer about the forthcoming invasion of Sicily. CREDIT: U.S. ARMY

White House transcript of Vichy French radio broadcast alleging Marshall's dismissal forwarded to him by Harry Hopkins, and Marshall's response, followed by Roosevelt's rejoinder. Credit: U.S. Army

Marshall's draft, from President Roosevelt's dictation in Cairo, for a cable to Stalin, December 6, 1943, announcing Eisenhower's appointment to command "Overlord." Only the signature is by the president. Marshall gave Eisenhower the document the next day. Credit: U.S. Army

Marshall and MacArthur (right) in New Guinea, December 1943. On Marshall's only personal inspection trip to the Southwest Pacific Theater he visited MacArthur's field headquarters. Others whose faces show, from left, are Lieutenant General George C. Kenney, commander of air forces in the SWP, Lieutenant General Walter Krueger, commanding general, Sixth Army, and Major General Stephen J. Chamberlin, SWP operations officer. CREDIT: NATIONAL ARCHIVES

Eisenhower on D-Day minus one, June 5, 1944, with troops of the 101st Airborne Division, prior to their jumping off for France. The 101st would later defend encircled Bastogne during the Bulge. CREDIT: NATIONAL ARCHIVES

Eisenhower (left, behind driver) and Admiral Ernest J. King compare notes while standing in the amphibious "duck" that brought them ashore for an inspection tour at the beachead in Normandy. At the far left, talking to an unidentified soldier on the beach, is General Marshall. CREDIT: NATIONAL ARCHIVES

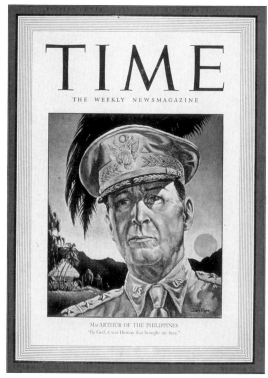

"MacArthur of the Philippines." General MacArthur appears on the cover of *Time,* December 29, 1941. Many readers thought he had been named "Man of the Year" for 1941 because it was the final issue of the year, but the next week's issue portrayed President Franklin D. Roosevelt as "Man of the Year." CREDIT: *TIME*

General George C. Marshall as "Man of the Year" for 1943, *Time*, January 3, 1944. Marshall would again be "Man of the Year" for 1947, for the Marshall Plan.
CREDIT: *TIME*

General Dwight D. Eisenhower as "Man of the Year" for 1944, *TIME*, January 1, 1945. Eisenhower, as president, would again be "Man of the Year" for 1959.
CREDIT: *TIME*

MacArthur wading ashore on Leyte in the Philippines, October 20, 1944, into the lenses of cameramen on the beach. Credit: U.S. Army Signal Corps

The Big Three at Yalta in the Crimea, February 10, 1945. Roosevelt, now very frail, is carefully seated between Churchill and Stalin. Marshall is behind Admiral Leahy, standing, center. Eisenhower did not attend the conference.
Credit: National Archives

Eisenhower in mid-March at the villa *Sous le Vent*, near Cannes, on the Riviera, on a brief recuperative holiday from the war. Kay Summersby is to his right.
CREDIT: U.S. ARMY

Katherine and George C. Marshall arriving at the White House late on the afternoon of April 12, 1945, following the death of President Roosevelt.
CREDIT: MARSHALL LIBRARY AND FOUNDATION.

Marshall with Secretary of War Henry Stimson leaving the White House after conferring with the new president, Harry S. Truman, April 13, 1945, the morning after the death of Franklin D. Roosevelt. CREDIT: MARSHALL LIBRARY AND FOUNDATION

Marshall and Eisenhower leaving National Airport, Washington D.C., following General Eisenhower's arrival, June 18, 1945, for a welcoming parade. CREDIT: MARSHALL LIBRARY AND FOUNDATION

MacArthur conferring with Lieutenant General Robert Eichelberger, commanding general of the Eighth Army, shortly after they arrive at Atsugi Airbase near Tokyo, August 30, 1945. CREDIT: U.S. AIR FORCE

As chief of staff of the army, succeeding Marshall, Eisenhower visited forces in China and Japan. Here he is with Marshall in Nanjing (then Nanking), May 9, 1946. Between them are Madame Chiang and Generalissimo Chiang Kaishek.
CREDIT: MARSHALL FOUNDATION AND LIBRARY

Ike and Marshall waiting to testify before Congress, July 1950. Marshall's glum expression may result from his understanding that he was to be called back as secretary of defense by President Truman.
CREDIT: JOHN S. D. EISENHOWER'S COLLECTION

The U.N. flag joins the American flag atop the Dai Ichi Building in Tokyo, July 14, 1950. Across the moat behind the viewer is the Imperial Palace. On the top floor of the Dai Ichi is MacArthur's office, overlooking the palace grounds. CREDIT: U.S. ARMY

MacArthur's cleared desk at his Dai Ichi office, his calendar at April 12, 1951. CREDIT: U.S. ARMY

President Truman pinning yet another Distinguished Service Medal on MacArthur, Wake Island, October 5, 1950. Looking on is Ambassador to South Korea, John Muccio. CREDIT: U.S. ARMY

MacArthur peering down from his Consellation aircraft at the Yalu River boundary between Manchuria and North Korea, November 24, 1950. Forward of MacArthur is Far East Air Force commander Lieutenant General Stratemeyer. CREDIT: U.S. ARMY

"We've Been Using More of a Roundish One"

A Herblock cartoon in The Washington Post, April 1951, satirizing MacArthur's view of the world.
CREDIT: HERBERT BLOCK FOUNDATION

A pro-MacArthur editorial cartoon in the New York *Journal-American*, April 1951. The general remains rocklike in the face of Truman's "political" slap. The cartoonist is Burris Jenkins.

MacArthur, with Jean and young Arthur, leaving the Dai Ichi after a final visit, April 15, 1951. They flew off to Hawaii and the United States the next day. CREDIT: U.S. ARMY

Ike and Mamie waving to a crowd of supporters from aboard their presidential campaign train in 1956. CREDIT: EISENHOWER CENTER PRESIDENTIAL LIBRARY, ABILENE, KANSAS, ADMINISTERED BY THE NATIONAL ARCHIVES AND RECORDS ADMINISTRATION

President Eisenhower greeting civilian business executive Douglas MacArthur at a White House luncheon, March 18, 1954. CREDIT: NATIONAL ARCHIVES.

A Bill Mauldin response, October 16, 1959, in the *St. Louis Post-Dispatch*, October 16, 1959, to the death of George C. Marshall. Mauldin had been the most famous service cartoonist in World War II. His GI characters Willie and Joe are here uniquely without words. CREDIT: REPRINTED WITH PERMISSION OF *ST. LOUIS POST-DISPATCH*, © 1959

A frail MacArthur entering Walter Reed Army Hospital in March 1964, on the arm of Surgeon General Leonard D. Heaton. To the left is Jean MacArthur. General MacArthur died at Walter Reed on April 5, 1964. CREDIT: MacARTHUR MEMORIAL AND ARCHIVE.

13

The End of the End

I N EARLY 1945, redeployments to the Pacific had become almost as high on the Pentagon agenda as rolling back the Wehrmacht. The Joint Chiefs set November 1, 1945, for "Olympic," MacArthur's landing on southern Kyushu. Beaches had been staked out on maps, with code names concocted by an early auto aficionado—"Maxwell," "Hupmobile," "Winton," "Essex," and "Stutz," among others. Nothing so prosaic as Eisenhower's "Utah" or "Omaha." Even before the German surrender, orders had gone to some of Eisenhower's generals and their staffs—those high on his reward list—to fight the other war. On MacArthur's list, probably to Eisenhower's surprise, was Matthew Ridgway and his XVIIIth Airborne Corps. Marshall had already radioed MacArthur when the war with Germany was a month from the end, "General Bradley asked me to have him in mind for service in the Pacific, incidentally, the only personal request of any kind he has ever made. Since then I have received formal applications from some of the leading officers in the European theaters; one came in a few days ago from Patton. . . ."

Although Patton was now flawed for further action, he had appealed to be redeployed, even if the assignment might cost him a star or two. "I should like to be considered for any type of combat command from a division up against the Japanese. I am sure that my method of fighting would be successful. I am also of such an age that this is my last war, and I would therefore like to see it through to the end." His public relations officer, Major James T. Quirk, knew of the plea and its poor prospects, writing to his wife that MacArthur had disparaged all of his commanders who had done the real fighting, but "Patton would be rather hard to play down. . . . I think we could give MacArthur a run for his money. We have never built up Patton at the expense of anyone and our divisions have gotten more credit for what they have done than any other army. That's the Old Man's policy. . . . I have no special yen for the Pacific, but I know that we could keep MacArthur's PRO awake a few nights worrying about us."

"Some superb commanders . . . and their staffs," Marshall urged MacArthur, had coped with "great masses of troops under rather extraordinary circumstances," and he suggested that several could be employed further "without too much of bitter disappointments on either side and hurt feelings generally." Marshall wanted "the ablest people in the Army" for the Pacific, and would "ease out" the others. In one of his last conversations with the president, FDR observed that politicians were lobbying him to keep their favorite National Guard generals. "Well, Mr. Roosevelt," Marshall said, "you just have to make a decision. You are going to have a reserve army and no Regular army. We'll demote all the Regular officers and keep all the other officers."

"Not that exactly," said Roosevelt.

"Well," contended Marshall, "will you let me handle it?" And Marshall did. On an earlier occasion he had thirteen senators in his office, he claimed, to lobby for retaining a division commander who Marshall regarded, however politically connected, as incompetent. "I'll put it to you this way," said Marshall: "if he stays, I go, and if I stay, he goes."

"Easing out" was easy with the ranks, and with reserve officers lacking career ambitions. Most GIs in European assignments were already adding up their "points"—measuring units of service time and awards—and yearned for home. If short in credits, a soldier was likely to face a sprawling camp in France named for his favorite smoke—a Camp Lucky Strike, Philip Morris, or Chesterfield—and shipment, possibly after a Stateside furlough, to the Pacific. Units redeployed to "Olympic" were often veteran outfits that even with high-point men homeward bound and off the roster could be counted upon to bolster untested troops.

Marshall had cautioned Eisenhower about wholesale reassignments to "please see that Staffs do not get too much into . . . designs without sufficient thought for human reactions," and Ike had responded on May 10 in a letter released by his office to the press. The *Stars and Stripes* quoted him as affirming that no one who served both in North Africa and Europe would have to go the Pacific. Then Corporal D. E. Jarvis of the 4378th Quartermaster Truck Company complained right to the top. Eisenhower had to hedge his promise by "limit[ing] it to soldiers who had fought in actual combat in both Theaters." Embarrassed, he wished Jarvis "God-speed and a safe return home after the final victory has been won."

Corporal Jarvis did not get his orders to the Pacific altered, but he might have consoled himself that few men wearing two stripes on their sleeves had ever received at mail call a letter from a general with five stars on his tabs. Some GIs in Jarvis's situation, Marshall felt, were "steamed up" by the press, which echoed local constituencies. Newspapers and newsmagazines mailed from home stirred up "what amounted actually to a form of mutiny."

Mutiny seemed everywhere. Marshal Josip Broz Tito had to be co-erced out of Italian territory on the Adriatic he took for Yugoslavia, and General De Gaulle had appropriated the Italian province of Cuneo, claiming it to be legitimate French territory. Eisenhower's authority was now limited by the peace. When Lieutenant General Willis D. Critten-berger, commanding U.S. troops in northern Italy, was told bluntly by De Gaulle not to interfere, the French ultimatum was forwarded to President Truman. It was June 6, 1945, and although he was still new at the game, he knew about legal frontiers. "You write it for me, General," he asked Marshall, "and make it as strong as you like. I'll sign anything you tell me to."

In the president's name, Marshall fired off a salvo via the American ambassador in Paris, Jefferson Caffery, which concluded, "While this threat from the French Government is outstanding . . . I regret that I have no alternative but to issue instructions that no further issue of military equipment or munitions can be made to French troops. Rations will con-tinue to be supplied. Truman." Since the embargo included fuel for French vehicles, De Gaulle knew that his armies everywhere would soon be immobilized. Shortly, through his foreign minister, Georges Bidault, De Gaulle informed Truman that French troops would begin withdraw-ing once they had the gasoline to get them out.

After six years of managing global war, Marshall wanted to "ease out" himself as soon as Japan could be coerced into surrender. Kay Summersby noted in her diary a message to "E" from Marshall that Bradley, who wanted a role in the Pacific, would be tapped by Truman to direct veter-ans' affairs, and that Marshall himself "is going to try very hard to get out of his present job. In about 2 months he's going to ask the President to re-lease him and then E. would have to become C/S. Confidentially, E. would loathe the job."

Although Eisenhower resisted what he termed to Churchill as "over-glorification," he had become the symbol of victory in the West much as

Marshal Georgy Zhukov, to Stalin's unease, had earned that role in the East. (In the Pacific, MacArthur openly encouraged glorification.) On June 12, Eisenhower flew to London for initial honors. At the venerable Guildhall, which like nearby St. Paul's had survived the Blitz, he was awarded honorary London citizenship (the "Freedom" of the City), and presented with a ceremonial sword replicating the symbol on the SHAEF shoulder patch. "Humility," he said in acceptance, "must always be the portion of any man who receives acclaim earned in the blood of his followers and the sacrifices of his friends."

Some of his staff were in the audience. Also Ike's son, detached from the 1st Division, was in the party, and a press photo shows John in a box at the theater (the revue was *Strike Up a New Note*) with an attractive date arranged by Lieutenant Summersby, who was seated next to Eisenhower. Behind them is Omar Bradley, with Kay's mother, Vera McCarthy-Morrogh. Kay had offered to sit discreetly with her mother, behind Eisenhower, but although he was recognized on entrance, and the audience applauded and whistled, he insisted (she recalled), "Come on, Kay. This is where I want you."

As if to prepare her indirectly for an unanticipated letdown, Eisenhower (on July 18) mentioned in responding to Mrs. McCarthy-Morrogh's thank-you note his forthcoming, and long postponed, reunion with his wife. Apparently he had been weighing the alternatives since the guarded euphoria of V-E Day. While not eager to relinquish Kay, he realized that he had to make the break or banish aspirations for further public life, military or otherwise. In the 1930s, MacArthur had somehow escaped scandal with his hidden teenage Filipina by avoiding being seen with her. Kay was highly visible in Eisenhower's European settings, but America remained puritanical about dalliance and divorce. A broad hint went to Marshall on June 4, when Ike proposed a policy which would permit wives to join their husbands assigned to the Occupation. "My own conviction," he explained less than obliquely, "is somewhat colored by personal desire. . . . I just plain miss my family." Yet John had been nearby since West Point. "Family" meant Mamie. Ike wrote of wanting to bring her to Europe "after three years of continued separation" if he were to remain much longer—as he knew was unlikely—yet two weeks later he was sentimentally visiting, with Kay, Telegraph Cottage, his suburban London residence in 1942.

At the cottage he talked (so she wrote) ambiguously about sharing their lives. A staff car arrived for them. "We'll be back," he promised. Then he called her inside again, she wrote almost thirty years later, when

Ike was dead and she was dying of cancer. "Come here," he said, opening his arms. "You've never given me a victory kiss." Clubbing afterward at Ciro's in London he danced—awkwardly—with her, and she whispered, "If anyone here tonight could guess how much I love you, they would not believe it."

"I would," he said. Although something had already triggered what was a cold career decision, letting go was awkward, long, and, finally, abrupt. In *Plain Speaking: An Oral Biography of Harry S. Truman*, published as Kay was hospitalized and near the end—she died in 1975—Merle Miller claimed to quote Truman, although the president had soured on Eisenhower, as intending to suppress potential scandal. The opportunity had allegedly come when Truman had authorized the assembly of Marshall's papers for a research library at VMI, the general's alma mater. "Right after the war was over, he [Eisenhower] wrote a letter to General Marshall saying that he wanted to come back to the United States and divorce Mrs. Eisenhower so that he could marry this English-woman."* Marshall, according to language Miller attributed to Truman, "wrote him back a letter, the like of which I never did see. He said that if Eisenhower even came close to doing such a thing, he'd not only bust him out of the Army, he'd see to it that for the rest of his life he wouldn't be able to draw a peaceful breath. . . . One of the last things I did as President, I got those letters from his file in the Pentagon and I destroyed them."

Most Eisenhower scholars have dismissed the intimacies in the second Summersby memoir as "salacious" and Miller's account as unsubstantiated by his interview tapes. (In Truman's lifetime he had indeed charged Miller on other grounds with "misstatements of fact.") Summersby's own accounts, where they can be documented in time and place, check out, and she provided facsimiles of some documents, and reproduced photographs, some from press agencies. Prior to Miller she could not have known of any of Eisenhower's exchanges with Marshall except those she handled as secretary.

Miller's source may have been Major General Harry H. Vaughan, Truman's garrulous crony and aide. "General Eisenhower asked General Marshall if he thought a divorce would hurt his military career," Vaughan explained to the Associated Press after Miller's book emerged. "Marshall

---

*The president—or Miller—was wrong. Although long resident in England, Kathleen Helen McCarthy-Morrogh Summersby was from Innis Beg, in the west of Ireland.

told him it certainly would, and would be a very stupid thing to do."
Vaughan guessed that the letters ("I saw them," he claimed) had once
been in the Pentagon files—allegedly the source of the "Pentagon" allu-
sion in *Plain Speaking*. Senator Robert Taft's agents, who had heard rumors about such correspondence, tried to get hold of them to discredit
Eisenhower when both were presidential aspirants. They failed.

Since Eisenhower was about to replace Truman in the White House,
and Truman had lost esteem for his successor, he may have been trying to
protect the dignity of the office. Patton claimed that Eisenhower had explained his feelings to Marshall so openly that the chief of staff wrote
back advising him to "take a cold bath and have [in] a masseur." If a blunt
Marshall-Eisenhower bargain occurred in the weeks just after V-E Day,
the only surviving evidence is the surprising Eisenhower letter of June 4,
which (as he knew he was to be recalled home and didn't need to bring
Mamie to Europe) could have been a covert response. Other alleged but
seemingly authentic letters from earlier years—from MacArthur to
Eisenhower and from Marshall to MacArthur—do not survive substan-
tively, and there is no reason why Eisenhower-Marshall letters could not
have also vanished. The exchange which Truman (or Miller) described
would have passed through secretive "eyes only" channels, carried by
couriers, the documented route taken when Ike's risky requests, first for a
medal and then for a commission for Kay, were denied. Marshall had intervened in potential scandals before, as with Brereton and Sutherland.
His agents brought him much that never made the files.

When, after London, Eisenhower (without Kay) left his relocated
headquarters in Frankfurt on June 16 for an official welcome in the
United States, to be greeted when his plane touched down by Marshall
and Stimson—and Mamie—the Summersby matter was already decided,
yet not over.

There was no such problem with the more distant MacArthur. While his
personal pilot, Weldon Rhoades, worried about what four years of war
had done to the general's staff, some of whom had precipitated extramar-
ital scandals that had reached Marshall's ears in Washington, "the General," Rhoades noted in his diary, "has his family with him and leads an
entirely normal life." That had not been the case with MacArthur's number two. Richard Sutherland was ordered to the U.S. on leave while

Robert Eichelberger, an authentic combat general, continued MacArthur's planning for "Olympic." In Manila, Eichelberger's planners were setting out landing sites in southern Kyushu for troops as far off as Hawaii. Their magnitude in personnel and equipment would dwarf Eisenhower's complex D-Day operation four times over.

Deviously, Sutherland had divided his time between his wife and WAC Captain Elaine Bessemer-Clarke, who MacArthur assumed had been sent home to Australia. Sutherland had arranged instead to get her posted to the San Francisco port of embarkation. When her papers reached the War Department in June they traveled on quietly from the Pentagon to the White House—and Elaine was ordered back to Australia and out of the army.

Convinced that there would be no Eisenhower scandal and that domesticity would prevail, Marshall made it official that as soon as the president would release him, Eisenhower would become chief of staff. In the interim, returned to Frankfurt, Eisenhower "often came to the WAC house," Kay wrote, sensing change, "for supper and bridge. . . . But Ike was growing restive. His old cronies, the ones who had been so close, were gradually leaving." By day he confronted a plethora of problems: the feeding and housing of millions of displaced persons, prisoners of war, and survivors in the debris of German cities; the outcries at home about the coddling of Nazi war criminals in a resort hotel in Luxembourg; the difficulties of filling civil and service positions everywhere in Germany by job-seekers without embarrassing Nazi pasts.

Also high on Eisenhower's agenda was the uncooperativeness and open duplicity of the Russians; the logistical nightmare of transferring much of the military to the Pacific war, or home; and the drastic downsizing (as in 1919) in which some top officers faced reduction from wartime ranks while others by accident of assignment kept their stars, eagles, and leaves.

When Eisenhower moved to the posh I. G. Farben chemical colossus at Frankfurt, Kay Summersby wrote happily of "no more schoolhouses"—as in Reims.* Rumors arose among GIs that the complex had escaped being flattened in air raids because the Supreme Commander had, early on, fancied the key establishment as his future headquarters. Blocks around it were rubble, with debris bulldozed aside to clear the streets. "It

*When Louisiana Representative F. Edward Hébert visited Reims he found "that this so-called 'Little Red School House' has probably more floor space than the House Office Building in Washington" and occupied "10 or more acres." He felt misled by the press.

was very elegant," according to Kay, "lots of marble and fountains and indoor flower gardens, great curving staircases and luxurious offices. Several tennis courts could have fitted into Ike's [suite of] office[s]."

By July 16, Eisenhower's challenges included carrying out decisions made by the altered "Big 3" at the Berlin suburb of Potsdam, where Truman was a feisty newcomer and deputy prime minister Clement Attlee in midconference—on July 26—surprisingly succeeded Churchill, who was voted out of office (with his party) by a weary electorate which wanted someone else to win the peace. The conference had been delayed by Truman into July because the Manhattan Project was about to test its first nuclear device. While Churchill and Roosevelt had already secured Stalin's agreement to enter the war against Japan, and the countdown had begun, an atomic bomb could mean the difference between invasion—an Okinawa in spades—and accepting a surrender before the Russians might seize more than the price already paid at Teheran and Yalta. Although it was recognizably Stalin's opportunity to Sovietize East Asia, the British embassy had cabled realistically from Washington to Whitehall as early as May 26, "The hard fighting on Okinawa has dispelled excessive optimism about a quick end to the Japanese war." Yet the Russians could not be kept out even if the conflict ended before they came in.

Postwar Soviet aggrandizement loomed in Europe as well as Asia. The negotiated European military boundaries might not hold, as—risking a new war—the Red Army, once Eisenhower's forces began to downsize, could roll across the Continent all the way to the Atlantic. The largest political parties in Italy and France were Communist. As Marshall and Eisenhower knew, Churchill only a few days after the German surrender had sent a "profoundly concerned" cable to Truman about a Soviet "iron curtain . . . drawn down upon their front." Churchill had not coined the term, which had first been applied to "Bolshevik Russia" in 1918, but his public usage of it the next year would give it new and frightening currency.

Two vast undertakings against the Japanese home islands had already been worked out to the last paper clip. Late in May, after consultations with MacArthur and Nimitz, the Pentagon was coordinating its plans for "Olympic," which would put three quarters of a million troops ashore on southern Kyushu on or about November 1. A follow-up landing, "Coronet," targeted central Honshu, in the vicinity of Tokyo Bay, and was planned for March 1, 1946. Collectively "Downfall," the end game for Japan had been approved by the Joint Chiefs of Staff on July 11, 1944, before the invasion of the Philippines, and refined by a joint services committee in Hawaii, and then Manila, through the months since.

MacArthur was pushing hard for the landings, having won, through Marshall, the battle of service rivals to command them. Truman had let it be known that his approval would depend upon what approach to defeating Japan would affect the fewest American lives. If a less costly war of attrition by sea and air took longer, so be it. In anticipation of an invasion, the army's monthly draft calls had gone up from 60,000 to 80,000 in January 1945, and in March to 100,000, and the levies for the navy and marines added a further 41,200. The navy ordered a crash program to turn out thousands of additional landing craft.

Impatient to keep his troops busy although the Philippines still required pacifying, MacArthur, fudging JCS policy to refrain from using American resources to restore European colonies, again put on his SWPA hat and ordered landings on Borneo. From the obviously American *Boise*, he watched the Australian 9th Division land on Brunei on June 10, and went ashore himself in midafternoon when the opposition seemed only token. He wanted to see dead Japanese, and strode beyond the beach after a firefight. While an Aussie cameraman tried to fit the general into his lens with two nearby enemy corpses, a sniper fired from the jungle. The photographer crumpled. General Kenney suggested urgently that the reconnaissance end, and they hurried back to the *Boise*. As the blockaded oil port of Balikpapan was taken by the Australian 7th Division on July 1, MacArthur, this time on the cruiser *Baltimore*, watched naval batteries destroy, in balls of fire, storage tanks filled with crude that might have been saved. Admiral Daniel Barbey tried to deter him from surveying the damage, claiming enemy mortar fire in the area. "Send barge at once," MacArthur ordered stubbornly, reluctant to end his war.

Ashore, he ignored the chattering of seemingly distant machine-gun fire until bullets flew past. As he backtracked down a ridge, he remarked to an accompanying Australian officer, "I think it would be a good idea to take out that machine gun before someone gets hurt." Returning to Manila, he found on July 5 a cable from Marshall, who was anticipating attacks on the home islands from Luzon, that George Kenney's bombers were to refrain from targeting Kyoto, Kokura, Niigata, and Hiroshima. Marshall offered no explanation.

Former president Herbert Hoover, in his early career an economist and engineer (and a pariah at the White House in Roosevelt's day), had been asked quietly by Stimson, once his secretary of state, for an estimate of invasion casualties. He met with Truman at the White House on May

28. Studying the rather vague problem with a cluster of knowledgeable colonels who were his informal think tank, Hoover predicted in a brief 700-word memo "500,000 to 1,000,000" American combat deaths over however long it took. It exceeded estimates in the planning document JCS 924, in mid-1944, which was predicated on facing 3,500,000 home islands troops and a "Saipan ratio" of 1 American killed and several wounded to exterminate 7 of the enemy.

The Japanese were mobilizing additional men now without work because their places of employment had been destroyed, and bringing troops home under cover of darkness from China and Manchuria. At least another million were in the home army, and millions of both sexes were being trained with whatever weapons existed, even kitchen knives and ceremonial swords. Collective suicide was no secret. Japanese radio boasted of it as a response to invasion.

The numbers haunted Stimson, who asked Hoover to tell Truman. Hoover insisted on a formal invitation, which came on May 24. On May 28, he saw the president, offered his data, and suggested that to ward off catastrophic casualties, unconditional surrender be modified in a face-saving manner to permit Japan to keep Formosa (seized in 1895) and Korea (seized in 1905). Hoover knew nothing, however, of Russian designs on Korea and Manchuria (seized in 1931). Truman asked for a written memorandum, which Hoover prepared.

With that somber estimate and others ranging from bleak to upbeat, Truman called for a definitive review. For the president and the service secretaries, Marshall outlined the alternatives at the White House on June 18, describing the damage already wreaked upon home islands infrastructure by B-29 raids from the Marianas since March and the state of the Imperial Navy and the Japanese air forces, both reduced largely to suicide tactics. Given demonstrated enemy will at Iwo Jima and Okinawa to fight to the end, Marshall emphasized in his low-key manner that bombing and blockade were unlikely to alter that resolve. He quoted Eisenhower and his staff that air power alone had not been sufficient "to put the Germans out." The Hoover estimates assumed fighting for all of Kyushu, which might require follow-up landings, while Pentagon planners intended seizure only of sufficient coastal and interior space for mobilizing the "Coronet" operation—an invasion of the Kanto (Tokyo) Plain on Honshu in early 1946.

A proponent of attrition who deplored both invasion and the Bomb (which he described, if it worked, as "un-Christian"), Admiral William D. Leahy observed that American forces still subduing Okinawa "had lost

35% in casualties," including, that very day, their commanding general, Simon Bolivar Buckner Jr.* Leahy asked how many men would initially be landed on Kyushu. A memo of the meeting quotes Marshall as estimating the "total assault troops" as 766,700, and Truman following with an "All right. . . . We can do this operation and decide as to the final action later." Calculating on Okinawa percentages to date, Leahy pencilled 268,345 casualties for the Kyushu phase, a conservative estimate, he thought, given *kamikaze* discipline and that the Japanese homeland itself was to be invaded.[†]

In balance, Marshall reported far more optimistic forecasts from MacArthur. "Olympic," he had cabled, might cost 50,000 dead and wounded in the first thirty days. His estimate, he explained, was a "purely academic and routine" one, as he did not anticipate "such a high rate of loss." Although he meant to reassure, using Luzon figures as yardstick, he took no account of the heightened intransigence which invading the home islands would create. Truman did not buy it. "I do not want another Okinawa," he said, "from one end of Japan to the other." (Privately, MacArthur predicted that in the likely event that enemy forces retreated into the mountainous spine of Japan, the war could go on for ten more years.)

A venerable cautionary voice like Leahy, Stimson sought "some fruitful accomplishment through other means." The adjective *nuclear* was conspicuously absent, but on July 2, he would send Truman a memorandum predicting that an invasion of Japan would require "a very long, costly, and arduous struggle on our part" and would result in "an even more bitter finish fight than in Germany." Western Europe had cost more than 760,000 casualties, nearly 600,000 of them American, including 131,965 battle deaths, although the Red Army had engaged the bulk of the Wehrmacht. A surrender of the Japanese short of invasion, eliminating need for the ultimate weapon, seemed the best possible outcome, but only the enemy could make that choice. Some in the military establishment wanted the investment in the atomic bomb paid off by its use, or in an overwhelming

---

*Buckner was killed by enemy fire on the 18th, Pacific time; Marshall would immediately dispatch "Vinegar Joe" Stilwell to replace him. At Okinawa 110,000 Japanese soldiers died, and 150,000 civilians. American casualties were about 50,000, including 13,000 dead.

[†]Although many pilots were still disciplined to die, an increasing number of them, trained little more than to cope with the controls, were being "carried and pushed into their planes" by ground maintenance crews, as Private Tsuneo Watanabe, who helped do it, recalled. Watanabe would become the editor in chief of *Yomiuri,* the leading Tokyo newspaper, in 1991.

invasion eclipsing that of D-Day. Either one would cap, or enhance, careers.

Buoyed by White House backing for the Kyushu operation, MacArthur radioed a revised plan to Washington three days later. While keeping his casualty projections unrealistically low, he now estimated twelve divisions to carry out the initial assault, with eleven more to follow and three in reserve, plus 22,300 airmen: an assault force up to Marshall's projection. Additionally, hundreds of thousands of supporting troops would handle the logistics from the Marianas, the Philippines, and Hawaii. One June 27, MacArthur added an intermediate Kyushu landing three months after "X-Day" on November 1, if enemy resistance had contained the "Olympic" beachheads. Two days later, the usually optimistic Major General Willoughby, MacArthur's intelligence chief, noted to him anxiously, from radio intercepts, new projections of Japanese forces massing on Kyushu, "This threatening development, if not checked, may grow to the point where we attack on a ratio of one to one, which is not the recipe for victory." MacArthur would keep that disquieting information to himself.

Had the general known how astute Japanese intelligence estimates were, he would have been further concerned. Major Eizo Hori, whose admiring colleagues called him "MacArthur's staff officer," had surveyed Kyushu's southern beaches on foot, and predicted landing sites on Ariake Bay, the Miyazaki Plain, and the Kushikino coast. He might have been reading the "Olympic" beaches planning map. Further, he realized that only with the end of the summer typhoon season would an invasion fleet be risked. He guessed that as late October. The JCS had already approved "X-Day" as November 1.

That the price for a home islands landing would be high became forcefully apparent when General Stilwell transmitted his closing casualty report from Okinawa. His July 2 communique declared that the campaign to take the island group of 922 square miles was over, although some pockets of resistance remained. In eighty-two days, about 2,500 Japanese troops, and civilians who were either suicides or caught in the crossfire, had—on average—died *each day*. Excluding airmen, American dead and wounded already exceeded 72,000. Navy casualties were more than 10,000, half of them dead, mostly from *kamikazes*.

In anticipation that both "Downfall" operations might be necessary, the Pentagon ordered hundreds of thousands of Purple Heart medals—for the wounded. The unused stocks (some later refurbished) outlasted Korea, Viet Nam, and wars thereafter. Nothing could evidence more dramatically what military planners expected would be the price of invading Japan.

On the morning of July 7, as the cruiser *Augusta* with Truman and entourage aboard left Newport News for Antwerp, and the conference at Potsdam, the president penned a note about his last meeting at the White House. Former Senate colleagues, vocal conservatives from both parties, some of them prewar isolationists, had come to urge him to pull Eisenhower's forces out of Europe. There was no hope for the Continent, they advised. "France would go Communistic, so would Germany, Italy, and the Scandinavians, and there was grave doubt about England." In his diary he called the blowhards "members of the famous 'Cave of the Winds.'"

As the *Augusta* entered the Scheldt Estuary, which for months Montgomery had failed to secure, and sailed upstream to Antwerp, the first and only uranium bomb, "Little Boy," was on its way to Tinian in the Marshalls. To drop only one nuclear device, whatever its dramatic effects (if it worked), might suggest that it was only an experimental weapon. To impress the Japanese hierarchy that the United States was capable of a super-bomb offensive, another, strategists thought, had to be delivered soon after. The second would have to be a plutonium bomb like its prototype then being fixed to a tower in the New Mexico desert. In two segments, the fissionable material for "Little Boy" made its way to Tinian with a covering letter from George Marshall authorizing its mission and whatever emergency assistance was necessary, anywhere, to get it there. Would it work? It could not be tested: there was no more U-235.

The welcoming delegation at Antwerp led by Eisenhower was sizable. The forty-seven-vehicle caravan motored thirty-five miles to the Brussels airport where the presidential C-54, *The Sacred Cow*, waited with two other transports to fly the party to Gatow Airfield in Berlin. Along the road to Potsdam, Eisenhower had arranged for an honor guard from the 137th Infantry Regiment, 35th Division, in which Truman had been an artillery captain in 1918. Completing his ceremonial duty in Antwerp, Eisenhower returned to Frankfurt. Marshall flew to Berlin with Hap Arnold separately after a day of salmon fishing in Quebec. In Frankfurt he teamed up with Omar Bradley for another day of fishing, in Bavaria. Then he felt ready for the conferences, as a military delegate attending none of the political sessions but meeting with other service chiefs in Babelsberg, across the Tetlow Canal from Potsdam, about twelve miles from the Brandenburg Gate in devastated central Berlin.

Since the 2nd Armored Division was in the Berlin area to protect the presidential party and project an American presence, Marshall invited the participants to inspect the showpiece unit, which formed on an *Autobahn*, with tanks, armored vehicles, and self-propelled guns. "A most impressive sight," Brooke conceded with his typical faint praise. "The efficiency of their equipment left a greater mark on one than the physique or turn-out of the men."

On the day they first met, July 16, the service chiefs discussed plans under way for Japan. Then after visiting the ruins of the Reichstag and the Chancellery with Hap Arnold and with Alan Brooke, Marshall learned from Stimson (who had been radioed by Groves) that the United States now possessed the capacity to outdo with a single bomb what had flattened Berlin. The prototype of "Fat Man," a plutonium device, had successfully detonated, creating a rising sun (and mushroom cloud) to the west of the scientific observers that rivaled the dawn in the east. A completed bomb to be airdropped was being rushed across the Pacific. When Marshall dined privately that evening with Churchill, who had been informed by Truman, there was no talk of the Bomb except by indirection. No one doubted that every room was bugged.

The next day Churchill would tell Foreign Office adviser Alexander Cadogan about Marshall, "That is the noblest Roman of them all. Congress always did what he advised. His work in training the American armies has been wonderful. I will pay tribute to it one day when occasion offers." He would have little more time. The general election results on July 26 (during a recess in the talks) would be a Labour landslide. Churchill would not be back.

Early conversations focused on how to finesse insistence on unconditional surrender with sparing Hirohito as figurehead sovereign. Anything drastic might be seen as threatening the fabric of Japanese culture and complicating the disarming of the military. Most Americans saw the emperor as a war criminal. Weakening the position on unconditional surrender might suggest to die-hards in Japan that their *kamikaze* position was paying off, yet Marshall as always wanted closure. He saw "war weariness" at home, and indeed the air offensive from the Marianas had been handicapped by shortages of spare parts—like tires—caused by industrial strikes. Labor unions feared the layoffs that would come with victory, and competition with the millions of returning servicemen who would swell the ranks of job-seekers. Also, the casualties anticipated from "Downfall" could become a political atomic bomb at home.

At the July 17 meeting of the Joint Chiefs of Staff in Potsdam, as a typhoon bore up the China coast, curtailing naval and air strikes on Japan, and British warships joined Admiral Halsey's fleet as Task Force 37,* Brooke asked Marshall for a greater role. His response, wrote Brooke, "was far better than I hoped for." A British corps commander would join MacArthur, with British, Australian, and Canadian divisions. No Indian troops, to preserve "homogeneity of language" (and culture). The British would be reequipped with American weapons. As for strategy, Brooke added, "There I see more trouble ahead. We want a greater share in the control of strategy in the Pacific and they are reluctant to provide this." The "they" was really MacArthur, for whom Marshall was speaking, but MacArthur offered to alter his operational boundaries to give Mountbatten's South East Asia Command responsibility for Dutch, French, British, and Portuguese colonies south and west of the Philippines. Japan seemed enough.

Brooke's meeting notes did not record that at one point when the American and British chiefs of staff were meeting separately from the Russians (as they were not at war with Japan), General Marshall cleared the room except for the chiefs themselves and reported the detonation of a nuclear device in New Mexico. It could make invasion unnecessary, but there was a serious hitch. A surrender in the home islands could strand millions of Japanese troops who might fight on across thousands of miles of occupied territories. Because Hirohito's nominal continuity might make possible his ordering a peaceable capitulation, overcoming the prevailing *kamikaze* mentality, Marshall had the Joint Chiefs draft a memo for Truman that hedged unconditional surrender with assurance that the Japanese people would then be free to choose their own form of government—obvious code for retaining the monarchy.

"I've not yet gone to Berlin," Eisenhower wrote to Mamie from Frankfurt early on the eighteenth, suggesting that although he was "busier these days than the proverbial one-armed paperhanger," he was puzzled not to be in the Potsdam deliberations. *"I love you, only,"* he closed, sealing the letter before it passed across the desk of Kay Summersby in the adjacent office. There was little business for Ike in Potsdam. The political lines for Germany and Austria had been laid out earlier, and decisions about reparations and the zonal economy were only peripherally military issues.

*Halsey's own TF-38 was larger than the entire Royal Navy, worldwide.

Eisenhower was also busy with feeding, clothing, and housing "Displaced Persons," a new refugee category; coping with charges about mistreatment of prisoners of war; and arranging for further transshipments of entire divisions to the Pacific. He had nominated Hodges to Marshall to take the First Army, minus long-serving troops to be released, to command MacArthur's forces in "Coronet," the March 1, 1946, amphibious landing on the Kanto Plain near Tokyo. Marshall had no idea how much of Hodges's paper record was a cover-up. Curiously, Eisenhower cabled Marshall to write off Bradley, claiming that his role in Europe had been too big to be reduced in scale for the other war. But Truman already had a job for him.

With a duplicity paralleling that of the Vatican, which was furnishing false papers to spirit Nazis in hiding to South America, the victors were busy sheltering—sometimes even abducting—German scientists who might furnish a technological edge for the next war, or to deter it. Some were physicians who had experimented brutally on Allied prisoners to test tolerance for high altitudes or for immersion in cold seawater. Others sought by the West were rocket engineers who might otherwise sell their services to the Soviets. On July 19 in Potsdam the undercover program was secretly approved by the JCS as "Operation Overcast," allowing 350 scientists to emigrate covertly to Texas with their hardware under renewable six-month contracts, with an additional hundred to include Wernher von Braun's rocketry team which had exploited slave labor. Clandestinely, the British were building a new V-2 launching pad at Cuxhaven on the North Sea using *their* Germans, a project Eisenhower had approved as "Operation Backfire." The "Cold War" in Europe had not begun with the close of the hot one: it had been under way all along.

While the army arranged unobtrusive berths for Nazi specialists in the U.S., Eisenhower's bureaucracy was expunging the concrete, if not the fleshly, vestiges of Hitlerism. "Any park, street, or public way, institution, building (public or privately owned), or industrial concern in the U.S. Zone of Occupation," the order mandated, "which was named for any person or thing associated with either Naziism or German militarism as herein defined, shall have its name removed from public display and use." Each would receive a sanitized replacement tag.

When the Potsdam conference adjourned temporarily because of the British election, and Churchill's contingent returned to London to await the results, Marshall and King planned to fly to Salzburg to look over Hitler's former eyrie at Bertchtesgaden. Then Marshall, with Frank McCarthy, planned some trout fishing. Before they left, Marshall approved a `directive which General Groves had drafted ordering the use of "the first special bomb . . . after about 3 August 1945." Marshall discussed the text with Stimson and with Truman. The deployment was to follow the close of the Potsdam sessions, now left to the politicians. On July 23, Truman asked Stimson to find out "whether Marshall felt we [still needed] the Russians in the war." The next day, Marshall, about to leave, sent a courier to Truman advising, "We feel that our departure tomorrow morning would have the advantage of indicating to the Russians that we were not . . . soliciting their support nor dependent upon their participation in the war in the Far East."

Stalin knew why his intervention was now superfluous. Long before Truman told him that the U.S. had a powerful new (but undescribed) weapon to use against the Japanese, the Manhattan Project had been infiltrated by Communist spies, both American and European. Foreign Minister Molotov urged Stalin, "We'll have to talk it over with [Igor] Kurchatov and get him to speed things up." The director of the Soviet atomic bomb program already had the purloined American designs. Stalin also rushed mobilization for war with Japan.

Marshall intended to inform MacArthur by courier about the implications of the atomic device successfully tested at Alamogordo in New Mexico. By radiogram on July 19 came the expected directive that his decks were being cleared for Japan by removing areas south and west of the Philippines from his command to that of Mountbatten. Since the admiral was planning to invade Singapore (which the New Mexico results would make unnecessary), the transfer of boundaries would follow. Also, Marshall reported to MacArthur from Potsdam, the Okinawa jurisdiction "has been settled reasonably to your satisfaction." The navy would let him take over the Ryukyu chain to jump off for Japan.

With his role now at the top of the war agenda and his further visibility in the ascendant, MacArthur was ebullient. He radioed Marshall, "The Okinawa solution is a good one and will undoubtedly facilitate OLYMPIC. Your sound professional judgment as usual prevailed to the ultimate benefit of all concerned."

Marshall also had delivered to MacArthur before leaving Potsdam secret reports from neutral nation observers in the diplomatic corps in Japan, and decrypted signals traffic with locations and strengths of Japanese home islands forces. These forty pages, too, would go by courier to MacArthur. "Training of all kinds, other than suicide training in tactical units," Marshall reported, "is believed to have been abandoned in view of the expected imminent invasion." Pages on army deployment identified thirty-six divisions with supporting units in eight headquarters areas, with upwards of 2,110,000 ground troops. The Kyushu defenses were overseen by the Second Army from Hiroshima, across the Suõnada Strait in lower Honshu. Harbor dispositions, radioed from Third Fleet headquarters in Okinawa waters, noted "remaining Japanese naval strength" as concentrated at Kure, just east of Hiroshima. The documents also observed that the Japanese were stockpiling thousands of *kamikaze* planes for use "during the amphibious phase of the expected invasion." Post-occupation surveys would confirm their numbers as more than 5,000.

After the concluding Combined Chiefs session, Marshall cabled MacArthur and Nimitz about business that would appear nowhere in the Potsdam minutes. Soviet entry into the war with Japan was scheduled for August 15, but for optimum spoils, Stalin had to rush mobilization. Since Japan might capitulate at any time, joint plans were being detailed for occupation and control of the home islands, China, and Korea. Coordinating attacks and accepting surrenders, if any, wrapped up the discussions. General Alexei Antonov proposed placing American "liaison groups" in Khabarovsk and Vladivostok—as long as Russian observers could be posted to Nimitz and MacArthur. Accepting the gesture, Marshall "hoped that there would develop such an intimacy in liaison that we would find later that the commanders in the field would develop an even greater intimacy." That was hardly what Antonov—or Stalin—had in mind.

When, asked Antonov, would the American invasion of Kyushu take place? (Although the U.S. had offered Russia no occupation zone in the home islands, Stalin planned to seize one if possible while Americans were preoccupied elsewhere.) Toward the end of October, said Marshall. It depended on the weather, on the arrival of troops from Europe, on rehabilitation of troops in Okinawa and the Philippines, and the movement of assault and supply vessels from as far away as the Solomons and Hawaii. He promised copies of the minutes to his counterparts and was given a Russian-drawn map of Soviet understandings that would be overtaken by events.

Brooke privately downplayed Churchill's news of the Bomb. "He had absorbed all the minor American exaggerations, and as a result was completely carried away!" But Brooke realized also that it was "no longer necessary for the Russians to come in," although they could not be persuaded otherwise. Similarly, Stimson told Truman "of my conference with Marshall, and the implication . . . that the Russians were not needed to subdue Japan." That intervention had been beyond doubt since Yalta. Bomb or no Bomb, Russia could not be kept out.

On July 20, before the generals departed their separate ways, President Truman had been driven to the headquarters of the United States sector of rubble-strewn Berlin to symbolically raise an American flag. He identified it in his diary as the same one "raised in Rome, North Africa, and Paris. Flag was on the White House when Pearl Harbor happened. Will be raised over Tokyo." In a brief address, chopping the air in emphasis, Truman hoped "for a better world, a peaceful world, a world in which all the people will have an opportunity to enjoy the good things in life and not just a few [people] at the top."

In the president's car on the drive back to Potsdam was Eisenhower, who had been invited as occupation chief. Perhaps acknowledging his situation as accidental president, Truman leaned toward Ike and confided, emotionally, "General, there is nothing you may want that I won't try to help you get. That definitely and specifically includes the presidency in 1948." In the other rear seat, Omar Bradley struggled to mask his surprise. Eisenhower searched for words. Finally he said, "Mr. President, I don't know who will be your opponent for the presidency, but it will not be I."

More down to earth, Truman's charge to Eisenhower was to prepare the western zones of Germany to survive the winter, and to rehabilitate stricken industries, by extracting as much as ten million tons of German coal, and to attempt to secure more from the Silesian mines in the Soviet (and Polish) zones. Unemployment and unrest could cause the West to go Communist by default. Eisenhower had learned little about such matters in nearly thirty years of military life, but he knew that Germany had to be the industrial engine for Europe if the Continent was to revive. He also knew that the Soviets, busy removing machinery from surviving German plants, ostensibly as war reparations, to haul to Russia, had no interest in German prosperity. His mission had been victory; Eisenhower was eager to have someone else cope with occupation.

A week after the Potsdam proceedings began, Brigadier General Thomas F. Farrell, Groves's deputy, who had been at a control site ten thousand yards from the "S-1" test blast, arrived in Manila to brief MacArthur on the Bomb, and to explain why four designated cities were being spared. Farrell would then fly to Tinian to prepare for the first drop, planned for Hiroshima. A few days later, on July 31, General Carl Spaatz, reassigned from Eisenhower's command to the strategic air forces in the Pacific, brought MacArthur a copy of the order to deploy the Bomb. While Marshall was in Germany, Spaatz had asked for written authorization. "Listen, Tom," he told Marshall's deputy, General Handy (according to Hap Arnold), "if I'm going to kill 100,000 people, I'm not going to do it on verbal [meaning "oral"] orders. I want a piece of paper." The Bomb was to be deployed "in operations against Japan, 5 to 10 August."

No one in Washington was eager to offer MacArthur such information any sooner than was necessary, as he would predictably insert his ego into the mission. Communiques were still emanating from his headquarters crediting achievements to almost no one but himself. One he had issued the day Spaatz had visited resulted in a *New York Times* headline, MACARTHUR FLIERS HIT 30 SHIPS. STRIKE OFF THE COAST OF MALAYA.

A few days earlier, General Eichelberger had written to his wife that he hoped that Japan would soon "fold up." Many in Manila believed, he added, that "the Japs will quit if Russia comes in, and I hope they do." It was not the cliché attitude of the professional soldier who wants his operation to come off in order to add to his career potential. One of the other breed was a new brigadier general, John Dudley, assigned to Krueger's Sixth Army. Dudley was peeved that his regiment was scheduled for the *second* invasion wave, but his indignation faded when he discovered that his assignment would be same as the first wave. "It was clear to me then," Dudley recalled thirty-five years later, "[that] they expected the first echelon to be wiped out in the invasion. The second echelon would get the thing done."

Whatever happened, Eichelberger recognized that the glory would go to "the Big Chief [who] writes his own communiqués." Although indebted to MacArthur's unpredictable patronage, he also recognized "the centralization of publicity around the man. . . . It hasn't been exactly fair for the many brave men who have died in winning those victories." Among other matters, the Joint Chiefs, hoping that nuclear shock could bring off a surrender without an invasion, would cable MacArthur about the "pressing necessity" of having an occupation plan in place. He turned the task, and the recommendations from Washington, over to Eichelberger.

MacArthur did not learn of the Potsdam ultimatum that would impact his mission until Truman released the text on July 26. In thirteen brief paragraphs, Allied governments, excluding Russia, still a nonbelligerent, declared that they were "poised to strike the final blows," but would give Japan "a final opportunity to end the war" by unconditional

surrender "of all the Japanese armed forces." The home islands would be
occupied and war criminals punished. Nowhere, deliberately, was any language about the future of Hirohito and the Imperial institution he symbolized. Only implicitly did it recognize that no one but the emperor
could proclaim and ensure surrender, for it permitted the Japanese to
freely choose their form of government, which seemed a sufficient hint.
By radio and leaflet drops the text was communicated to the Japanese, but
public opinion existed only through the contagion of rumor.

"Magic" decrypting specialists soon intercepted a cable to Premier
Kantaro Suzuki from Minister Shuichi Kase in Switzerland urging careful examination of the Potsdam offer, for the signatory governments
"seem to have taken pains to save face for us." But despite Kase's cautionary words, Suzuki convened a press conference in Tokyo on July 28 to declare that the ultimatum leaves "no other recourse but to ignore it entirely,
and resolutely fight for the successful conclusion of this war."

That afternoon in Washington, Maxwell Taylor, at the Pentagon after
leaving the 101st Airborne, and George Patton, on leave but to return to
Munich, were told by Marshall—so Taylor noted in his diary—"about
the . . . experimental atom bomb at Alamogordo and the plans for its use
against the Japanese." To Patton and Taylor, Marshall guessed that two
bombs would convince Japan to end the war; "however this estimate was
not shared by the War Department because a few days later the [101st
Airborne] Division was ordered to withdraw to the Auxerre region in
France as the first leg of its movement to the Far East." All options remained open.

The command lines to deploy the atomic bombs originated and remained at the Pentagon in the "Office of Secretary of War." Generals
Arnold and Groves, under Marshall, controlled their use. Covertly,
Groves attached to the 509th Composite Group on Tinian dozens not on
the manning charts: scientists and technicians, liaison and security officers. Some test and supply flights in and out were not recorded. Since deception was also an integral part of "Olympic" strategy, MacArthur's
command distributed, on July 30, with deliberately sloppy secrecy, a
phony "Pastel Two," which set October 1 for landings on the Chinese
coast to create airfields from which to attack Japan, and December 1 for a
landing on the home island of Shikoku.

On the last day of July, Marshall fielded a request from Spaatz on Guam that Nagasaki be eliminated from the target list for the Bomb. Its surface contours were wrong for optimal blast effect, and a POW camp was located nearby. Marshall again reaffirmed the four designated cities, as "practically every major Japanese city" had such camps. The only amendment in the original orders came from Truman, shifting the first drop date to "no sooner than August 2"—to give him time to exit Germany. "We have not done too badly, I think," Alexander Cadogan, now advising Prime Minister Attlee, wrote on leaving Potsdam. "Joe [Stalin] got most of what he wants, but then the cards were mostly in his hands."

With the countdown now beginning for the Bomb, and MacArthur's planning both for invasion and occupation handled at the staff level— principles for ruling Japan had come from the White House—he sought some personal visibility. Soon he would have all he could want. On August 1 he announced the invasion of tiny Fuga Island, off the northern Luzon coast from Aparri. The entire garrison of two Japanese was captured. Unrelated to the achievement, on August 2, under Marshall's signature, a member of his staff asked MacArthur what further assistance he needed from the War Department. "It was not easy to draft a cable to General MacArthur," recalled Robert Cutler, a lawyer in civil life then a colonel. "He was regarded in the Pentagon and elsewhere, not as a Person but as a Personage. Cables to him, like his own replies, were often works of art. One did not cable to MacArthur by ringing for a secretary and saying, 'Take a cable, Miss Jones.'"

The weather off the home islands began to cooperate with the mission of the 509th, beyond MacArthur's oversight, on August 6. Three weather planes and a standby B-29 to remain at Iwo Jima for emergencies took off at 1:37 A.M. Tinian time. At 2:45 A.M. the *Enola Gay*, carrying "Little Boy," and its two accompanying observation planes, began to roll. The six-and-one-half-hour flight proved uneventful. At 8:15 A.M. local time the 9,000-pound bomb dropped toward the Aioi Bridge in Hiroshima. Pretending it was a letter home, Robert Lewis, Paul Tibbets's co-pilot, was keeping a log for *New York Times* science reporter William Laurence, who had been scratched from the mission because of weight limitations. "My God," Lewis recorded piously for press release, "what have we done?" What he had actually shouted as the explosion erupted 1,890 feet above Hiroshima was, "God, look at that son-of-a-bitch go!"

"Bingo!" radioed Richard Nelson to Tinian. Deak Parsons, the navy ordnance expert who armed the bomb, noted in his terse log, "Flash followed by two slaps on plane. Huge cloud." To Lewis, Tibbets remarked as the plane lurched upward and twisted away from the blast, "I think this is the end of the war."

The strike message from Parsons reached Washington at 11:30 P.M. on the 5th. Additional details came in at 4:30 A.M. At 6:58 A.M., having finished a two-page report for Marshall, Groves was waiting in the general's Pentagon office when the chief of staff arrived. Marshall scanned the pages, then rang up Secretary Stimson at his home on a secure scrambler telephone. Stimson authorized release of a statement prepared for the president, and asked them to notify Truman aboard the *Augusta* en route home. Groves had prepared a separate news release, and Marshall cautioned him to look it over once more to ensure that there was no element of gloating in it. "I replied," Groves recalled, "that I was not thinking so much of those casualties as I was about the men who had made the Bataan death march."

Both releases stressed (it has been forgotten since) that Hiroshima was a major army headquarters not attacked until the Potsdam ultimatum had been rejected. "It is an atomic bomb," said Truman's statement, released from Washington at 11:00 A.M. "It is a harnessing of the basic power of the universe. The force from which the sun draws its power has been loosed against those who brought war to the Far East. . . . Let there be no mistake: we shall completely destroy's Japan's power to make war. . . . If they do not accept our terms they may expect a rain of ruin from the air, the like of which has never been seen on this earth."

In Tokyo, informed by his deputy, Marquis Koichi Kido, the emperor expressed his grief and conceded that the dread new circumstances required "bow[ing] to the inevitable." He asked for an emergency meeting of the War Cabinet. In the U.S., even some of the scientists who made the bomb possible deplored its use, regretting that the weapon had not been employed in a demonstration to dismay the enemy. Yet the realities were that a unique piece of ordnance could not have been chanced as intimidating theater. (What if its untried detonation mechanism did not work? Would a remote, harmless explosion awe a militarist-dominated culture in which suicide was glorious and surrender base?) Further, only one untested uranium device had existed. The Alamogordo plutonium weapon ("Fat Man"), entirely different in composition and triggering device, had itself only been tested on a tower by wired circuitry, not in timed air release.

Before the news of Hiroshima broke, MacArthur summoned twenty-five correspondents to Manila City Hall for a rare off-the-record press conference. From a leather armchair he radiated confidence that Japan would quit the war, but perhaps not before the Russians entered it. "Every Russian soldier killed," he said coldly, "is one less American death." He foresaw no more wars like the one now ending. "Atomic disintegration bombs" launched from the air, he predicted (from certain knowledge), would magnify the horrors of war. Only a decade earlier the first Pan Am Clipper had flown the Pacific to Manila. Planes that now dwarfed it crossed the Pacific by the hundreds to bomb Japan. The newsmen returned to their desks to find teletypes from Washington about a single atomic bomb that had just destroyed a city.

A few days later, MacArthur met privately with Theodore White of *Time*. On the afternoon of December 7, 1941, White had dropped slips of paper down twenty-nine floors to the street from the *Time* offices at Rockefeller Center to inform bewildered Christmas shoppers below that Japan had attacked Pearl Harbor. Before the war he had interviewed the general in Manila, and again after his arrival in Australia. To White, MacArthur, whose earlier blunders were now buried under victories, blamed the Bomb as likely to end the era of heroic warfare. "Scholars and scientists" had stolen future wars from military professionals and made "men like me" obsolete.

As the *Enola Gay* turned homeward (the roundtrip, 3,000-mile flight would take twelve hours and thirteen minutes) Parsons began encoding a message to Brigadier General Farrell at Tinian: "Results in all respects clear-cut. Immediate action to carry out further plans [for the second bomb] is recommended." By order, bombs were to be deployed as they became available. Assembly of "Fat Man" would begin as Stalin's government hurried a declaration of war on Japan, delivered to its ambassador in Moscow at five in the afternoon of August 8. The Soviet claim was that it hoped to shorten the war and speed the onset of peace, but it was an undisguised rush for spoils, for which a Japanese surrender would be irrelevant. At Potsdam, Truman had refused to write a begging letter to Stalin to ask for Soviet intervention.

The Bomb had so disrupted communications to Tokyo that the War Cabinet learned belatedly that the device which had leveled a city of a third of a million was indeed nuclear. Nearly nonstop meetings of courtiers and militarists remained deadlocked about surrender. Even in the face of Russian intervention, Japanese war minister Korechika Anami contended that the atomic bomb was an unique experimental weapon, unlikely to be repeated. Despite food shortages and burned-out cities, Japanese morale elsewhere was allegedly strong. The much-propagandized "suicide of a hundred million"—a population exaggeration—was still a prospect.

At 3:49 A.M. Tinian time on August 9, the strike planes of Special Bombing Mission 16 began lifting off once more. Their target was Kokura, on the northern coast of Kyushu, east of Yawata. *Bock's Car*, the B-29 carrying "Fat Man," had left with a defective auxiliary transfer pump that made 600 gallons of fuel in a reserve bomb bay inaccessible. To fix or change it would have aborted the operation for days, as a typhoon was moving toward Iwo Jima and Japan. Unlike "Little Boy," the plutonium bomb could not be armed while airborne. It had to be detonated by an implosion resulting from the simultaneous explosion inward of sixty-three lenses that surrounded the plutonium core.

Over Kokura the crew paid the price for earlier missions to pound the heavy industry of nearby Yawata. Wind-blown smoke obscured the aiming point. After three tries round, with fifty-five minutes and precious fuel wasted, *Bock's Car* turned toward its alternative target, the busy port city, Nagasaki. Ground zero was the Mitsubishi Shipyards, and with thirty seconds left to release, a hole in the cloud layer opened and the bomb bay unfolded for the fourth time. It was 11:58 A.M. in Tinian—an hour earlier in Nagasaki. Within minutes, burned and blackened survivors struggled out of the devastation.

Eisenhower had learned about the Bomb in Potsdam, and when Stimson visited him in Frankfurt, the general noted his misgivings about employing it, observing that the Japanese were already trying to surrender "with a minimum loss of 'face.'" Rare to show anger, Stimson argued for its necessity—that however lost was their war, the Japanese were not as likely as the Germans to surrender.* Eisenhower had fought a very different militarist culture. Later he called his views "merely personal and immediate reactions; they were not based on any analysis of the subject." Ironically he was preparing to leave for Moscow, to be honored by the Soviets, when the two bombs were dropped, and he was in Russia during the first days of the abbreviated Russian war. Stalin had stonewalled Japanese pleas for mediation as counter to his territorial designs.

Careful to say very little of substance, Eisenhower accepted his lionization gracefully, and appeared with Stalin on the reviewing stand above Lenin's tomb during a Red Army parade. Eisenhower's special honor, never before accorded a foreigner, masked Stalin's secret orders to his Far East Command that on going to war with Japan the Red Army was to in-

---

*At an international conference in Japan in 1995 marking the fiftieth anniversary of the end of the war, most Japanese participants conceded that at least one atomic bomb had been a necessary catalyst for the surrender. The War Cabinet record is that it took two.

vade southern Sakhalin (relinquished after the war with Japan in 1904), then strike southward into Hokkaido before the Americans invaded the lower islands, establishing a presence there to demand a share in the occupation.

Just before Eisenhower flew to Moscow, Marshall cabled, assuming that Japanese peace feelers from intermediaries were genuine, "When you are formally notified of the capitulation of Japan, we want you immediately to reverse the priorities for movement of organizations and men. . . . My thought is that when Japan surrenders the return of personnel from your theaters for discharge will have priority over all but MacArthur's most urgent requirements. . . ."

For Russia, the first days of the Japanese war did not go entirely as anticipated, although the Red Army swamped the depleted Kwantung Army, taking hundreds of thousands of prisoners, many transported to slave-labor camps where they worked under terrible conditions well into the 1950s, if they survived at all. As Red Army radio signals sent urgently in the clear revealed, the haste of veteran Marshal Aleksandr Vasilevsky's invasion left mechanized units from Outer Mongolia without fuel three days into the war. Occupying the vastness of Manchuria would take more time than anticipated, but the double blow of the new enemy and the new weapon shocked and divided Hirohito's War Cabinet. Still, War Minister Anami claimed, to general disbelief, "It is far too early to say the war is lost." Premier Suzuki, and Foreign Minister Shigenori Togo, on five separate visits on August 9, and marathon meetings thereafter, pleaded with the emperor to intervene. Since the interval between bombs had been three days, a third bomb was anticipated with growing fear. Without much official news, rumors raced through the panicky civilian population that the Americans had a huge signboard already painted, stored because of its size on an offshore battleship. It allegedly read: "There was a city here called Tokyo."

Marshall would shortly instruct Groves that "F-102," the third atomic bomb, which would be ready by August 16, should not be deployed without the express authority of the president. No more fissionable material was to be shipped to the Pacific. Truman was appalled at "wiping out" another "100,000" people unless necessity intervened. Decrypts from Japan made it clear that despite the stubbornness of the hard-liners, the will to continue was now a minority view, and dwindling further. On both sides, the war was now beyond the generals and the admirals. "Unconditional surrender" meant "without conditions," but as Secretary Stimson observed on August 10, "We would have to continue the Emperor ourselves under our command and supervision" in order to persuade "the many scattered armies of the Japanese" to lay down their arms, for the emperor was "the only source of authority in Japan."

Secretary of State James F. Byrnes enlisted Departmental Counselor Benjamin Cohen to develop phraseology that would acknowledge that the emperor could remain yet not guaranteeing what prerogatives he could keep. "Subject to the authority of the Supreme Commander of the Allied Powers.... the Emperor would be required to authorize and ensure the signature of the Government of Japan and the Japanese Imperial General Headquarters of the surrender terms necessary to carry out the provisions of the Potsdam Declaration...."

The succeeding paragraphs were to cause more dismay to Japanese authorities, as they put the "national polity" (*Kokutai*) at risk although the subtle language was intended to sidestep that. The "ultimate form of government of Japan," it directed, should be "established by the freely expressed will of the Japanese people." Further, the armed forces of the Occupation would remain until "the purposes set forth in the Potsdam Declaration"—demilitarization and democratization—"are achieved." The Washington assumption, in the face of opinion polls that most Americans wanted Hirohito tried as a war criminal, was that the Japanese would freely choose to retain the Imperial facade.*

At four in the afternoon of August 10, Tokyo time, with its war under way, Soviet envoy Jacob Malik formally delivered his overdue declaration of war, quoting the Potsdam manifesto which Russia had not signed. In return, Togo immediately handed Malik an offer to surrender. No such exchange had ever occurred in the annals of war. Malik rejected the appeal. The Russians eyed more territorial spoils. The next day, while Eisenhower was still in Moscow, Foreign Minister Molotov suggested smugly to Ambassador Averell Harriman that Emperor Hirohito be subordinated to a joint high command of an American and a Russian general. Harriman scoffed that the proposal was "unthinkable." After "heated discussion," as Harriman put it, he agreed to forward it to Washington, warning Molotov that it would be unacceptable.

China remained a problem difficult to separate from Manchuria. The theater commander, now Lieutenant General Albert Wedemeyer, cabled Marshall suggesting that Manchurian and Chinese seaports—specifically Darien and Shanghai—be occupied to keep them from Mao's Commu-

---

*Serenely, Hirohito told Marquis Kido, "I think it's perfectly all right to leave the matter up to the people."

nists. East Asia, Wedemeyer warned, was "an enormous pot, seething and boiling," and likely to waste away the gains made by "Allied sacrifices." Both Nimitz and MacArthur opposed the idea of venturing into someone else's civil war. As potential Supreme Commander in Tokyo, MacArthur wanted nothing in the way of "the prompt occupation of Japan proper," although he advised as an exception that two divisions of Marines be sent to Shanghai.

Just before midnight on August 10, Tokyo time, the Supreme War Council of six, with aides, gathered in the emperor's sweltering *Gobunko* (library) underground shelter. Three favored acceptance of the Potsdam ultimatum if the Imperial house were preserved; War Minister Anami and the service chiefs of staff stubbornly laid down unrealistic further terms: "that the occupation of Japan should if possible be avoided or, if inescapable, should be on a small scale and should not include such population centers as Tokyo; and that disarmament should be carried out on our own responsibility; and that war criminals should be dealt with by Japan." The holdouts knew they would not prevail but preferred dramatic self-destruction to ignominious defeat.

Marshall's staff recommended that all forces in the Pacific keep wary. In a memorandum on the 11th, "Ultra Intelligence during and after Arrangements to Terminate the Japanese War," his G-2, Major General Clayton Bissell, warned that covert enemy orders for "general or isolated repudiation of the surrender" were predictable. Although he added that given the state of mind of the Japanese military, a decisive effect from the atomic attacks might take as much as thirty days, three days after Nagasaki the airwaves carried surrender rumors. Concerned about suicidal Japanese intentions, Marshall again considered the Bomb's potential as a tactical weapon supporting the invasion. Grove's aide Colonel L. E. Seeman advised that at least seven devices would be ready for "Olympic," and could clear the beaches while troops stayed about six miles offshore. After two or three days, he estimated, much in error, as later tests would prove, that landing sites impacted by nuclear explosions would be radioactively weak, and viable.

Not waiting for the playing out of peacemaking, which MacArthur now assumed was inevitable, he confidently told Weldon Rhoades to plan to fly him to Tokyo as the new *Shogun* to "officially accept the surrender of Emperor Hirohito." It would not be that simple, as to save face the emperor would only be required to validate surrogates, but a military-diplomatic committee in Washington recommended that MacArthur be the sole American authorized to sign a surrender document. He began planning a grandiose one-man show with a gargantuan supporting cast. To cheering troops in the streets of Manila on Sunday evening August 12 he declared that he hoped, from the bottom of his heart, that the end was coming without an amphibious assault.

Publicly, the posture from Japan, largely deduced from government hand-outs on Tokyo radio, remained one of belligerent defiance. With new caution, MacArthur welcomed the recommendation in Washington that the formal surrender take place on Admiral Halsey's flagship, the battleship *Missouri*. Still, he contemplated a dramatic *deus ex machina* preliminary arrival on Japanese soil, but safely distant from Tokyo. As Eichelberger described the MacArthur scenario to his wife in the disparaging racist caricature that had underestimated the Japanese in 1941 and beyond, "As soon as the bomb craters [on the airstrips] are filled, we will fly in." But first, "the monkeys will come to Manila where final peace terms probably will not be signed." Eichelberger would "accompany a certain person on a boat" where "we would receive a number of goggle-eyed little buck-toothed birds and settle things."

Again calling in Rhoades, MacArthur directed him to get Richard Sutherland back from his indefinite leave in the States. Preparing to run Japan was a tall order, and the former deputy, although in the doghouse, was a cool administrative hand. No one, however, could keep MacArthur from the imperial ways he had adopted long before he knew what his next role would be. On the 13th, Truman approved the final details for the surrender ceremony and on August 15, Marshall's team working on the surrender flew an Operations Division colonel to Manila with the sealed packet. The courier was asked on his return about his "high-level conversation." He did have one "high-level conversation," he said. "I walked into his headquarters and stepped into the elevator, and General MacArthur came along, and stepped into the same elevator. He turned to me and said, 'You will take the next elevator [down], I presume.' That was my high-level conversation with General MacArthur." Still, the Operations directive prepared for the president's signature would inform the general that "the authority of the Emperor and Japanese Government to rule the state will be subject to you." MacArthur would not need to adjust his style.

"It was a hard job to do," Marshall recalled, "to have MacArthur put in command in Japan, because the navy wanted to control that and they put up quite a battle to get it. But we managed to control it for MacArthur." When Washington's paperwork for the signing was hand-carried by another colonel to MacArthur, according to Dean Rusk, then at the Pentagon, the liaison officer hurried from his plane to motor-launch out to the *Missouri* "with the surrender documents in hand. One of MacArthur's staffers met him at the foot of the gangway and said, 'General MacArthur says you will not be needed on board.'"

The ritual of Japanese defiance concluded on August 14. The twenty-four members of the full Cabinet, most in street clothes, arrived at 10:30 A.M. Hirohito entered the clammy *Gobunko* at 10:55, wearing a military uniform and white gloves. Premier Suzuki apologized for having him confront the ministerial deadlock. As Hirohito spoke, the others wept, recognizing, without the word *surrender* ever being used, what they were being ordered to do on the moral authority of the emperor. "If the war were to continue," he explained with the second Bomb in mind, "our country would be reduced to rubble, and I cannot bear to have my people suffer more anguish. I could not face the spirits of my ancestors." To rebuild Japan, they had to preserve something, "be it ever so little." He expected the Cabinet to approve an Imperial Rescript and called for a draft to be prepared "as soon as possible." If it would assist in maintaining calm, and order, he offered, "I shall be glad to stand before a microphone."

In Moscow, where it was just past midnight on the 14th, Ambassador Harriman, Eisenhower's host at a formal reception responding to a glittering Soviet gala two evenings before, was called to the telephone. When he returned, it was with news that Japan had surrendered. Again, vodka glasses were raised.*

The people of Japan had never heard the Imperial voice. For practice and for security, Hirohito would record it—a wise choice, it turned out, as army mutineers would try to prevent the broadcast as part of a vain attempt to forestall the surrender. Yet to force events, new orders came from General Arnold to bomb the hell out of the Japanese. He sent a thousand

---

*Two evenings before, Stalin at dinner had asked Ike what he would like as a remembrance of Russia. Eisenhower thought a diplomatic moment and suggested a portrait of Stalin. It would, indeed, arrive, via Harriman, inscribed "To the famous strategist General of the Army D. Eisenhower with very best wishes. I Stalin" (*I* the Russian for *J*).

aircraft over Japan on the 14th. Coming within ten miles of Tokyo, some Eighth Air Force planes caused an alert that delayed the six-minute recording of the Rescript, but it was made, hidden, then broadcast at noon on the 15th. The emperor would accept the Potsdam terms, noting ambiguously that "the war situation has developed not necessarily to Japan's advantage." He cited the unfavorable "general trends of the world," and noted that the enemy had begun "to employ a new and more cruel bomb, the power of which to do damage is indeed incalculable." All business and traffic ceased as he spoke; in their homes, people stood reverently.

Some die-hards, like Anami, would commit formal *seppuku*. Most Japanese, however willing to die to resist invasion, were relieved. Less resigned to Hirohito's reluctance to intervene until catastrophe had come, Tatsuichiro Akizaki composed a bitter, laconic *tanka*,

> While I read the Emperor's Rescript that came too late,
> Atomic bomb victims writhe on the scorched ground.

Ready to move on the occupation, MacArthur's headquarters radioed a first message in the clear to Japan in his name as Supreme Commander. He directed that a station be designated to handle communications at a specified frequency and in English text. A second message in the clear ordered "the immediate cessation of hostilities" and directed "the Japanese Imperial Government to send . . . a Competent Representative empowered to receive . . . certain requirements for carrying into effect the terms of surrender." The emissary would have to carry "a document authenticated by the Emperor of Japan empowering him." Ranking officers of the Japanese army, navy, and air forces were to accompany the Imperial envoy. In elaborate detail the message set out time and procedure for the Japanese to fly south to Ie Shima, just off the northwestern coast of Okinawa, in an unarmed plane painted white with green crosses. From there they would be flown to Manila in an American plane. "In communications regarding this flight," the instructions concluded, "the code designation *Bataan* will be employed." The directive was vintage MacArthur.

Marshall drafted a statement on the surrender for Secretary Stimson which closed, "The next war might destroy the world. It must not come." The Kyushu operation rendered moot by events was formally disposed of by radiogram to MacArthur from Marshall's Joint Logistics Plans Committee at the Pentagon under the subject heading, "Cancellation of Directive."

14

Postwar Postings

O F THE BIG THREE in the postwar military, only MacArthur would close out 1945 as he wanted. As emperor of Japan in fact if not in name, at sixty-five and lacking American ties of home and family, he had a post tailored to his personality. Without postwar ambition after six exhausting years, Marshall looked to his fishing rod and his garden. (Katherine confided that the compost heap at Leesburg was the pride of his heart.) While Eisenhower, not yet fifty-five, intended to remain in the military, the only position possible for his five stars was chief of staff. Downsizing of the army into a lean 1 million that could run the occupations and keep the peace was a no-win assignment. Under a budget-cutting Congress, Eisenhower would oversee the reduction to 1,891,000 men in 1946; to 992,000 in 1947, when the draft law expired; and to 554,000 in 1948.

At Potsdam, Eisenhower had asked Truman to expedite citizenship for Kay Summersby. Keeping his misgivings to himself, Truman recommended that she write to Secretary of State James F. Byrnes. Eisenhower offered to send a covering letter. "I wanted very badly to be an American citizen," Kay recalled. "There was no other way that I could see for me to stay with Ike." She did not know that her separation from him had already been arranged.

Early in October, Harry Hopkins received a letter from Eisenhower about a suggestion that he write a book. Some in his former circle were already doing that. The results would become a major irritation and minor embarrassment. Major General Alexander Surles, who handled public relations for Marshall, had cabled Eisenhower about Harry Butcher's typescript on his years with him. As Surles put it, regardless of Butcher's attempts at tact, "he obtained the data while in [a] highly confidential position." Marshall himself refused all memoir bait and was uninterested in what others wrote about him. "I have made a vow," he confided to his old VMI roommate Major General Philip B. Peyton, "never to commit the error of writing any memoirs." Eisenhower wanted to keep his hands off all reminiscences mentioning him—and he knew that more were sure to come. To read over Butcher's pages "would give a tacit approval to everything said." From Frankfurt, Ike wrote to "Butch" not to fly over with his typescript, for the book should be "exclusively your product."

Even Mickey McKeough, Ike's enlisted aide, was writing (with help) *Sgt. Mickey and General Ike,* for which Eisenhower permitted a letter of commendation from him as a foreword. In 1946, *San Francisco Chronicle* humorist Paul Speegle, commenting on both *My Three Years with Eisenhower* and *Sgt. Mickey,* predicted more such books, including "*I Opened the Door,* by Cholmondeley Thames. This will be an intimate study of the Supreme Commander . . . by the doorman at Eisenhower's favorite London hotel." The most painfully discreet of Ike-related memoirs would be by a yet-to-be discharged WAC, Kay Summersby.

To Hopkins, Eisenhower confessed that although he had been putting publishers off, he had been "draft[ing] a bit of a narrative just to satisfy myself that I had something to say that was worth hearing." He hadn't yet convinced himself. "I need not tell you," he went on, "that this job [in Germany] is an unholy mixture of irritations, frustrations, and bewildering conflicts. Nevertheless I try to keep my sense of humor and keep swinging with both hands. . . . In a job such as this we are particularly vulnerable to day by day criticism. An administrative blunder, even if local and temporary, is news; constructive progress is not dramatic."

Some of Eisenhower's vulnerability related to his ongoing tendency to distance himself from awkward matters for which deputies fronted for him. On his official watch were thousands of sick and malnourished "Displaced Persons," considered by his subordinates as troublesome misfits to be closeted for convenience in the very concentration camps from which they had been liberated. Protests from Washington finally got Eisenhower's attention. To survey the situation, Stimson had sent Earl Harrison, dean of the University of Pennsylvania Law School, to Germany. He found Jewish DPs still "living under guard behind barbed wire in camps . . . built for slave laborers." Stimson relayed the "grim" Harrison report to Frankfurt, adding firmly, "I want to emphasize the importance we attach to this problem."

Irritated, Eisenhower responded that he saw the situation as "completely different. . . . I should call your attention to the fact," he lectured the sophisticated former secretary of state, "that problems of this nature must not be oversimplified because each Jewish individual is presumably a national of some European country, and it is impossible to consider them as stateless." Whatever his forced technicality, Eisenhower must have realized that the problem would not go away. When Stimson insisted on action, Eisenhower finally decreed that "overcrowding" be eliminated by creating new facilities, and that "sanitation and wholesomeness of food" and medical care were to become "adequate."

Although Eisenhower preferred to have evacuated the DPs, as the press referred to them, elsewhere, most nations, including his own, didn't want them, and the British, fearing Arab volatility, refused to open Palestine, the goal of many Jewish DPs. "Aryan" Germans had less difficulty adjusting to peace, while protesting questionnaires limiting civil jobs to those who were *"Persilschein"*—clean of Nazi pasts in the language of the popular laundry soap. In Bavaria, where he was military governor, Patton publicly condemned denazification screening. American papers headlined, "American General Says Nazis Are Just Like Republicans and Democrats." It was routine in the U.S., he contended, to join the party in power to become a postmaster, just as jobs under Hitler had required, as a sort of political blackmail, surface Nazi loyalties. Once the *New York Times* editorialized, "General Patton belittles the very purpose for which the war was fought," Marshall wired Eisenhower bluntly, "Please take action."

Patton was summoned to Frankfurt. In his diary he deplored that he could not explain at the raucous press conference resulting from his newest public relations flap that the only overtly *Persilschein* job-seekers were Communists unemployable after 1933, and that his "chief interest in establishing order in Germany was to prevent Germany from going communistic." Ugly Russians were just across his occupation frontier. Even with the office door closed, Kay Summersby wrote, "I heard one of the stormiest sessions ever staged in our headquarters." Eisenhower relieved Patton of his Bavarian command, reassigning him to an innocuous position in which he could not make policy. Lucian Truscott Jr. took over Third Army.

Few questioned that Eisenhower would soon succeed Marshall in Washington. Although Eisenhower did not want the job, Marshall had made that request specific in a letter to Truman the week after the Japanese surrender. A copy went to Eisenhower, who agreed reluctantly to accept the appointment until Bradley could be released from his new Veterans Administration post. Truman called Marshall in and asked how soon he hoped to "get away." "Oh," said Marshall, "something like ten days." The president said he would be sorry to see Marshall leave, and would like him to "go along a little further" while he thought over the general's effective departure date. Marshall amended his estimate to early September. The formal end of the war, with MacArthur presiding, would take place on the decks of the *Missouri* on September 2. It seemed appropriate to Marshall to put a period to his own service then.

With the surrender, the Pentagon had ordered all possible resources extended to furnish food, medicines, and clothing to Pacific area prisoners of war, who would remain technically under Japanese control until the official signing. Enemy officers had already begun turning over the camps to senior POWs, and air evacuations began late in August. Jonathan Wainwright had been among those plucked from a camp in Manchuria. As soon as Marshall learned of his safe arrival in China on August 28, he telephoned Mrs. Wainwright, then radioed the gaunt general "reaffirm[ing] the expressions of my last message to you a few hours before the fall of Corregidor in deepest appreciation of all that you did and have done for the honor of the Army." Marshall also ordered that all POW officers held by the Japanese and being flown Stateside be informed, as William E. Brougher noted in his diary in Mukden, "that our wives will be brought to meet us in Wash'n or wherever desired."

Marshall's message of May 5, 1942, to Wainwright had concluded, "You and your devoted followers have become the living symbols of our war aims and the guarantee of victory." Wainwright replied from Chungking that he had kept the original copy of the message "since it came to my hand and it will always be one of my most cherished possessions." Marshall drafted a citation for a Medal of Honor—which MacArthur had opposed earlier, claiming that Wainwright had not fought effectively and had exceeded his authority when he surrendered all of the Philippines. Marshall and Stimson also proposed a fourth star for him. In Washington on September 10, after an emotional welcoming parade, Wainwright, now a full general, received his Medal of Honor at the White House from President Truman.

MacArthur saw Wainwright for the first time since 1942 when he and Arthur Percival, the British general who had surrendered Singapore, were brought to the New Grand Hotel in Yokohama on the evening of September 1, where the American command awaited boarding the *Missouri* the next morning. The two generals embraced, and ignoring his earlier imprecations about Wainwright as an incompetent old drunk, MacArthur impulsively offered him command of a corps. Both knew that it was only a gesture toward the near-skeleton that Wainwright now was, but it confirmed his immunity from charges made by MacArthur from the safety of Australia that Wainwright had violated orders. Marshall had already taken care of that.

However reluctantly made, Truman's appointment of MacArthur ("Mr. Prima Donna" to the president) to be viceroy of Japan had conceded the general's dominating personality and overwhelming prestige. Defeated Japan, to be left with only a puppet prime minister under a nominal emperor, needed an imperious substitute. No one in the military hierarchy but MacArthur would do. His initial instructions from Washington, later assumed to be his own policy, included the key line, "The Emperor of Japan is not at present a liability and may later become an asset." When Marshall asked about accepting American political advisers who would possess no "executive capacity," and liaison officers in Tokyo representing other nations, from Britain to Russia, MacArthur radioed regally that he would "welcome" such people and groups in Japan provided that he could "pass upon individual acceptability before assignment."

The general, in effect *Shogun*, relished his vast dimension of authority, some of it soon self-assumed. The bypassed Russians seethed. The Soviet representative in Manila, Lieutenant General Kuzma Nikolaevich Derevyanko, a chunky man with oversized shoulderboards, arrived bearing Stalin's Potsdam understandings. MacArthur brushed off any implied dismemberment of the home islands into occupation zones. A midlevel Pentagon scenario for shared occupation had been submitted to the Joint Chiefs of Staff the day after Hirohito's surrender broadcast, recommending a Soviet zone in Hokkaido and northern Honshu, a Chinese presence in small Shikoku, a British occupation of Kyushu, and a four-power Berlin-like occupation of Tokyo. Lessening the American burden of policing Japan in such fashion met total rejection. Marshall recognized that Truman, the State Department, and MacArthur all flatly opposed diluting American authority. "I was determined," Truman later wrote, "that the Japanese occupation would not follow in the footsteps of the German experience. I did not want divided control."

Russia had proposed the return of former czarist territories, and occupation of Hokkaido and all of Honshu southward to the 38th parallel at Niigata. "Why are you wasting your time with those ridiculous demands?" MacArthur asked Derevyanko, threatening to return him to Moscow. When he reported his rebuff, Stalin cabled Truman on August 22, having even been denied the backwater of Hokkaido, "I have to say to you that I and my colleagues did not expect such an answer from you." The Red Army had been at war for all of a week. Derevyanko remained, preferring impotence under MacArthur, whose high-handedness he loyally deplored to Moscow, to anything under Stalin.

Despite Truman's rejection, Marshal Vasilevsky ordered his East Asian Army, about to move into southern Sakhalin, although they did not have landing craft or protective vessels for an invasion in depth, to cross the Soya Strait into Hokkaido. As late as August 21 the operation was scheduled for August 23. Then Stalin communicated sudden misgivings. Nimitz belligerently controlled Japanese home waters. "To avoid the creation of conflicts and misunderstandings," General S. P. Ivanov, Vasilevsky's chief of staff, backed down, "it is categorically forbidden to send any ships or planes at all in the direction of Hokkaido." Occupying Sakhalin and the Kuriles to the north, Stalin settled for what he had been guaranteed at Yalta.

MacArthur's deputies pressed for a surrender ceremony on August 26, but were put off by the need for the Japanese to suppress breakouts of *kamikaze* mutinies. Fortunately for both sides, a typhoon moved across the home islands, delaying the formalities further. On the Asian mainland, however, the Red Army continued taking territory with its usual brutality, prompting Tokyo to appeal to MacArthur, who could do nothing. The Russians fudged that as yet there was no formal surrender.

On August 28, the first American transport planes from Okinawa put down forty miles southwest of Tokyo at Atsugi Airfield. Its bomb-cratered runways roughly repaired, Atsugi soon handled hundreds of unarmed aircraft with maintenance and communications equipment, troops and vehicles. There were no hostile incidents. On the 29th, Nimitz arrived by air to board the *South Dakota*, and MacArthur flew in with a stream of unarmed C-54s. His entourage proceeded to the Yokohama customs house (temporary GHQ) and the New Grand Hotel in a motley fleet of barely workable vehicles led by an ancient red fire engine. Many were charcoal-retrofitted as there was little gasoline. The Supreme Commander rode in a rackety old Lincoln. The route was guarded by armed Japanese troops standing at attention, their backs turned and eyes averted from the motorcade—a mark of respect (and security) until then reserved for the Imperial family.

The new signing date of August 31 proved overly optimistic, perhaps chosen by MacArthur for its symbolism. The war had begun on the other side of the globe on September 1, 1939, and might end dramatically at the six-year mark. But the logistics for the arrival of dignitaries and the press, and for the theatrical display of military power, took a further day. Ceremonially, MacArthur would outdo Eisenhower in spades. As Theodore White, covering the event, put it, "This was to be no cloistered surrender, as . . . at Reims three months earlier. MacArthur wanted everyone there, and the world to watch."

Tokyo Bay was crowded with 258 Allied vessels. On Sunday morning, September 2, still evening on September 1 in Washington, where the ceremonies were heard on radio, MacArthur boarded the *Missouri* at 8:43. Three minutes later, the Japanese delegation mounted the starboard gangway. Delicately, no members of the Imperial family participated, not even the interim prime minister, Naruhiko Higashikuni, a royal prince and Hirohito's cousin. Rather, the defeated were led by Mamoru Shigemitsu, the foreign minister, who walked with painful difficulty, limping on an inadequate artificial leg and leaning on a cane. Their credentials authorized their signatures on behalf of "Hirohito, by the Grace of Heaven, Emperor of Japan, seated on the Throne occupied by the same Dynasty changeless through ages eternal." Permitted nine representatives, the delegation included three each from the foreign office, army, and navy. As Shigemitsu's side was Toshikazu Kase, who recalled "standing in the public gaze"—under newsreel cameras—"like penitent schoolboys awaiting the dreaded schoolmaster."

On deck, a mess table covered with a green felt cloth displayed the documents to be signed. As the proceedings opened at 9:08 A.M., 450 aircraft from TF-38 roared overhead. Flanking MacArthur, in his familiar suntan uniform and scrambled eggs cap, at a standing microphone, were Generals Wainwright and Percival,* frail in their fresh, too-large, uniforms. "We are gathered here," MacArthur intoned sepulchrally, "to conclude a solemn agreement whereby Peace may be restored." He asked for a disavowal on both sides of "distrust, malice, or hatred," and hoped "that

---

*Arthur Percival, a POW like Wainwright, had abjectly surrendered Singapore.

both victors and vanquished . . . [would] rise to that higher dignity which alone befits the sacred purposes we are about to serve."

The Japanese signatories walked forward and bent over the papers looking for their places. Seated because of his infirmities, Shigemitsu slowly removed his silk top hat and yellow gloves and placed them on the table. As he fumbled, MacArthur snapped to Sutherland, "Show him where to sign!" As General Yoshijiro Umezu, with his chief of staff's gold-braid cord over one shoulder, completed the endorsements for the defeated, the morning sun broke through the grey overcast. Once MacArthur signed for the Allied Powers, other representatives came forward, including the stolid Derevyanko, with some confusion following when the Canadian delegate signed on the line for France. Observing the disorder, Sutherland walked over and drew arrows to identify appropriate nations.

The two copies of the instrument of surrender would win no prizes for neatness, but after six years and two days, with peace already producing nearly as many crises as the terminated conflict, the Second World War was formally over. In a ringing voice that seemed to require no microphone, MacArthur declared, "These proceedings are closed." Then he added in a quiet aside to Admiral Halsey, "Bill, where the hell are those airplanes?" As if stage-managed—and it was—a cloud of 400 B-29s and 1,500 carrier aircraft swept over Tokyo Bay from the north and thundered toward the mists overhanging Mount Fuji. Japan was now officially under what would be an orderly occupation.

The postwar chaos in the temporarily recovered European colonies, and China, would continue; and the surrender and return of millions of stranded Japanese troops from posts thousands of miles apart would take months, and even years. Colonial forces from the West would find even their abbreviated reoccupancy difficult—and unwelcome. While losing the war, the Japanese had indirectly liberated much of East Asia.

No message from Eisenhower exists congratulating MacArthur, but he was not out of mind. Eisenhower still had much on his European plate, and was also thinking ahead to his next post, at the Pentagon. Marshall had cabled that there was not "a shadow of a doubt regarding your appointment to succeed me." Three days after the *Missouri* ceremonies, Ike wrote to Marshall to ask MacArthur through channels about releasing "able men from his theater" for the future War Department staff. "We must find some important positions to be filled by personnel from the Pacific." He hoped "to avoid at any cost the growth of a European versus a Pacific clique." In particular he sought Robert Eichelberger (his 1926 Leavenworth classmate), Stephen Chamberlin, and Hugh Casey (of the Army Service Command). He got only Chamberlin, MacArthur's G-3, who would become Eisenhower's director of intelligence in 1946.

Eisenhower wanted the able Eichelberger as deputy chief of staff, which would bring the general the coveted fourth star denied him under MacArthur's thrall. But the general's grievances were many, and were likely to be aired Stateside. While cautiously agreeing to let him go, MacArthur made the conditions such that Eichelberger stayed, which meant that in the downsizing Occupation to come, his *bête noire,* Krueger, would be deactivated instead, along with his Sixth Army. With his own Eighth Army intact, Eichelberger would nurse his bitterness in Tokyo for two more years.

MacArthur settled only briefly in a suite at Yokohama's less-than-grand New Grand Hotel. He had been cautioned by Japanese authorities to keep troops out of Tokyo until the capital was quiet, but even from a distance he realized that direct rule would only delay a placid takeover. As Foreign Minister Shigemitsu pointed out to him the day after the formal surrender, an overwhelmingly visible intrusion into Japanese life "will be relieving the Japanese Government from the responsibility of seeing that the Occupation policy is faithfully carried out." Shigemitsu's approach coincided with Washington's recommendation two days later about governing indirectly in practice as well as principle.

Unlike Germany, when at its *Stunde null*—"Hour Zero"—the Nazi government ceased to exist, Japan maintained civil authority at every level. Above town and village administrations were a Cabinet, a Diet, and an Imperial House—a visible institutional continuity. MacArthur's chief task, which his characteristic remoteness made more difficult, was to keep his occupation troops from behaving like conquerors. Rapes, robberies, vandalism, and even murder were more often covered up or cautiously ignored than disciplined. It did not help that when MacArthur had the Stars and Stripes hoisted over Tokyo, he banned the display of "the meatball"—the Rising Sun flag in GI parlance. It was unusually negative symbolism for a benign beginning.

MacArthur knew little of the situation throughout Japan from his grand apartments on the wooded American embassy grounds, to which he moved with his family and retainers on September 17. Seldom venturing beyond central Tokyo, he was chauffeured each morning in his pre-war Cadillac, shipped from Manila, to the Supreme Command Allied Powers (SCAP) offices only minutes away on the sixth floor of the Dai Ichi ("Number One") Mutual Life Insurance Building. Overlooking the moat and Imperial Palace grounds in Hibaya, the imposing (for its day) building had survived the firebombings because aircrews had been ordered to spare the palace.

The boulevard which SCAP headquarters faced was renamed First Avenue. MacArthur decreed further that street signs and public notices in central Tokyo were to appear only in English lettering. He would see very little of the script of the vanquished as he traveled his restricted route, and saw few, even eminent, Japanese in his spartan office who did not speak passable English. Yet his public image had to contrast sharply with a put-down attributed to him that venerable Japan was immature—a nation of twelve-year-olds.

Made public on September 22, Washington's "Initial Post-Surrender Policy for Japan" declared that although the U.S. would consult with other Allies on Occupation matters, "in the event of any differences among them, the policies of the United States will govern." In effect, within presidential guidelines, MacArthur executed policy. Often initiating his own, on September 17, without consultation with Washington, he announced that within six months, depending upon shipping, he would reduce the American garrison in Japan to 200,000 men, less than half the initial presence. Undersecretary of State Dean Acheson complained to the press that MacArthur was dictating the Occupation. Whatever the merits of the downsizing, he had chosen a good time to announce it. Secretary of War Stimson handed his resignation to the president the next day, just before his seventy-eighth birthday. Too much was going on in the Capital for anyone to take much notice—anyone but Marshall, who rebuked MacArthur for not consulting the Pentagon. In a rare apology which perhaps only Marshall could elicit, MacArthur radioed, "Your WD 65406 distresses me. There was not the faintest thought that my statement . . . would cause the slightest embarrassment."

Although MacArthur often overstepped his prerogatives, he could have been reversed at any time by Washington. Marshall objected to the assumption of authority, but force reduction made sense. Surplus troops bred indiscipline, and further downsizing was being urged in Congress. Soldiers long abroad wanted to go home. Although Americans pulled the strings, the nation of 74 million was largely running its own domestic affairs. (The Japanese authorities would brazenly post spies in GHQ to read internal Occupation documents.) MacArthur would not even criticize the deliberate failure of the Japanese to use the words *defeat* and *surrender* and *occupation. Termination of war* satisfied pride, as did *garrison force.*

In adept public relations, MacArthur had already established the internal realities by what became known as "the Photograph." Early on September 27, 1945, Emperor Hirohito arrived at MacArthur's embassy home in his ancient Rolls-Royce, formally dressed in cutaway coat and top hat, and accompanied by carloads of court attendants. Brigadier General Bonner Fellers and Major Faubion Bowers (whose Japanese was excellent) saluted the emperor. His Imperial Highness bowed and shook their hands, and Bowers took the emperor's hat. MacArthur materialized, in tieless khaki shirt and suntans, greeting Hirohito with a baritone "You are very, very welcome, sir!" (Fellers had never heard MacArthur "sir" anyone.) The viceroy reached out to clasp the emperor's hand just as Hirohito bowed so deeply that the handshake happened above his head.

Leaving the court retainers with Bowers and Fellers, MacArthur led the emperor inside with his official interpreter Katsuzō Okumura. They agreed to keep their discussions private, to enhance the inviolability of the relationship. (Much later, Okumura reported that MacArthur had praised Hirohito for his "great prompt decision" to spare his people further suffering by ending the war.) After forty minutes they parted, with MacArthur encouraging the emperor to transmit any advice he had through officials of his choice, as "Needless to say, there is no one else who knows as much about Japan and its people as you."

They would meet in much the same fashion ten more times, but only one photograph—the first—symbolizes the postwar shogunate. MacArthur, towering over the emperor, stands casually. Hirohito, slight and forty-four, is stiffly at his left. Although the symbolism of overwhelming authority appalled the Home Ministry, censorship of the American regime was impossible. Japanese officialdom saw in the image only defeat and *lèse-majesté,* yet "the Photograph" also confirmed that the Supreme Commander Allied Powers would literally stand by Hirohito.

Deftly, the emperor's retainers followed "the Photograph" with an Imperial Rescript on New Year's Day 1946, in which Hirohito formally renounced his divinity. Defeat had made the myth absurd. "The ties between Us and Our people," the Rescript pronounced confidently, "are not predicated on the false assumption that the Emperor is divine and that the Japanese people are superior to other races and fated to rule the world." He pledged a peaceful reconstruction of Japan. An early index to relative status was Hisako Iwabuchi's first-grade class in Niigata. Her teacher passed out sheets of paper for writing practice and directed, "Write down the person you most respect." Hisako recalled, "I wanted to write down the Emperor, but I thought I shouldn't write that. So I wrote down General MacArthur."

On January 25, 1946, in response to a request from Eisenhower as chief of staff for results of an investigation of Hirohito's war culpability, MacArthur, having conducted no such thing, cabled, "Investigation has been conducted." No evidence had ostensibly been found linking Hirohito to political decisions leading to war. With doomsday rhetoric, MacArthur warned that if the emperor were indicted, "a tremendous convulsion" would agitate Japan, resulting in "guerrilla warfare, the disintegration of democracy, and communism."* Eisenhower dropped the subject. Exporting democracy to an alien culture required compromises.

Beyond the home islands, MacArthur's warrant included decolonizing the "Greater Japanese Empire" and disarming forces at home and abroad, repatriating overseas Japanese, and ending Japan's powers to deal independently with foreign governments. On September 6, 1945, he had ordered the closure of foreign embassies and consulates. When compliance was slow, on October 25 he directed the recall of all diplomatic personnel accredited to Japan, and on November 4 he ordered the severance of all diplomatic ties with other nations and the transfer of such functions to SCAP. After that, GHQ handled Japan's foreign relations, a task given to a new Diplomatic Section in April 1946.

The final days overseeing the German occupation passed quickly if not easily for Eisenhower. On October 14, Ike's fifty-fifth birthday, he celebrated privately with Kay at his official residence; she remained by night at the WAC house in Frankfurt. He confided that he was arranging a flight to Washington for her in his command B-17 to enable Kay to take out her first citizenship papers, giving her a personal letter to Bradley, which she delivered on November 2. The gesture seemed to validate their wartime affection, but when she returned to Frankfurt, to her surprise he

*Later, when former prime minister Hideki Tojo was being tried as a war criminal and testified that had Hirohito not assented to the Pacific war, "none of us would have dared to act against the Emperor's will," MacArthur had the English translation protectively watered down.

was packing for Washington himself. He told her that Marshall was undertaking a mission to China for the president, which made an Eisenhower presence urgent at the Pentagon. "It's just for a few weeks, though; I'll be back." They'd be together, he promised, "around the first of the year." Having made his career bargain, he knew otherwise. He would write in 1947, of someone else's emotional torment, that it "makes one wonder whether any human ever dares to become so wrapped up in another that all happiness and desire to live is determined by the actions, desires—or life—of the second."

Eisenhower's arrival and Marshall's exit were preceded by Stimson's retirement. On September 18, he wrote to Truman urging "properly recognizing the services of General Marshall" as the person who "has dominated the global strategy of the war."* He cited Marshall's "intellectual power, his selfless integrity, and his inflexible habit of considering only the general interest and never his own," and proposed that Congress vote Marshall "a special supreme medal such as they did to General Ulysses Grant. Certainly a DSM would be insufficient. He already has one from the last war." The president read the statement to the Cabinet at the last meeting which Stimson attended, and feeling was unanimous that something unique should be done. On September 19, at his final press conference, Stimson devoted most of his farewell statement to Marshall, whose "position of public trust . . . has given me a new gauge of what such service should be." He was puzzled when no appropriate recognition followed. But for his ineligibility in rank, as an officer, Marshall was at least worthy of the ubiquitous Good Conduct Medal. From Truman's feelers to both parties in the Congress, he learned that he could do nothing for Marshall without a commensurate accolade for someone else. Curiously, the someone else turned out to be not General MacArthur, but Admiral King, and Truman agreed to such an amendment in the House to elicit a watered-down Thanks of Congress. A politician since forgotten spitefully blocked a vote on the joint resolution to ensure Marshall's promised testimony to yet another Pearl Harbor investigating committee then being organized.

Much of Marshall's concluding weeks at the Pentagon were filled with briefings for Eisenhower by memorandum, including the recommendation that Ike take on the unpopular cause of Universal Military Training long espoused to no effect by Marshall himself. American unreadiness had been costly, and had prolonged the war. Yet as always,

---

*Churchill, despite his wartime differences with Marshall, lauded him as "the organizer of victory."

Americans preferred to be unprepared. That kept taxes down—but also international deference. Winning the war, he explained bluntly to the *New York Herald-Tribune* Forum (October 29, 1945), was "but a negative return for our tremendous investment of blood and money." Although America had also won "the respect of the peoples of the earth," he reminded listeners that such regard was only an "intangible." Consider what it would have meant in reality, he proposed, "had we commanded the military respect of Germany, Italy, and Japan in 1939." Prestige was "fleeting, unless we bend our efforts to preserve it." He was deliberately worrying aloud that demobilizing wholesale would jeopardize the peace. "The business of dissipating the political benefits that a nation may derive from victory," he observed ruefully, "is in the American tradition."

Among Marshall's last decisions was his painful acceptance of the relief of his old friend Patton from his Bavarian post to the largely paper 15th Army, primarily a "Theater Board" to compile a history of the ETO. Patton knew why he was removed. No one at the command level was happy about it. He had been the most effective fighting general the Americans had, but unsuited to be a military governor, or to any peacetime desk role. Not wanting to sever their old friendship, Eisenhower invited Patton, whose relocated headquarters was in Heidelberg, to a football game in Frankfurt between players from two divisions in the area. At halftime, to demonstrate impartiality, Eisenhower crossed the former soccer pitch to the opposite side, Patton with him. The GI spectators cheered wildly; but when they realized that Ike's companion, in tailored riding breeches and gleaming cavalry boots, was Patton, the cheers changed abruptly to jeers. They were not his troops, and knew him only by clouded reputation.

Patton's death in December after a paralyzing automobile accident in Mannheim ended any question of a new peacetime posting. From Chungking, Marshall drafted a press release confessing his "shock" and recognizing Patton's "utterly fearless" leadership in battle, and "driving energy and tactical skill" that made him "one of the greatest military leaders in our history." Perhaps typical of how things happened in postwar China, the draft release vanished.

Decisions before flying to China were tough to make, but Marshall took comfort in such reminders as that from former secretary of state Edward

Stettinius, a good friend now working in London on setting up United Nations administration, "At the time you become a country gentleman. . . ."* Marshall's letters for many months had been full of dreams about gardening at his Leesburg home in Virginia, and riding—and fishing—at his winter retreat in Pinehurst, North Carolina. Wherever he was in wartime, he had tried to get his lines into the water.

Eisenhower left Frankfurt on November 10. He never returned. General Joseph McNarney, another Marshall product, took his place as military governor of the American Zone. Almost as soon as Ike returned to the U.S. he came down with a disabling bronchial infection. He had to cancel a forthcoming Scottish honorary degree ceremony, and a formal farewell planned for staff and troops in Germany—although that might have been a relief, given the Summersby dilemma. On November 22, just before he entered an army hospital in West Virginia, he wrote to Beetle Smith in Frankfurt, who was also about to leave the command, "I think you should make arrangements to transfer Kay to General [Lucius] Clay [in Berlin], who wants her and has promised her a very good job with the promotion [to Captain] she is now entitled." She could not be reassigned to the U.S., he contended, although no such regulation existed, because as a foreigner she had been commissioned for a specific theater. "Since Kay has become too widely published to hope to escape notice," he confessed, acknowledging references to her, and him, in the press, "there is nothing to do but continue her. . . ."

On the same day he wrote similarly to Clay, and added that he would "attempt to do so in a letter to Kay herself." He did, claiming as he opened, "I am terribly distressed. . . ." Otherwise quite impersonal, his letter of November 22 had been dictated. According to Summersby, "He said that it had become impossible for him to keep me as a member of his personal official family. . . . There would be opposition to anyone who was not a completely naturalized American citizen working in the War Department, and it also appeared that I would be discharged from the WACs promptly upon arriving in the United States. . . . It seemed to contradict everything that we had been talking about for so long. It closed 'With lasting and warm regard.' There was a handwritten postscript . . . [which] ended, 'Take care of yourself—and retain your optimism.'"

"Nana wrote it up for me," Ike's postscript had begun. WAC Chief

*Former U.S. Steel executive Edward R. Stettinius Jr., Cordell Hull's replacement until Truman replaced him with James F. Byrnes, was "Ed" to Marshall—a rare first-name intimacy.

Warrant Officer Nana M. Rae, a friend of Kay's who had been a secretary to Eisenhower since 1942, had flown back with him, and must have understood what lay between the lines—that it was all over.

Arrivals, farewells, and departures agitated the War Department through the autumn. Marshall had referred to the courtly Stimson until his retirement as "Mr. Secretary." Now he was to be "Colonel." The efficient if rigid John McCloy* also left as assistant secretary on November 24, and Frank McCarthy, Marshall's all-purpose deputy, moved to the State Department, but worn out at thirty-three, soon resigned and was hospitalized for low blood pressure and anemia. Marshall's own retirement as chief of staff took effect on November 18. Eisenhower took over on the 20th. Symbolically, Marshall accepted one speaking invitation for that week, and turned down another. He left the conspicuous annual meeting of the American Legion in Chicago for Eisenhower, and instead addressed the eightieth anniversary meeting of the Salvation Army in Kansas City. Marshall admired their men and women for "their standards of loyalty and discipline and their simplicity and selfless devotion to duty. . . . There is one quality of greatness that a soldier appreciates perhaps more than any other, that is, the selfless willingness to be of service to others without thought of personal reward or danger."

His introductory words reflected his past. He had no idea yet that his envoi would also anticipate his future, as he longed to be the unassuming country gentleman Ed Stettinius had described. (Marshall would be sixty-five on the last day of the year.) "The distracted people of devastated Europe and Asia . . . look to us," he told the Salvation Army delegates. "They do not view us with suspicion as to our motives. They trust and like our soldiers. They probably have an exaggerated conception of our strength in resources, in our capacity to get things done and in our strength as a nation. As a consequence we have virtually been elected by the acclamation of the harassed and suffering people of the world to the leadership of the greatest and most beneficent movement in world history for the good of mankind."

It was a tall order for a people weary of efforts beyond their vision,

---

*Stimson's leaving things to McCloy meant a hard line on mass interments of Japanese and on the air force's refusal to bomb rail lines to, and furnaces in, the death camps.

and Marshall was in the innocent fashion of his generation little aware that even the most openly selfless Americans might be viewed elsewhere with cynicism or suspicion. In a remarkable salute, the British chiefs of staff understood what drove Marshall by quoting from a 1720 tribute by Alexander Pope to an otherwise forgotten royal official, James Craggs, who was

> . . . of soul sincere,
> In action faithful, and in honour clear;
> Who broke no promise, served no private end,
> Who gained no title, and who lost no friend.

Marshall received his meager second Distinguished Service Medal from Harry Truman at the White House on November 28, enlarging in his acceptance what he had begun to say in Kansas City—that "along with the great problem of maintaining the peace we must solve the problem of the pittance of food, of clothing and coal and homes. Neither of these problems can be solved alone." He had refused all decorations and awards in wartime. An oak leaf cluster to his first DSM was not much of a retirement bauble, but he already knew that it would not be much of a retirement.

Already relocated from government quarters at Fort Myer, Katherine Marshall wrote to a friend, "The post-war reconversion seems to be more difficult than the war. . . . I shall be so glad to get to Pinehurst for a little rest." But at a Cabinet meeting the day before the retirement ceremony, Truman had been blindsided by the resignation of Patrick Hurley as ambassador to China. The chaotic nation of many hundreds of millions, known to many Americans only through the sentimental pathos of Pearl Buck's *The Good Earth* (1931) and the political slant of the China Lobby press, had known little peace for decades, and was close to, if not already, in a civil war. In July 1944, at Marshall's urging, even to his drafting the message, President Roosevelt had cabled Chiang Kai-shek through General Stilwell that it was essential for Stilwell to "take command of all Chinese and American forces . . . including the Communist forces." Since the Chinese were fighting each other rather than the Japanese, Marshall hoped that a coalition under a tough outsider might create the conditions for a settlement. "Vinegar Joe" personally took the cable to Chiang ("Peanut" to the disgusted Stilwell), who agreed, then did nothing. Since the war was over, except among the Chinese, Truman's Cabinet unanimously urged sending Marshall, who had just shed his uniform.

The telephone rang at Leesburg just as Katherine and George were unlocking their front door. "General," said Truman without any preliminaries, "I want you to go to China for me."

"Yes, Mr. President," said Marshall. He put down the phone. Any attempt of his to balance mutual mistrust and juggle alternative evils in seething China would be an utterly futile and thankless assignment, but he would give it all he had. He had no intention of breaking the news to his wife so abruptly, but Katherine soon heard about it on the radio. "How could you?" she sighed. As Marshall told the president two days later, there was "the devil to pay." At least he had time to respond to an already obsolete telegram in characteristic biblical blather (yet personally sincere) from MacArthur in Tokyo: "The entire command sends sincere greetings and hopes you will find full contentment in green pastures and by still waters."

"Thanks for your message . . ." Marshall replied tersely. "My retirement was of rather short duration and the outlook does not indicate still waters."

Perhaps his preparation to testify before the Joint Committee on the Investigation of the Pearl Harbor Attack was a useful initiation into the partisan rancor he would encounter in China. There had already been three congressional hearings on Pearl Harbor during the war—and none on the unpreparedness and incompetence relating to the attack on the Philippines. MacArthur would continue to escape scrutiny. The hatchetmen of the right, from both parties, still determined to tarnish the dead Franklin Roosevelt by again raking over Pearl Harbor: this effort included holdovers from prewar days whose myopia and penny-pinching votes had kept the armed forces unready.

Marshall had cabled Chiang Kai-shek that he hoped to depart for the wartime capital of Chungking by December 7, an ironic date, given the focus of the hearings. Responding to questions in laborious, rambling, and repetitious detail would take seven days, filling 407 pages of the printed record. The inquisition tried his soul. Enduring badgering intended to twist into suspicion precise details in prewar messages, Marshall explained wearily to Representative Frank Keefe of Wisconsin, now only a name in an index, that at one point he would have had "a lively recollection. But there are some rather great events that have intervened." Asked about the vagueness of his war warning to Lieutenant General Short in Hawaii ten days before Pearl Harbor, he told Keefe sharply, "I feel that General Short was given a command instruction to put his command on the alert against a possible hostile attack by the Japanese. The command was not so alerted."

"Remember," he told Forrest Pogue eleven years later, "that the investigation was intended to crucify Roosevelt, not to get me. There was no feeling in the War Department that we had anything to hide." Marshall's testimony added little, but every page of the hearings would furnish something for exploitative conspiracy theorists who coin lucrative mysteries from assassinations, accidents, and catastrophes.

Marshall had little opportunity, or time, to relearn the Mandarin he had picked up with the 15th Infantry in Tientsin twenty years earlier. He flew from the hearings to China to attempt (according to his instructions) a "reconciliation" of the Chinese government with its political adversaries and manage "a cessation of hostilities." Eisenhower went to the airport on December 15 to see him off. Although it was a hopeless mission, Truman, under pressure in the press and in Congress, hoped that Marshall's immense prestige and powers of persuasion might bring irreconcilables together. As the cynical, ill-disposed Stimson told Marshall, keeping the presidential charge strictly military was impossible, and the Kuomintang (or Nationalist) administration was "a mere surface veneer (more or less rotten) over a mass of Chinese people" to whom it offered little hope. Generalissimo Chiang was largely the facade for a cabal of corrupt relatives and warlords protecting personal fiefdoms.

The Communist forces under Mao Zedong, burgeoning in numbers and expanding areas they controlled, seemed intent only in a coalition government which they could subvert and dominate. Both sides planned to bargain with Marshall only to gain time. Mao called it privately "a tactic of expedience." From Moscow, Averell Harriman warned of Red deceit. During the war just concluded, Communists and Nationalists fought each other more than they did the Japanese, and now both sides co-opted unrepatriated Japanese prisoners and appropriated enemy weapons.

Urged by Truman to be frank with Chiang, Marshall warned the "Gimo" again and again that his government would self-destruct. Yet every shaky truce, entered into dishonestly by both sides, would collapse and be followed, after Marshall's urgent intervention, by another. The decision by what he described to Dean Acheson (July 2, 1946) as Chiang's "inner Kuomintang bureaucracy" seemed only "a sop to me preliminary to launching a[nother] military campaign." Explaining what he saw, Marshall added, "I am so closely engaged and so close to the trees that I may lack perspective." Certainly the Chiang faction lobbied for by Henry Luce of Time Inc. and by congressmen whose names evoked prewar isolationism thought so. Massive aid to "legitimate" China, they urged, however much would be diverted into corruption, might impede otherwise inevitable Communism, its contagion likely to spread through Asia. Anything short of that, even Lieutenant General Albert Wedemeyer—who in 1941 was a major under Marshall and who as last American chief of staff to Chiang had conceded the sinkhole of warlord misfeasance—was objected to as "outrageous appeasement of the Communists." Pacific-focused once his military posting took him there, and aspiring to become the next ambassador to Chiang's China, Wedemeyer saw no compromise possible with Communism—and indeed there was none. To his frustration, Marshall warily postponed, then blocked, the appointment.

Chairman Mao remained nearly invisible, massaging his personal myth while pulling the Communist strings. His deputy, Chou En-lai, whose suave mien and references to a future democracy "based on the American style" concealed his apparatchik ruthlessness, understood that time was on the Red side.* Chiang's moving into territory in the north which his Kuomintang could not control only overextended his government's dwindling resources. If the U.S. pulled out its remaining troops and further limited support, the "Gimo's" facade of government would collapse. Marshall warned Chiang about his empty successes with war-supplied American arms seldom used against the Japanese: the Communists had "lost cities but not armies."

Marshall's futile efforts to mediate involved months of immense and exhausting travel across the vast Chinese distances. One trip took him to Mukden in Manchuria, with General Lin Biao of the Communist side and the Nationalist Chiang Ch'un. To learn about the obviously wretched local conditions, Marshall called aside the conductor on their railway carriage. He had little opportunity to talk to ordinary people, and wanted to learn whatever he could between the party lines. Writing of the commute from the summer capital of Kuling back and forth to fetid, overcrowded Nanking, he explained to Frank McCarthy (September 30, 1946) that it was "something of a trip—2 hours by plane, 3/4 hours by gun boat down the [Yangtze] river and across [to a] fantastic path with frequent stretches of stone steps, one of 937 [steps] at about a 40° angle. Down the mountain required one hour but was rather exciting with running coolies and precipitous steps and sheer drops of hundreds of feet at one's elbow."

In the heat of summer, Marshall's hair-trigger temper grew even shorter. When accused of pro-Chiang bias, he exploded at Chou, "I don't belong to the Kuomintang Party and I do not belong to the Communist

*Much later (July 14, 1971), Henry Kissinger would gush about Chou's "heroic stature" to President Richard M. Nixon.

Party, and I don't enjoy my job. I am merely doing the best I can." The only consolation was the charm, whatever her "Dragon Lady" reputation, of Madame Chiang. Since his postwar months in Paris in 1919, Marshall had savored the company (the attraction was more cosmopolitan than carnal) of shrewd, sophisticated women. One of his favorite people was the beautiful, serene Lady Mary Burghley, wife of the royal governor of Bermuda, one of the few women he called by her first name. On transatlantic flights he looked forward to refueling stops on the island. Another Circe would be the enchanting young queen of Greece, Frederika. Marshall's warm affection survived his dislike of her unpopular husband, King Paul. The exotic, American-educated Mei-Ling Soong Chiang would even be a house-guest at Pinehurst, helping to tend to the general's garden.

On a brief trip home Marshall had brought Katherine back to China with him, but he wanted to be recalled altogether "for consultation," as civil war had become an unavoidable reality. That meant only leaving the fire for the frying pan. Secretary of State Byrnes had long wanted to leave Washington, crediting a heart condition rather than continuing policy differences. Truman again needed a distinguished replacement above party. The compost heap at Leesburg was much closer to Washington than the compost aggregate that was China.

Early in Marshall's mission he had written a friend (January 11, 1946), "I long for personal freedom and my own home and simple pleasures. My shooting trips were all arranged for the winter along with horseback rides on the lively Pinehurst trails. . . ." In April, Truman sent for Eisenhower, who conferred with him on the presidential yacht, *Williamsburg*, anchored at Quantico, Virginia, about carrying a message to Marshall about replacing Byrnes, on Ike's forthcoming inspection trip to the Pacific. When they met, to keep the correspondence secret, Marshall scrawled out on a slip of paper a simple code for key words. PINEHURST stood for the State appointment; AGENT for Byrnes; COURIER for Truman; AGREEMENT for confirmation. Eisenhower folded up the scrap and put it in his coin purse.

While Byrnes dragged his feet about resigning, and Marshall reluctantly remained in China until his summons to State, cryptic messages went back and forth to Ike about an agent to rent Pinehurst. Referring in cables to Truman, Marshall agreed, once Byrnes finally signed off, to rush back without being able to "rest up" after a 10,000-mile flight and more than a year of unremitting discouragement. He confessed wearily on January 4, 1947, "I think I fully understand matter to be discussed.

My answer is in the affirmative if that continues to be his desire. My personal reaction is something else."

Even his exit from China would be bungled by a White House that, whatever its good intentions, would handle many sensitive matters awkwardly. Marshall wanted news of his new post withheld until he exited China. Instead, Byrnes's resignation leaked to the press and on January 8 came the announcement that Marshall would be secretary of state effective January 10. The cover story that he was returning "to report to the president in person on China" had exploded. It was the final frustration in a doomed mission.

Marshall had received hints as early as mid-February 1946 that Truman wanted him in Foggy Bottom. Wedemeyer had even offered to join him at State, then clashed over funding the futile Chiang. Reviewing the worldwide downsizing of the army, Eisenhower had begun a tour of army installations in the Pacific late in April, relieved to escape what he called "the squirrel cage." As he wrote to Lucius Clay in Germany on March 4, "The job here is fully as onerous and dreary as we had figured it would be. . . . The further one can be from Washington these days the better off he is." Since there was no other job for five stars in the army, his old friend Everett "Swede" Hazlett suggested politics but noted that he saw no leaning on Ike's part toward "any political party." Eisenhower (March 13, 1946) agreed "100 per cent. . . . I cannot conceive of any set of circumstances that could ever drag out of me permission to consider me for any political post from Dog Catcher to 'Grand High Supreme King of the Universe.'"

Disassembling an army once upwards of 8 million, and its appurtenances, from vehicles rusting on distant atolls to surplus training camps that had driven local economies, meant managing the drab downside of victory. The Cold War, nameless but real during the interwar years, had surfaced even earlier in the continuing suspicion and wary cooperation from 1941 into 1945. It would not go away, yet Eisenhower saw no hot one likely to involve ordinary Americans. Although the Soviet empire was at its most extensive and absolutist, it had an infrastructure to repair and readjustments to manage after 20 million or more casualties. Eisenhower assured Truman and the service chiefs in June 1946, "I don't believe the Reds want a war. What can they gain now by armed conflict? They've gained just about all they can assimilate."

Eisenhower would report to Marshall on his return from the Pacific that COURIER was "more than pleased"; Truman, unnamed, saw AGREEMENT as "a wonderful ace in the hole." En route, flying on to

Tokyo on May 10, Eisenhower called on MacArthur, who had no intention of leaving unless it were for the White House. With no home in the U.S., no circle of Stateside cronies, no hobbies or avocations, and aside from resurfacing political ambitions, no interest in anything but his wife, son, and reputation, inevitable vegetation into honorific corporate directorships seemed a bore to be put off.

MacArthur had paid little attention to messages from the Pentagon. Among other things, Eisenhower had warned that Congress and the clergy were puritanically unhappy that the army was sanctioning "so-called GI houses of prostitution in Japan—and that it might affect some of our legislative projects." Prostitution had long been legal in Japan. The Occupation had looked the other way. Although MacArthur ordered the Japanese to abrogate laws licensing prostitution, nothing realistically changed, for the Home Ministry with rare bureaucratic sensitivity would declare that it was a human right to permit a woman to ply her trade, whatever it was.

Having run his own war, MacArthur was now running another personal show. When unwanted junketing congressmen came, he made them feel important without ever jarring his personal routine. Cultivating a youthful look although he was officially of retirement age, he stood ramrod straight, combed his dyed black hair across his head, and wore an open khaki shirt without his rows of medal ribbons. While Marshall had chafed at the frustrations of fetid Chungking, as miserable in winter as in summer, MacArthur in Tokyo lived in the parklike American embassy compound in the stately ambassador's home available because resumption of formal diplomatic relations awaited a peace treaty. Aside from entertainment space, the mansion had even more bedrooms and service rooms than his prewar eyrie at the Manila Hotel. None of his lunches or dinners were formally elaborate, and few included a Japanese guest. No alcoholic beverages were served. The cuisine, a visitor claimed out of earshot, "was just what you would expect from a good army mess sergeant."

The routine was that all the guests, when there were any, would gather in the entrance hall to await the viceroy. Then Mrs. MacArthur would announce, "Oh! I hear the General coming." He would stride down the sweeping stairway from their quarters above and kiss Jean (so one of his staff recalled) "as though he hadn't seen her for 100 years." After a short greeting "just like he was making a speech," he would lead the assemblage into the dining room, and on occasion he invited the men to remain for cigars and the women to join them after coffee. The rare official dinners would be followed by a film in the drawing room: newsreels to start, then a light comedy, musical, or Western. Sometimes his projectionist included newsreel-like footage of Japan shot by Signal Corps cameramen, affording MacArthur indirect acquaintance with the unvisited island domain he governed.*

After lunch, he often left his guests to climb the broad, curving staircase for a nap, or to dig into his military memoirs and histories. Jean MacArthur would remain until it became time to announce that she had better join the general. His social activities in Japan, but for occasionally meeting visiting dignitaries at Haneda Airport, were limited to dining, and, on occasion, postprandial conversation. He went once to the Soviet embassy to mark the anniversary of the October Revolution. He went once to a Bastille Day ceremony at the French embassy. On a day in early June he went to the British embassy in honor of the official birthday of George VI. Jean did the rest. He left Tokyo only twice, for ceremonial visits to Manila and Seoul. As for his future, he told one of his guests, Hugh Baillie, head of United Press, "I have stated before and reiterate now that I started as a soldier, and shall finish as one. I am on my last public assignment which, when concluded, will mark the definite end of my service."

Just before Eisenhower visited, MacArthur gave Major Bowers a sour lowdown on his relationship with the general who was now ostensibly his boss. "He used to be an aide of mine in the Philippines, and he hasn't changed a whit. If I had to know something that I had forgotten, he made a good enough aide-mémoire, but if I wanted a plan of something, a scheme worked out, he would always turn up some crackbrain scheme that wouldn't work in years. Hopeless." Then he turned to the European Theater, where "Ike let his generals in the field fight for him. They were good and covered up for him. He drank tea and coffee with kings and queens. Just Eisenhower's alley, and that's why Rosenfeld—Roosevelt—put him in there. . . . His only instructions were, in case of doubt, to sell the American soldier down the drain. Keep on good terms with the Allies. He did that all right. Look who our allies were. Russians and English. Roosevelt didn't care how the war was fought, so long as the Allies

---

*His understanding of the country and its people was sometimes peculiar. He thought—so he wrote Eisenhower on February 20, 1947—that the Occupation had begun moving the Japanese "from the immaturity that comes of mythical teaching and legendary ritualism to the maturity of enlightened knowledge and truth," and claimed that 2 million Japanese had already turned to Christianity, although he went nowhere and saw no physical evidence of it. MacArthur's Occupation staff routinely inflated the number of purported converts to humor their boss.

were happy. Luckily he [Ike] had Patton. Poor old Patton. I and him are the only generals they persecute. The press hauls us over the coals, and for what? Without us they wouldn't have a paper to write for."

Nevertheless, MacArthur gave Eisenhower the rare accolade of a private dinner. Before it was served, the two, seated in large armchairs, reminisced about old times. Then they switched to demobilization, the imminent expiration of the Selective Service Act, and the unification of the armed services. Dinner was delayed until ten o'clock, as Eisenhower was awaiting a cable from Washington about further demobilization. Veterans still overseas were objecting noisily, and MacArthur was eager to send many more of his own restless troops home.

For coffee, they returned to MacArthur's study. What he wanted to discuss before Eisenhower flew home was politics. Next time around, he predicted, either he or Ike would be president. Both seemed to him more popular than Truman. Since MacArthur expected to be too busy running Japan to be available in 1948, that made Eisenhower a sure thing. The military, Eisenhower declared, ought to keep out of politics. He had achieved, personally, all he could possibly hope for, or deserve, from the public sector. He had no aspirations for the White House.

"That's right, Ike," said MacArthur, slapping Eisenhower's knee. "You go on like that and you'll get it sure." MacArthur, Eisenhower recalled, "kept me in his study from dinner until 1:00 a.m. trying to persuade me to run for President in 1948. When I suggested that he was the one to be a candidate, he merely dismissed the notion with the remark that he was too old for the job." Truman told James Forrestal, then secretary of the navy, that he had been amused by Eisenhower's report that he expected MacArthur's "returning here . . . to launch a campaign for himself." But when postmaster general and Democratic power Robert E. Hannegan proposed to visit Japan and asked for MacArthur's OK to do so, the general, in consenting, advised Robert Eichelberger, "Tell Hannegan that I said if the Republicans nominate any Army officer for the next election it will not be MacArthur but will be Eisenhower." Truman joked that both generals seemed to be suffering from "either Potomac fever or brass infection."

While sending out covert signals that Eisenhower was likely to run, possibly to suggest to Truman that it would be prudent to declare that he would not be a candidate himself in 1948, MacArthur continued to sound out the competition. Visiting Tokyo, Herbert Hoover urged him to make a speaking tour in the States in 1947 to stir interest in a MacArthur presidential candidacy—that it would be a "transcendent service." Yet the general hoped for a personal call in 1948 that would be a draft rather than an inducement to be dragged into a remote primary campaign. He told Eichelberger that he expected a Republican draft, and "to stand by to take over Japan." Yet MacArthur was unwilling to return to the U.S. for so much as a speech or parade.

The general was already recognized beyond Japan as a great lawgiver. The country had a new constitution, and although its thin veil was Japanese, he had promulgated it. Most of the reforms had been recommended by Washington, in JCS 1380-15, the Basic Directive for Post-Surrender Military Government in Japan. On MacArthur's orders to supersede the Prussian-inspired Meiji Constitution of 1890, Japanese politicians evaded reality by papering over the country's feudal society and the role of the emperor. The viceroy rejected their drafts. A four-power agreement signed in Moscow in December 1945 had assigned any charter revision to a Far Eastern Commission to meet late in February 1946. To evade Russian input, a document had to be in place before that, and on sheets of yellow legal notepaper MacArthur outlined to his assistant for civil government, Courtney Whitney, the three essentials. The emperor would be head of state subject to the will of the people. Japan would renounce the right to wage war. The feudal system would be abolished.

On February 4, Whitney called in the Public Administration specialists. "Ladies and Gentlemen," he announced, "you are now a constitutional assembly and you will now write a new draft of the Japanese Constitution, and it has to be ready in seven days." His three deputies, able lawyers, at least one with a Rooseveltian past, preserved the appearance of continuity with Meiji legal structure. It had to look Japanese. Yet it became almost a New Deal document, establishing social welfare and civil rights, even enfranchising women. At the end of the week the head of the committee of twenty-five, Lieutenant Colonel Charles Kades, told Beate Sirota, twenty-two, fluent in Japanese and the only woman in the room, "My God, you have given Japanese women more rights than in the American Constitution."

"That's not very difficult to do," she retorted, "because women are not in the American Constitution." But she could say nothing publicly about the shaping of the document because MacArthur swore members of the drafting group to secrecy.

On February 13 Japanese old-line parliamentarians reacted to the document with dismay. Whitney warned them for his boss, "General MacArthur feels that this is the last opportunity for the conservative groups, considered by many to be reactionary, to remain in power. . . . I cannot emphasize too strongly that acceptance of the draft Constitution is your only hope of survival."* Since the draft implied preservation of big business—the entrenched *zaibatsu* financial-industrial entities—there was something for everyone. Legislators caved in, then artfully manipulated Japanese translations to shade many interpretations their way. Only they had the linguistic and technocratic capacity to govern the country from city to village level.

On February 22, Emperor Hirohito gave it his "full approval" and MacArthur announced that "the decision of the Emperor and the Government of Japan" also had his "full approval." On March 6 the document was made public. Had MacArthur campaigned for the American presidency with the Japanese charter as his platform, he would have had to run as candidate of a different political party than the one which considered him its own.

Where the viceroy was rigidly hard-line was in his doctrinaire anti-Communism. Accordingly, Japanese Reds were legally marginalized. The Japanese press loved him, and Stateside reporters ensconced in Tokyo were more often MacArthur boosters than reporters. For the expatriate elite, life in late-1940s Japan was as good as it got, and journalistic toadying meant preferential treatment in accommodations, amenities, and access to exclusive stories and interviews. Eisenhower found everything laid on for him "splendid." Eichelberger escorted him to spiffed-up army installations and scenic spots, and Eisenhower found "all ranks . . . fully alive to their responsibilities and . . . meeting them without complaint." MacArthur, who did not accompany Ike to any of his inspections, would sneer, privately, in West Point lingo, "He came out and told the soldiers he would get them home to mother, and they gave him 'Three cheers and a Tiger. Hip, hip, hooray.' So our army dissolved."

When Eisenhower departed, the two generals exchanged appreciative letters. On the anniversary of the Japanese surrender, Eisenhower as chief of staff praised MacArthur's victories, "repeatedly proved against staggering odds," and his "unprecedented task of guiding the Japanese nation toward a new way of life." Later in his memoirs, MacArthur reminisced about the "pleasant reunion," and added, "I have always felt for him some-

---

*Even now, irreconcilable and influential nationalists send sound trucks about Japanese cities screaming diatribes against the "peace constitution." History textbooks continue to distort and glorify Japanese militarism, and prime ministers and other politicians pay obeisance to the war dead "in defense of the empire," including executed war criminals, at the Yasukuni Shrine in Tokyo. Yet the MacArthur constitution, however tweaked in practice, survives.

thing akin to the affection of an older man for a younger brother. His amazingly successful career has filled me with pride and admiration." However he also quoted the bitter and vindictive Alan Brooke as assessing MacArthur as "the greatest general and the best strategist" of the war, who "outshone Marshall, Eisenhower, and all other American and British generals including Montgomery." He had kept "a very careful watch on MacArthur's strategy in the Pacific," Brooke claimed, although his wartime diaries fail to document it. MacArthur reciprocated by calling the British chief of staff "the finest strategic mind" of the war, but there is little evidence that he cared much about the campaigns in the West other than to object that they drew resources away from him.

Although MacArthur issued directives framing the Occupation, he never left the Tokyo area. To oversee his divisions, his chiefs of staff were accompanied by Mrs. MacArthur. An assistant deputy G-3, John "Mike" Michaelis, then a lieutenant colonel fresh from the Pentagon, arranged for MacArthur to inspect his army by running "four or five" reviews of about 20,000 troops on the Imperial Palace plaza near the Dai Ichi. Michaelis recognized "the absolute necessity for timing. . . . We knew, for example, that it took exactly so many seconds from the embassy compound where he lived to the reviewing stand. . . . General MacArthur was very courteous about it and very careful to thank us." He never materialized at field exercises, where pampered garrison soldiers for whom much was done by Japanese labor could not recall from basic training how to erect tents, break down a rifle, assemble equipment, or maintain themselves in any way without indigenous assistance. A later chief of staff, Edward Almond, admitted their unreadiness and indiscipline but blamed it on the poor quality of peacetime recruits and the dregs of draftees.

Michaelis became "heartsick" at the condition of most occupation troops and their officers. Following policy from the Dai Ichi, he recalled, by the time a transport with replacements docked at Yokohama, SCAP already had the personnel records of all officers aboard. According to Michaelis, headquarters in Tokyo kept prime candidates, whether needed or not. Rejects shipped to Eighth Army "were known as 'Reject Ones.' The rest were released to corps and became 'Reject Twos.' If corps didn't want them they became available to divisions and became 'Reject Threes.'" The top prospects remained "sitting up at GHQ four-deep."

MacArthur would arrive at the Dai Ichi at about 10:30 in an MP convoy. The ten-minute drive at his instructions took a stately twenty minutes. At the entrance, white-gloved MPs in white helmets restrained crowds of camera-happy Japanese gawkers as he emerged from his Cadillac—license plate number 1—accompanied by aides Sidney Huff or Laurence E. Bunker. Returning salutes, he strode inside, his corncob pipe, unlit, clamped in his mouth. The routine, Brigadier General (then Lieutenant Colonel) John Chiles remembered, was "like the changing of the guard at Buckingham Palace."

At about two the general would return through more crowds to his embassy quarters for lunch, and (if there were no guests), after listening to the three o'clock news on the Armed Forces Radio Network he would nap until 5:30 or six, then return to the Dai Ichi. Business discussions were held in a deputy's office where he met with members of his "Bataan gang" of subordinates whose elevated ranks were earned by loyalty and who competed for his attention. He had no personal secretary and drafted letters in longhand on lined legal pads. He permitted no telephone. Often his only company were the portraits of Washington and Lincoln on the walls. When he left for a late dinner his desk was usually bare.

In March 1947, MacArthur made his only visit to the Tokyo Press Club. Journalists could hardly believe he had accommodated them—and, relaxed, he permitted quotes on the record. He had planted the questions he wanted. Would control of Japan be transferred to the United Nations? The military purpose of the Occupation had been accomplished, he said. "The political phase is approaching such completion as is possible under the Occupation. . . . The third phase is economic. . . . But this is not a phase the Occupation can settle." What was needed was a peace treaty— "as soon as possible."

Although it might take many months, or more, to fashion a treaty that would be internationally applicable, why would MacArthur promote himself out of the post of a lifetime? No one asked, but the calendar offered the answer. In November 1946 the American electorate unsettled the last wartime Congress by voting in Republican majorities. Harry Truman's days in office appeared numbered. A presidential election was due in November 1948. Truman might be dropped by the Democrats for a fresh candidate. To Eisenhower, MacArthur claimed that in 1948 he might be busy, still, in Japan, but if then at the peak of his prestige, a Republican convention might happily draft him home. All he needed was a home, and he would quietly arrange for an hotel address in what he called "my ancestral home in Milwaukee." His grandfather, the first Arthur MacArthur, had been acting governor of Wisconsin in 1856.

In the summer of 1946 he had joked to George Kenney, who had described seeing enthusiastic welcoming parades for returning heroes in New York and Washington, "I expect to settle down in Milwaukee, and on the way to the house I'm going to stop at a furniture store and buy the biggest rocker in the shop. I'll set it up on the porch and alongside it put a good-sized pile of stones. Then I'll rock."

"What are the stones for?" Kenney asked. "To throw at anyone," said MacArthur, pleased with himself, "who comes around talking politics."

Eisenhower, too, was flirting with alternatives. In 1935, as outgoing chief of staff, MacArthur envisioned no further role in the pallid peace-time army. Since 1945, Eisenhower had wondered what would come next for him after the chief of staff job he despised. He enjoyed foreign inspections, golfing with the moneyed and the mighty, speaking to major organizations, accepting honorary doctorates, and what he described as "high-powered resting." What he didn't enjoy was the nitty-gritty of the Pentagon. To his wealthy father-in-law, John Sheldon Doud, who would have liked Ike to settle down nearby in Colorado, he explained on January 31, 1947, that under physician's orders, Mamie had to "avoid more and more the higher altitudes." He was being offered lucrative positions in "the financial and commercial world"; one he didn't mention was to succeed David Sarnoff as head of RCA. He did not want to be accused of just "selling a name" and did not want to be confined again to a desk at high pressure. He might "tie up with something like an educational institution or a foundation, . . . but it would have to be on my own terms." Friends suggested that he "remain in Governmental life in any capacity." He did not elaborate further. But he expected to "take off my uniform."

Although he seemed unsure as yet what he would do sans uniform, others continued to tout him for the presidency as Republican alternative to MacArthur. Later in 1947, Drew Pearson would write melodramatically in his syndicated "Washington Merry-Go-Round,"

> Stocky, scowling Speaker [of the House] Joe Martin bluntly admitted to close friends recently that the "Eisenhower boom has politicians worried." Darkly he added that "an undercurrent for MacArthur also is rustling across the country. . . ." Joe didn't seem happy about this either.
>
> "What if MacArthur should suddenly step off the boat at San Francisco? Next he would be riding down Fifth Avenue. What then? Can't you visualize it? The idea of MacArthur for President could take the country by storm."
>
> "Let me tell you," continued the little man from Massachusetts. "If things get worse in Europe, the people may turn to a military man like Eisenhower or MacArthur." The Eisenhower boom already has penetrated the grass roots

and is gaining strength, Martin continued, citing as his source ex-GOP candidate Alf Landon. "I don't think Alf would kid me," he added.

"I am a politician, and I know how these booms can pick up momentum," explained the Speaker. The Eisenhower boom was not starting too early, he said, and hinted [that] the chief of staff might not be so reticent about politics once out of uniform. Eisenhower, Martin agreed, was more popular than MacArthur, but "if chaos should develop, the people will look for an iron hand. Then they would naturally turn to MacArthur."

"But what about the bonus march?" said his friend. "I can't forget how MacArthur ejected veterans from the capital."

"The public has a short memory," shrugged Martin. "That was 15 years ago."

"You mustn't forget that MacArthur is getting along in age," pointed out another of Martin's friends. He is 67, if I remember right. "Isn't that a little too old to be running for President?"

The Speaker shook his head. . . . "A man is as young as he feels." . . . As for Martin's own designs on the Republican nomination, . . , he admitted that he had outlined a speaking tour that would cross the paths of other Presidential candidates, but claimed it was no Presidential scouting trip. ". . . We could stop to shoot pheasants in South Dakota."

Ironically, the five-star general only a heartbeat from the White House early in 1947 was George Catlett Marshall. Under the succession law of the time, in force since 1886, if the office of vice president were vacant, as it was then, next in line for the presidency was the secretary of state. Marshall took the oath of office as secretary on January 21, 1947.* "You will not find it an easy task," Henry Stimson, once secretary of state himself, wrote. ". . . Surprise bombshells from the outside world will drop upon you with much greater frequency than in the War Department even in time of war." Beetle Smith, now ambassador in Moscow, wrote that it was "good to be serving directly under you again, but they certainly passed the baton to you in the final lap of the race." Out of the information loop in China, Marshall would learn belatedly that the baton meant bad news. A lot of it.

---

*Later in the year, in new legislation, the Speaker of the House, followed by the president pro tempore of the Senate, were placed in the presidential succession, as elected officials, ahead of the secretary of state.

15

Postwar Bureaucracies

I N PEACE, AND EVEN IN WAR, the most effective adversaries can be unarmed bureaucracies—even one's own. In occupied Japan, MacArthur was proconsul and the former enemy was without weapons, but much of the defeated regime was run by Japanese technocrats of whose language he understood only a few words. Eisenhower would find that through unification of the armed services, the military establishment would be run by a secretary of defense, James Forrestal, who as navy secretary had campaigned against the merger. After running an army he had shaped and disciplined, Marshall discovered that the Department of State was sloppy, disorganized, and often disloyal except to entrenched careerists. "You will feel yourself," Stimson warned him, "far more often standing alone than you did as head of the General Staff."

Marshall reined in the State secretariat along the lines of his War Department experience, achieving greater control at the top for strategy while giving lower officials more tactical leeway. He did not want a troop of assistants bringing everything in to be signed off. He also created an in-house Policy Planning Staff, his think tank.

In wartime, Marshall had blocked Churchill's aspirations east of Italy, where there was little chance for freedom. The Balkans, but for Tito's contrary Yugoslavia, and Greece and Turkey, were postwar Stalinist satellites. Marshall genuinely liked the young Greek queen, Frederika, great-granddaughter of Victoria and granddaughter of Kaiser Wilhelm, but the unpopular rightist government now under her husband, Paul, had been reimposed by the British after the German occupation.* Marshall would maintain a long, friendly correspondence with Frederika. The king's Greek supporters were few, but the alternative was Communism. Assisted by the breakdown of the economy, as almost everywhere else in devastated Europe, Russian-backed guerrillas had destabilized the country. Civil war loomed. Coveting influence but unable to afford the cost, the British were pulling out of Greece. Truman knew, from Potsdam, Stalin's designs on the Dardanelles, and realized that Turkey also had to be kept from the Soviet bloc to maintain the precarious postwar alignment.

Inheriting such crises, Marshall spoke confidentially to congressional leaders about forestalling the Russians. Over a weekend he and Dean Acheson, then undersecretary, worked on a document for Congress to support military aid to Greece and Turkey, presaging an extended international role for the U.S. Then, as Acheson put it, they "drank a martini or two toward the confusion of our enemies." The president followed with his "Truman Doctrine," declaring that "it must be the policy of the United States to support free peoples who are resisting attempted subjugation by armed minorities or by outside pressures." Marshall—in April 1947 about to leave for Moscow—quietly criticized the language as unhelpfully belligerent.

George Kennan, chairman of Policy Planning, also deplored what seemed an open invitation to almost any country with internal problems to turn to America. The White House response was that getting action from Congress required overheated Cold War rhetoric. Yet he was rarely disregarded by Marshall or Truman. Kennan's "long telegram" from Moscow in February 1946 had been an influential prescription for armed patience, which he labeled "containment." He expected the paranoid and inefficient Soviet empire, after peaking through brutality belying its utopian propaganda, to decay, and that the West, utilizing political rather than military responses, and covert action, would outlast it. While Truman's anti-Communist political excesses played to the Congress, Marshall, conceding that the Stalinist system was a corrosive evil, tried to develop a lower-key and nonpartisan approach to confrontation.

Western Europe remained Marshall's priority. A brutal winter and spring floods in 1947 had been followed by a drought portending a torrid summer. Almost every agricultural commodity would experience crippling shortfalls. MacArthur was overseeing Japan, where postwar reha-

---

*Paul had succeeded his elder brother, George. Frederika at twenty-nine first met Marshall in 1947 in London.

bilitation faced economic crisis, and Marshall wanted the Chinese situation to sort itself out without useless and costly American meddling. The
Moscow foreign ministers' conference proved a learning experience. In
China he had patiently encouraged small compromises that both Mao
and Chiang accepted, then violated. Marshall assumed that Stalin was a
realist: that he needed time to recover from the war and rebuild Russia,
and would not intervene expensively in China. In a long meeting with
Marshall in the Kremlin, Stalin claimed that compromise was possible on
"all the main questions." It was only necessary "to have patience and not
become pessimistic." Yet Marshall's reservoir of patience had run out in
China. Like Mao, Stalin sought further instability which Communists
could exploit. He pressed for further reparations from the western sectors
of Germany, and unity of the Occupation zones under restrictions promoting Soviet control. Marshall, with Britain's Ernest Bevin, and France's
Georges Bidault, refused. Russian designs would have shifted the Iron
Curtain to the Rhine.

Home or abroad, wherever Marshall sat in on foreign policy meetings
he was likely to find former subordinates in key diplomatic or military
posts: Bedell Smith, Lucius Clay, Albert Wedemeyer, Dwight Eisenhower, Omar Bradley, Mark Clark, Tom Handy, Wade Haislip, Matthew
Ridgway, Joseph McNarney, John McCloy. Prior to discussing German
affairs in Russia, he paused in Paris to deal with alleged dread, in part a
political ploy, that Germany might be resuscitated to French disadvantage. Yet the German zones, separately or together, had to be assisted into
economic viability. He had nothing devious in mind, Marshall explained
to President Vincent Auriol, whose post–De Gaulle government seemed
as uncooperative as were the Russians. Keeping the peace required wean-
ing Europe from American welfare doles. "I am not a diplomat," Marshall
told Auriol. "I mean exactly what I say and there is no use trying to read
between the lines because there is nothing to read there."

Conferring with Stalin in the Kremlin, Marshall soon understood
that Soviet obstruction on almost every issue was calculated to encourage
European deterioration and crisis, both political and economic, from
which local Communist parties could inhabit the ruins. Impairing the
economies of the defeated, and perpetuating disorder, were tactics which
Marshall wanted to reverse to Western advantage. Europe had to regain
control of its destiny.

Secretary Byrnes had made it a practice on returning from international conferences to report to the nation by radio. Marshall broadcast on
Monday evening, April 28, 1947, deploring that peace treaties with Ger-

many and Austria remained out of reach, yet that Russia considered the Potsdam rearrangements of Europe final. He saw "disintegrating forces" everywhere. "The patient is sinking while the doctors deliberate. . . . I believe that action cannot await compromise through [exploiting] exhaustion." Indirectly he courted Senator Vandenberg, a Republican foreign policy power in the Senate and a belated convert from isolationism, turning him toward a bipartisan program that would be predicated on self-help rather than giveaway.

Instead of extending the Truman Doctrine, largely military in thrust and predicated upon resisting Communist pressure, Marshall wanted, as a popular wartime song went, to accentuate the positive—to involve as much of Europe as would work collectively in its own interest. Eisenhower recommended assistance predicated on the trendy tag of "National Security." As that would confront "ideological enemies"—political parties and governments under Soviet control—Congress was likely to support it. Meeting with key advisers on May 24, Marshall fielded questions about likely Russian reaction to a European-based American initiative. Suppose, like Mao in China, Stalin seemed to cooperate, obviously in bad faith, in order to wreck European recovery? Would Moscow, rather, maintain its closed economy, and bar its satellites? Marshall proposed tempting the Soviets to contribute to, rather than exploit, the opportunities.

To air innovative ideas in a widely public forum, he explored venues which had already offered him honorary doctorates. Ruling out Madison, Wisconsin, as "Bert McCormick's [*Chicago Tribune*] area" and Amherst College because the mid-June ceremony would be too late (". . . things change so much in Europe"), Marshall settled on a commencement address at Harvard on June 5, 1947.

On that sunny Thursday afternoon, among such honorees as J. Robert Oppenheimer, Omar Bradley, T. S. Eliot, and I. A. Richards, Secretary Marshall was introduced by President James Bryant Conant in Washingtonian terms lost on few as "an American to whom Freedom owes an enduring debt of gratitude, a soldier and statesman whose ability and character brook only one comparison in the history of the nation."

Marshall's brief address, accruing ideas from Kennan on containment, had its origins in talks he had made during the war itself, when he was missionary for the gospel that victory was not mere winning. Walking away from wartime dislocation would undermine any gains. "Our policy," he proposed at Harvard, "is directed not against any country or doctrine but against hunger, poverty, despotism, and chaos. Its purpose shall be the revival of a working economy in the world so as to permit the emergence of political and social conditions in which free institutions can exist." He contended that the initiative had to come from Europe, rather than be imposed. "The program should be a joint one, agreed to by a number of if not all European nations." And with Russia in mind he warned that governments, groups, or parties seeking instead "to perpetuate human misery in order to profit therefrom" would be unwelcome.

As the press the next morning dealt also with a ruthless Communist coup in Hungary, it was immediately clear that Marshall's continental approach to economic recovery, however generous in spirit, would be closed by Stalin to such needy satellites as Czechoslovakia and Poland. Under the heading "Marshall Doctrine," a hostile editorial in the Ukraine edition of *Pravda* condemned the proposal the next day as representing the "black forces of reaction." It was America's design for "the wholesale purchase of the whole European continent." That morning, however, British foreign minister Ernest Bevin, seeing the proposal as a lifeline, described Marshall's reaching out as "one of the greatest speeches in world history." Bevin telephoned his French counterpart, Georges Bidault, to call for a conference of interested nations. Molotov was dispatched to Paris to find out more for Stalin, and soon grasped that the program would resuscitate Germany and undermine Soviet hegemony in Eastern Europe if its satellites were permitted to participate.

By September 12, representatives of Austria, Belgium, Britain, Denmark, Ireland, France, Greece, Iceland, Italy, Luxembourg, the Netherlands, Norway, Portugal, Sweden, Switzerland, and Turkey had prepared a preliminary response which Bevin, as conference secretary, forwarded to Marshall and Truman. Marshall's deputy Robert Lovett began gathering data and convening committees, and on October 23 the president called Congress into special session to initiate hearings on a European recovery bill. Marshall traveled across the country to lobby "tobacco people, cotton people, New York eastern industrialists, Pittsburgh people, the whole West Coast." He worked, he recalled, "as though I was running for the Senate or the presidency." Such apparent American self-interest attracted the Republican Congress. European economies could not afford to draw further on the vast American trade surplus without creative help.

In London for a Council of Foreign Ministers conference, Marshall received a wry but positive report from Lovett on December 4, 1947, that prospects for passage were good despite tacked-on special interest amendments and a session by the familiar die-hards "devoted almost entirely to attacks on past Lend-Lease shipments to Russia, Communism, grain shortages, previous relief abuses, German plant dismantling and reparations deliveries, and the German currency system. . . . While no direct attack was made on sin, I judge that the [Appropriations] Committee omitted that, feeling that the State Department was an adequate substitute."

The landmark legislation passed on December 15, and was signed by the president two days later. The first appropriation bill followed on December 23, 1947, adding on a political and irrelevant $18 million for Chiang's China.* Recognizing the role of the secretary of state in making the initiative palatable, the president began referring to the "Marshall Plan." Not only was there already a "Truman Doctrine," but, the president remarked to intimates, "Can you imagine its chances of passage in an election year† in a Republican congress if it is named for Truman and not Marshall?" *Time* again named Marshall its "Man of the Year," featuring him on its cover on January 5, 1948, above the caption, "Hope for those who needed it."

The first delivery of Marshall Plan sugar to the London docks from the Caribbean on February 3, 1949, made headlines, and by Christmas 1949, photos of Greek orphans receiving bread made from Marshall Plan flour boosted morale across the troubled country. The program proved so popular that in General Franco's Spain, ineligible for the aid, a hit film appeared in 1952, *Bienvenido, Mister Marshall,* in which a small and impoverished Spanish town geared up enthusiastically to welcome a Marshall Plan representative. In Russia, posters showed a worker indignantly refusing Marshall Plan eggs wrapped in a document labeled "North Atlantic Pact" from a rifle-carrying tough in Uncle Sam regalia.

Ostensibly an economic program, the Marshall Plan was inherently political. It forced nations involved in multilateral cooperation to negotiate among themselves the control of their own destinies, sharing resources and planning. Indirectly it would lead to the European Economic Com-

---

*Although Eisenhower later would go along with Republican charges that Democratic administrations had "lost" China, he wrote to Robert Lovett on July 10, 1948, that he recognized the uselessness of aid given to Chiang since 1945, the regime's "sad deterioration," and the "impossibility of the United States doing anything except by direct involvement—almost engaging in full scale war." He would make many such partisan backtracks as candidate and after.
†The presidential election year of 1948 was, at passage of the bill, eight days away.

munity, and even to the future euro unit of currency, which would flourish against the American dollar. In 1953, recognizing his achievement, as the program had already succeeded beyond all expectations, Marshall would be awarded the Nobel Prize for Peace.

The first of Marshall's high-pressure two years at State was relatively routine for MacArthur in Japan, who was determined to do nothing that might derail a presidential draft in 1948. Cold War priorities began to turn the Occupation more conservative, which pleased Japanese big business. Under General Willoughby's intelligence umbrella, where any criticism could be labeled Communist, censorship of the media, including films, remained rigid, especially casualty details about Hiroshima and Nagasaki. When physician Takashi Nagai completed his graphic, eyewitness book, *The Bells Toll for Nagasaki* (1948), publication was withheld until a vindictive appendix on the sack of Manila, which he did not write, was imposed.

Myopically, because stage plots included faked violence, traditional Kabuki theater was under ban. MacArthur's aide Faubion Bowers, a prewar aficionado, appealed personally to the general, but MacArthur had no interest in theater in any language. Resigning his commission, Bowers arranged to work for SCAP's Press, Pictorial, and Broadcast Division, managing to lift the Kabuki prohibition in November 1947. After that, he encouraged benign SCAP neglect of literature and the arts. MacArthur did not notice.

Eisenhower's official calendar suggested a very busy chief of staff, but he built into it a great deal of golf, bridge, and fishing—not only the rod-and-reel variety but exploration for post-Pentagon occupations. A plethora of possibilities emerged via such influential golfing cronies who cultivated him as IBM chairman Thomas B. Watson and Coca-Cola chairman Robert W. Woodruff. By June 1947 Eisenhower seemed settled on the presidency of Columbia University, provided, he told Watson, that he would have "a minimum of concern with details" and be "largely master of my own time and activity."* That he was not going to sell his repu-

---

*The aged and overpraised Nicholas Murray Butler, an empty gown, was retiring, and would die in December. Frank Fackenthal, an academic dean, became acting president.

tation seemed a less rigid matter now. He professed interest in academic leadership, and in promoting university goals.

After meeting with Truman to set a release date from the army early in 1948, he sent a formal letter of acceptance on June 23, 1947, to search committee chair Thomas I. Parkinson. Eisenhower expected to have two military aides accompany him to Columbia, one of whom he was entitled to for his lifetime as a five-star general, and he began brief exploratory trips to New York. (Eisenhower as a five-star general would also retain his salary.) Truman agreed to have Bradley, still with the Veterans Administration, succeed as army chief of staff.

Writing to Beetle Smith (usually now softened to "Beedle") in Moscow early that July, Eisenhower seemed to be relieved by his imminent freedom from broad responsibilities. "General Marshall," he noted, "is having his own troubles, some of them involving the Congress. However he seems to keep his disposition fairly well and I understand he maintains the same personal schedule that he always did when Chief of Staff. I wish I could do the same but I don't happen to be built in quite that fashion." To Swede Hazlett he confided on July 19, "Mamie and I both hate New York City and recoil from the thought of living there permanently." From the start it should have been obvious to the Columbia trustees that they were purchasing a part-time, prestige president—very likely only temporarily, as a transition to a further presidency.

Eisenhower first sat at his Columbia desk on February 8, 1948, largely to work on his *Crusade in Europe*. Publisher Douglas Black of Doubleday offered a no-royalty outright payment of $500,000 to buy the unwritten war memoir. William Robinson of the *New York Herald-Tribune* added $135,000 for prepublication rights. While flabbergasted by the numbers, Ike signed on.* In preparation he read the magisterial two-volume *Personal Memoirs of Lieutenant General Ulysses S. Grant*. Before formally assuming his title, he intended to deliver on his contracts.

Eisenhower had been in army service for thirty-six years, tapering off with a long leave, and he had open-ended preliminary time from the university. With army researchers and publisher's editorial assistants to arrange and glean from his collected military papers, he paced back and forth in his grand office in Low Library over seven weeks, often in sixteen-hour days beginning at seven in the morning, dictating rather than drafting what would become five hundred printed pages. Each day after

---

*Had he taken royalties rather than a flat payment he would have earned twice as much.

lunch he read through the previous day's transcript and dealt with queries from his six-person editorial team, four of them on Doubleday's payroll.

Doubleday enlisted editor in chief Ken McCormick and Joseph Barnes, foreign desk editor of the *Herald Tribune,* and historian Arthur Seymour Nevins (who also prepared the footnotes), and employed the efficient Douglass Wallop III, a journalist, to take down the shorthand on steno pads and spin it into narrative Eisenhowerese. The pace was hectic. On March 26 Eisenhower wrote to McCormick about a chapter revise, "Today Major McCann's daughter is typing it so that I may have it tomorrow morning for a final check." Marie Loughran, stepdaughter of Kevin McCann, a Pentagon speechwriter for Eisenhower who would remain as Ike's assistant at Columbia, had been drawn into the project.

On March 29 Eisenhower met with Black and Robinson to go over finished copy and apply suggestions for revisions. There were more pages to dictate and review. In mid-April, Eisenhower two took weeks off to golf at the posh Augusta National club where he was offered free use of its facilities indefinitely and where his moneyed new friends could join him. (Fat cats were falling over themselves to host his holidays, buy his civilian suits, pick up the tabs for his dinners, and reward his corporate speechmaking.) Nevins's fact-checking continued into June.

While Columbia at first would get little from Eisenhower but a tie-in to his fame, the book was a guaranteed winner for Doubleday—and Eisenhower. He was already an icon. *Crusade* would sell more than a million copies and make him financially secure. After being taxed for capital gains, Eisenhower would net $476,250. Wallop only got a salary as the work progressed, but assured Eisenhower that he found himself "absorbed, often downright excited, in following the thread of the book merely from the day-to-day dictation."

One of Eisenhower's aides, soon to join MacArthur in Tokyo, was Lieutenant Colonel Mike Michaelis, who was coping with Ike's most sensitive correspondence. Letters related to the forthcoming general election on November 3, 1948, were a priority. The political season was already heating up, and on January 9 a group of New Hampshire Republicans formally entered into the March 9 primary a slate of delegates pledged to Eisenhower. By no coincidence, Leonard Finder, publisher of the state's ultraconservative *Manchester Union-Leader,* printed his endorsement the same evening, and sent the newspaper to Eisenhower. Mulling over a response with Michaelis, he produced a statement released by General Floyd Parks, chief of the army's Publication Information Division, that Eisenhower had "reiterated on many previous occasions that he wants nothing to do with politics. He has not changed his mind." The *New York Times* and other media published the response on January 13, 1948.

With apparent relief, President Truman wrote that had he been in Ike's place his reaction would have been "just as it was. . . . I am sure that you and I understand what politicians are doing." Despite deep concern in the Democratic Party since their congressional losses in 1946 that Truman could not win reelection, he expected to run, and now was confident that it would not be against Eisenhower, who owned up publicly to having never voted, and told inquirers that he would not endorse anyone. Finally, Ike asked the director of the Department of Public Information at Columbia, where he considered himself, so he told Marshall, a "freshman President," to issue a follow-up that he would not identify himself with any party nor run for any public office—yet that it "implies no intention of maintaining silence on any issue of importance to my country on which I may feel qualified to express an opinion."

Mail urging him to be a candidate on either party's ticket kept coming anyway. James Roosevelt, FDR's eldest son, offered to put Ike's name in nomination at the Democratic convention. Eisenhower warned him off. When Drew Middleton of the *New York Times* wrote from Frankfurt that Germans were eager for strong American leadership, hinting at Ike, he replied that his own dreams were very different. "I still believe that heaven will be constituted primarily of quiet streams, and good fishing, with golf courses handy and easy to play."

Just before Eisenhower had exited the Pentagon, a personal and political embarrassment with the potential to affect whatever presidency he aspired to threatened to surface. After a year in Berlin escorting VIPs, Captain Kay Summersby, taking their dog, Telek, with her, flew to Washington, where she was not discharged, as she expected to be, by alleged "precedent." At social gatherings in the capital she encountered officers she knew, "looking nervous" or "absolutely white" because they were with their wives, and she had known some of their wartime diversions. At the Pentagon she and Telek visited Eisenhower, who "got all red, and it was not just from bending over to scratch Telek's tummy." Still in uniform, she told him that she would look for civilian employment in New York City. "Good, good," he said. "That sounds sensible. If there's anything I can do to help you about the job, I hope you will let me know when the time comes." He invited her to drop in again with Telek. "Anytime. I can always find a few minutes." She wrote that she did, but that their meetings were few and brief.

In a letter to Margaret ("Peg") Chase, who worked for the Red Cross and knew Ike in France, he wrote in December 1947, "I saw Kay the other day. I thought she looked very well, in spite of the many difficult things she has encountered in the past two or three months. I am sure there is going to come a time soon when she will get herself established and really settled in something she will like, and where she will be happy."

Despite Eisenhower's letter to Margaret Chase, an interview by Marshall's biographer, Forrest Pogue, with Cora Thomas, who remained as secretary to the new chief of staff after Marshall's departure, is fiercely protective and in extreme denial. Kay Summersby is also a nonperson to Forrest Pogue, who never mentions her. Kay's own reminiscences parallel the few careful footnotes, references, and letters to her in the volumes of Eisenhower's then-unpublished papers. According to Miss Thomas, Kay's sole visit to the Pentagon, where she gained admission only because she had shown guards the collar on "Felix" on which was engraved "This dog belongs to Kay and Ike," had caused an anxious flurry to keep her from the general. (Although she was a WAC captain, the misleading implication is that she was in civilian dress.) Thomas dates the flap as occurring on September 11, 1946, when Field Marshal Montgomery was in Washington, and Mamie was expected at Eisenhower's office to join him in greeting Monty at the airport.*

Apprised of Kay's presence, one of the general's aides reportedly shrilled, "Get her out of here!" Kay was supposedly spirited to a back office until it became clear that Ike was not returning. "The next day she left Washington and got out of Eisenhower's life," Thomas claimed. On the alleged morning of Kay's visit, Ida Eisenhower, the general's mother, died in Kansas. When he learned of it, Ike and Mamie entrained for the funeral. Kay may very well have turned up with Telek when she arrived in the U.S., precipitating office anxiety, but her appearance on that hectic September day, or any other day that September, is a fiction.

Other details from Cora Thomas are also more than suspicious. Kay goes for "a visit" to California, leaving the Scottie behind. "She never saw the dog again." Kay was then in Berlin, working for General Clay, and six days after the supposed flurry in the Pentagon, Eisenhower cabled Clay to ask that Captain Summersby type up for him her diary entries about Eisenhower's movements for June through December 1944. Obviously the story of her being protectively hustled out of Washington didn't happen then, or that way.

Kay's new WAC orders when she did fly to the U.S. posted her to

*Monty actually arrived the day before.

Hamilton Air Force Base in California, where she worked unhappily in military public relations, then applied for a discharge and returned to New York. She found an apartment, shopped for civilian clothes, and wrote the commercially successful but cautiously unrevealing *Eisenhower Was My Boss*. By then Eisenhower had left the Pentagon for Columbia. Before the book appeared, but once he was on campus, she began seeking ways to encounter him there, ostensibly by accident. He tried to evade her, but finally said, frankly, "Kay, it's impossible. There's nothing I can do." She conceded that she understood.

She saw Eisenhower again at an Anglo-American event in Manhattan where he spoke at the Seventh Regiment Armory. Kay left before the reception, but she had been recognized, and the *New York Times*, reporting on the speech and reawakening dormant gossip, noted that she had departed without speaking to him. Her book tour of forty states fed upon the undercurrent of their relationship, but the press was discreet. When Telek died at seventeen, he was her last link to Eisenhower, then at the close of his White House years.

The success of the Summersby book prompted the *New York Daily News* to ask Marshall if he would consent to having Sergeant Marjorie Payne, the chauffeur who had replaced James Powder when he took on additional duties, write a parallel account. The intensely private Marshall said he would not object. Having written her own memoir of life with her husband—without his assistance—Katherine Marshall even agreed to help Marjorie. But Sergeant Payne would have second thoughts, and postponed a decision.

Before Eisenhower exited the Pentagon he was being consulted on the first stirrings of the North Atlantic Treaty Organization that was an outgrowth of Cold War tensions, especially the Berlin crisis and the Czech coup. (NATO would not materialize until 1949.) Most nonmilitary issues in Washington did not reach Ike's Morningside Heights desk, and he was preoccupied anyway with Columbia—when he was there. Still, the past remained part of the present. When Bradford Chynoweth, a retired brigadier general who knew him in Philippines days, stopped by to talk of old times, he was surprised to find Eisenhower "fulminating about George Patton and Douglas MacArthur, whom he called 'megalomaniacs.'" Chynoweth understood the slap at MacArthur, but was "astounded"

at the attack on their late friend "Georgie," unaware of the load of wartime anxiety which Patton had laid on his chief.

Eisenhower's first speeches as Columbia's president offered platitudes that did not foreshadow a dynamic approach to the job. "As a fellow freshman at Columbia," one address began, "let me just say this: I have learned on the field of battle what I think you can learn more easily in these pleasant surroundings. Our need is for moral rectitude and a spiritual rededication to the principles upon which this great nation was built." Although at Columbia through the year, he would not be installed formally until October 12, 1948, and soon after took a leave of absence to mediate interservice rivalries in the wake of unification. Even when not away altogether he would often catch up on correspondence at Columbia by day, take a night train to Washington, and spend the next day at the Pentagon, then return to New York. Columbia was quickly receding into irrelevance.

Perhaps the most nagging matter then in Marshall's purview but not yet Ike's was the issue of Israel. Eisenhower's army involvement with the Jewish Agency for Palestine, which would become the womb of the State of Israel, largely concerned Displaced Persons and death camps. As chief of staff he fielded, warily, a memo left on June 24, 1947, by Judge Simon Rifkind of New York, who had served as staff representative for Ike in handling such matters in the ETO. Rifkind contended that a Jewish state in Palestine would be in the American interest politically and militarily. Eisenhower gave copies to Marshall and to General Tom Handy (for the secretary of war), and asked General Lauris Norstad for a General Staff opinion. Norstad replied that "Rifkind's arguments are not convincing" and that given Arab hostility (and Arab oil) there would be "an adverse strategic impact on the security interests of the U.S." He advised against a formal submission of Rifkind's memo to State. Eisenhower kept out of it.

Just as Britain had withdrawn from Greece, it was to abandon Palestine, effective May 15, 1948. For months, the United Nations had been debating partition. Arab nations warned that a Jewish attempt to form a nation would be suicidal. Arabian king Ibn Saud warned Truman (and thus Marshall) on October 26, 1947, that American support of partition was an unfriendly and useless act: "The Arabs will isolate such a state from the world and lay siege to it until it dies by famine." Professional Arabists had managed Middle East policy at State for decades. As May

15, 1948, neared, the official American position at the U.N. was to back away from partition. Yet for two months there had been open war in Palestine. Every Arab army was already involved or poised to attack, and the imminent (and nameless) Jewish state had no agreed-on boundaries.

On May 12, beset by other problems, Marshall bluntly told Moshe Sharett, head of the Jewish Agency's U.N. delegation, that the issue was best left on hold, under U.N. trusteeship. There was insufficient international support for a state. Further, the U.S. would not intervene. "I advise you not to go ahead [with declaring independence]. Your military people feel that they can make it. My advice is don't take military advice. But fundamentally, it is your decision. If you make the decision to go ahead, and succeed, then good luck to you. You will probably be recognized by us.* But we are not going to take any responsibility for the decision itself."

Marshall perceived some subtle complications. A Communist coup had overthrown the coalition Czech government in February 1948 and a Red regime was now in power. Flexing Cold War muscle to exploit the isolation of Allied Occupation zones in Berlin from the West, the Russians, after failing to impose a single local currency, had left the Allied Control Commission and were harassing surface movement in and out of Berlin, intending to slowly strangle the beleaguered city. (To the Soviets the real threat from the West, however, was the expectation that Allied sectors of Germany would be combined into an economically viable whole.) In a curious way, Berlin's predicament paralleled that of what would be proclaimed as *Israel* on May 14, and would be recognized eleven minutes later by President Truman. A messenger had to be sent to the White House to identify the name of the besieged new nation. Truman was not going to let Stalin beat him to it—and the Soviet Union, and little Guatemala, did recognize Israel later the same day.

The Soviet Union had already been voicing support for the isolated Jewish state (as Communism had no friends then in the Arab world), and its recognition was anticipated. Israel's government, the Russians realized, had socialist origins. Through satellite Czechoslovakia, the Soviets were openly selling military equipment to Jewish emissaries, and training volunteer pilots and paratroop recruits arriving from the West. The first Soviet arms shipment arrived by air via Turkey on April 1. In a postwar irony, Israel would soon be painting six-pointed stars on thirty Czech-supplied Messerschmidts. How much Mideast advantage could Moscow

---

*Marshall meant recognition by Truman as president, rather than by State.

take of American indecision? David Ben-Gurion, provisional Israeli president, had told a hastily summoned press conference in Tel Aviv, "The Jewish State exists because we defend it." However remote from Berlin, Israel would be another, if only implicit, front in the Cold War. (Even difficult France, responding to Arab support of the rebellion in Algeria, began delivering Mystère jets to Israel.)

Immediately on recognition, angry aides from the Middle Eastern desk at State had gathered round Marshall to urge that he had no choice but to resign. "Who has made *me* the president?" he asked. Truman occupied the White House, Marshall reminded them, and policy decisions were his. The secretary of state's role was to offer his best advice, and he had done so, unsuccessfully. To covertly counter Soviet assistance, State and the military began looking the other way as private groups began sending contraband World War II arms and equipment to compete with Communist gear—and potential influence. Even "surplus" B-17 Flying Fortresses were flown "illegally" to Israel.

Later in the year, when U.N. membership came up for Israel and the balloting seemed likely to be close, the General Assembly was meeting in Paris when Count Folke Bernadotte of Sweden, the U.N. envoy to what had been Palestine, and the architect of partition, was assassinated by Jewish extremists. The utter stupidity of the shooting seemed likely to doom Israel's U.N. chances. Ernest Bevin of Britain lobbied Marshall to instruct the American delegation to vote no. Dramatically, Swedes appeared at the U.N. in mourning garb. Suddenly Marshall's painful kidney problem flared up and he had to leave the sessions, going to Greece to recuperate. He was advised to have surgery on his return to the U.S.

The Palestine issue dragged on as John Foster Dulles of the bipartisan delegation took his place. Marshall had left no instructions. (On May 11, 1949, almost a year after the fledgling nation declared its existence, the hard-line anti-Communist Dulles, who had expected to be President Dewey's secretary of state, would vote U.N. membership for Israel.)

In the first weeks of the Palestinian crisis in 1948, the Western allies, meeting in London, announced the partial solution of another partition: the imminent establishment of a separate German state unifying the British and American zones. (France would join soon after.) On June 18, a new currency was formalized, the *Deutsche Mark*, secretly printed earlier in the U.S., brought to Germany by army escort, and placed in circulation three days later. On June 23 the Soviets retaliated with a new East German currency, and cut rail links from the West into Berlin. The complete ground blockade of West Berlin, effective on June 24, created the necessity to supply 2,500,000 Germans by air, or to force ground traffic, by rail or truck, whatever the consequences, through Russian-controlled territory.

To avoid a hostile land incident that might precipitate open war, the Pentagon determined to fly in tons of supplies. In a postwar agreement with the Soviets on November 30, 1945, three air corridors to Berlin, each twenty English miles wide, afforded the West access to its sectors. It was the legal basis for the Berlin Airlift, which Russia could only hope would fail. General Clay estimated he would need 4,500 tons of food and fuel daily, but if the blockade continued into cold weather, massive supplies of coal would also have to be flown in. Lieutenant General Curtis LeMay, who had overseen the deployment of the Hiroshima and Nagasaki bombs, was now commanding air forces in Germany. He began with what he had—one hundred twin-engine C-47s, which each carried safely only 2½ tons of cargo. The workhorse planes, which had supplied Bastogne, began flying the next day. To handle heavier loads, LeMay called for all available four-engine C-54s worldwide.

At Walter Reed Army Hospital, tests confirmed that Marshall required surgery for a tumor on his right kidney. He put it off. Too much was happening, and he wanted to avoid overkill which might precipitate a shooting incident. He and Lovett vetoed Clay's recommendation that a truck convoy call Stalin's bluff. Russia was eager to see the entire American economic house of cards in Europe—if it proved that—collapse with Berlin.

London was nervous. Truman met with his key advisers and Marshall proposed that the English and French, with the Americans, warn the Soviets that "coercion, irrespective of its motivation, obviously can lead to war if the Government applying such methods continues to pursue them to the end." Bevin, for Britain, agreed that the abandonment of Berlin could lead to the communizing of Western Europe. Since a single shot downing a plane, however, could trigger war, Washington made it clear to Moscow that war could mean the Bomb. Yet on October 5, Marshall, in Paris on State business, learned that Truman was sending Chief Justice Fred Vinson to Moscow to assure Stalin of America's desire for mutual understanding. To Marshall, the usually feisty president, behind in the polls a month before election day, was undercutting the message of the airlift. Lovett rushed to the White House to explain that if Vinson went—suggesting waffling on Berlin—the secretary of state would resign. Marshall even flew back hurriedly on Truman's own plane, but it was too late to recall what a French reporter described cynically as "an electoral operation." In any case, Vinson, whose judicial role made his mission inappropriate, had no effect.

From the outside hopefully looking in as the presidential year of 1948 began was Douglas MacArthur. His rocking chair witticism aside, he was covertly encouraging his candidacy while claiming the opposite. With Japanese industrial infrastructure destroyed, getting the nation back on its economic feet was outside his interests, and the Occupation could not go on indefinitely. A Marshall Plan for Japan was politically out of the question. When Herbert Hoover had visited MacArthur, whom he had made chief of staff in 1930, the two talked economics and politics, and Hoover had urged the general to return and campaign for the presidency. "I want none of it," said MacArthur.

Some months later, Hoover tried again, and MacArthur ticked off his reasons to avoid an overt candidacy. He would have to retire from the army. He did not want to leave Japan prior to a peace treaty. He would not campaign. And aside from military matters, diminishing now in importance, "is the very definite feeling on my part that no one would seriously listen to me. . . ."

MacArthur wanted to be coaxed into believing that was not the case—that his popularity was as deep as it seemed broad. The sentiments in right-wing Midwest newspapers could always be counted upon, but did they translate into political convention ballots? Could he run by remote control, without campaigning? In October 1947 he wrote to Sears, Roebuck chairman Robert E. Wood, long an admirer, "I certainly do not covet nor actively seek any other office, but should the movement [for me] become more expressive of the desire of good and loyal friends and well wishers, and take on the character of popular will, I should be left no alternative but to consider it a mandate which I could not in good conscience ignore."

MacArthur expected such sentiments to be quoted and exploited, as with his response to Los Angeles lawyer Joseph Choate, to whom he wrote philosophically, as if he were not directing a one-man government in Japan, "The need is not in the concentration of greater power in the hands of the state, but in the reservation of much more power in the people as intended by constitutional mandate—more leadership and less direction." Choate thought that the final five words made a cogent, if vague, campaign slogan, and he read the letter to a meeting in Milwaukee of ardent MacArthur-for-President supporters from sixteen states, getting a slate of delegates to enter the Wisconsin primary in April 1948. William Randolph Hearst got his string of newspapers to run pro-MacArthur editorials as "Man of the Hour," but Hearst no longer had his old clout, and the rival *Examiner* in Los Angeles sneeringly forecast from photo-op war memories that MacArthur "will wade ashore at San Simeon"—Hearst's castle-like coastal estate—"when he comes home."

When the *New York Times* predicted "wide support in a national election" for Eisenhower, Ike wrote to the *Manchester News-Leader* to again refuse to consider "high political office," but added, certainly with MacArthur in mind, "It is my conviction that the necessary and wise subordination of the military to civic power will be best sustained . . . when lifelong professional soldiers, in the absence of some obvious and overriding reason, abstain from seeking political office." That Eisenhower included a clause keeping the door open, probably for himself, but not just then, seemed overlooked.

To keep his own political pot boiling, as MacArthur thought it was, the general had Courtney Whitney release a statement on March 9, 1948, that he was "profoundly stirred" by the "public movement" to put him on the Wisconsin ballot on April 6. He acknowledged it with "due humility," as "I would be recreant to all my concepts of good citizenship were I to shrink . . . from accepting any public duty to which I might be called by the American people." It was front-page news—in Japan. Shopkeepers hung "We Want MacArthur for President" in their windows, and ordinary citizens exuberantly wore MacArthur buttons. An editorial in the Tokyo *Nihon Kezai* offered to share him with the American people.

As likely nominee, the losing candidate in 1944, Governor Dewey, invested no campaign money in Wisconsin, assuming it was lost, and it was, but to Governor Harold Stassen of neighboring Minnesota, who had the support of an ambitious new Wisconsin senator. Joseph P. McCarthy, a war veteran with dubious credentials who siphoned rumors from the sewer and spouted virulent anti-Communism, bafflingly called MacArthur the choice of Stalin. Nineteen of Wisconsin's twenty-seven delegates went to Stassen; the other eight went to the general. When foreign affairs adviser William Sebald arrived at the Dai Ichi the next morning on a routine appointment, he was turned away by Major General Paul J. Mueller. "The general," Mueller said, "is as low as a rug. He's very disappointed."

A week later the Nebraska primary drew a humiliating blank for

MacArthur. He asked supporters to withdraw his name—which they did not—and he rejected an invitation by Senators Kenneth Wherry and H. Styles Bridges to return in May to testify at an Appropriations Committee hearing, a ploy to get him back for a belated hero's welcome just before the June convention in Philadelphia. Although Robert Taft of Ohio saw a chance for himself if Dewey failed to get an early majority, the governor's managers controlled the convention.

While Jonathan Wainwright waited loyally to deliver a nominating speech for MacArthur, his address and an arranged demonstration were delayed until 3:40 A.M., when few delegates remained on the floor. MacArthur received eleven votes (out of nearly eleven hundred) on the first ballot, seven on the second ballot. Dewey was overwhelmingly renominated, and MacArthur was sounded out by the nominee's camp on becoming secretary of defense if Dewey became president. It looked like good politics if the governor could announce it during the campaign. The general declined to jeopardize his proconsulship.

Very different plans were being hatched for MacArthur should Truman remain president. He sounded out Lucius Clay in Berlin, whose profile had been raised by the success of the airlift, about taking the SCAP post in Tokyo. Truman would then order the *shogun* home. But Clay, at fifty-one and archconservative, knew he had his pick of lucrative corporate careers now waiting, and wanted to be out of uniform and the military bureaucracy. John J. McCloy, who had been head of the World Bank, was now high commissioner for Germany, and Omar Bradley, now chief of staff, and no MacArthur fan, urged a nonmilitary appointee for Japan. Learning of it, MacArthur fired off diatribes to Bradley and to Dean Acheson, by then Marshall's successor at State. Nothing like it could have gone to Marshall. MacArthur stayed.

Marshall had expected to remain at State only until the conclusion of Truman's term ("the end of my run"), whatever the election results. Since he had never voted, it made no difference to him that he would be at United Nations meetings in Paris on election day. A photo taken there shows him with delegate Warren Austin and adviser John Foster Dulles soberly listening to the election returns by radio. A second photo evinces no change in Marshall's expression, but much alteration in the reaction of the two Republicans. Dulles had learned that he would not be Marshall's successor as President Dewey's secretary of state.

Although the Democratic Party had split into three factions, each with a candidate, Truman's feistiness and the failures of the Republican Congress confounded the pollsters. He carried twenty-eight states and

Dewey only sixteen. It was a great personal victory for the underrated president. More than dutifully, Marshall sent a congratulatory message to Truman. He had not forgotten the dour Dewey's suspicions about pre–Pearl Harbor codebreaking and warmongering during the 1944 campaign. When Marshall returned to Washington, a large banner still hung at the *Washington Post*'s offices: a large black crow with its feet stiffly in the air. The caption read, "Welcome home, Mr. President, from the Crow Eaters." The *Post* had predicted Truman's defeat.

Eisenhower had quietly voted for the first time, breaking the career service tradition. He told several intimates before the election that he was voting for Dewey, and expected him to win. MacArthur had long identified himself as a Republican; Eisenhower was finding it more difficult to maintain political neutrality, as his clubby circle of wealthy associates was almost entirely Republican, and pressed for him to come out publicly as one. But he was also traveling regularly to Washington to consult on service unification, which required him to appear above politics. He waited two weeks before offering congratulations to Truman on his electoral triumph, "until after the initial commotion . . . should have died down." Obviously biting his tongue, he called the president's "accomplishment" unique in political history in that it could be "traced so clearly to the stark courage and fighting heart of a single man."

Eisenhower assured Truman "that I always stand ready to attempt the performance of any professional duty for which my constitutional superiors believe I might be especially suited." Truman would take him up on the offer, responding, "Of course you didn't have to reaffirm your loyalty to me. I always know exactly where you stand." Truman very likely did. Still, he invited Eisenhower to the White House, and Ike, with Mamie, boarded a night train on November 29 and met with the president (and James Forrestal) on December 1. It seemed the apogee of their curious relationship.

Eisenhower's publishers had waited until after the election (but timed before Christmas) to release *Crusade in Europe*. Of the special limited edition, the first ten were for Eisenhower's family. Eleven and twelve went to Truman and Churchill; number thirteen went to Marshall with an understated message of gratitude "for wise leadership, friendly advice, and warm support during a great national crisis." No signed copy seems to have been sent to Douglas MacArthur.

Much as Eisenhower would have preferred not sending one to Bernard Montgomery, Monty asked for it, and he also requested, from Ike, Kay Summersby's *Eisenhower Was My Boss*, which had appeared that

September, as it was unavailable in England and, he claimed, he was being asked questions about it. "So far as Mrs. Summersby's book is concerned," Eisenhower responded blandly, then with asperity, on November 3, "I have not read it* and do not know where it can be obtained. If I run into a copy somewhere I will forward it to you. I am forced to say, however, that I do not see why you should be called upon to answer inquiries aris- ing from inconsequential, personal accounts of anything that was as big as the war was." Monty would have to find Kay's opus some other way.

Montgomery would be further troublesome—but only after he read Eisenhower's book. The first dissonant notes came in the London press, prompted by an anonymous review in the *Sunday Times* on November 21 by the paper's "military correspondent," who sounded like a clone of Sir Alan Brooke. "General Eisenhower," the critic carped, "considers that the war was really won by America, that every American view was right, every British idea wrong." A panelist on BBC radio reviewing the book at- tacked the American politicians and generals for allegedly caving in to the Communists on European Occupation boundaries, charging that the Russians, to naive Yanks like Roosevelt, Marshall, and Eisenhower, were only "Americans with dirty fingernails." The American naïveté of the title was also sniffed at. Anticipating more British patronizing, Hastings ("Pug") Ismay, who hadn't yet seen *Crusade* because of an eighteen-day longshoremen's strike in New York, wrote a letter to the *Sunday Times* de- fending Eisenhower. Ike lamented that its review "was practically a post- war low point for me."

Although reactions were largely admiring on both sides of the At- lantic, Eisenhower received protests from American commanders who felt badly treated. In one case he revised a sentence for a second edition. Even a line on the loathsome Pierre Laval, executed for treason by the French, and described as "Hitler's most evil puppet," was objected to by his son- in-law. Eisenhower had the phrase expunged, perhaps because there was a plethora of candidates for that ignominy, possibly because in France one could libel the dead.

Once Montgomery received his copy, Eisenhower heard from him al- most instantly. "I think it is a pity," Monty wrote, "that you should have thought it necessary to criticise me and my ways." But he was "quite used to having my ideas, and methods of working, misrepresented and twisted to convey an untrue picture: and even described as 'fantastic.'" Eisenhower

---

*To Harry Butcher on January 4, 1949, he wrote unconvincingly, "I never got to read Kay Summersby's book except for the first and last chapters."

claimed to be "regretful." Montgomery responded, "I fear you have lost many friends in England."

Authorship also made Eisenhower more legitimate as a university president, although his charge was less with professors and students than with administrators, trustees, and potential benefactors. Whatever his intentions to be a hands-on executive, he was drawn elsewhere for his more relevant expertise. With the legislatively unified armed services bickering over budgets and strategic assignments, and influential members of Congress backing their favorites, Secretary Forrestal asked Truman to bring Eisenhower, with his prestige, to Washington as military adviser, effectively the Joint Chiefs of Staff chairman. "With Ike here for sixty days I think we can get the pattern set and prove its workability by pragmatic experience. . . ."

"My basic objective in all the work I have undertaken since last fall with the JCS," he explained in July 1949, "has been to develop a peacetime military program and budgetary structure that would be related as closely as possible to an agreed strategic plan." In August, the new executive of the Department of Defense would reduce the authority of the individual services, but by then Forrestal was gone. Plagued by depression and frustrated by the military bureaucracy, he was admitted to the U.S. Naval Hospital in Bethesda, Maryland, on April 2, 1949. Recognizing his condition as irreversible, Truman asked him to resign in March, replacing him with the ambitious Louis Johnson, a Democratic fund-raiser and American Legion stalwart who had lobbied for the job.

Arrogant, and efficient at budget cutting, Johnson would run into an admirals' revolt when he canceled construction of a supercarrier. Privately, Eisenhower considered the stubbornly tactless Johnson—although an assistant secretary of war in 1937—a child in a man's job, but Ike continued to offer advice when asked. To Swede Hazlett, he faint-praised, "Louis Johnson may make mistakes, but I believe he is thoroughly and completely determined to turn in the finest performance that he can."

Ike's last letter to the suicidal Forrestal reached him in Bethesda in mid-May. On the night of May 21 he plunged from his hospital room window, his bathrobe cord tied round his neck. Eisenhower mused about him in a diary entry on June 11 that when Forrestal had visited him in Normandy in 1944 he advocated a vigilant "modus vivendi" with the Soviets, and warned, "Never believe we have changed their basic purpose." Now, in the aftermath of the Berlin crisis in which Stalin's bluff had been called, Eisenhower thought, those who were "asleep" about Russian designs have become "professional patriots & Russian haters."

On occasion his military and academic identities merged, as when two Columbia graduate students on fellowships to conduct research in Japan were refused entry permits by SCAP. Eisenhower asked army secretary Kenneth Royall to intervene with MacArthur, who was letting in "very considerable numbers of missionaries, businessmen, and journalists," while permission was withheld "from a mere handful of scholars."

Although his political ambitions in the U.S. were still thwarted, MacArthur was enjoying his clout in Japan. The military phase of the occupation was on automatic pilot, and he was unsure whether he wanted to prolong his proconsulship or bring it to an end via a peace treaty. As State and Defense were at odds over it, he had maneuvering room. The State Department wanted to return the Ryukyus chain to Japan on the signing, and in a cable to Marshall, then still at State, MacArthur, seeking protracted American rule for Okinawa, appealed, "Control over this group must be vested in the United States as absolutely essential to the defense of our Western Pacific Frontier. It is not indigenous to Japan ethnologically, does not contribute to Japan's economic welfare, nor do the Japanese people expect to be permitted to retain it. . . . Failure to secure it for control by the United States might prove militarily disastrous."

Despite the emperor's depoliticized status under the 1947 constitution, even Hirohito was put to backing MacArthur, writing an "Imperial Note" that American presence in Okinawa would protect Japan. After the occupation ended, the emperor wrote, Russia would be the primary menace to Japan's security. U.S. control of the Ryukyus would discourage Moscow from interference. He suggested a long-term lease with Japan retaining nominal sovereignty. By May 1950, Shigeru Yoshida, then prime minister, had conceded, recognizing Cold War tensions, long-term American bases in Japan in exchange for a peace treaty.

MacArthur was under increasing pressure from the prewar "Japan Crowd" in the U.S., which wanted the powers of SCAP curbed, and his routine was continually disturbed by special missions urged on Washington by the informal lobby of old Japan hands led by former ambassador Joseph Grew. It exasperated many with other agendas that MacArthur's remote proconsulship, in which the defeated enemy largely ran the government, worked. Almost certainly he never read the leadership dictum of the great *shogun* Iyeyasu Tokugawa, but MacArthur's style paralleled it: "The right use of a sword is that it should subdue the barbarian while lying gleaming in its scabbard. If it leaves its sheath it cannot be said to be used rightly."

One Cold War mission led by George Kennan promoted a shift away from MacArthur's democratic reforms toward economic stability and internal security, and led to purges of suspected Communists, which under General Willoughby's intelligence office came to mean almost any sort of labor or teacher activist. The purged did not take it lightly. When on May 30, 1950, allegedly Communist-affiliated groups demonstrated in the People's Plaza near the Imperial Palace and shouted anti-American slogans, MacArthur would have to intervene. "I direct you," he ordered Yoshida, "to take the necessary administrative measures to remove and exclude . . . the full membership of the Central Committee of the Japan Communist Party from public service and render them subject to the prohibitions, restrictions, and liabilities of my directive of January 4, 1946." The twenty-four members were prohibited from further political activity or public office.

Some of Willoughby's earlier tactics, exploiting MacArthur's aloofness, had backfired. He had tried to set up under a former Japanese colonel, once military secretary to General (and wartime prime minister) Hideki Tojo, a cadre of former officers to be the nucleus of a future Japanese army. When MacArthur ordered formation of a Police Reserve, Willoughby saw his opportunity, but Colonel Laurence Bunker alerted his chief to the subterfuge. The initiative was quashed although Willoughby escaped any censure. He was part of the "Bataan Gang." Although MacArthur was becoming bored by the job, going home was no option. He had no home.

Expecting another attempt by Truman to keep him on, Marshall determined nevertheless on private life, following hospitalization for kidney surgery. He had postponed it too long. After he again collapsed in pain, as he had in Paris, he was taken quietly—he insisted on that—to Walter Reed Army Hospital. His procedure on December 7, 1948, was no longer elective. The diseased kidney had to go. Through a State Department press officer he would warn Moscow from his hospital bed, "We are in Berlin as a result of agreements between the Governments on the areas of occupation in Germany and we intend to stay." It was his last intervention as secretary of state.

But for Katherine, hospital visitors were turned away. When Sergeant Marjorie Payne's turning down of an offer to write about her years with Marshall reached the media, she went to see him, to explain, but was not permitted in. Learning of her visit, he wrote to her, "I appreciated your calling and I wanted to tell you of my respect and admiration for your judgment. . . . I did not want to limit you in any way and I am afraid you have denied yourself a fair sum. However, you have shown a great deal of character, for which I have high regard."

Marshall read Ike's *Crusade in Europe* while hospitalized. When Eisenhower had tried to see him, Marshall's doctors had also kept him out, suggesting that if the nation's first soldier could not be admitted, recovery at best was slow. After Marshall's release, on December 28, he confided to Eisenhower, "Confidentially, I had a pretty rough time." By December 31, 1948, his sixty-eighth birthday, he was recuperating, but could not carry on. Undersecretary Robert Lovett was filling in, and the urbane Dean Acheson, briefly back in law practice, would take over the top job. On January 3, 1949, Marshall sent his resignation to the White House, effective on January 20, inauguration day. At a dinner for him, the Overseas Press Club recognized his willingness, always, to be forthcoming with the press, and presented him with a gold-plated typewriter, which he affably promised to use—and he did.

On January 10, Acheson wrote to Marshall of his great privilege in having worked under him. Twice in his life, he confided, he had been understudy to greatness: working as a young man under Justice Oliver Wendell Holmes Jr., "and once with you. Greatness is a quality of character and is not a result of circumstances." He would "take comfort in thinking from time to time that if what I am doing is what you would have done, then it meets the highest and surest test I know."

Following his letter to Truman, Marshall wrote a parting message to Lovett, asking that it be read to the staff at State. After convening the deputies and aides and secretaries, Lovett, no sentimentalist, wrote to him,

> If you ever feel that I can ever be of any conceivable help,
> in anything, it would be a great favor if you would let me
> lend a hand. This open-ended request, which comes from
> deep inside me, has only two reservations. I have neither
> the stamina nor the courage to join you in putting dead
> fish-heads under your tomato plants, and I might have to

think twice about joining you on a Zionist mission to Tel Aviv. Otherwise, the sky is the limit. I send you my very dear love and affection,

                                        Yours, ever . . .

A similar tribute had arrived on an earlier retirement from Frank McCarthy, who had left the government in October 1945 for ten weeks of hospitalization. When he had learned that Marshall was delaying retirement to undertake a mission to China, McCarthy had volunteered from his hospital bed, at whatever cost to his career plans,* "I would gladly, even eagerly, forego any other future possibility, if I could be of assistance to you." Marshall had replied that much as he would like to have McCarthy with him, it would be "doing you a very bad service to shorten your convalescence." It again illustrated the level of loyalty and affection drawn by the stoic Marshall.

While he rested in the sun in Puerto Rico and Florida with Katherine, his mail was forwarded, and he politely turned down all invitations and honors—but for a trip to Washington, to see Winston Churchill, who had asked for him. "I was pretty well knocked out for several days," he told Dean Acheson. Eisenhower was also ill again, just after returning to Columbia in March 1949. He had long endured painful digestive ailments, attributed to emotional strain but now diagnosed as ileitis, an inflammation of the small intestine. His physician, Howard Snyder, whom he would later make surgeon general, warned him that to ward off surgery he would have to give up his compulsive smoking, which, with great reluctance, he did. For recovery, Truman offered him, as he had Marshall, the "Winter White House" at the Key West naval station. Then Eisenhower went to Augusta for golf, now an addiction, becoming more and more Columbia's absentee president. He hated the job, confiding that it made more "demands" on his time than he anticipated, with all of the meetings and committees and interviews and paper-pushing being boring in the extreme. Although he was an admirer, biographer Stephen Ambrose quotes an acid allegation popular among the Columbia faculty that one learned never to send the general a memorandum of more than one page, or Eisenhower's lips would get tired.

In April 1949 Marshall, still unwell, agreed to a summons from Acheson to support legislation for the North Atlantic Treaty Organiza-

---

*McCarthy, with prewar Hollywood connections, would become assistant to the president of the Motion Picture Association, and then a producer.

tion before the Foreign Relations Committee of the Senate. Although "getting up and sitting down" was still "an uncomfortable business" for Marshall, the president was concerned that Marshall's lifestyle was constrained by his decades of living on army pay, and looked for a sinecure to offer him. But no job for Marshall was a sinecure. He took his work seriously.

Basil O'Connor, an old Roosevelt associate, was about to retire as president of the American Red Cross. His administrative passivity had produced an expensive mess, ridden by regional faction. Marshall had long admired the selfless service in wartime of the Salvation Army, and had less to do with the Red Cross, although he had known many who had served it since 1917. Realizing that the job would take more than the esteem in which he was held, Marshall agreed to take over as of October 1, 1949. Some regretted his willingness to put overdue retirement aside. Ambassador James Bruce recalled that Marshall had told him that he had promised Katherine he would take a postwar rest. "A few days later, I picked up the paper and you were on your way to China." Another ambassador who had served under him, Stanton Griffis, called him unjokingly "a glutton for punishment" but added that it increased his pride in the Red Cross. To ease the strain of the new job he was sending Marshall some bottles of vintage bourbon. Marshall's former secretary at State, Mildred Asbjornson, wrote that his former staff hoped that the new job would not "seriously curtail or limit his tomato growing, Japanese beetle warfare and other agricultural pursuits at Leesburg."

It took a visit by Clare Boothe Luce to Eisenhower's university office late in September 1949 to get him to own up, if only to himself, where his ambitions lay. Increasingly uneasy, Ike could only wait for something to happen. Bored with business lunches and dinners, and answering uninteresting business mail, yet comfortable and well-connected, Eisenhower *could* make something happen. Something did when Paul Fitzpatrick, the Democratic state chairman of the party in New York, offered him the Democratic nomination for senator. Through their mutual friend George Allen, Tom Dewey had just tried to persuade Eisenhower to run for governor as his successor—as a Republican—and advised against a run for the Senate. In both cases Ike reiterated his conviction that he was uninterested in political office—but in a diary entry on September 27, 1949, recalling the offers, he wondered why Fitzpatrick had considered him a Democrat. "No one," Eisenhower wrote, "has condemned paternalism—yielding to pressure groups—raiding the Federal Treasury in favor of any class—etc. etc., more than I have. The answer is that political bosses don't care what a man thinks—they just want to know whether he is probably a man who can get votes. . . ."

The recollection had been triggered by Mrs. Luce's visit earlier that Tuesday. The charming if chilly former congresswoman from Connecticut claimed to be "downhearted" about the future of the Republican Party after Truman's surprise victory, and "believes I *may*"—he underlined the word twice—"turn out to be the one who could provide the leadership she believes to be mandatory." She didn't tell him that she had been a proponent of MacArthur, and went on to castigate paternalism, federal subsidies, and the weakening of individual initiative, and prophesied a slide toward "Dictatorship." She thought that eventually Eisenhower would be unable to resist "personal involvement in political struggles."

The situation, he went on in his diary, is now "far different" than it had been a year earlier. "Then, all Republicans thought they'd win easily. So—no 'leaders' wanted me or bothered me. All the 'Republican' pressure on me was truly from the grass roots, because the [party] bosses wanted the top man to be someone they could control." But he looked back on the preconvention pressure in 1948 for him to run on the Democratic side as coming from "the bosses—all except H.S.T. & his personal crowd. They were desperate, and I was a possible port in a storm." Now, he thought, "everything is reversed!"

He chose to forget that in Berlin, in July 1945, Harry Truman, new to the presidency and far from desperate politically in that victory year, had offered to propose Ike for nomination in 1948. Had he taken it seriously and followed it up, he would be in the White House rather than in Morningside Heights. Now he closed, "Well—nothing to do now but continue to fight for what I believe in—which is decentralization of both responsibility and authority in govt."

In early November he had a visitor pleading the cause of Christian Arabs in embattled Bethlehem, and he noted Yusif el Bandak's "rather naive conviction that *I* can do something decisive about it." Since such questions were now posed to him often, he found himself asking to his diary, "What are *you* going to do about an alarming situation which only *you* can correct?" He could then effect nothing beyond Columbia, other than to make as many speeches as he cared to. Yet he was clearly talking himself into political candidacy as a Republican, a fit in which he felt increasingly comfortable.

He kept telling himself in his diary that he didn't want a political future and didn't want to be "publicly associated with any political party." Yet he had registered and voted Republican in 1948 and confessed to his diary in April 1950 that his "Republican connections in Kansas . . . know of course that I believe we must have a Republican victory in '52." His corporate connections in New York who played Monday evening bridge at his home at 60 Morningside Drive, and hosted him for golfing, fishing, and hunting excursions nationwide, listened hopefully to his criticisms of Truman's domestic policies. He recorded the results of every political poll, each showing him regularly far ahead of Taft in one party and Truman in the other. Once he noted, "I hope that [the] Pres. is too philosophical to take real note of the 60–30 report against him." Every public speaking appearance he made—and there were many—was interpreted as a preview of his candidacy, and he noted, "*every* luncheon & dinner, some, even, that appear to be social only—seems certain to bring around the moment when a host declares—'I'm sure Gen. E. will. . . .' How I hate it!" Yet did he?

To give him time for other pursuits while he was the magnetic public face of Columbia University, he arranged with the ever-compliant board of trustees to combine the offices of vice president and provost in the person of Grayson L. Kirk, long a Columbia stalwart, to "take over," as Eisenhower wrote to Kirk on June 13, 1950, "the major portion of the University administrative load." He itemized a laundry list of dreary duties "to which you should give personal attention and supervision." It was how MacArthur operated at the Dai Ichi, and the way that Eisenhower had employed his staff system since 1942. Kirk would be his academic Beetle Smith.

One disturbing letter came to Morningside Heights from retired general George Van Horn Moseley, Eisenhower's early 1930s War Department colleague. Clinging as always to the fringe of the radical right while imagining Robert Taft as America's only hope, Moseley wrote to Eisenhower in May 1950 out of concern that former backers of Willkie and Dewey, even the gossipy, much-listened-to radio reporter Walter Winchell, would come out for Eisenhower in 1952. For the general's own good, Moseley warned, Eisenhower should eschew politics. "You just cannot afford to be in such company, or to permit the public at large to feel you are accepting any such support." Further, Moseley warned with an undisguised sneer, Eisenhower should not "let anything happen now to

set you back in[to] the George Marshall class—our dear friend—who
made a great record as a soldier and killed himself completely as Secretary
of State. Today he is, in fact, a 'pathetic figure.'"

Lunatic attacks on Marshall to which Eisenhower failed to respond
would later haunt his reputation. Ignoring the extremist diatribes and the
election still two years away, he replied obliquely that he had an "almost
fanatical belief in the American system—that is in a capitalistic economy
and a political republic." If Moseley quoted him, that seemed safe enough.

Marshall was no longer a heartbeat from the White House. Revised succession legislation and the election of Senator Alben Barkley of Kentucky
as Truman's vice president had altered that even before his retirement
from Foggy Bottom. As chief of staff and as secretary of state Marshall
had traveled constantly on authentic rather than photo-opportunity inspections but he now understood that a dimension of his Red Cross job
was public relations. For the first time he dealt with local people everywhere he traveled, and had his picture taken with them to promote regional fund drives, blood banks, and volunteer programs. At Katherine's
insistence he spent some of the winter of 1949–50, three years late, at
Pinehurst. Then he traveled another twenty thousand miles on Red Cross
business, much increased by late in June 1950 when the Korean War
erupted. But it was on MacArthur's watch, not his. He took some time off
in August for fishing along Lake Huron in Michigan.

At a country store near the lake he was called to take a telephone
from the White House. Aware he was being overheard by a gathering clot
of the curious, he responded, even more laconic than usual, "Yes, Mr.
President" several times, then hung the phone up. His holiday—and his
holiday from government service—was over.

16

MacArthur's War and Eisenhower's Peace

P ERSISTENT INTELLIGENCE that Communist North Korea was up to no good finally pushed Omar Bradley, JCS chairman, to ask MacArthur on June 20, 1950, whether an invasion of South Korea seemed imminent. Almost daily for two years, incursions from the north and attacks from the south had agitated the "temporary" postwar frontier of the 38th Parallel. During MacArthur's lone visit to South Korea, in August 1948 for the installation of hawkish autocrat and former exile Syngman Rhee, seventy-five, as president, the general promised effusively that if the forces of Kim Il Sung in the north attacked the south, "I would defend it as I would California." But to Bradley, MacArthur privately brushed Korea off. Assisted by the Korean Military Advisory Group (KMAG) of 482 Americans, the Republic of Korea forces (ROK) were allegedly able to take care of themselves. And in March 1949, MacArthur told a *New York Times* interviewer, Ward Price, that only "the chain of islands" on the Asian rim should be "our line of defense" in the Pacific.

As G-2, Charles Willoughby informed MacArthur only what he thought the general wanted to hear. Mike Michaelis of the SCAP staff, seeing the departing KMAG general, a MacArthur toady, off for the States, was also assured that the South Koreans could handle the Communists. Yet Syngman Rhee was so distrusted by the Pentagon, Michaelis knew, that his ROK forces were given no offensive aircraft and no heavy artillery. He recalled MacArthur's overconfident description of his Philippine Scouts to Washington before Pearl Harbor: "who were really like Boy Scouts. . . . They just weren't soldiers, period."

On Sunday morning, June 25—it was fourteen hours earlier across the International Date Line in Washington—the North Koreans, using plans drawn up by Soviet advisers, attacked in force all across the 38th Parallel, claiming that they were repelling an invasion. It was before dawn in Tokyo when a Dai Ichi duty officer took an hysterical call from Rhee, who was told that MacArthur was asleep. Rhee exploded on the phone, "Our people are dying, and they don't want to wake up the General!" He was put through.

"You must save Korea," he screamed to a very sleepy MacArthur. Although MacArthur had no authority to save Korea, he promised help. That got Rhee, eager to evacuate southward to Suwon, off the phone. As MacArthur would write in his memoirs, he experienced "an uncanny feeling of nightmare. . . . It couldn't be, I told myself." It seemed déjà vu—another Pearl Harbor. Then came a call to the embassy residence from Major General Edward Almond, his chief of staff, who had also been alerted. "Any orders, General?"

MacArthur reported that Rhee was very excited, more than usual, and asked for some fighter planes. Some P-51 Mustangs should be offered, MacArthur advised, although that would have only psychological impact. Rhee's pilots couldn't fly them. Until MacArthur had more information and authority there was little he could do from Tokyo. "If Washington will not hobble me," he said, "I can handle it with one arm tied behind my back."

Truman had been home in Missouri. Even before he flew back to Washington, the Joint Chiefs had given MacArthur operational control of the few U.S. troops in Korea. Truman authorized further support from Japan for the South Korean military. It seemed obvious that Russia was pulling the North Korean strings, and he did not want to be drawn into a direct confrontation. On Monday, June 27, in emergency session, the U.N. Security Council voted to aid South Korea and called for member nations to assist in repelling North Korean aggression. The decision was spared a veto because the Soviets were boycotting the Council for its refusal to award Mao's China the seat occupied by Chiang's rump regime, now driven offshore to Taiwan.

MacArthur communicated with the Pentagon from the Dai Ichi by teletype, with a coded teleprinter and screen on each end. Since the time zones reversed night and day, arranging conferences was awkward. Through J. Lawton Collins, now army chief of staff, Truman explained that for external political reasons he was not ready to name MacArthur to command in Korea—the U.N. Security Council would have to authorize that, as it quickly did—but in advance of that he wanted MacArthur to send "a survey group" to get as close to the front as possible to see what could be done. It seemed a prerequisite to justifying the use of American forces against bullying Communism. MacArthur looked up from his screen to remark to aides, "I don't believe it!" It contradicted his assumptions about Truman's weak commitments to Asia.

MacArthur reported that the Republic of Korea military felt that the fall of Seoul was imminent. The weak ROK army was close to collapse, and running away. As Drew Pearson's deputy, Jack Anderson, quickly discovered after slipping into the Pentagon, the general's communiques as the situation worsened were widely at odds with the realities flashed on the secret screen. MacArthur had not changed: only the new technology differed.

SCAP's first exploratory mission proved useless. MacArthur's underlings, while loaded with campaign and medal ribbons, included few with relevant experience. Early on the 28th MacArthur flew to Suwon, below Seoul, taking with him in his C-54 (now christened *SCAP*) four of his "palace guard" of favored correspondents. Soviet-built NK Yaks had strafed the airfield earlier. RF-80A jets from Japan kept bare control of the air over the field and the nearby schoolhouse where MacArthur met with ROK and American officers, and with President Rhee, who had fled farther south to Taejon but returned with U.S. ambassador John Muccio.

With the briefing over, MacArthur proposed, buoyantly, "Let's go up to the front and have a look." Minus Rhee and Muccio, they jolted north in two jeeps and a battered black Dodge to the lower banks of the Han River while desperate refugees streamed in the opposite direction, hauling their possessions on their backs and atop their heads. Smoke rose from the ruins of Seoul. Seeing in the distance a railway bridge still intact and another buckled but usable by foot soldiers, he turned to his air chief, Major General George Stratemeyer, and waving at the bridges with his field glasses ordered, "Take them out."

MacArthur had hardly left when columns of smoke arose from the direction of both bridges. Nothing from a command level happens that quickly, but his order and the explosions made the wire services. The bridges nevertheless remained viable for crossings. To *Life* photographer David Douglas Duncan, the general appeared keyed up. The two-hour jostle, except for Inchon in September, would be the closest he would get to the war. Willoughby would later fictionalize colorful details about the Suwon visit for his fulsome MacArthur biography.

North Korean forces would occupy most although not all of the peninsula by August. The defenders, soon including several inadequate American divisions diverted from light occupation duty, reeled back toward what became known as the Pusan perimeter. Without the rackety southeastern port of Pusan as the Antwerp of the theater, MacArthur could not have poured into Korea much of his underemployed and undertrained Eighth Army from Japan, and additional forces soon shipped from the States. He was warned against precipitating "a general Asiatic war," but his JCS mandate to repel the invasion was clear: "Restrictions on use of Army Forces imposed by JCS 84861 are hereby removed and authority granted to utilize Army Forces available to you as proposed [in] your C 56492 subject only to requirements for the safety of Japan in the present situation which is a matter for your judgment."

Eisenhower's first involvement came early. On the day that MacArthur flew to Suwon, Ike had gone to Walter Reed Army Medical Center for a checkup, afterward meeting old colleagues in the Pentagon, including Collins, Haislip, and deputy chiefs of staff Matthew B. Ridgway and Alfred M. Gruenther. They knew very little, as MacArthur's intelligence system had been less effective than his cover-ups. Recalling post–Pearl Harbor days in Washington with Marshall, Eisenhower queried Gruenther sharply, without naming names, "Has it occurred to you that the G-2 Division in Japan is headed by the same man who headed the G-2 Division in the Philippines in 1941? Is it possible that he is not very alert? This is something that might cause you and your associates a little head scratching." But there was no way that the Pentagon could dump Willoughby without relieving his patron.

"I went in[to the Pentagon]," Eisenhower noted for his diary, "expecting to find them all in a dither of effort—engaged in the positive business of getting the troops, supplies, etc. that will be needed to settle the Korean mess. They seemed indecisive—which was natural in view of the indecisiveness of political statements." It was a curious criticism, as U.S. effort had to be based upon a collective United Nations will to counter aggression, and Truman would authorize all the support he could muster under that international framework. "I have no business talking about the basic political decision," Eisenhower conceded. However, he saw more such challenges to come: "It happens that I believe we'll have a dozen Koreas if we don't take a firm stand."

Before going off on a two months' Western vacation from Columbia, Eisenhower made another flying visit to Washington. Representing the university, he testified to a congressional committee on July 5 in support of international education programs. He also intended to discuss Korea, conferring afterward with Averell Harriman, White House adviser on foreign affairs, lunching at Blair House* with Truman, Marshall, and Bradley, and going on to the Pentagon for a private session with Louis Johnson. Eisenhower and Marshall "encountered good intentions" from the president, according to Ike's diary, "but I'm not sure that we met full comprehension." They urged "speed & strength" in assisting South Korea, but Ike thought he saw from both the president and the Pentagon "no disposition to begin serious mobilizing."

Congress needed the mobilizing. Eisenhower was oversimplifying Truman's dilemmas. Washington may have been at war, but to the rest of the nation, Korea was almost off the map. History, demography, the Berlin Airlift, and the Cold War had reinforced America's focus on Europe. Although much of the Korean burden would be American, the world beyond Washington needed concrete evidence of the U.N. character of the effort, and its urgency, in order to support it. Britain, much diminished as an empire but still with a global reach, exemplified the problem. When the Labour Cabinet met, Korea was only the fourth agenda item, and not all present were even certain where it was. Prime Minister Clement Attlee asked one of the senior officials sitting in, who advised that Korea "lies between China and Japan." In the Opposition since mid-1945, elderly MP Winston Churchill approved of confronting Communism in Korea but claimed never to have heard of the "bloody country."

It was difficult for Truman to raise American consciousness, mobilize its industries to return to military priorities, and increase the armed forces (and its budget) that Secretary of Defense Louis Johnson had been paring down. Incurring more debt and raising taxes to pay for the war was politically hazardous. Even so, army ground forces ceilings were incrementally raised, by August to a million. Unable to count on flag-and-country feelings, the army had to cease being a volunteer force and resort to reactivating the wartime draft. With reluctance, on September 12, Truman also called up four National Guard divisions and two regimental combat teams. The draft call, a political liability, had been recommended by Marshall and Eisenhower.

Allegations of unpreparedness were lodged at Secretary Johnson, and media attacks on Soviet Russia as covert perpetrator of the war acceler-

*Blair House, across Lafayette Park from the White House, was being used as a presidential residence while the Executive Mansion was undergoing long-postponed renovations.

ated a domestic anti-Communism encouraged by the China Lobby, which saw Mao's regime as a surrogate for Stalin. Although Chiang's loss of the mainland was the inevitable result of ineptitude and corruption, die-hards blamed Marshall's failed mediation. Truman wanted not another "nickel" given to Chiang—about the only area of agreement he and his Cabinet had with Johnson. The only one, it seemed, who didn't want him booted from the Pentagon was Johnson himself, who saw his highly visible job imaginatively as a launching pad for the presidency in 1952.*

Rightist opinion was that war with Russia was unavoidable, and backed MacArthur's proposals to "unleash" Chiang's aging and incompetent army on Taiwan at the allegedly puppet North Koreans. The "Gimo" even offered to put his worthless troops under MacArthur, who visualized Taiwan falling under his shogunate into an arc of Pacific Rim anti-Communism. He even flew with a party of his courtiers to Taipei to assess the Nationalist potential, an intrusion into foreign affairs beyond his brief and only the beginning of a new round of subverting civilian authority. Truman would not buy into that risk of a greater Asian war. Nor would a skeptical JCS delegation which flew to Tokyo and heard MacArthur urge, "If we win here, we improve the chances of winning everywhere."

Eisenhower's mail and telephone calls were forwarded to Colorado. Responding to a fellow Kansan who predicted war with Russia, he would not "minimize the grimness of the present situation." It was August 14, and the North Koreans were reaching their deepest penetrations into the hapless Eighth Army of Lieutenant General Walton ("Johnny") Walker, a self-styled Patton facsimile who had commanded a corps in France. Eisenhower furnished a history lesson that evidenced his reading beyond pulp Westerns. "In the same area where the great Russian dictatorship now rules with an iron hand lived once a man who was probably the greatest dictator of all time, Genghis Khan and his immediate successors in power. That dictatorship finally fell apart, not through defeat in war or as a result of war, but because of internal difficulties. Certainly I do not give you this thought with any contention that the same result will be repeated—I merely give it to you to show why I cannot agree with your word 'inevitable.'" Eisenhower would have had to live to be ninety-nine to see that prescience validated—but it was.

MacArthur seemed cornered in Korea. He had to face down critics in the Pentagon to force his amphibious Inchon initiative. The designated

---

*Johnson had been campaign finance chairman for Truman in 1948. His Cabinet appointment in March 1949 rewarded his success.

field commander of the marine force he was offered, Major General Oliver Prince Smith, objected that Inchon, just above Seoul and subject to extreme tide falls of more than thirty feet twice a day, was "a terrible place to land." MacArthur contended that exploiting a window of tidal opportunity would trap much of the North Korean army below Seoul. The Inchon landing on September 15 proved more personally glorious for MacArthur than the Côte-de-Châtillon in France in 1918 or Leyte in 1944. Tens of thousands of North Korean People's Army (NKPA) troops cut off in the south surrendered. After hard fighting, Seoul was retaken. With pressure relieved, Walton Walker's divisions holed up near Pusan broke out easily from the "perimeter." What remained of the NKPA withdrew northward across the 38th Parallel. The war seemed won.

One of Marshall's first acts as secretary of defense (Johnson had been forced to resign on September 12) was to send congratulations on Inchon by air to MacArthur, in a handwritten personal letter intended to get the renewed relationship off to a good start. "Please accept my personal tribute," Marshall opened with uncharacteristic effusiveness, "to the courageous campaign you directed . . . and the daring and perfect strategical operation." Surprised, MacArthur began his reply warmly with an unprecedented "Thanks, George, for your fine message." A MacArthuresque spin on their shared past followed. "It brings back vividly the memories of past wars and the complete coordination and perfect unity of cooperation which has always existed in our mutual relations and martial endeavors."

Marshall had seen Truman on September 6 after returning from his fishing trip, knowing why he was called in. He agreed to stay at Defense for six months to a year—if he could get confirmed by the Senate. Candidly, he predicted that opportunistic administration critics would charge that he, not Chiang's mafia, had "lost" China to Mao, and would blame Marshall for everything from Pearl Harbor to the Iron Curtain. The only condition for acceptance was that his deputy secretary be the efficient Robert Lovett, who had been with Marshall at State.

The Marine Corps League on September 8 had blasted Secretary Johnson as "short-sighted, inefficient, and dictatorial" when Truman hesitated firing him. Although Johnson wept as he resigned, on presidential orders he recommended that Marshall succeed him—which had already been arranged. Immediately after, Truman telephoned Marshall to exit the Red Cross.

While the *Washington Post* editorialized helpfully that Marshall was a military man with a civilian mind, he was still a lifetime general, ineligible according to the services unification act. Congress voted Marshall an exemption. It passed the House 220–105. One hundred of the nays came from the Republican side. Although the Senate had approved him unanimously as secretary of state, raw partisanship had escalated. Under the guise of anti-Communism, several extremist senators attacked Marshall's patriotism. In a frenzied diatribe, William Jenner of Indiana libeled Marshall as "a front man for traitors" and "an errand boy . . . for Communist fellow-traveling appeasers." Eleven Republicans voted against confirmation.

Eisenhower telephoned Marshall from Denver, then wrote to offer his "continued admiration and loyalty." Marshall on September 18 responded realistically, "I accept your good wishes but I think I am entitled to your sympathy too because there are going to be hard days ahead." MacArthur's open-ended ambitions initiated the hard days. Although Major General O. P. Smith's 1st Marine Division had achieved the tough landing, MacArthur had public relations motives for having Edward Almond's X Corps forces (augmented by marines) take Seoul, which could have been isolated and bypassed while the NKPA was pursued northward beyond the 38th Parallel. He wanted his loyal chief of staff (now with three stars) to earn a fourth, and he wanted a showpiece return of the South Korean capital "three months to the day after the North Koreans launched their surprise attack." To make that date he ordered a frontal attack on Seoul that was bitter and bloody. The NKPA contested nearly every street. Then MacArthur issued a communique claiming falsely that the wrecked city had been taken (rather than entered) on time.

To stage-manage his Seoul extravaganza, MacArthur, accompanied by Jean and GHQ staffers, flew in from Tokyo to Kimpo airfield on the 29th. (Offshore for the Inchon operation, he had made a photo-op landing and inspection, then returned to the *Mount McKinley* for dining and sleeping. Several days later he was back at the Dai Ichi.) Rhee and his wife, with Ambassador Muccio, were brought from refuge in Pusan. Five Chevrolet staff cars flown in by Almond, and forty jeeps, proceeded from Kimpo to smoking Seoul over hastily linked bridging sections and a road bulldozed through the rubble. Dai Ichi spit-and-polish MPs stood outside the blasted shell of the capitol, its interior hung hurriedly with velvet drapes from Japan to disguise some of the damage. Attendees blanched at the strong smell of charred wood and, from the uncollected corpses in the area, the sweet stench of death.

Conducting the reinstallation of Rhee to his seat of government, a gesture approved reluctantly by the State Department, MacArthur spoke through concussions from artillery and small-arms fire which loosened weakened panes of glass from overhead panels. The audience dodged the shards as the glass shattered. Then he intoned the Lord's Prayer, asking everyone to join him. Tears coursed down his face. It was a consummate performance, although perhaps a colonialist affront in a country pervaded by Buddhism, Confucianism, and shamanism. Rhee, however, was a Christian, and missionaries of both Roman and Protestant persuasions flocked over liberated Korea. In a separate exercise outside the capitol, MacArthur awarded cheap Distinguished Service Crosses to Almond and Walker "for their fearless example."

On JCS recommendation, Marshall authorized MacArthur to cross the 38th Parallel to chase down and destroy the NKPA, but setting limits. "We want you to feel unhampered strategically and tactically to proceed north of the 38th Parallel," he began. If Red Chinese or Russian forces entered North Korea, however, he was to go on the defensive and request further instructions from Washington. Nor, since North Korea abutted on Manchuria and Siberia, was he to violate those frontiers. Only ROK troops were to be used near the international borders.

Ignoring any limits, or likelihood of intervention, MacArthur responded sweepingly that until the NKPA capitulated, "I regard all of Korea open for our military operations." In his library of military histories in Tokyo, where he had been replacing books destroyed in Manila, he may not have had the writings of Sun Pin. According to the Chinese sage there are five "postures" for a commander. MacArthur would have rejected only the fourth and fifth. "The first is being strong and imposing; the second is being haughty and arrogant; the third is being unbending and obstinate; the fourth is being apprehensive and timid; and the fifth is being sluggish and weak." Sun Pin also listed twenty-eight "fatal mistakes," among them,

> If he has a lot of favorites, and, as a result, his troops become indolent in their duties, this can lead to defeat.
> If he dislikes to hear about his own faults, this can lead to defeat.
> If he associates with incompetents, this can lead to defeat.

MacArthur's usually clean desk at the Dai Ichi when he returned was piled high with congratulatory cables from President Truman on down. Success encouraged the obstinacy deplored by the astute Sun Pin. Candidly, General Almond said later, "MacArthur was fully capable of making up his own mind without benefit of advice." Whatever advice he solicited came from tame staff who understood what MacArthur wanted.

As O. P. Smith, who was with MacArthur at Inchon and later at Chosin, recalled, "With that staff MacArthur was God. . . . It didn't make any difference how logical you were if the General said otherwise. You know, General George Marshall sure put that in perspective. . . . MacArthur said to me, 'My staff tells me so and so.' Marshall had said to him, 'You don't mean your staff. You mean your court.'"* Matthew Ridgway would observe of that heady post-Inchon moment that had MacArthur "suggested that one battalion walk on water to reach the port, there might have been somebody ready to give it a try."

The port in question was Wonsan, across the peninsula from the Communist capital of Pyongyang. General Walker, bringing up his Eighth Army from the south, suggested a simple overland movement through central and coastal Korea. Almond's X Corps, invented by MacArthur, which Walker contended should come under Eighth Army, was positioned to pursue the NKPA northward to Pyongyang. In prolonging the division of troop strength, to give Almond continued command visibility, MacArthur may have forestalled an ending to the war. Fantasizing another dramatic Inchon, this time to trap what remained of the North Korean army, he ordered X Corps to reassemble laboriously, and sail to Wonsan, its marine component south from Inchon and then north round the peninsula, its army units by rail to Pusan in order to board ships there to sail up the Sea of Japan. The complicated logistics eliminated for weeks the opportunity to rout the demoralized NKPA. Walker's depleted Eighth Army could not do it alone. Exhausted by its slog from the perimeter, much of its fuel and supplies diverted to Almond's X Corps, it was resuming a hobbled offensive soon to run down.

Conducting the war from the Dai Ichi by remote control, MacArthur would make occasional photo-ops to an air base, inspect some nearby troops, confer for the cameras with generals, then reboard the *SCAP* for dinner in Tokyo. He discounted all threats and forecasts of Chinese intervention as bluff. Warned by the visiting Ridgway in August, MacArthur maintained, "I pray nightly that they will—I get down on my knees." (In his last years he would deny that.) On October 8, the day after an overreaching U.N. resolution empowering its forces in Korea (eleven nations supplied at least some token troops) to unite the country, the intervention he claimed to wish for began. Secretly, Mao had the "Northeast Border Defense Force" in Manchuria christened the Chinese People's Volunteers" and ordered it to "get ready to move immediately." Stalin had

---

*He was recalling a comment by Marshall while visiting New Guinea late in 1943.

agreed to accept a specific shopping list of arms and equipment from Mao, but would do nothing openly.

On the same day, Truman cabled MacArthur—the message written by Marshall—warning of "the possible intervention of Chinese Communist forces." Four days later, on October 12, a contrary CIA assessment argued that "barring a Soviet decision for global war," Chinese involvement "will probably be confined to continued covert assistance." With the contradictory forecasts in hand, the president flew west to meet with MacArthur.

Roosevelt had once conferred with the general on Oahu, as MacArthur claimed it was urgent for him to be no farther away from his command. Now he tried to beg off another meeting in Hawaii as, reasonably, he felt that he was being exploited for political reasons. Congressional elections were the first Tuesday in November. Ignoring the timing, Truman would always claim higher motives, writing in his memoirs that "the first and simplest reason" for a meeting "was that we had never had any personal contacts at all."

The JCS suggested that the president offer an alternative site, and Truman cajoled that if the situation in Korea was "such that you should not absent yourself for the time involved in such a long trip," he would go to Wake Island. MacArthur gave in, perhaps aware that any newspaper reader would realize that the president would have to fly more than seven thousand miles to an isolated Pacific atoll, while for MacArthur it was a mere 1,900 miles. It was one of Truman's hasty political mistakes. He could have arranged a photo opportunity on the 38th Parallel. He could have grandstanded his anti-Communism for the press, pinned medals on draftee privates, and shaken hands with U.N. soldiers from Britain or Greece or Turkey who had given a politically significant coloring to the war. Instead he appeared to be going, hat in hand, to MacArthur.

The general's skepticism was reinforced when he received no agenda for the meeting and learned that Marshall would not be present. (He claimed he was needed at the Pentagon.) MacArthur's diplomatic adviser William Sebald saw nothing in the trip but a "political junket" for the president. When MacArthur's request to bring his claque of GHQ correspondents was turned down on security grounds, he realized that the White House wanted no Dai Ichi briefing spin. He came with several aides and with Ambassador Muccio, who saw the general looking "mad as hell." Muccio had been requested, Marshall radioed, because the president, anticipating Korean unification, wanted to discuss the country's "rehabilitation." The war seemed nearly over. Truman's oversized party of twenty-four included only Bradley as military representative.

On Sunday, October 15, on the Wake side of the Date Line, Mohammed and the mountain met, Truman dapper in business suit and hat and the general in open shirt and squashed cap. They posed for photographers, pretended conviviality, and conferred in a small pinkish concrete-and-frame building near the airfield. According to an accompanying Secret Service agent, as they were driven to the meeting site Truman asked the general whether he thought that the Chinese would intervene. Confidently, MacArthur said that his own intelligence people didn't think so (Willoughby kept the CIA out), but that if the Communists did, his forces could handle them. "Organized resistance," he predicted, according to the notes stamped TOP SECRET made by MacArthur's aide Larry Bunker, "will be terminated by Thanksgiving. . . . They are thoroughly whipped. The winter will destroy those we don't. . . . In North Korea, unfortunately, the government is pursuing a forlorn hope."

Since the North Atlantic Treaty Organization was in formation, Bradley raised the question of troops made surplus by success becoming available for NATO. "Could the Second or Third Division be made available to be sent over to Europe by January?" MacArthur offered to manage it—and added that he would also not need a French battalion already in the pipeline. The meeting drifted on for another ninety minutes, Truman closing by asking again about Chinese or Russian intervention. MacArthur was no longer "fearful" of that. The Chinese, he claimed, would have difficulty getting across the Yalu River and then getting supplied. They "have no air umbrella. There would be the greatest slaughter if China tried to put ground troops across. They would be destroyed." Then he looked at his watch, which he had kept on Japan time, three hours later, and announced, "There are many pressing matters awaiting my return to Tokyo." Their aircraft were ordered ready, and lunch on the ground canceled.

Returning to the airstrip in Wake's only civilian auto, a Chevrolet, Averell Harriman asked MacArthur about his future plans. Once the Japanese peace treaty was concluded, he said, he would return for good. He hoped to be back in a year. Truman brought up the matter of generals in politics, trying to draw MacArthur out. Eisenhower, Truman scoffed, "doesn't know the first thing about politics. Why, if he should become President, his administration would make Grant's look like a model of perfection." There was no reaction from MacArthur. Near the ramp of the *Independence*, Truman, his light fedora gleaming in the intense noonday sun, smilingly pinned a Distinguished Service Medal (the recipient's fifth) on MacArthur. Shaking hands for the cameras, the general said, "Goodbye, sir, and happy landings. It's been a real honor to talk to you." He remained courteously at his own plane, not boarding until the president did.

Despite the pleasantries, MacArthur claimed in his memoirs to have detected a sinister aspect to the meeting. Truman had made it clear that he wanted no war, even by accident, with China or Russia, and in retrospect MacArthur read timidity and defeatism with respect to the Communists, "a deliberate underestimating of the importance of the conflict." He had hoped to have word, for bragging rights, before parting from Truman, of the capture of Pyongyang. The North Korean capital was occupied two days later, on the 17th.

General Willoughby's sweeping intelligence summary on October 20 appeared to confirm earlier estimates. "Organized resistance on any large scale has ceased to be an enemy capability," he declared for MacArthur. But that resistance was taking on an unanticipated dimension as the Chinese—260,000 by mid-September—began slipping by night across the Yalu. Some used the concrete road atop the Suiho power plant, shared by both countries. MacArthur had been ordered to leave it unbombed, to avoid a provocation with China. Most troops moved across on wooden bridges painted "the color of the water" and submerged just below its surface. Trucks could cross it at night at wheeltop depth, and troops could wade at kneetop height through the icy water. By day, soldiers concealed themselves. They wore padded earth-hued coats which could be turned inside out, the white lining matching the snowy surfaces to come.

Unaware, MacArthur flew to Pyongyang and traveled conspicuously through a city so new to occupation that North Korean flags still flew, and posters of Stalin and Kim Il Sung adorned buildings and light standards. It was an opportune time for MacArthur to stretch his JCS limitations. Walker and Almond were ordered to push to the Yalu, but first, Almond had to disembark his X Corps troops in the Wonsan area, and expand their beachhead, which took almost until early winter arrived in North Korea. General Willoughby's intelligence summary for October 28 explained smugly that the few Chinese forces so far detected south of the Yalu had no experience fighting "a major power" and possessed little modern equipment. Yet they had foot power, iron discipline, and the ability to march and fight at night.

On the same day, Eisenhower sent MacArthur belated congratulations for his succession of victories. "I have not wanted to bother you with correspondence during the more active phases of your recent campaign," he wrote, "but I can no longer stay the impulse to express the conviction that you have again given us a brilliant example of professional leadership. . . . My very best wishes to you and your family. With warm personal regard. . . ." MacArthur replied that Ike's message had "brought back so vividly the memories of our intimate relationships over so many hard years of effort and travail."

Marshall actually worried on the basis of MacArthur's optimism that fighting could end too soon, with a North Korean collapse. Conferring with Army Secretary Frank Pace, who had been to Wake with Truman, Marshall spoke of a "too precipitate ending to the war." Do you mean, Pace asked, that Americans would then fail "to grasp the implications of the Cold War?"

"I certainly do," said Marshall. "You didn't live through the end of World War II the way I did, and watch people rush back to their civilian jobs and leave the tanks to rot in the Pacific and the military strength that was built up to fade away."

"Would you say I was naive if I said that the American people had [now] learned their lesson?"

"No, Pace," Marshall shot back. "I wouldn't say you were naive; I'd say you were incredibly naive."

Lieutenant Colonel John H. Chiles of X Corps later observed, when a general, "Anything MacArthur wanted, Willoughby produced intelligence for." He scorned, as disinformation, claims from the daily interrogation of Chinese prisoners already across the Yalu that their orders were to go all the way to Pusan. There were only a few of them. With the Pacific Rim situation apparently stabilizing (as Washington bought into MacArthur's estimates), Truman and the Pentagon turned the lens upon Europe, where the outlook remained bleak. The success of the Berlin Airlift had not resulted in the Iron Curtain's lifting so much as a millimeter. Rebuffing the Marshall Plan aspirations of the Russian buffer of satellites, the Stalin regime preferred secure stagnation to the risks of openness. Communist parties in the West—such as in Italy and France—remained potential gravel in the gears of economic recovery. The North Atlantic Treaty Organization was a paper tiger, needing a military dimension. Unlike the Marshall Plan, conceived to be European in focus whatever its American backing, NATO required American military presence to deter a Soviet attack, and a commander with wide respect in Europe. Its commander initially, at least, had to be an American.

Eisenhower had little choice but to accept the role. Refusal would throw NATO into prenatal disarray. At Wake, Truman had asked MacArthur for divisions for NATO, and the general confidently had agreed. His war was over. No number of American divisions in Europe realistically could deter Soviet aggression, Truman realized, unless it was recognized as, effectively, an attack upon the United States. Returning home, Truman telephoned Eisenhower at the Blackstone Hotel in Chicago; Ike was on a tour of Columbia alumni groups. It was clear that Truman wanted to offer the NATO command. On Friday evening October 27, 1950, the day before his congratulatory cable to MacArthur, Ike had been flown to Washington from an alumni dinner at Charleston, West Virginia. The next day he saw General Collins, Deputy Chief of Staff Gruenther, Army Secretary Pace, and the president. Truman was frank. NATO needed Eisenhower's prestige at home and his organizing skills abroad—and immediately.

He expected to leave Columbia "temporarily," Eisenhower told his diary, assuming that his "alleged prestige" would diminish once the "organizational phases . . . begin to show results." After that he wanted younger blood and brains to carry on: "I would not want to see the habit started of assigning successive commanders who had almost reached the end of their usefulness as soldiers." While preparations went on for his NATO assignment, he continued to conduct Columbia business, primarily promotional travel exploiting his star-quality glamour. Rumors leaked about the NATO assignment nevertheless, and Governor Dewey added complications by announcing that he would work on New York Republicans to nominate Eisenhower in 1952. Was Eisenhower willing? In his diary for November 6, 1950, he noted dismissively about Truman, who was allegedly over his head in problems—there was already "some hysteria" in Washington about both Europe and Asia—that "poor H.S.T.—[is] a fine man who, in the middle of a stormy lake, knows nothing of swimming. Yet a lot of drowning people are forced to look to him as a life guard. If his wisdom could only equal his good intent!!"

Although NATO seemed likely to restrain Eisenhower politically by returning him to uniform, on campus and off, and while wearing suit and tie, he continued to blow his nonpartisan cover. At a St. Andrews Society dinner in the Waldorf-Astoria he defined a liberal for his fat-walleted audience as "a man in Washington who wants to play Almighty with your money,"* and chided such misguided folk—certainly Democrats—for en-

---

*Eisenhower remained close with his own money, perhaps a farm-family trait. Kyriacos Demetriou, proprietor of a fashionable Upper West Side barbershop, recalled sending five of his crew in turn to Morningside Heights to give Ike a back-and-sides trim. None were willing to return. "Mr. Kay" then went himself and discovered why. "You see, the General did not tip."

couraging ordinary Americans to aspire to "champagne and caviar when they should have beer and hot dogs." The student-run *Spectator* at Columbia scolded,

> General Eisenhower, who doubles as president of this University, delivered himself of several remarkable statements last Wednesday evening. . . . Being content with beer and hot dogs has never been a part of the American tradition we know. The one we know assures any citizen that he may some day eat champagne and caviar, and in the White House at that. We don't know, of course, but we are willing to bet that beer and hot dogs weren't on the menu at the Waldorf-Astoria last Wednesday night either.

A week later the *New York Times* reported that eight fresh frankfurters, with rolls, had mysteriously appeared in the large right hand of the statue of Alexander Hamilton on campus. Soon after, probably to the discomfiture of *Times* publisher Arthur H. Sulzberger, a trustee in the Eisenhower cabal, a dispatch appeared, almost certainly furnished by a *Times* stringer from Columbia, that at a campus Christmas party Ike joked that he couldn't offer a sermon because the chaplain was present, and couldn't address "scholarly things" because scholars were present— and "certainly I'm not going to talk about politics. . . . I never have."

Talking frankly to the man in Washington he most admired, George Marshall, left Eisenhower depressed about the looming catastrophe in Korea which MacArthur had flagrantly failed to foresee. The Chinese had driven south in force. MacArthur's divisions were reeling. Marshall had taken the job at Defense only reluctantly, and expected his deputy designate, Robert Lovett, still to be confirmed, to replace him as soon as military conditions warranted—yet conditions were getting worse. "General MacArthur's messages had shown that he believed the whole mess to be largely over," Ike wrote to Mike Michaelis, now a colonel and commander of the 27th Regiment of the 25th Division. Michaelis had written on October 24 as North Korea seemed to be succumbing, that the war was in "its final stages." By the time the letter arrived, the war had taken a different turn. "I do hope that the senseless bloodshed soon can stop," Ike commiserated. "But if we have to be in it, I cannot tell you how gratified

I am that soldiers of the caliber of yourself and Johnny Walker, and others like you, are on the job."* "Marshall—the best public servant of the lot—obviously wants to quit," Ike wrote in his diary. "I don't blame him."

When MacArthur ordered B-29s from Japan to bomb the Yalu bridges, Washington forbade the strike, warning, despite the intervention, that not an inch of Chinese soil was to be violated. The war was to be kept to Korea. Cabling the JCS on November 7, MacArthur warned of "a calamity of major proportions for which I cannot accept the responsibility. . . ." The alarmist message led to rethinking from the Pentagon that the bridges might be targeted from their Korean sides. It made little difference. In the first days of November, once the Yalu froze, the "Chinese People's Volunteers" could walk across by dark of night. Yet first they deceived MacArthur's command by releasing some American and Korean prisoners who reported, without evoking suspicion, that from what they saw, the Chinese were backtracking toward the Yalu in response to continuing air strikes and superior U.N. firepower. "To hook a big fish," General Peng Dehuai explained to Mao, "you must let the fish taste your bait."

Encountering little resistance, elements of Major General David Barr's 7th Division reached the icy Yalu two days before Thanksgiving. MacArthur radioed congratulations to Ned Almond that they had "hit the jackpot." Some troops expressed their jubilation in a manner seemingly taken from Patton's playbook at the Rhine in March 1945. Standing at the snowy riverbank, officers and enlisted men alike urinated into the river. Almond and Barr flew in to focus field glasses on impassive Chinese sentries in quilted brown uniforms on the other side.

Although MacArthur and Almond were convinced that some symbolic presence along the Yalu would intimidate the Chinese, soon troops on both Korean fronts would not need field glasses to see Mao's conscripted volunteers. Somehow no one had noticed the movement and dispersal across the Yalu of masses of Chinese troops, and thousands of supply porters with laden shoulder poles, or A-frames on their backs. Two legs were better than four wheels, went a Maoist saying. A week earlier, Beetle Smith of the CIA had finally warned that the Chinese had moved three armies from South China to Manchuria. Before long, many times that number would be camouflaged in Korea. Yet American patrols cautiously probing only a thousand yards beyond their lines—little more than half a mile—reportedly found no signs of the enemy.

In Washington, as the state and defense secretaries met with the JCS,

*He would ask for Michaelis, a brigadier general in 1951, to assist him at NATO.

MacArthur's upbeat reassessments dominated the discussion. Even the cautious Secretary Acheson agreed that troops should press forward to the border, to end the war. Marshall agreed. Army Chief of Staff Collins radioed to MacArthur, "There should be no change in your mission."

In his standard self-promotion for announcing an offensive, MacArthur flew to the airstrip at Sinanju, about fifty miles north of Pyongyang, early on November 24. Even before he touched down, he had a smug communique released from the Dai Ichi. It seemed a next-to-last declaration about the course of the conflict. (The final one, then, would confirm the close of his war.) He was unleashing a "massive compression development." General Almond in the northeast, in a "brilliant tactical movement" by X Corps, MacArthur claimed, had "reached a commanding enveloping position." With Walker's Eighth Army in the west already at the Yalu, the pincers, "if successful, should for all practical purposes end the war and restore peace and unity to Korea."

MacArthur predicted to correspondents, as he had done earlier to Truman at Wake, that troops could begin returning home by Christmas. On departure, as he returned salutes from atop his plane's ramp, Walton Walker, beset by misgivings, could be heard below murmuring "Bullshit!" Via Brigadier General John H. Church, Walker hurried a message to Colonel Richard W. Stephens, whose 21st Regiment would lead the 24th Infantry Division's advance, "You tell Stephens that the first time he smells Chinese chow, [he should] pull back immediately."

En route to Tokyo from his photo-op, MacArthur ordered Lieutenant Colonel Anthony Story to stretch the three-hour flight. "Head for the west coast and fly up the Yalu." He wanted to skirt the border for personal confirmation that no enemy buildup was in progress. Korea resembled an upside-down boot with its heel near Sinanju in the west and its toe toward the Siberian border in the east. "I don't think we should do it, General," Story worried. The plane was unarmed.

"I don't care," said MacArthur—and from 5,000 feet in the brilliant sun, peering through sunglasses, he saw what the Chinese would have expected him to see—a merciless wasteland and the black waters of the Yalu now locked in snow and ice. The Chinese did not move by day. After dark, soldiers and bearers crossed the ice unseen; before dawn a small army of dragooned villagers and farmers emerged with brooms and swept away any telltale tracks.

For Eighth Army and X Corps, turkey for Christmas would be only metaphorical. There was almost no contact between armies. Liaison at MacArthur's order was conducted by radio through Tokyo. By the second morning of the end-the-war offensive, to the sounds of bugles, the Chinese emerged by daylight in six armies equivalent to eighteen American divisions, heaving grenades from long wooden launchers. The surprise was total. ROK troops on the American flanks fled. A Turkish brigade sent to assist the South Koreans was ambushed. Despite the bitter cold, many GIs discarded their helmets, guns, coats, blankets, and even boots to unburden themselves for flight. The lightly armed, sneaker-clad Chinese would be the beneficiaries. Walker telephoned the Dai Ichi to report that he was in full retreat. Almond's X Corps, including tough Marines trapped near the Chosin Reservoir, would have to conduct a painful, fighting withdrawal to the coast for evacuation.

In the predawn of November 28, Washington time, early evening in Tokyo, MacArthur urgently radioed the Pentagon,

> All hope of localization of the Korean conflict to . . . NK troops with alien token elements can now be completely abandoned. The Chinese military forces are committed . . . in great and ever-increasing strength. . . . We face an entirely new war. . . . The resulting situation presents an entirely new picture . . . beyond the sphere of decision by the theater commander. This command has done everything possible within its capabilities but is now faced with conditions beyond its control and strength.

MacArthur was describing an unanticipated attack on the order of Pearl Harbor and in the surface strength of the Bulge offensive in the Ardennes in December 1944. The indicators had been out there for him to see—and ignore—for more than a month. The Pentagon's duty officer awakened Lieutenant General Ridgway. He telephoned General Collins with MacArthur's frantic appeal. Collins contacted Bradley, who described the message to Truman as "rather hysterical" but conceded that the Chinese had "come in with both feet."

Addressing the National Women's Press Club as scheduled, Marshall described the world and Korean outlook as "critical," and predicted that "a long period of tension" loomed, "during which we must maintain a posture of sufficient strength that the situation won't go into full war." Privately, Eisenhower wrote to General Gruenther in Germany, "I am now grasping at any news that shows that we are not at the very bottom of the hole."

Without heavy artillery, tanks, or an air force, China had suddenly emerged as a world power, threatening the U.N. position in Korea. Ridgway urged preparing for a possible evacuation to Japan. Unwilling to have Washington put its own interpretation on events, MacArthur issued a communique to the world press which evaded any personal responsibility, declaring that "an entirely new war" had to be faced as a result of the "surprise assault." Then, reversing course to have it both ways, he twisted the fiasco into a cunning strategic initiative of his own, contending that his own blunted offensive had "forced upon the enemy a premature engagement."

Captain John Eisenhower had been visiting his father at Columbia that Thanksgiving weekend. As John was leaving on Monday morning, Ike confided that he had never been so depressed about the Korean War. When a newscaster on John's car radio reminded listeners of MacArthur's "home by Christmas" statement, both realized that he had overreached.

MacArthur had no idea how precarious the situation would be for both his armies when, poised, he thought, to end the war, he had agreed to an interview with Henry Luce's flagship magazine, *Life*, often a conduit for the general's views. Sudden caution caused him to substitute an indirect, third-person pseudointerview, published as "Yardstick from Tokyo" (December 4, 1950), and probably prepared by Courtney Whitney, who often assumed his master's voice. In the altered circumstances, the canned questions and answers were, by publication date, a public relations embarrassment. "Must the United Nations forces go all the way to the Yalu border? Is there anything good in the idea of offering the Chinese Communists a 'buffer zone?'"

"General MacArthur believes," the ventriloquist in *Life* contended melodramatically, "that to give up any portion of North Korea to the Chinese Communists would be the greatest defeat of the free world in modern times. To yield to so immoral a proposal would bankrupt our leadership and influence in Asia...."

MacArthur hurriedly summoned Walker and Almond to Tokyo to discuss alternatives beyond withdrawal. In the circumstances, his own return to Korea was out of the question. He had been there six times since the war began, five of those (Inchon excepted) flying visits of a few hours. Walker's headlong reversal was nothing less than a breaking off of contact, while Almond had to withdraw toward the coast at Hungnam over frozen terrain that made haste impossible. For MacArthur the reassignment of responsibility rather than the reassignment of troops became top priority. In a cable to Arthur Krock of the *New York Times*, he claimed that "every major step" had been approved by Washington. To

Hugh Baillie of the United Press, an old friend, he cabled, imaginatively covering his posterior, "It is historically inaccurate to attribute any degree of responsibility for the onslaught of the Chinese . . . to the strategic course of the campaign itself." To the supportive *U.S. News & World Report* he claimed, "The tactical course taken was the only one which the situation permitted."

MacArthur's beleaguered generals met with him late at night at the embassy compound. After four hours during which MacArthur insisted on holding a line above Pyongyang and Hungnam, Walker and Almond flew back to their commands to find further withdrawal urgent. In Washington, the Pentagon hesitated about ordering MacArthur to do anything. The facts on the ground were unclear and fudged. Integration of ROK troops into American units was failing badly. They were a logistical burden of little use. The Chinese were coming, one GI recalled, "out of nowhere, hundreds of them, all lined up, screaming and yelling, bugles blowing, shouting and rushing at us. I am scared out of my mind."

The JCS had no idea how chaotic the Eighth Army "front" had become. Remote from the action, MacArthur knew little more, yet understood that unintended consequences were in play. There was no front. Some blacks and Puerto Ricans of the segregated and white-officered 24th and 65th Regiments had already "bugged out." The ugly incidents, and the subsequent court-martials, were largely covered up until official unit histories were researched and published decades later. Truman's Executive Order 9981 of July 26, 1948, had ordered equal opportunity within the armed forces, but granted time to effect the changes without damaging efficiency. In a Jim Crow culture, the commands down to battalion level had dragged their feet.

Further damaging morale, supplies of winter gear were woefully short. MacArthur had not expected, after Inchon, to be fighting in Korea after the first snows fell. Many soldiers were limited to one fur-lined or pile-lined garment: a field jacket or parka, cap with ear flaps, gloves, or winterized boots, whether or not they fit. Prisoners of war, however, were often issued warm World War II–vintage officers' overcoats deemed surplus, to be painted with the letters "PW." Chilled GIs often stole them before they could be marked.

MacArthur again appealed to Washington for the unleashing of Chiang's discredited troops from Formosa. The contention that exploiting them might draw the Red Chinese into the war was no longer valid, but rather than acknowledge the useless Nationalists as an unwise military bet, Truman approved a cautious reply from Acheson and Marshall that although MacArthur's request was "being considered," it involved broader worldwide consequences. "The utmost care will be necessary to avoid the disruption of the essential allied lineup."

"I should have relieved General MacArthur then and there," Truman conceded in his memoirs. "The reason I did not was that I did not wish to have it appear as if he were being relieved because the offensive failed. I have never believed in going back on people when luck is against them. . . ." More than luck was against MacArthur. Dividing his forces, attempting to control them from Tokyo, and going deep into North Korea although warned of the consequences, were all tempting "luck." As troops continued to reel back, and X Corps began evacuating by sea, MacArthur asked on December 9 that Washington grant him field discretion to employ nuclear weapons as necessary. He wanted atomic stockpiles in Okinawa, within his Japanese jurisdiction, to cover the ultimate fallback—to Japan. His request was denied. Two weeks later—no one was coming home for Christmas—he proposed a blockade of the coast of China, and air and sea bombardment of China's "industrial capacity to wage war," even—wildly ignoring the map—an invasion against "vulnerable areas of the Chinese mainland."

Undaunted by refusal, he listed thirty-four targets for atomic bombs, radioing a shocked Pentagon that his armies were "facing the entire Chinese nation in an undeclared war," and that without immediate action from Washington, "speedy attrition leading to final destruction can reasonably be contemplated." In reality the Eighth Army, rather than confronting the Red Chinese, was in flight and disarray, abandoning huge supply dumps of equipment, ammunition, and fuel. Only exhaustion slowed the Chinese down.

In that atmosphere the president formally asked Eisenhower to command collective NATO defense. "I am half way to Europe," Ike told his diary on December 16. In words that were awkwardly chosen, Truman told a press conference on December 19 that Eisenhower's position in Europe would be analogous to that of MacArthur in Asia. Two days later, Marshall offered to Ike to be "at your disposal in any way I can. . . . There are a great many men of wisdom and of courage, men of reputation in the world, but your combination of these qualities together with a rare ability to work harmoniously with other people and control their efforts, capped by . . .

the high degree of integrity which has characterized your every action, makes you rather unique in the world."

Despite the warmth of the accolade, Eisenhower could not unbend to a first-name basis any more than could his old mentor. His letter of thanks, on December 29, on taking on the "extraordinary task," began, "Dear General . . ." The same day, he wrote to Grayson L. Kirk, Columbia vice president and all-duties deputy, "I soon go on indefinite leave of absence on military duty. . . . Effective with my departure to Europe and pending my return to the University, you . . . are to exercise the chief executive power of the University."

On December 23—Seoul had not yet been evacuated again—General Walker mounted his personal, Patton-style jeep to ride forward against the crawl of vehicles fleeing in the opposite direction. South Koreans seemed always headed south. An ROK weapons carrier clipped Walker's jeep, hurtling him off the icy road. He and his driver died instantly. When MacArthur in Tokyo was informed, he radioed Washington, lavishing more praise on Walker in death than he had ever offered in life. Truman, Marshall, Collins, and Army Secretary Frank Pace agreed on sending the deputy chief of staff, Lieutenant General Ridgway, to replace Walker at EUSAK (Eighth U.S. Army in Korea), and MacArthur cabled Ridgway in rosy hyperbole that he looked forward to "the resumption of a comradeship which I have cherished through long years of military service." In the early 1920s, when MacArthur was commandant at West Point, Ridgway, now fifty-five, had served as a young instructor.

With her faith in MacArthur fading, Francesca Rhee, wife of the autocratic South Korean president, charged in her diary on December 29 "that the Pentagon or the State Department put this man [Ridgway] in purposely . . . so as to counteract MacArthur's highhanded way of running this war." She could not have been more on the money. Contemptuous of cronyism and with a reputation for rigidity, Ridgway was what the dispirited forces in Korea needed. An agonized MacArthur admirer at the Dai Ichi, Lieutenant Colonel James H. Polk, wrote to his wife, diffusing the blame, "Why oh why oh why does MacA put up with some of the people that he does? Why does he keep people around him that will lead him into pitfalls?"

Ridgway was at the Dai Ichi by the day after Christmas, as

MacArthur was issuing an Olympian communique announcing the completion of the Hungnam evacuation, the close of the horrendous if heroic X Corps fighting withdrawal below the icy Chosin Reservoir. The retreat was actually a "redeployment" that had "served a very significant purpose—possibly in general result the most . . . fortunate of any conducted during the course of the Korean campaign." With a rhetorical whitewashing of the catastrophe which no one else could have written, he added, "We exposed before too late secret [Communist] political and military decisions of enormous scope and threw off balance enemy preparations aimed at surreptitiously massing the power capable of destroying our forces with one mighty extended blow."

Although warning Washington that a Dunkirk to Japan loomed, MacArthur hoped that Ridgway could shore up some line of defense across South Korea. "Form your own opinions and use your own judgment," he said in rare concession of weakness. "I will support you. I will assume responsibility. You have my complete confidence."

To Ridgway, the force of MacArthur's personality overshadowed his obvious failures, but the new EUSAK commander wanted to leave for Korea on his own dramatic high note. "If I find the situation to my liking," he asked surprisingly as they parted, "would you have any objections to my attacking?"

"The Eighth Army is yours, Matt," MacArthur conceded. "Do what you think best."

Ridgway confronted "a dismaying spectacle." ROK troops, including their officers, having abandoned everything but vehicles in which to flee, were streaming south to put distance between them and the Chinese. Ridgway set up no-nonsense straggler posts to stop the hemorrhaging and restore order, and reported to the Pentagon that arming more Koreans was a bad investment. In an evaluation that was overly generous, he blamed American indiscipline on ROK retreats. Yet, undermining him, MacArthur sent the Joint Chiefs on January 7, 1951, a gloomy last-resort "general emergency" plan to redeploy troops from Korea "to the Ryukyus, to the Philippines, as well as Japan."

Fortunately for Ridgway, the Red Chinese, drained by the pace of their advance, and handicapped by winter weather, had paused at the Han River line below retaken Seoul to bring down supplies from Manchuria, a laborious task by laden A-frames on the back, and slogging foot power. Eighth Army could rehabilitate itself. At the top, that meant sacking some brass for command failures. Ridgway's implied message trickled down—and up. He was in charge, and no complaints about the house-cleaning came from the Dai Ichi, where the Supreme Commander's seven-days-a-week schedule seemed more and more a facade.

On January 26, 1951, MacArthur turned seventy-one. To the Japanese, who venerated great age, length of years exemplified a continuing increase in wisdom. Admiring officials of Kanagawa prefecture, just south of Tokyo, presented him with a bust of himself. The general was sculpted wearing the open-collar shirt he affected, and flattered by having years shaved from his jowls and strands added to his combed-across pate. To suggest that he was still capable of commanding from Japan, he had renewed flying visits to Korea, landing in Suwon, below Seoul, on January 20. "This is exactly where I came in seven months ago to start this crusade," he told waiting correspondents. The "stake," he insisted, was a "free Asia." Rebutting his own pessimism to the Pentagon he added, "This command intends to maintain a military position in Korea just as long as the statesmen of the UN decide we should do so." But that sarcasm about the UN, and his "free Asia" remark, were intentional political intrusions certain to raise displeasure in Washington. Truman's government was decidedly not interested in widening the war with unwinnable ideological crusades.

In little more than an hour the *SCAP* was again airborne to Tokyo. MacArthur had seen nothing on the ground in Korea not visible from the air. The meddling left Ridgway furious. War was serious business. Still, flying photo-ops from Tokyo would become a nearly weekly routine to counter appearances of MacArthur's increasing irrelevancy. His strategy, he told tame newsmen on February 13, "involving a rapid withdrawal to lengthen the enemy's supply lines with resultant pyramiding of his logistical difficulties and an almost astronomical increase in the destructiveness of our air power, has worked well." At Wonju on February 20 he told the press to Ridgway's "surprise then and even my dismay" that *he* had "ordered a resumption of the offensive." Nothing in its planning had come from Tokyo. To substantiate MacArthur's hands-on command, the loyal Ned Almond invented for his diary an operation ordered in conference *in* Korea, *after* which Ridgway "joined" them. "No such order was ever issued," Ridgway wrote, for he was present from the moment MacArthur's plane touched down.

Self-serving interviews at the Dai Ichi were now offered to impress bigwigs and prominent visitors who would credit MacArthur's clever string-pulling for Ridgway's successes in moving Eighth Army gradually northward. The politics of again crossing beyond the 38th parallel came up in Washington, where Marshall and Acheson agreed that no South

Korean soil should be conceded to the Communists, and that limited buffer-zone advances should be continued to reach a secure cease-fire line. Although Ridgway reoccupied devastated and depopulated Seoul, the fourth time since July 1950 that it had changed hands, Cold War tactics ruled out such absolutes as victory. Yet not to MacArthur. His fiasco south of the Yalu could only be expunged by retaking the entire Korean peninsula.

MacArthur had been on notice from the White House for months to refrain from foreign policy pronouncements that might wreck momentum toward peace. Having long considered himself a reigning sovereign rather than a mere field commander—wasn't he also viceroy of Japan?—he gave little heed to restrictions formulated a hemisphere away. Some of his proposals, continuing fantasies about unifying Korea and defying China that he had purveyed to rightist foreign diplomats, had been intercepted by Washington. Tempting new opportunities to sabotage negotiating a way out of the war kept arising: a message to an "Anti-Communist Convention" in New York at Carnegie Hall declaring, "Predatory Communist adventures must be decisively defeated"; a meeting in Tokyo with the ultraconservative national commander of the American Legion; an interview with the editor in chief of the International News Service, and with the head of United Press. MacArthur also continued his flying visits to Korea. His twelfth, on March 17, included a four-hour photo-op jeep runabout of 1st Marine units above Wonju, where he claimed to correspondents that recrossing the 38th Parallel would be his decision to make.

For a chance at some kind of closure, MacArthur had to be leashed, or let go. On March 19, 1951, Marshall, Acheson, and the Joint Chiefs reviewed a peace proposal to go out under Truman's signature. A cable to MacArthur requesting his views accompanied a copy of the draft, which suggested that "further diplomatic efforts towards settlement should be made before any advance with major forces north of 38th parallel. Recognizing that [the] parallel has no military significance, State has asked JCS what authority you should have to permit sufficient freedom of action for [the] next few weeks to provide security for the United Nations forces and maintain contact with [the] enemy. Your recommendations desired."

Objecting that Washington's restrictions made it "completely impracticable to clear North Korea," MacArthur ordered Ridgway to move forward in west-central Korea, to create new facts on the ground to out-fox Washington. "Will see you at Seoul airfield Saturday." At his next photo-op he told correspondents that Eighth Army would cross the 38th Parallel again when "tactically advisable." Although State wanted to en-hance the U.N. bargaining position, having MacArthur brag about it in advance seemed as unhelpful as his communique from the Dai Ichi the same day which suggested that if no settlement were reached, his forces might expand operations to Chinese "coastal areas and interior bases." Also, that he was ready "to confer in the field" with the enemy comman-der to realize "the political objectives of the United Nations."

Promotion of a personal foreign policy that was clearly off-limits fi-nally prompted the Pentagon, despite the domestic consequences, to con-sider relieving MacArthur. When asked by *Newsweek* whether he was violating presidential orders, he cabled the editors dishonestly that he had never received such a policy statement "and do not know if it even exists." Truman was livid. A close reader of history, he was well aware that he might have to replay the conflict between Lincoln and Major General George McClellan, who went on after his sacking to become the presi-dential candidate for the opposition.

Set on his collision course, MacArthur looked for further opportuni-ties to subvert Washington. Primary season for the next general election was only a year away, and he may have imagined himself as the McClellan of popular anti-Communism. The issue had already split Democratic ranks while energizing the Republican right wing. In an interview with the military correspondent of the *London Daily Telegraph,* MacArthur complained about being "circumscribed by a web of artificial conditions." The right-wing journal *Freeman* published an interview in which he charged that rather than give South Koreans weapons to defend their own soil, Washington preferred to have its own soldiers die. Then came the general's response to a speech by Representative Joseph Martin, minority leader of the House. Martin read the response on the floor early in April. The rhetoric was vintage MacArthurese. "It was strangely difficult for some to realize," the general argued dramatically, "that here in Asia where the Communist conspirators have elected to make their play for global conquest, . . . we fight Europe's war with arms while the diplomats there still fight it with words; that if we lose this war to Communism in Asia the fall of Europe is inevitable; win it and Europe most probably would avoid war and yet preserve freedom. As you point out, we must win. There is no substitute for victory."

It was the culminating indiscretion. Under Eisenhower at NATO, the U.S. was organizing a deterrent dimension in Europe against the Soviets. On the other side of the world, MacArthur was playing his own game, seemingly plotting with a leader of the political opposition. "This looks like the last straw," Truman told his diary. "Rank insubordination. I've come to the conclusion that our Big General in the Far East must be recalled."

While the global press saw MacArthur as irresponsible, Field Marshal Montgomery claimed to peripatetic *New York Times* foreign correspondent Cy Sulzberger that generals "are never given adequate directives. This was the case with MacArthur. First, he was told to hold on to South Korea and to drive the North Koreans out. Then he was told to reunite Korea, which meant conquering all of North Korea. One cannot blame him. . . . The records will show he never received any truly logical instructions." But realizing how Montgomery, like MacArthur, was wont to evade instructions, Sulzberger added in his diary, "[Monty] tends to bring to mind Clemenceau's remark that war was entirely too important to be left in the hands of generals."

On the morning of April 6, the day after Martin's reading of the combative letter, Acheson, Marshall, Bradley, and Harriman were closeted with the president to determine how to dispose of MacArthur. As the sacking would be explosive, Marshall warned that Congress was practically a MacArthur fan club. "I'm going to fire the son of a bitch *right now*," Truman insisted. But endorsing Marshall's caution, Acheson seconded, "If you relieve MacArthur, you will have the biggest fight of your administration."

That afternoon, a Friday, the group met again, but without Truman, in Acheson's office. Marshall suggested that MacArthur be called home "for consultation." He could not refuse without resigning his posts. Since the others were opposed to giving the general any options, Marshall withdrew his motion. On Sunday morning the four met again with Truman at Blair House, but postponed a recommendation until the Joint Chiefs met. In the interim, Truman proposed, Marshall should reexamine the cable traffic between MacArthur and Washington.

Anticipating MacArthur's dismissal, Marshall that Sunday, already Monday, April 9, in Japan, fired off a cryptic cable to Army Secretary

Frank Pace, then on his first day in Tokyo en route to Korea on a routine inspection. "This is explicit. Repeat, this is explicit. You will proceed to Korea and remain there until you hear from me." Ridgway was to escort the Pentagon party to the front for a review. Marshall's intention was to have Ridgway learn of MacArthur's relief and his own appointment as SCAP from an authority who represented civilian control over the military—a concept which MacArthur had long been flouting.

Truman's crisis team met again on Monday morning, this time with the addition of Bradley. He reported JCS unanimity on dismissal. Marshall confided that he had "gone over all those telegrams and communications . . . over the past two or three years," and had reluctantly "come to the conclusion that the general should have been relieved two or three years ago."

"Thank you," said Truman. "Now will you write me the order relieving General MacArthur of his command, and I will have him brought home." Written in Bradley's name as JCS chairman by Paul Nitze and Colonel Chester Clifton, it largely quoted an earlier message to MacArthur signed by the president but penned by Marshall, about making no pronouncements on policy. "The only question," Truman instructed the group, was "how to do it with the least fuss." He wanted no opportunity for MacArthur's martyrdom. After preliminary language about continued violation of presidential directives, the message closed, bluntly, "You will turn over your command at once to Lieutenant General Matthew B. Ridgway. You are authorized to have issued such orders as are necessary to complete desired travel to such place as you may select."

A means of confidentially notifying MacArthur was the next order of business. Using military channels, Acheson cautioned, "would be a grave humiliation and embarrassment" to the general as "almost everyone in his headquarters [would] know he was relieved before he knew." State Department code was agreed upon. The White House comings and goings on a weekend presaged something really big to astute Washington newsmen, and only one matter could account for them. Earthquakes are impossible to keep secret. No one in newspaperdom was a greater admirer of MacArthur than crusty Robert R. McCormick of the *Chicago Tribune,* a 1st Division veteran of France in 1918. In Walter Trohan, his Washington bureau chief, he had the most indefatigable snooper in the Capital. On

the evening of April 9, Truman signed the replacement orders for Ridgway, to be radioed via Ambassador Muccio in Korea to Secretary Pace.
Trohan's assistant, Lloyd Norman, was busy investigating talk of a "major
resignation" rumored in Tokyo.

Bad news is often bungled in delivery. No one considered where
MacArthur might order himself to go. A statement from the White
House to damp down the expected firestorm was to be released once it
was certain that the proud old soldier was duly notified. Anticipating it,
Trohan confronted Truman's press secretary, Joseph Short, who panicked
the president into rushing his announcement. Panic even engulfed the
Pentagon high brass. Everyone denied everything, after which General
Bradley hurried to the White House to warn that if MacArthur sniffed
out his pink slip before it reached him officially, he might resign with an
extravagant, politically damaging polemic. "The son of a bitch isn't going
to resign on me," Truman said angrily. *"I want him fired."* He ordered an
unprecedented White House press conference for one in the morning on
April 11, early afternoon in Japan.

Reporters who crowded in found only Joe Short and several secretaries, who distributed copies of Truman's announcement at 12:57 A.M.,
with background papers giving the chapter-and-verse of the general's insubordination. "Military governors," Truman declared, "must be governed
by the policies and directives issued to them in the manner provided by
our laws and Constitution." By 1:03 the statement was being aired on
late-night radio: MacArthur's unwillingness to "give his wholehearted
support" to American and U.N. instructions required "a change of command." The president regretted that one of the nation's "greatest commanders" had to be relieved, but civilian (and elective) authority over the
military was at stake.

A call to Korea for Frank Pace was first rebuffed by an army switchboard jockey who denied the existence of any such soldier in the 5th
Regimental Combat Team. Finally, as early spring hail rattled loudly on
the roof of Pace's hut, his windup field telephone jangled in its green
canvas holder. It was Major General Leven C. Allen, EUSAK chief of
staff, who read a cable to Pace that should not have been transmitted in
the clear in any manner: "Disregard my cable 8743. You will advise General Matthew Ridgway that he is now supreme commander of the Pa-

cific, vice General MacArthur relieved. . . ." Pace was in shock. So, soon, was Ridgway. Hours later, the original message arrived belatedly via Ambassador Muccio.

The eviction notice which MacArthur had been expecting—even courting—reached Tokyo when the White House handout was broadcast on Armed Forces Radio. MacArthur's aides were prepared. A cooperative correspondent had been alerted by his home office. "Be sure to listen to the three o'clock broadcast," he advised Colonel Sidney Huff. "We think President Truman is going to say something about MacArthur."

The general was at his usual late lunch at the embassy residence. Huff listened, then relayed the relief message to Jean. MacArthur accepted the news impassively. When Huff's phone rang again, it proved to be the Signal Corps, asking for someone to receive "an important message for the general": Bradley's much-delayed cable. With the general absent, no one at the Dai Ichi had been willing to accept responsibility for the brown envelope stamped in red letters ACTION FOR MACARTHUR. Reporters were already clustering at the embassy gate.

MacArthur telephoned Courtney Whitney, who rushed to the embassy quarters and was given orders to begin the business of preparing for departure. He had handled all personal business for the general through the long occupation. William Sebald, informally the American ambassador, called at the Dai Ichi and found that MacArthur had returned. Having held his tongue earlier with intimates, the general found that his stiff upper lip was breaking down. "Publicly humiliated after fifty-two years of service in the Army . . ." he began to Sebald, but he could not complete the sentence.

Tactfully, Sebald suggested that MacArthur consider preparing a parting statement to the Japanese people to support his successor. All the general would respond was that his sacking was part of a plot to weaken the American position in the Far East, but that he would obey orders. Sebald had nothing further to offer, and left MacArthur to himself. Loyalists in Tokyo marveled at his poise when they came, one by one and in small groups, to the embassy residence to offer condolences mixed with praise. Although the general's hawklike, waxen face appeared serene, he was seething with rage. Receiving his senior courtiers in his shabby old West Point bathrobe he told them that although he didn't know who had been "the firing squad" in Washington, the dismissal language convinced him that "George Marshall pulled the trigger."

One of MacArthur's alternatives for months had been to resign dramatically while airing his differences with Truman and the Pentagon, but

April 1951 may have seemed too soon to initiate the domestic outrage he coveted as a springboard for his unquieted ambitions for the presidency. He hadn't yet plotted the logistics of a return, but expected Whitney to work it out. A leisurely progress toward the Golden Gate, through the locales of his Pacific war glory, might build momentum for a politically timed arrival in the United States, where he had not set foot since the late 1930s. That would bring him "home" just a year before the presidential nominating conventions in 1952.

Former president Hoover, seventy-seven and still nursing his electoral rejection in 1932, telephoned Tokyo that Republicans in Congress wanted the general to come "straight home as quickly as possible, before Truman and Marshall and their crowd of propagandists can smear you." Hoover even offered a "home." The posh Waldorf-Astoria in Manhattan, where Hoover resided, was prepared to offer MacArthur an American domicile. And Republican stalwarts had arranged, early on Wednesday, April 11, to pressure the Democratic leadership in Congress, which could hardly refuse to host a hero, to offer an address to a joint session.

Quoting pro-MacArthur editorials from around the nation, recently elected Senator Richard M. Nixon declared that since Americans were "shocked, disheartened, and angered" by Truman's action, he would introduce a resolution asking the president to restore MacArthur to his command. Joe Martin, whose grandstanding in the House had precipitated the dismissal, told newsmen that he would demand a congressional inquiry into Korean War policy certain to embarrass the administration. Further exploiting MacArthur as an icon of anti-Communism, Senator McCarthy of Wisconsin offered his support for Truman's impeachment.

To evade any hostile demonstrations by imagined enemies, MacArthur asked Tony Story, his pilot, to plan a flight to the States via Honolulu that would arrive late in the evening. "We'll just slip into San Francisco after dark, while everybody's at dinner or the movies." In the U.S., however, the policy clash that led to his dismissal was already overshadowed by the demeaning manner by which MacArthur's relief was inadvertently accomplished. The White House switchboard was clogged with irate calls, and the anticipated contrary opinions enlivened the pro-MacArthur press. Truman, Acheson, and Marshall had to endure weeks of indignation until emotions had run their course. Marshall, at least, would see a striking and supportive Herblock cartoon on the editorial page of the *Washington Post*. In it a stubborn MacArthur (in five-star uniform) and a stern Marshall (in civilian garb) are seated before large "globes" of the Earth. While the defense secretary's is the familiar sphere,

MacArthur's, containing only East Asia, is square and flat. Marshall explains, "We've been using more of a Roundish One."

The general's staff orchestrated a triumphal exit via Haneda Airport. Given a holiday for the occasion and furnished with small flags, Japanese schoolchildren were bused and trucked to the departure route. Their elders were both curious and tearful. NHK radio broadcast an account of the procession live. Although aloof as a viceroy, he had filled a vacuum left when the even more remote Hirohito had been diminished by defeat. The Japanese had another and more material reason to celebrate MacArthur's reign. A resolution of the Japanese Diet cited the general as a leader "who helped our country out of the confusion and poverty prevailing at the time the war ended." Nothing helped more than MacArthur's current war, which Prime Minister Shigeru Yoshida would describe as "a gift from the Gods." In effect it was an informal Marshall Plan for Japan, rejuvenating industry and commerce and creating millions of jobs, as the islands became a logistical and staging depot of mammoth proportions for the American (and U.N.) military effort. Even Red China had quiet cause to appreciate MacArthur, although contenting itself with the usual vituperation. His miscalculations had given China military credibility as a world power, international standing beyond East Asia, and the impetus for industrial revival.

A congressional inquiry into the dismissal was in the works even as the general's C-54, now renamed *Bataan,* was in the air over the Pacific, and Eisenhower, in Paris with NATO, was pressed for comment. He told Cy Sulzberger that he would resign his commission if forced to testify. Eisenhower knew it would be impossible to defend MacArthur's mishandling of the war in Korea, while unadmitted ambition required that he not offend the Republican right wing. He waited until the hearings were over, and then some, returning only in November.

17

General to President

J UST AFTER MIDNIGHT on Thursday, April 19, 1951, MacArthur's sleek Lockheed Constellation, with *Bataan* painted boldly on its nose, touched down in Washington. Despite the hour, Cabinet members (including Marshall), representatives of both parties in Congress, and General Bradley waited to greet him. Absent—as expected—was President Truman, who delegated Brigadier General Harry Vaughan, his military aide, to stand in for him.

Escorted after the ceremonies (with Jean and young Arthur) to a suite at the Statler Hotel, MacArthur postponed sleep in order to review his valedictory address, to be delivered at noon to a joint session of Congress. He had drafted it in longhand en route; aides had it typed and retyped. Millions would hear him on radio, or see him on their flickering, state-of-the-art television screens. Old-fashioned, rolling phrases came easily to MacArthur. He wanted his words to be memorable as well as mischievous to the administration that had sacked him.

At 12:31 P.M., to thunderous applause, MacArthur was ushered into the House. For thirty-four minutes, in a resonant, lingering voice which recalled the radioed Japanese surrender ceremony on the *Missouri* in September 1945, he kept his Capitol and nationwide radio and television audience spellbound. "I address you with neither rancor nor bitterness, in the fading twilight of life," he declared, "with but one purpose in mind: to serve my country." Although he had been criticized for insisting upon victory rather than accommodation, he insisted that his ideas were "fully shared" by the Joint Chiefs of Staff. The falsehood won him a cheering, hand-clapping, foot-stamping ovation.

MacArthur never mentioned the U.N., whose forces he had commanded. He denied that he was a warmonger. The nation was mired in a war with world Communism which it did not initiate, and "in war there is no substitute for victory." The blackmail of appeasement would beget more wars, and he would not settle for a "sham peace." His soldiers had asked him, he said, why military advantages in the field had to be surrendered to the enemy, and, his voice turning husky, he revealed, "I could not answer." Enraptured audiences did not pause to imagine opportunities when the aloof general might have exchanged such views with men in the ranks.

He looked back upon the fifty-two years since he had been a West Point plebe. The world had "turned over many times since I took the oath," MacArthur said, his voice trembling. "But I still remember the refrain of one of the most popular barracks ballads of that day, which proclaimed, most proudly, that 'Old soldiers never die; they just fade away.' And like the old soldier of that ballad, I now close my military career and just fade away—an old soldier who tried to do his duty as God gave him the light to see that duty. Good-bye."

After listening in his suite at the Waldorf, former president Hoover described MacArthur to a reporter effusively as "the reincarnation of St. Paul into a great General of the Army who came out of the East." Republican Representative Dewey Short of Truman's home state declared, "We heard God speak here today, God in the flesh, the voice of God." Had the occasion been a quadrennial party convention, MacArthur might have been nominated for president by acclamation. Not intending to click on his radio, Truman asked Secretary Pace to get a text to him. "I read it," the president recalled. "It was nothing but a bunch of damned bullshit."

Six days later, on April 25, the Senate voted to hold hearings on MacArthur's dismissal and the military situation in the Far East. As opening witness the general testified more strongly than persuasively for three days. Although Laurence Bunker had taken, for him, minutes at Wake Island recording the opposite, he denied that he had told Truman that the Chinese would not intervene in Korea and would be crushed if they did. Asked about the chief executive's authority to relieve him, he conceded that the president did not even have to furnish a reason. Although he found no enthusiasm among his questioners for carrying the war to Chairman Mao, a Republican senator, very likely on cue, asked MacArthur about the effect of General Marshall's mission there in 1946. It lost us China, MacArthur claimed. Abandoning Chiang was "the greatest political mistake we made in a hundred years. We will pay for it for generations. . . ."

Despite the orchestration of conservative press barons, once MacArthur left the stand, media interest declined. White House and congressional mail began shifting away from the general, especially after Marshall's testimony, which followed, and that of Joint Chiefs chairman Bradley, who charged that MacArthur would push the United States into "the wrong war, at the wrong place, at the wrong time and with the wrong enemy."* Army Chief of Staff Collins noted MacArthur's flouting JCS instructions to use only South Korean troops near the Yalu River. Although Ridgway had turned retreat into advance, Collins added, MacArthur, in his usual fashion of barring any competition for the limelight, had overruled Ridgway's promotion to a fourth star. The fourteenth and final witness, General Emmett "Rosie" O'Donnell, would not appear until June 23. By then the inquiry had ceased being news.

The Korean question, Marshall had contended in the hearings, was the price of world peace. Taking the war directly to the Chinese mainland would "risk involvement not only in an extension of the war with Red China, but in an all-out war with the Soviet Union. He would have us do this even at the expense of losing our allies . . . [and] even though the effect of such action might expose Western Europe to attack." Still, he praised his old contemporary, despite MacArthur's career-long penchant for insubordination, for a lifetime of "brilliant" service. As Marshall left the hearings, Senator Wayne Morse commented to Richard Nixon, "I know which of those generals I trust."

"And I know," Nixon rejoined, "which one of them is going to win us the next election!"

By then, MacArthur, his family, and the forty-seven tons of personal belongings he had shipped from Japan had found a home on the thirty-seventh floor of the Waldorf Towers assembled from three apartments by hotelman Conrad Hilton and presented at a token $450 a month. The ten-room suite included a drawing room forty-seven feet by twenty-eight

---

*Major General Samuel W. Koster, who would lose a star after the My Lai débacle in Viet Nam in 1968, would say late in life, "Before you fight on the continent of Asia, you ought to have an overwhelming reason to be there."

feet, which would become an informal museum of Asian artifacts. MacArthur's former deputy in Tokyo, Major General Courtney Whitney, continued to prepare press releases, but for a dwindling number of reporters. In an idle hour, several bored newsmen composed "The Battle Hymn of the Waldorf":

> Here is the Waldorf-Astoria.
> The home of the rich and the odd,
> Where the press speaks only to Whitney
> And Whitney speaks only to God.

In Paris, Eisenhower had been photographed hearing the news of MacArthur's dismissal with an expression interpreted in the press as a suppressed smile. His old aspersions about MacArthur were dredged up, but as early as April 13, retired general Lucius Clay had telephoned Eisenhower to keep silent about the sacking. Clay, now a corporation executive, wrote a follow-up assessment that MacArthur was beyond White House ambitions and could only be a stalking horse for Taft, whose supporters "are definitely aligned with MacArthur who, because of his age, no longer seeks office but is determined to obtain vindication. Their OFFICIAL strategy (this is not hearsay) is to maneuver you into taking a position on the MacArthur issue, thus aligning you with the President and indirectly with his party and its inept conduct of government. . . . We cannot let the true isolationists gain control. . . . This may depend on you and whether you like it or not, you must be prepared to meet that challenge."

Eisenhower had already said, cautiously, yet obviously backing the president, "When you don a uniform, there are certain inhibitions that you assume." After pondering further clarification, he tried to defuse the awkwardness at the source. Without directly referring to MacArthur's sacking, on May 15, 1951, he cabled him, in lines that could be quoted safely,

> Dear General:
> Sometimes I think that we shall never see the end of the persistent efforts of some sensation-seeking columnists to promote the falsehood that you and I are mortal enemies. . . . Of course, I need not tell you that, through these years, I have truly valued your friendship. But I do want to express my appreciation of the fact that, during all the stresses and strains to which you have been

subjected since the beginning of World War II, you have never, even accidentally, uttered a word that could give an atmosphere of plausibility to this curious lie.

The preoccupations of my job are such that it will probably be months before I can ever find opportunity to return, even briefly, to the United States. But I must say that I look forward, as I hope you do, to indulging again on some quiet evening in the kind of conversation on absorbing military subjects that we had at our most recent meeting—almost exactly five years ago today, at your home in Tokyo. . . .

MacArthur assured Eisenhower on May 18 that he paid "absolutely no attention to scuttlebut[t]s who would like to make sensational headlines." His esteem for Eisenhower, "born of . . . many years of intimate association," was "well known and understood by everyone." Yet their scornful comments about each other had been current for decades. In 1948, when MacArthur had been asked about Eisenhower as possible president, he had derided him as too limited "to tackle the job."

Now, welcoming parades and "MacArthur for President" rallies suggested more popular support than really existed. George Gallup's polling figures setting Eisenhower against MacArthur (while ignoring the Republican establishment's solid backing of Taft) showed 51 percent for Eisenhower, 27 percent for MacArthur. Clay would report again to Ike in June after several confidants had spoken to MacArthur about his aspirations that he was "what you and I have always thought, which makes him most vindictive." In Taft's behalf, Clay claimed, the general was expected to "remove himself" just before the nominating conventions, "and announce that no military man should be considered."

With MacArthur out of the equation in Asia, movement toward a ceasefire began to stir. Ridgway had been given leeway to cross the 38th Parallel wherever he could put pressure on the Chinese. As hopeful signs appeared, mostly through third parties like India, Marshall began a quiet visit to Japan and Korea, slipping away from Washington on June 5. In Korea, rain squalls and high winds should have limited him to a jeep, but he insisted on flying with Ridgway in a light liaison plane to the fronts, to see the situation for himself. Near-stalemate breeds casualties seldom worth the acreage involved, and the hilly terrain itself was brutal. Marshall told Colonel James T. Quirk, Ridgway's aide, that on returning to Washington he would recommend to the president that unless the shooting stopped, "we are going to give them a taste of the atom." As a threat it was mere rhetoric. President Truman, who had authorized the Hiroshima and Nagasaki bombs that had ended World War II, had no desire to precipitate World War III with a first strike. Stalin also now had the Bomb. Mutually assured destruction, even unspoken, was a more persuasive armed bluff than NATO and its Warsaw Pact counterpart.

Two days after Marshall returned, on June 14, Joseph McCarthy rose on the Senate floor to deliver a twisted, bullying three-hour diatribe that accused the defense secretary not only of having "lost" China to Communism, but of having made common cause with Stalin since 1943. Marshall's career allegedly included "black" conspiracy and was "steeped in falsehood." (In a novel about the period, a character exclaims, "Marshall, by God! Might as well indict Abe Lincoln for Communism!") No response, predictably, came from Marshall, who was phasing out of his office—he had told Truman he would serve only six months to a year—and intended to turn the job over to Robert Lovett, his deputy. Marshall's visit to the 38th Parallel would be his last to any front line. Since his kidney surgery late in 1948 he had grown frail and susceptible to viral ailments. His vegetable garden in Virginia beckoned.

No response came, either, from leading Senate Democrats like Brien McMahon of Connecticut, who decided cravenly not to attack Republicans on the Marshall allegations, although they were entirely false. If they helped nominate Taft in 1952, some Democrats thought, Taft's weakness as a candidate would cost his party the election. Marshall was expendable.

Although Eisenhower had cautiously remained aloof and abroad during the turbulence in Washington, a delegation of congressmen ostensibly reviewing the progress of NATO turned up in Paris and met with him on June 19. His key task, he realized, but couldn't say, was not so much a military one, but to "inspire [a sense of urgency in] a somewhat apathetic civilization in Europe, as well as the United States," regarding collective defense against the Soviet bloc, which was likely to rely on cunning and deception more than on force. He prepared a formal statement on the "global" situation. What was happening East and West, he contended, were not "isolated, unrelated events." He guessed at a "relationship between the time that the Marshall Plan was really reaching fruition in Europe and the beginning of the Korean War. It was time, I think, the

Soviets felt they had to create a diversion.* They just didn't like a growing
strength and unity here." He also imagined the strife in Indo-China not
as an anticolonialist rebellion but a Communist strategy to keep France
from committing its military forces to NATO.

Eisenhower's informal remarks seemed so surprising to the Washington bureau of the *New York Herald-Tribune* that they were held up for
confirmation, and a month later, his deputy in Paris, General Alfred Gruenther, confirmed that "Eisenhower did say substantially what he is reported to have said." The indiscretions would not be declassified until
August 1976, for, seemingly echoing both MacArthur and McCarthy,
Eisenhower labeled "the loss of China to the Communists the greatest
diplomatic defeat in this nation's history." Although Chiang had proved
militarily beyond rescue, for future political leverage against the Republican right, Eisenhower was implicitly attacking the man who had made
him. Urged on by new and old friends in business and government who
would be his financial backers, he was coldly establishing his anti-
Communist credentials for the primaries in 1952.

At a staff meeting in the Pentagon on September 1, Marshall observed,
"At eleven o'clock I cease to be Secretary of Defense." He had been asked
to stay on until June 30, then until the first day in September. His five-star
rank was for a lifetime, and entitled him to an office, an aide, a secretary,
and an orderly; however his primary support systems were Katherine,
Leesburg, and Pinehurst. He tilled his gardens, rode and walked, and
went fishing. On Sundays he and Katherine attended Episcopal churches
in whichever town he happened to be and he often read the lesson from
Scripture. Like Pershing, he accepted the chairmanship of the American
Battle Monuments Commission. He also chaired the VMI Foundation,
another nonpaying position. He accepted no invitations to sit on the
boards of corporations.

Marshall continued to decline attractive sums to write his memoirs.
Alistair Cooke recalled, certainly from the source, that "a very distin-

---

*Most views now discount the diversion concept as only a by-product of Stalin's assis-
tance to Kim Il Sung's invasion of South Korea. Destabilization of Japan through the
occupation of all Korea may have been more intended than destabilization of western
Europe.

guished, very lordly, American magazine publisher" who could only have been Henry Luce of *Time* and *Life* "badgered" Marshall "in the early fifties" to see him on what was described as "a serious professional mission." The publisher was invited to Leesburg for lunch. Retiring afterward to Marshall's study they chatted amiably until Luce came to the point. He wanted the general's war memories, and would furnish any assistance needed. He planned to do the magazine serialization in parallel with a national newspaper, and the settlement for book publication alone would be "handsome indeed." For two hours Luce pressed his case, noting that the "personal testaments" of such luminaries as Eisenhower and Churchill and Stimson had already appeared, and that others were coming, including that of Montgomery, but all of them still left "one yawning gap."

When Marshall failed to take the bait, the publisher appealed, "General, I will put it on the line. I will tell you how essential we feel it is to have you fill that gap, whether with two hundred thousand words or ten thousand. I am prepared to offer you one million dollars after taxes for that manuscript."

"But sir," said Marshall, embarrassed at the large numbers, "you don't seem to understand. I am not interested in one million dollars."

Eisenhower remained under intense pressure to announce for the White House, but he could not merely leave military life, like Marshall, nor be effectively retired, as was MacArthur. He had to evade being seen as slipping out of a major international task he had only taken up that January; nor could he be visualized as exploiting the NATO appointment for political gain. Further, Army Regulation 600-10 stipulated that active duty members of the regular army could neither solicit nor accept political office. He was also keeping his Columbia presidency (including his only American residence) on what was a lengthening string. He had to hang in a little longer, while hoping that MacArthur's shallow popularity would fade, and that Taft's esteem among Republicans would diminish as his limitations were exposed. Ike's backers expected that Taft's extreme positions would force Eisenhower into the open. His very NATO role was at odds with Taft's residual isolationism. Yet Eisenhower, in Europe, could not merely accept a call from a political convention, and return. The primary system might lock up the nomination in advance for Taft, or even MacArthur.

Two days before Taft was to declare his candidacy, October 14, 1951, came Eisenhower's sixty-first birthday. In Paris, General Gruenther and his wife, Grace, gave him (and Mamie) a surprise birthday party. Eisenhower expected to play bridge, and did, but while he was sitting gloomily as dummy, guests arrived. Minister to Luxembourg Perle Mesta brought a cake she had baked; Averell and Marie Harriman brought a bestselling novel, *The Cruel Sea*; *New York Times* correspondent Cy Sulzberger, back from Poland, brought a bottle of Persovka—pepper vodka, which Eisenhower said he had drunk only once before, in Moscow with Stalin. Birthday cards and cables were piled up—one from President Truman. A few days later, in his NATO office, Eisenhower showed Sulzberger a larger pile of messages, most of them begging him to run for the White House. Also brochures from "Ike for President" clubs. It was not the gesture of someone reluctant to run.

On October 18, MacArthur was to speak at the national convention of the American Legion, a core constituency for his long-shot chances. As he had already done, he was expected to attack the Atlantic Pact under which NATO was formed, for ignoring the supreme importance of Asia. Ignoring regulations, under the date of the 14th, Eisenhower sent a handwritten, clandestine letter to Senator James Duff of Pennsylvania, who represented a cabal of supporters, confirming that he was a Republican (as no one now doubted), and that if nominated, he would resign from the army and campaign for the presidency. It did not surface until 1993. The message implicitly authorized primary activity in his behalf in any state where he did not have to personally disavow his candidacy. State delegations pledged to him were already in formation. Publicly, he disclaimed little, including maneuvering in his behalf, while insisting to those importuning him that he would do nothing overtly political to hinder his effectiveness as American commander in Europe. If someone quoted him otherwise, he would "make a negative statement of complete repudiation."

Although he had earlier offered Ike his support for a White House bid (as a Democrat), Truman now privately scoffed at an Eisenhower campaign, claiming to his press secretary that a military career did not prepare someone for the presidency, which required a talent for persuasion rather than for issuing orders. But he thought that if MacArthur's chances rose, Eisenhower would leave NATO and declare his candidacy. "Eisenhower hates MacArthur as much as anyone." Accepting plaudits at public gatherings, especially in states where delegates might be picked up, MacArthur remained active. Lucius Clay reported to Eisenhower about an alleged increase in MacArthur percentages in New Hampshire, which traditionally held the first primary, and about Colonel McCormick's support of Taft in a *Chicago Tribune* editorial. While holding Eisenhower's feet to the fire, Clay had no intention himself of abandoning big corporate money to join a future Eisenhower government. Rather, he wanted to be in a position to influence it. As he exchanged coded messages with Eisenhower, agents for Ike's candidacy flew back and forth between New York and Paris to report on organization and strategy to counteract any chance that Taft might sew up the nomination before Eisenhower felt ready to commit himself.

The "personal and secret" letter to Duff, delivered by courier and read by the general's intimates, was concealed in a specially rented safe deposit box. A confidant since *Crusade in Europe* days, *Herald-Tribune* executive editor William Robinson ran a front-page editorial on October 25, 1951, declaring that the paper's resources would be devoted to Eisenhower's undeclared candidacy. Soon after, Eisenhower flew back to Washington ostensibly on NATO business, and quietly followed through on his brother Milton's suggestion for a personal advisory committee. He still professed not to be a candidate but he led the public opinion polls.

As the New Hampshire primary approached, he still had to deal officially with Truman, who on December 19, 1951, sent Ike a handwritten appeal hoping that Eisenhower would run as a Democrat, or not all. "As I told you in 1948 and at our luncheon in 1951"—it was still 1951 for two more weeks!—"do what you think best for the country. . . . I must keep the isolationists out of the White House. I wish you would let me know what you intend to do. It will be between us and no one else. I have the utmost confidence in your judgment and patriotism."

Eisenhower answered on January 1, 1952, squirming out of admitting that he was about to announce his Republican identity, to permit his name on the New Hampshire primary ballot. He did not feel, he lied to Truman, that he had "a duty to seek a political nomination, in spite of the fact that many have urged to the contrary. Because of this belief I shall not do so." His abstention from politics would be "meticulously observed by me unless and until circumstances would place a mandate upon me that . . . would be deemed a duty of transcendent importance." Then, again evading army regulations, he dictated a letter under Senator Henry Cabot Lodge Jr.'s signature, to Governor Sherman Adams of New Hampshire, that Massachusetts delegates "are completely secure in their signed sworn statement that General Eisenhower is a member of their party." Rather than keep isolationists out of the White House in the manner that Truman hoped, Eisenhower would do it his way, in a pseudo-draft bankrolled by internationalist businessmen.

On the evening that the "Lodge" letter appeared in the press, an Ike backer found himself in an elevator in the Waldorf-Astoria with General MacArthur, who had to unburden himself to someone—even a stranger. "Well," said MacArthur, "General Eisenhower dropped a bomb today, didn't he?" On schedule, in a full-page editorial in *Life* dated January 8, 1952, came Henry Luce's "The Case for Ike." Having the leading candidate out of the country and not speaking for himself was a problem for his sponsors, but the press, other than the predictable McCormick papers, seemed little short of "I Like Ike" paid advertising. Arthur H. Sulzberger of the *New York Times* suggested that Eisenhower find a terminal point to his NATO role before June, "to stimulate the campaign prior to convention time."

A possible land mine lurked in Eisenhower's path. Rumor, if not reality, about the Kay Summersby episode could still damage his reputation as embodiment of the traditional American virtues. Discussing strategy in Paris with Howard Chase, a Republican strategist close to Roy Larsen, Time Inc. president, Ike was asked whether he could stomach the personal abuse inevitable in a campaign, especially about his wartime relationship with Kay Summersby. He could take it, Eisenhower said. Although he would not respond to scandalous allegations, he "never saw Kay," he claimed, "except while she was driving, or in groups, and that was that." Also in Paris, John Bennett of Drew Pearson's staff—the "Washington Merry-Go-Round" column was still widely read—confronted Eisenhower in December 1951 with the rumor that Beatrice Patton planned to publish extracts from the general's diaries and letters that alluded to divorcing Mamie. Bennett questioned what the public reaction would be if she released anything relating to Mrs. Summersby. Eisenhower refused to be drawn in. Offered the unfounded rumors by supporters in the U.S., MacArthur reportedly scoffed, "That boy will back out in the final showdown."

Nothing would come of it. But William Loeb of the *Manchester Union-Leader* passed along a suggestion to Senator Taft's leading sponsor, Colonel McCormick. In his fashion, he sent out sleuths from the *Chicago Tribune*—who returned empty-handed. Kay would later write, wryly, "I have felt like the girl in the hair-coloring advertisement, the one that asks the question, 'Does she or doesn't she?' In my case, they were not speculating about my hair-color."

There was always something. Arthur Krock wrote in his influential

Times column in February 1952 that Eisenhower, still avowedly nonpolitical, had become "associated with an inevitable attack on the President's record." Truman wrote to the general in what was little short of a plea that whatever "the pathological columnists may have to say, you and I understand each other." Yet that "understanding" had always been one-sided.

Although Eisenhower maintained a public pretense of resisting candidacy, he claimed to Milton that if he did not run, the country would either be "overtaken by socialism" or—if Taft or MacArthur won out—America's foreign affairs would be "bungled" by isolationists or skewed by Asia-firsters. Ike's planned excuse for returning late in May was to dedicate a foundation already initiated in Abilene in memory of his parents: the expected keystone of his own future library and museum. By mid-March he had won the New Hampshire primary and the state's fourteen delegates. A week later, Minnesota went to Governor Harold Stassen, but Eisenhower, not even on the ballot, received nearly as many write-in votes. He could not stay out any longer.

Eisenhower sent his resignation from NATO to Secretary of Defense Robert Lovett on April 5, effective June 1. "I deem it necessary to seek early termination of my military assignment," he also wrote to Truman, as if only a spectator to his candidacy, "so that any political activity centering about me cannot possibly affect the military service." Leaving Paris with Mamie on May 16, he planned to use Abilene as a springboard for ostensibly nonpolitical speeches until he was out of uniform and could openly rally Republicans away from Taft.

Recognizing that he would be the issue, Truman had already announced on March 29, 1952, that he would not seek reelection. To his own satisfaction he guessed that despite stalemate in Korea, inflation in America, and McCarthyite allegations of "softness" on Communism, he could defeat Taft, who seemed to have sewn up 500 delegates out of the 604 needed for nomination. Truman speculated that many votes were less than firm, and would fall away to Eisenhower unless MacArthur was also on Taft's ticket. A liability to the Democrats after two stormy terms, the first of them accidental, Truman understood that he could not be nominated again, whatever the opposition.

MacArthur had not quite faded away as he had forecast in his farewell speech to Congress a year earlier. At his suite in the Waldorf Towers, the general saw few guests, but he was flown off now and then to deliver speeches at high fees; chauffeured to board meetings of Sperry Rand, an hour away; and received bundles of mail and newspapers from an office furnished by the army on Church Street in Brooklyn, to which

Courtney Whitney and Sidney Huff were assigned. MacArthur went to boxing matches, and also watched them on television along with baseball and football. He attended Broadway musicals and holiday shows, and enjoyed the audience applause his entrances evoked. He translated them all into a misconstrued public esteem.

Such old acquaintances as Robert E. Wood and Herbert Hoover, eager for Taft to win, urged MacArthur to announce for the vice presidential nomination. At seventy-two he was little older than Taft, who had long waited, past Willkie in 1940 and twice afterward past Dewey, for his chance. Though a geriatric ticket, the pairing seemed a possible back door to the presidency. The strategy was to ignite Republicans with the kind of oratory MacArthur had used to wow Congress as well as the millions who heard him by radio and television that April afternoon the year before. On June 10 the Taft machine offered him the keynote address, and he accepted, although three weeks earlier he had told the Michigan legislature that no soldier should be president. Henry Luce's *Time* commented that MacArthur's anti-Ike thrusts "failed to create any great stir. Among the great man's well-deserved laurels nestled a bunch of slightly sour grapes."

Since even a small MacArthur supplement might put Taft over if Eisenhower's support surged dangerously, a quiet deal seemed to have been arranged. A penciled note was found in Taft's desk after his death: "If Senator Taft receives the Republican nomination, in the course of his acceptance [speech] he will announce his intention to appeal to General MacArthur's patriotism to permit his name to be presented to the convention as his [Taft's] choice for running mate." Taft also offered MacArthur the additional role of "deputy commander-in-chief" for issues relating to "national security." According to Earl Warren's memoirs, despite that secret arrangement, Taft then appealed to him too. "This is my last chance," he said. For the California delegation's votes, Warren could have "anything I desired."

"There was only one thing that could cause any embarrassment," Taft conceded, as if it were not a done deal—"that Douglas MacArthur wanted the vice-presidency. But he could even take care of that." Warren insisted nevertheless that as governor he was to have his delegation's "favorite son" votes on the initial ballot, and that arrangement would stick.

Just before the convention opened, when it appeared that Taft would not have enough delegates for a first-ballot decision, after which he might fade, Hoover attempted to persuade him to step aside and authorize a switch of his delegates to MacArthur. Apparently Taft was only willing to do so only if he actually failed on the first ballot, after which it might be too late. Observing the American scene from Downing Street, through his informants in Washington, Churchill would write to Clementine, on holiday in Italy, "Either Ike or the Democrat wd be all right. A Taft-MacArthur combine wd be vy bad."

Herbert Brownell, a slick New York pro and former party chairman who had managed Dewey's campaigns, was Eisenhower's handler. At Lucius Clay's suggestion, he had flown to Paris on March 24 under an assumed name to spend ten hours with Eisenhower, technically still a noncandidate, advising him that a draft was out of the question. Delegates were up for grabs. Long before convention time the Chicago papers had chosen sides. Predictably, McCormick's *Tribune* promoted Taft, while the *Daily News* was the Eisenhower organ. Perhaps by default, the low-circulation *Herald-American* was staunchly for MacArthur. From his hotel suite, Eisenhower, a novice at hardball politics, would ask Brownell, who sat at his side by the telephones and the television receiver, "What do we do next, Herb?"

MacArthur's lackluster keynote address, at three in the afternoon on July 7, 1952, his first significant appearance in civilian garb, was, according to his usually admiring biographer William Manchester, "probably the worst speech of his career—banal and strident in content, wretchedly delivered, a bungling of his chance to become a dark horse. Whenever he mentioned God, which was often, his voice had a disconcerting way of rising an octave and breaking, and he had developed a peculiar habit of jumping up and down and pointing his right forefinger toward the ceiling for emphasis." He was interrupted by cheers nevertheless, especially when castigating the "party of noble heritage" that had "become captive to the schemers and planners" who "set the national course unerringly toward the socialistic regimentation of a totalitarian state."

As sometimes happens when audiences become uncomfortable, delegates soon began talking among themselves. The general was almost unheard. Cy Sulzberger wrote sadly, "He said nothing but sheer baloney. One could feel the electricity gradually running out of the room. I think he cooked his own goose and didn't do much to help Taft."

Although he had exited the Corps under a cloud, Senator Joseph McCarthy, described as "that fighting Marine," was being introduced to spew his familiar vitriol as MacArthur slipped away to confer with party faithful at the nearby Stock Yard Inn. Discouraged, MacArthur then flew back to New York. He ordered the Waldorf switchboard to put no calls through to him. Some further maneuvering toward MacArthur, particularly by oilman J. Howard Pew, boss of the Pennsylvania delegation, failed, and the first ballot left Eisenhower only nine votes short of nomination, Taft trailing by 104. MacArthur had only ten votes. A telephone call from Taft to MacArthur in New York was too late to matter. When Stassen's favorite-son twenty delegates in Minnesota were switched to Eisenhower, the tallying of other shifted ballots became mere paperwork.

Eisenhower's leverage, Governor Dewey had assured him, and as the ubiquitous red, white, and blue campaign buttons reading I LIKE IKE validated, was because he was "someone of great popularity . . . who has not frittered away his political assets by taking positive stands." With the nomination settled, however, he had to embody more than "good government." As Anne O'Hare McCormick observed in the *New York Times*, the speeches at the convention "set" by the Republican hierarchy were "keyed to proclaim a policy completely at odds with many of the ideas for which General Eisenhower stands." That became even more evident when Eisenhower accepted Richard Nixon, the rather callow and shrill California senator the party leadership handed to him, as his running mate, for Nixon represented McCarthyite anti-Communism and Taft-tinctured domestic doctrine. Still, the foreign policy platform condemning "godless Communism," drafted largely by John Foster Dulles, rejected isolationism.

In Denver, where Eisenhower worked on the campaign with his political handlers, he met with Earl Warren, to voice his concern that an independent write-in candidacy mounted by MacArthur admirers might swing a close election in California to the Democrats. Should he meet with the general to head that off? He had sent MacArthur a cordial telegram after the convention and received a reply that he was "not in politics." Warren advised against it. In the end, MacArthur received 3,326 write-in ballots in California.

Keeping to himself and tending to his tomatoes in Leesburg, George Marshall offered Eisenhower congratulations on the "fine victory." Marshall had remained "incommunicado," he explained, because "any communication with you" might have been "detrimental to your cause."

Eisenhower responded on July 17 that if he had suggested to his old boss in the spring of 1942 that what had just happened could happen, "you would have had me locked up as a dangerous character." He was "buoyed up" by the belief that he was "performing a real service and I am doing my duty." It was vital, he contended, to end the domination of government by a party with which he disagreed "on so many points of policy."

As candidate, Eisenhower had to break any remaining bonds to that party, and his rhetoric, fashioned largely by C. D. Jackson of *Life* magazine and his Time-Life Inc. deputy, Emmet Hughes, attacked Truman's record, foreign and domestic. One Hughes phrase coined for a televised speech, "I shall go to Korea," mesmerized voters and outraged Truman—who had not gone there when he could have and should have. Yet it was not the president's irretrievable failure to have gone to Korea himself that was crucial, nor the opposition candidate's promise to go. Adlai E. Stevenson, the articulate governor of Illinois, who had been a wartime civil servant for the navy in Washington, did not possess the impalpable magic of a five-star hero. "Ike" radiated a D-Day aura that guaranteed the shooting would stop. Still, he had no formula unavailable to Truman. Despite MacArthur's mantra that there was no substitute for victory, the war would have to end in the near-stalemate that had followed reversal of the failed invasion. Truman saw betrayal. "I am extremely sorry," he wrote to Eisenhower, "that you have allowed a bunch of screwballs to come between us."

More of a betrayal was Eisenhower's failed response to the witchhunting of the man who put him on the world stage. In retirement, Marshall had not wanted to be "detrimental" to Eisenhower's candidacy, and in return Ike had written that in his campaign he would fight with "honor, fairness, and decency." Senator McCarthy's demagoguery about the "treason" of Marshall, however, cried out for the candidate's response. To McCarthy, Marshall had conspired with Roosevelt to provoke Japan into war. Marshall had also abandoned the saintly Chiang, and democratic China, to Chairman Mao's Reds. He had lost the Korean War by refusing to unleash General MacArthur, who was "the contemporary George Washington." Marshall purportedly had been the tool of soft-on-Communism Democrats. To promote Communism he would "sell out his grandmother." Robert Welch, bizarre founder of the well-financed, extreme right John Birch Society,* outdoing McCarthy, charged that Eisenhower had spent his military career "knowingly accepting and abiding by

*MacArthur's former deputy, Colonel Laurence E. Bunker, was vice president.

Communist orders, and consciously serving the Communist conspiracy."
Further, brother Milton allegedly was Eisenhower's "superior and boss
within the Communist Party."

A campaign appearance in Milwaukee, Wisconsin, McCarthy's home
state, was scheduled, with McCarthy and his blowhard colleague, Senator Jenner (who had called Marshall "not a living legend but a living lie"),
on the platform with Eisenhower. Ike asked Emmet Hughes, who as
usual was writing the speech, to type in a tribute to Marshall "right in
McCarthy's back yard." Hughes happily did. He praised Marshall's self-
lessness and patriotism, and characterized attacks upon his imagined
"disloyalty" as "a sobering lesson in the way freedom should *not* defend itself." The lines were leaked to Governor Walter J. Koehler of Wisconsin,
who, with McCarthy, flew to Peoria, Illinois, the campaign stop preceding Milwaukee, to argue that the rebuke would damage Republican
chances.

In Milwaukee, Jenner opened the rally by throwing his usual Red
meat to the crowd, and Koehler, an heir to the plumbing fixtures firm,
then announced the featured speaker. Reporters and broadcasters were
present in large numbers for the expected denunciation of McCarthy.
They had the advance text. Eisenhower skittishly bypassed the key
paragraph, evading any defense of Marshall. Media people were astonished.

Only twelve years later did Eisenhower attempt an explanation. "You
know the story of that, don't you?" he fictionalized to Forrest Pogue. "It
was that damned McCarthy gang, and some of the newspaper people,
who played that up. I had made a strong statement in [Marshall's] defense at Denver a short time before. Then I put it in my speech for Wisconsin. When the governor saw it, he said it was dragging it in by the tail
and would be regarded as something dragged in. So I said, 'Well, I will
take it out, since I have already made clear my feelings about General
Marshall.'"

From beginning to end Eisenhower's alibi was false. Marshall refused
comment, but, Truman recalled, "When I found out [about Eisenhower's
omission] . . . I skinned him from his head to his heels." The general, he
said, "doesn't know any more about politics than a pig knows about Sunday." But he did. Anti-Communism meant votes. George Marshall was

yesterday. As a result, Eisenhower's stonewalling continued at every campaign stop. At a press conference in Wilmington, Delaware, WDEL radio reporter Nick Clooney (brother of Rosemary and father of George) asked, "Do you owe George C. Marshall an apology?"

"I got no answer," Clooney remembered, "but only several dirty looks from Mr. Eisenhower's handlers." Katherine Marshall was livid. Her husband shrugged and said it was all politics. He had never voted, and still would not. He said he was neither Republican nor Democrat, but an Episcopalian.

After Eisenhower's solid victory in November, Marshall mailed his congratulations. "I [will] pray for you," he wrote, "in the tremendous years you are facing. I pray especially for you in the choice of those to be near you. That choice, more than anything else, will determine the problems of the years and the record in history. Make them measure up to your standards." Eisenhower replied that he was "touched" by the letter. If he had not expected it after the Wisconsin affair, he did not really know Marshall.*

One choice which Eisenhower did not make was to confront the malignancy of McCarthy during the first presidential years. Others had to do it. Eisenhower had his excuses, such as demeaning his office. But he also had White House advisers and a Cabinet dominated by partisans who wanted him to keep his distance from anyone connected to the Roosevelt and Truman administrations. Always outside politics, Marshall was nevertheless a political liability.

Eisenhower could not maintain a distance from the continuing Joint Chiefs of Staff, and received a briefing from them before he made good his promise to go to Korea. The JCS offered him two military options other than merely bringing the troops home and letting Syngman Rhee shift for himself. Beyond negotiation, he could continue the costly near-stalemate or seek a more costly solution that might lead to a bigger war on the mainland of Asia. Running for office, he had gifted Mao—and Stalin—with some leverage, because whatever he did, he

---

*Marshall wrote to Stevenson, "You fought a great fight. In my opinion your political speeches reached a new high in statesmanship. You deserved far better of the electorate and you will be recognized increasingly as a truly great American."

had to fulfil his implied campaign promises of ending the war and bringing the troops home.*

With the press and the public watching, and Truman, still president, irate on the sidelines, Eisenhower flew, with aides, to Korea. He was in battered Seoul on December 2. A "piece of demagoguery," Truman called it. The U.N. commander was now Ike's old friend Mark Clark, who was almost as conservative and as militantly anti-Communist as Syngman Rhee. Clark wanted victory as much as had MacArthur, and would have damned the cost. So would the militant Eighth Army commander James A. Van Fleet, who had lost a son in Korea. Eisenhower, however, did not need maps or jeepings round the fronts to recognize that enduring further casualties "without any visible results" had to stop. "Small attacks on small hills will not end this war." A nuclear alternative was unimaginable and a limited war was unwinnable.

"I know just how you feel, militarily," he told Clark, "but I feel I have a mandate from the people to stop the fighting. That's my decision." After three days, including two brief meetings with the implacable Rhee, and a press conference in which he declared vaguely that America "will see it through," Eisenhower left for home. Meanwhile, to preempt the president-elect, MacArthur used an opportunity, on December 5, to speak to the National Association of Manufacturers, blasting "the indecision of our leaders" and announcing that he had a plan (which he would not publicly reveal) to end the war with victory.

Returning with deliberate lack of urgency on the cruiser *Helena* as an opportunity to meet quietly with Republican advisers flown out to Guam for the purpose, Eisenhower cabled MacArthur from shipboard. He asked for a meeting "to obtain the full benefits of your thinking and experience." They would confer at the upper East Side home of Secretary of State–designate John Foster Dulles on December 17. Priggish and addicted to sermonizing, Dulles tested nearly everyone's tact, but he was Eisenhower's foreign policy payoff to his Republican base. Dulles wanted to break off the truce talks in Korea and "fight the Communists everywhere"—much like MacArthur's big stick formula for the Cold War. One of the major problems of Eisenhower's presidency would be to determine when it was useful to unleash Dulles's

---

*The author recalls, as his unit's "voting officer" in Korea to countersign sealed mail ballots, being told by many of his men, although he could not talk politics to them, that they were voting for Eisenhower because he had guaranteed that he would bring them home.

hard-line rhetoric, for the president had to make certain that it remained rhetoric.

MacArthur brought with him a multipage memorandum which among other impossible enormities proposed delivery of an ultimatum to Mao threatening atomic bombings of his cities. Eisenhower realized that such action risked worldwide opprobrium and likely extension of the war to the Soviet Union. The other MacArthur solution was to airdrop a swath of nuclear waste across North Korea south of the Yalu, to keep Chinese troops from escaping or from their resupply. Amphibious landings would then wipe out the enemy. Although the off-the-wall plan had actually been proposed in Congress earlier by Tennessee Representative (later Senator) Albert Gore Sr., it was clear that MacArthur had no conception of the hazards to U.N. troops, or of the likelihood that the ground and atmosphere over unpredictably vast distances would also be impacted. A member of the Joint Committee on Atomic Energy, Gore had probably received the idea from a hawkish physicist at the Oak Ridge atomic facility in his home state. The JCS had already discussed and rejected the concept of a radioactive *cordon sanitaire.*

As Eisenhower prepared to leave, MacArthur told him with exaggerated pomposity, "This is the last time I shall call you 'Ike' and speak to you on equal terms. Hereafter you will be 'Mr. President.' So now I say that you have the opportunity to be perhaps the greatest man since Jesus Christ, as only you can dictate the peace of the world. I beg you to take the initiative with bold action." With that he folded his memo and tucked it into Eisenhower's breast pocket, patting it down as he bid goodbye with a soft "God bless you." A public farewell followed outside. Reporters and curious onlookers listened as Eisenhower blandly summed up the meeting: "We had a very fine conversation on the subject of peace, not only in Korea but in the world in general." Linking arms with the president-elect for the cameras, MacArthur added, "I haven't seen him for nearly six years. It is the resumption of an old friendship that has existed for thirty-five years." There would be no resumption of an intimacy which had never existed. From his internal exile at the Waldorf Towers.

Although the future secretary of state politely but vaguely called MacArthur's ideas "bold and imaginative," MacArthur realized that was as far as they would go. They even frightened Dulles. "The trouble with Eisenhower," MacArthur explained to his acolytes, "is that he doesn't have the guts to make a policy decision. He never did have the guts and never will."

Eisenhower and Dulles would quietly threaten the Chinese with nuclear attack to end the war, an empty warning, Mao realized, yet the White House may have credited it with getting negotiations moving. In reality, Eisenhower received a post-inauguration gift from the gods. On March 5, 1953, Marshal Stalin suffered a massive stroke and was dead by the next morning. As Mao had almost no industrial base, and his weaponry came either by capture from Chiang or by purchase from the Soviets, Stalin had pulled the strings. Mao was now freed to look after China's interests rather than Stalin's. Despite further haggling, China and North Korea settled, basically on Truman's terms, with Eisenhower, who could again be Atlantic-minded. The Korean truce ended the war on the existing battle lines, and authorized the repatriation of only those prisoners of war who chose to return.

Stalin had already stirred the NATO rearmament of free Europe which, but for the trappings, was as much bluff as fact. The truce in Korea and the economic revival of Western Europe, anchored by the Marshall Plan, would give Eisenhower's presidency a strong start. He moved into the White House on January 20, 1953, directly from his official Columbia residence on Morningside Drive. On Friday evening, January 16, he had turned up at the university's McMillin Theater on upper Broadway to bid farewell to thirteen hundred faculty and staff, some of whom had never seen him before. He was awarded a small bronze Columbia lion, a university key, and a plaque signed by the university trustees. In a typical bromide, he said he had found, and was leaving, a university engaged in developing "fine citizens to serve in a free democracy." America remained at war with its opposite. "This is a war against darkness, freedom against slavery, Godliness against atheism." The applause was polite.

As with his vice president, Eisenhower's Cabinet was recommended to him by the tight circle of party advisers who had steered him into office. He knew few of his appointees. Dulles had waited for years for State. Ike wanted a token woman, and got Oveta Culp Hobby, the Texas publisher once head of the Women's Army Corps. He wanted someone from a labor background, and Martin Durkin of Chicago, head of the AFL's plumber's union, was found. (He would last a year.) The liberal *New Republic* exaggerated only slightly in calling it a Cabinet "of eight millionaires and one plumber."

When young Elizabeth II had succeeded her father in 1952, she responded to Marshall's letter of condolence by recalling meeting him "during the war." She would do so again when President Eisenhower, perhaps as a gesture of reconciliation, asked Marshall in the early summer of 1953 to head a commission, including General Bradley, to represent the nation at her coronation. The Marshalls sailed on the liner *United States*, the general's first ocean voyage to Europe in forty-three years. In Westminster Abbey, as Marshall walked toward his seat near the altar, he noticed that the throng of nobility, heads of state, and other eminent invitees was rising to its feet. "Who are they rising for?" he whispered.

"You," said Bradley.

As Churchill, nearly eighty and again prime minister, passed Marshall's seat on the way to the altar he stopped the procession briefly to shake hands, and Montgomery and Alanbrooke* followed. If Wisconsin had privately troubled Marshall, Britain had removed some of the sting.

Following his return, both he and Katherine were ill at Pinehurst, Marshall coming down with pneumonia. His kidney surgery had permanently debilitated him, and at a frail seventy-two he was infection-prone as never before. The White House arranged for a plane to fly him to Walter Reed Army Hospital. From his sickbed he wrote to Madame Chiang (a guest at Pinehurst when in the States) that he would have to miss a state dinner for another of his favorite ladies, Queen Frederika of Greece—"a very beautiful and most interesting woman and you might consider her 'working royalty.' . . ." Frederika visited him instead at Walter Reed, as did Madame Chiang, who spurned any suggestions that Marshall had not done his best for her China.

He was still hospitalized when the Nobel Prize Committee announced that he would be conferred the Prize for Peace, for the Marshall Plan, on December 10. Eisenhower telephoned his congratulations. He often wondered how and why some people were picked for awards, but "this time I thoroughly approve." Marshall wrote back that he was surprised by "this recognition," which he would accept "on behalf of the

---

*Now a viscount, Alan Brooke had conflated his names in his title. Montgomery had been created an earl.

American people, for it was they who made it possible." He planned to travel by ship, and "on the Southern route [to Genoa] to avoid heavy weather." Still, he would have to cross Europe to get to Oslo for the ceremony.

Interviewed on television by Edward R. Murrow, on a program which Marshall watched, former president Truman expressed his delight, and Marshall wrote to him, "I hope you will share this distinction with me because it was through your guidance and leadership that the European Recovery Plan was made possible." He hoped to make that case in his acceptance speech, which he planned to write on board the *Andrea Doria,* but after eight sunless days of "cold and damp," he arrived, he told Truman, "without a line." His former deputy, Tom Handy, now commanding in Germany, sent a plane to fly Marshall to Heidelberg. In Paris, where another former aide, Alfred Gruenther, had replaced Eisenhower at NATO, Marshall dictated "for an hour and an quarter, rather in desperation," from bed, "as my time was running out." Colonel Andrew Goodpaster, much later a successor to Gruenther's job but soon to become an assistant to Eisenhower at the White House, spread out bits of dictation on the floor at Marshall's bed, and stitched together a draft address.

In Oslo on December 10, the awards for both 1952 and 1953 were presented. Medical missionary and theologian Dr. Albert Schweitzer, too frail to travel from Africa, received the Prize for Peace for 1952 via the French ambassador to Norway. As Marshall was called forward to accept his award, not as a general but as an enabler of European recovery, three youths, screaming "Murderer! Murderer!"—it was already an era of disruptive radical outrages in Europe—began dropping handbills from the balcony which accused Marshall of wartime crimes. In response, as he looked calmly on, Norwegian king Haakon VII and the Nobel committee, followed by the audience in the hall, rose to give Marshall a compensatory ovation. Sitting close to the demonstrators in the balcony were the aircrew who had flown Marshall from Paris. They quietly overpowered the hotheads and handed them over to guards outside.

At the formal dinner afterward, Marshall, in white tie and tails, referred to the protest he had anticipated. "The awarding of a Nobel Peace Prize to a soldier," he said, ". . . does not seem so remarkable to me as it quite evidently appears to others. . . . The cost of war is constantly spread before me, written neatly in many ledgers whose columns are gravestones. I am greatly moved to find some means or method of avoiding another calamity of war." That would not come only through "material things," he closed. What the world needed beyond that was "a spiritual regeneration which would establish a feeling of good faith among men. . . ."

With Katherine he flew back to Germany, recuperating further under Tom Handy's roof. But for his two days in Oslo he had been invalided during his entire stay in Europe. On returning to Pinehurst he remained bedridden through February. Marshall's visits to the Washington area thereafter were as often to Walter Reed as to Leesburg. Public life was over.

18

Fading Away

FOR THE FIRST TIME since 1937, at 12:15 on March 18, 1954, Douglas MacArthur was ushered into the White House. He arrived for a meeting, and luncheon, with President Eisenhower and selected Cabinet secretaries and congressmen. Even General Ridgway, who had succeeded MacArthur rather awkwardly in Tokyo, was present. But for a miscalculation, the White House roles might have been reversed. MacArthur had turned down the opportunity to be the vice presidential candidate on a ticket with Robert Taft, who espoused traditional party values. The general might have swung the few votes necessary for the senator, the front-runner before the nominating convention in 1952, to best Eisenhower in the early balloting. In a Republican year, despite Taft's negatives as a campaigner, he might have achieved his life's ambition—like his father in 1908. Senator Taft died of cancer on July 31, 1953, six months after the inauguration, which might have been his own. Had that scenario played out, MacArthur would have occupied the Oval Office.

The general's circle had lobbied Sherman Adams, the president's chief of staff, for an invitation, offering to have MacArthur meet with Eisenhower on "anything." The red carpet treatment proved short on substance. MacArthur might have sought support for Chiang's hold on the outpost islands of Quemoy and Matsu, off Taiwan, threatened by mainland China, but the issue was moot. Congress had offered Eisenhower a blank check for retaliation that was largely bluff, and Mao's government, busy with assimilating the vast mainland nation, backed off.

A White House photographer captured their firm handshake for history. Eisenhower, ten years younger, looked much the elder of the two. MacArthur, with his dyed, dark hair combed across his pate, and dapper double-breasted civilian suit set off by a flamingo-decorated necktie, held a large cigar in his left hand and looked like the high-salaried corporation executive he now was.

The meeting had no news consequences and warranted only a few lines in the press. The talk of Washington in 1954 would be the McCarthy hearings, which would leave the senator's ugly career in ruins. While evading confrontation himself, Eisenhower had written to his brother Milton that there would be "far more progress made against so-called 'McCarthy-ism' if individuals of an opposing purpose would take it upon themselves to help sustain and promote their own ideals, rather than wait and wail for a blasting of their pet enemies by someone else." Yet Ike was among those waiting. Like millions of Americans, Marshall could watch what he wanted of the seventy-two televised hearings from Leesburg—gripping political theater about which he, a former target, made no public comment.

McCarthy had charged the army with being "soft" on Communism and the army had accused McCarthy of interfering in personnel matters to promote a soft deal for a draftee who had been one of the senator's toadies. Inevitably the inquiry ranged beyond the initial issues. The army's chief counsel, Joseph Nye Welch, let McCarthy spew his self-destructive slander at length until finally interrupting him with "Have you no sense of decency, sir?" Following the hearings, and three days of acrimonious debate, the Senate voted, on December 2, 1954, to censure him. Although the lopsided 67–22 verdict ended McCarthy's effective political career and freed Eisenhower from him, it failed to end McCarthyism in politics. Security issues and "disloyalty" charges with a Communist taint would continue to preoccupy the administration.

Among McCarthy's dwindling defenders was Vice President Richard Nixon, whom Eisenhower ordered to disassociate himself from the senator. Cautiously having it both ways, Nixon, naming no names, was quoted as conceding, "Men who have in the past done effective work exposing Communists in this country have, by reckless talk and questionable methods, made themselves the issue rather than the cause they believe in so deeply." Nixon also courted the right through visits to MacArthur. "I did not report them to the President," he later said, "and in fact I cannot recall ever discussing MacArthur with Eisenhower. I always had the distinct impression that any mention of MacArthur would be unwelcome."

In the immediate post-McCarthy years, the administration, taking its cues from Eisenhower's passivity, treated Marshall shabbily. Even before his physical decline, Marshall had no desire for further influence, although his wealth of experience could have been valuable. He was only twenty miles away in Leesburg. MacArthur was more openly ignored. He told such old cronies as his West Point roommate George Cocheu, who had been on his prewar staff in the Philippines, "It is no secret that the present administration is as hostile to me as was the past." A few MacArthur devotees in Congress, like Representative Martin, tried to organize support for honorific six-star rank for the general, but as that would have been a slap at Eisenhower, such legislation had no chance.

Elected more as emblematic American than as politician, Eisenhower attempted to remain above criticism by keeping aloof from partisan battles. An outsider, he leaned upon Republican political professionals and the business elite who had become his bridge and golfing buddies. Harking back to the Hoover tradition, he saw their roles as policy advocates governing indirectly through men of means from the corporate sector in appointive posts. Theoretically they were all wealthy, above ambition, and targeted only the public good. Invariably they were fiscal conservatives, Eisenhower's surrogates as he confronted, and often co-opted, members of Congress on both sides of the aisle whom he referred to as "spenders."

In bullish economic times, the Eisenhower management style of appearing to be reigning rather than ruling often worked. After a heart attack in September 1955 incapacitated him for several months, the perception of a cruise control presidency continued. Although he considered giving way to a successor, cardiac specialist Dr. Paul Dudley White advised him that he could cope with a second term. On November 5, when doctors were ready to release him from Fitzsimons Army Hospital in Denver—he had become ill on vacation in Colorado—he learned that he would be taken to his plane for the flight to Washington in a wheelchair. It would be another week before he would be permitted to walk. In that case, Eisenhower said, he would remain another week. He wanted to appear in public on his feet.

Lobbying by trucking and automotive interests for a toll-free national highway system early in 1956 recalled Eisenhower to his military past. As an aging postwar junior officer in 1919 he had been on the staff of an 81-vehicle army convoy attempting to traverse the length of Route 1 from Washington, D.C., to San Francisco, to test the possibilities of a highway network for efficient mobilization in a future war. The roads were so hopelessly rotten—"dust, ruts, pits and holes," he wrote—that the journey took sixty-two days. Nine trucks had to be abandoned in the mud and muck. Twenty-five years later as supreme allied commander in the west he observed, and exploited, the efficiency of the German *Autobahn* system of divided highways, on-off ramps, and signals-free traffic. Congress, however, balked at paying for an equivalent with politically off-putting tolls, until Representative Hale Boggs of Louisiana proposed a highway trust fund via less obtrusive federal gasoline surcharges. It was a spending bill that did not require appropriated funds. On June 29, 1956, while again recuperating from a major medical setback, Eisenhower signed the bill for a "National System of Interstate and Defense Highways." A zero milestone on the Ellipse in Washington marks in triumphal fashion the place where Eisenhower's 1919 convoy began. The 47,000 miles of interstate concrete proved the death knell for efficient national railways, and magnified fuel consumption into utter dependence on foreign sources of supply, with all its policy consequences.

Intestinal bypass surgery (for ileitis) in June 1956 had changed little for Eisenhower: he resumed at least the appearance of activity six weeks later. The anxiety about subjecting a cardiac patient to two hours of bowel surgery was more public than private. The procedure was essential, and Eisenhower put his worries off until recovery. Nixon and Dulles, each eager to act for him, were fended off. At a press conference later he compared his medical emergency to the Battle of the Bulge, which he once wanted to downplay and even forget. "I didn't get frightened until three weeks after it had begun, when I began to read the American papers and found . . . how near we were to being whipped."

A "dump Nixon" campaign escalated as Eisenhower's illnesses made Republican moderates nervous, but buying the vice president off the ballot with a Cabinet office and promises of support for his own candidacy in 1960 failed. Eisenhower could not face up to defying the party orthodoxy which Nixon represented. As an activist Cold War president, he encouraged that base with psychological warfare and security initiatives, while promoting nonlethal competition with the Soviets, and cultural exchanges. However much Eisenhower believed in these, they were window dressing for the deeper realities. He called his mix of long-range missile silos and people-to-people programs "waging peace." On the surface the strategy seemed to work, and his policies were continued with few exceptions (like the Cuba standoff) by later administrations. The chief embarrassment was his personal denial of secret high-altitude spying, a contention which came apart when a U-2 reconnaissance plane was shot down over Soviet airspace. The incident blew over after some Kremlin bluster, because beneath the belligerent rhetoric of Soviet policy, Communism was a failing patchwork, covertly on the defensive, as the Berlin Wall in 1961 would evidence.

On the domestic front, the era of good feeling was even more a surface. Americans were not living blissfully in a color-blind society, and Eisenhower's election had been the first success of what would be a Republican "Southern strategy" of supporting "states' rights" as code for stonewalling civil rights. To the discomfort of the White House, which preferred the status quo, the federal judiciary was beginning to address the inequities. (When, reluctantly, the president had to order federal troops to Central High School in Little Rock, he explained it to himself on a notepad as "*not* to enforce integration, but to prevent opposition by violence to orders of a court.") Spurred by the president's most crucial appointment, that of former California governor Earl Warren as Chief Justice, civil rights would never leave the judicial agenda during the Eisenhower years, and ruefully, he would intimate privately that Warren (and the "Warren Court") was his greatest mistake. According to Eisenhower's own *The White House Years,* his first choice had been John Foster Dulles, but the hard-line secretary of state preferred presiding over foreign policy.

Prosperity as Eisenhower took office was real, and would get even better, thanks to jobs created by two wars and the consumer demands they inspired. Further, the war of 1941–45 had triggered the immediate postwar "GI Bill of Rights," an engine of immense social mobility. Millions out of uniform whose schooling otherwise would have been over were able to move up professionally, and also to acquire "GI" mortgages which turned Americans into homeowners, stoking an economic boom in everything related to owning and equipping a residence—and its garage. A Truman-era "GI Bill" extension offered similar benefits to Korean War veterans. The Eisenhower administration inherited the results: a triumph of undeclared social engineering.

As the presidential election in 1956 approached, Marshall, in rare personal candor, wrote to Queen Frederika, "Important groups of the Republican Party are extremely hostile to me in their pre-election endeavor[s] to tear down everything the Democratic Administration did, and are now attacking foreign relief assistance. . . . You may not be aware of the fact that I have been more viciously attacked than any public figure in this generation. . . . They count all the billions my policies have already cost the American tax payer and, in this pre-election demagogic scramble, they want no more of my influence or interference." He was writing, he closed, with "my heart as well as my head."

Although unhappy with the manner in which his isolation had occurred, Marshall was free, at seventy-five, to look back. In 1952, as Truman, nearing the close of his presidency, was planning a library on the Roosevelt precedent, he had proposed a Marshall Library at VMI, and prepared a directive requesting government departments to supply copies of relevant documents for the collections. A George C. Marshall Foundation had been established by former colleagues to assemble papers and artifacts, and to plan a library and museum. Private funding was necessary, and only in 1956 did it materialize through John D. Rockefeller Jr., who furnished $150,000 as start-up. Since Marshall would not write a memoir, his former deputies planning the library urged him to permit a biographer to interview him at length. He agreed on Forrest Pogue, a former army combat historian with a 1939 doctorate who had been a sergeant during the Battle of the Bulge. Marshall directed that any royalties from books based upon his interviews and papers go to the foundation.

Preliminary work began in September 1956, with Pogue visiting the Pentagon or traveling to Leesburg or Pinehurst. Frail, and finding it difficult to walk, Marshall wanted only to be questioned afternoons, once he descended the stairs from his second-floor bedroom in Leesburg. Pogue's sessions began none too soon. Although Marshall had a lifetime of forgetting names, he was also beginning to forget dates, except for the distant past. He recalled his boyhood in detail, and with delight. Lengthy interviews began on November 15, 1956, and nineteen sessions in all, each over many hours, were recorded on tape. When Marshall at first was reluctant to field questions he felt were too personal, Pogue warned, jocularly, "If you decline to answer me, the Freudians will get you." One winter day when Pogue arrived bundled in hat, scarf, gloves, and overcoat, Marshall said with a grin, "You look just like John Foster Dulles coming up there!"

"Is that good?" Pogue asked. Dulles had been reported as recovering from cancer surgery. "You have to admire a man who has beaten a thing like that," said Marshall. There was little else about Eisenhower's dour and militant secretary of state, whose policies were labeled "brinkmanship," and "MAD" (Mutually Assured Destruction"), that Marshall found admirable.

Often appearing to be more a sovereign setting policy than a chief executive carrying it out, Eisenhower blandly furnished placebos to an indulgent public while his Cabinet officers and other advisers from the corporate world shifted the governmental gears. Examining his style, an historian of Eisenhower's presidency described it as adroitly "veiled" leadership fronted by "gaff-taking subordinates, . . . [and Eisenhower] casting himself as an uncontroversial head of state." Yet that historian also quotes Henry Cabot Lodge Jr.'s memo urging that the president should be photographed less on the golf course and more in carrying out his official duties. Even so, Eisenhower seemed to have the public on his side, for when a Gallup Poll asked whether he was "taking too much time off to play golf," only 17 percent of the respondents agreed. He was reluctant to draw on his popularity to deplete it, as he had to do on such occasions as directing federal authority to enforce Supreme Court decisions for which he had little sympathy. But everywhere he went, at work or at play, a military officer could be seen a few steps away carrying "the football"—a euphemism for the otherwise unidentified black case containing codes and communications gear to unleash, in minutes, nuclear weapons against predetermined enemy targets. As much theater as reality, it symbolized, worldwide, presidential power.

The power of the White House, however, had its domestic limits. One of Eisenhower's perks since emerging as a political comer had been his honorary membership in the elite Augusta National Golf Club. Rising 210 yards from the tee to the left of the fairway on the seventeenth hole, a sixty-foot loblolly pine stood in the path of par four. Eisenhower launched so many drives into its broad trunk that at a club governors' meeting in 1956 he requested that the tree be cut down. Ruling the president of the United States out of order, Clifford Roberts, the club chairman (an Ike intimate, and his investment adviser), promptly adjourned the meeting. The venerable swamp pine became known as the Eisenhower Tree.

On larger issues, Eisenhower mustered his popular clout with more success. Backing Dulles during the Britain-France-Israel débacle over Suez late in October 1956, he forced the blundering British and French to withdraw from Egypt. However that inadvertently gave a maneuvering bonus to the Russians,* for almost simultaneously, Nikita Khrushchev's Soviet troops, with tanks, forced their way into Budapest after some ini-

---

*The Israelis withdrew only in March 1957 after guarantees of passage to the Red Sea.

tial hesitation and overwhelmed the fragile independence of Hungary. In the failed uprising against their overbearing Stalinist rulers, thousands died while awaiting American intervention, which was never in the White House playbook. But Eisenhower was sometimes kept out of the loop. Before issuing regrets, he had a pained conversation with Dulles, observing that the Hungarian people had been encouraged by such militant broadcasts as those by Radio Free Europe, an arm of the intelligence effort. Inflaming the situation, the broadcasts implied American assistance for a rising. "We have excited Hungarians for all these years," Eisenhower charged. "Now [we] are turning our backs on them when they are in a jam." Ignoring 1775, Dulles shrugged, "We have always been against rebellion."

Eisenhower's reelection on November 6, 1956 was made even easier by Suez and its display of international American muscle inappropriate to apply to Hungary. Moscow was implicitly conceded its free hand east of the Iron Curtain, and the satellite nations descended further into an Orwellian twilight of subjection and stagnation. Hungary waited another thirty-three years for its freedom.

With the advent of the first Eisenhower administration, MacArthur learned that Harry Truman had signed to write his memoirs. With little but his government pension to live on, Truman needed the income and wanted to put his own stamp on his presidential years. He expected a MacArthur "blow-up" when it appeared, Truman told a newsman, because "when an egoist is punctured, a lot of noise and whistling always accompanies the escaping air." Certain of attack, MacArthur planned a pre-emptive strike, but honor required that his name not be attached to it. Rather, he threw his courtiers, Charles Willoughby and Courtney Whitney, into battle. Willoughby was signed by Henry Luce's Time-Life Inc. and through his easy access to MacArthur began an account that was more admiring than accurate. Yet his pace was so slow that journalist John Chamberlain was hired by McGraw-Hill to make a book of it, which he did by historical abbreviation—opening with the Japanese subjection of the Philippines and closing with MacArthur's return from Japan.

Willoughby's *MacArthur, 1941–1951* had its greatest success in being appropriated from by Whitney for what was labeled as his biography of his boss. A memo writer over his career with MacArthur, he had never produced an extensive narrative. To get him going, MacArthur dictated paragraph after paragraph of self-serving recollections in the third person, some of it willfully inaccurate, some of it bolstered by documents often altered by omissions. Since the work would have MacArthur's imprimatur, Henry Luce loyally bought the serial rights for Time-Life, and Alfred Knopf the book rights. But it took Luce's staff, drawing substantially from Willoughby's effusive book, to stitch the text into coherence, which was not easy as MacArthur spurned corrections to his spin of events. With a florid title suggesting its sponsor, it became *MacArthur: His Rendezvous with History*. However flawed in details and without competition, it stood from 1955 until 1978 as the standard one-volume life.

Toward the close of Eisenhower's second term, as MacArthur approached eighty, he proceeded to write his own memoirs. He knew the task would not be onerous, as he could adapt his own words from the books of his courtiers and turn them back into the first person. "His" became "my" and "he" became "I." With renewed loyalty, Henry Luce paid $900,000 for the rights, then a huge sum. Most important for MacArthur's ego, it was more than Eisenhower had received for *Crusade in Europe*.

Marshall's last taped interview was on April 11, 1957, at Pinehurst. The exchange began with the 1917–18 war and its close. Forrest Pogue followed up by asking about what lessons the general had learned in 1918–19 that influenced his actions in World War II. "The big thing," said Marshall, was "the urgent necessity of frequent [theater] visits." Was he indirectly regretting that, in order to bolster Eisenhower against Churchillian domination, he had made only one flying visit to MacArthur's expanse, leaving him free to run his private war?

MacArthur came up for the last time when Pogue asked about something that a reporter who had published a fulsome pseudo–campaign biography of the general in 1944 had written. With "a note of asperity," Marshall said, "Well, Frazier Hunt knows a lot more than I do." And Marshall went on about drafting a Medal of Honor citation for MacArthur, and what "damn nonsense" it was for writers to claim that he had been "hostile" to MacArthur during the war, and after. "I did everything in the world I could for him. . . . It was a hard job to do to have MacArthur put in command in Japan, because the navy wanted to control that and they put up quite a battle. . . . But we managed to control it for MacArthur."

When the tape ran out, Marshall was talking about the postwar years. "I thought the disintegration [of the armed services] in '46 and '47 was the most amazing thing. I was out of the country most of the time in China, and I didn't realize how complete it was till I went over as secretary of defense and I just found literally nothing." He offered to continue recording in May, on returning to Leesburg, but the interviews were never resumed. Marshall was failing. In August 1958, he was back at Walter Reed, from which he thanked Eisenhower for the "gracious gesture" of making available the suite always reserved for the president. After minor surgery for a cyst on his eye, Marshall fell in his hospital room and fractured a rib. Recovering at Pinehurst a few weeks later, he was considered so fragile that medical corpsmen from nearby Fort Bragg were assigned round the clock outside his bedroom.

By Christmas he seemed improved, but early in 1959 a medic on hallway duty heard sounds of strangling. Marshall had suffered a crippling stroke. An ambulance rushed him to Fort Bragg, where he remained until he could be moved to Walter Reed on March 11. The presidential suite was occupied then by John Foster Dulles, whose colon cancer had returned and would be fatal in a few months. Dulles offered to switch rooms with Marshall, who declined. Katherine remained nearby at a cottage on the hospital grounds.

From Athens, Queen Frederika cabled, "ALL MY THOUGHTS AND BEST WISHES ARE WITH YOU CONSTANTLY. A VERY SPEEDY RECOVERY. FREDERIKA R." There would be no recovery. Marshall sat occasionally in a wheelchair and for a time could receive visitors. When beyond writing, he dictated messages to his last aide, Colonel C. J. George. One note, to General Charles Herron, recalled a Christmas when they were both young officers. To General Harold Bull, who had been with Eisenhower in France, he reminisced amiably about their times at Fort Benning. Retired Master Sergeant James W. Powder came up from Florida to see him, and as they chatted Marshall confided from bed, "I slipped and broke a couple of ribs, and I don't want Mrs. Marshall to know."

"I ain't going to tell her," said his wartime factotum.

"I just wanted to warn you," Marshall said. "I know you wouldn't, but it might come out."

When Powder arose, Marshall asked if he was in a hurry to leave. "Are you tired of looking at me?"

"No, sir," said Powder, "I don't want to tire you. Besides, there are others out there waiting to see you."

"Those are people who come and go," said Marshall. "They don't have anything in common, like you and I have." Powder stayed until Marshall dozed off, then stole away.

Not long after, Marshall had two further strokes, and when the city of Aachen awarded him its International Charlemagne Prize that summer, he could only gaze quietly as the ceremony was conducted in his hospital room without his comprehending what was going on. When Churchill was at the White House, and MacArthur to his certain surprise was invited for dinner to meet him, Churchill and Eisenhower looked in afterward on both Dulles and Marshall. The general did not know who the plump old man with the unlit cigar was, nor his ruddy, bald companion.* Churchill left in tears. Eisenhower told Tom Handy, "I'd hate like hell to be in the shape General Marshall is."

An old friend and physician, Major General Morrison Stayer, who had been with Marshall at Benning, drove down regularly from retirement in Carlisle, Pennsylvania, finally acknowledging, "I can't come down any more. He is paying the price of a strong physical constitution." General Richard Sutherland, MacArthur's estranged former deputy, to whom Marshall had radioed to Corregidor about the Medal of Honor citation, came confessing to an aide that he respected the general above anyone else. Taken aback by Marshall's lingering helplessly in a tangle of wires and tubes, Sutherland left, cursing to himself at the "indignity." Marshall was beyond sight, hearing, and speech.

When the general's vital signs ceased on October 16, 1959, Harry Truman, learning the news, said, "He was the greatest of the great in my time. I sincerely hope that when it comes to my time to cross the great river, Marshall will place me on his staff, so that I may try to do for him what he did for me."

Although an old hand at state funerals, including those of Roosevelt and Pershing, Marshall in 1956 had prepared very different instructions for his own obsequies. He wanted no eulogies, no lying in state, no panoply, and a private interment. He drew up a short list of honorary pallbearers, to include Sergeant Powder and the general's postwar orderly, Sergeant William Heffner. He also listed C. J. George (his last aide), Frank McCarthy and Robert Lovett, Beetle Smith and Ambassador

---

*Eisenhower would look in three times, but each time Marshall failed to recognize him.

James Bruce. Among the invitees he proposed was his longtime Pentagon barber, Joseph Abbate. Sergeant Richard C. Wing, a cook at Fort Myer who became Marshall's orderly during the mission to China, also asked Colonel George if he could be at the general's side, as did retired sergeant John Semanko, who was with Marshall when, at Fort Myer, he first learned about Pearl Harbor.

The pallbearers gathered in Marshall's Pentagon office on the morning of October 20, after the coffin had rested, unopened, in the Bethlehem Chapel of the National Cathedral and they accompanied it to the brief service at the Fort Myer chapel. In the front pew were Mrs. Marshall, her daughter and family, and Allen Brown's widow and son. Also Harry Truman, with the omnipresent General Vaughan. Once they were seated, Dwight Eisenhower arrived with two aides, and greeted Truman with "How do you do, Mr. President?"

"How are you, Mr. President?" Truman returned, and they shook hands. They had nothing further to say to each other until the ceremonies were over, and then each said, "Goodbye, Mr. President." The animosities of 1952 had not faded.

Marshall had wanted no public formalities. An undertaker's limousine took the casket to Arlington, where, down the hill from the Tomb of the Unknown Soldier, a bugler in an honor guard played taps. The low-key ceremonies were in character. Marshall, who always eschewed fuss, would have been seventy-nine in December.

Not present, and uninvited, was Douglas MacArthur, in 1959 in his eightieth year. He was still penning his memoirs—a slow task by a non-typist although he was exploiting his earlier dictation to Willoughby and Whitney. Writing as always on legal-size yellow ruled pads, he had found a project to keep him busy without his having to emerge from the Waldorf Towers.

The general's birthday party at the Waldorf was organized and paid for by Jack Sverdrup, his deputy chief engineer in the Pacific and now a millionaire businessman. MacArthur's health was failing. Some of his circle thought the birthday might be his last. Eisenhower sent an awkward message, with his "warm personal regard," that the event "brings to all our people a renewed feeling of gratitude for your dedicated services to our common country." Other than aged Herbert Hoover, the guests were all

ex-military. The next day, MacArthur was rushed to St. Luke's Hospital
for prostate surgery. It took him a year to recover, but he stubbornly did.

Eisenhower had been ill yet again, with a stroke late in 1957. He briefly
lost control of speech function, and the nation seemed rudderless when it
emerged that Nixon and Dulles were again quarreling over temporary
presidential powers neither would employ. Recovery may have been assisted by Eisenhower's knowledge of the imbroglio, but before Dulles's
final illness early in 1959, after six years in office, White House secretary
Ann Whitman was complaining in her diary that "the State Department
[Dulles, obviously] regards the President as its chattel."

Although coping with the cumbersome executive branch of government was difficult for a weakened president, once his rather authoritarian
original Cabinet secretaries began to depart he appeared more in control
of policy, foreign and domestic. His strong farewell address on January 17,
1961, written in his own longhand, with scratched-out phrases, may have
made the nationwide radio and television audience forget gossip about his
golfing away his presidency while others ran the country. Although the
ongoing Cold War, Eisenhower declared, seemed of "indefinite duration,"
and the maintenance of freedom was costly, he warned presciently—but,
it turned out, with futility—about the dangers of a "military-industrial
complex" that could tilt the nation toward "misplaced power" and military
adventurism.

When Richard Nixon was anointed predictably in 1960 as the next Republican presidential candidate and another young veteran of World War
II became his Democratic opponent, a generational shift loomed. Eisenhower's support of his vice president appeared more nominal than zeal-
ous, and after a tight election, John Fitzgerald Kennedy, a junior senator
as Nixon had been, claimed the White House. The new president had
been seriously injured in August 1943 in MacArthur's Southwest Pacific
domain when the PT boat he commanded was rammed and sunk by a
Japanese destroyer. Before being invalided out of the war, Kennedy had
written to his parents, great admirers of the general, that MacArthur was

"very, very unpopular. His nick-name is Dug-out-Doug. . . . He sat out in his dug-out in Australia." Young Kennedy had no idea then that the epithet dated back to Bataan.

Since MacArthur nevertheless was a living icon, the new president paid a courtesy call to the general's bedside. They talked about Communist inroads in East Asia, and MacArthur warned about the errors of Kennedy's predecessors, "All the chickens are coming home to roost and you are living in the coop." Kennedy would visit a second time, after which MacArthur received his only official assignment following his relief in 1951. (Eisenhower had ignored him.) A jurisdictional feud between the two major amateur athletic associations, the AAU and the NCAA, was jeopardizing the eligibility of potential Olympic participants for 1964, and Attorney General Robert. F. Kennedy asked West Point football coach "Red" Blaik to recommend a mediator. Blaik suggested his old friend MacArthur, and the groups, under White House pressure, agreed to the negotiations. In the general's Waldorf suite, with Whitney and Blaik also in attendance, the dispute was settled.

By July 1961, MacArthur seemed marginally up to a return to Manila for the fifteenth anniversary of national independence. His presence—he was considered the savior of the republic—was the occasion for a special holiday in the Philippines. Although he was less well early in 1962 when he accepted West Point's Sylvanus Thayer Award, he had been determined to make the rather brief trip because the distinction had gone to Eisenhower the year before. A painful gall bladder condition had left MacArthur gaunt, fragile, and jaundiced, but he resisted surgery, assuming that at his age and state of health, he would not survive the knife. He insisted to Jean that he would go to the Academy "if I have to crawl there on my hands and knees."

In brilliant sunlight on May 12, 1962, hawklike, waxy, and shrunken, and in dark mufti and fedora, MacArthur stood before the awed Corps of Cadets. Only a miniature medal pin in his lapel remained of his rows of ribbons, but he was his country's military history personified, and his magnetic voice, however wan, was amplified waveringly by microphone. At eighty-three and failing, he had little new to say, and had assembled, from characteristically orotund passages he had employed before, much of what would be his last public address. In his memory he was reliving not 1941–51, but 1899–1903 and 1917–18. "I listen vainly," he closed, mixing his metaphors, "but with thirsty ear, for the witching melody of faint bugles blowing reveille, of far drums beating the long roll. In my dreams I hear again the crash of guns, the rattle of musketry, the strange mournful mutter of the battlefield. But in the evening of my life, I always come back to West Point. Always there echoes and re-echoes in my ears—Duty, Honor, Country. Today marks my final roll call with you. But I want you to know that when I cross the river my last conscious thought will be of the Corps . . . and the Corps . . . and the Corps. I bid you farewell."

He was nearly finished, then, with his vivid, self-justifying, and sometimes imaginative *Reminiscences*, written with hardly an erasure. His propensity to fictionalize would be as obvious as his borrowings from himself via Willoughby and Whitney. On the day he was relieved by Truman, April 11, 1951, Whitney—or his master—had observed that the sun rose "upon this land of the chrysanthemum with its deep shadows and brilliant hues . . ." (Yet it rained heavily that morning.) On April 16, the day that MacArthur left Japan, he recalled in his imaginative *Reminiscences*, "We took off as the sun rose. . . . Beneath us lay this land of the chrysanthemum with its deep shadows and brilliant hues." John Chamberlain would quip, "MacArthur is the only ghost who ever ghosted for some unadmitted ghosts."

When Whitney delivered the 220,000-word manuscript to *Life* in April 1963, he claimed that he had been unaware until then that MacArthur had been working on it. It would have been difficult for Whitney, who saw MacArthur nearly every day, not to have known of the project, unless the general was concealing the manuscript under his bed. With more than his earlier dictation to Whitney at hand, MacArthur had employed, selectively, what survived of his correspondence and what copy he had furnished to Willoughby; and he also made use of his quotes to effusive wartime biographers. He wrote of "my forces," and "my plan," of how he never made a mistake, and how he was beset, over a lifetime, by unnamed enemies, small men, and governments infiltrated by Communists. As for the commander in chief who directed his relief, and who understood humbly that he was an ordinary person in an extraordinary time, MacArthur wrote, "Among President Truman's many weaknesses was his inability to discriminate between history and histrionics."

MacArthur was also pleased that Field Marshal Earl Montgomery, who had visited him in New York, and his compatriot Field Marshal Viscount Alanbrooke, lauded him as the most able American wartime commander. One knew nothing of the Pacific war and the other very little, and both disliked Marshall and abhorred Eisenhower. Monty had asked through Freddy de Guingand whether Ike would be his host in the States, and Eisenhower replied, "It would likely be bad judgment, at this particular time, for Monty to make any attempt to visit me."

Montgomery "would scarcely stand much chance of going down in history as one of the great British captains," Eisenhower wrote to Lord Ismay, detailing Monty's sluggishness in Sicily and then Italy; his failure to capture Caen and lies about the Normandy breakout, which Monty owed to Patton and Bradley; and the catastrophe at Arnhem "even after I had promised and given to him everything he requested." Even worse was the "preposterous proposal to drive on a single pencil-line thrust straight through to Berlin."

By early 1964, there was again a new president. John Kennedy had been assassinated in Dallas in November 1963. Pale and drawn at a reunion birthday dinner of his "Bataan Gang" at the Waldorf on January 26, 1964, MacArthur looked wraithlike. Learning at the White House late in February about MacArthur's alarmingly worsening health, Lyndon Johnson asked the army surgeon general, Leonard Heaton (who as a young physician had been on emergency duty at Schofield Barracks Hospital in Honolulu on December 7, 1941), to look in urgently on the general. When Heaton recommended immediate surgery, President Johnson ordered a plane to La Guardia Airport to fly MacArthur (who had reluctantly assented) to Walter Reed. He was hospitalized for four weeks. Johnson visited and was offered advice on foreign policy.

Although MacArthur's gall bladder was removed, along with gallstones and other internal obstructions that had exacerbated his misery, he was eighty-four, and past recovery. A second operation was necessary to stanch severe bleeding. Then a third. He died on April 5, 1964.

On Monday afternoon, April 6, at the Seventh Regiment Armory at Park Avenue and 66th Street in Manhattan, a military funeral proceeded according to MacArthur's instructions, which directed that he was to be interred in his trademark faded suntans. The next day his flag-draped coffin was drawn to Pennsylvania Station by six Fort Myer horses in a caisson used for VIP funerals—not long before for John Kennedy. The traditional riderless horse with reversed boots in its stirrups symbolizing the fallen warrior followed. The Military Academy band with the Corps of Cadets came next, and finally an honor guard of generals and admirals.

In Washington, MacArthur lay in state in the Capitol Rotunda. Only months before, Defense Department officials revising rites for state funerals had asked diplomatically whether MacArthur would want one, and noted that four days would be set aside for the Rotunda bier. He requested seven days for himself. Military ceremony according to the new formula stipulated a closed casket, but Whitney insisted that MacArthur would have wanted it open.

The general's coffin was then flown to the Naval Air Station in Norfolk, Virginia, from which it was taken to the venerable former city courthouse, which MacArthur had permitted the city fathers to rededicate that January as a memorial and museum. Crypts were ready under its imposing dome for the general and, in time, for Jean.*

At MacArthur's death, new controversies erupted. Two near-legendary newsmen, from the Hearst and the Scripps-Howard press, released interviews withheld for a decade. Bob Considine, an Overseas Press Club awardee, reported that MacArthur claimed that British "perfidy" had undermined him in Korea by relaying his plans to the Chinese Communists, that Truman was a "little bastard [who] honestly believes he is a patriot," and that Eisenhower, "once a man of integrity," was "naive" and "does not want to offend anyone." In Washington, timid "fools" had failed to support him. Jim Lucas, who won a Pulitzer Prize for Korean War reporting, had also interviewed MacArthur in January 1954. In his memorandum, Truman and Eisenhower were excoriated in similar terms, and General Ridgway was dismissed as a "chameleon" who had performed "poorly." Ridgway's successors, John E. Hull and Maxwell Taylor, both once deputies to Marshall, were treated with even more contempt. Courtney Whitney, who claimed that he was present at both interviews, called the derogatory comments "fictional nonsense." Editors for Considine and Lucas stood by the stories. From Viet Nam, Lucas commented, "General Whitney's a liar."

The last prepublication installment of MacArthur's *Reminiscences* would appear in *Life* on July 24, 1964, and included a postscript about the radioactive barrier, rejected by Eisenhower, which MacArthur had proposed for ending the Korean War. When the lines appeared in the book version by McGraw-Hill (which had published Whitney) in September, six additional pages followed that were not in the proofs sent to reviewers. They described political and economic views far to the right of MacArthur's declared principles and practice, certainly at odds with the Japanese Constitution he had sponsored at perhaps the pinnacle of his long career. If his last words were not his own, he was beyond disavowing them.

---

*Jean Faircloth MacArthur died at 101 on January 22, 2000.

There the intersected lives end. Only the youngest, Dwight Eisenhower, remained, now a gentleman farmer looking over his pedigreed cattle at his splendid Gettysburg spread, and dabbling on his personal putting green until complications accruing from his abdominal surgery in 1956 intervened. As he would write in his own gossipy reminiscences (1967) two years before his death,* he was, in more than the military terms of its title, *At Ease.*

---

*On March 28, 1969.

Afterword:
Opportunity, Celebrity, Personality

Men at some time are masters of their fates:
The fault, dear Brutus, is not in our stars,
But in ourselves. . . .

F ROM 1918 ONWARD, when George Marshall vanished into two decades of obscurity and Dwight
Eisenhower was still an unknown junior officer
hoping to survive in a shrunken postwar army, Douglas MacArthur was
already a celebrity. A dashing wartime hero and the youngest wartime
general, he achieved further visibility as superintendent of West Point,
then as husband of an immensely wealthy socialite, and finally, in the early
1930s, as the youngest chief of staff. He even saw a future beyond the military, in national politics. FDR would classify him, on a par with Huey
Long, as one of the most dangerous men in America. As the reelection
candidacy of Herbert Hoover gained momentum in 1932, MacArthur
even thought that he might be the Republican vice presidential nominee,
to add glamour to Herbert Hoover's ticket.

When such hopes failed to materialize, and Hoover then sank from
sight, MacArthur rejected domestic subservience following his tenure as
chief of staff. Not willing to be second to anyone, he relocated nine thousand miles westward to head an infant army in the Philippines. Celebrity
faded—until the Japanese attacked and he commanded the only American troops in actual combat with the enemy. Opportunity then reappeared, and with his public relations skills, he made the most of the bad
hand he had dealt himself. Despite multiple miscalculations and defeats
early on, he promoted himself into the most famous military figure in
America—without being anywhere near America.

Marshall doggedly pursued his seemingly impossible goals: to rise to
the general's rank denied him by the armistice in 1918, to stave off aging

into mandatory retirement, and to become chief of staff himself. When he became the nation's first soldier in 1939, literally on the first day of World War II in Europe, his ramrod integrity was already the president's lifeline to a Congress still inhibited by Depression and isolationism. There might have been no peacetime draft, or its extension, without Marshall's intervention, and far less momentum in mobilizing for an inevitable role in the war. As Franklin Roosevelt began pursuing an extraordinary third term in 1940, some politicians reluctant to break precedent proposed Marshall as an alternative candidate, and did so again in 1944. Marshall quietly headed off such intrusions into his future, insisting he had no political loyalties. Neither Republican nor Democrat, he became, paradoxically, closer to achieving the presidency than MacArthur ever would. During the first Harry Truman term, the vice presidency was vacant, and until the succession law was amended, Marshall as secretary of state (replacing James F. Byrnes) was next in line for the White House.

Beyond party, Marshall was a persuasive speaker to governors, journalists, and public service groups, even to jaded university audiences. It was at Harvard that he proposed the crucial Cold War "Marshall Plan" he would never identify with himself, but for which he—paradoxically as a general—earned the Nobel Prize for Peace. Never having attended a political rally, he would have been uncomfortable at one, and rejected any idea of elective anything. Whatever his platform skills, running for office was not his style. In Marshall, opportunity and celebrity were trumped by a rigid personality. What he radiated was an off-putting integrity.

Winston Churchill saw Marshall, in his military role which he sweepingly enlarged to global dimensions, as the "organizer of Victory." He could have exchanged his realm in Washington for the command of "Overlord," the D-Day landing and its aftermath that was the greatest combined military operation in history. The opportunity could have made him whatever he wanted to be afterward. It might have brought him back to Washington—not to the Pentagon, but to the White House. Although "Overlord" was Marshall's for the asking, and most of the top civilian and military guns wanted him to take it, he refused to promote himself. The appointment went elsewhere and would make Eisenhower.

At a summit conference in 1943 planning the future of the worldwide war, had MacArthur flown in dramatically to press his own strategic plans, he might have, by force of personality, found himself delegated to command "Overlord" the next year—and the immense celebrity which D-Day would gain for its Supreme Commander. Rather than argue, in person, for his own theater of operations, and never conceiving a possibility for himself in Europe then, he sent a deputy disliked by everyone. MacArthur would not be a supplicant for anything, and the mountain would not come to Mohammed. "Overlord" went to his prewar clerk and assistant.

As postwar viceroy of Japan, and one of the most famous men in the world, MacArthur rejected entreaties to return to the U.S. for parades in his honor, as other military celebrities coming home from overseas had enjoyed. Former president Hoover envisioned such populist circuses as propelling MacArthur inevitably to the presidency. In an excess of hubris MacArthur wanted to be recalled by acclamation—by being drafted from afar as Republican presidential candidate in 1948. It did not happen. He was too remote from politics, and had not been "home"—where in reality he had no home—since 1937. In 1952, he might have headed off Eisenhower by allying himself with Robert Taft as the ticket's vice presidential candidate, and if elected, becoming president when Taft died shortly after. It was also not to be.

Only one of the three generals whose careers intersect here would gain the White House. Eisenhower exploited the openings thrust upon him by his senior mentors. His celebrity was the product of opportunity, but his compelling personality converted celebrity into the presidency. At fifty, before Pearl Harbor, Eisenhower would have considered himself fortunate to earn a single star. In just three years he had four more.

Although Eisenhower, in wartime, might have been derailed by rumor, potential crises were plowed under by Marshall, who would not abandon the intended successor whose career he had groomed. Even when aspiring himself for the ultimate prize of the presidency, MacArthur could not covertly eliminate his younger nemesis, now his five-star equal.

"The nature of history," writes László Jakab Orsós, ". . . is no more than a chain of stories and lives, all interwoven, often in the most unexpected ways." Opportunity passed by becomes opportunity past retrieval. MacArthur penned his claims and his cavils into his memoirs. Marshall, in character, wrote none, and mulched his garden. Only Eisenhower closed his career at 1600 Pennsylvania Avenue.

Source Notes

Preface: Intersected Lives

MacArthur, Marshall, and Eisenhower were portrayed in wartime on the covers of *Time* on December 29, 1941; January 3, 1944; and January 1, 1945. Marshall appeared again on January 5, 1948, and Eisenhower in 1959. All three appeared on postage stamps, posthumously. The first was MacArthur, on a six-cent stamp in 1964; Eisenhower followed on a six-cent stamp in 1970; then Marshall, on a twenty-cent stamp in 1976. Details only sketched out in this preface appear more fully in later chapters, where they are described more completely. Many sources are identified in the narrative itself.

Substantial documentary archives exist for all three principals. The Eisenhower Presidential Library is in Abilene, Kansas. The Marshall Library is on the VMI campus in Lexington, Virginia. The MacArthur Memorial and Archive is in Norfolk, Virginia. No scholarly edition of MacArthur's letters exists, but many not quoted in biographies survive in originals or copies at the MacArthur Archive, or appear in exchanges with General Marshall published in his papers. Very few surface in the Eisenhower collections. The key source for MacArthur in print, although now dated by subsequent scholarship, remains D. Clayton James's three-volume *The Years of MacArthur, 1880–1941* (Boston, 1970), *1941–1945* (Boston, 1975), and *1945–1964* (Boston, 1985). James's interviews and working papers, a mine of additional information, are in the MacArthur Archive in Norfolk.

The multivolume *Papers of Dwight David Eisenhower*, edited by Alfred D. Chandler and his successors and associates, began to appear via Johns Hopkins University Press in 1970 and reaches to the end of his presidency. The 21 volumes (1970–2001) are now digitized, with index and rudimentary search engine. *The Papers of George Catlett Marshall*, edited by Larry I. Bland and Sharon Ritenour Stevens, began via Johns Hopkins University Press in 1981 and also now approaches completion. All these volumes are utilized throughout. The most complete biography, although with some reticences, is Forrest Pogue's three-volume *George C. Marshall* (New York, 1963, 1966, 1973). Also referred to throughout is Leonard Mosley's *Marshall* (see below, chapter 4), which includes documentation unavailable to or unused by Pogue. Letters and papers from other sources are cited where they appear.

1. "Our Tails Are in the Air"

Eisenhower's role in anticipating war mobilization, and the descriptions of prewar unpreparedness, are from Kerry E. Irish, "Apt Pupil: Dwight Eisenhower and the 1930 Industrial Mobilization Plan," *The Journal of Military History*, 70 (January 2006). The Louisiana maneuvers are fully detailed in G. Patrick Murray, "The Louisiana Maneuvers: Practice for War," *Louisiana History*, 13 (1972).

Eisenhower's diaries, extracted from his papers in a volume by Robert Ferrell, also appear chronologically in his published letters. Marshall's reminiscences, when not in his published letters, are from Forrest C. Pogue, ed., *George C. Marshall: Interviews and Reminiscences* (Lexington, Va., 1991), where his memory of Mindoro appears. For the background to December 7, 1941, see S. Weintraub, *Long Day's Journey into War* (New York, 1991 and 2001). Henry Stimson's diary, *On Active Service in Peace and War*, edited by Henry Stimson and McGeorge Bundy (New York, 1947), and Robert Sherwood's *Roosevelt and Hopkins* (New York, 1948, rev. 1950), are both utilized throughout. John J. McCloy's work at the War Department and beyond is chronicled in Kai Bird, *The Chairman: John J. McCloy and the Making of the American Establishment* (New York, 1992). MacArthur's responses and nonresponses to the Japanese attacks are described in *Long Day's Journey* (see above) and in D. Clayton James, *The Years of MacArthur, II* (Boston, 1975).

Louis Morton's "War Plan ORANGE: Evolution of a Strategy," *World Politics*, II (1959) notes the lack of funding by Congress to back it up, and Marshall's charges to Eisenhower to work on war plans for the Pacific, also dealt with in chapter 2. Vice Admiral Greenslade's remark to Earl Warren is in the *Memoirs of Earl Warren* (Garden City, N.Y., 1977). Antonio Quintos was interviewed by SW in Manila; SW also saw for himself the 1898 inscription on the huge surviving mortars on Corregidor.

2. Managing the Shop

The fullest account of the Arcadia Conference is David J. Bercuson and Holger H. Herwig, *One Christmas in Washington* (Woodstock and New York, 2005); also referred to is Lord Moran, *Winston Churchill: The Struggle for Survival, 1940–1965* (London, 1966). Hopkins is quoted from Sherwood (above). Marshall's reminiscences, including the charge to Patrick Hurley, are from his *Interviews* (above). Eisenhower's diary entries are in Ferrell and in the Eisenhower *Papers*, referred to throughout. For McCloy, see above. The late E. Willard Miller, a civilian geographer assigned to the War Department, told SW about the minimal prewar geographical intelligence on file about Japan and the Pacific. Wainwright and Townsend are quoted from James's *Years of MacArthur*. The British embassy reports to the Foreign Office in London were made by Isaiah Berlin, and collected in H. G. Nicholas, ed., *Washington Despatches 1941–1945* (Chicago, 1981). That Marshall did not bypass Stimson on strategy as FDR suggested is noted by Pogue in his biography of Marshall.

Idaho attorney general Bert Miller's racist remark to Eisenhower about Japanese "relocation" is quoted by Ed Cray in his *Chief Justice: A Biography of Earl Warren* (New York, 1977).

3. Sea Changes

For MacArthur's *Reminiscences,* see text in, and notes to, chapter 18. For his evacuation from the Philippines, see James; also Geoffrey Perret, *Old Soldiers Never Die: The Life of Douglas MacArthur* (New York, 1996). The cargo of the *Don Esteban,* including MacArthur's and Sutherland's automobiles, is described in the diary of Lewis Beebe for December 24, 1941, in John M. Beebe, ed., *Prisoner of the Rising Sun: The Lost Diary of Lewis Beebe* (College Station, Texas, 2006). The bitter prison camp memorandum by William E. Bougher is in his diary, edited by D. Clayton James, *South to Bataan, North to Mukden: The Prison Diary of Brigadier General W. E. Bougher* (Athens, Ga., 1971). The award of the Medal of Honor to MacArthur is best described in the Marshall *Interviews.* For Hopkins, see Sherwood, above. Alan Brooke's diaries are Alex Danchev and Daniel Todman, eds., *War Diaries, 1939–1945: Field Marshall Lord Alanbrooke* (London, 2001). All references to Brooke are from this edition. The earlier version, edited by Arthur Bryant (London, 1957, 1959), is unreliable.

Kay Summersby's two memoirs, the second published after Eisenhower's death, are *Eisenhower Was My Boss* (New York, 1948) and (as Kay Summersby Morgan) *Past Forgetting: My Love Affair with Dwight D. Eisenhower* (New York, 1976). For further citations on the relationship, see later chapter notes, especially chapter 9.

The definitive biography of FDR is Conrad Black, *Franklin Delano Roosevelt: Champion of Freedom* (New York, 2003). Marshall's comment about FDR to Mrs. Churchill is quoted by her in a letter to her husband, December 24, 1947, in Mary Soames, ed., *Winston and Clementine: The Personal Letters of the Churchills* (Boston and New York, 1999). MacArthur's unrecovered letter from Roosevelt, and MacArthur's reference to it in a similarly lost letter to Eisenhower, are recalled by John Eisenhower in *General Ike* (New York, 2003), and in his follow-up letter to SW, July 17, 2004. FDR's comment to Beaverbrook about the rarity of his handwritten presidential letters is in *Christmas in Washington* (see above).

4. Dreaming of Commands

Quezon's offers of bonuses to MacArthur and lesser fry on his staff through to Eisenhower was first revealed by Carol Petillo in *Douglas MacArthur: The Philippine Years* (Bloomington, Ind. 1981). Eisenhower's exchanges with Marshall about it are in both the Marshall and Eisenhower papers, above. Eisenhower's years with MacArthur in Washington and Manila are recounted in the Eisenhower papers, John Eisenhower's *General Ike,* Perret's *Old Soldiers Never Die,* and other major biographies, including that by Clayton James.

Entire books deal with the Bonus Army fiasco, most recently Paul Dickson and Thomas B. Allen, *The Bonus Army: An American Epic* (New York, 2005). None are kind to MacArthur. His melodramatic and empty suicide threat to T. J. Davis is described in the introduction to Joseph C. Goulden's *Korea: The Unknown Story of the War* (New York, 1982). The effort of the Frieder brothers from the Philippines to relocate refugee German Jews is told, beyond the Eisenhower diaries, in Joseph Berger, "A Filipino-American Effort to Harbor Jews is Honored," *New York Times,* February 14, 2005.

Marshall's Great War experience is recalled in his papers and interviews as well as in a posthumously published memoir, *Memories of My Services in the World War 1917–18* (Boston, 1976). It was found after his death by his stepdaughter, Molly Winn. Barringer Crater was located for me (Mrs. Marshall recalled it wrong in *Together: Annals of an Army Wife,* Atlanta, 1946), and described in a letter from David Weintraub, November 3, 2004. Katherine Marshall's letter to FDR on her husband's appointment is in the Marshall *Papers* (above); I. Marshall's long slog up from postwar cutbacks is detailed in Pogue, *George C. Marshall: I. Education of a General 1880–1939* (1969), and Leonard Mosley, *Marshall: A Hero for Our Times* (New York, 1982). Hopkins's comment about assisting relations between Marshall and FDR is in James Leutze, ed., *The London Journal of General Raymond E. Lee* (Boston, 1971). For much more on Hopkins and Marshall, see Sherwood (above).

John Eisenhower recalls his father's final year with MacArthur in Philippines in *General Ike* (above).

5. Counterparts

Marshall's postwar upward climb, continued from chapter 4, is described in the Marshall *Interviews,* in Pogue, I, and in Mosley, and in the Marshall papers. His accommodation to marriage with Lily is in Mosley, both text and source notes. Eisenhower's relations with Conner and Rickenbach are best detailed in Jerome H. Parker IV's "Fox Conner and Dwight Eisenhower: Mentoring and Application," *Military Review,* July–August 2005. (Elsewhere, Conner is often misspelled as Connor.) Eisenhower's return to the U.S. is described in his *Papers,* in his *At Ease: Stories I Tell My Friends* (New York, 1967), and in John Eisenhower's *General Ike.*

For Churchill during the later war years, when the U.S. was a combatant, see Martin Gilbert, *Winston Churchill: VII, Road to Victory 1941–1945* (Boston, 1986). For Churchill's alteration and rewriting of his history and his wartime role, noted throughout these pages, see David Reynolds, *In Command of History: Churchill Fighting and Writing the Second World War* (New York, 2005). Brooke is quoted from his *Diaries* (above). FDR is quoted from Conrad Black and from Robert Sherwood (both above). Marshall's Great War experience is from Weintraub, *A Silence Heard Round the World* (New York, 1985), and from Pogue. MacArthur's Great War experience is largely from James and from Perret. Wilmot's experience with MacArthur in Australia and New Guinea, including the Tubby Allen episode, is from *Chester Wilmot Reports: Broadcasts That Shaped World War II,* edited by Neil McDonald (Sydney, 2001). Eisenhower's outburst to Bedell Smith about "fifty MacArthurs" is recorded in his office diary for October 5, 1942, in *Papers.*

6. Turning to Offense

For more on MacArthur and the Australians, see Wilmot, above, and the Marshall *Papers,* where, also, the exchanges with MacArthur appear. Also see Jack Gallaway's *The Odd Couple: Blamey and MacArthur at War* (St. Lucia, Queensland, 2000), an Australian perspective. Eddie Rickenbacker's memoir, in which he recognizes Wiedenfeld-Willoughby, is *Rickenbacker* (Englewood Cliffs, N.J., 1968). A more detailed biography based upon his unpublished 8,000-page *Life Story of Edward V. Rickenbacker* is in the Ohio State University Library. There his secret mission to MacArthur for Stimson is documented. The manuscript is the basis for Finis Farr's *Rickenbacker's Luck: An American Life* (Boston, 1979) and W. David Lewis's *Eddie Rickenbacker: An American Hero in the Twentieth Century* (Baltimore, 2005).

Marshall on Edward Martin of Pennsylvania is from the Pogue *Interviews.* FDR's note to Marshall, "You win again," is quoted by Katherine Marshall in her *Together: Annals of an Army Wife.* Patton's diary entry on the abortive dinner with Marshall in Casablanca is in Martin Blumenson, ed., *The Patton Papers, II* (Boston, 1974). Douglas Porch's comprehensive *Hitler's Mediterranean Gamble: The North African and Mediterranean Campaigns in World War II* (London, 2004) is the source for Marshall's personnel arithmetic for "Torch," the reference to Ike's "charmed life," and Fredendall's "hurting a Kraut." Marshall's and Eisenhower's *Papers* detail much of the North African campaign. Butcher's memoir concedes that the Americans "stand humiliated" after Kasserine. Brooke's diary quotes Montgomery's appraisal of the ragged American performance in Tunisia.

Reynolds, in his *In Command of History,* quotes Churchill on Eisenhower's "horrible bad temper" because Mrs. Summersby had not been invited to the PM's dinner. He also notes that she never appears in Churchill's memoirs. Reynolds also quotes the devious Macmillan on political strategy in co-opting the Americans.

7. Running a War, and Running for Office

Marshall recalls the LaFollette visit to the Pentagon in his *Interviews.* Brooke is quoted from his *Diaries.* Churchill conceding privately to his wife Marshall's "masterly" planning is from the PM's letters to Clementine (above), this one from May 28, 1943. Marshall's employment of Red Reeder and collaboration with Hap Arnold are from Pogue's *George C. Marshall: Organizer of Victory* (New York, 1973). Pogue himself, in the preface to his service diary, *Pogue's War: Diaries of a WWII Combat Historian* (Lexington, Ky., 2001), writes about Marshall's formation of a team of writers to describe wartime actions to servicemen. W. P. Yarborough's obituary describing his wartime exploits is in the *New York Times,* December 9, 2005. MacArthur's running of his war is drawn from his cables to and from Marshall in *Papers,* and from James and Perret, above. Marshall's heading off Truman on investigating A-bomb development is from *Interviews.*

The Sicily campaign, told mainly from the perspectives of Eisenhower and Marshall, is drawn largely from Eisenhower's and Marshall's *Papers* and their annotations, and from Porch (above). Russian skepticism about a Second Front is from *A Writer at War: Vasily Grossman with the Red Army, 1941–1945,* edited and translated by Anthony Beevor and Luba Vinogradova (New York, 2005). Marshall's public relations speeches are in his *Papers.* Eichelberger's often caustic comments about his relations with MacArthur are from his letters to his wife in Jay Luvaas, ed., *Dear Miss Em* (Westport, Conn., 1972).

Stimson's campaign to make Marshall the commander of "Overlord" is in his diaries (above), in Sherwood (above), and in Pogue (above).

8. The Best Man

Brooke is quoted from his *Diaries.* Marshall is quoted on 1917–18 from a speech in his *Papers.* His communications to Eisenhower are also from his *Papers.* Isaiah Berlin is quoted from his *Despatches* (above). The "Quadrant" Quebec conference is taken from Black, Gilbert (*VII*), and Pogue. Eisenhower's activities and communications are from his *Papers.* Controversies over Marshall's proposed "Overlord" role, including the participation of Hopkins and Stimson, are largely from Sherwood. George VI and Churchill are quoted from communications dated October 14 (the King), October 17, and October 22 (Churchill) from Gilbert (*VII*).

Katherine Marshall writes about her role in *Together* (above). Thomas Parrish in *Roosevelt and Marshall* (New York, 1989) also describes Mrs. Marshall's partial departure from Fort Myer. Marshall's stormy private dinner with Churchill is described in *Interviews.* Kay Summersby's recollection of Cairo with Eisenhower is from her memoir, which includes her Cairo photographs and others related to her boss.

9. Goodenough Island to Grosvenor Square

Marshall's Red Cross Christmas greeting to POWs is in Lewis Beebe's diary (see chapter 3). The "MacArthur will save us" assertion from May 1944 is recalled by the speaker, Horiguchi Itsurō in Frank Gibney, ed., *Senso: The Japanese Remember the Pacific War* (New York, 2000). MacArthur's "Well, you win," to Admiral William Halsey, is from *Admiral Halsey's Story* (New York, 1947).

Japanese ambassador Oshima's conversation with Hitler is found in David Irving's *The War Between Generals* (New York, 1981). Marshall's flight to the Pacific theaters, and later oversight of Italy, are detailed in his *Papers.* The war in Italy is from Porch. Eisenhower's shooting prowess is described by Summersby and Butcher from their proximity to the episode. General Morgan's visit is described by Mrs. Marshall and by Pogue. The praise of Morgan is from *Crusade in Europe.* Marshall's Christmas is from his *Papers.* Churchill's Christmas is from Gilbert (above). Eisenhower's is from his *Papers* and from Carlo d'Este, *Eisenhower: A Soldier's Life* (New York, 2002). Goebbel's boast about the invasion to come is quoted by Victor Klemperer in his diary entry for May 24, 1944, in *I Will Bear Witness* (New York, 1999).

The story of Liddell Hart's report on the "Overlord" beach sites only broke in September 2006, and was reported in *The Times* of London on September 4, 2006. Liddell Hart had shown his paper to Duncan Sandys, Churchill's son-in-law, then a junior minister, who tipped off Ismay.

The Summersby relationship is described by Kay herself, most fully in her second memoir; by Patton in his diaries and letters to his wife in *The Patton Papers* (Boston, 1971); by the diary of Everett Hughes (February 5, 1943, MS. Division, Library of Congress); James Gavin from his memoirs; by Drew Pearson in his *Diaries*, edited by Tyler Abell (New York, 1974); and by David Reynolds in *Rich Relations: The American Occupation of Britain, 1942–1945* (London and New York, 1995). Stephen E. Ambrose in the admiring *Eisenhower, I* (New York, 1983) reports the gossip but explains that "loving Mamie did not necessarily preclude loving Kay" in their special wartime situation. Eisenhower's letter to Mamie, March 2, 1943, denying any "emotional involvements," is in his *Letters to Mamie* (Garden City, N.Y., 1978). Colonel Hobby is quoted from an interview, August 28, 1965, in Pogue's biography. According to FDR's adviser Tom Corcoran, as quoted by Conrad Black (above), the president also "concluded . . . that the general and his chauffeuse were sleeping together." Summersby is circumspectly unmentioned in Pogue's Marshall *Interviews* and (but for Hobby) otherwise largely bypassed by Pogue.

Churchill is quoted from Gilbert, *V* (Boston, 1980), and from Reynolds (on Churchill's war memoirs), as well as by Brooke in his *Diaries*. Eisenhower's reluctant visit to the States, to which he was ordered by Marshall, is described in Pogue, in d'Este, and in the Marshall *Papers*, and by Black. Eisenhower's letters are negative about Devers. His lack of interest in "Ultra" is from F. W. Winterbotham, *The Ultra Secret* (New York, 1974). Chester Wilmot on Marshall is quoted from his notes (15/15/134/1) in the Liddell Hart Archives, University of London. The February 12, 1944, CCS directive is in the Gale papers, Liddell Hart Archives. The loss of Hopkins's son is in Sherwood. The background of Monty's St. Paul's School is detailed, December 11, 2005, in a letter to me from A. H. and Eileen Hanley-Browne.

10. "A Satisfactory Foothold"

"Overlord" is chronicled in hundreds of accounts. The special sources are largely identified in the narrative. Generals Hastings Ismay and Humfrey Gale are quoted from their papers and diary accounts in the Liddell Hart Archives, University of London. Grossman is quoted on Red Army reactions to the Second Front in *A Writer at War*. Eisenhower on Monty's "preposterous proposal to go to Berlin" in September 1944 is from his diary dictation to Ann Whitman, his secretary, on September 10, 1959, in his *Papers*.

The confidential memoranda among officials at the Pentagon about Eisenhower's request to commission Mrs. Summersby are quoted from General

Staff files by Mosley in his *Marshall*. Mosley also quotes T. T. Handy on De Gaulle's desire to arrive in France grandly on a capital ship. Marshall's keeping FDR's consciousness raised on casualties by sending graphic memoranda every few days is from the general's *Interviews*. General Aurand's attempted inspection of the SHAEF supply situation is described by Pogue in his Marshall bio. Pogue's own diary, *Pogue's War* (above), in an entry for January 25, 1945, suggests from the standpoint of a Third Army soldier that Patton may have been deliberately shortchanged in matériel by SHAEF to keep him in his place.

MacArthur's setting foot on Leyte is described for me by radioman Dan L. Laurence in a letter, quoting his "pocket notes" of the day, on January 31, 2005. The MacArthur negotiations with Nimitz over theater boundaries is detailed in Robert S. Burrell, "Breaking the Cycle of Iwo Jima Mythology: A Strategic Study of Operation Detachment," *Journal of Military History,* 68 (October 2004). Robert Leckie in *Delivered from Evil: The Saga of World War II* (New York, 1987), and many others, quote selectively from the FDR-MacArthur conversations in Hawaii. Tom Pitoniak's recollection of the MacArthur and Roosevelt drive-by in Hawaii is from a letter to SW from Thomas Pitoniak Jr., November 26, 2006. George Nakhnikian's recollection of "300%" Hürtgen Forest casualties is from a letter to SW, November 22, 2006. Diller is quoted on the upcoming election in *The Odd Couple* (above).

11. Victory Delayed

Ike's wager with Monty is in the Eisenhower *Papers*. The "three trees a day" is quoted by Hugh M. Cole in *The Ardennes: Battle of the Bulge* (Washington, D.C., 1965, 1972), volume 8 in the subseries *The European Theater of Operations of the United States Army in World War II*. The Hemingway attack on American leadership in the Hürtgen is from *Time,* "Hemingway Is Bitter about Nobody—But His Colonel Is," September 11, 1950. Hemingway was using his fictional colonel in the novel *Across the River and into the Trees*, published that month, to condemn the way the war, just before the Bulge, was being carried out. *Time* had cabled him in Cuba.

Nigel Hamilton, *Monty: The Battles of Field Marshal Bernard Montgomery* (New York, 1997), quotes Major Bigland's reports to Monty. William Desobry's oral history is in the United States Army Military History Institute, Carlisle Barracks, Pa.—hereafter USAMHI. Hitler's plans for the Ardennes offensive are in Ian Kershaw, *Hitler, 1936–1945: Nemesis* (New York, 2000). For Skorzeny, see John Toland, *Battle: The Story of the Bulge* (New York, 1959).

Marshall describes his uneasiness about five-star titles in his *Interviews*. FDR's appeal about using the Bomb against the Germans is from Stimson's diaries (above) and from Robert S. Norris, *Racing for the Bomb* (New York, 2002).

Gavin's memoir is *On to Berlin: Battles of an Airborne Commander* (New York, 1979); Ridgway's is *Soldier: The Memoirs of Matthew B. Ridgway* (New York, 1956). Omar N. Bradley's *A General's Life* (New York, 1983) was ghostwritten by his aide, Chester Hansen, whose notes for the bio are at USAMHI. Noel Annan's memoir-history is *Changing Enemies: The Defeat and Regeneration of Germany* (London, 1989). Bruce Clarke's oral history is in the Truman

Presidential Library, Independence, Mo. The German artillery lieutenant is quoted in Max Hastings, *Armageddon* (London, 2004). Russell Weigley's cavalry metaphor is from his *Eisenhower's Lieutenants* (Bloomington, Ind., 1981). The only correspondent on the scene was Fred Mackenzie, whose *Men of Bastogne* (New York, 1968) is crucial as a comprehensive first-person account, including the "Nuts!" episode.

Brooke is a key source for Montgomery, who regularly communicated with him. Patton's Third Army chaplain, Colonel James O'Neill, wrote about Patton's request for a prayer in "The True Story of the Patton Prayer," *Review of the News*, October 6, 1971. Patton would write to Beatrice after Christmas to note that his prayer had been answered.

Kay Summersby's thank-you letter to Colonel McCarthy, for her WAC lieutenancy (intended for Marshall), is quoted in full in Mosley's *Marshall*.

Edgar Eisenhower's letter of January 11, 1945, to Dwight, responded to by DDE on March 7, is in the Raab Collection, Ardmore, Pennsylvania.

12. Reclaiming the Lost Ground

Marshall on Dill is from Pogue's *Organizer of Victory*. Irène Némirovsky, who died in Birkenau in 1942, is quoted from her posthumously published *Suite Francaise* (New York 2006), translated by Sandra Smith. The Führer's comments to von Below are from Kershaw's *Hitler*. The murder of German POWs by the 11th Armored is described in Peter Schrijvers, *The Unknown Dead: Civilians in the Battle of the Bulge* (Lexington: Ky., 2005), a source earlier (chapter 11) for the atrocities of the Peiper SS unit.

The statistics on Lee's expropriation of Paris hotels are from Ambrose. All of Marshall's recollections are from his *Interviews*. The Yalta and post-Yalta episodes are largely from Pogue's *Marshall*, Mosley's *Marshall*, and Black's *Roosevelt*. Eisenhower is quoted from his *Papers*. His letter to General Harold Bull, June 5, 1951, and explanatory editorial note following, also in *Papers*, deal with the Remagen Bridge controversy. Victor Brombert describes the "Jim Crow" misuse of black troops in his memoir, *Trains of Thought* (New York, 2002). Hundreds of other accounts document the political background of the "Jim Crow" military, including the U.S. Army Center of Military History's own *Black Soldier, White Army*, by W. T. Bowers, W. M. Hammond, and G. L. MacGarrigle (Washington, D.C., 1996), largely about the Korean War but with extensive background on earlier failures to integrate African-American soldiers into combat units.

Eichelberger is quoted from *Dear Miss Em*. MacArthur is quoted from James and Perret, and from his messages to Marshall. Sherwood on visiting MacArthur is quoted from his *Roosevelt and Hopkins*. MacArthur's health and aloofness from doctors is from Perret.

Frank McCarthy on Marshall is quoted from Mosley. Eisenhower's holiday in Cannes is most detailed in Summersby's *Past Forgetting*. Messages on Patton's Hammelburg misadventure and its fallout are in the Marshall *Papers* and the *Patton Papers*. A diary entry in *Patton Papers* describes hearing the BBC broadcast news of FDR's death. In a letter in the Eisenhower *Papers*, February

20, 1952, to Forrest Pogue, Eisenhower explains his decision to stop at the Elbe and not go on to Prague or Berlin as not "political" and "strictly military." He wanted "the best possible positioning of Western Troops in those areas of which political agreements had made no mention."

The little-known operation in April 1946 concluding the German war is described in S. Weintraub, *The Last Great Victory: The End of World War II* (New York, 1995). For *Cartridge Carnival*, see also *The Last Great Victory*. Patton's letter to McCloy on Buchenwald is in Kai Bird, *The Chairman* (above). Kay Summersby describes the signing of the surrender in *Past Forgetting*. Although she was present, she was airbrushed from most photographs.

13. The End of the End

The code names of the invasion beaches are in the "Downfall" landing chart in the National Archives. These undertakings are divided into "Olympic"—a vast file—and "Coronet." The planning for them is described in SW's *The Last Great Victory;* in John Ray Skates, *The Invasion of Japan: Alternative to the Bomb* (Columbia, S.C., 1994), which downplays the likely casualties; and in a less reliable book by Richard Frank, *Downfall: The End of the Imperial Japanese Empire* (New York, 1999), which also questions the casualty estimates. Hoover's prediction of casualties, "The Japanese Situation," is his Memorandum 4 in the Truman Library. The most reliable review of the projected cost of invading Japan, and the sources of the estimates, is D. M. Giangreco, "'A Score of Bloody Okinawas and Iwo Jimas': President Truman and Casualty Estimates for the Invasion of Japan," *Pacific Historical Review,* 72 (February 2003). Based largely on Truman Library papers, and including facsimiles of the Hoover memos, it also makes the case for the atomic bombing to forestall invasion. Giangreco quotes the Stimson memorandum to Truman from "Stimson 'Safe File' Japan" (7/41), box 8, Records of the Secretary of War, Record Group 107, National Archives and Records Administration, College Park, Md. The figure of 131,965 battle deaths in the ETO, including aircrews, from D-Day through to the end of the war in Europe, is from *Army Battle Casualties and Nonbattle Deaths in World War II: Final Report: 7 December 1941–31 December 1946* (Washington, D.C., 1987).

MacArthur's attempts to have active campaigns ongoing as the buildup for "Olympic" continued are described in James, in Perret, and in Manchester, *American Caesar* (Boston, 1978). MacArthur's postwar contention that he did not want the Russians in the Pacific war, and that he was against the deployment of the atomic bomb, have both been dealt with throughout this text as false. That Japan would have surrendered without the Bomb, and that it was used—twice—to forestall Soviet entry into the war is the thesis of Tsuyoshi Hasegawa's *Racing the Enemy: Stalin, Truman, and the Surrender of Japan* (Cambridge, Mass., 2005). I have noted in detail in "The Three-Week War," *Military History Quarterly,* 7 (Spring 1995), that Stalin would have seized Japanese spoils in Asia regardless of the surrender, went to war earlier than intended when the Hiroshima bomb fell, kept his troops fighting after the surrender, and had to be warded off an invasion of Hokkaido. He received largely what he had been offered at Yalta. In the same issue, David M. Glantz, in "The Soviet Invasion of Japan," also documents the Soviet plan to invade Hokkaido before "Olympic" jumped off. Also, in *Last Great Victory*, I referred to Hirohito's own plea to his War Council to surrender—but only after the Bombs fell.

Marshall's debate with FDR about the postwar future of political generals is recalled in *Interviews*. Patton's failed plea to Marshall to be sent to fight in the Pacific, March 13, 1945, is recalled in the Marshall *Papers*. Eisenhower's successful request to the blindsided Marshall to permit Hodges and his First Army staff to go to fight under MacArthur is dated April 26, 1945, in the Eisenhower *Papers*. MacArthur's request to employ Ridgway's XVIII Airborne Corps in the invasion of Japan is in *Ridgway's Paratroopers*.

Corporal Jarvis's complaint to Eisenhower is quoted in *Last Great Victory* (above), as is the general's response. Marshall's drafting strong letters for the new president, Truman, is in Pogue, and in the Marshall *Papers*. Ike's Guildhall speech is printed in full as an appendix to *General Ike* (above). Mrs. Summersby's account of the London visit, and its aftermath, is in *Past Forgetting*, illustrated with UPI press photos.

Whether Eisenhower was planning on divorce at cost to his career, and whether Marshall intervened, will remain a matter of controversy. Eisenhower's request to Marshall to have Mamie join him in Germany, which would have required a sea voyage as she would not fly, and her departure from Washington, closing down her household only a few months before he was to return to the U.S. after years away, is suspicious on its surface. Merle Miller's charges in *Plain Speaking* (New York, 1975) are unsubstantiated by his notes or tapes. Documents, if any, have disappeared. That itself was not unique in the self-protective bureaucracy. Truman's military aide, Harry Vaughan, claimed that there was something to Truman's alleged involvement, and that he saw the actual exchanges. To the contrary, Robert H. Ferrell and Francis H. Heller, in "Plain Faking?" (*American Heritage*, 3, 1995), set out examples of Merle Miller's alleged inventions of Truman's words in his "oral biography," noting that tapes of his interviews in the Truman Library do not include Summersby and several other issues put into Truman's words in *Plain Speaking*.

Much controversy has been generated by the decision to drop the Bomb rather than to invade at great cost, or to wait out attrition of the Japanese ability to wage war. Most of it focuses on the morality of the Bomb, ignoring the immorality of the brutal Japanese waging of war since 1931. The most succinct review of the Purple Heart medal orders anticipating invasion casualties—nearly 500,000 medals remained at the surrender—is "Half a Million Purple Hearts," *American Heritage*, December 2000, co-authored by D. M. Giangreco and Kathryn Moore.

The experience of Tsuneo Watanabe in a *kamikaze* crew is described by Norimitsu Onishi in "Shadow Shogun Steps Into Light, to Change Japan," *New York Times*, February 11, 2006. The cancellation of the directive for "Olympic" is in the Marshall *Papers*. The preparations for the surrender and the ceremony aboard the *Missouri* are in *Last Great Victory*.

Both the Marshall and Eisenhower papers deal with the winding down of their wartime assignments. Marshall's "lost" press release on Patton's death is reproduced in corrected draft form in volume 5 of the *Marshall Papers*.

14. Postwar Postings

Papers of both Marshall and Eisenhower continue to document this chapter. The surrender ceremony itself is in *Last Great Victory*. For the Hokkaido episode, see notes to chapter 13, above. The Marshall offer to POW officers freed by the Japanese to speed reunions with spouses is in the Beebe diary (see chapter 3).

The details of the administration of the Occupation are strikingly set out in Eiji Takemae, *Inside GHQ: The Allied Occupation of Japan and Its Legacy*, translated and augmented by Robert Ricketts and Sebastian Swann (London, 2002). The "photograph" episode is described there, largely from Faubion Bowers in "The Late General MacArthur, Warts and All," *Esquire*, January 1967. Hisako Iwabuchi recalls her school essay placing MacArthur over Hirohito in Gibney, ed., *Sensō* (above). Also in *Sensō* is the recollection of the railway conductor in Manchuria, Toshio Kawano, of his conversation with Marshall.

Bowers also reports conversations with MacArthur, his daily routine, and the visit of General Eisenhower to Tokyo, a meeting followed up by Eisenhower's correspondence in his *Papers*, where the code on the impending State vacancy appears in diary recollections in 1959. Other details on MacArthur's routine in his residence and at the Dai Ichi are from William Manchester's interview with Clayton James (MacArthur Archive); Laurence Bunker's recollections (MacArthur Archive); John Michaelis's 1977 interview with James (MacArthur Archive); Mrs. W. A. Smith, wife of an Occupation officer (on the general's theatrical luncheon entrances and Jean's complicity) in an interview with James (MacArthur Archive); Sid Huff's *My Fifteen Years with General MacArthur* (New York, 1975); and William Sebald's *With MacArthur in Japan* (New York, 1965).

The shaping of the MacArthur constitution for Japan is recalled by one of the makers, Beate Sirota, in her *The Only Woman in the Room: A Memoir* (Tokyo and New York, 1997), and in James Brooke's "Fighting to Protect Her Gift to Japanese Women," *New York Times*, May 28, 2005. MacArthur's conversations with visitors were apparently gossiped after the fact to Eichelberger, who reported them to "Miss Em" or to his diaries. MacArthur's conversations with Hoover are in Hoover papers utilized by Michael Schaller in his *Douglas MacArthur: The Far Eastern General* (New York, 1989). The "transcendent service" appeal from Hoover is from a follow-up letter to MacArthur quoted by Schaller. That Eichelberger should "stand by to take over Japan" is reported by Drew Pearson in his *Diaries* (see above) in May 1951 from a conversation with Eichelberger, who by then had broken with MacArthur.

For Stimson, see his diaries (above) and volume 5 of the Marshall *Papers*. Patton and Ike at the service football game in Frankfurt was recalled for me by a spectator, Harold Segal, then an army sergeant at SHAEF headquarters. Eisenhower's covert parting from Mrs. Summersby is described in her *Past For-*

getting. Her letter from him, then unpublished but for her extracts, is now in the Eisenhower *Papers.* The salute to Marshall on his retirement by the British chiefs of staff is in the Pogue biography. Katherine Marshall is quoted from her memoir. Marshall's China experience is memorably described in his letters, in *Papers* (above), and in *Interviews.* His Pearl Harbor testimony is in the Pogue and Mosley biographies.

Drew Pearson's exposure of Representative Martin's thinking about the prospective candidacies of MacArthur and Eisenhower, and about his own White House ambitions, appears in the "Washington Merry-Go-Round" column syndicated in the American press on September 25, 1947.

15. Postwar Bureaucracies

Marshall's experience in State is largely drawn from volume 5 of his *Papers,* and from Mosley and Pogue, whose lives preceded publication of this volume in the series. Truman's account of the appointment is from the transcripts in the Harry S. Truman Presidential Library of a 1947 diary discovered in its archives late in 2005 and transcribed by Raymond H. Geselbracht. Marshall and Frederika, here and later, is from Mosley. Kennan's "Long Telegram" was a cable in code from Moscow, which evolved into an even longer article, "The Sources of Soviet Conduct," published under the anonymous byline "X" in the July 1947 issue of *Foreign Affairs.* Marshall's development of the "Truman Doctrine" and the European Recovery Plan is covered in Dean Acheson's own *Present at the Creation* (New York, 1969); Hugo Young, *This Blessed Plot: Britain and Europe from Churchill to Blair* (London, 1999); and Tony Judt, *Postwar: A History of Europe Since 1945* (New York, 2005). The "martini" quote is from Acheson.

The suppression of *The Bells Toll for Nagasaki,* and other heavyhanded responses by General Willoughby, are detailed in *Inside GHQ* (above). Eisenhower's move to Columbia University and preparation of *Crusade in Europe* are documented in his *Papers.* Reactions to *Crusade* are in the *Papers,* and also commented upon in a BBC "Third Programme" broadcast of February 5, 1949, quoted from the transcript in the Liddell Hart Archives (above). Eisenhower's speech to Columbia students as "a fellow freshman" is reported by Max Frankel in *The Times of My Life* (New York, 1999). Arrangements to find work for Kay Summersby in army offices in Germany are also in the *Papers.* Her unwelcomed arrival in the U.S. is described in her *Past Forgetting.* The guarded response of the chief of staff's office is partly cover-up falsehood (as press photos evidence) and partly an anxiety reaction, but accepted as fact by Mosley, and passed over lightly, if at all, in Eisenhower biographies. Bradford Chynoweth's oral history referring in part to visiting Ike in his Columbia office (but mostly on his army service) is in the USAMHI.

Marshall's cautious handling of the Palestine issue, under career State Department influence, is detailed by Pogue and Mosley and in the *Papers.* The Truman Cold War agenda to counter the Soviets would undercut Arabists at State.

MacArthur's presidential politics is largely from James, Manchester, Perret, and from Michael Schaller's "Occupied Japan and American Politics, 1945–1949," in his *Douglas MacArthur: The Far Eastern General*. Eisenhower's covert presidential politics are recounted in detail in his diaries (*Eisenhower Papers*), and most comprehensively in Herbert S. Parmet, *Eisenhower and the American Crusade* (New York, 1972).

Marshall's appreciation that Sergeant Payne would not prepare any memoir for sale is recorded in Pogue and in *Papers*. The gold-plated typewriter presented to Marshall by the Overseas Press Club is in museum storage at the Marshall Library in Lexington, Virginia.

16. MacArthur's War and Eisenhower's Peace

For a detailed examination of the MacArthur phase of the Korean War, and the role of Marshall in attempting to keep him from being sacked, but finally conceding its necessity, see S. Weintraub, *MacArthur's War* (New York, 2000). MacArthur's statement (later denied and blamed on the State Department) that Korea belonged *outside* the American defense perimeter was made in an interview with Ward Price published in the *New York Times*, March 2, 1949. Jack Anderson's quiet and unrevealed visit to the Pentagon to observe the "newfangled" screen by which MacArthur communicated with Washington was described in his *Confessions of a Muckracker*, a memoir written with James Boyd (New York, 1979). The October 12, 1950, CIA memo predicting that although the Chinese Reds might intervene, they would have no "decisive" effect, *was* in the National Archives but withdrawn under a once-secret program to reclassify documents already in public access. General Almond is quoted from his oral history at USAMHI. Much further documentation substantiating the misadventure is in the MacArthur Archives. Recently surfaced material supplementing *MacArthur's War* appears in this chapter.

Eisenhower's receding presence at Columbia and his taking on the NATO command is documented in his *Papers, XI*. His feeling about the Korean "mess" made by MacArthur appears in his *Papers* and their editorial notes. His published correspondence includes his political mail from Clare Boothe Luce and others who would be closer than she was to his strategy for the nomination. His emerging politically conservative views in speeches and conversations are also clear from the *Papers* and the press, and from Parmet and Ambrose (both above). The student-run *Spectator* at Columbia is quoted from Max Frankel (above). Kyriacos Demetriou is quoted from his obituary in the *New York Times*, May 18, 1999. Marshall's return to the Cabinet as defense secretary is documented in Pogue (vol. 4, *Statesman*) and in Mosley (both above).

17. General to President

For MacArthur's return, address to Congress, and aftermath, see *MacArthur's War*. General Koster's remark about going to war in Asia is quoted in his obituary, *New York Times*, February 12, 2005. Eisenhower's post-Korea meeting with MacArthur is described graphically in Manchester. See also Weintraub, *MacArthur's War* (above), and the Eisenhower biographies above for Ike's campaign promise to go to Korea, and the aftermath.

For Eisenhower's, MacArthur's, and Taft's positioning for the 1952 nomination, see Parmet (above). For Eisenhower at center stage, see Ambrose, II *The President* (New York, 1984), and Geoffrey Perret, *Eisenhower* (New York, 1999). Earl Warren's recollections are in his *Memoirs* (Garden City, N.Y., 1977). Eisenhower's letter to MacArthur is in the DDE *Papers*. For the right-wing efforts to discredit Marshall, see Pogue and Mosley, and Tom Wicker's *Shooting Star: The Brief Arc of Joe McCarthy* (New York, 2005). Robert Welch's bizarre attack on Eisenhower is quoted by Ed Cray in his *Chief Justice: A Biography of Earl Warren* (New York, 1997). Kai Bird in *The Chairman* (above) also deals with Ike and McCarthyism. George Clooney describes his father's efforts to question Eisenhower about Marshall and McCarthy in Joan Darvish-Rouhani's "Clooney: Recalling McCarthyism's Dark Days," *Wilmington News-Journal,* November 1, 2005. Alistair Cooke writes about Marshall's turning down serious money to write his memoirs in his *Talk about America* (New York, 1969). The "Abe Lincoln" remark about Marshall is from Robert Elegant's novel *Cry Peace* (London, 2005). Elegant had covered the war in Korea and was a correspondent elsewhere in Asia afterward.

C. L. Sulzberger in *Seven Continents and Forty Years* (New York, 1977) recalls the sixty-first birthday party for Eisenhower in Paris. His covert political tactics, flouting service regulations, with Duff, Lodge, Brownell, Clay, and others to seek the nomination are in Blanche Wiesen Cook, *The Declassified Eisenhower* (Garden City, N.Y., 1981); Parmet (above), Herbert Brownell, with John P. Burke, *Advising Ike: The Memoirs of Attorney General Herbert Brownell* (Lawrence, Kans., 1993); Ambrose, *II* (above), and Pickett (below). Also, Eisenhower's *Papers, XII, XIII: NATO and the Campaign of 1952* (1970). Eisenhower's denial to Howard Chase of improprieties with Mrs. Summersby is in William B. Pickett's *Eisenhower Decides to Run: Presidential Politics and Cold War Strategy* (Chicago, 2000), much the best book on the lead-up to the 1952 nomination. Pickett also deals with the Duff letter concealed for decades. John Bennett's talk with Eisenhower at Christmas 1951 which touched on his Summersby concerns is reported in the Drew Pearson *Diaries* on March 18, 1952, and December 4, 1952. MacArthur's alleged statement, "That boy will back out in the final showdown," is quoted in the March entry. Churchill's letter to Clementine on "Ike or the Democrat" is in *Winston and Clementine* (above).

The attempt of the Taft handlers to arrange a deal with MacArthur is in Pickett. MacArthur's "lackluster" keynote address and its aftermath is described in Manchester (above). Truman's calling it "a dud" is in a letter to Russ Stewart, general manager of the *Chicago Sun-Times,* July 10, 1952, facsimile in Autograph Catalog 37, item 86, Profiles in History, Beverly Hills, Calif. Eisenhower's campaigning betrayal of Marshall is in Pogue, *Statesman.* Marshall's responses are in Mosley (who publishes the frank letter to Queen Frederika) and Pogue. Marshall's attendance at the coronation of Elizabeth II, and the audience response, are in Pogue and Mosley. Madame Chiang as well as Queen Frederika are in Mosley. Marshall's difficult Nobel Prize journey, dogged by illness, is described in Pogue and in Mosley.

18. Fading Away

For Eisenhower's early presidency, see bios above and Robert H. Ferrell, *The Diary of James C. Hagerty* (Bloomington, Ind., 1983), and Eisenhower, *Papers, XIV: The Presidency, The Middle Way. Papers, XX and XXI*, conclude the presidency. His leadership style is interpreted by Fred I. Greenstein in *The Hidden-Hand Presidency* (New York, 1982). Greenstein also quotes Henry Cabot Lodge Jr. on golf, and the Gallup Poll on public perceptions of the president's golfing. Eisenhower's failed attempt to get a tree removed at the Augusta National Golf Club is reported in *USA Today*, April 6, 2006.

The conversation between Eisenhower and Dulles over Hungary is recorded in a Dulles memorandum of November 9, 1956, quoted by Roger Cohen in "In a Long-Ago Revolt, Echoes for Today," *New York Times*, October 8, 2006. In a letter to the editor, October 15, 2006, Wes Pedersen, who was then with the CIA, confirms the "deadly and shameful" anomaly.

For Marshall's last years, Pogue and Mosley supplement each other. Truman describes meeting Eisenhower at the obsequies in *Talking with Harry*, edited by Ralph E. Walker (Wilmington, Del., 2001). Richard Sutherland's visit to the dying Marshall is described in Paul P. Rogers, *The Bitter Years: MacArthur and Sutherland* (New York, 1990). A letter from MacArthur to Katherine Marshall, February 12, 1957, is in the sale catalogue of Kenneth W. Rendell in the *New York Times Book Review*, 1999. The young Jack Kennedy is quoted on the unlikable MacArthur from the South Pacific by Nigel Hamilton in *JFK: Reckless Youth* (New York, 1992). Louis Morton describes the posthumous additions to MacArthur's *Reminiscences* in "Egotist in Uniform," in *MacArthur and the American Century*, edited by William M. Leary (Lincoln, Neb., 2001).

Eisenhower's last years and death are described in Ambrose, *II*, and Perret (above).

Afterword: Opportunity, Celebrity, Personality

The Afterword, but for the epigraph from Shakespeare's *Julius Caesar*, and the concluding quotation, is grounded in the eighteen previous chapters. The final line quotes László Jakab Orsós, the director of the Hungarian Cultural Center in New York, from the *New York Times*' "News of the Week in Review," October 8, 2006.

Acknowledgments

I am indebted to the following archivists, veterans, scholars, editors, and other resource persons for helping to make *15 Stars* possible: James M. Barkley, Michael Birkner, James Brady, Tom Branigar, Robert Clark, Robert C. Doyle, William H. Duncan, John S. D. Eisenhower, Robert S. Elegant, Raymond H. Geselbracht, Dennis M. Giangreco, Gladys Greenfield, Robert Guinsler, A. H. and Eileen Hanley-Browne, John Hill, Paul M. Kennedy, Dan H. Laurence, Octave C. Merveille, Patricia J. Methven, Kadzi Mutizwa, George Nakhnikian, the late Nigel Nicolson, Bruce Nichols, Michel Pharand, Tom Pitoniak Sr., Tom Pitoniak Jr., Harold Segal, Nigel Streel, Richard Sommers, Richard Swain, David A. Weintraub, Rodelle Weintraub, Meriel Wilmot-Wright, Richard E. Winslow, and Peter Zimmerman.

Index

About the Author

Stanley Weintraub is Evan Pugh Professor Emeritus of Arts and Humanities at Pennsylvania State University. He is the author or editor of more than fifty histories and biographies. He has been a National Book Award finalist and a Guggenheim Fellow. He currently lives in Newark, Delaware, where he is an adjunct professor at the University of Delaware.